THE VISUAL ENCYCLOPEDIA
OF SCIENCE FICTION

Editor:
Brian Ash

Introductions to 02 Thematics:
Brian Aldiss
Poul Anderson
Isaac Asimov
J. G. Ballard
Ken Bulmer
John Brunner
Arthur C. Clarke
Lester del Rey
Philip José Farmer
Harry Harrison
Fritz Leiber
Larry Niven
Frederik Pohl
Keith Roberts
Josephine Saxton
Robert Sheckley
A. E. van Vogt
James White
Jack Williamson

Contributors to 03 Deep Probes:
Edmund Cooper
Damon Knight
L. Sprague de Camp
George Turner

Principal Research Consultant:
Mike Ashley

Researchers:
John Eggeling
Walter Gillings
James Goddard
Jon Gustafson
Philip Harbottle
George Hay
Colin Lester
Philip Strick
Gerry Webb

THE VISUAL ENCYCLOPEDIA OF SCIENCE FICTION

EDITED BY BRIAN ASH

HARMONY BOOKS
NEW YORK

Created, designed and produced by Trewin Copplestone Publishing Ltd, London

Filmsetting by Jolly & Barber Ltd, Rugby. Origination by Positive Plus, London. Printed in Hong Kong by South China Photo-Process Printing Co Ltd.

First published, 1977, in the United States by Harmony Books, a division of Crown Publishers, Inc.

Harmony Books, a division of Crown Publishers, Inc. One Park Avenue, New York, New York 10016.

Published simultaneously in Canada by General Publishing Company Ltd.

ISBN: 0-517-531747 (hardcover)
0-517-531755 (paperback)

Library of Congress Cataloging in Publication Data:
Main entry under title:
The Visual Encyclopedia of Science Fiction
1. Science Fiction – Dictionaries.
I. Ash, Brian
PN3448S45V5 1977
ISBN: 0-517-531747 (hardcover)
0-517-531755 (paperback)

First published in Great Britain in 1977 by Pan Books.

THE VISUAL ENCYCLOPEDIA OF SCIENCE FICTION

BRIEFING

This encyclopedic guide has been compiled with the help of contributors from all over the world. It is a truly international effort. In addition to many of the well-known sf authors whose work appears on the following pages, a host of other fans, devotees and similarly interested people have played their part in putting together this book. To them all thanks are due.

In this general introduction there is no need to attempt to spell out the grand panorama which science fiction has spread across its own area of literature during the last fifty years. In the following pages the newcomer will discover it for himself. The devotee will find much which he already knows—and further or additional delights. The long-standing fan will search for the highlights which particularly appeal to his personal interest—and find more besides.

In short there is something for everyone. No other compilation of such scope has ever been undertaken in the sf field; and in that sense this book is unique. However, anyone at all familiar with science fiction will surely agree that a single volume, even of the complexity of the text that follows, may give a comprehensive picture but would hardly pretend to be definitive. In fact, it is highly unlikely that any definitive work in the genre could appear at this stage in its development. Science fiction, at its best, is an on-going process. To describe it as an exclusively literary endeavour would be to misunderstand both science fiction and the general body of outside literature. The great value of the good science fiction tale is that its bounds can extend far beyond the scope of the conventional novel or short story. This introduction is no place to elaborate on such a statement. The reader will find ample justification for the claim in the pages that follow. If he wishes to learn of the editor's personal views, he can read them in the 'Deep Probes' section.

He will also find in the 'Thematics' section the personal comments of many of the world's leading science fiction writers. In their great variety, they provide much insight into the motivations which persuade writers to enter the science fiction field. In the 'Deep Probes' section more extended arguments and personal opinions are given.

In endeavouring to include, in an intended reference book, a less formal and personal touch, we have tried to convey some of the atmosphere of individual involvement and cross-fertilisation of ideas which is so significant a part of the world of science fiction. This book is not expected to end its days as a dusty tome on some forgotten reference shelf, although much of the nature of the information which needs to be presented must obviously take the form of simple and factual statements.

The contents page indicates how this guide is presented. No 'Who's Who' of authors has been attempted for there are already several noted reference works in existence, providing all the information required in this area. They range from the straightforward academic format of Donald Tuck's *The Encyclopedia of Science Fiction and Fantasy*, through Robert Reginald's less formal *Stella Nova: The Contemporary Science Fiction Authors*, to the present editor's own popular, but selective, *Who's Who in Science Fiction*. The serious student will find most that he needs to know about the personal history and background of writers in these existing books.

The concluding indexes cover authors and artists, together with titles of books and short stories. Details of films, television programmes and comics, and those responsible for them, can be found in the appropriate sub-sections in 04 Fandom and Media. All important information regarding magazines and their publishers is given year-by-year in 01 Program, supplemented by further facts in sub-section 04.05.

Here it all is, then. We hope it will provide many hours of lasting pleasure and enlightenment to all who know, or wish to learn about the fascinating world of what Robert Heinlein—among many others—has called the only worthwhile literature of the twentieth century.

CHECKLIST

ALL SCIENCE FICTION TERMS – SOME PURELY IMAGINARY, SOME USED IN HARD SCIENCE TODAY – PLUS EXPLANATIONS WHERE NECESSARY, ARE LISTED BELOW ALPHABETICALLY.

A

B

C

D

E

F

I

J

L

M

N

P

R

S

T

U

V

01

PROGRAM

This opening section represents a major attempt to provide a broadly based science fiction chronology. It is designed to give a year-by-year coverage of important events in all areas of the genre so that they can be appreciated at a glance. As such, it is bound to be selective – but the intention has been to record as many noted stories, magazine details, movies, TV series, fan events, and any other items of significance, as space will allow.

The format has been designed for ease of assimilation, and is presented in the form of a space mission program. Fandom is shown throughout as a below-the-line support activity. A full explanation of how this information is presented is given overleaf.

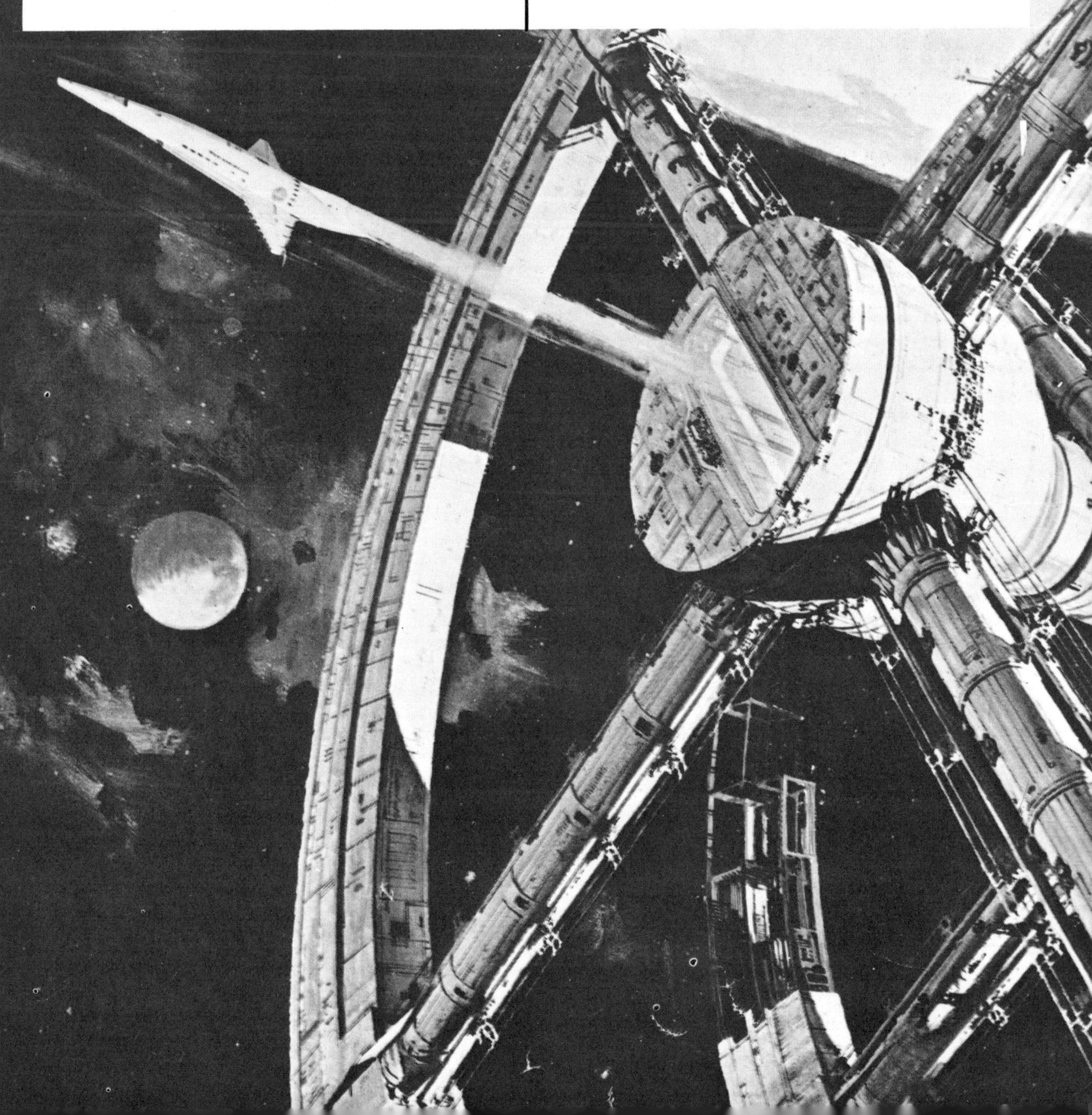

01. PROGRAM

The Program begins at the beginning of the nineteenth century, the first year of note being 1805. The critical observer may argue that earlier examples of what has been called 'prototype science fiction' should merit inclusion. However, they are covered elsewhere in the later Thematics section.

To identify the basic stages in the development of the modern genre, the Program is set out in three parts. 'Countdown' covers the nineteenth century, when the majority of stories were set on Earth, until 1895 where 'Lift Off' begins with the first novel of H. G. Wells.

During the next thirty years sf writers ventured into the solar system, but rarely farther. Not until the advent of the pulp magazines was the reader regularly taken to the stars. This third period, dating from 1926, is labelled 'Trans-Galactic Insertion', and brings the reader up to 1976.

A concise explanation must be given regarding the way in which facts have been marshalled. A list of visual symbols is given to identify the various highlights from 1926 onwards. Magazine stories appear, naturally, against the names of the authors and issues of the publications concerned. Works listed in italics – the great majority of them serialisations – are regarded as novels, even if some subsequently failed to appear in book form. Short stories are denoted by single quotation marks.

Wherever possible a writer's debut in the sf magazine field has been included, together with an indication of whether this was his or her first story, or a first effort at science fiction after published successes in other fields. In this context a certain distinction has been made in the case of *Weird Tales*, which for the purpose of this flow-chart is not regarded as a genuine sf magazine, even though it is recognised that it often carried the fantasy work of those who were to become well known as sf writers. Only where acknowledged classics, or first appearances of noted authors are concerned, does *Weird Tales* receive attention.

Occasionally a writer's first *sale* is overtaken chronologically by a later story because of delay in publication. In such instances where the distinction is known, it has been made clear.

Apart from first stories, which may be of significance only because they mark individual debuts, the inclusion of subsequent tales by each writer is based on the merit of the work. For reasons of space, few sequels have been listed; this principle also applies in the books, movies and TV categories. A selection of noted novels, which from their first appearance have only been published in book form, is also included.

In the listing of the many magazine launches, amalgamations and changes of name, details have normally been taken from title pages rather than covers, which may not necessarily coincide. Magazines are given their full titles, or single name abbreviations where it is clear that no confusion can arise, eg *Amazing* for *Amazing Stories*. *The Magazine of Fantasy and Science Fiction*, because of the length of its title, is identified by the commonly accepted initials '*F&SF*'.

Magazine publishing companies are also referred to by their most familiar names; any changes in these, or in those of a company's subsidiaries under which sf magazines were published, are not generally given. The term 'aborts' generally signifies the date of the last issue of a magazine (or fanzine). Foreign reprint editions of professional sf magazines are not listed.

In the Fandom section, it should be noted that the numbering of fan history periods was originated by Jack Speer in his 'Up to Now' articles in 1939. He named the periods 'First Fandom', 'Second Fandom', and so on. Later Sam Moskowitz produced an alternative system in the first of his 'Immortal Storm' articles, naming the periods 'First Fan Era', etc. His First Era extended back beyond Speer's First Fandom, and Speer, belatedly recognising earlier fan activity, named the First (Moskowitz) Era 'Ecofandom'.

Speer's system, which has been followed in the Program, has received wider acceptance than the Moskowitz version, and has been extended by Robert Silverberg up to Sixth Fandom. Elliot Weinstein continued the numbering up to Thirteenth Fandom, though without any description of the features identifying each stage.

For the benefit of newcomers, certain fan expressions used in the Program must be defined:

Blitzkrieg: An activity by certain factions in the fan world to explore areas and initiate action which they feel should have been undertaken by the various organisations to which they are affiliated. In other words, an unofficial attempt to force the organisations to change either their attitudes or direction.

Combozine: An expression used to describe the composite binding into one volume of several issues of individual fanzines.

Conventions (Cons): Generally defined as fan meetings which (a) have been arranged beforehand, and (b) include a business meeting. However, little agreement exists in fandom as a whole on this definition, various commentators claiming more than one historic meeting as 'the first true convention'.

Fanzine: Denotes an amateur or semi-professional publication, usually in some kind of magazine format – either duplicated, mimeographed or occasionally printed when the organisations/clubs find themselves in sufficient funds, or when offered free facilities.

Gafiate: Means 'to get away from it all' – essentially to abandon one's involvement in fandom, but not necessarily forever.

Lettercol: An abbreviation of 'letter columns' – an area in which feedback between reader and writer has played a substantial part.

Prozine: The fan term for a professionally published sf magazine as compared with the amateur offerings.

Conflicting opinions among fans themselves make it difficult to detail authentically many activities over the last few years. There is no published fan history for the post-1950 period, although Harry Warner Jr has written a volume covering the 1950s and early 1960s which has yet to appear at the time of going to press. However, enough reasonably indisputed facts have now emerged regarding the earlier years to allow a broad representation.

• 1805 • • • • • • • • • • • • • • • • • • • 1894 •

1805 *The Last Man; or Omegarus and Syderia. A Romance in Futurity* by Jean-Baptiste Cousin de Grainville

1818 *Frankenstein* by Mary Shelley

1827 *The Mummy! A Tale of the Twenty-Second Century* by J. Webb

1828 Jules Verne born in Nantes, France

1835 *Hans Phaal – A Tale* by Edgar Allan Poe

'Moon Hoax' by Richard Adams Locke

1838 *The Narrative of Arthur Gordon Pym's Adventures* by Edgar Allan Poe

1844 'The Artist of the Beautiful' and 'Rappacini's Daughter' by Nathaniel Hawthorne

'A Tale of the Ragged Mountains' and 'The Balloon Hoax' by Edgar Allan Poe

1845 'The Facts in the Case of M. Valdemar' by Edgar Allan Poe

1849 'Mellonta Tauta' by Edgar Allan Poe

1855 'The Bell-Tower' by Herman Melville

1858 'The Diamond Lens' by Fitz-James O'Brien

1859 'The Wondersmith' and 'What Was It? A Mystery' by Fitz-James O'Brien

1863 *Five Weeks in a Balloon* by Jules Verne

1864 'How I Overcame My Gravity' by Fitz-James O'Brien

Journey to the Centre of the Earth by Jules Verne

1865 *From the Earth to the Moon* by Jules Verne

1866 H. G. Wells born in Bromley, Kent

1868 *The Steam Man of the Prairies* by Edward F. Ellis

1869 'The Brick Moon' by Edward Everett Hale

1870 *Round the Moon* and *Twenty Thousand Leagues Under the Sea* by Jules Verne

1871 *The Coming Race* by Sir Edward Bulwer-Lytton

'The Battle of Dorking' by Sir George Tomkyns Chesney

1872 *Erewhon* by Samuel Butler

1875 *The Mysterious Island* by Jules Verne

1876 *Frank Reade and His Steam Man of the Plains* by Harry Enton (who began the series)

1877 *Hector Servadac* and *The Underground City* by Jules Verne

1878 *Oxygen och Aromasia* by Claës Lundin

1879 *The Begum's Fortune* by Jules Verne

Frank Reade, Jr, and His Steam Wonder by Louis P. Senarens (who took over the series)

1880 *The Steam House* by Jules Verne

1884 *Flatland: A Romance of Many Dimensions* by Edwin Abbott

Hugo Gernsback born in Luxembourg

1886 *The Strange Case of Dr Jekyll and Mr Hyde* by Robert Louis Stevenson

Robur the Conqueror (*The Clipper of the Clouds*) by Jules Verne

1887 *A Crystal Age* by W. H. Hudson

The Twentieth Century War by Albert Robida

1888 *Looking Backward 2000–1887* by Edward Bellamy

1889 *A Connecticut Yankee in King Arthur's Court* by Mark Twain

Urania by Camille Flammarion

Freeland: a Social Anticipation by Theodor Hertzka

1893 'The Advent of the Flying Man' and 'A Slip Under the Microscope'. First stories by H. G. Wells

Le Fin du Monde by Camille Flammarion

1894 'Aepyornis Island', 'The Diamond Maker', 'The Flowering of the Strange Orchid', 'The Lord of the Dynamos' and 'The Stolen Bacillus' by H. G. Wells

A Journey in Other Worlds by John Jacob Astor

A Traveller from Altruria by William Dean Howells

The Great War in England in 1897 by William Le Queux

1895

1895 *The Time Machine* 'The Argonauts of the Air' and 'The Remarkable Case of Davidson's Eyes' by H.G. Wells

Propeller Island by Jules Verne

The Crack of Doom by Robert Cromie

1896 *The Island of Dr. Moreau*, 'In the Abyss', 'The Plattner Story', 'The Purple Pileus', 'The Sea Raiders', 'The Story of the Late Mr. Elvesham' and 'Under the Knife' by H. G. Wells

For the Flag by Jules Verne

Argosy, as the first important all-fiction 'pulp' magazine, redesigned by Frank A. Munsey

1897 *The Invisible Man*, 'The Crystal Egg', 'The Star', 'A Story of the Days to Come' and 'A Story of the Stone Age' by H. G. Wells

Auf Zwei Planeten by Kurd Lasswitz

1898 *The War of the Worlds* and 'The Man Who Could Work Miracles' by H. G. Wells

Edison's Conquest of Mars by Garrett P. Serviss

The Yellow Danger by M. P. Shiel

1899 *When the Sleeper Wakes* by H. G. Wells

1900 *The Moon Metal* by Garrett P. Serviss

The Honeymoon in Space by George Griffith

1901 *The First Men in the Moon*, 'The New Accelerator' and 'A Dream of Armageddon' by H. G. Wells

The Purple Cloud and *The Lord of the Sea* by M. P. Shiel

1902 *A Voyage to the Moon*, based on Verne's stories, filmed by Georges Méliès in France

1903 'The Land Ironclads' and 'The Valley of Spiders' by H. G. Wells

1904 *The Food of the Gods* and 'The Country of the Blind' by H. G. Wells

Master of the World by Jules Verne

Hugo Gernsback emigrates from Luxembourg to the US

1905 *A Modern Utopia* and 'The Empire of the Ants' by H. G. Wells

'With the Night Mail' by Rudyard Kipling

Gulliver of Mars by Edwin L. Arnold

Jules Verne dies

1906 *In the Days of the Comet* and 'The Door in the Wall' by H. G. Wells

Before Adam by Jack London

1907 *The Iron Heel* by Jack London

1908 *The War in the Air* by H. G. Wells

The House on the Borderland by W. H. Hodgson

Hugo Gernsback launches *Modern Electrics*

1909 *A Columbus of Space* by Garrett P. Serviss

'The Machine Stops' by E. M. Forster

'Moxon's Master' by Ambrose Bierce

The Invisible Thief. Based on Wells's *The Invisible Man*, filmed by Pathé in France

1910 'My First Aeroplane' by H. G. Wells

First silent film of *Frankenstein* produced by Thomas Edison

1911 *Ralph 124C 41 +* by Hugo Gernsback

The Hampdenshire Wonder by J. D. Beresford

The Elixir of Hate by George Allan England

1912 *The Second Deluge* by Garrett P. Serviss

The Lost World by Sir Arthur Conan Doyle

Under the Moons of Mars. First novel by Edgar Rice Burroughs (under pen name Norman Bean)

Darkness and Dawn and *The Golden Blight* by George Allan England

1925

1913 *The Poison Belt* by Sir Arthur Conan Doyle

The Gods of Mars, The Warlord of Mars and *The Man Without a Soul* by Edgar Rice Burroughs

The Dragon by M. P. Shiel

1914 *The World Set Free* by H. G. Wells

'At the Earth's Core' by Edgar Rice Burroughs (first story in the 'Pellucidar' series)

First silent *Golem* movie made by Paul Wegener

1915 *The Scarlet Plague* and *The Star Rover* by Jack London

Pellucidar by Edgar Rice Burroughs

1916 Otto Witt launches *Hugin*, the world's first sf magazine, in Sweden

'The Alchemist'. First story by H. P. Lovecraft

1917 *The Messiah of the Cylinder* by Victor Rousseau

'Through the Dragon Glass'. First story by A. Merritt

1918 *The Gods of Mars* by Edgar Rice Burroughs (book)

'The People of the Pit' and 'The Moon Pool' by A. Merritt

Palos of the Dog Star Pack by J. U. Giesy

1919 'The Runaway Skyscraper' First sf story by Murray Leinster

The Girl in the Golden Atom. First sf story by Ray Cummings

The Flying Legion by George Allan England

The Conquest of the Moon Pool by A. Merritt

Hugin magazine ceases publication in December

H. G. Wells's *The First Men in the Moon* filmed by Gaumont

Precursor of US sf magazines, Street & Smith Inc's *The Thrill Book*, has sixteen issues; successive editors, Harold Hersey & Ronald Oliphant

1920 *We* by Yevgeny Zamyatin

Beyond the Planet Earth by Konstantin Tsiolkovsky

The Metal Monster by A. Merritt

A Voyage to Arcturus by David Lindsay

'The Mad Planet' by Murray Leinster

E. E. ('Doc') Smith completes *The Skylark of Space*, begun in 1914 and unpublished until 1928

1921 *R.U.R.* First performance of Karel Čapek's play in Prague introduces the word 'robot'

'The Grisly Folk' by H. G. Wells

The Blind Spot by Homer Eon Flint and Austin Hall

1922 *The Absolute at Large* by Karel Čapek

1923 *Men Like Gods* by H. G. Wells

Weird Tales magazine launched by Rural Publishing Corporation of Chicago, Editor: Edwin Baird

'The Thing of a Thousand Shapes'. First appearance in *Weird Tales* of Otis Adelbert Kline

'Dagon'. First appearance in *Weird Tales* of H. P. Lovecraft

Hugo Gernsback publishes August issue of *Science & Invention* as special 'Scientifiction' number

1924 *The Dream* by H. G. Wells

The Radio Man by Ralph Milne Farley

'Death Waters'. First story by Frank Belknap Long

Hugo Gernsback's proposal for sf magazine *Scientifiction* fails

Anniversary issue of *Weird Tales* (editor Otis Adelbert Kline)

Popular Fiction Publishing take over *Weird Tales*, Farnsworth Wright becomes editor

1925 *Krakatit: An Atomic Fantasy* and *The Makropoulos Secret* by Karel Čapek

Conan Doyle's *The Lost World* filmed by First National

01. PROGRAM

1926

Magazine Dates

Apr Hugo Gernsback's Experimenter Publishing (editor: Gernsback; associate editor: T. O'Conor Sloane) launches first US specialist sf magazine AMAZING STORIES

Magazine Stories

June 'The Malignant Entity' – first appearance in an sf magazine by Otis Adelbert Kline, AMAZING (reprinted from WEIRD TALES, March/April 1924)

June 'The Coming of The Ice' by G. Peyton Wertenbaker, AMAZING

July 'The Eggs from Lake Tanganyika' – first translated story by Curt Siodmak, AMAZING

Aug 'The Monster-God of Mamurth' – first story by Edmond Hamilton, WEIRD TALES

Oct *Beyond the Pole* – first story by A. Hyatt Verrill (two-part serial), AMAZING

Books

Films/Television/Radio

Metropolis (based on the book by Thea von Harbou) directed by Fritz Lang for UFA

Fandom

1927

June Experimenter Publishing produce 1 issue of AMAZING STORIES ANNUAL

Jan 'The Man with the Strange Head' – first story by Miles J. Breuer, AMAZING

June 'The Fate of the Poseidonia' – first appearance in an sf magazine by Clare Winger Harris, AMAZING

June 'The Four-Dimensional Roller-Press' – first story by Bob Olsen, AMAZING

June Gernsback announces results of cover story contest to encourage new writers

June *The Master Mind of Mars* by Edgar Rice Burroughs, AMAZING STORIES ANNUAL

Aug 'The Tissue Culture King' by Julian Huxley, AMAZING (reprinted from CORNHILL MAGAZINE)

Sept 'The Colour out of Space' by H. P. Lovecraft, AMAZING

Oct 'Around the Universe' by Ray Cummings, AMAZING (reprinted from SCIENCE & INVENTION)

Oct '*The Metal Emperor* by A. Merritt (eleven-part serial), SCIENCE & INVENTION

Nov 'The Machine Man of Ardathia' – first story by Francis Flagg, AMAZING

Nov 'Back to the Beast' – first story by Manly Wade Wellman, WEIRD TALES

Play

The Absolute at Large by Karel Čapek

Jan Hugo Gernsback starts 'Discussions' column in *Amazing Stories*

Code:

 Magazine Launch

 Magazine Abort

 Writer's first SF work

1928

Jan Experimenter Publishing launch AMAZING STORIES QUARTERLY

Feb 'The Revolt of the Pedestrians' – first story by David H. Keller, AMAZING

Apr 'The Miracle of the Lily' – by Clare Winger Harris, AMAZING

June 'The Golden Girl of Munan' – first story by Harl Vincent, AMAZING

July *The Sunken World* – first story by Stanton A. Coblentz, AMAZING STORIES QUARTERLY

July 'The Menace' – first story of 'Taine of San Francisco' series by David H. Keller, AMAZING STORIES QUARTERLY

July 'Out of the Sub-Universe' – first story by R. F. Starzl, AMAZING STORIES QUARTERLY

Aug *Crashing Suns* – first 'Interstellar Patrol' series by Edmond Hamilton (two-part serial), WEIRD TALES

Aug 'Armageddon – 2419 AD' – first story by Phil Nowlan initiating 'Buck Rogers' series, AMAZING

Aug *The Skylark of Space* – first story by E. E. ('Doc') Smith (three-part serial), AMAZING

Dec 'The Metal Man' – first story by Jack Williamson, AMAZING

Mr. Blettsworthy on Rampole Island by H. G. Wells

The Girl in the Moon filmed by Fritz Lang

1929

Spr Experimenter Publishing declared bankrupt, Teck Publishing buy AMAZING titles (editor: Arthur H. Lynch)

T. O'Conor Sloane becomes sf editor at Teck Publishing

May Hugo Gernsback forms Stellar Publishing (editor: Gernsback; managing editor: David Lasser)

June Stellar Publishing launch SCIENCE WONDER STORIES

July Stellar Publishing launch AIR WONDER STORIES

Oct Stellar Publishing launch SCIENCE WONDER QUARTERLY

Jan 'The Roger Bacon Formula' – first story by Fletcher Pratt, (with Irvin Lester), AMAZING

Mar 'The Airlords of Han' – second in 'Buck Rogers' series by Phil Nowlan, AMAZING

July 'Futility' – first story by S. P. Meek, AMAZING

Aug 'Beyond Gravity – first story by Ed Earl Repp, AIR WONDER

Fall 'The Shot into Infinity' by Otto Willi Gail, first story using Hermann Oberth's scientific rocket principles, SCIENCE WONDER QUARTERLY

Nov 'The Crystal Ray' and 'The Space Dwellers' – first stories by Raymond Z. Gallun, respectively in AIR WONDER and SCIENCE WONDER

Nov 'The Darkness on Fifth Avenue' by Murray Leinster, ARGOSY

Dec 'A Baby on Neptune' by Clare Winger Harris and Miles J. Breuer, AMAZING

The Maracot Deep and Other Stories – collection by Arthur Conan Doyle

First recorded fanzines, *Cosmic Stories* and *Cosmic Stories Quarterly*, produced briefly by Jerome Siegel and Joseph Shuster

01. PROGRAM

1930

MD

Jan Clayton Publications (sf editor: Harry Bates) launch ASTOUNDING STORIES OF SUPER SCIENCE

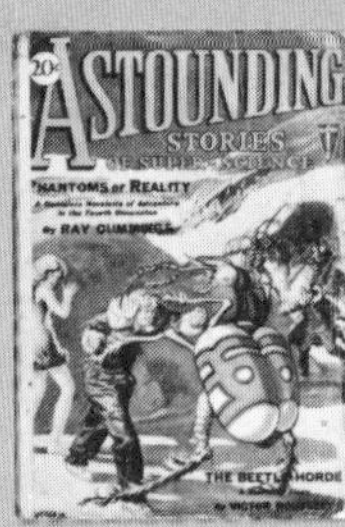

Jan Stellar Publishing launch SCIENTIFIC DETECTIVE MONTHLY (editor: Hector Gray)

June SCIENTIFIC DETECTIVE MONTHLY becomes AMAZING DETECTIVE TALES

June AIR WONDER STORIES and SCIENCE WONDER STORIES combine as WONDER STORIES

July SCIENCE WONDER QUARTERLY becomes WONDER STORIES QUARTERLY

Oct Stellar Publishing's AMAZING DETECTIVE TALES aborts

MS

Jan 'When the Atoms Failed' – first story by John W. Campbell, Jr, AMAZING

Jan 'The Death's Head Meteor' – first story by Neil R. Jones, AIR WONDER

Jan 'The Perfect Counterfeit' – first of 'Dr Bird' series by S. P. Meek, SCIENTIFIC DETECTIVE

Jan *White Lily* – first appearance in an sf magazine by John Taine, AMAZING STORIES QUARTERLY

Feb 'Spawn of the Stars' – first sf story by Charles Willard Diffin, ASTOUNDING

Feb 'The Man with the Silver Disc' – first story by Lloyd Arthur Eshbach, SCIENTIFIC DETECTIVE

Mar *Brigands of the Moon* by Ray Cummings (four-part serial), ASTOUNDING

Mar 'The Green Girl' by Jack Williamson (two-part serial), AMAZING

Apr 'Monsters of Moyen' – first story in an sf magazine by Arthur J. Burks, ASTOUNDING

May 'The City of the Living Dead' – first story by Laurence Manning (with Fletcher Pratt), SCIENCE WONDER

June 'Piracy Preferred' – first of the 'Arcot, Wade and Morey' stories by John W. Campbell, Jr, AMAZING

June 'The Flashlight Brigade' – first story in an sf magazine by Ralph Milne Farley, AMAZING DETECTIVE

July 'The Red Plague' – first story by P. Schuyler Miller, WONDER STORIES

Sum 'The Tower of Evil' – first story by Nat Schachner, WONDER STORIES QUARTERLY

Aug *Skylark Three* by E. E. ('Doc') Smith (three-part serial), AMAZING

Fall *The Black Star Passes* by John W. Campbell, Jr, AMAZING STORIES QUARTERLY

Sept 'Marooned Under the Sea' – first story in an sf magazine by Paul Ernst, ASTOUNDING

Sept 'In 20,000 AD' by Nat Schachner (with Arthur Leo Zagat), WONDER STORIES

Oct 'The Man Who Saw the Future' by Edmond Hamilton, AMAZING

Oct 'Marooned in Andromeda' and 'Murder in the Fourth Dimension' – first stories in sf magazines by Clark Ashton Smith, respectively WONDER STORIES and AMAZING DETECTIVE

B

Gladiator – first novel by Philip Wylie

Last and First Men – first sf novel by Olaf Stapledon

FR

Fin du Monde (based on the book by Camille Flammarion) filmed in France by Abel Gance

Fan

1930 Ecofandom starts (Speer)

May First fan organisation, Science Correspondence Club, started from suggestion of Raymond A. Palmer with the aid of Hugo Gernsback; launches first mimeographed fanzine, *The Comet* (later *Cosmology*)

July The Scienceers and *The Planet* (editor: Allen Glasser) launched

1931

Feb ASTOUNDING STORIES OF SUPER SCIENCE becomes ASTOUNDING STORIES

Apr Good Story Publishing launch MIRACLE SCIENCE AND FANTASY STORIES (editor: Douglas M. Dold) – it aborts in June

May 'The Voice from the Ether' by Lloyd Arthur Eshbach, AMAZING

May 'Worlds to Barter' – first story by John Beynon Harris (John Wyndham), WONDER STORIES

June 'The Light Bender' – first story by Frank K. Kelly, WONDER STORIES

June 'The Power Planet' by Murray Leinster, AMAZING

July 'The Jameson Satellite' – first of 'Professor Jameson' series by Neil R. Jones, AMAZING

July *Spacehounds of IPC* by E. E. ('Doc') Smith (five-part serial), AMAZING

Fall 'Dramatis Personae' – first appearance in an sf magazine by Joe W. Skidmore, AMAZING STORIES QUARTERLY

Fall *Seeds of Life* by John Taine, AMAZING STORIES QUARTERLY

Nov 'Hawk Carse' – first of series by Harry Bates and Desmond W. Hall (under pseudonym Anthony Gilmore), ASTOUNDING

Dec 'Lord of the Lightning' – first story by Arthur K. Barnes, WONDER STORIES

Dec 'The World of the Red Sun' – first story by Clifford D. Simak, WONDER STORIES

Lo! by Charles Fort (non-fiction)

Frankenstein directed by James Whale for Universal

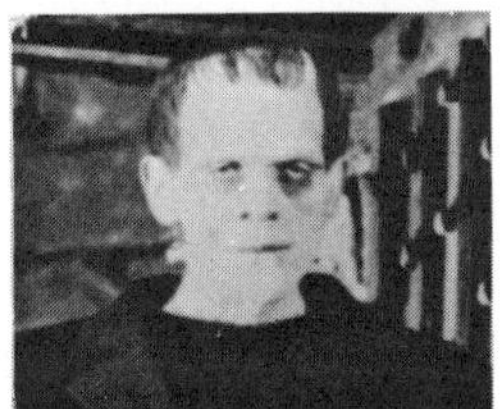

Dr Jekyll and Mr Hyde directed by Rouben Mamoulian for Paramount

Jan Fortean Society started

June Daniel McPhail launches *The Science Fiction News*

Fall Charles D. Hornig launches *Science Fiction Monthly*

Oct Walter H. Gillings launches first UK club, Ilford Science Literary Circle

1932

Feb *Wandl, the Invader* by Ray Cummings (four-part serial), ASTOUNDING

Apr 'The Lost Machine' by John Beynon Harris (John Wyndham), AMAZING

Sum 'Exiles of Mars' by Frank K. Kelly, WONDER STORIES QUARTERLY

Sept 'The Romance of Posi and Nega' – first of series by Joe W. Skidmore, AMAZING

Sept 'Raiders of the Universe' – first appearance in an sf magazine by Donald Wandrei, ASTOUNDING

Oct 'The First Martian' – first story under pseudonym Eando Binder (Otto O. Binder and Earl A. Binder), AMAZING

Nov 'The Venus Germ' – first story by Festus Pragnell (with R. F. Starzl), WONDER STORIES

Wint 'Moss Island' – first appearance in an sf magazine by Carl Jacobi, AMAZING

When Worlds Collide by Philip Wylie and Edwin Balmer

Wild Talents by Charles Fort (non-fiction)

Brave New World – first sf novel by Aldous Huxley

The Island of Lost Souls (based on Wells's *The Island of Dr Moreau*) directed by Erle C. Kenton for Paramount

US radio serialisation of *Buck Rogers* begins transmission

1932 Conrad Ruppert starts below-cost printing of several fanzines

Jan Allen Glasser launches *The Time Traveller* from suggestion by Mort Weisinger and Julius Schwartz; Forrest J. Ackerman becomes involved; staff organise Arra Publishers

Sept Science Fiction Digest group formed, launches *Science Fiction Digest* (editor: Maurice Ingher) – Bob Tucker runs two issues only of *The Planetoid*

01. PROGRAM

1933 / 1934

MD

1933

Jan Stellar Publishing's WONDER STORIES QUARTERLY aborts

Jan ASTOUNDING STORIES reverts to ASTOUNDING STORIES OF SUPER SCIENCE

Mar Clayton Publications collapse

Mar Street & Smith Inc launch fantastic-fiction single-hero magazine DOC SAVAGE

May Frank R. Paul (already Gernsback's regular illustrator for many years) officially becomes art editor of WONDER STORIES

Sum Street & Smith Inc (sf editor: F. Orlin Tremaine) buy ASTOUNDING STORIES OF SUPER SCIENCE, which reverts to ASTOUNDING STORIES

Nov Charles D. Hornig becomes managing editor of Stellar Publishing

1934

Feb Pearsons launch first UK sf periodical, the weekly SCOOPS (editor: Haydn Dimmock)

MS

1933

Mar 'The Man Who Awoke' – first of series by Laurence Manning, WONDER STORIES

Jun *The Intelligence Gigantic* – first story by John Russell Fearn (two-part serial), AMAZING

Nov 'The Call of the Mech-Men' – first of 'Stranger Club' series by Laurence Manning, WONDER STORIES

Nov 'The Price of Peace' – first story by Mort Weisinger, AMAZING

Nov 'Shambleau' – first story by C. L. Moore, WEIRD TALES

Dec 'Ancestral Voices' by Nat Schachner, first 'thought variant' story in ASTOUNDING

1934

Jan *Triplanetary* by E. E. ('Doc') Smith (four-part serial), AMAZING

Jan 'The Man from Ariel' – first story by Donald A. Wollheim, WONDER STORIES

Mar 'The Man Who Stopped the Dust' by John Russell Fearn, ASTOUNDING

Apr 'A Matter of Size' – first story by Harry Bates under his own name, ASTOUNDING

Apr *The Legion of Space* by Jack Williamson (six-part serial, first in series), ASTOUNDING

June 'Sidewise in Time' by Murray Leinster, ASTOUNDING

June 'Crater 17, Near Tycho' by Frank K. Kelly, ASTOUNDING

July *Life Everlasting* by David H. Keller (two-part serial), AMAZING

B

1933

The Shape of Things to Come by H. G. Wells

F

1933

King Kong directed by Ernest Schoedsack and Merian C. Cooper for RKO

The Invisible Man directed by James Whale for United Artists

Fan

1933

1933 Start of First Fandom (Speer)

1933 End of First Fan Era, start of Second and Third Fan Eras (Moskowitz)

Sept Charles D. Hornig launches *The Fantasy Fan*

Oct Formation of British Interplanetary Society by P. E. Cleator, with Leslie J. Johnson as secretary

Wint *The Time Traveller* merges with *Science Fiction Digest*

Science Correspondence Club becomes International Scientific Association (ISA); *Cosmology* aborts

1934

1934 First sf agency, Solar Sales Service, started by Mortimer Weisinger and Julius Schwartz

Jan *Science Fiction Digest* becomes *Fantasy Magazine*; Julius Schwartz becomes editor

Mar William H. Crawford's semi-professional *Unusual Stories* has brief run

1935

May William H. Crawford's Fantasy Publications (editor: Crawford) launch MARVEL TALES

Jun Pearsons' SCOOPS aborts

Oct Teck Publishing's AMAZING STORIES QUARTERLY aborts

July Fantasy Publications' MARVEL TALES aborts

July 'A Martian Odyssey' – first story by Stanley G. Weinbaum, WONDER STORIES

July 'Zero as a Limit' – first story by Robert Moore Williams (as Robert Moore), ASTOUNDING

July 'Before Earth Came' by John Russell Fearn, ASTOUNDING

Aug *The Skylark of Valeron* by E. E. ('Doc') Smith (seven-part serial), ASTOUNDING

Oct 'Inflexure' – first story by H. L. Gold (as Clyde Crane Campbell), ASTOUNDING

Oct 'The Bright Illusion' by C. L. Moore, ASTOUNDING

Nov 'The Mole Pirate' by Murray Leinster, ASTOUNDING

Nov 'Twilight' – first of the Don A. Stuart (John W. Campbell) stories, ASTOUNDING

Dec *The Mightiest Machine* – by John W. Campbell (five-part serial), ASTOUNDING

Dec 'Old Faithful' – first in series by Raymond Z. Gallun, ASTOUNDING

Dec 'The Rape of the Solar System' by Leslie F. Stone

Mar 'Proxima Centauri' by Murray Leinster, ASTOUNDING

May *The Liners of Time* by John Russell Fearn (four-part serial), AMAZING

June 'Alas, All Thinking' by Harry Bates, ASTOUNDING

July *The Green Man of Graypec* by Festus Pragnell (three-part serial), WONDER STORIES

July 'Parasite' by Harl Vincent, AMAZING

Aug 'Man of Iron' – first story by Ross Rocklynne, ASTOUNDING

Aug 'The Star that Would Not Behave' – first story by R. R. Winterbotham, ASTOUNDING

Sept 'Earth Minus' by Donald Wandrei, ASTOUNDING

Nov 'The Red Peri' by Stanley G. Weinbaum, ASTOUNDING

Man Who Could Work Miracles directed by Lothar Mendes for London Films

May Hugo Gernsback and Charles D. Hornig at *Wonder Stories* start Science Fiction League (SFL)

Sept John B. Michel, Frederik Pohl and Donald A. Wollheim launch *International Observer*

Oct Los Angeles SFL Chapter (LASFL) incorporated

1935 Overseas SFL Chapters incorporated in Nuneaton, Leeds, Liverpool (UK) and Sydney (Australia)

1935 ISA takes over International Cosmos Science Club; William S. Sykora becomes director

1935 Science Fiction Syndicate (D. R. Welch and William H. Crawford) produce *The Science Fiction Bibliography*

1935 First fan deity, 'Ghu', invented

Jan Philadelphia SFL Chapter (PSFL) incorporated

Feb Conrad Ruppert stops below-cost fanzine printing; *The Fantasy Fan* aborts; William H. Crawford takes over some printing

Spr Arthur Wilson (Bob) Tucker launches *The D'Journal*

Spr Donald A. Wollheim and others feud with *Wonder Stories*

June Donald A. Wollheim, William S. Sykora and John B. Michel temporarily expelled from SFL

July *Terrestrial Fantascience Guild Bulletin* (editor: Donald A. Wollheim) becomes *The Phantagraph*

Fall Bob Tucker's *The D'Journal* mothballed

Oct PSFL becomes Philadelphia Science Fiction Society (PSFS)

Nov James Blish launches *The Planeteer*

Nov Claire P. Beck launches *The Science-Fiction Review*, which becomes *The Science Fiction Critic*

01. PROGRAM

1936

MD

Apr Charles D. Hornig leaves Stellar Publishing, WONDER STORIES aborts

Aug Standard Magazines (sf editor: Mortimer Weisinger) buy WONDER STORIES, which becomes THRILLING WONDER STORIES

Fall Shepherd and Wollheim produce one issue only of FANCIFUL TALES OF TIME AND SPACE

Dec Stephen Slesinger Inc issue FLASH GORDON STRANGE ADVENTURE MAGAZINE (one issue)

MS

Feb *At the Mountains of Madness* by H. P. Lovecraft (three-part serial), ASTOUNDING

Feb 'Mathematica' by John Russell Fearn, ASTOUNDING

Mar 'The Graveyard Rats' – first story by Henry Kuttner, WEIRD TALES

Mar 'Earth's Lucky Day' – first story by Forrest J. Ackerman (with Francis Flagg), WONDER

May *The Cometeers* by Jack Williamson (four-part serial), ASTOUNDING

June 'The Shadow Out of Time' by H. P. Lovecraft, ASTOUNDING

Aug 'He Who Shrank' – first solo appearance in an sf magazine by Henry Hasse, AMAZING

Dec 'Devolution' by Edmond Hamilton, AMAZING

Dec 'The Flame Midget' by Frank Belknap Long, ASTOUNDING

B

The Croquet Player by H. G. Wells

Odd John by Olaf Stapledon

F

Things to Come (H. G. Wells's script) directed by William Cameron Menzies for Alexander Korda's London Films

Flash Gordon directed by Frederick Stephani and Ray Taylor for Universal

Fan

1936 Bob Tucker gafiates after hoax obituary in *Astounding Stories*

1936 *The Canadian Science Fiction Fan* launched

Mar Maurice K. Hanson and others at Nuneaton SFL Chapter launch *Novae Terrae*

Mar Jack Speer and Daniel McPhail start first state-wide club, the Oklahoma Scientifiction Association

May Morris Dollens launches *Science Fiction Collector*

July Olon F. Wiggins launches *The Science Fiction Fan*

July The Terrestrial Fantascience Guild aborts; *The Phantagraph* goes independent

July Roy Test produces preliminary issue of *Imagination!*

Oct Nils Helmer Frome launches first Canadian fanzine, *Supramundane Stories* (two issues only)

Oct First convention; New York fans meet fans in Phila delphia, starting an annual convention

1937

June World's Work (UK) launch TALES OF WONDER (editor: Walter H. Gillings)

Oct John W. Campbell, Jr becomes sf editor for Street & Smith Inc

Jan 'The Blue Spot' by Jack Williamson (two-part serial), ASTOUNDING

Feb 'The Saga of Pelican West' – first story by Eric Frank Russell, ASTOUNDING

Mar 'The Dawn of the Conquest of Space' – first article in an sf magazine by Willy Ley, ASTOUNDING

Apr 'Down the Dimensions' – first appearance in an sf magazine by Nelson Bond, ASTOUNDING

Apr 'The Sands of Time' by P. Schuyler Miller, ASTOUNDING

July 'Seeker of Tomorrow' by Eric Frank Russell and Leslie J. Johnson, ASTOUNDING

July *Frontier of the Unknown* – first story by Norman L. Knight (two-part serial), ASTOUNDING

Sept 'The Isolinguals' – first story by L. Sprague de Camp, ASTOUNDING

Sept 'Past, Present and Future' – first of series by Nat Schachner, ASTOUNDING

Sept *Galactic Patrol* by E. E. ('Doc) Smith (six-part serial), first of 'Lensman' novels, ASTOUNDING

Oct 'Elegy to a Dead Satellite: Luna' (poem) – first contribution by Frederik Pohl (as Elton V. Andrews), AMAZING

Dec *Zagribud* by John Russell Fearn (three-part serial), AMAZING

Adventures to Come – first true 'original' sf anthology, edited by J. Berg Esenwein

Star Maker by Olaf Stapledon

Star Begotten by H. G. Wells

1937 Second Fandom starts (Speer)

1937 Fifth Fan Era starts (Moskowitz)

1937 SFA (UK) incorporate first overseas branch, in Los Angeles

early Leslie A. Croutch (Canada) launches *Croutch Magazine Mart News*

Jan Science Fiction Association (SFA) launched in UK

Jan *Science-Fantasy Correspondent* absorbs *Fantasy Magazine*

Jan Walter H. Gillings (UK) launches *Scientifiction: The British Fantasy Review*

Jan First UK convention, in Leeds

Feb ISA-sponsored convention in New York City

May *Science Fantasy Correspondent* becomes *Amateur Correspondent*; Corwin F. Stickney becomes editor

June Donald A. Wollheim disbands ISA after William S. Sykora resigns; *International Observer* aborts

Spr SFA (UK) launch *Science Fiction Gazette* and *Tomorrow*

July Donald A. Wollheim and John B. Michel start Fantasy Amateur Press Association (FAPA), first sf APA; first mailing included *The Fapa Fan* (editor: Wollheim)

Aug James V. Taurasi launches *Cosmic Tales*

Aug SFA issues first *British Science-Fiction Bibliography*

Sum Second Philadelphia convention; John B. Michel's 'Mutation or Death' speech starts 'Michelism'

Oct Sam Moskowitz starts first sf Manuscript Bureau

Oct LASFL launch *Imagination! (Madge)* (editors: Bruce Yerke, Forrest J. Ackerman and Morojo Douglas)

Oct Ray Bradbury joins LASFL

Oct SFA (UK) launch *Amateur Science Stories* (editor: Douglas W. F. Mayer); London branch launched

Nov John V. Baltadonis and Oswald Train launch *PSFS News*

Nov Corwin F. Stickney's *Amateur Correspondent* aborts

Nov Robert A. Madle launches *Fantascience Digest*

Dec Richard Wilson launches first regular weekly newszine, *The Science Fiction News-Letter*

Late Jack Speer starts Oklahoma Institute of Private Opinion, first serious sf poll-takers

01. PROGRAM

1938

MD

Mar ASTOUNDING STORIES becomes ASTOUNDING SCIENCE FICTION

Apr Ziff-Davis Publishing (sf managing editor: Raymond A. Palmer) buy AMAZING STORIES (editor: B. G. Davis)

May A. A. Wyn produce one issue only of CAPTAIN HAZZARD

May Red Circle Publications (sf editor: Robert O. Erisman) launch MARVEL SCIENCE STORIES (dated August)

MS

Jan 'Red Heritage' by John Russell Fearn, ASTOUNDING

Mar 'Dead Knowledge' by Don A. Stuart (John W. Campbell), ASTOUNDING

Spr 'Lunar Lilliput' – first magazine story by William F. Temple, TALES OF WONDER

Apr 'The Faithful' – first story by Lester del Rey, ASTOUNDING

Apr 'Hollywood on the Moon' – first of series by Henry Kuttner, THRILLING WONDER

Apr *3000 Years* by Thomas Calvert McClary (three-part serial), ASTOUNDING

May *Legion of Time* by Jack Williamson (three-part serial), ASTOUNDING

June 'Seeds of the Dusk' by Raymond Z. Gallun, ASTOUNDING

July 'The Dangerous Dimension' – first sf story by L. Ron Hubbard, ASTOUNDING

B

Out of the Silent Planet by C. S. Lewis

Anthem by Ayn Rand

R

Fan

1938 Second Fandom ends (Speer)

1938 Sixth Fan Era starts (Moskowitz)

1938 Moskowitz-Wollheim feud reaches FAPA

1938 James Taurasi forms Cosmic Publications

1938 E. J. (Ted) Carnell and Leslie J. Johnson start Science Fiction Service

1938 Erle Korshak starts sales service

1938 Bob Tucker produces *1st Science, Weird and Fantasy Fiction Yearbook*

1938 Bill Veney launches Junior Australian Science; Fiction Correspondence Club, recruits many fans

Jan Moskowitz-Wollheim feud starts

Jan Harold Gotliffe launches *Bulletin of the Leeds Science Fiction League*

Jan James V. Taurasi launches *Fantasy News*

Mar *Tomorrow* (UK) absorbs *Scientifiction: The British Fantasy Review*

Mar SFA's (UK) *Amateur Science Stories* aborts after 3 issues

Apr National Fantasy Fan Federation starts, and launches *Bonfire* (first editor: Harry Warner, Jr)

Spr FAPA launch *The Fantasy Amateur*

Apr SFA holds London convention

Apr SFA's Manchester branch launched

May Sam Moskowitz and William S. Sykora organise the first national, large convention, in Newark

May Larry B. Farsace launches *The Fantasy Collector*

June *Bulletin of the Leeds Science Fiction League* becomes *The Futurian*; J. Michael Rosenblum becomes editor

Sept George Newnes Ltd (UK) launch FANTASY (editor: T. Stanhope Sprigg)

Aug 'Hell Ship' by Arthur J. Burks, first in 'Josh McNab' series, ASTOUNDING

Aug 'Who Goes There?' by Don A. Stuart (John W. Campbell), ASTOUNDING

Aug 'Eviction by Isotherm' – first story by Malcolm Jameson, ASTOUNDING

Aug 'The Smile of the Sphinx' by William F. Temple, TALES OF WONDER

Oct 'The Command' by L. Sprague de Camp, first in 'Johnny Black' series, ASTOUNDING

Oct 'Of Jovian Build' – first sf story by Oscar J. Friend, THRILLING WONDER

Dec 'Helen O'Loy' by Lester del Rey, ASTOUNDING

Wint 'Man's Empire of Tomorrow' – first professional article by Arthur C. Clarke, TALES OF WONDER

US radio serialisation of *Superman* begins transmission

Oct Orson Welles's radio adaptation of *The War of the Worlds* terrifies New York

July Claire P. Beck's *Science Fiction Critic* aborts

Aug Sam Moskowitz, William S. Sykora and James V. Taurasi start New Fandom, which absorbs Science Fiction Advancement Association, and launches *New Fandom* and other fanzines

Aug Arthur C. Clarke, William Temple and Maurice K. Hanson move into 'The Flat' in London

Sept SFA's Liverpool branch launch *The Satellite* (editors: David McIlwain and John F. Burke)

Sept Michelists, with Isaac Asimov, Cyril M. Kornbluth and others, form Futurian Scientific Literary Society (Futurians)

Sept Jack Speer produces the first *hourly* fanzine, *The Chronoton* (9 am-3 pm; second series 16 October, 11 am-midnight)

Fall Bob Tucker launches new series of *D'Journal*, *Le Zombie*, *Science Fiction Advertiser* (first serious advertising-only fanzine) and other fanzines

Fall Jack Speer launches *Sustaining Program* (in FAPA)

Oct LASFL's *Imagination!* aborts

Oct New Fandom form Queens SFL Chapter (QSFL)

Oct Robert D. Swisher starts first large-scale fanzine index, *The SF Checklist*

Nov Cyril M. Kornbluth and Richard Wilson launch *Voice of the Vombis*

Nov Harry Warner Jr and James S. Avery launch *Spaceways*

Dec Robert W. Lowndes launches first regular free fanzine besides APA's, *Le Vombiteur*

Wint Vincent Clarke (UK) launches *Science Fantasy News*

01. PROGRAM

1939

MD

Jan Short Stories Inc buy WEIRD TALES

Jan Standard Magazines launch STARTLING STORIES (editor: Mort Weisinger)

Feb Red Circle Publications launch DYNAMIC SCIENCE STORIES

Feb Standard Magazines launch STRANGE STORIES (overall editor: Leo Margulies)

Mar Columbia Publications (sf editor: Charles D. Hornig) launch SCIENCE FICTION

Mar Street & Smith Inc launch UNKNOWN (editor: John W. Campbell)

Apr Komos Publications launch SUPERWORLD COMICS

MS

Jan 'The Black Flame' by Stanley G. Weinbaum, STARTLING

Jan 'I, Robot' by Otto O. Binder, first of 'Adam Link' series, AMAZING

Mar 'Marooned off Vesta' – first story by Isaac Asimov, AMAZING

Mar *Sinister Barrier* by Eric Frank Russell, UNKNOWN

Apr 'The Broken Axiom' – first story by Alfred Bester, THRILLING WONDER

Apr *One Against the Legion* by Jack Williamson (three-part serial), ASTOUNDING

July 'The Golden Amazon' by John Russell Fearn (as Thornton Ayre), first in 'Golden Amazon' series, FANTASTIC ADVENTURES

July 'Black Destroyer' – first story by A. E. van Vogt, ASTOUNDING

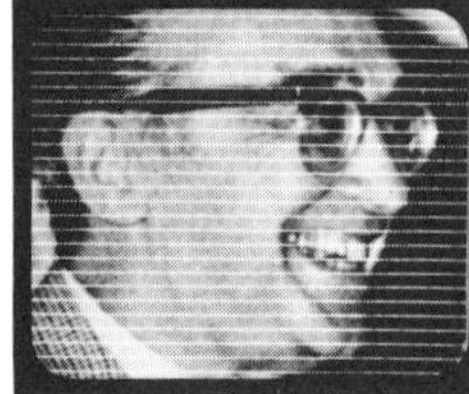

B

War with the Newts by Karel Čapek

F

First episode of *Buck Rogers* movie serial filmed by Beebe and Goodkind

Fan

1939 August Derleth and Donald Wandrei form Arkham House semi-professional publishers

1939 Frederik Pohl launches Fantastory Sales Service

1939 Jack Speer produces first extensive fandom history, *Up To Now*, in his fanzine *Full Length Article* (in FAPA)

Jan Forrest J. Ackerman and Morojo continue *Imagination!*'s lettercol as *Voice of the Imagi-Nation* (*VOM*)

Mar *Novae Terrae* (UK) becomes *New Worlds*; E. J. Carnell becomes editor

Mar James Blish's *The Planeteer* aborts (last issue edited by James V. Taurasi)

Apr C. S. Youd (John Christopher) launches *The Fantast* (UK)

May Leslie J. Johnson, L. V. Heald, Ron Holmes and J. F. Burke (UK) launch *Science Fantasy Review*

01. PROGRAM

Apr Red Circle Publications' DYNAMIC SCIENCE STORIES aborts

May Ziff-Davis Publishing launch FANTASTIC ADVENTURES (editor: Raymond A. Palmer)

June George Newnes Ltd's FANTASY THRILLING SCIENCE FICTION (UK) aborts

Sept Frank A. Munsey Co (sf editor: Mary Gnaedinger) launch FAMOUS FANTASTIC MYSTERIES

Nov Columbia Publications launch FUTURE FICTION (editor: Charles D. Hornig)

Dec Love Romances Publishing (sf editor: Malcolm Reiss) launch PLANET STORIES

Dec MARVEL SCIENCE STORIES becomes MARVEL TALES

July 'Trends' by Isaac Asimov, ASTOUNDING

Aug 'Life-Line' – first story by Robert A. Heinlein, ASTOUNDING

Aug 'Two Sought Adventure' – first story by Fritz Leiber, UNKNOWN

Sept 'Ether Breather' – first story by Theodore Sturgeon, ASTOUNDING

Oct 'The Scourge Below' – first story by Sam Merwin Jr, THRILLING WONDER

Oct *Grey Lensman* by E. E. ('Doc') Smith (four-part serial), ASTOUNDING

Nov 'The 4-Sided Triangle' by William F. Temple, AMAZING

Dec *Lest Darkness Fall* by L. Sprague de Camp, UNKNOWN

May SFA hold first London (third British) convention

May Richard Wilson's *Science Fiction News-Letter* aborts

July First world convention (Nycon); Moskowitz-Wollheim feud at its height

July Adverse feature on fandom in TIME MAGAZINE

Aug Bob Tucker's *D'Journal* aborts

Aug E. J. Carnell's *New Worlds* aborts (continued post-war as prozine)

Aug Futurians move into 'Futurian House' in New York

Sum Ray Bradbury launches *Futuria Fantasia*

Oct Larry B. Farsace launches *Golden Atom*

Oct Several Australian fanzines launched, including *Ultra*

Oct C. S. Youd (UK) launches *Fantasy War Bulletin*

Dec William S. Sykora becomes editor of *Fantasy News*

01. PROGRAM

1940

MD

Jan Standard Magazines launch CAPTAIN FUTURE (editor: Mort Weisinger)

Feb Popular Publications (sf editor: Frederik Pohl) launch ASTONISHING STORIES

Feb Gerald G. Swan (UK) start YANKEE SF (a reprint magazine)

Mar Popular Publications launch SUPER SCIENCE STORIES (editor: Frederik Pohl)

May Dorothy McIlwraith becomes editor of WEIRD TALES, having assumed her duties in January

MS

Feb 'Martian Quest' – first story by Leigh Brackett, ASTOUNDING

Feb 'Locked Out' – first story by Horace B. Fyfe, ASTOUNDING

Feb *If This Goes On . . .* by Robert A. Heinlein (two-part serial), ASTOUNDING

Mar 'Emergency Refueling' – first story by James Blish, SUPER SCIENCE STORIES

Apr 'Stepsons of Mars' – first story by C. M. Kornbluth (with Richard Wilson, jointly as Ivar Towers), ASTONISHING

Apr 'Murder From Mars' by Richard Wilson, ASTONISHING

Apr *Final Blackout* by L. Ron Hubbard (three-part serial), ASTOUNDING

B

F

Fan

Third Fandom starts (Speer)

During the year, David McIlwain (UK) launches hectograph *Gargoyle*

Jan J. Michael Rosenblaum's *The Futurian* becomes *Pseudo-Futurian*

Feb Leslie J. Johnson et al's *Science Fantasy Review* (UK) becomes *Science-Fantasy Review War Digest*

Feb The Nameless Ones (later the Strangers Club), launched by Arthur L. (Art) Widner, produce *Fanfare*

Mar LASFL becomes Los Angeles Science Fantasy Society (LASFS), affiliated with SFL and Science Fictioneers, with Walter J. Daugherty president; produced *Shangri-La* (*Shaggy*)

Spr The Decker Dillies launch first multi-coloured mimeographed fanzine, *Pluto*

May Damon Knight launches *Snide*

June Jack Speer, Milton A. Rothman and Elmer Perdue carry out FAPA 'blitzkrieg' to ensure mailing

Sum Ray Bradbury's *Futuria Fantasia* aborts

Aug Eric Frank Russell (UK) launches *Hermes*

01. PROGRAM

July  Frank A. Munsey Co launch FANTASTIC NOVELS MAGAZINE

July  Columbia Publications launch SCIENCE FICTION QUARTERLY (editor: Charles D. Hornig)

Nov MARVEL TALES becomes MARVEL STORIES

Dec Ziff-Davis Publishing reactivate AMAZING STORIES QUARTERLY (a combination of three monthly issues bound together, not a new magazine)

Dec  H-K Publications launch COMET STORIES (editor: F. Orlin Tremaine)

Dec Asam Publishing launch Canada's first fantastic-fiction magazine, UNCANNY TALES (editor: Lyle Kenyon Engel)

May 'Mad Hatter' – first story by Winston K. Marks, UNKNOWN

June 'The Roads Must Roll' by Robert A. Heinlein, ASTOUNDING

June 'Into the Darkness' by Ross Rocklynne, ASTONISHING

July 'Before the Universe' – first story by Frederik Pohl (with C. M. Kornbluth, jointly as S. D. Gottesman), SUPER SCIENCE STORIES

Aug 'Vault of the Beast' by A. E. van Vogt, ASTOUNDING

Sept *The Kid From Mars* by Oscar J. Friend, STARTLING STORIES

Sept 'Blowups Happen' by Robert A. Heinlein, ASTOUNDING

Sept *Slan* by A. E. van Vogt (four-part serial), ASTOUNDING

Oct 'Farewell to the Master' by Harry Bates, ASTOUNDING

Oct 'The Voyage that Lasted 600 Years' by Don Wilcox, AMAZING

Nov *Typewriter in the Sky* by L. Ron Hubbard (two-part serial), UNKNOWN

Nov 'The Outpost at Altark' – first story by R. W. Lowndes, SUPER SCIENCE STORIES

Dec *Darker than You Think* by Jack Williamson, UNKNOWN

Wint *Captain Future and the Space Emperor* – first in series by Edmond Hamilton CAPTAIN FUTURE

Sept SFA (UK) aborts

Sept Second world convention (Chicon), sponsored by Illini Fantasy Fictioneers

Sept Attempt to unite Australian fans fails; Futurian Society of Sydney aborts

Oct Julius Unger launches *Fantasy Fiction Field*, with bibliographical inserts by A. Langley Searles

Oct *Pseudo-Futurian* (UK) and *Science-Fantasy Review War Digest* combine as *Futurian War Digest* (*Fido*) (editor: J. Michael Rosenblum)

Nov Clifford D. Simak and others launch Minnesota Fantasy Society; produce *The Fantasite* (editor: Phil Bronson)

Dec First Australian convention leads to launching of new Futurian Society of Sydney

Dec *Croutch Magazine Mart News* becomes *Croutch News*

Dec Franklyn Brady and A. Ross Kuntz produce *The Imag-Index*

Dec Robert W. Lowndes's *Le Vombiteur* aborts

Wint Oswald Train's *The Fantasy Collector* aborts

Australian government ban on import of prozines and institution of paper controls lead to restricted fanac

Fan and artist, Joseph Shuster, joins Jerome Siegel to start professional *Superman Comics*

01. PROGRAM

1941

MD

Feb Standard Magazines' STRANGE STORIES aborts

Feb  Albing Publications (sf editor: Donald A. Wollheim) launch STIRRING SCIENCE STORIES

Mar Albing Publications launch COSMIC STORIES

Mar SUPER SCIENCE STORIES becomes SUPER SCIENCE NOVELS MAGAZINE

Apr Red Circle Publications produce one issue of UNCANNY STORIES

Apr Red Circle Publications' MARVEL STORIES mothballed

Apr Robert W. Lowndes becomes editor at Columbia Publications

May COSMIC STORIES becomes COSMIC SCIENCE FICTION

June FAMOUS FANTASTIC MYSTERIES absorbs FANTASTIC NOVELS MAGAZINE

July Albing Publications' COSMIC SCIENCE FICTION aborts

July Oscar J. Friend becomes editor of STARTLING STORIES and THRILLING WONDER STORIES

July H-K Publications' COMET STORIES aborts

MS

Jan 'John Carter and the Giant of Mars' by Edgar Rice Burroughs, AMAZING

Jan 'Not Yet the End' – first story by Fredric Brown, CAPTAIN FUTURE (Winter)

Jan 'A Yank at Valhalla' by Edmond Hamilton, STARTLING STORIES

Feb 'Oscar' – first story by Cleve Cartmill, UNKNOWN

Feb 'Resilience' – first story by Damon Knight, STIRRING SCIENCE STORIES

Feb 'Bad Medicine' – first story by William Morrison (Joseph Samachson), THRILLING WONDER

Mar 'Genus Homo' by L. Sprague de Camp and P. Schuyler Miller, SUPER SCIENCE STORIES

Apr 'Microcosmic God' by Theodore Sturgeon, ASTOUNDING

Apr 'Reason' – first significant robot story by Isaac Asimov, ASTOUNDING

May 'Solution Unsatisfactory' by Robert A. Heinlein (as Anson MacDonald), ASTOUNDING

May 'Jay Score' by Eric Frank Russell, ASTOUNDING

May 'Interstellar Way-Station' – first story by Wilson Tucker (as Bob Tucker), SUPER SCIENCE STORIES

May 'Universe' by Robert A. Heinlein, ASTOUNDING

July 'The Seesaw' – first of 'The Weapon Makers' series by A. E. van Vogt, ASTOUNDING

July *Methuselah's Children* by Robert A. Heinlein (three-part serial), ASTOUNDING

July 'The Vortex Blaster' – first of series by E. E. ('Doc') Smith, COMET STORIES

Sept 'Nightfall' by Isaac Asimov, ASTOUNDING

Sept 'Test of the Gods' by Raymond F. Jones, ASTOUNDING

B

The Other Worlds – first significant sf anthology, edited by Phil Stong

The Books of Charles Fort – collection of all Fort's works

F

Fan

1941 Feuds split Futurians and LASFS

1941 Damon Knight's *Snide* aborts

1941 Revised *Science Fiction Checklist* produced

1941 Philadelphia convention cancelled

1941 Last *Science, Weird and Fantasy Fiction Yearbook* produced

Wint Morris Dollers' SCIENCE FICTION COLLECTOR aborts

Feb First Boston convention (Boskone)

Mar *Shangri-L'Affaires* launched as *VOM* insert

Apr Ken Bulmer launches *Star Parade*

Apr Convention in Sydney (Australia)

June Fred Hurter launches *Rocket* (Canada); becomes *Censored*

July Third world convention (Denvention); first convention awards made privately by Walter J. Daugherty; Robert A. Heinlein makes 'superior fans' speech; *Denventioneer* (combozine) produced

Aug James V. Taurasi's *Cosmic Tales* aborts

1942

Sept FUTURE FICTION and SCIENCE FICTION combine as FUTURE COMBINED WITH SCIENCE FICTION

Oct SCIENCE FICTION launched (Canada), editor: William Browne-Forbes

Oct UNKNOWN becomes UNKNOWN WORLDS

Nov SUPER SCIENCE NOVELS MAGAZINE reverts to SUPER SCIENCE STORIES

Nov Alden H. Norton becomes overall sf editor at Popular Publications; Frederik Pohl becomes assistant editor

Dec Ziff-Davis Publishing launch FANTASTIC ADVENTURES QUARTERLY (three monthly issues combined)

Mar Albing Publications' STIRRING SCIENCE STORIES aborts

Apr World's Work's TALES OF WONDER (UK) aborts

June SCIENCE FICTION (Canada) aborts

June YANKEE SF (UK) aborts

June Norman Book Co (Canada) buys UNCANNY TALES

Fall Malcolm Reiss becomes managing editor, and Wilbur S. Peacock editor, of Love Romances Publishing

Oct FUTURE COMBINED WITH SCIENCE FICTION becomes FUTURE FANTASY AND SCIENCE FICTION

Dec Howard Browne becomes associate editor of FANTASTIC ADVENTURES

Oct 'By His Bootstraps' by Robert A. Heinlein (as Anson MacDonald), ASTOUNDING

Oct 'Plants Must Grow' – first of 'John Carstairs, Botanical Detective' series by Frank Belknap Long, THRILLING WONDER

Nov 'Pendulum' – first story by Ray Bradbury (with Henry Hasse), SUPER SCIENCE STORIES

Nov *Second-Stage Lensman* by E. E. ('Doc') Smith (four-part serial), ASTOUNDING

Nov 'Lost Legion' by Robert A. Heinlein (as Lyle Monroe), SUPER SCIENCE STORIES

Feb 'The Star Mouse' by Fredric Brown, PLANET STORIES

May 'Foundation' – first of series by Isaac Asimov, ASTOUNDING

May 'Asylum' by A. E. van Vogt, ASTOUNDING

June 'Proof' – first story by Hal Clement (H. E. Stubbs), ASTOUNDING

June 'Heritage' – first story by Robert Abernathy, ASTOUNDING

June 'Time Will Tell' – first story in a sf magazine by Emil Petaja, AMAZING

Sum *The Comet Kings* – in 'Captain Future' series by Edmond Hamilton, CAPTAIN FUTURE

July 'Collision Orbit, – first of 'Seetee' series by Jack Williamson (as Will Stewart), ASTOUNDING

Aug 'Waldo' by Robert A. Heinlein (as Anson MacDonald), ASTOUNDING

Sept *Nerves* by Lester del Rey, ASTOUNDING

Oct 'QRM-Interplanetary' – first story by George O. Smith, initiating the 'Venus Equilateral' series, ASTOUNDING

Dec 'The Flight that Failed' – first story by E. Mayne Hull, ASTOUNDING

Dec 'The Weapon Shop' by A. E. van Vogt, ASTOUNDING

Sept James V. Taurasi launches *Fantasy Times*, first photo-offset fanzine, which becomes *Science Fiction Times*

Nov First Michigan Annual Science Fiction and Fantasy Convention (Michicon); Midwest Fantasy Federation launched

Fall *New Fandom* aborts

Dec LASFS's *Shangri-La* becomes *Shangri-L'Affaires* on merger

Dec E. Everett Evans launches *A Tale of the Evans* (ATOTE)

late *Ultra* (Australia) aborts

1942 Midwest Fantasy Fan Federation fades

1942 Walter J. Daugherty produces first national fan directory, *Directory of Fandom*

1942 Canadian Amateur Fantasy Press launched

June J. Michael Rosenblum, E. J. Carnell and others from British Fantasy Society (BFS), produce *BFS Bulletin*

July *The Fantast* (UK), then edited by D. R. Webster, aborts

Fall Francis T. Laney and Duane Rimel launch *The Acolyte*

01. PROGRAM

1943

MD

Mar Popular Publications take over Frank A. Munsey Co; Mary Gnaedinger remains sf editor

Apr Popular Publications' ASTONISHING STORIES aborts

Apr FUTURE FANTASY AND SCIENCE FICTION becomes SCIENCE FICTION STORIES

Apr Columbia Publications' SCIENCE FICTION QUARTERLY mothballed

May Frederik Pohl leaves Popular Publications

May SUPER SCIENCE STORIES mothballed

July Columbia Publications' SCIENCE FICTION STORIES mothballed

Sept Norman Book Co's UNCANNY TALES (Canada) aborts

Oct Street & Smith's UNKNOWN WORLDS aborts

Dec Ziff-Davis Publishing's AMAZING STORIES QUARTERLY mothballed

MS

Feb *The New Adam* by Stanley G. Weinbaum (two-part serial), AMAZING

Feb 'Mimsy Were the Borogroves' by Lewis Padgett (Henry Kuttner and C. L. Moore), ASTOUNDING

Mar 'Q.U.R.' by Anthony Boucher (H. H. Holmes), ASTOUNDING

Apr 'Abdication' – first of 'Arthur Blord' series by E. Mayne Hull, ASTOUNDING

May *Gather, Darkness!* by Fritz Leiber (three-part serial), ASTOUNDING

Aug 'Greenface' – first story by James H. Schmitz, UNKNOWN

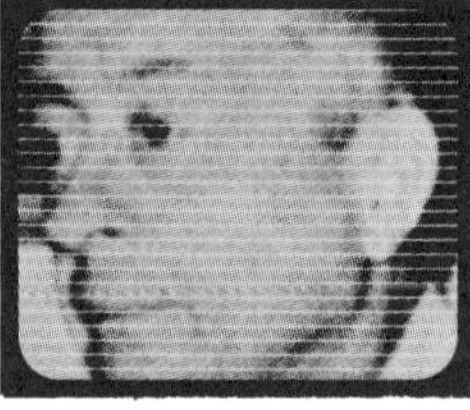

Sept 'Robinc' by Anthony Boucher (H. H. Holmes), ASTOUNDING

Oct *The Book of Ptath* by A. E. van Vogt, UNKNOWN WORLDS

Oct 'Fifty Million Monkeys' by Raymond F. Jones, ASTOUNDING

B

The Pocket Book of Science Fiction – first anthology to be edited by Donald A. Wollheim

Perelandra by C. S. Lewis

Donovan's Brain by Curt Siodmak

F

Fan

1943 Jack Speer makes tour of US fandom

1943 Larry B. Farsace's *Golden Atom* aborts

1943 Forrest J. Ackerman holds Staplecon 1 convention in his Staples Avenue home

1943 NFFF hold first ballot for awards

Feb Beak Talor (Canada) launches *8-Ball*

Apr Splinter groups split LASFS

Apr BFS sponsor UK con in Leicester (Midvention)

early Futurians expel Isaac Asimov, Leslie Perri and Robert G. Thompson

July *8-Ball* becomes *Canadian Fandom*

July Bob Tucker launches *Fanewscard*

July Francis T. Laney launches *Fan-Dango*

Sum Claude Degler hitch-hikes round US fandom organising Cosmic Circle; feuds with LASFS and NFFF

Sept Claude Degler launches *Cosmic Circle Commentator* and large number of other fanzines

Oct Third Michicon becomes house-warming for Slan Shack as Al and Mrs Ashley, Walt Liebscher and Jack Weidenbeck move in

Nov Francis T. Laney moves to Los Angeles, starts crusade to clean up LASFS

Dec A. Langley Searles launches *Fantasy Commentator*

1944

Apr Gerald G. Swan (UK) produce one issue of FUTURE (a reprint magazine)

Spr Standard Magazines' CAPTAIN FUTURE aborts

Fall Sam Merwin, Jr becomes editor at Standard Magazines

Jan 'Far Centaurus' by A. E. van Vogt, ASTOUNDING

Mar 'The Children's Hour' by Lawrence O'Donnell (Henry Kuttner and C. L. Moore), ASTOUNDING

Mar 'Deadline' by Cleve Cartmill, ASTOUNDING

May 'This Means War' – first story by A. Bertram Chandler, ASTOUNDING

May 'City' – first of series by Clifford D. Simak, ASTOUNDING

June 'Arena' by Fredric Brown, ASTOUNDING

Fall 'Shadow over Mars' by Leigh Brackett, STARTLING

Nov 'Killdozer!' by Theodore Sturgeon, ASTOUNDING

Dec 'No Woman Born' by C. L. Moore, ASTOUNDING

Sirius by Olaf Stapledon

Ape and Essence by Aldous Huxley

The Lady and the Monster (based on Siodmak's *Donovan's Brain*) filmed by Republic

End of Third Fandom (Speer)

1944 Futurians elected to FAPA offices, but set up competing Vanguard APA

Jan *Cosmic Circle Commentator becomes The National Futurian Weekly*

Feb Phil Bronson's *The Fantasite* aborts

Spr Jack Speer exposes Claude Degler in *Investigation in New-castle*; FAPA suspends Degler, who apologises for fraud

Mar Cosmic Circle dies

Mar New Fandom-Futurian feud cools

Spr LASFS feud intensifies

Spr Cosmos Club (UK) organises convention at Teddington (Eastercon)

Jun Donald A. Wollheim's *The FAPA Fan* aborts

July Claude Degler's *The National Futurian Weekly* aborts

Oct Convention in Chicago (Little Chicon)

Oct Philadelphia Futurians merge with PSFS

Nov Bob Tucker's *Le Zombie* becomes irregular

Dec NFFF's *Bonfire* becomes *The National Fantasy Fan*

1945

Wint Chester Whitehorn becomes editor at Love Romances Publishing

Mar 'I Remember Lemuria' – first story by Richard S. Shaver in 'Shaver Mystery' series, AMAZING

May 'First Contact' by Murray Leinster, ASTOUNDING

Sum 'The World-Thinker' – first story by Jack Vance, THRILLING WONDER

Aug *World of Ā* by A. E. van Vogt (three-part serial), ASTOUNDING

Fall 'Aftermath' by John Russell Fearn, STARTLING

Oct 'Giant Killer' by A. Bertram Chandler, ASTOUNDING

Dec 'Let Freedom Ring' – first story by Rog Phillips, AMAZING

Wint 'The Ultimate World' – first story by Bryce Walton, PLANET STORIES

That Hideous Strength by C. S. Lewis

Portable Novels of Science – anthology compiled by Donald A. Wollheim

1945 Fourth Fandom starts (Silverberg)

1945 Splits in Futurians; C. M. Kornbluth and others expelled

1945 Futurians elected out of FAPA

1945 *British Fantasy Society Bulletin* aborts

1945 Dagmar launches first Lemurian fanzine, *Maxin-96*

1945 SFL and New Fandom peter out

Jan J. Michael Rosenblum produces first British national fan directory

Feb Boskone 4, Last Boston convention until 1960s

Mar J. Michael Rosenblum's *Futurian War Digest* aborts

July William S. Sykora's *Fantasy News* mothballed

July Jack Speer launches *Stefnews*

July Fifth and last Michicon held at Slan Shack

mid-year Jack Speer moves to Seattle, holds first Seattle Con-fabulation

mid-Sum Crisis in NFFF and Slan Shack; E. Everett Evans leaves both

Aug Fanewscard becomes *The Fanews*; Walt Dunkelberger becomes editor

Sept Slan Shack break up

Dec Julius Unger's *Fantasy Fiction Field* aborts

Dec Bob Tucker launches *Bloomington News Letter*

01. PROGRAM

1946

MD

Feb Utopian Publications (UK) launch STRANGE TALES (editor: Walter H. Gillings)

Mar Utopian Publications' STRANGE TALES (UK) aborts

Apr Pendulum Publications (UK) launch NEW WORLDS (editor: E. J. Carnell)

June Hamilton & Co (sf editor: Dennis H. Pratt) launch AMAZING ADVENTURES (UK)

Aug William L. Hamling becomes assistant editor at Ziff-Davis Publishing

Fall Paul L. Payne becomes editor at Love Romances Publishing

Oct Outlands Publishing (UK) produce one issue of OUTLANDS (editor: Leslie J. Johnson)

Oct Hamilton & Co (UK) launch FUTURISTIC STORIES

Oct AMAZING ADVENTURES becomes STRANGE ADVENTURES

Nov Hamilton & Co's FUTURISTIC STORIES (UK) aborts

Dec Temple Bar Publishing (UK) launch FANTASY, (editor: Walter H. Gillings)

MS

Mar 'The Valley of Flame' by Keith Hammond (Henry Kuttner), STARTLING

Apr 'Loophole' – first story by Arthur C. Clarke, ASTOUNDING

May 'Placet is a Crazy Place' by Fredric Brown, ASTOUNDING

May 'Alexander the Bait' – first story by William Tenn (Philip Klass), ASTOUNDING

Sum 'The Dark World' by Henry Kuttner, STARTLING

Sum 'The Million Year Picnic' – first in 'Martian Chronicles' series by Ray Bradbury, PLANET STORIES

Nov 'Rocket to Limbo' – first story by Margaret St Clair, FANTASTIC ADVENTURES

Dec 'Metamorphosite' by Eric Frank Russell, ASTOUNDING

B

Slan by A. E. van Vogt

Adventures in Time and Space – milestone sf anthology, edited by Raymond J. Healy and J. Francis McComas

The Shade of Time – first sf novel by David Duncan

H. G. Wells dies 13 August

The Best of Science Fiction – first anthology compiled by Groff Conklin, another milestone

F

Fan

1946 Thomas P. Hadley founds one of the earliest 'fan' publishing houses (Hadley Publishing Co) to print hardbound books of fantasy classics; issues the *Skylark of Space* by E. E. ('Doc') Smith

1946 'White Horse' fan meetings begin in London

1946 Forrest J. Ackerman launches Big Pond Fund

1946 Lloyd A. Eshbach launches Fantasy Press

1946 Chet Geier and others launch Shaver Mystery Club and Shaver Mystery Magazine

Jan Donald A. Wollheim's *The Phantagraph* aborts

Mar Sam Moskowitz, the Null-A Men and others launch the Eastern Science Fiction Association, which holds first big post-war convention (Newarkon)

Spr Francis T. Laney and Duane Rimel's *The Acolyte* aborts

Apr Gus Willmorth Launches *Fantasy Advertiser*

July Fourth world convention (Pacificon), Los Angeles, sponsored by LASFS; Forrest J. Ackerman launches Fantasy Foundation; Walter Liebscher produces *Combozine*

Aug Jack Speer's *Stefnews* aborts

Fall Algis Budrys launches *Slantasy*

Oct Philadelphia annual conventions restart

Nov Convention in Chicago (Contracon)

Nov Montreal Science Fiction Society launched at McGill University

1947

Feb Avon Publishing (sf editor: Donald A. Wollheim) launch AVON FANTASY READER

Mar Gerald G. Swan launches AMERICAN FICTION (UK) which aborts in May

Spr Pendulum Publications (UK) collapse; NEW WORLDS mothballed

July Fantasy Publishing launch FANTASY BOOK (Editor: William H. Crawford, under the pseudonym of Garrett Ford)

Aug Temple Bar Publishing's FANTASY (UK) aborts

Dec Hamilton & Co's FUTURISTIC STORIES and STRANGE ADVENTURES (UK) abort

Dec Ziff-Davis Publishing re-launch AMAZING STORIES QUARTERLY (yet more reissues)

Mar 'Tomorrow's Children' – first story by Poul Anderson (in collaboration with F. N. Waldrop), ASTOUNDING

Apr 'Time and Time Again' – first story by H. Beam Piper, ASTOUNDING

May 'E for Effort' – first story by T. L. Sherred, ASTOUNDING

May *Fury* by Lawrence O'Donnell (Henry Kuttner and C. L. Moore) (three-part serial), ASTOUNDING

July 'With Folded Hands . . .' by Jack Williamson, ASTOUNDING

Sept 'Lord of the Storm' by Henry Kuttner (as Keith Hammond), STARTLING STORIES

Sept 'The Star Kings' by Edmond Hamilton, AMAZING

Nov *Children of the Lens* by E. E. ('Doc') Smith (four-part serial and final novel of the 'Lensman' series), ASTOUNDING

Nov 'Thunder and Roses' by Theodore Sturgeon, ASTOUNDING

Nov 'The Man in the Iron Cap' by Murray Leinster, STARTLING

Dec 'Age of Unreason' – first story by Alfred Coppel, ASTOUNDING

Of Worlds Beyond! The Science of Science Fiction Writing edited by Lloyd Arthur Eshbach

Greener Than You Think by Ward Moore

1947 Prime Press founded by James Williams, Oswald Train, Alfred Prime and Bud Waldo

1947 Hydra Club – a semi-professional fan club – founded in New York City by Frederik Pohl, Lester del Rey and others

1947 Algis Budrys's *Slantasy* aborts

1947 Science Fantasy Society (UK) launched, Vincent Clarke later (1949) revives pre-war *Science Fantasy News* as its organ

1947 British Fantasy Society fades

1947 Portland Science fantasy Society sponsors Northwest Fantasy convention

Jan *PSFS News* aborts

Feb Walter H. Gillings (UK) launches *Fantasy Review*

Apr Art Rapp launches *Spacewarp*

July Forrest J. Ackerman's *VOM* aborts

Mid year Don Wilson launches *Dream Quest*

Sum Jack Speer's *Sustaining Program* aborts

Sum Marion Zimmer Bradley launches *Astra's Tower*

Aug Australian fandom expands, Futurian Society of Sydney restarts

Aug Sept PSFS's Philcon Society sponsor fifth world convention, in Philadelphia; *Philcon Memory Book* produced

Sept Beak Taylor's *Canadian Fandom* aborts

Sept Vernon Coriell launches *The Burroughs Bulletin*

Sept Ken Slater participates in a revival of UK fandom, launches *Operation Fantast* and organisation of same name

Fall Ron Maddox launches *The Spectator*

1948

MD

Jan William L. Hamling becomes sf managing editor of Ziff-Davis Publishing

Jan Arkham House launch ARKHAM SAMPLER (editor: August Derleth)

Mar Popular Publications reactivate FANTASTIC NOVELS MAGAZINE

Spr Raymond A. Palmer establishes Clark Publishing Co and issues FATE

Oct Lila E. Schaffer becomes sf associate editor of Ziff-Davis Publishing

MS

Jan 'Guaranteed' – first story by E. Everett Evans, STARTLING STORIES

Mar *. . . and Searching Mind* by Jack Williamson (three-part serial), ASTOUNDING

Mar 'The Endochronic Properties of Resublimated Thiotimoline' – first (humorous) article by Isaac Asimov, ASTOUNDING

May 'The Strange Case of John Kingman' by Murray Leinster, ASTOUNDING

June 'That Only a Mother' – first story by Judith Merril, ASTOUNDING

June *Dreadful Sanctuary* by Eric Frank Russell (three-part serial), ASTOUNDING

July 'Hard Luck Diggings' – first of 'Magnus Ridolph' series by Jack Vance, STARTLING STORIES

Aug 'Time Trap' – first story by Charles L. Harness, ASTOUNDING

Sept *What Mad Universe* by Fredric Brown, STARTLING STORIES

Sept 'Dreams are Sacred' – first story by Peter Phillips, ASTOUNDING

Oct *The Players of $\bar{A}$* by A. E. van Vogt (four-part serial), ASTOUNDING

Nov *Against the Fall of Night* by Arthur C. Clarke, STARTLING STORIES

Nov 'In Hiding' by Wilmar H. Shiras, ASTOUNDING

Dec 'Bureau of Slick Tricks' – first in series by Horace B. Fyfe, ASTOUNDING

B

A Treasury of Science Fiction – anthology compiled by Groff Conklin

F TV

First of the *Superman* film serials begins

Fan

1948 James and Virginia Blish begin to dominate VAPA

1948 Art Rapp and others launch Michigan Science-Fantasy Society (The Misfits) and *The Michifan*

1948 LASFS and NFFF veer from fandom to science fiction interests

1948 Many Canadian groups formed, including Lakehead Science Fiction Society (Hamilton, Ontario) and Canadian Science Fiction Association, by Jack Bowie-Reed and others

1948 Forrest J. Ackerman, Redd Boggs and Richard Wilson, at Fantasy Foundation, produce *Fantasy Annual*

1948 Erle Korshak, Mark Reinsberg and T. E. (Ted) Dikty launch Shasta Publishing, produce Everett Bleiler's *The Checklist of Fantastic Literature*

1948 Francis T. Laney produces fan-memoirs *Ah! Sweet Idiocy!*

1948 Fan consortium launch Nova Publications (UK)

1948 Richard Abbott launches International Science Fiction Correspondence Club

Jan Walt Dunkelberger's *The Fanews* aborts

Jan *Shangri-L'Affaires* reverts to *Shangri-La*

Apr Oswald Train reactivates *The Fantasy Collector*

May First post-war UK convention, Whitcon, in London

July Bob Tucker's *Le Zombie* becomes infrequent

July Charles Lee Riddle launches *Peon*

July Sixth world convention at Toronto (Torcon) – first world convention outside USA

Aug William S. Sykora reactivates *Fantasy News*

Sept LASFS sponsors first West Coast Science-Fantasy Conference (Westercon), which becomes large annual regional convention

Oct Outlander Society launched as splinter from LASFS

Minnesota convention

Nov Walter A. Willis (UK) launches Irish fandom and produces *Slant* with James White and others

Wint Redd Boggs launches *Sky Hook*

1949

Jan Ejler Jacobsson becomes sf editor of Popular Publications, who reactivate SUPER SCIENCE STORIES

Feb Nova Publications (UK) reactivate NEW WORLDS (editor: Edward J. Carnell)

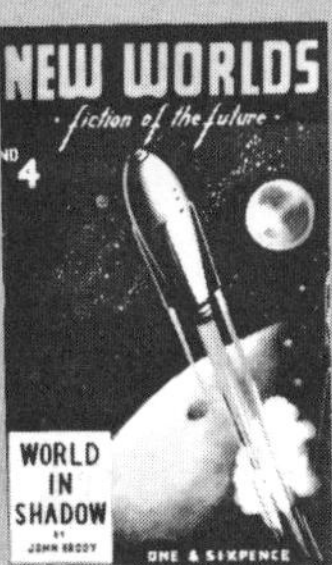

Fall ARKHAM SAMPLER aborts

Oct Mercury Press launch THE MAGAZINE OF FANTASY (general manager: Joseph W. Ferman; managing editor: Robert P. Mills; editors: Anthony Boucher, J. Francis McComas)

Nov Popular Publications launch CAPTAIN ZERO

Nov Clark Publishing launch OTHER WORLDS SCIENCE STORIES (editor: Raymond A. Palmer, in the first issues as Robert N. Webster)

Dec Popular Publications launch A. MERRITT'S FANTASY MAGAZINE

Jan 'Forbidden Voyage' – first of 'Conquest of Space' series by L. Ron Hubbard (as René Lafayette), STARTLING STORIES

Feb 'Christmas Tree' – first published story by Christopher Youd (chiefly known as John Christopher), ASTOUNDING

Feb *Seetee Shock* by Jack Williamson (as Will Stewart) (three-part serial), ASTOUNDING

May *Flight into Yesterday* by Charles L. Harness, STARTLING

May 'History Lesson' by Arthur C. Clarke, STARTLING STORIES

May *Needle* by Hal Clement (two-part serial), ASTOUNDING

July 'The Hand from the Stars' – first story by Kris Neville, SUPER SCIENCE STORIES

July 'The Animal Cracker Plot' by L. Sprague de Camp (two-part serial), first in 'Viagens Interplanetarias' series, ASTOUNDING.

Fall 'The Wheel is Death' – first story by Roger Dee, PLANET STORIES

Oct 'Defense Mechanism' – first story by Katherine MacLean, ASTOUNDING

Dec 'The Witches of Karres' by James H. Schmitz, ASTOUNDING

Wint 'Tubemonkey' – first story by Jerome Bixby, PLANET STORIES

The Best SF Stories, 1949. First annual sf anthology edited by E. F. Bleiler and T. E. Dikty

Nineteen Eighty-four by George Orwell

Captain Video TV series begins transmission in US

Fifth Fandom starts (Silverberg)

Apr Robert Silverberg and Saul Diskin launch *Spaceship*

Apr 'Loncon' Convention in London (UK)

Apr Donald B. Day and others hold Northwest Fantasy convention

Sum The Elves, Gnomes and Little Men's Science Fiction, Chowder and Marching Society launch *Rhodomagnetic Digest*

Sept Seventh world convention at Cincinnati (Cinvention); Big Pond Fund brings E. J. Carnell from UK; first ballots for following year's bid

Fall Outlander Society launches *The Outlander*

Aug *Fantasy Review* becomes *Science-Fantasy Review*

Aug Ken Bulmer launches *Nirvana* (UK)

Oct Art Rapp launches *Postwarp*

Nov *Misfits* aborts

Late Gnome Press launched by David Kyle and Martin Greenberg

01. PROGRAM

1950

MD

Jan Howard Browne becomes sf editor of Ziff-Davis Publishing

Jan THE MAGAZINE OF FANTASY becomes THE MAGAZINE OF FANTASY AND SCIENCE FICTION (F&SF)

Mar Associated General Publications launch first Australian sf magazine, THRILLS INCORPORATED

Mar CAPTAIN ZERO aborts

Apr Standard Magazines launch FANTASTIC STORY QUARTERLY

May Magabooks Inc launch FANTASY FICTION (editor: Curtis Mitchell)

May Columbia Publications launch new series of FUTURE COMBINED WITH SCIENCE FICTION STORIES

June Standard Magazines launch WONDER STORY ANNUAL

June John Spencer & Co (UK) launch WORLDS OF FANTASY

June Popular Press (UK) produce one issue of COSMIC SCIENCE STORIES (a reprint)

July Nova Publications (UK) launch SCIENCE-FANTASY, edited by Walter H. Gillings (hyphen dropped in 1954)

MS

Jan 'Scanners Live in Vain' – first story by Cordwainer Smith, FANTASY BOOK No 6

Feb 'No Teeth for the Tiger' – first story by Paul Fairman, AMAZING

Feb *The Dreaming Jewels* by Theodore Sturgeon, FANTASTIC ADVENTURES

Mar 'Trespass!' – first story by Gordon R. Dickson (in collaboration with Poul Anderson), FANTASTIC STORIES QUARTERLY (Spring)

Apr 'Okie' – first of 'Cities in Flight' series by James Blish, ASTOUNDING

Apr 'Isolationist' – first story by Mack Reynolds, FANTASTIC ADVENTURES

May 'Dianetics, the Evolution of a Science' by L. Ron Hubbard (non-fiction), ASTOUNDING

Sum 'Born of Man and Woman' – first story by Richard Matheson, F&SF

B

The Martian Chronicles, collection by Ray Bradbury

Pebble in the Sky by Isaac Asimov

Shot in the Dark – first anthology compiled by Judith Merril

The Voyage of the Space Beagle by A. E. van Vogt

F TV

Destination Moon (based on Heinlein's *Rocketship Galileo*) directed by Irving Pichel for Universal International

Tom Corbett: Space Cadet TV series begins transmission in US

Fan

1950 Sixth Fandom starts (Silverberg)

1950 L. Ron Hubbard launches Dianetics

1950 Futurian Society of Sydney finally aborts; Australian Science Fiction Society launched; *Omara* launched in New South Wales

1950 Vernon Coriell's *The Burroughs Bulletin* aborts

1950 *The National Fantasy Fan* becomes infrequent

1950 Manly Bannister launches *Nekromantikon*

1950 The Nameless launch *Cry of the Nameless* (later *Cry*)

July Avon Publishing launch OUT OF THIS WORLD ADVENTURES (editor: Donald A. Wollheim)

Sum Jerome Bixby becomes editor at Love Romances Publishing

Aug John Spencer & Co (UK) launch FUTURISTIC SCIENCE STORIES

Sept John Spencer & Co (UK) launch TALES OF TOMORROW

Oct Galaxy Publishing (sf editor: Horace L. Gold) launch GALAXY SCIENCE FICTION

Oct Clark Publishing launch IMAGINATION (managing editor: Beatrice Mahaffey; editor: Raymond A. Palmer)

Oct Popular Publications' A. MERRITT'S FANTASY MAGAZINE aborts

Nov Beatrice Mahaffey becomes managing editor of OTHER WORLDS SCIENCE STORIES

Nov Red Circle Publications reactivate MARVEL SCIENCE STORIES

Nov John Spencer & Co (UK) launch WONDERS OF THE SPACEWAYS

Nov Magabooks Inc's FANTASY FICTION becomes FANTASY STORIES, then aborts

Dec Hillman Periodicals launch WORLDS BEYOND (editor: Damon Knight)

Dec Love Romances Publishing launch TWO COMPLETE SCIENCE ADVENTURE BOOKS (editor: Malcolm Reiss)

Dec Avon Publishing's OUT OF THIS WORLD ADVENTURES aborts

June 'Incommunicado' by Katherine MacLean, ASTOUNDING

July 'The Little Black Bag' by C. M. Kornbluth, ASTOUNDING

July 'City at World's End' by Edmond Hamilton, STARTLING

July *Earth's Last Citadel* by Henry Kuttner and C. L. Moore, FANTASTIC NOVELS

Sept 'The Eternal Eve' by John Wyndham, AMAZING

Nov 'The Land of Lost Content' – first published story by Chad Oliver, SUPER SCIENCE FICTION

Dec 'The Mindworm' by C. M. Kornbluth, WORLDS BEYOND

Dec 'The Curfew Tolls' – first story by J. T. McIntosh, ASTOUNDING

Wint-Spr 'Elephas Frumenti' and 'The Gift of God' – first stories in 'Gavagan's Bar' series by L. Sprague de Camp and Fletcher Pratt, F&SF

1950 Harlan Ellison joins Cleveland fan club

1950 First Midwestcon held (later called Relaxicon)

Apr *Bloomington News Letter* becomes *Science Fiction News Letter*

June William S. Sykora's *Fantasy News* aborts

July First Southern US convention in Florida

July Three-day convention organised by ESFA and the Hydra Club in New York City

July *Science-Fantasy Review* (UK) turns professional

Aug Lee Hoffman launches *Quandry*

Sept Eighth world convention in Portland, Oregon (Norwescon), sponsored by The Nameless (organised by Donald B. Day)

Dec Marion Zimmer Bradley's *Astra's Tower* aborts

Dec VAPA aborts

01. PROGRAM

1951

MD

Jan William L. Hamling leaves Ziff-Davis Publishing, forms Greenleaf Publishing (editor: Hamling), buys IMAGINATION STORIES OF SCIENCE AND FANTASY

Jan Hamilton & Co (UK) launch AUTHENTIC SCIENCE FICTION SERIES (editor: L. G. Holmes)

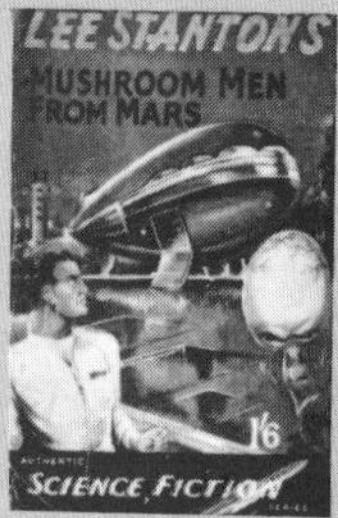

Jan Fantasy Publishing's FANTASY BOOK aborts

Feb Hillman Periodicals' WORLDS BEYOND aborts

Feb AUTHENTIC SCIENCE FICTION SERIES (UK) becomes SCIENCE FICTION FORTNIGHTLY; H. J. Campbell becomes technical editor

Mar Avon Publishing produce one issue only of 10 STORY FANTASY

Mar Pembertons (UK) launch AMAZING SCIENCE STORIES

Mar Ziff-Davis Publishing's FANTASTIC ADVENTURES QUARTERLY aborts

Mar Lila E. Schaffer becomes managing editor of Ziff-Davis Publishing

Apr Avon Publishing launch AVON SCIENCE FICTION READER

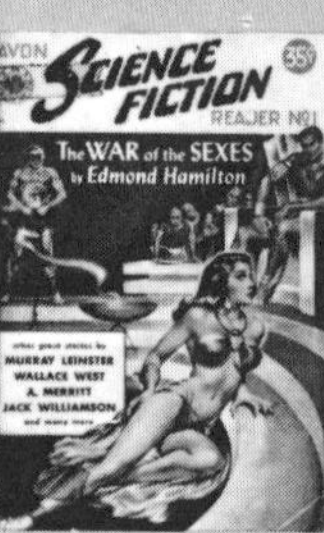

MS

Jan '"The Devil, You Say?"' – first story by Charles Beaumont, AMAZING STORIES

Jan 'The Secret of the Death Dome' – first sf magazine story by Walter M. Miller, Jr, AMAZING STORIES

Feb 'Rock Diver' – first story by Harry Harrison, WORLDS BEYOND

Feb 'The Fireman' by Ray Bradbury, GALAXY

Mar 'Protected Species' by H. B. Fyfe, ASTOUNDING

Mar 'High Threshold' – first story by Alan E. Nourse, ASTOUNDING

Mar 'Sentinel of Eternity' by Arthur C. Clarke, 10 STORY FANTASY

Apr 'In This Sign' by Ray Bradbury, IMAGINATION

Apr 'The Marching Morons' by C. M. Kornbluth, GALAXY

B

The Sands of Mars by Arthur C. Clarke

The Weapon Shops of Isher by A. E. van Vogt

F

When Worlds Collide directed by Rudolf Mare for Paramount

The Day the Earth Stood Still directed by Robert Wise for Twentieth Century-Fox

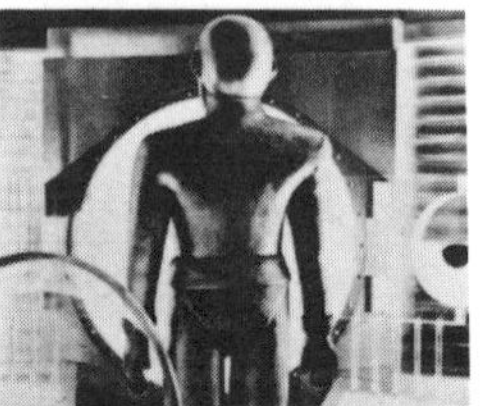

Fan

01. PROGRAM

Apr Pembertons' AMAZING SCIENCE STORIES (UK) aborts

Apr FANTASTIC STORY QUARTERLY becomes FANTASTIC STORY QUARTERLY/MAGAZINE

May Columbia Publications launch new series of SCIENCE FICTION QUARTERLY

May SCIENCE FICTION FORTNIGHTLY (UK) becomes SCIENCE FICTION MONTHLY

June Popular Publications' FANTASTIC NOVELS MAGAZINE mothballed

June FANTASTIC STORY QUARTERLY/MAGAZINE becomes FANTASTIC STORY MAGAZINE

Aug Popular Publications' SUPER SCIENCE STORIES aborts

Aug MARVEL SCIENCE STORIES becomes MARVEL SCIENCE FICTION

Sept Malcolm Reiss becomes editor at Love Romances Publishing

Sept SCIENCE FICTION MONTHLY (UK) becomes AUTHENTIC SCIENCE FICTION

Nov Sam Mines becomes editor at Standard Magazines

Dec Ziff-Davis Publishing's AMAZING STORIES QUARTERLY aborts

Wint E. J. Carnell becomes editor of SCIENCE-FANTASY (UK)

May 'Izzard and the Membrane' by Walter M. Miller, ASTOUNDING

June 'Angel's Egg' by Edgar Pangborn, GALAXY

June 'No Short Cuts' – first story by E. C. Tubb, NEW WORLDS

July '''You'll Never Go Home Again''' by Clifford D. Simak, FANTASTIC ADVENTURES

Aug 'Beyond Bedlam' by Wyman Guin, GALAXY

Aug 'The Monkey Wrench' by Gordon R. Dickson, ASTOUNDING

Sept 'Welcome, Stranger!' – first story by Alan Barclay, NEW WORLDS

Sept 'If I Forget Thee, Oh Earth' by Arthur C. Clarke, FUTURE

Sept *The Puppet Masters* by Robert A. Heinlein (three-part serial), GALAXY

Oct 'Of Time and Third Avenue' by Alfred Bester, F&SF

Oct *Iceworld* by Hal Clement (three-part serial), ASTOUNDING

Nov 'Betyann' by Kris Neville, NEW TALES OF SPACE AND TIME (editor: Raymond J. Healy)

Dec 'Come on Wagon' – first sf magazine story by Zenna Henderson, F&SF

The Day of the Triffids by John Wyndham

1951 Donald B. Day produces *Checkindex* (with help from others)

1951 Russ Watkins launches Crusade to Clean up Fandom (CCF)

1951 Science Fantasy Society (UK) aborts

Apr Recently-formed Fantasy Veterans Association (Fan-Vets) hold their first convention

Spr Bob Shaw (UK) becomes associate editor of *Slant*

May European International Convention (Festivention) in London launches International Fantasy Awards

Sept Ninth world convention in New Orleans (Nolacon)

01. PROGRAM

1952

MD

Jan Avon Publishing's AVON FANTASY READER and AVON FICTION READER mothballed

Jan FUTURE COMBINED WITH SCIENCE FICTION STORIES becomes FUTURE SCIENCE FICTION STORIES

Feb Derrick Rowles becomes editor of AUTHENTIC SCIENCE FICTION (UK)

Mar James L. Quinn's Quinn Publishing launch IF, WORLDS OF SCIENCE FICTION (editor: Paul W. Fairman)

Mar Jack O'Sullivan becomes editor, Malcolm Reiss managing editor, at Love Romances Publishing

Apr FAMOUS FANTASTIC MYSTERIES reabsorbs FANTASTIC NOVELS MAGAZINE

May John Raymond launches SPACE SCIENCE FICTION (editor: Lester del Rey)

May Red Circle Publications' MARVEL SCIENCE FICTION aborts

May FUTURE SCIENCE FICTION STORIES becomes FUTURE SCIENCE FICTION (reverts to previous title in Sept and back to new title in Nov)

June Associated General Publications' THRILLS INCORPORATED (Australia) aborts

June Malian Press (Australia) launch AMERICAN SCIENCE FICTION SERIES

July Ziff-Davis Publishing launch FANTASTIC

MS

Jan 'Alien Analysis' – first story by Dan Morgan, NEW WORLDS

Jan *The Demolished Man* by Alfred Bester (three-part serial), GALAXY

Feb 'Bridge' by James Blish, ASTOUNDING

Mar 'Rebirth' – first sf story by Daniel F. Galouye, IMAGINATION

Apr 'Letters to the Editor' – first sf magazine story by Ron Goulart, F&SF

Apr 'Looking for Something' – first story by Frank Herbert, STARTLING STORIES

May 'What Have I Done?' – first story by Mark Clifton, ASTOUNDING

May 'Precedent' – first story by Daniel Keyes, MARVEL SF

May 'Final Examination' – first sf magazine story by Robert Sheckley, IMAGINATION

May *Gravy Planet* (*The Space Merchants*), GALAXY (three-part serial) by Frederik Pohl and C. M. Kornbluth

June 'The Spectre General' – first story by Theodore R. Cogswell, ASTOUNDING

June 'The Business, as Usual' by Mack Reynolds, in F&SF

July 'Beyond Lies the Wub' – first sf story by Philip K. Dick in PLANET STORIES

B

Jack of Eagles by James Blish

Player Piano by Kurt Vonnegut Jr

F TV

Fan

1952 First regular annual Australian national convention held

1952 W. Max Keasler and Bill Venable launch Fanvariety Enterprises; Harlan Ellison becomes involved

1952 Donald B. Day publishes *The Index to the Science Fiction Magazines, 1926–1950*

May Walt Willis and Chuck Harris (UK) launch *Hyphen*

Aug Capitol Stories launch FANTASTIC SCIENCE FICTION (Editor: Walter B. Gibson)

Sept Paul W. Fairman leaves Quinn Publishing, becomes associate editor at Ziff-Davis Publishing

Sept Peter Hamilton's Crown Point Publications (UK) launch NEBULA SCIENCE FICTION (editor: Hamilton)

Sept Willy Ley becomes science editor of GALAXY SCIENCE FICTION

Sept Fanny Ellsworth becomes managing editor of Standard Magazines

Oct Standard Magazines launch SPACE STORIES

Nov John Raymond launches SCIENCE FICTION ADVENTURES (editor: Lester del Rey, as Philip St John)

Nov Robert W. Lowndes becomes sf editor of Columbia Publications

Dec Columbia Publications launch DYNAMIC SCIENCE FICTION

Dec Capitol Stories' FANTASTIC SCIENCE FICTION aborts

Dec H. J. Campbell becomes editor of AUTHENTIC SCIENCE FICTION (UK)

Aug 'The Lovers' – first sf story by Philip José Farmer, STARTLING

Aug 'Counterfeit' by Alan E. Nourse, THRILLING WONDER

Aug 'Surface Tension' by James Blish, GALAXY

Sept 'The Fly' by Arthur Porges, F&SF

Sept 'Big Planet' by Jack Vance, STARTLING

Oct 'In a Day of Victory' – first story by Irving E. Cox, Jr, FANTASTIC ADVENTURES

Oct 'Ararat' – first 'People' story by Zenna Henderson, F&SF

Oct 'Baby is Three' by Theodore Sturgeon, GALAXY

Oct *The Currents of Space*, by Isaac Asimov (three-part serial), ASTOUNDING

Nov 'Walk to the World' – first sf story by Algis Budrys, SPACE SF

Nov 'The Martian Way' by Isaac Asimov, GALAXY

Nov 'Bring the Jubilee' by Ward Moore, F&SF

Nov 'Command Performance' by Walter M. Miller, GALAXY

Dec 'What's it Like Out There?' by Edmond Hamilton, THRILLING WONDER

Dec 'The Reluctant Weapon' – first story by Howard L. Myers, GALAXY

Dec 'Sail On! Sail On!' by Philip José Farmer, STARTLING

Tales of Tomorrow TV series begins transmission in US

The Thing from Another World directed by Christian Nyby for Winchester Pictures

Sum Nor'west Science Fantasy Club (UK) launches *Astroneer* (edited by Paul L. Sowerby and Harry Turner)

Aug-Sept Tenth world convention in Chicago (10th Worldcon); Willis Fund brings Walt Willis from Northern Ireland

01. PROGRAM

1953

MD

Jan Avon Publishing launch AVON SCIENCE FICTION AND FANTASY READER from AVON FANTASY READER and AVON SCIENCE FICTION READER (editor: Sol Cohen)

Jan AUTHENTIC SCIENCE FICTION (UK) becomes AUTHENTIC SCIENCE FICTION MONTHLY

Feb John Raymond launches FANTASY MAGAZINE (editor: Lester del Rey)

Feb Standard Magazines' WONDER STORY ANNUAL aborts

Feb Damon Knight becomes book editor of SCIENCE FICTION ADVENTURES

Mar Hugo Gernsback's Gernsback Publications launch SCIENCE FICTION PLUS (managing editor: Sam Moskowitz; editor: Gernsback)

Mar Love Romances Publishing launch TOPS IN SCIENCE FICTION

Mar NEW WORLDS (UK) becomes NEW WORLDS SCIENCE FICTION

Apr John Raymond launches ROCKET STORIES (editor: Lester del Rey as Wade Kaempfert)

Apr Avon Publishing's AVON SCIENCE FICTION AND FANTASY READER aborts

May Specific Fiction Corp (sf editor: Chester Whitehorn) launch VORTEX SCIENCE FICTION

May Larry T. Shaw becomes associate editor of IF, WORLDS OF SCIENCE FICTION

May FANTASTIC absorbs FANTASTIC ADVENTURES

June Leo Margulies' King-Size Publications launch FANTASTIC UNIVERSE SCIENCE FICTION (editor: Sam Merwin, Jr)

June Popular Publications' FAMOUS FANTASTIC MYSTERIES aborts

June Standard Magazines' SPACE STORIES aborts

June FANTASY MAGAZINE becomes FANTASY FICTION MAGAZINE

Sum OTHER WORLDS SCIENCE STORIES splits to form SCIENCE STORIES (editor: Raymond A. Palmer) and UNIVERSE SCIENCE FICTION (editor: George Bell)

July Galaxy Publishing launch BEYOND FANTASY FICTION

MS

Jan 'Chessboard' – first sf magazine story by Jonathan F. Burke, NEW WORLDS

Jan 'Assisted Passage' first story by James White, NEW WORLDS

Feb 'The Nine Billion Names of God' by Arthur C. Clarke, STAR SF STORIES (editor: Frederik Pohl)

Mar *Police Your Planet* by Erik Van Lhin (Lester del Rey) (four-part serial), SF ADVENTURES

Mar 'Thou Good and Faithful' – first sf magazine story by John Brunner (as John Loxmith), ASTOUNDING

Mar 'The Rose' by Charles L. Harness, AUTHENTIC

Mar 'The Moon is Death' by Raymond F. Jones, FUTURE

Apr 'Unready to Wear' – first sf magazine story by Kurt Vonnegut, Jr, GALAXY

Apr 'Made in USA' by J. T. McIntosh, GALAXY

Apr *Mission of Gravity* by Hal Clement (four-part serial), ASTOUNDING

May 'Lot' by Ward Moore, F&SF

May 'Liberation of Earth' by William Tenn, FUTURE

May 'Jupiter V' by Arthur C. Clarke, IF

June 'Imposter' by Philip K. Dick, ASTOUNDING

June 'Nightmare Planet' by Murray Leinster, SF PLUS

B

Fahrenheit 451 by Ray Bradbury

Childhood's End by Arthur C. Clarke

Bring the Jubilee by Ward Moore

More Than Human by Theodore Sturgeon

F

Journey Into Space radio series begins transmission in UK

Quatermass TV series begins transmission in UK

Fan

July Frew Publications (Australia) launch FUTURE SCIENCE FICTION and POPULAR SCIENCE FICTION (editorial adviser: Vol Molesworth)

Aug Hanro Corp launch ORBIT SCIENCE FICTION (editor: Jules Saltman)

Sept Star Publications launch COSMOS SCIENCE FICTION AND FANTASY MAGAZINE (editor: L. B. Cole)

Sept John Raymond's ROCKET STORIES and SPACE SCIENCE FICTION abort

Sept Malcolm Reiss becomes editor of TOPS IN SCIENCE FICTION

Oct Love Romances Publishing's TOPS IN SCIENCE FICTION aborts

Oct Clark Publishing launch SCIENCE STORIES

Oct Specific Fiction Corp's VORTEX SCIENCE FICTION aborts

Nov John Raymond's FANTASY FICTION MAGAZINE aborts

Nov One issue only of WORLDS OF THE UNIVERSE (UK)

Dec Fantasy Publications launch SPACE WAY STORIES OF THE FUTURE

Dec Columbia Publications launch new series of SCIENCE FICTION STORIES

Dec Gernsback Publications' SCIENCE FICTION PLUS aborts

Dec Raymond A. Palmer becomes editor of UNIVERSE SCIENCE FICTION

Dec Sam Merwin Jr becomes associate editor of Galaxy Publishing

Dec Harry Harrison becomes editor of SCIENCE FICTION ADVENTURES

Wint Katherine Daffron becomes editor of TWO COMPLETE SCIENCE ADVENTURE BOOKS

Wint Paul W. Fairman becomes sf managing editor of Ziff-Davis Publishing

July 'A Bad Day For Sales' by Fritz Leiber, GALAXY

July 'Babel II' by Damon Knight, BEYOND

Aug 'Common Time' by James Blish, SF QUARTERLY

Aug 'Spacebred Generations' by Clifford D. Simak, SF PLUS

Sept 'The Wall Around the World' by Theodore R. Cogswell, BEYOND

Sept 'Repulsion Factor' – first sf magazine story by Charles Eric Maine, AUTHENTIC

Sept 'A Case of Conscience' by James Blish, IF

Oct 'Keyhole' and 'Women Only' – double debut of Marion Zimmer Bradley in VORTEX

Oct 'The Gulf Between' – first story by Tom Godwin, ASTOUNDING

Oct 'Freedom of the Race' – first story by Anne McCaffrey, SF PLUS

Oct 'The Haunting' – first story by Arthur Sellings, AUTHENTIC

Oct *The Caves of Steel* by Isaac Asimov (three-part serial), GALAXY

Nov 'Expatriate' – first sf magazine story by Larry M. Harris (Laurence Janifer), COSMOS

Dec 'Sustained Pressure' by Eric Frank Russell, NEBULA

Dec *The Syndic* by C. M. Kornbluth (two-part serial), SF ADVENTURES

War of the Worlds directed by Byron Haskins for Paramount

1953 Seventh Fandom starts (Weinstein – including The Phony Seventh

1953 Ron Smith launches *Inside Science Fiction*

1953 Max Keasler's *Opus* aborts

Sept Eleventh world convention in Philadelphia (11th World-con); first Science Fiction Achievement (Hugo) Awards made

Nov Lee Hoffman's *Quandry* aborts

01. PROGRAM

1954

MD

Jan Scion Ltd. (UK) launch VARGO STATTEN SCIENCE FICTION MAGAZINE (editor: Alistair Paterson)

Jan Columbia Publications' DYNAMIC SCIENCE FICTION aborts

Jan Beatrice Jones becomes editor of FANTASTIC UNIVERSE SCIENCE FICTION

Feb Specific Fiction Corp launch SCIENCE FICTION DIGEST

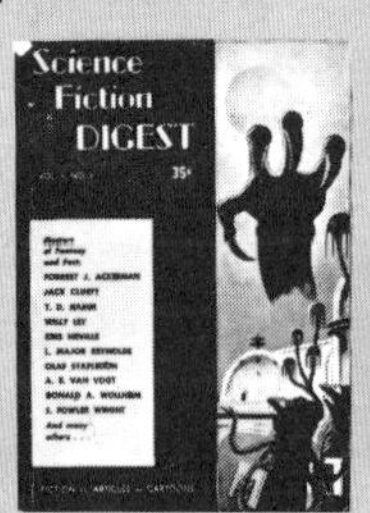

Mar Gerald G. Swan (UK) launch SPACE FACT AND FICTION

Mar Nova Publications (UK) absorbed by MacLarens Publishing, though name retained

Mar Love Romances Publishing's TWO COMPLETE SCIENCE ADVENTURE BOOKS aborts

Mar Larry T. Shaw leaves IF, WORLDS OF SCIENCE FICTION

Apr Clarke Publishing's SCIENCE STORIES mothballed

Apr John Spencer & Co's WONDERS OF THE SPACEWAYS (UK) aborts

May Specific Fiction Corp's SCIENCE FICTION DIGEST aborts

May Leo Margulies becomes editorial director of FANTASTIC UNIVERSE SCIENCE FICTION when Beatrice Jones leaves

May AMERICAN SCIENCE FICTION SERIES (Australia) becomes AMERICAN SCIENCE FICTION MAGAZINE

MS

Jan 'It's a *Good* Life' by Jerome Bixby, *Star SF 2* (anthology edited by Frederik Pohl)

Jan 'Anachron' by Damon Knight, IF

Feb 'The Prodigy' – first sf magazine story by Thomas N. Scortia, SF ADVENTURES

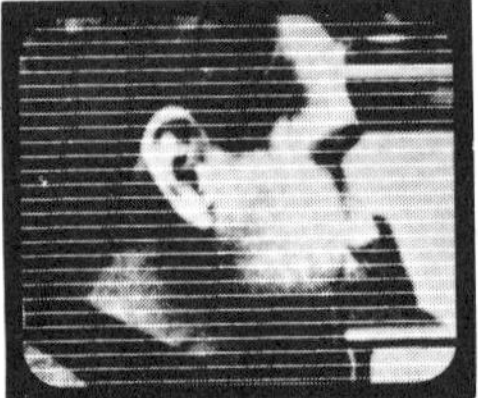

Feb 'Gorgon Planet' – first story by Robert Silverberg, NEBULA

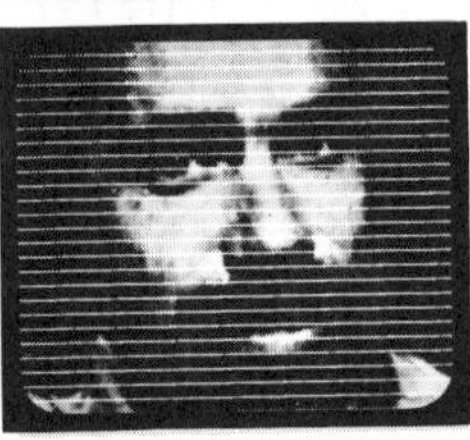

Feb *Sucker Bait* by Isaac Asimov (two-part serial), ASTOUNDING

Mar 'Stop-Over' – first sf magazine story by Robert F. Young, STARTLING

Mar 'The Draw' by Jerome Bixby, AMAZING

Apr 'First Down' – first sf magazine story by Ken Bulmer, AUTHENTIC

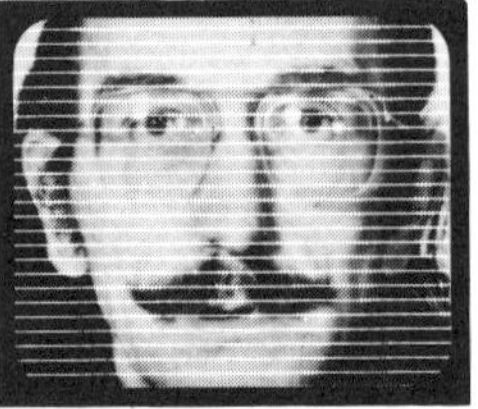

Apr 'The Midas Plague' by Frederik Pohl, GALAXY

May 'Combat's End' – first story by Barrington J. Bayley, VARGO STATTEN SF MAGAZINE

May 'At Death's End' by James Blish, ASTOUNDING

June 'Balaam' by Anthony Boucher, *9 Tales of Space and Time* (anthology edited by Raymond J. Healy)

B

I Am Legend by Richard Matheson

A Mirror for Observers by Edgar Pangborn

F

Fan

1954 Sam Moskowitz produces *The Immortal Storm*

1954 Richard Eney produces revised *Fancyclopedia*

1954 Donald H. Tuck (Australia) produces *Handbook of Science Fiction and Fantasy*

1954 Ken Bulmer, Vincent Clarke and others (UK) form Off-Trail Magazine Publishers Association (OIMPA)

01. PROGRAM

May VARGO STATTEN SCIENCE FICTION MAGAZINE (UK) becomes VARGO STATTEN BRITISH SCIENCE FICTION MAGAZINE

June John Raymond's SCIENCE FICTION ADVENTURES aborts

June John Spencer & Co's TALES OF TOMORROW (UK) aborts

June John Spencer & Co's WORLDS OF FANTASY (UK) aborts

July Star Publications' COSMOS SCIENCE FICTION AND FANTASY MAGAZINE aborts

Aug John Spencer & Co's FUTURISTIC SCIENCE STORIES (UK) aborts

Sept Francis W. McComas becomes advisory editor at Galaxy Publishing

Sept VARGO STATTEN BRITISH SCIENCE FICTION MAGAZINE (UK) becomes BRITISH SCIENCE FICTION MAGAZINE

Sept Short Stories Inc's WEIRD TALES aborts

Sept Greenleaf Publishing launch IMAGINATIVE TALES

Oct SPACE FACT AND FICTION (UK) aborts

Fall Alexander Samalman becomes sf editor of Standard Magazines

Nov BEYOND FANTASY FICTION becomes BEYOND FICTION

Nov Scion Press (UK) collapse; their printers, Dragon Publications, continue BRITISH SCIENCE FICTION MAGAZINE; John Russell Fearn becomes editor

Nov Hanro Corp's ORBIT SCIENCE FICTION aborts

Dec SPACEWAY STORIES OF THE FUTURE becomes SPACEWAY SCIENCE FICTION

Dec Sam Merwin Jr leaves Galaxy Publishing

June *Gladiator-at-Law* by Frederik Pohl and C. M. Kornbluth (three-part serial), GALAXY

July 'Criminal Record' – first published sf magazine story by Brian W. Aldiss, SCIENCE FANTASY

July 'My Boy Friend's Name is Jello' – first sf magazine story by Avram Davidson, FANTASY AND SCIENCE FICTION

Aug 'Fondly Fahrenheit' by Alfred Bester, F&SF

Aug 'The Cold Equations' by Tom Godwin, ASTOUNDING

Aug 'The Joy of Living' – first story by William F. Nolan, IF

Aug 'Aspect' – first story by Bob Shaw, NEBULA

Aug *They'd Rather Be Right* by Mark Clifton and Frank Riley (four-part serial), ASTOUNDING

Sept 'The Jar of Latakia' – first sf magazine story by Edmund Cooper, AUTHENTIC

Sept *For I am a Jealous People* by Lester del Rey, *Star SF Short Novels* (anthology edited by Frederik Pohl)

Oct 'Mister Fuller's Revolt' – first story by Roger Zelazny, LITERARY CAVALCADE

Oct 'The Big Rain' by Poul Anderson, ASTOUNDING

Nov 'How-2' by Clifford D. Simak, GALAXY

Dec 'And Gone Tomorrow' – first story by Andrew J. Offutt, IF

20,000 Leagues under the Sea directed by Richard Fleischer for Walt Disney Productions

Them! directed by Gordon Douglas for Warner Bros

Spr J. Michael Rosenblum (UK) launches *The New Futurian*

Sept Twelfth world convention in San Francisco (SFCon)

Nov *Inside Science Fiction* combines with *Science Fiction Advertiser* to become *Inside & Science Fiction Advertiser*

Dec Ethel Lindsay (UK) launches *Scottishe*

01. PROGRAM

1955

MD

Jan — Galaxy Publishing's BEYOND FICTION aborts

Jan — Standard Magazines' THRILLING WONDER STORIES aborts

Jan — SCIENCE FICTION STORIES assumes volume numbering of FUTURE SCIENCE FICTION

Mar — Frew Publications' FUTURE SCIENCE FICTION and POPULAR SCIENCE FICTION (Australia) aborts

Apr — Standard Magazines' FANTASTIC STORY MAGAZINE aborts

Apr — FANTASTIC becomes FANTASTIC SCIENCE FICTION

May — Malian Press (Australia) launch SELECTED SCIENCE FICTION

May — SCIENCE STORIES and UNIVERSE SCIENCE FICTION recombine as OTHER WORLDS SCIENCE STORIES (editor: Beatrice Mahaffey)

June — Fantasy Publishing's SPACEWAY SCIENCE FICTION mothballed

June — BRITISH SCIENCE FICTION MAGAZINE (UK) becomes BRITISH SPACE FICTION MAGAZINE

July — Love Romances Publishing's PLANET STORIES aborts

Sept — Atlas Publishing (Australia) launch SCIENCE FICTION MONTHLY

Sept — Malian Press's SELECTED SCIENCE FICTION (Australia) aborts

Sept — Malian Press's AMERICAN SCIENCE FICTION MAGAZINE (Australia) aborts

Sept — SCIENCE FICTION STORIES becomes THE ORIGINAL SCIENCE FICTION STORIES

Oct — IMAGINATION STORIES OF SCIENCE AND FANTASY becomes IMAGINATION SCIENCE FICTION

Oct — Standard Magazines' STARTLING STORIES aborts

Nov — Royal Publications (sf editor: Larry T. Shaw) launch INFINITY SCIENCE FICTION

Nov — Beatrice Mahaffey leaves Clarke Publishing

MS

Jan — 'The Darfstellar' by Walter M. Miller, ASTOUNDING

Jan — 'Tunnel Under the World' by Frederik Pohl, GALAXY

Feb — 'Grandpa' by James H. Schmitz, ASTOUNDING

Mar — 'Sense from Thought Divide' by Mark Clifton, ASTOUNDING

Apr — *A Canticle for Leibowitz* – first of series by Walter M. Miller, F&SF

May — 'Allamagoosa' by Eric Frank Russell, ASTOUNDING

May — 'Time Patrol' – first of series by Poul Anderson, F&SF

June — 'Final Weapon' by Everett B. Cole, ASTOUNDING

July — 'Father' by Philip José Farmer, F&SF

Aug — 'The Two-Handed Engine' by Henry Kuttner and C. L. Moore, F&SF

Sept — 'Blessed are the Meek' – first sf magazine story by G. C. Edmondson, ASTOUNDING

Sept — 'The Statics' – first story by Philip E. High, AUTHENTIC

Sept — 'The Brat' – first sf magazine story by Henry Slesar, IMAGINATIVE TALES

Oct — 'A Ticket to Tranai' by Robert Sheckley, GALAXY

Oct — 'The Game of Rat and Dragon' by Cordwainer Smith, GALAXY

Oct — 'The Light on Precipice Peak' – first sf story by Stephen Tall, GALAXY

Nov — 'The Star' by Arthur C. Clarke, INFINITY

Nov — *Under Pressure* by Frank Herbert (three-part serial), ASTOUNDING

Dec — 'Delanda Est' by Poul Anderson, F&SF

B

The End of Eternity by Isaac Asimov

Earthman Come Home by James Blish

The Long Tomorrow by Leigh Brackett

This Fortress World by James Gunn

Hell's Pavement by Damon Knight

Star Bridge by Jack Williamson and James Gunn

The Chrysalids (Re-birth) by John Wyndham

F

This Island Earth directed by Joseph Newman for Universal International

Forbidden Planet directed by Fred McLeod Wilcox for MGM

1984 directed by Michael Anderson for Holiday Productions

Fan

1955 — Eighth Fandom starts (Weinstein)

1955 — Ken Slater (UK) produces *British Science Fiction Book Index 1955*

1955 — Bob Tucker produces *The Neo-Fan's Guide* (publisher: Dean Grennell)

1955 — William Danner launches Fantasy Amateur Tape Exchange (FATE)

1955 — Pete Vorzimer launches The Cult (an apa)

1955 — Trans-Atlantic Fan Fund (TAFF) launched

Apr — Annual British convention becomes Eastercon

June — Greg and Jim Benford launch *Void*

Aug — Robert Silverberg's *Spaceship* aborts

Sept — Thirteenth world convention in Cleveland (Clevention); Hugo Awards become annual

Nov — *Inside & Science Fiction Advertiser* absorbs *Kay-Mar Trader*

Late — Ken Slater's Operation Fantast (UK) turns professional as Fantast (Medway) Ltd; *Operation Fantast* aborts

Late — Gnome Press launch *The Science-Fiction World* (editors: Robert Bloch and Bob Tucker)

1956

Feb Dragon Publications' BRITISH SPACE FICTION MAGAZINE (UK) aborts

Feb E. C. Tubb becomes editor of AUTHENTIC SCIENCE FICTION MONTHLY

Sept Paul W. Fairman becomes sf editor, and Cele G. Goldsmith sf associate editor, at Ziff-Davis Publishing

Oct Leo Margulies leaves King-Size Publications; Hans Stefan Santesson becomes editor

Oct J. Francis McComas leaves THE MAGAZINE OF FANTASY AND SCIENCE FICTION

Oct Leo Margulies's Renown Publications launch SATELLITE SCIENCE FICTION (editor: Sam Merwin, Jr)

Dec Royal Publications launch SCIENCE FICTION ADVENTURES

Dec Headline Publications launch SUPER SCIENCE FICTION (editor: W. W. Scott)

Jan 'Brightside Crossing' by Alan E. Nourse, GALAXY

Feb 'The Prisoner' – first story by Christopher Anvil, ASTOUNDING

Feb 'Glow-worm' – first story by Harlan Ellison, INFINITY

Feb 'Love Me Again' – first sf magazine story by Carol Emshwiller, SF QUARTERLY

Feb *Double Star* by Robert A. Heinlein (three-part serial), ASTOUNDING

Mar 'Exploration Team' by Murray Leinster, ASTOUNDING

Mar *Slave Ship* by Frederik Pohl (three-part serial), GALAXY

Apr 'Legwork' by Eric Frank Russell, ASTOUNDING

May 'Two by Two' by John Brunner, NEW WORLDS

June 'Blind Lightning' by Harlan Ellison, FANTASTIC UNIVERSE

July 'Gypped' – first story by Lloyd Biggle, Jr, GALAXY

Aug 'Time in Advance' by William Tenn, GALAXY

Sept 'Dust Rag' by Hal Clement, ASTOUNDING

Oct 'Jackpot' by Clifford D. Simak, GALAXY

Oct *The Naked Sun* by Isaac Asimov (three-part serial), ASTOUNDING

Oct *The Door into Summer* by Robert A. Heinlein (three-part serial), F&SF

Oct *The Stars My Destination* by Alfred Bester (four-part serial), GALAXY

Nov 'T' – first sf sale by Brian W. Aldiss, NEBULA

Dec 'Prima Belladonna' and 'Escapement' – double debut of J. G. Ballard, in SCIENCE FANTASY and NEW WORLDS respectively

The Death of Grass by John Christopher

The Pawns of Null-A by A. E. van Vogt

The Incredible Shrinking Man directed by Jack Arnold for Universal International

Invasion of the Body Snatchers directed by Don Siegel for Allied Artists

1956 Damon Knight, Judith Merril and James Blish organise first Milford Science Fiction Writers Conference

1956 Ken Bulmer's *Nirvana* aborts

1956 Lee Hoffman launches *Science-Fiction Five-Yearly*

1956 Ron Smith's *Inside* aborts

Mar Arthur Thomson (ATOM) becomes artist for *Scottishe* (UK)

June-July Terry Carr launches *Innuendo*

Sept Fourteenth world convention in New York (Newyorcon); World Science Fiction Society launched (re-formed annually at worldcons)

Sept Tom Perry launches *Logorrhea* (*Log*)

Oct LASFS hold their one-thousandth meeting

1957

MD

Jan Mercury Press launch VENTURE SCIENCE FICTION (editor: Robert P. Mills; advisory editor: Anthony Boucher)

Feb Cylvia Kleinman becomes editor of SATELLITE SCIENCE FICTION

Feb Atlas Publishing's SCIENCE FICTION MONTHLY (Australia) aborts

Feb Cele G. Goldsmith becomes sf managing editor at Ziff-Davis Publishing, who launch DREAM WORLD, STORIES OF INCREDIBLE POWER

Mar Robert C. Sproul's Cander Publishing launch SATURN, THE MAGAZINE OF SCIENCE FICTION (editor: Sproul; editorial consultant: Donald A. Wollheim)

Mar Republic Features Syndicate launch SPACE SCIENCE FICTION MAGAZINE (editor: Lyle Kenyon Engel)

Apr Frank P. Lualdi resurrects WONDER STORIES (continuing the old numbering) for one issue (editor: Jim Hendryx, Jr)

May SATURN, THE MAGAZINE OF SCIENCE FICTION becomes SATURN, MAGAZINE OF FANTASY AND SCIENCE FICTION

June OTHER WORLDS SCIENCE STORIES becomes FLYING SAUCERS FROM OTHER WORLDS

July SATURN, MAGAZINE OF FANTASY AND SCIENCE FICTION becomes SATURN, MAGAZINE OF SCIENCE FICTION AND FANTASY

Aug Ziff-Davis Publishing's DREAM WORLD, STORIES OF INCREDIBLE POWER aborts

Aug Republic Features Syndicate's SPACE SCIENCE FICTION MAGAZINE aborts

Sept Palmer Publishing's FLYING SAUCERS FROM OTHER WORLDS becomes a ufo magazine

Oct Hamilton & Co's AUTHENTIC SCIENCE FICTION MONTHLY (UK) aborts

MS

Jan 'Virgin Planet' by Poul Anderson, VENTURE

Feb 'Omnilingual' by H. Beam Piper, ASTOUNDING

Mar 'Survival Type' – first sf story by J. F. Bone, GALAXY

Apr 'Call Me Joe' by Poul Anderson, ASTOUNDING

Apr 'The Mile-Long Spaceship' by Kate Wilhelm, ASTOUNDING

May 'Ask Me Anything' by Damon Knight, GALAXY

June 'The Cage' by A. Bertram Chandler, F&SF

June *The Sky is Falling* by Lester del Rey, SATELLITE

July '. . . And then She Found Him' by Algis Budrys (as Paul Janvier)

Aug 'The Stainless Steel Rat' by Harry Harrison, ASTOUNDING

Sept 'Genius Loci' by Thomas N. Scortia, SCIENCE FICTION STORIES

Oct 'The Grandfather's War' by Murray Leinster, ASTOUNDING

Oct *Wolfbane* by Frederik Pohl and C. M. Kornbluth (two-part serial), GALAXY

Nov 'Sector General' – first of series by James White, NEW WORLDS

Dec 'Routine Emergency' – first sf magazine story by David R. Bunch, IF

Dec *The Languages of Pao* by Jack Vance, SATELLITE

B

Earthman's Burden, the 'Hoka' tales of Poul Anderson and Gordon R. Dickson

They Shall Have Stars by James Blish

The Deep Range by Arthur C. Clarke

The Black Cloud by Fred Hoyle

Atlas Shrugged by Ayn Rand

The Andromeda Nebula by Ivan Yefremov (USSR)

F TV

Fan

1957 Last International Fantasy Awards made

1957 Five Chicago fans launch Advent Press; first production: Damon Knight's *In Search of Wonder*

1957 Cheltenham SF Circle (UK) launch The Order of The Knights of St Fantony

1957 Bjo Trimble reactivates LASFS

1957 UK fandom slumps after worldcon

Apr *Fantasy-Times* becomes *Science-Fiction Times*

Sept Fifteenth world convention in London (Loncon I) – first worldcon held outside North America

1958

Jan Ballantine Magazines produce one issue only of STAR SCIENCE FICTION (editor: Frederik Pohl)

Jan Isaac Asimov becomes contributing science editor of VENTURE SCIENCE FICTION

Feb Columbia Publications' SCIENCE FICTION QUARTERLY aborts

Mar SATELLITE SERIES launched in Australia

Mar AMAZING STORIES becomes AMAZING SCIENCE FICTION

Mar Candar Publishing's SATURN, MAGAZINE OF SCIENCE FICTION AND FANTASY becomes a detective magazine

June Vanguard Science Fiction Inc produce one issue only of VANGUARD SCIENCE FICTION (editor: James Blish)

June Royal Publications' SCIENCE FICTION ADVENTURES aborts

July THE MAGAZINE OF FANTASY AND SCIENCE FICTION absorbs VENTURE SCIENCE FICTION

July IMAGINATIVE TALES becomes SPACE TRAVEL

Aug SATELLITE SERIES (Australia) aborts

Sept GALAXY SCIENCE FICTION becomes GALAXY MAGAZINE

Sept Robert P. Mills becomes editor, William Tenn consulting editor, and Anthony Boucher book editor, of THE MAGAZINE OF FANTASY AND SCIENCE FICTION

Oct Greenleaf Publishing's IMAGINATION SCIENCE FICTION aborts

Oct Damon Knight becomes editor of IF, WORLDS OF SCIENCE FICTION

Nov Royal Publications' INFINITY SCIENCE FICTION aborts

Nov Greenleaf Publishing's SPACE TRAVEL aborts

Nov Edward L. Ferman becomes editorial assistant at Mercury Press

Dec William Tenn leaves THE MAGAZINE OF FANTASY AND SCIENCE FICTION

Dec Norman Lobsenz becomes editorial director, Cele G. Goldsmith editor, at Ziff-Davis Publishing

---

Jan 'Lemmings' by Richard Matheson, F&SF

Jan *And Then the Town Took Off* by Richard Wilson (two-part serial), INFINITY

Feb 'Drog' – first sf magazine appearance by John Rackham, SCIENCE FANTASY

Feb 'The Feeling of Power' by Isaac Asimov, IF

Feb *The Man Who Counts* – first story on 'Nicholas Van Rijn and the Polytechnic League' by Poul Anderson (three-part serial), ASTOUNDING

Mar 'A Big, Wide, Wonderful World' by Charles E. Fritch, F&SF

Mar *The Big Time* by Fritz Leiber (two-part serial), GALAXY

Apr 'Poor Little Warrior' by Brian W. Aldiss, F&SF

May 'Or All the Sea with Oysters' by Avram Davidson, GALAXY

May 'The Iron Chancellor' by Robert Silverberg, GALAXY

May *Close to Critical* by Hal Clement (three-part serial), ASTOUNDING

June 'But Who Can Replace a Man?' by Brian W. Aldiss, INFINITY

July 'Two Dooms' by Cyril Kornbluth, VENTURE

July 'Winged Victory' – first sf magazine story by Thomas Burnett Swann, FANTASTIC UNIVERSE

Aug 'The Million Cities' by J. T. McIntosh, SATELLITE

Aug *Have Space Suit – Will Travel* by Robert A. Heinlein (three-part serial), F&SF

Sept 'That Hell-Bound Train' by Robert Bloch, F&SF

Sept 'From an Unseen Censor' – first sf story by Rosel George Brown, GALAXY

Sept 'Casey Agonistes' – first story by Richard McKenna, F&SF

Oct 'The Yellow Pill' by Rog Phillips, ASTOUNDING

Oct 'The Big Front Yard' by Clifford D. Simak, ASTOUNDING

Nov 'Life Plan' – first story by Colin Kapp, NEW WORLDS

Nov 'Unhuman Sacrifice' by Katherine MacLean, ASTOUNDING

Dec 'The Immortals' by James E. Gunn, *Star SF 4* (anthology edited by Frederik Pohl)

The Triumph of Time by James Blish

Rod Serling's *Time Element* paves way for *Twilight Zone* TV series in US

1958 Ninth Fandom starts (Weinstein)

1958 EASTER. E. C. Tubb and others (UK) at Cytricon III (Kettering Eastercon) launch British Science Fiction Association (BSFA) from suggestions by Ken Bulmer, Vincent Clarke and others to revive UK fandom

Feb Terry Carr and Ron Ellik launch *Fanac*

Sum BSFA launch *Vector* (editor: E. C. Tubb)

Nov Sixteenth world convention in Los Angeles (Solacon)

Richard Eney produces *Fancyclopedia II*

H. P. Sanderson launches *Apporheta*

Berkeley Bhoys (Terry Carr and Ron Ellik among them) produce many fanzines

International Science Fiction Society launched in Vienna (short-lived)

01. PROGRAM

1959

MD

Jan Nova Publications (UK) launch SCIENCE FICTION ADVENTURES as continuation of previous reprint edition

Feb Galaxy Publishing buy IF, WORLDS OF SCIENCE FICTION; Horace L. Gold becomes editor, Damon Knight book editor, Frederik Pohl feature editor

Apr Anthony Boucher leaves THE MAGAZINE OF FANTASY AND SCIENCE FICTION; Damon Knight becomes book editor

May Renown Publications' SATELLITE SCIENCE FICTION aborts

June Peter Hamilton's NEBULA SCIENCE FICTION (UK) aborts

Sept FANTASTIC SCIENCE FICTION becomes FANTASTIC SCIENCE FICTION STORIES

Oct Headline Publications' SUPER SCIENCE FICTION aborts

Oct GALAXY MAGAZINE reverts to GALAXY SCIENCE FICTION

MS

Jan 'The Quest for Saint Aquin' by Anthony Boucher, F&SF

Feb 'The Wind People' by Marion Zimmer Bradley, IF

Mar '"All You Zombies—"' by Robert A. Heinlein, F&SF

Apr 'Flowers for Algernon' by Daniel Keyes, F&SF

Apr 'Greylorn'—first story by Keith Laumer, AMAZING

Apr 'The Whole Man' by John Brunner' SCIENCE FANTASY

May 'The Outstretched Hand' by Arthur Sellings, NEW WORLDS

May *Dorsai* by Gordon R. Dickson (three-part serial), ASTOUNDING

June 'Visitor at Large' by James White, NEW WORLDS

July 'If the Red Slayer' by Robert Sheckley, AMAZING

Aug 'Echo in the Skull' by John Brunner, SCIENCE FANTASY

Sept 'A Grain of Manhood'—first sf story by Phyllis Gottlieb, FANTASTIC

Sept 'Nor Custom Stale'—first story by Joanna Russ, F&SF

Oct 'The Man Who Lost the Sea' by Theodore Sturgeon, F&SF

Oct *Starship Soldier* (*Starship Troopers*) by Robert A. Heinlein (two-part serial), F&SF

Nov 'Grapeliner' by James White, NEW WORLDS

Dec 'Peace on Earth'—first story by Michael Moorcock (in collaboration, as Michael Barrington), NEW WORLDS

B

Level Seven by Mordecai Roshwald

The Sirens of Titan by Kurt Vonnegut Jr

F

The Time Machine directed by George Pal for MGM

Fan

Feb Ted White takes over *Void*

Apr Terry Jeeves (UK) launches *Erg*

Seventeenth world convention in Detroit (Detention)

Bill Donaho launches *Habakkuk*

Dec Thomas D. Clareson launches *Extrapolation*, Newsletter of the Conference on Science Fiction of the Modern Languages Association

Wint Michael Moorcock (UK) joins editorial staff of *Vector*

1960

MD

Feb ASTOUNDING SCIENCE FICTION becomes ASTOUNDING (ANALOG) SCIENCE FACT & FICTION

Feb GALAXY SCIENCE FICTION reverts to GALAXY MAGAZINE

Mar King-Size Publications' FANTASTIC UNIVERSE SCIENCE FICTION aborts

Apr Columbia Publications' FUTURE SCIENCE FICTION aborts

MS

Jan 'Day of the Glacier'—first story by R. A. Lafferty, SCIENCE FICTION

Jan *Deathworld* by Harry Harrison (three-part serial), ASTOUNDING

Feb 'A Long Way Back'—first story by Ben Bova, AMAZING

Feb 'The First Men' by Howard Fast, F&SF

Mar 'All the Traps of Earth' by Clifford D. Simak, F&SF

Apr 'Crazy Maro' by Daniel Keyes, F&SF

B

Rogue Moon by Algis Budrys

Corpus Earthling by Louis Charbonneau

The Genetic General by Gordon R. Dickson

1961

May Columbia Publications' THE ORIGINAL SCIENCE FICTION STORIES aborts

Oct FANTASTIC SCIENCE FICTION STORIES becomes FANTASTIC, STORIES OF IMAGINATION

Oct AMAZING SCIENCE FICTION STORIES becomes AMAZING STORIES FACT & SCIENCE FICTION

Oct ASTOUNDING (ANALOG) SCIENCE FACT & FICTION becomes ANALOG SCIENCE FACT & FICTION

Oct Alfred Bester becomes book editor of THE MAGAZINE OF FANTASY AND SCIENCE FICTION

May 'A Pride of Islands' – first story by C. C. Macapp, IF

June 'Chronopolis' by J. G. Ballard, NEW WORLDS

June . . . *And All the Stars a Stage* by James Blish (two-part serial), AMAZING

June *Drunkard's Walk* by Frederik Pohl (two-part serial), GALAXY

July 'Time Enough' by Damon Knight, AMAZING

July *The High Crusade* by Poul Anderson (three-part serial), ASTOUNDING

Aug 'Imprint of Chaos' by John Brunner, SCIENCE FANTASY

Sept 'Ironhead' by E. C. Tubb, SF ADVENTURES

Sept 'The Six Fingers of Time' by R. A. Lafferty, IF

Oct *The Trouble with Tycho* by Clifford D. Simak, AMAZING

Nov 'Donor' by James E. Gunn, FANTASTIC

Nov 'Sunspot' by Hal Clement, ANALOG

Dec 'The Longest Voyage' by Poul Anderson, ANALOG

Flesh by Philip José Farmer

The Haunted Stars by Edmond Hamilton

A Canticle for Leibowitz by Walter M. Miller

Venus Plus X by Theodore Sturgeon

1960 Eighteenth world convention in Pittsburgh (Pittcon)

1960 Earl Kemt produces *Who Killed SF?*

1960 H. P. Sanderson's *Apporheta* aborts

1960 John White revives *Inside*

May BSFA launches *BSFA Newsletter* (editor: James A. Green)

Sept Pat and Dick Lupoff launch *Xero*

Sept Roy Tackett launches *Dynatron*

Mar Theodore Sturgeon becomes features editor of IF, WORLDS OF SCIENCE FICTION

May Frederik Pohl becomes managing editor of Galaxy Publishing when Horace L. Gold leaves

Nov IF, WORLDS OF SCIENCE FICTION becomes WORLDS OF IF SCIENCE FICTION

Dec ANALOG SCIENCE FACT & FICTION becomes ANALOG SCIENCE FACT-SCIENCE FICTION

Jan 'The Sources of the Nile' by Avram Davidson, F&SF

Feb 'Hothouse' – first of series by Brian W. Aldiss, F&SF

Feb 'Volume Paa-Pyx' – first story by Fred Saberhagen, GALAXY

Mar 'Prometheus' by Philip José Farmer, F&SF

Apr 'The Ship Who Sang' – first of series by Anne McCaffrey, F&SF

May 'Join Our Gang?' – first story by Sterling E. Lanier, ANALOG

June 'The Dreaming City' – first 'Elric' story by Michael Moorcock, SCIENCE FANTASY

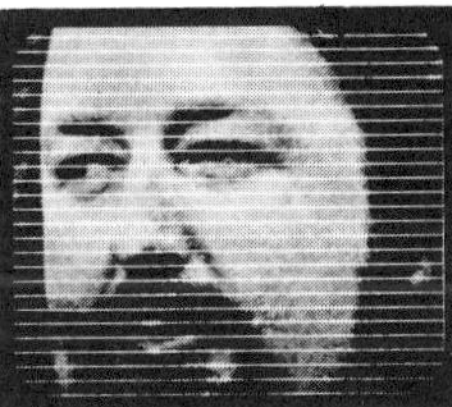

June 'Before Eden' by Arthur C. Clarke, AMAZING

July 'Whatever Gods there Be' by Gordon R. Dickson, AMAZING

Aug 'The Moon Moth' by Jack Vance, GALAXY

Sept 'Tongues of the Moon' by Philip José Farmer, AMAZING

Oct 'A Planet Named Shayol' by Cordwainer Smith, GALAXY

Nov 'At the End of the Orbit' by Arthur C. Clarke, IF

Dec 'Evergreen' by Brian W. Aldiss, F&SF

Dec *The Day after Doomsday* by Poul Anderson (two-part serial), GALAXY

Some Will Not Die by Algis Budrys

A Fall of Moondust by Arthur C. Clarke

Dark Universe by Dan Galouye

Stranger in a Strange Land by Robert A. Heinlein

Solaris by Stanislaw Lem

The Day the Earth Caught Fire directed by Val Guest for Melina

1961 Nineteenth world convention in Seattle (Seacon)

1961 First Deep South Con Held

1961 Earl Kemp produces *Why Is a Fan?*

Aug Terry Carr's *Innuendo* merges with Ted White's *Void*

Sept Greg Calkins's *Oopsla* aborts

01. PROGRAM

1962

MD

Feb Condé Nast Inc take over Street & Smith Inc

Apr Robert P. Mills becomes consulting editor, Edward L. Ferman managing editor, Avram Davidson executive editor of THE MAGAZINE OF FANTASY AND SCIENCE FICTION

July Alfred Bester leaves THE MAGAZINE OF FANTASY AND SCIENCE FICTION

Dec Robert M. Guinn hires Sol Cohen as publisher at Galaxy Publishing

MS

Jan 'The Towers of Titan' by Ben Bova, AMAZING

Feb ❶ 'The Engineer' – first story by Joseph L. Green, NEW WORLDS

Mar 'Flame in the Flux Field' by Kenneth Bulmer, NEW WORLDS

Mar *Joyleg* by Ward Moore and Avram Davidson (two-part serial), FANTASTIC

Apr 'Thirteen to Centaurus' by J. G. Ballard, AMAZING

May ❶ 'Who Sups with the Devil?' – first story by Terry Carr, F&SF

May 'The Stars, My Brothers' by Edmond Hamilton, AMAZING

June 'Novice' – first of 'Telzey' series by James H. Schmitz, ANALOG

June *Here Gather the Stars* (*Way Station*) by Clifford D. Simak, (two-part serial), GALAXY

July 'Listen! The Stars' by John Brunner, ANALOG

Aug ❶ 'The Mynah Matter' – first story by Larry Eisenberg, FANTASTIC

Aug 'Horseman!' and 'Passion Play' – double sf magazine debut by Roger Zelazny in FANTASTIC and AMAZING respectively

Aug 'The Dragon Masters' by Jack Vance, GALAXY

Sept ❶ 'April in Paris' – first story by Ursula K. Le Guin, FANTASTIC

Sept 'The Streets of Ashkelon' by Harry Harrison, NEW WORLDS

Sept *A Life for the Stars* by James Blish (two-part serial), ANALOG

Oct 'The Ballad of Lost C'mell' by Cordwainer Smith, GALAXY

Oct ❶ 'The Double-Timer' – first story by Thomas M. Disch, FANTASTIC

Nov *Space Viking* by H. Beam Piper (four-part serial), ANALOG

Nov 'The Sundered Worlds' by Michael Moorcock, SF ADVENTURES

Nov *Podkayne of Mars* by Robert A. Heinlein (three-part serial), IF

Dec 'Lambda 1' by Colin Kapp, NEW WORLDS

B

A Clockwork Orange by Anthony Burgess

The Eleventh Commandment by Lester del Rey

The Man in the High Castle by Philip K. Dick

Island by Aldous Huxley

F TV

The Day of the Triffids directed by Steve Sekely for Security Pictures

A for Andromeda serialised on TV in UK

Out of this World TV series begins transmission in UK

Fan

Robert Bloch produces *The Eighth Stage of Fandom*

Joe Pilati launches *Enclave*

Twentieth world convention in Chicago (Chicon III); Tenth Anniversary Fund brings Walt Willis and wife to the convention

1963

Feb Robert P. Mills leaves Mercury Press

Apr Galaxy Publishing launch WORLDS OF TOMORROW

Apr Frank P. Lualdi produces a second and last issue of resurrected WONDER STORIES

May Nova Publications' SCIENCE FICTION ADVENTURES (UK) aborts

Spr Star Press launch GAMMA (publishers/editors: Charles E. Fritch and Jack Matcha)

Jan 'The Putnam Tradition' – first story by Sonya Dorman, AMAZING

Feb 'Phoenix' – first story by Ted White (in collaboration), AMAZING

Feb 'Some Lapse of Time' by John Brunner, SCIENCE FANTASY

Mar *Chocky* by John Wyndham, AMAZING

Apr 'Possible to Rue' – first story by Piers Anthony, FANTASTIC

Apr *Window on the Moon* by E. C. Tubb (three-part serial), NEW WORLDS

May 'The Last of the Romany' – first story by Norman Spinrad, ANALOG

June 'Another Rib' – first story by Juanita Coulson (in collaboration, as John Jay Wells), F&SF

June 'No Truce with Kings' by Poul Anderson, F&SF

July 'Down to the Worlds of Men' – first story by Alexei Panshin, IF

July *The Reefs of Space* by Frederik Pohl and Jack Williamson (three-part serial), IF

Aug 'The Pain Peddlers' by Robert Silverberg, GALAXY

Sept 'The Expendables' by A. E. van Vogt, IF

Oct 'Breakdown – first story by Hilary Bailey, NEW WORLDS

Nov 'A Rose for Ecclesiastes' by Roger Zelazny, F&SF

Nov 'Savage Pellucidar' by Edgar Rice Burroughs, AMAZING

Dec 'No Great Magic' by Fritz Leiber, GALAXY

Dec *Dune World* by Frank Herbert (three-part serial), ANALOG

Dec *The Star King* by Jack Vance (two-part serial), GALAXY

Planet of the Apes by Pierre Boulle

Fail-Safe by Eugene L. Burdick and J. H. Wheeler

Cat's Cradle by Kurt Vonnegut, Jr

Dr Strangelove directed by Stanley Kubrick for Hawk Films

Lord of the Flies directed by Peter Brook for Allen Hodgdon Productions/Two Arts

Dr Who TV series begins transmission in UK

The Outer Limits TV series begins transmission in US

Tenth Fandom starts (Weinstein)

1963 First Doc Weir Award (UK) given at Eastercon, administered by Terry Jeeves

1963 *Hyphen*, issued by Walt Willis and Chuck Harris (UK), aborts

1963 *Fanac*, issued by Terry Carr and Ron Ellik, aborts

1963 Langdon Jones launches *Tensor*

1963 Tom Perry launches 'his' *Quark*

1963 Twenty-first world convention in Washington DC (Discon)

May Charles Partington and others (UK) launch *Alien*

May Pat and Dick Lupoff's *Xero* aborts

Nov Andrew Porter launches *Algol*

Oct Peter Weston (UK) launches *Speculation*

01. PROGRAM

1964

MD

Mar Theodore Sturgeon leaves WORLDS OF IF SCIENCE FICTION

Apr Frank P. Lualdi's Popular Library launch A TREASURY OF GREAT SCIENCE FICTION STORIES (series edited by Jim Hendryx, Jr)

May Roberts & Vinter Ltd's Compact SF take over Nova Publications (UK); Michael Moorcock becomes editor of NEW WORLDS SCIENCE FICTION, which becomes NEW WORLDS SF; Kyril Bonfiglioli becomes editor of SCIENCE FANTASY

MS

Jan 'The Eyes Have It' – first Lord Darcy story by Randall Garrett, ANALOG

Feb 'Time of Passage' by J. G. Ballard, SCIENCE FANTASY

Mar 'The Graveyard Heart' by Roger Zelazny, FANTASTIC

Apr 'Problem Child' by Arthur Porges, ANALOG

Apr *The Dark-Light Years* by Brian Aldiss, WORLDS OF TOMORROW

May 'The Imperial Stars' by Edward E. Smith, IF

June 'Tin Lizzie' by Randall Garrett, AMAZING

July *Farnham's Freehold* by Robert A. Heinlein (three-part serial), IF

July 'The Fall of Frenchy Steiner' by Hilary Bailey, NEW WORLDS

July 'Stormwater Tunnel' – first story by Langdon Jones, NEW WORLDS

July 'The Silkie' by A. E. van Vogt, IF

Aug 'Two's Company' – first story by Douglas R. Mason (as John Rankine), *New Writings in Sf1* (anthology edited by E. J. Carnell)

Sept 'Escapism' – first published sf story by Keith Roberts, SCIENCE FANTASY

Oct 'Soldier, Ask Not' by Gordon R. Dickson, GALAXY

Nov 'Gunpowder God' by H. Beam Piper, ANALOG

Dec 'Coldest Place' – first story by Larry Niven, IF

Dec 'One of those Days' – first sf magazine story by Charles Platt, SCIENCE FANTASY

B

The Rest of the Robots (collection) by Isaac Asimov

The Wanderer by Fritz Leiber

Hard to be a God by Boris and Arkadi Strugatski (USSR)

F TV

Fail Safe directed by Sidney Lumet for Max E. Youngstein-Sidney Lumet

The First Men in the Moon directed by Nathan Judd for American British

Fan

1964 Twenty-second world convention in Oakland, California (Pacificon II)

Feb Hank and Lesleigh Luttrell launch *Starling*

Aug Brian W. Aldiss and Harry Harrison launch *SF Horizons*

Aug Leland Sapiro takes over *Inside*, renames it *Riverside Quarterly*

1965

May Sol Cohen leaves Galaxy Publishing to form Ultimate Publishing

May ANALOG SCIENCE FACT-SCIENCE FICTION becomes ANALOG SCIENCE FICTION/SCIENCE FACT

May Judith Merril becomes book editor of THE MAGAZINE OF FANTASY AND SCIENCE FICTION

Aug Ultimate Publishing (editor: Sol Cohen) buy AMAZING STORIES FACT & SCIENCE FICTION, which reverts to AMAZING STORIES; and FANTASTIC, STORIES OF IMAGINATION, which becomes FANTASTIC STORIES

Sept Star Press's GAMMA aborts

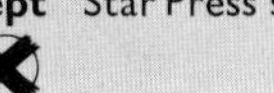

Jan 'Day of the Great Shout' – first 'Riverworld' story by Philip José Farmer, WORLDS OF TOMORROW

Jan *He Who Shapes* by Roger Zelazny (two-part serial), AMAZING

Jan *The Prophet of Dune* by Frank Herbert (five-part serial), ANALOG

Feb 'On the Storm Planet' by Cordwainer Smith, GALAXY

Mar 'The Doors of His Face, the Lamps of His Mouth' by Roger Zelazny, F&SF

Apr 'Brighteyes' by Harlan Ellison, FANTASTIC

May 'Trouble Tide' by James H. Schmitz, ANALOG

June 'Stand-In' – first story by Greg Benford, F&SF

June *Mindswap* by Robert Sheckley, GALAXY

June *Skylark DuQuesne* by E. E. ('Doc') Smith (five-part serial), IF

Aug 'Preliminary Data' – first 'Jerry Cornelius' story by Michael Moorcock, NEW WORLDS

Sept 'The Saliva Tree' by Brian W. Aldiss, F&SF

Sept 'Traveller's Rest' – first story by David I. Masson, NEW WORLDS

Sept 'Computers Don't Argue' by Gordon R. Dickson, ANALOG

Oct 'Three to a Given Star' by Cordwainer Smith, GALAXY

Oct . . . *And Call Me Conrad* by Roger Zelazny (two-part serial), F&SF

Nov 'Beyond Time's Aegis' – first story by Brian Stableford (in collaboration, as Brian Craig), SCIENCE FANTASY

Dec '"Repent, Harlequin!" said the Ticktockman' by Harlan Ellison, GALAXY

Dec *The Moon is a Harsh Mistress* by Robert A. Heinlein (five-part serial), IF

The Three Stigmata of Palmer Eldritch by Philip K. Dick

The Genocides by Thomas M. Disch

The Ship that Sailed the Time Stream by G. C. Edmondson

Crack in the World directed by Andrew Marton for Security Pictures

Star Trek TV series begins transmission in US

Out of the Unknown TV series begins transmissions in UK

1965 Twenty-third world convention in London (Loncon II)

1965 Harold Palmer Piser reprints *Fanzine Index*

1965 OMPA (UK) suffers temporary collapse

1965 Joe Pilati's *Enclave* aborts

Jan Damon Knight and others launch Science Fiction Writers of America (SFWA), *SFWA Bulletin* and *SFWA Forum*

Aug *SF Horizons* (UK), issued by Brian W. Aldiss and Harry Harrison, aborts

Sept Philip Harbottle produces *The Ultimate Analysis*, a biography of John Russell Fearn

01. PROGRAM

1966

MD

Jan Ultimate Publishing launch GREAT SCIENCE FICTION MAGAZINE

Mar SCIENCE FANTASY (UK) becomes IMPULSE (new numbering)

Apr Popular Library's TREASURY OF GREAT SCIENCE FICTION STORIES becomes GREAT SCIENCE FICTION STORIES; then aborts

June Ultimate Publishing launch MOST THRILLING SCIENCE FICTION EVER TOLD

Aug IMPULSE (UK) becomes SF IMPULSE

Oct Harry Harrison becomes editor of SF IMPULSE (UK)

Oct Compact SF (UK) lose distribution facilities

Nov Health Knowledge Publications launch FAMOUS SCIENCE FICTION

MS

Jan 'Representative from Earth' by Greg Benford, F&SF

Feb 'A Two-Timer' by David I. Masson, NEW WORLDS

Mar 'The Signaller' – first 'Pavane' story by Keith Roberts, IMPULSE

Mar 'For a Breath I Tarry' by Roger Zelazny, NEW WORLDS

Apr 'The Last Castle' by Jack Vance, GALAXY

Apr 'The Secret Place' by Richard McKenna, ORBIT 1

May 'The Run' – first story by Christopher Priest, IMPULSE

May 'Mountains Like Mice' – first sf magazine story by Gene Wolfe, IF

May 'Call Him Lord' by Gordon R. Dickson, ANALOG

June 'Mandroid' by Piers Anthony, Robert E. Margroff and Andrew J. Offutt, IF

July 'Just Like A Man' by Chad Oliver, FANTASTIC

Aug 'Light of Other Days', first 'slow glass' story by Bob Shaw, ANALOG

Aug 'The Keys to December' by Roger Zelazny, NEW WORLDS

Aug *Make Room! Make Room!* by Harry Harrison (three-part serial), IMPULSE

Sept 'The Empty Man' – first story by Gardner R. Dozois, IF

Sept 'Behold the Man' by Michael Moorcock, NEW WORLDS

Sept 'Rocket to Gehenna' – first story by Doris Piserchia, AMAZING

Oct 'Neutron Star' by Larry Niven, IF

Oct 'Prisoners of Paradise' by David Redd, NEW WORLDS

Nov 'A Code For Sam' by Lester del Rey, IF

Dec 'At the Bottom of a Hole' by Larry Niven, GALAXY

Dec *Echo Round His Bones* by Thomas M. Disch (two-part serial), NEW WORLDS

B

The Crystal World by J. G. Ballard

Babel-17 by Samuel R. Delany

Doomstar by Edmond Hamilton

F TV

Fahrenheit 451 directed by François Truffaut for Anglo-Enterprise-Vineyard

Fan

Mar First Nebula Awards made by SFWA, at banquets

June John Bangsund launches *Australian Science Fiction Review*

Twenty-fourth world convention in Cleveland (Tricon)

Ron Bennett produces fan directory

Tom Perry's *Quark* aborts

July *Alien* (UK) becomes semi-pro *Alien Worlds*

July Semi-pro *Alien Worlds* aborts

1967

Mar Michael Moorcock forms New Worlds Publishing (UK), continues NEW WORLDS SF with Arts Council grant; it reverts to NEW WORLDS and absorbs SF IMPULSE

June Ultimate Publishing launch SCIENCE FICTION CLASSICS

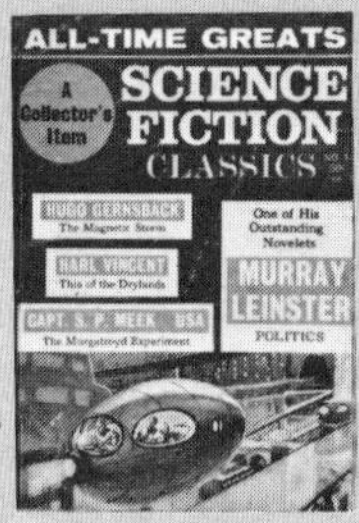

Aug WORLDS OF IF SCIENCE FICTION absorbs WORLDS OF TOMORROW

Nov Galaxy Publishing launch INTERNATIONAL SCIENCE FICTION

Nov I.D. Publications produce one issue only of BEYOND INFINITY (Editor: Doug Stapleton)

Dec Harry Harrison becomes editor at Ultimate Publishing

Popular Library start SF YEARBOOK, A TREASURY OF SCIENCE FICTION (editor: Helen Tono)

Jan 'Supernova' by Poul Anderson, ANALOG

Feb 'There is a Crooked Man' – first story by Jack Wodhams, ANALOG

Mar 'I Have No Mouth, and I Must Scream' by Harlan Ellison, IF

Apr 'To Love Another' by James Blish and Norman L. Knight, ANALOG

June 'Driftglass' by Samuel R. Delany, IF

July 'The Narrow Land' by Jack Vance, FANTASTIC

July *Camp Concentration* by Thomas M. Disch (four-part serial), NEW WORLDS

Aug 'Soft Come the Dragons' – first story by Dean R. Koontz, F&SF

Aug 'We're Coming Through the Window' – first story by Barry Malzberg (as K. M. O'Donnell), GALAXY

Sept 'A Bowl Bigger than Earth' by Philip José Farmer, IF

Oct *An Age* by Brian W. Aldiss (three-part serial), NEW WORLDS

Oct 'Weyr Search' by Anne McCaffrey, ANALOG

Oct 'Damnation Alley' by Roger Zelazny, GALAXY

Oct 'Winter of the Llangs' by C. C. MacApp, IF

Nov 'Prostho Plus' – first 'Dillingham' story by Piers Anthony, ANALOG

Dec 'The Cloud-Sculptors of Coral D' by J. G. Ballard, F&SF

Dec *All Judgement Fled* by James White (three-part serial), IF

Dec *Bug Jack Barron* by Norman Spinrad (Six-part serial), NEW WORLDS

Dec *Dragonrider* by Anne McCaffrey (two-part serial), ANALOG

The Einstein Intersection by Samuel R. Delany

Lords of the Starship by Mark S. Geston

Lord of Light by Roger Zelazny

Dangerous Visions (edited by Harlan Ellison), containing such stories as:
'Aye and Gomorrah' by Samuel R. Delany
'Gonna Roll the Bones' by Fritz Leiber
'Riders of the Purple Wage' by Philip José Farmer

The Prisoner TV series begins transmission in UK

1967 Twenty-fifth world convention in New York (Nycon 3)

1967 US fandom in doldrums

Nov BSFA becomes a limited company

01. PROGRAM

1968

MD

June Galaxy Publishing's INTERNATIONAL SCIENCE FICTION aborts

June Lester del Rey becomes managing editor of Galaxy Publishing

Sept Galaxy Publishing launch WORLDS OF FANTASY

Fall Sam Moskowitz and Robert A. Madle become editorial consultants at FAMOUS SCIENCE FICTION

Nov Barry N. Malzberg becomes editor at Ultimate Publishing

Dec M. John Harrison becomes book editor of NEW WORLDS, which is jointly edited by Michael Moorcock, Charles Platt, Langdon Jones, Graham Hall, Graham Charnock, James Sallis and others at different times; science editor: Christopher Evans

MS

Jan 'In His Own Image' by Lloyd Biggle Jr, F&SF

Feb 'Stranger in the House' by Kate Wilhelm, F&SF

Mar 'Birth of a Salesman' – first story by James Tiptree Jr, (Alice Sheldon), ANALOG

Mar 'Sunbeam Caress' by David Redd, IF

Apr 'Mother to the World' by Richard Wilson, *Orbit 3*

Apr 'The Planners' by Kate Wilhelm, *Orbit 3*

May 'A Quiet Kind of Madness' by David Redd, F&SF

June 'The Beast that Shouted Love at the Heart of the World' by Harlan Ellison, GALAXY

June 'The Secret of Stonehenge' by Harry Harrison, F&SF

July 'The Sleeper with Still Hands' by Harlan Ellison, IF

July *Sos the Rope* by Piers Anthony (three-part serial), F&SF

Aug 'Getting Through University' by Piers Anthony, IF

Sept *Nightwings* by Robert Silverberg, GALAXY

Oct 'The Pirate' by Poul Anderson, ANALOG

Nov 'Split Personality' by Jack Wodhams, ANALOG

Dec 'The Sharing of Flesh' by Poul Anderson, GALAXY

Dec 'Time Considered as a Helix of Semi-Precious Stones' by Samuel R. Delany, NEW WORLDS

Dec 'Passengers' by Robert Silverberg, *Orbit 4*

Dec 'Sweet Dreams, Melissa' by Stephen Goldin, GALAXY

B

Barefoot in the Head by Brian W. Aldiss

The Last Starship from Earth by John Boyd

Stand on Zanzibar by John Brunner

Five to Twelve by Edmund Cooper

Do Androids Dream of Electric Sheep? by Philip K. Dick

The Ring of Ritornel by Charles L. Harness

Rite of Passage by Alexei Panshin

Pavane by Keith Roberts

Dimension of Miracles by Robert Sheckley

F

2001: A Space Odyssey directed by Stanley Kubrick for MGM

Fan

1968 Twenty-sixth world convention in Oakland, California (Baycon); Trans-Pacific Fan Fund (TPFF) brings Takumi Shibano from Japan

1968 ANZAPA launched

Jan Susan Tompkins and Linda Bushyager launch *Granfalloon*

Apr Charles Brown, Ed Meskys and Dave Vanderwerf launch *Locus*

Spr John Bangsund (Australia) launches *Philosophical Gas*

Fall Guy Snyder and others launch Wayne Third Foundation

Dec Peter Roberts (UK) launches *Checkpoint*

Dec Guy Snyder launches *Seldon's Plan* for Wayne Third Foundation

1969

Wint SCIENCE FICTION CLASSICS becomes SCIENCE FICTION ADVENTURE CLASSICS

Wint GREAT SCIENCE FICTION MAGAZINE becomes SCIENCE FICTION GREATS

Jan Fantasy Publishing relaunch SPACEWAY SCIENCE FICTION

Mar Ted White becomes editor at Ultimate Publishing

Spr Health Knowledge Publications' FAMOUS SCIENCE FICTION aborts

Spr Ultimate Publishing launch STRANGE FANTASY

May Mercury Press relaunch VENTURE SCIENCE FICTION

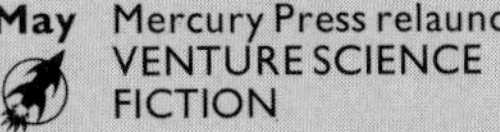

Sum Universal Publishing & Distributing Corp buy Galaxy Publishing's sf magazines; Lester del Rey becomes features editor, Judy-Lynn Benjamin managing editor, Ejler Jakobsson editor

Aug Ronald E. Graham Ltd (Australia) launch VISION OF TOMORROW (edited in England by Philip Harbottle)

Aug Universal Publishing & Distributing Corp relaunch WORLDS OF TOMORROW

Jan 'A Meeting of Minds' by Anne McCaffrey, F&SF

Feb 'A Womanly Talent' by Anne McCaffrey, ANALOG

Mar 'The Frozen Summer' by David Redd, IF

Mar *A Cure for Cancer* by Michael Moorcock (four-part 'Cornelius' serial), NEW WORLDS

Apr 'A Boy and his Dog' by Harlan Ellison, NEW WORLDS

May 'Hour of the Horde' by Gordon R. Dickson, VENTURE

June 'Artifact' by J. B. Clarke, ANALOG

July *Dune Messiah* by Frank Herbert (five-part serial), GALAXY

July 'Ship of Shadows' by Fritz Leiber, F&SF

July 'The City that Was the World' by James Blish, GALAXY

July *Up the Line* by Robert Silverberg (two-part serial), AMAZING

Aug 'The Time Sweepers' by Keith Laumer, ANALOG

Sept 'Your Haploid Heart' by James Tiptree, Jr, ANALOG

Sept 'Out of Phase' – first story by Joe Haldeman, GALAXY

Oct 'The Electric Ant' by Philip K. Dick, F&SF

Nov 'Roof Garden under Saturn' – first story by Ian Watson, NEW WORLDS

Dec 'Oracle for a White Rabbit' – first sf magazine story by David Gerrold (and first 'Harlie' story), GALAXY

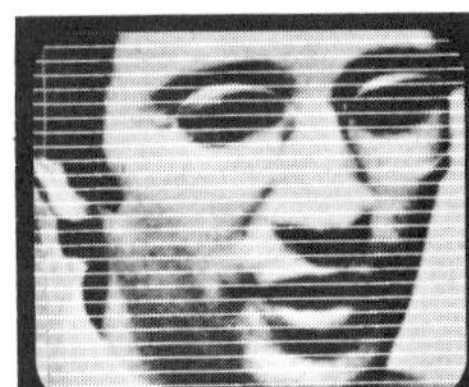

The Compleat Werewolf (collection) by Anthony Boucher

When Harlie Was One by David Gerrold

The Left Hand of Darkness by Ursula K. Le Guin

The Ship Who Sang by Anne McCaffrey

1969 Twelfth Fandom starts (Weinstein)

1969 Bruce Gillespie (Australia) launches *SF Commentary*

1969 *SF Commentary* (Australia) absorbs *Australian Science Fiction Review*

1969 Harry Warner, Jr, produces *All Our Yesterdays*

1969 Twenty-seventh world convention in St Louis (St Louiscon)

1969 International Science Fiction Symposium held in Rio de Janeiro

1969 First Clarion Science Fiction Writers Workshop held

1969 Australian National Convention in Melbourne launches Ditmar Awards

Jan Ted White's *Void* mothballed after first issue for seven years

Jan Mike Ashley (UK) launches *Monolith* (first of two issues)

Feb Walter H. Gillings (UK) launches *Cosmos*

Aug Edward C. Connor launches *Moebius Trip*

Sept Ann F. Dietz and Franklin M. Dietz, Jr, launch *Luna Monthly*

Nov Peter Roberts's *Checkpoint* (UK) mothballed

Nov Walter H. Gillings's *Cosmos* (UK) becomes *Cosmos Tape-Magazine*

01. PROGRAM

1970

MD

Jan Charles Platt becomes editor of NEW WORLDS (UK)

Jan Ultimate Publishing produce one issue only of SCIENCE FICTION ADVENTURES YEARBOOK

Jan Ultimate Publishing launch SPACE ADVENTURES (CLASSICS)

Feb Ultimate Publishing produce one issue only of FANTASTIC ADVENTURES YEARBOOK

Mar Ultimate Publishing produce one issue only of SCIENCE FICTION CLASSICS ANNUAL

Spr SCIENCE FICTION GREATS becomes SF GREATS

May Ultimate Publishing launch ASTOUNDING STORIES YEARBOOK

June Fantasy Publishing's SPACEWAY SCIENCE FICTION aborts

June Ultimate Publishing launch SCIENCE FANTASY YEARBOOK

June Ultimate Publishing produce one issue only of THE STRANGEST STORIES EVER TOLD

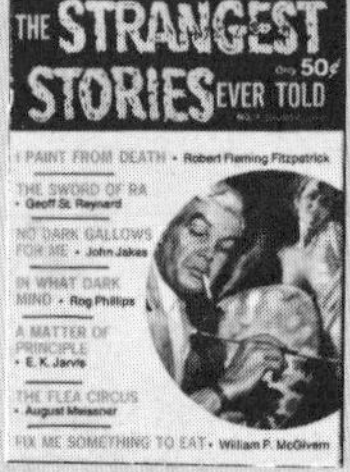

Aug Mercury Press's VENTURE SCIENCE FICTION aborts

Sept Ronald E. Graham Ltd's VISION OF TOMORROW (Australia/UK) aborts

Fall ASTOUNDING STORIES YEARBOOK becomes ASTOUNDING SF, then after one issue, aborts

Fall Ultimate Publishing's STRANGE FANTASY aborts

Fall SCIENCE FANTASY YEARBOOK becomes SCIENCE FANTASY

Oct Nectar Press launch FORGOTTEN FANTASY (editor: Douglas Menville)

Oct Sharon Moore becomes editor of SCIENCE FICTION YEARBOOK

MS

Jan *Whipping Star* by Frank Herbert (four-part serial), IF

Jan 'By the Falls' by Harry Harrison, IF

Jan 'Sending the Very Best' – first story by Ed Bryant, NEW WORLDS

Feb 'Breaking Point' – first story by Vonda N. McIntyre, VENTURE

Feb 'Slow Sculpture' by Theodore Sturgeon, GALAXY

Mar 'The Region Between' by Harlan Ellison, GALAXY

Apr 'Dear Aunt Annie' – first story by Gordon Eklund, FANTASTIC

Apr 'Ill Met in Lankhmar' by Fritz Leiber, F&SF

May 'Hijack' by Edward Wellen, VENTURE

June 'The Moon of Thin Reality' – first 'Interface' story by Duncan Lunan, GALAXY

July 'Invasion of Privacy' by Bob Shaw, AMAZING

July *I Will Fear No Evil* by Robert A. Heinlein (four-part serial), GALAXY

Aug 'Brillo' by Harlan Ellison and Ben Bova, ANALOG

Aug 'Beastchild' by Dean R. Koontz, VENTURE

Sept 'Fimbulsommer' by Avram Davidson and Michael Kurland, IF

Oct 'Through a Glass – Darkly' by Zenna Henderson, F&SF

Nov 'Dogman of Islington' by Hilary Bailey, *Quark 1*

Dec 'Darkside Crossing' by James Blish, GALAXY

B

Tau Zero by Poul Anderson

The Year of the Quiet Sun by Wilson Tucker

F TV

THX 1138 directed by George Lucas for Zeotrope Productions

Doomwatch TV series begins transmission in UK

Fan

1970 Thomas Clareson and others launch Science Fiction Research Association at Secondary Universe Convention

1970 John Bangsund and Leigh Edmonds launch rival Australian organisations: Communication Organization of Australian Science Fiction (COMORF) and Australian SF Information Organization (ASIO)

1970 Twenty-eighth world convention in Heidelberg (Heicon '70)

1970 International Science Fiction Symposium held in Tokyo

Jan Peter Roberts (UK) launches *Egg*

Jan William L. Bowers launches *Outworlds*

Mar Arnie Katz and Rich Brown launch *Focal Point*, presaging resurgence of US fandom

June James Goddard (UK) launches *Cypher*

June Peter Weston and others (UK) hold first Speculation Conference in Birmingham

Sept Greg Pickersgill and Roy Kettle (UK) launch *Fouler*

Oct Richard Bergeron's *Warhoon* mothballed

Oct George Hay, John Brunner, Ken Bulmer, James Blish and others (UK) launch Science Fiction Foundation at North East London Polytechnic

Nov Ian Williams (UK) launches *Maya*

1971

Mar New Worlds Publishing's NEW WORLDS (UK) aborts after withdrawal of Arts Council grant (continued as non-subscription paperback)

Apr MOST THRILLING SCIENCE FICTION EVER TOLD becomes THRILLING SCIENCE FICTION

Spr Ultimate Publishing's SF GREATS and SCIENCE FANTASY abort

Spr Universal Publishing & Distributing Corp's WORLDS OF FANTASY and WORLDS OF TOMORROW abort

June Nectar Press's FORGOTTEN FANTASY aborts

July John W. Campbell, Jr, dies

Sum Ultimate Publishing's SPACE ADVENTURES aborts

Nov Popular Library's SCIENCE FICTION YEARBOOK aborts

Jan 'The Telzey Toy' by James H. Schmitz, ANALOG

Feb 'This is My Country' by Stephen Tall, GALAXY

Mar 'The Missing Man' by Katherine MacLean, ANALOG

Mar *The Lathe of Heaven* by Ursula K. Le Guin (two-part serial), AMAZING

Apr 'The Eight Thirty to Nine Slot' – first published story by Geo. Alec Effinger, AMAZING

Apr 'Queen of Air and Darkness' by Poul Anderson, F&SF

May 'The Bear with the Knot in His Tail' by Stephen Tall, F&SF

June 'There's a Wolf in My Time Machine' by Larry Niven, F&SF

July 'Good News from the Vatican' by Robert Silverberg, *Universe 1*

Aug 'Occam's Scalpel' by Theodore Sturgeon, IF

Sept 'A Collector of Ambroses' by Arthur J. Cox, F&SF

Oct 'The Autumn Land' by Clifford D. Simak, F&SF

Oct *The Dramaturges of Yan* by John Brunner (two-part serial), FANTASTIC

Nov 'Rammer' by Larry Niven, GALAXY

Dec 'The Real People' by J. T. McIntosh, IF

To Your Scattered Bodies Go by Philip José Farmer

Gold the Man by Joseph L. Green

A Time of Changes by Robert Silverberg

Slaughterhouse Five directed by George Roy Hill for Universal Film/Vanadas

Clockwork Orange directed by Stanley Kubrick for Warner Bros/Polaris

1971 Twenty-ninth world convention in Boston (Noreascon); BoSh Fund brings Bob Shaw from Northern Ireland

1971 Donald A. Wollheim founds DAW Books

1971 Jack Williamson produces *Science Fiction Comes to College*

1971 Richard E. Geis's *Science Fiction Review* (first series) aborts

Mar British Weird Fantasy Society (BWFS) launched by Keith Walker and others

Mar Lisa Conesa launches *Zimri*

Apr Peter Roberts (UK) relaunches *Checkpoint* as only UK newszine

May Keith Walker launches *BWFS Bulletin*

June Birmingham (UK) SF Group relaunched by Peter Weston and others after five-year lapse; launches *Newsletter*

June Down-Under Fan Fund (DUFF) launched

Sept SFWA launch Science Fiction Writers Speakers Bureau

Nov First Novacon (UK) held in Birmingham

Dec Rosemary Pardoe launches *Dark Horizons* for BWFS

01. PROGRAM

1972

MD

Jan Ben Bova becomes editor of ANALOG SCIENCE FICTION/SCIENCE FACT

July Theodore Sturgeon becomes contributing editor of WORLDS OF IF SCIENCE FICTION

MS

Jan 'Rorqual Maru' by T. J. Bass, GALAXY

Feb 'Goat Song' by Poul Anderson, F&SF

Mar 'And I Awoke and Found Me Here on the Cold Hill's Side' by James Tiptree, Jr, F&SF

Mar 'The Gold at Starbow's End' by Frederik Pohl, ANALOG

Mar *The Gods Themselves* by Isaac Asimov (three-part serial), GALAXY (the April episode appeared in IF)

Apr 'Midsummer Century' by James Blish, F&SF

Apr *A Transatlantic Tunnel, Hurrah!* by Harry Harrison (three-part serial), ANALOG

May 'That Man Who Walked Home' by James Tiptree, Jr, AMAZING

June 'In The Ocean of Night' by Greg Benford, IF

June 'Hero' by Joe Haldeman, ANALOG

July 'For G.O.D.'s Sake' by David Gerrold, GALAXY

July *Dying Inside* by Robert Silverberg (two-part serial), GALAXY

Aug 'Basilisk' by Harlan Ellison, F&SF

Sept 'The Symbiotes' by James H. Schmitz, ANALOG

Oct 'The Star Hole' by Bob Buckley, ANALOG

Nov 'The Meeting' by Frederik Pohl and Cyril Kornbluth, F&SF

Nov *Cemetery World* by Clifford D. Simak (three-part serial), ANALOG

Dec 'The Second Kind of Loneliness' by George R. R. Martin, ANALOG

B

The Sheep Look Up by John Brunner

334 by Thomas M. Disch

Beyond Apollo by Barry N. Malzberg

Breakfast in the Ruins by Michael Moorcock

F

Solaris directed by Andrei Tarkovsky for Mosfilm

Planet of the Apes TV series begins transmission in US

Fan

1972 Thirteenth Fandom starts (Weinstein)

1972 Mass influx of crudzine-publishing neofans

1972 SFRA make first Pilgrim Award

1972 Thirtieth world convention in Los Angeles (LACon)

1972 Eleventh Australian National Convention in Sydney hosts first DUFF-funded fan guest Lesleigh Luttrell

Feb BWFS (UK) make first August Derleth Fantasy Award

Mar Science Fiction Foundation (UK) Launches *Foundation: the Review of Science Fiction*

Apr BWFS becomes British Fantasy Society (BFS; *not* a continuation of the earlier BFS)

May Nick Shears (South Africa) launches *African* to replace *Entropion*, which becomes ANZAPAzine only

June CANADAPA launched

June Last Speculation Conference (UK) held in Birmingham

June Fantasy Association launched in Los Angeles

July First European Convention (Eurocon) held in Trieste

Oct First annual Milford (British) SF Writers Conference held

Oct Phyllis Eisenstein and George R. R. Martin hold first Windy City SF Writers Conference in Chicago (eight per year)

Nov First annual Fantasy Film Convention (Filmcon) held in Los Angeles; first convention devoted entirely to science fiction and fantasy films

1973

Apr Mankind Publishing launch VERTEX, THE MAGAZINE OF SCIENCE FICTION (editor: Donald J. Pfeil; contributing editor: Forrest J. Ackerman)

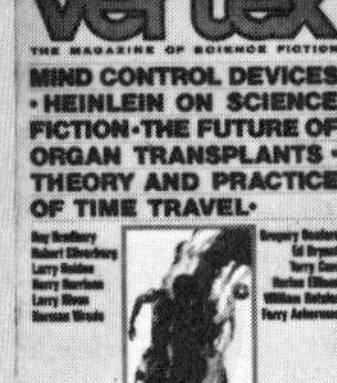

Sum Sam Moskowitz resurrects WEIRD TALES (continuing the old numbering)

Dec Forrest J. Ackerman leaves VERTEX

Wint Sam Moskowitz's WEIRD TALES aborts

Jan 'Case and the Dreamer' by Theodore Sturgeon, GALAXY

Feb 'Eurema's Dam' by R. A. Lafferty, *New Dimensions 2*

Feb 'Construction Shack' by Clifford D. Simak, IF

Mar 'The Deathbird' by Harlan Ellison, F&SF

Apr 'Love is the Plan, the Plan is Death' by James Tiptree, Jr, *The Alien Condition* (anthology edited by Stephen Goldin)

Apr 'Icarus Descending' by Greg Benford, F&SF

Apr 'Doomship' by Frederik Pohl and Jack Williamson, IF

May 'Parthen' by R. A. Lafferty, GALAXY

June 'The Alibi Machine' by Larry Niven, VERTEX

July 'Luna 1' by Ernest Taves, GALAXY

Aug 'The Invaders' by Stephen Tall, IF

Aug 'All the Bridges Rusting' by Larry Niven, VERTEX

Sept 'In the Problem Pit' by Frederik Pohl, F&SF

Sept *Rendezvous with Rama* by Arthur C. Clarke (two-part serial), GALAXY

Oct 'Of Mist, and Grass, and Sand' by Vonda N. McIntyre, ANALOG

Oct *The Dream Millennium* by James White (three-part serial), GALAXY

Nov 'The Death of Dr Island' by Gene Wolfe, *Universe 3*

Nov 'Epicycle' – first story by P. J. Plauger, ANALOG

Dec 'Moby, Too' by Gordon Eklund, F&SF

Dec *Inverted World* by Christopher Priest (four-part serial), GALAXY

Crash by J. G. Ballard

Rendezvous with Rama by Arthur C. Clarke

The Cloud Walker by Edmund Cooper

Star Smashers of the Galaxy Rangers by Harry Harrison

Tim Enough for Love by Robert A. Heinlein

Hellstrom's Hive by Frank Herbert

Soylent Green (based on Harry Harrison's *Make Room! Make Room!* directed by Richard Fleischer for MGM

1973 Thirty-first world convention held in Toronto (Torcon 2); includes 'All Our Yesterdays' fan-history room; first John W. Campbell Award made

1973 First beneluxcon (Continental Europe) held in Ghent

Jan AFRICAPA launched

Jan *Richard E. Geis becomes The Alien Critic*

Feb Dave and Mardee Jenrette launch *Tabebuian*

early Mike Glyer launches *Prehensile*

Spr R. D. Mullen and Darko Suvin launch *Science Fiction Studies*

Apr First John W. Campbell Memorial Awards made at Illinois Institute of Technology

Nov First Nova Award (UK) made at Novacon

Nov Oct- Beyond This Horizon Festival of Science Fiction and Space Exploration (UK) held in Sunderland

01. PROGRAM

1974

MD

Jan  New English Library (UK) launch SCIENCE FICTION MONTHLY (editor: Anne Batt)

Jan James Baen becomes managing editor of Universal Publishing & Distributing Corp, and in March becomes editor in the same organisation

MS

Jan 'The Hole Man' by Larry Niven, ANALOG

Feb 'The Girl Who Was Plugged In' by James Tiptree, Jr, *New Dimensions 3*

Feb 'The Ones Who Walk away from Omelas' by Ursula K. Le Guin, *New Dimensions 3*

Mar 'If the Stars Are Gods' by Gordon Eklund and Greg Benford, *Universe 4*

Mar *Frankenstein Unbound* by Brian W. Aldiss (two-part serial), FANTASTIC

Apr 'Hot Spot' by Brenda Pearce, ANALOG

May '—That Thou Art Mindful of Him!' by Isaac Asimov, F&SF

May 'On the Street of the Serpents . . .' by Michael Bishop, *SF Emphasis 1*

May *Berserker's Planet* by Fred Saberhagen (two-part serial), IF

June 'A Song for Lya' by George R. R. Martin, ANALOG

June *Orbitsville* by Bob Shaw (three-part serial), GALAXY

July 'Threads of Time' by Greg Benford, *Threads of Time* (anthology edited by Robert Silverberg)

Aug 'The Legend of Hombas' by Edgar Pangborn, *Continuum 2*

Sept 'Mephisto and the Ion Explorer' by Colin Kapp, IF

Oct 'Adrift just off the Islets of Langerhans . . .' by Harlan Ellison, F&SF

Nov 'The Night Wind' by Edgar Pangborn, *Universe 5*

Dec 'Encounter below Tharsis' by Bob Buckley, ANALOG

Dec *Venus on the Half-Shell* by Philip José Farmer as Kilgore Trout (two-part serial), F&SF

B

The Soul of a Robot by Barrington J. Bayley

Extro by Alfred Bester

The Dispossessed by Ursula K. Le Guin

First volume of Mike Ashley's *The History of the Science Fiction Magazine* (UK) appears

F

Fan

1974 Thirty-second world convention held in Washington DC (Discon II); Mae Strelkov's Friends' Fund brings her from Argentina; Fantasy Association make first Grand Master of Fantasy (Gandalf) Award

Jan Linda Bushyager launches *Karass*

Feb International Star-Trek Convention held in New York

Mar First French national convention

Mar *Fouler* (UK) splits into *True Rat* and *Ritblat* (later *Stop Breaking Down*)

May USIA-sponsored sf Conference held in USSR

Sum John Bangsund's *Scythrop* (Australia) aborts

Aug Second Eurocon held in Grenoble

Late ERB Society (UK) and *Burroughsiana* launched

Dec Elliot Weinstein completes *The Fillostrated Fan Dictionary*

1975

Spr GALAXY MAGAZINE absorbs WORLDS OF IF SCIENCE FICTION

Jul THRILLING SCIENCE FICTION absorbs SCIENCE FICTION ADVENTURE CLASSICS, then aborts

Aug Paul Collins's Void Publishers (Australia) launch VOID (editor: Collins)

Aug Mankind Publishing's VERTEX, THE MAGAZINE OF SCIENCE FICTION aborts

Jan 'The Borderland of Sol' by Larry Niven, ANALOG

Feb 'The Tax Man' by Stephen Robinett, ANALOG

Feb *Lifeboat* by Harry Harrison and Gordon R. Dickson (three-part serial), ANALOG

Mar 'Child of All Ages' by P. J. Plauger, ANALOG

Mar 'Second Creation' by Gordon Eklund, AMAZING

Apr 'Crazy Oil' by Brenda Pearce, ANALOG

Apr 'Eyes of the Blind' by Rachel Cosgrove Payes, VERTEX

Apr *The Stochastic Man* by Robert Silverberg (three-part serial), F&SF

May 'The Storms of Windhaven' by Lisa Tuttle and George R. R. Martin, ANALOG

July 'The Black Hole Passes' by John Varley, F&SF

July 'The Way of Our Fathers' by Daphne Castell, AMAZING

Aug 'Nobody Here but Us Shadows' by Sam Lundwall, GALAXY

Sept 'Coda and Finale' by Anne McCaffrey, *Continuum 4*

Oct 'Gibraltar Falls' by Poul Anderson, F&SF

Oct 'Nuisance Value' by James White, ANALOG

Nov 'Home is the Hangman' by Roger Zelazny, ANALOG

Nov 'The Ministry of Children' by Keith Roberts, NEW WORLDS 9

Dec 'Unfaithful Recording' by Bob Shaw, ANALOG

The Shockwave Rider by John Brunner

The Hellbound Project by Ron Goulart

Rollerball directed by Norman Jewison, Alonguin production for United Artists

Space 1999 TV series begins transmission in UK

The Survivors TV series begins in UK

1975 Thirty-third world convention held in Melbourne (Aussiecon) – first worldcon held in Southern Hemisphere; Tucker Fund brings Bob Tucker to it; first Fan Activity Achievement (FAAn) Awards made

1975 First World Fantasy Convention held in Providence, Rhode Island; first World Fantasy (Howard) Awards made

1975 H. G. Wells Society makes first H. G. Wells Award

1975 Mike Glicksohn and others produce large number of Canadian fanzines

Feb *The Alien Critic* becomes *Science Fiction Review* (second series)

Feb BFS holds Fantasycon 1, first annual UK Fantasy convention

Mar *Science Fiction Review Monthly* launched

Apr Richard Delap launches *Delap's F&SF Review*

May Keith L. Justice launches *Universe SF Review*

May David A. Kyle and Keith Freeman launch *Science Fiction International News*

July James Gunn organises first annual Intensive English Institute on the Teaching of Science Fiction, a summer school at the University of Kansas

Oct-Nov Instructors of Science Fiction in Higher Education make first Jupiter Awards

Nov Tom Reamy and Ken Keller launch *Nickelodeon* to replace *Trumpet*

Dec LASFS hold LA2000 convention to celebrate 2000th meeting

Dec New Hope Publishing buy semi-professional *Eternity*, issued by Stephen Greg and Scott Edelstein

Dec F. Macskasy, Jr, (New Zealand) launches National Association for Science Fiction (NASF)

01. PROGRAM

1976

MD

Spr Webb Offset launch ODYSSEY SCIENCE FICTION (editor: Roger Elwood)

June New English Library (UK) produce one issue only of SF DIGEST

Spr New English Library's SCIENCE FICTION MONTHLY (UK) aborts

Sept  GALILEO (editor: Charles C. Ryan) launched

MS

Jan 'The Dark Destroyer' by Jack Williamson, AMAZING
Feb 'Unsilent Spring' by Richard & Clifford D. Simak, STELLAR 2
Feb 'The Samurai and the Willows' by Michael Bishop, F&SF
Mar 'Field Test' by Keith Laumer, ANALOG
Mar 'Piper at the Gates of Dawn' by Richard Cowper, F&SF
Apr 'Transfigurement' by Bob Buckley, ANALOG
May 'Speculation' by George O. Smith, ANALOG
June 'Starhiker' by Jack Dann, AMAZING
June 'Chlorophyll' by Stephen Tall, F&SF
July 'Tricentennial' by Joe Haldeman, ANALOG
Aug 'The Cinderella Machine' by Michael G. Coney, F&SF
Sept 'The End's Beginning' by Vonda N. McIntyre, ANALOG
Oct 'Hero's Moon' by Marion Zimmer Bradley, F&SF
Oct 'Bagatelle' by John Varley, GALAXY
Nov 'I See You' by Damon Knight, F&SF
Dec 'The Funhouse Effect' by John Varley, F&SF

B

My Name Is Legion by Roger Zelazny

Deus Irae by Roger Zelazny and Philip K. Dick

F

Logan's Run directed by Michael Anderson for MGM

The Star Wars, directed by George Lucas for Twentieth Century Fox, nears completion

Fan

1976 Thirty-fourth world convention held in Kansas City (MidAmericon)
1976 Third Eurocon held in Poland
1976 BSFA (UK) issue first *Yearbook*
1976 Science Fiction Foundation (UK) announce James Blish Award to be made from 1977
Jan *Universe SF Review* becomes *SF Booklog*
May Brian Thurogood (New Zealand) launches *Noumenon*
Spr Frederik Pohl becomes contributing editor of *Algol*
July August Derleth Fantasy Award (UK) becomes the British Fantasy Award
July Peter Weston's *Speculation* (UK) mothballed after first issue for three years
Sept Harry Harrison and others organise World SF Writers Conference in Dublin; world coalition of sf writers proposed
Oct First Orbit British Science Fiction Award made (UK)

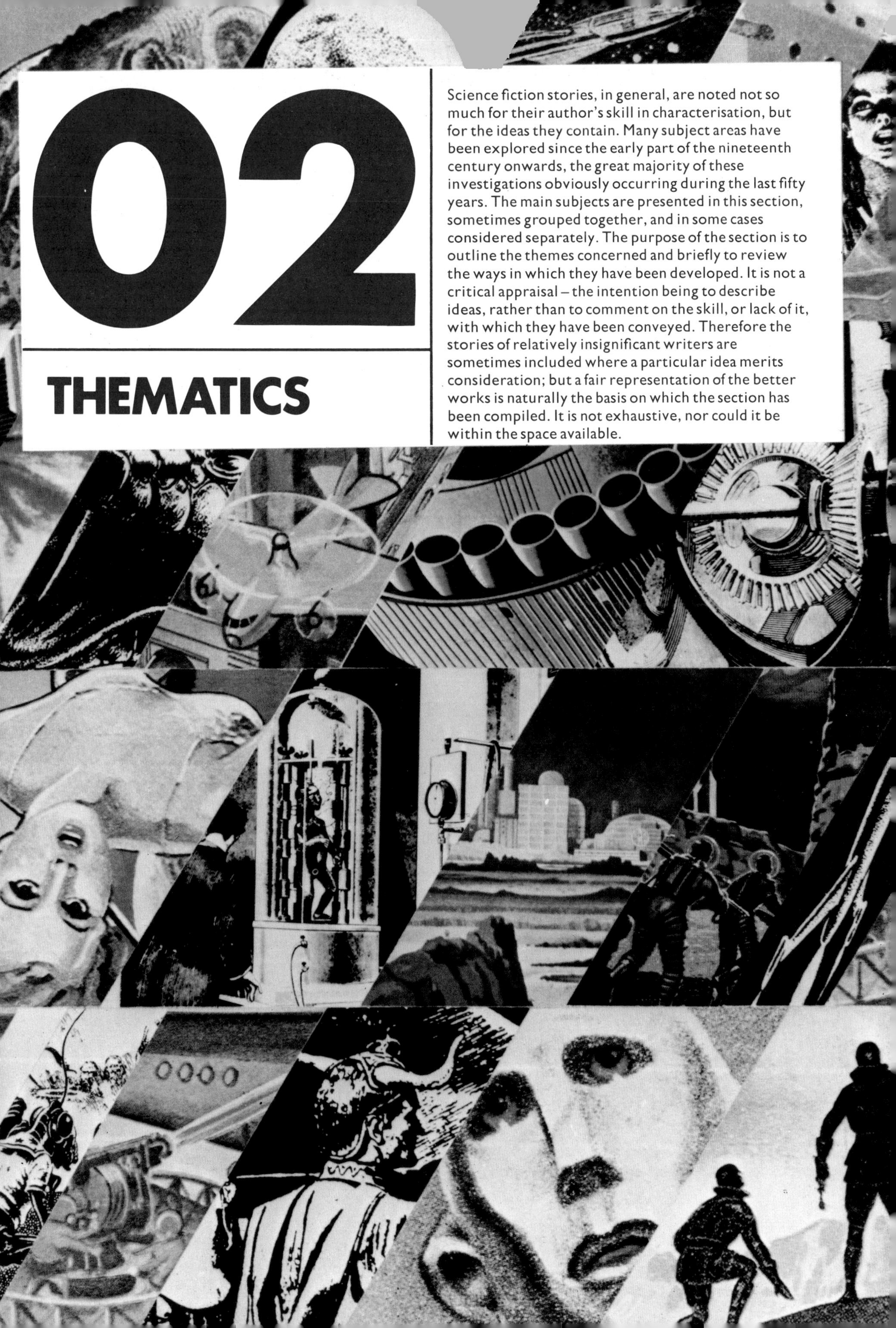

02

THEMATICS

Science fiction stories, in general, are noted not so much for their author's skill in characterisation, but for the ideas they contain. Many subject areas have been explored since the early part of the nineteenth century onwards, the great majority of these investigations obviously occurring during the last fifty years. The main subjects are presented in this section, sometimes grouped together, and in some cases considered separately. The purpose of the section is to outline the themes concerned and briefly to review the ways in which they have been developed. It is not a critical appraisal – the intention being to describe ideas, rather than to comment on the skill, or lack of it, with which they have been conveyed. Therefore the stories of relatively insignificant writers are sometimes included where a particular idea merits consideration; but a fair representation of the better works is naturally the basis on which the section has been compiled. It is not exhaustive, nor could it be within the space available.

02.01 SPACECRAFT AND STAR DRIVES

Where possible, the stories are grouped in a logical order so that the general development of ideas in the field can be viewed sequentially. In one or two areas, however, it has made more sense to approach a theme through the personal development of particular authors – 'Inner Space' is a case in point. Because a great many stories explore more than a single theme, a certain amount of overlap between various sub-sections is inevitable. At the same time, some tales which could easily have appeared in several sub-sections are dealt with principally under one heading. The section is designed to be read as a whole for its overall coverage of stories and ideas. Individual sub-sections are given more for general guidance and ease of presentation than for rigid categorisation. And each section is prefaced by a personal note from an established sf writer.

For bibliographic details of all stories mentioned in this section the reader is referred to the published checklists and indexes listed at the end of sub-sections 04.05 and 04.08. Lists of stories at the end of each sub-section in 'Thematics' provide a guide to additional reading.

When you read this, Viking One will be history, half-forgotten by all save those of us who care. But as I write, its landing upon Mars is only a few days old. And for the company who were there at the Jet Propulsion Laboratory, waiting out that long night, cheering when the news came that she had landed safely, and then, strip by strip, seeing built up man's virgin view of a country on Mars (*Mars!*) – among us Robert Heinlein, Theodore Sturgeon, Ray Bradbury, Larry Niven, Jerry Pournelle, Gene Roddenberry – surely it will live in us while *we* live, as vividly as man's first step onto the Moon, or the first Sputnik passing eerily overhead before dawn, or the first child or the first love.

That final word suggests to me what drives the whole enterprise. We have been tormentedly curious about the cosmos beyond our sky, yes; we have seen opportunities there, too, for adventure of material advancement or even the preservation of humanity; but seventh and last, as they say in Danish, we have loved the universe and yearned to become one with it. English, otherwise so rich, has only a single term for a whole spectrum of feelings. But Greek, which distinguishes three kinds of love, would still have to use all three to come anywhere near saying what the exploration of space *feels like*.

Eros: The fashion among intellectuals is to deride the rocket as a phallic symbol. And in truth, when a big one rises, like Apollo Seventeen which filled a whole night with glory, the experience can be as intense for the onlooker as any climax between man and woman. Yet physical sex is just a part of sexual love; there are also tenderness, loyalty, shared laughter, shared grief, shared discovery, the creation of new life and the nurturing of it. Religions traditionally use such imagery to express our relationship to God. Why should we not feel likewise about our relationship to the stars?

Phile: In the bluntest economic language, the space effort has already returned far more than its cost to mankind as a whole, simply through the revolution in meteorology which it has brought about, with all that that implies for agriculture, storm warnings and pollution abatement. It would take a book to list the other existing benefits – and I do not refer to any fakery about 'spin-off', but to major advances in everything from biomedical science to management techniques. Either we keep our high-energy industrial civilisation going, or at least 90 per cent of mankind perishes in horrible ways. Without calling in extra-terrestrial resources, the civilisation cannot much longer endure.

Agape: We need to know, or to believe that we know, what we are within reality and what the meaning of reality may be. Uncounted martyrs, soldiers and common folk who died well have shown that the wish in them to play their parts in the world as they understood it was stronger than the wish to live. Today science is our chief means towards that understanding. This has not always been the case and may not always be, but it is today, and our search outside the Earth is a huge part of our whole search. Think what a rebirth we can find on new planets and in the works and dreams of intelligences upon them. Think what we ourselves might become if given the freedom of yonder suns.

Thus, is it strange that writers write so many stories about travel into space?

Poul Anderson

Poul Anderson

02.01 SPACECRAFT AND STAR DRIVES

02.01.1 The Space-Travel Concept

With the whole of the universe at their disposal, it is not surprising that some of the most inventive – and successful – sf writers have been largely occupied with the space-travel theme. Since science fiction began to develop as a specialised form, the interplanetary story has always been the most popular and, in spite of endless repetitions, probably remains so today.

The notion of a 'cosmic voyage' is probably as ancient as the study of the stars themselves, leading to speculations about 'other earths' and the possibility of making contact with their inhabitants. Although the devices conceived by early chroniclers of such voyages were invariably so quaint as to seem ridiculous to us (and even more so to their contemporaries), at times they were remarkably prophetic.

In his *Somnium* (1634), the inspired astronomer Kepler went a long way to solve problems which came to be associated with astronautics. He suggested what might be the effect of gravity changes on the human body; and he visualised the conditions that might exist on the Moon with a genuine appreciation of astronomical data which were only just being discovered. He is also credited with having anticipated, however cynically, the eventual colonisation of the Moon, a development clearly reflected in the accounts of imaginary voyages which proliferated at this period.

Along with the visions of utopia which it frequently incorporated, the space-travel theme lent itself admirably to poetry and satire. Following Cyrano de Bergerac, who had poked fun at both Church and State in his *The Comical History of the States and Empires of the World of the Moon* (1656), and had also speculated on the potentialities of the rocket as a means of propulsion, Daniel Defoe wrote *The Consolidator* (1705), in which he advanced the whimsical idea that the secret of space travel had been given to the ancient Chinese by a visitor from the Moon – a suggestion used, with variations, by latter-day writers. His 'engine formed in the shape of a chariot, on the backs of two vast bodies with extended wings', provided the first hints of powered flight by liquid fuel, together with a promise of the enormous spaceships conceived much later. The anti-gravity devices of Defoe's and other people's imaginings had their origin in the 'lodestone of prodigious size' which sustained the flying island of Laputa in Swift's *Gulliver's Travels* (1726).

Regardless of such precedents, Jules Verne relied on a vast cannon sunk in the ground in Florida to fire his three travellers *From the Earth to the Moon* in 1865 – but their trajectory was such that they could not make an exploratory landing. His space capsule was the first to be scientifically conceived, even though the padded walls and hydraulic shock-absorbers would hardly have saved his crew from a violent death in the take-off explosion of 400,000 tons of gun-cotton. That the projectile was equipped with rockets only for steering indicates a certain lack of imagination (and is somewhat untypical of Verne) but in the balance can be placed his shrewd anticipations of space travel and the mathematical approach he adopted.

A rather more serviceable vessel was the one in which the engineer hero of Percy Greg's *Across the Zodiac* (1880) journeyed to Mars, aided by a newly found electric force which nullified gravity. The metal walls were insulated with cork and cement, and the elaborate fittings even included a small garden. Again, there is intelligent anticipation of essential equipment for spacecraft. Such ideas were developed to a far greater extent by the Russian 'father of astronautics' Konstantin Tsiolkovsky, who actually presented his concepts in the form of science fiction. He firmly believed that man's destiny lay in space, and his *Beyond the Planet Earth* (1920) tells of a journey to the Moon and the asteroid belt in a rocket-ship built by an international team of scientists in the year 2017. Initially they establish 'colonies' in artificial satellites circling outside Earth's atmosphere. (This, to Tsiolkovsky, was the cure for all man's ills). Although he began writing this story in 1896, it did not see complete book publication until 1920 – and by then other imaginative dreamers were indulging in similar dreams.

Rather more readable than Tsiolkovsky's convoluted prose (it may have suffered in translation) was the work of such authors as George Griffith, which appeared in English and American magazines around the turn of the century. His 'Stories from Other Worlds,' first published in *Pearson's* in 1900, were later brought together as a novel entitled *A Honeymoon in Space* (1901). The honeymooning couple toured the solar system in a spacecraft propelled by the mysterious 'R Force'. Four months sufficed to complete the round trip of 2000 million miles, largely due to the quiet efficiency of an engineer who kept the engines supplied with the vital, gravity-defying 'fluid'.

Jules Verne's From the Earth to the Moon *1889 (Sampson Low, Marston, Searle and Runnyton).*

H. G. Wells (the heroes of whose *The First Men in the Moon*, 1901, made their famous voyage in the same year) ventured no farther into space than Earth's natural satellite, but he outdid Verne by enabling his pioneers to land and explore the inner caverns where the Selenites lurked – like Kepler's lunar monsters before them. Ever insistent on scientific accuracy (in spite of his improbable moonshot), Verne called Wells to task for 'inventing' the anti-gravity material 'cavorite' as a means to propel his space sphere. Yet he wrote a laudatory introduction to the work of his 'English disciple' Robert Cromie – actually a Belfast bank clerk – who had used very much the same principle as Wells in *A Plunge into Space* (1890).

Wells, however, was at one with Verne in insisting that their work was quite different in approach; he said his own novels 'do not pretend to deal with possible things'. There seems to be no record of what he thought, if anything, about the work of the American journalist-astronomer Garrett P. Serviss who, having read Wells's *The War of the Worlds* in serial form in 1897, wrote a cliff-hanging sequel to it for the New York *Evening Journal* early the following year. Unusual because it featured living personalities as characters, *Edison's Conquest of Mars* (1898) is also notable for its bold treatment of the interplanetary-travel theme. Graphically illustrated, it depicted encounters between massed spaceships armed with atomic disintegrators, astronauts in vacuum-suits, and all the apparatus which later became the property of so-called 'space opera' and the Marvel comics. The story of how the versatile inventor, assisted by Britain's Lord Kelvin and Germany's Dr Roentgen, saved the Earth from a second Martian invasion later became so legendary among sf fans that, half a century after it was written, it had to be exhumed from the files of the Library of Congress and published in book form.

Though many countries – with the notable exception of Great Britain – helped to finance Baltimore Gun Club's moonshot, the Edison expedition to Mars would seem to be the first truly international project envisaged up to that time; the world's treasuries gladly subscribed a total of $25,000 million to finance it. Considering that 100 spaceships and 2000 picked men were involved, the investment appears modest. However, the great majority of the pioneering vessels of the turn-of-the-century stories were built by inventors who, if they were not millionaires themselves, were usually able to count on a rich relative or sympathetic friend to cover the construction bill.

As early as 1894, the American John Jacob Astor, in *A Journey in Other Worlds*, depicted Jupiter as an eventual haven for Earth's overspilling population. More often than not, however, these early wanderers of the spaceways were motivated solely by the spirit of adventure. They had little thought of the consequences, which could easily be their involvement in a perilous romance with a Martian princess or Venusian queen. A good example of thi type of blind voyager is the central character of another Serviss epic, *A Columbus of Space* (1909); he took his friends on a voyage to Venus in a vessel, driven by atomic energy, which he had built himself. Very often encounters which appeared romantic at the outset came to unhappy conclusions, once it had been established that one planet's bacteria might prove deadly to the life of another. Learning the lesson of earlier writers, Mark Wicks obliged his young hero in *To Mars via the Moon* (1910) to return home without the seven-foot-high Martianess who had made him so welcome.

Many interplanetary novels of this period were written not so much to entertain as to impart the facts of popular astronomy or, more frequently, to stimulate political ideas in readers' minds. Wicks's 'astronomical story' was largely based on Professor Percival Lowell's theories on the Red Planet in *Mars and Its Canals* (1906), which furnished the background for many tales once science fiction had become an accepted feature of the story magazines. Although several writers followed Edgar Rice Burroughs in constructing worlds of their own, to which their characters were often conveyed by no more than wishful thinking, the insistence on scientific plausibility became more marked as the early stages of the genre progressed.

Most influential in this respect was the 'sugar-coated science' policy of editor-publisher Hugo Gernsback, who launched *Amazing Stories* in 1926 after featuring what he termed 'scientifiction' in his earlier

Illustration by Layzell.

Grey Lensman *by E. E. ('Doc') Smith,* Astounding *October 1939. Cover by Rogers.*

magazines. As early as 1911, in *Modern Electrics*, he had serialised his own story *Ralph 124C41+*, the account of a superman in AD 2660 who pursued a Martian villain across the solar system to rescue his girl-friend. The gyroscopic 'anti-gravitators' with which Ralph's space-flyer is equipped are among the few devices predicted in this remarkable tale which – unlike radar, television and solar-power plants – have not since materialised.

Almost as influential – and equally naïve in the telling – is *The Skylark of Space*, the first of the famous interplanetary novels of Edward E. ('Doc') Smith, which found a place in *Amazing* in 1928 after many rejections. Before long, 'Skylark' Smith was producing ever more audacious 'epics', sending his copybook heroes and villains to the ends of the universe at speeds exceeding the velocity of light, a contradiction of Einstein's theories which provoked much argument in *Amazing*'s correspondence columns. The 'Skylark' series was followed by the stories of the 'Lensmen', which appeared in *Astounding* over a ten-year period, beginning with *Galactic Patrol* (1937–38). Since it was first presented in book form in the late 1940s, Smith's work has acquired an enthusiastic following extending throughout the world. Every one of his galactic dramas is still in print.

Smith's influence on the evolution of 'space opera' (of which he was the acknowledged progenitor), has tended to obscure the contributions of other writers who also developed the concept of interstellar travel and cosmic conflict while their colleagues were confining their explorations to the solar system. Edmond Hamilton, whose debut was made in *Weird Tales*, extended his horizons in 1928 with *Crashing Suns*, and by 1929, in *Outside the Universe*, was anticipating Smith with a series featuring the 'Interstellar Patrol', basically a police force to keep galactic order on behalf of a federation of worlds. It was a concept which, in due course, became grossly overworked; and the idea of protecting the spaceways against pirates and alien marauders littered the tales of later writers.

In addition to the space he devoted to many notable writers, both British and American, Gernsback also brought international renown to several French and German authors, whose works he presented in translation. The quickening interest in space-travel theory and rocket experiments in Europe and the US was duly reflected in articles and editorials in *Science Wonder Stories*, featuring an abridged version of *The Problems of Space Flying* (July-September 1929), a book by an Austrian army engineer based on the ideas of Hermann Oberth, the German pioneer of astronautics. The same ideas were originally advanced in 1923, and inspired the novels of Otto Willi Gail (whose work appeared in *Science Wonder Quarterly*). *The Shot into Infinity* (Fall 1929), first published in Breslau in 1925, related the rivalry between a German and a Russian for the honour of piloting the first rocket-ship to the Moon. Unsurprisingly, the winner is the German, who also comes out well in the sequel, *The Stone from the Moon* (Spring 1930).

Moving into the direction of more modern feelings and the lure of gold, we may view with some sympathy the crew of Thea von Harbou's *Rocket to the Moon* (1930), a film which achieved worldwide distribution after Fritz Lang had directed the story as *The Woman in the Moon*. The latter, also, owed something to the works of Oberth as interpreted by Gail and Willy Ley, both of whom were associated with the German Society for Space Travel.

Ley's textbook, *Rockets*, first published in 1944 and updated later as *Rockets, Missiles and Space Travel* (1952), became the accepted post-war reference work on astronautics and its connected literature. He was well versed in the subject. Until then, only two popular works on space travel had seen light of day. One was *The Conquest of Space* (1931) by David Lasser, managing editor of *Wonder Stories*, who had enlisted the support of several prominent sf writers in founding the American Interplanetary Society, later renamed the American Rocket Society. Among these was Fletcher Pratt, who translated many of the manuscripts Gernsback imported from Europe. Laurence Manning, author of some of the most realistic tales of the early 1930s was another; so too was G. Edward Pendray, a science journalist who wrote fiction for *Wonder* as Gawain Edwards, and also wrote a book on *The Coming Age of Rocket Power* (which did not appear until 1945). Secretary of that society was Nathan Schachner, a lawyer and biographer, who injected some new life into *Astounding* when it changed hands in 1933.

As the era grew, the astronautics 'movement' spread to England. The British Interplanetary Society (BIS) was launched in Liverpool by Philip E. Cleator, a research scientist, but his book, *Rockets through Space* (1936), aroused characteristically little interest in the popular press. In the UK, as in the US, the few dedicated enthusiasts who were most identified with science fiction revealed themselves in the persons of Arthur C. Clarke, Eric Frank Russell and William F. Temple, supported by editor Walter H. Gillings, who boosted their efforts in *Tales of Wonder*. Earlier, Cleator had contributed a modest news feature, 'To the Planets', to the short-lived sf weekly, *Scoops*, which also featured a serial, 'Space', by Professor A. M. Low, a writer noted for his popular science offerings. As editor of *Armchair Science*, Low encouraged both the BIS and the British Science Fiction Association, formed in 1937, and became president of both of them.

The Complete Venus Equilateral *by George O. Smith (Ballantine). Cover by Sternbach.*

Not until after the war was the BIS accepted as a learned society, then gaining several hundred members, mainly due to the energetic proselytising of Arthur C. Clarke, who shortly became a leading authority on astronautics and one of science fiction's best-known writers. Other British writers who made notable contributions to the space-travel theme were Australian-born J. M. Walsh, who found the American magazines more receptive to his work, and John Beynon Harris (the real name of John Wyndham), who made his mark in *Wonder Stories* before he appeared as John Beynon in the magazine *Passing Show*. His *Stowaway to Mars* (1936) was serialised in this family weekly only after the magazine had featured the first of Burroughs's series of 'Carson Napier on Venus'. It was indicative of the growing understanding of space flight that Burroughs's new hero was, by then, obliged to make the journey in a two-stage rocket 'torpedo' and land on Venus by parachute – although his intended destination was meant to be Mars.

With a few exceptions, most of the stories in the magazines paid scant heed to technical details, their authors being more concerned with new problems as their heroes ventured further into space. Among the notable exceptions were the tales of John W. Campbell, which rivalled those of 'Doc' Smith whom he admired so much. It was on the reputation he made in *Amazing Stories*, to which he contributed such favourites as *Islands of Space* (1931) and *Invaders from the Infinite* (1932), that Campbell was invited to write for Street & Smith's *Astounding*. Later he was appointed editor of that magazine.

Under Campbell's predecessor, F. Orlin Tremaine, established contributors such as Murray Leinster and Jack Williamson were encouraged to produce fresh variations on the space-travel theme, some of which were highly implausible. Among the most enduring tales of this period are Williamson's classic adventures regaled in *The Legion of Space* (1934), which had the virtue of introducing credible characters. When Campbell assumed the editor's chair of *Astounding* in 1937, the accent on genuine story values became more pronounced, and new writers of the calibre of Lester del Rey and Heinlein brought a sense of realism to

Starman Jones *by Robert A. Heinlein (Ballantine). Cover by Rosenblatt.*

02.01 SPACECRAFT AND STAR DRIVES

the interplanetary tale. Meanwhile, other newcomers, A. E. van Vogt and Isaac Asimov among them, combined with many old-established writers to preserve the flow of original treatments that kept *Astounding* buoyant during the 'golden years' of the 1940s.

Since then, many other magazines have aided the continued development of the space-travel theme by many gifted writers, not least among them being Ray Bradbury, who dispensed with the established conventions to produce tales of universal appeal, but not necessarily to meet with the approval of the readers or writers of science fiction. With the dawning of the Space Age, those sceptics who had earlier refused to admit the possibility of man ever attaining the Moon took refuge in the supposition that Apollo 11 ended science fiction. In fact, the genre has flourished as never before. As Arthur C. Clarke pointed out as long ago as 1953, 'without some foundation of reality, science fiction would be impossible, and therefore exact knowledge is the friend, not the enemy, of fancy and imagination.'

'I caught a glimpse of whirling black bodies, a trail of them bearing down upon us.' From 'Vanguard to Neptune' by J. M. Walsh, Wonder Stories *Spring 1932. Illustration by Paul.*

ADDITIONAL INPUT

02.101.1 The Space Travel Concept

Asimov, Isaac. 'Trends', *Astounding* July 1939; 'Half Breed', *Astonishing Stories* February 1940

Bailey, J.O. *Pilgrims through Space and Time*, Argus (US) 1947

Beynon, John (J.B. Harris). 'Sleepers of Mars', *Tales of Wonder* No 2, 1938

Bloch, Robert. 'The Strange Flight of Richard Clayton', *Amazing* March 1939

Bounds, Sydney J. 'Portrait of a Spaceman', *New Worlds* October 1954

Bradbury, Ray. *The Martian Chronicles*, Doubleday (US) 1951; as *The Silver Locusts*, Hart-Davis (UK) 1951

Bretnor, Reginald (ed). *Modern Science Fiction*, Coward-McCann (US) 1953

Burroughs, Edgar Rice, *Pirates of Venus*, *Argosy* 17 September to 22 October 1932; Burroughs (US) 1934

Burroughs, Edgar Rice, *Lost on Venus*, *Argosy* 4 March to 15 April 1933; Burroughs (US) 1935

Campbell, John W. *The Planeteers*, Ace (US) 1966

Clarke, Arthur C. *The Exploration of Space*, Temple (UK) 1951

Clarke, Arthur C. *The Other Side of the Sky*, Harcourt (US) 1958

Clarke, Arthur C. *An Arthur C. Clarke Omnibus (Childhood's End; Prelude to Space; Expedition to Earth)*, Sidgwick and Jackson (UK) 1965

Clarke, Arthur C. *An Arthur C. Clarke Second Omnibus (Sands of Mars; Earthlight; A Fall of Moondust)*, Sidgwick and Jackson (UK) 1968

Clarke, Arthur C. (ed). *The Coming of the Space Age* Gollancz (UK) 1967

Clarke, Arthur C. *The Promise of Space*, Hodder & Stoughton (UK) 1968

Clarke, Arthur C. *2001 : a Space Odyssey*, Hutchinson (UK) 1968

Cleator, P. E. 'Martian Madness', *Wonder* March 1934

Cleator, P.E. *Rockets through Space*, Unwin (UK) 1936

Cleator, P.E. *Into Space*, Unwin (UK) 1953

Del Rey, Lester. 'The Stars Look Down', *Astounding* August 1940

Del Rey, Lester. *And Some Were Human*, Prime (US) 1948

Del Rey, Lester. *Rockets through Space*, Winston (US) 1957

Del Rey, Lester. *Outpost of Jupiter*, Holt (US) 1963

Del Rey, Lester. *Mortals and Monsters*, Ballantine (US) 1965

Edwards, Gawain (G. Edward Pendray). 'A Rescue from Jupiter', *Science Wonder Stories* February to March 1930

Edwards, Gawain. 'The Return from Jupiter', *Wonder Stories* March to April 1931

Gallun, Raymond Z. 'Passport to Jupiter', *Startling* January 1951

Heinlein, Robert A. 'Requiem', *Astounding*, January 1940

Heinlein, Robert A. 'Logic of Empire', *Astounding* March 1941

Heinlein, Robert A. *Space Cadet*, Scribner (US) 1948; Gollancz (UK) 1966

Heinlein, Robert A. *The Moon Is a Harsh Mistress*, *If*, December 1965 to April 1966; Putnam (US) 1966; Dobson (UK) 1967

Heinlein, Robert A. 'Skylift', *Imagination* March 1953

Lear, John. *Kepler's Dream*, University of California (US) 1965

Leinster, Murray (Will Fitzgerald Jenkins). 'The Power Planet', *Amazing* June 1931

Ley, Willy. *Rockets, Missiles and Space Travel*, Viking (US) 1951

Ley, Willy. (and Chesley Bonestell). *The Conquest of Space*, Viking (US) 1949

Ley, Willy. *Beyond the Solar System*, Viking (US) 1964

Ley, Willy. (and Wernher von Braun). *The Exploration of Mars*, Viking (US) 1956

Locke, George (ed). *Worlds Apart: an Anthology of Interplanetary Fiction*, Cornmarket (UK) 1972

Manning, Laurence. 'The Voyage of the Asteroid', *Wonder Stories Quarterly* Summer 1932

Manning, Laurence 'The Wreck of the Asteroid', *Wonder Stories*, December 1932 to January/February 1933

Nicholson, Marjorie Hope. *Voyages to the Moon*, Macmillan (UK) 1948

Oberth, Herman. *Man into Space*, Harper (UK) 1957

Philmus, Robert M. *Into the Unknown*, University of California (US) 1970

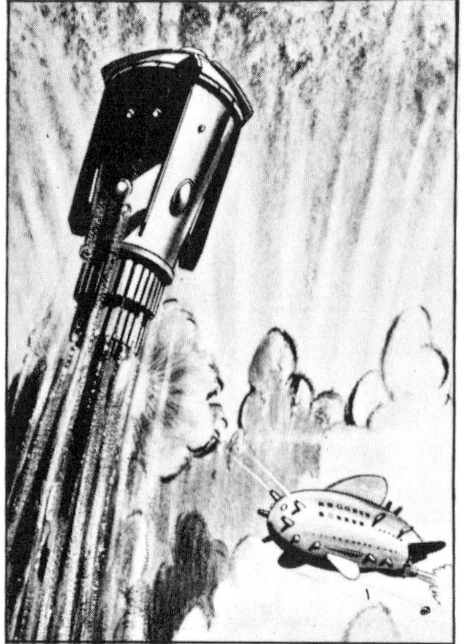

Frontispiece from Adrift in the Stratosphere *by Prof. A. M. Low (Blackie & Son, 1937).*

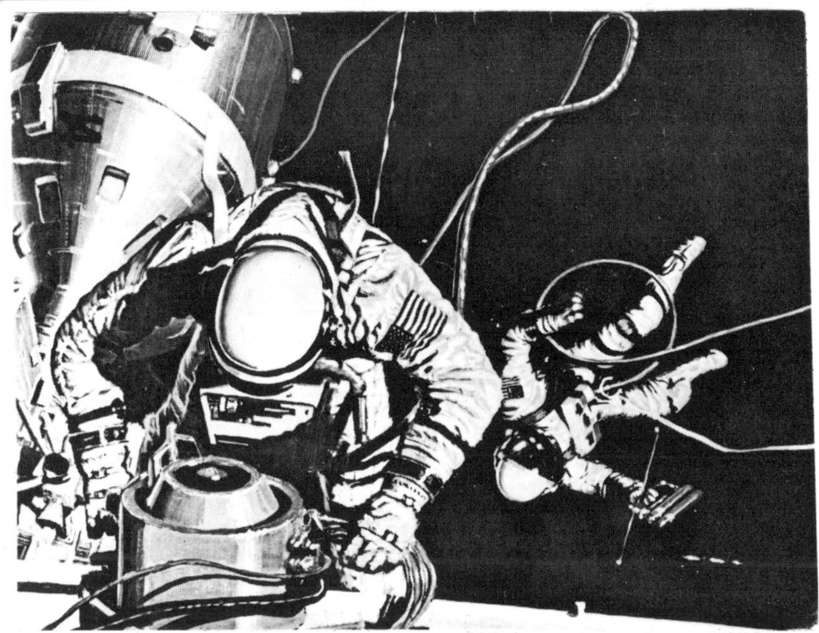

Vertex *August 1973. Illustration by Newsom.*

Pratt, Fletcher. 'Asylum Satellite', *Thrilling Wonder* October 1951
Pratt, Fletcher. 'The Wanderer's Return', *Thrilling Wonder*, December 1951
Pratt, Fletcher. *Double in Space* (two novels–see above), Doubleday (UK) 1951
Russell, Eric Frank. *Dreadful Sanctuary*, *Astounding* June to August 1948; Fantasy (UK) 1951
Russell, Eric Frank. 'Jay Score', *Astounding* May 1941
Schachner, Nathan. 'Emissaries of Space', *Wonder Stories Quarterly*, Fall 1932
Schachner, Nathan, *Space Lawyer*, Gnome (US) 1953
Smith, Edward E. *Triplanetary*, *Amazing*, January to April 1934; Fantasy (US) 1948
Smith, Edward E. *Galactic Patrol*, *Astounding* September to December 1937; Fantasy (US) 1950
Smith, Edward E. *The Best of E.E. 'Doc' Smith*, Futura (UK) 1975
Statten, Vargo (J.R. Fearn). *Odyssey of Nine*, Scion (UK) 1953
Temple, William F. 'Lunar Lilliput', *Tales of Wonder* No 2 1938
Temple, William F. *Shoot at the Moon*, Whiting (UK) 1966
Tubb, E.C. 'Homecoming', *Universe* May 1954
Tubb, E.C. 'Into the Empty Dark' *Nebula* July 1956
Tubb, E.C. 'Umbrella in the Sky', *SF Adventures* January 1961
Walsh, J.M. *Vandals of the Void*, *Wonder Stories Quarterly* Summer 1931; Hamilton (UK) 1931
Walsh, J.M. *Vanguard to Neptune*, *Wonder Stories Quarterly* Spring 1932; Cherry Tree (UK) 1952
Willey, Robert (Willy Ley). 'At the Perihelion', *Astounding* February 1937
Williamson, Jack. 'The Prince of Space', *Amazing* January 1931
Williamson, Jack. 'Born of the Sun', *Astounding* March 1934
Williamson, Jack. *The Cometeers*, *Astounding* May to August 1936; Fantasy (US) 1950
Williamson, Jack. *Bright New Universe*, Ace (US) 1967
Wyndham, John (John Beynon Harris). *The Outward Urge*, Michael Joseph (UK) 1959
Wyndham, John *The Best of John Wyndham*, Sphere (UK) 1973)

02.01.2 Interstellar Flight

While the exploration of our own solar system has now begun in earnest, planetary probes, manned or unmanned, represent only the very beginning of stellar exploration to the sf enthusiast. Many of the more thoughtful sf writers have seen man's confinement to a single world as a brake against his ultimate development.

As a result, a great number of interesting stories of interstellar flight have been concerned with the possibilities of man establishing colonies in other solar systems which may harbour Earthlike worlds. Writers have concerned themselves with the problems of getting their small colonies safely across the stellar abyss.

The standard device evolved for this purpose is the generation ship (or travelling ark), a small world in itself, travelling to the stars on a journey that may take centuries. The first working of the idea can be found in Laurence Manning's 'The Living Galaxy' (1934), and more particularly in Don Wilcox's 'The Voyage That Lasted 600 Years' (1940). But, as with so much else of his work, it was Robert A. Heinlein who wrote two evocative stories which proved highly influential: 'Universe' (1941) and 'Common Sense' (1941), later published as the book *Orphans of the Sky* (1963).

'The Voyage That Lasted 600 Years' by Don Wilcox, Amazing *October 1940. Illustration by Krupa.*

The tales are distinguished by Heinlein's conception of a huge ship containing a closed-cycle ecology where entire generations have born and bred, and died, on a voyage so long that they have forgotten their origins and purpose.

In the wake of Heinlein's example many authors have wrestled with variations on the travelling-ark theme, among the most notable being Brian Aldiss with *Non-Stop* (1958), E. C. Tubb with *Space-Born* (1956) and Clifford D. Simak in a number of magazine stories epitomised by 'Spacebred Generations' (1953).

There is a certain wistful appeal to these tales, in which the crew set out in the knowledge that not only will they never see the Earth again, but that they will also never see the planet of their destination. Entire generations are sacrificed in space for the ideal of spreading mankind to the stars.

One has only to consider the tremendous time-scale involved. A spaceship leaving our solar system en route to the binary star Alpha Centauri, some 4.3 light years distant, and travelling at a constant velocity of seven miles per second, would take about 110,000 years to achieve landfall. The idea of attempting such a journey is mainly academic. To bring it near feasibility it is necessary to increase the velocity of the starship until it can attain a speed of about 6000 miles per second. Obviously, known chemical propellants are inadequate for this purpose. But the controlled application of nuclear energy, or the invention of a genuine plasma drive, could provide a propellant system thousands of times more powerful than any existing now.

To deal with this shortcoming, many writers and (respectable scientists) have talked of an ion-drive, in which a high-velocity exhaust jet is produced by accelerating electrically charged atoms (ions) in an electric field. Such a drive could *conceivably* allow a velocity of 6000 miles per second; and one of its most intriguing aspects is that the engines would literally devour themselves. As parts became worn out, they would be fed to the ion producers and disintegrate, disappearing in the form of exploded fuel. In such a way, the mass of a ship could be quickly reduced as it moved further along its course.

A notable problem in this type of tale, as writers were quick to realise, is the effect of so closed an environment on the crew. In many sf stories, this results in some kind of barbarism or oppressive priesthood in which all knowledge of the purpose of the mission is lost. Edmund Cooper's *Seed of Light* (1959) is a good example.

A much-favoured way of overcoming the time problem is to place the human crew in suspended animation – the art of freezing the human body into a state of indefinite hibernation. The advantages of the technique are obvious; not only is the psychological difficulty removed, but many of the physical ones. The amount of air, food and water required for recycling is much smaller. Each member of the crew can periodically be awakened to check the ship's course and life-support systems and the onboard computer can be programmed to awaken the entire crew at journey's end.

Such tales of suspended animation are frequent in the annals of science fiction, as, for example, A. E. van Vogt's 'Far Centaurus' (1942). This well-known story concludes ironically with a crew, having slept in suspended animation for 500 years, finding a reception committee of Earth colonists awaiting them in the Centauran system. A faster-than-light drive had been discovered soon after they set off.

Frequently the sleeping crews are depicted as monitored by robots or machines, but this can lead to tragic results if the programming goes awry as in Arthur C. Clarke's *2001* (1968), where the master computer attempts to destroy the crew members mistakenly to protect itself. An earlier and more grisly variant is David S. Gardner's 'Cold Storage' (1954), in which the ship's robots have been programmed at the beginning of a 400-year voyage that 'the women are for the men', and take this literally. When the hungry male sleepers are revived near journey's end, they are fortified with roast meat in rich, brown gravy. Later, they learn what it was they ate!

A further development of the theme is Cordwainer Smith's 'The Lady Who Sailed the Soul' (1960). Smith imagined a form of motive power produced by vast solar space sails, thousands of square miles in area – an unlikely sounding device, but one which is now technically feasible. Similar types of spaceships have appeared in other tales, notably in Poul Anderson's *Orbit Unlimited* (1961) and Larry Niven and Jerry Pournelle's *The Mote in God's Eye* (1973).

Because story plots normally demand continuity in the actions of characters, sf authors have continually looked for ways and means of overcoming the relativistic light-speed barrier of 186,000 miles per second. Many, unconcerned with scientific validity, have taken their cue from E. E. ('Doc') Smith's *Skylark of Space* (1928), where Smith intimated that the Theory of Relativity was after all only a theory and that Einstein's calculations were arguable at best. His famous characters, Seaton and Duquesne, roamed the universe at whatever supra-light speed his epic plots demanded. Much the same line was taken in

Right: Illustration by Chris Foss (top) and cover by McKie for Rhapsody in Black *by Brian Stableford (Pan).*

Edmond Hamilton's *Crashing Suns* (1928).

In general, most writers of the time recognised the light-speed barrier, and at least paid lip-service to the need for some device to overcome it. Smith himself invented an 'inertialess drive' for use in his famous 'Lensman' series, beginning with *Tri-planetary* in 1934.

Subsequently, his fellow galactic roamer, Edmond Hamilton, proposed an alternative instellar drive in *The Star Kings* (1951), which overcame the speed of light by storing mass as it accumulated, in the form of energy that could be utilised as and when it was needed. The flaw in such reasoning, as James Blish later made clear, was that an object which reaches the speed of light attains *infinite* mass, according to Einstein's principles. However, Hamilton had also touched on a quite different possibility for stellar travel – the ram-jet principle, which will be discussed below. One of the earliest FTL (*f*aster *t*han *l*ight) drives that writers developed is also the one that has achieved the most widespread popularity in the genre – the use of hyper-space. In countless stories it has become the standard method of transporting characters from star A to star B in the shortest time. Occasionally, the idea has bred half-hearted variants, among them nulspace, overspace or subspace, but they are all essentially part of the same concept.

It is a late work of Murray Leinster's which perhaps best typifies the modern treatment. In *Talents, Incorporated* (1962) he referred to an alien space fleet operating in 'overdrive', and described how each vessel stressed, or warped, the space immediately around it so that it transfigured its surroundings into a separate space-time continuum. In such a situation the laws of Einstein no longer apply, because the laws refer to a natural area of space that has not been distorted by some unnatural means.

It is possible to identify the forerunner of Leinster's instellar drive in Jack

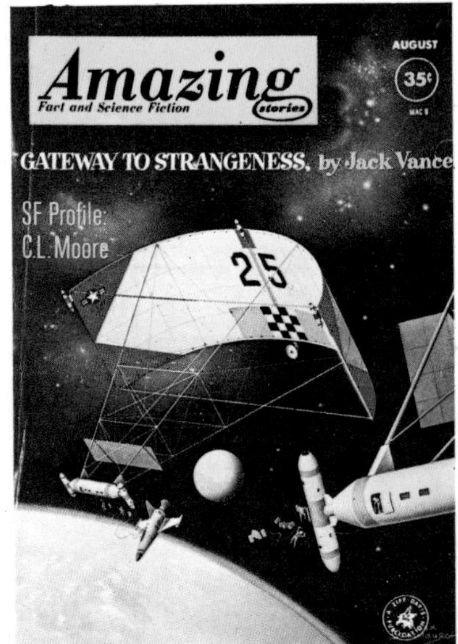

'*Gateway to Strangeness*' *by Jack Vance, August 1962. Cover by Schomburg.*

Halcyon Drift *by Brian Stableford (Pan). Illustration by McKie.*

Williamson's popular space opera, *The Legion of Space* (1934), the first of a trilogy. Here, spaceships are able to break the light barrier by means of an engine generating fields of force which react against the curvature of space itself, so that it drives the ship *around* space rather than through it. Although Leinster's and Williamson's versions of the FTL drive are three decades apart, there is little to distinguish between them – nor between many of the stories which came later. If the method of entry into hyper-space has changed little, the mode of navigation within it has changed even less. The standard procedure consists of 'jumps', as portrayed with dramatic effect in Isaac Asimov's *Foundation* series (1942–49). Spaceships are shown as bounding through the galaxy, their paths a widespread punctuated line across the interstellar gulf. The punctuation marks are the scant stretches of some ten to sixty light-seconds spent in normal space, while between them stretch the hundred and more light-year gaps that represent the 'jumps' through hyper-space. Each jump is supposedly aimed at a Target Star.

The Target Star system has remained the standard of interstellar navigation for most sf writers. But it has often been depicted as precarious – several stories have been written around the idea of a ship losing its way after an unchecked jump through hyper-space. Such a problem was posed in Frederik Pohl's 'The Mapmakers' (1955). It was 'solved' by the fortuitous presence of a blind man who could 'see' in hyper-space and act as navigator.

A British author who has done much to further hyper-space lore is E. C. Tubb. As the original Volsted Gridban, then as Charles Grey, and on through a plethora of pseudonyms and house names including Carl Maddox (*The Living World*, 1953), King Lang (*Saturn Patrol*, 1952) and Roy Sheldon (*The Metal Eater*, 1953), he has written a long series of space operas with hyper-space as their central theme. Among his stock characters is the engineer, forever struggling to tune his sub-tensor coils to their seven-place decimal similarity – a necessary prelude to the interstellar jump.

In general, the physical environment of hyper-space is presented as nothing more than 'a swirling grey mist', a limbo region quite unrelated to the cosmos we actually know. Only rarely has it been seen as populated. Two examples of its unlikely inhabitants can be found in Tubb's *Dynasty of Doom* (1953) and John Russell Fearn's 'Waters of Eternity' (1953), respectively featuring space dragons and living geometrical symbols. Usually, however, a ship in hyper-space can proceed without interruption. The major hazards arise when it re-enters ordinary space; if the navigation has been at fault, it may materialise inside a planet or star. In K. Houston (John) Brunner's 'Fiery Pillar' (1955), the first returning star-ship re-emerges within the Earth itself, causing an atomic chain reaction. The result is a column of fire which persists for decades, spawning mutations and disrupting scientific research.

Certain writers have attempted at least a 'pseudo-scientific' approach to the possible outcomes of travelling in hyper-space. Blish's 'Common Time' (1953) is a case in point, accentuating the 'time dilation' effect of interstellar travel. Another novel which takes time lags into account in the plot, is Poul Anderson's *No World of Their Own* (1955). E. C. Tubb pointed out another likely anomaly in his *Alien Universe* (1952) where he suggested that the use of rockets would be impractical in hyper-space, because the exhaust would fail to escape from the surrounding forcefield. Tubb's interstellar vessels accordingly 'drift' in hyper-space propelled by their initial velocity, and re-enter normal space by collapsing the energy field. If many authors have chosen to ignore such problems, it can be said in their favour that they have frequently created others to

02.01 SPACECRAFT AND STAR DRIVES

Cover by Donnell (Fantasy Press).

avoid making life too easy for their characters. Some have argued that a hyper-space field cannot be created close to a strong gravity source, such as our Sun's, and spaceships would need to reach the rim of the solar system before attempting the 'Big Jump'. The idea occurs in Thomas N. Scortia's 'Sea Change' (1956) and in Niven and Pournelle's *Mote in God's Eye* (1973).

In general, it can be said that the concept of hyper-space has been accepted amongst authors as a mere convention, a device to achieve continuity in a story's action, and not one to be taken very seriously. However, recent factual speculation in the physical sciences has indicated that it may indeed be possible. What such speculations involve is examined at the end of this section.

The greatest rival to the hyper-space concept of interstellar travel has come to the fore comparatively recently. It has been developed from observational evidence confirming early predictions of Einstein's theories. Scientists have been able to track cosmic particles invading the Earth's atmosphere at near-light speeds, and have come to the conclusion that they last longer than they should before disintegrating. Their observations suggest that for the speeding particles, time is slowed down. Consequently, the idea of near-to-light-speed flight, resulting in a time dilation effect on the travellers, has been increasingly favoured by sf writers. In fact it was a theme which had already received some attention as early as 1930, in Miles J. Breuer's 'The Fitzgerald Contraction' and its sequel 'The Time Valve', and, perhaps better known, in L. Taylor Hansen's 'Prince of Liars'. But it was rarely taken up by other writers until twenty years later, when genuine evidence began to accumulate.

Einstein had predicted that clocks on a moving vehicle close to the speed of light will appear to an outside observer to be running slow. To the observer, watching a spaceship moving relative to himself at the velocity of 0.99c (using c as the symbol for the velocity of light), the activities on board the ship will seem to be functioning at only 0.142, or one seventh, of their normal rate. The importance, for the purposes of star travel, of this slowing down of the tempo of events upon the moving ship relative to the same events if they were taking place in the 'stationary' universe soon becomes apparent.

If a space traveller were to fly from Earth to the star Procyon (10.4 light years distant) and back, at a velocity of 0.99c, the result would be that Earth records his return twenty-one years later, while the traveller has aged no more than three years! In fact, if he could get close enough to the speed of light, he could circumnavigate the universe in a single lifetime; but he might find on returning that perhaps ten billion years had elapsed and that the Earth was no longer there. Such a journey can only be regarded as travelling through time itself.

It was exactly such a situation which Poul Anderson handled brilliantly in *Tau Zero* (1970). His spaceship, carrying a crew of fifty, sets off towards a planet in the star system of Beta Virginis. Travelling at near-light speed, the ship is damaged in an accident and fails to slow down when it reaches its intended destination. The crew decide to accelerate the vessel so that they can reach the relatively matterless areas of intergalactic space, where they will be able to make the necessary repairs. But the author has plotted the story so that the crew are compelled to continue the acceleration. The ship comes nearer and nearer to the speed of light. Time slows down on board, to the point where the crew are able to witness the death of the present universe and its own rebirth. Eventually, they make planetfall in a new cosmos.

On a less exalted scale, the time-dilation factor in voyages to stars in our own galaxy has led authors to contemplate its disadvantages. Returning travellers have been depicted as finding the friends and loved ones they left behind already dead or in their dotage. Their reactions have been portrayed in such stories as L. Ron Hubbard's 'To the Stars' (1950), where those returning become the outcasts of humanity, and Poul Anderson's 'Ghetto' (1954) and its sequels, where the results are much the same.

At speeds lower than those of light, the problems of refuelling have also demanded attention. Among the serious suggestions are those of the photon-rocket and the nuclear pulse-jet. In the case of the former, interspatial matter is converted into radiation, which is then directed into a beam projected from the tail of the rocket. Such energy conversion could be 100 per cent efficient, if all the radiation was beamed in the same direction. The second method, involving the detonation of H-bombs at the rear of a starship, has often been regarded as too dangerous for manned expeditions.

Several stories develop the idea of a starship actually drawing its fuel *en route*, from space itself – an inversion of the principle conceived in Hamilton's *Star Kings* (1950), where it was proposed to use the ship's increased mass. Possibly a more practical source would be a ram-jet running on interstellar gas. The idea, originally postulated by R. W. Bussard in 1960, is simple in outline at least. The Bussard ship would be fronted by a scoop, probably consisting of an enormous electro-magnetic field, which can collect the interstellar gas and funnel it into a reaction chamber, there to be burned as fuel. Such vessels are now becoming part of contemporary science fiction, for example Larry Niven's 'Known Space' series; Anderson's *Tau Zero* ship also utilised this principle.

Meanwhile, the sf writer continues to dream. The perfect space drive would almost certainly dispense with the rocket principle altogether. Magazine editor John W. Campbell persuaded himself to think he might have uncovered such a method in the 1960s when he editorially promoted the 'Dean Drive', an anti-gravity device which turned out not to work. But, within the genre, the dream of establishing a negative gravity force continues.

One writer who took the idea to its farthermost limits was James Blish. In 'Bridge' (1952) he tells of scientific research on Jupiter which leads to the discovery of an anti-gravity propulsive device. Nicknamed the 'spindizzy', the invention made it unnecessary to design ships specially for space travel, since both mass and aerodynamic lines became unimportant. In the story which followed 'Okie' (1950), the most massive objects are lifted and hurled off the Earth. Whole cities, including New York, move into interstellar space in a search for new worlds. They are embraced by spindizzy force-fields, which hold in atmosphere and shield against cosmic

'The Problems of Space Flying' by Captain Herman Noordung, Science Wonder Stories *August 1929. Illustrations by Paul.*

radiation. The further discovery of a means to prolong life enables even the farthest interstellar journey by the nomad cities. Blish developed the theme across a span of 2000 years and through four novels, beginning with *Year 2018!* (1957), and by the series close whole planets were being shifted from orbit – a theme which is itself a sub-category of science fiction.

Rapid communications across the depths of space are a further sub-theme in the area of starflights. A few years ago, Gerald Feinberg, professor of physics at Columbia University, pointed out that Einstein's equations did not forbid particles to exceed light-speed *provided* they had a mass that could be described by an imaginary number. Such ghost particles have been dubbed 'tachyons', and Feinberg's theory holds that they would travel faster and faster the *less*

'The Long Way Home' by Poul Anderson, Astounding *April 1955. Illustration by Freas.*

energy they had, making the speed of light a barrier in reverse for them, since it would require infinite energy to slow them down to it. Although there is no observational evidence for the existence of tachyons, sf writers have often used the concept as window-dressing for tachyon radio transmitters which allow instant galactic communication. The idea of matter transmitters has also been revived, by using tachyons, notably in a series of novels by Frederik Pohl, jointly with Jack Williamson, which includes *Farthest Star* (1975).

Equally in the realms of present-day fantasy are other sf devices such as space-warps, in which the structure of interstellar space is distorted at some point so that it acts as a gateway to another cosmos or another part of the universe. The venerable principle of the Möbius Strip has frequently been evoked. Among modern treatments are *Starman Jones* (1953) by Robert A. Heinlein and Bob Shaw's *Night Walk* (1967).

In the same category can be classed the theoretical conception of black holes, dramatically outlined in John Nicholson's non-fiction work *Black Holes: the End of the Universe?* (1973), but first suggested half a century earlier by Karl Schwarzchild as an extrapolation from Einstein's General Theory of Relativity. The possible factual existence of black holes has lent an aura of some respectability to the sf writers' original hyper-space and space-warp conceptions. A black hole results from the collapse of a largish star. Instead of settling as a neutron star, the gravity of its compacted mass increases until it is so high that nothing, including light, can escape from it. Reputable scientists now believe that where a black hole exists, the normal laws of the cosmos may break down.

The force of gravity is regarded as infinite at the centre of a black hole, a force known as its singularity. However, in the case of a rotating black hole, the singularity would probably not be at its centre, but take the form of a ring at the equatorial plane. In this region, quantum mechanics have been quoted to conceive an area of super-space where it is possible to travel from point to point without crossing the space between. Such an instantaneous jump might be via a warp, often called a 'wormhole'. That wormholes, if they exist at all, are likely to be of subatomic dimensions has rarely deterred the sf writer from allowing his spaceship to dive into the singularity of a rotating black hole and emerge somewhere else – perhaps on the other side of the universe. Joseph Haldeman's 'Hero' (1972) made use of this idea, which was developed through several stories to become the theme of *The Forever War* (1975). The same device was employed by E. C. Tubb in *Breakaway* (1975), the first in the *Space: 1999* series, to explain Earth's runaway Moon reaching the interstellar spaces its TV-series plots demanded.

Such ideas still require much research and development, but they have undoubtedly opened up new fields of speculation. At least to the sf writer, the gate to the stars has swung wide open, and in fact it was the actual term 'Star Gate' which Arthur C. Clarke employed in several of his attempts at the script of the movie *2001*. At the other end of the scale, the continuing popularity of such tales as A. E. van Vogt's *Voyage of the Space Beagle* (1950), which can be seen as a forerunner to TV's *Star Trek*, indicates that the traditional idea of the giant rocketship travelling through space, with much adventure on the way, will retain a dominant role in the genre.

02.02 EXPLORATION AND COLONIES

ADDITIONAL INPUT

02.01.2 Interstellar Flight

Bounds, Sydney J. 'Project Starship', *Nebula* October 1954
Brackett, Leigh. *The Big Jump*, *Space Stories* February 1953; Ace (US) 1955
Brackett, Leigh. 'The Starmen of Llyrdis', *Startling* March 1951; as *The Starmen*, Gnome (US) 1952
Chandler, A. Bertram. *Bring Back Yesterday*, Ace (US) 1961
Chandler, A. Bertram. *The Rim of Space*, Avalon (US) 1961
Gallun, Raymond Z. 'Ten to the Stars', *SF Adventures* March 1953
Hawkins, Willard. 'Look to the Stars', *Imagination* October 1950
Hough, Stanley Bennett (as Rex Gordon). *Flight to the Stars*, Ace (US) 1959
Hubbard, L. Ron. 'To the Stars', *Astounding* February to March 1950
Leinster, Murray (Will F. Jenkins). *Colonial Survey*, Gnome (US) 1957
Leinster, Murray. *Operation: Outer Space*, Fantasy (US) 1954
Leinster, Murray. 'Proxima Centauri', *Astounding* March 1935
Leinster, Murray. *The Wailing Asteroid*, Avon (US) 1961
McIntosh, J.T. (J.T. McGregor). 'To the Stars', *Worlds of Tomorrow* August 1963
McIntosh, J.T. *200 Years to Christmas*, *Science Fantasy* June 1959; Ace (US) 1961
Morgan, Dan. 'The Lesser Breed', *Authentic* February 1955
Phillips, Rog (R.P. Graham). 'Starship from Sirius', *Amazing* August 1948
Russell, Eric Frank. *The Great Explosion*, Dobson (UK) 1962
Russell, Eric Frank. *Men, Martians and Machines*, Dobson (UK) 1955
Russell, Eric Frank. 'Ultima Thule', *Astounding* October 1951

Neutron Star *by Larry Niven* (Ballantine). *Cover by Rick Sternbach.*

We all long to see what lies beyond the hill. The rovings of early men seem to have been surprisingly wide. In my own life, I recall the vast excitement of moving by covered wagon from Texas to New Mexico the year I was seven. Crossing the Pecos. Camping each night in a new place. Claiming a new homestead.

Out of high school in 1925, I was longing for another move. Our land was poor and times were hard; I felt trapped by harsh circumstance. When at last I escaped from dull farm labour, it was into science fiction.

Into the spells of Poe's language and imagination. Into time, with Mark Twain's Connecticut Yankee. Into Tarzan's remarkable Africa and John Carter's stranger Mars. Finally, into the inviting far-off worlds I found in *Amazing Stories*, when it was new and I was young.

The first issue I owned – a free sample from the publisher – featured 'The Green Splotches', a fine novelette by T. S. Stribling about green-blooded plant-men. I will never forget the wonder of the cover by Frank R. Paul, which shows their ship taking off for Jupiter.

Fascinated with science fiction – 'scientifiction' then – I began writing my own. The next year I had the unforgettable thrill of seeing a dream-world of my own made real in another Paul painting. (The story was 'The Metal Man', in *Amazing* for December 1928. My first news of its publication was seeing my explorer-hero on the cover.)

Science fiction has been half my life since then, with the discovery and exploration and colonisation of new worlds its most appealing theme. The following section recalls forgotten stories of my own. *The Birth of a New Republic* (1931), a novel written with Miles J. Breuer about the coming colonisation of the Moon. 'The Prince of Space' (1931), about an orbital city. 'Salvage in Space' (1933), about mining the asteroids. 'Dead Star Station' (1933), about commerce between the stars. 'Operation Gravity' (1953), about the dangerous close-range study of a neutron star.

The word 'terraform' delights me when I see it in print, because it is a term I coined myself for the planetary engineers who were adapting new worlds for human colonists in the stories about anti-matter – then called CT or 'seetee', for contraterrene – that I began writing for John Campbell in 1942.

Even now, after nearly half a century, designing new worlds is still an exciting intellectual game. In the trilogy I am writing with Fred Pohl, *The Farthest Star* and *Wall around a Star* and another not yet titled, we are exploring a Dyson sphere – a habitable object so large that it would just fit inside the orbit of the Earth.

A thousand other writers have been gripped, as I always was, by the drama of the conquest of space.

Jack Williamson

Jack Williamson

02.02 EXPLORATION AND COLONIES

A substantial body of science fiction follows logically from the development of the idea of starships and concerns itself with the exploration of space and the colonisation of other worlds. Some of the earliest stories in literature (for instance, *Gilgamesh* and *The Odyssey*) tell of fantastic voyages on Earth; but even among ancient writers there were those who chose to escape the limitations of man's home planet and to set their fantasies in space. Among the works of such authors is *Of Wonderful Things Beyond Thule* by a little-known Greek, Antonius Diogenes, who lived in the first century AD, which tells of explorers who find they have walked to the Moon. Better remembered among the first accounts of lunar journeys are *Icaromenippos* and the *True History* (c180 AD) by Lucian of Samosata. The latter saw an English translation by Francis Hicks in 1634 which aroused some interest in scholarly circles. Its appearance in England was shortly followed by Bishop Francis Godwin's *The Man in the Moon* (1638) and, in France, by Cyrano de Bergerac's *The Comical History of the States and Empires of the World of the Moon* (1656), both outlandish fantasies – although in Cyrano's tale the idea of multi-stage rockets was touched on, together with predictions of the gramophone and the electric light-bulb.

Little space need be devoted here to detailing many such early fictional voyages; they are rarely relevant to the modern genre. Students and researchers will find all they are likely to want in three informative commentaries: *Voyages to the Moon* (1948) by Marjorie Hope Nicolson, *Into Other Worlds* (1957) by Roger Lancelyn Green and *Moon Travellers* (1960) by Peter Leighton. The modern science fiction writer, armed with the latest knowledge about our own solar system and, more speculatively, about the universe as a whole, is expected to extrapolate from accepted facts in his stories of exploration. The Apollo missions, the unmanned Mars and Venus probes, and the refinement of the radio telescope have to some extent curbed what might once have been, even in the 1950s, flights of the imagination.

Omnivore *by Piers Anthony (Ballantine).*

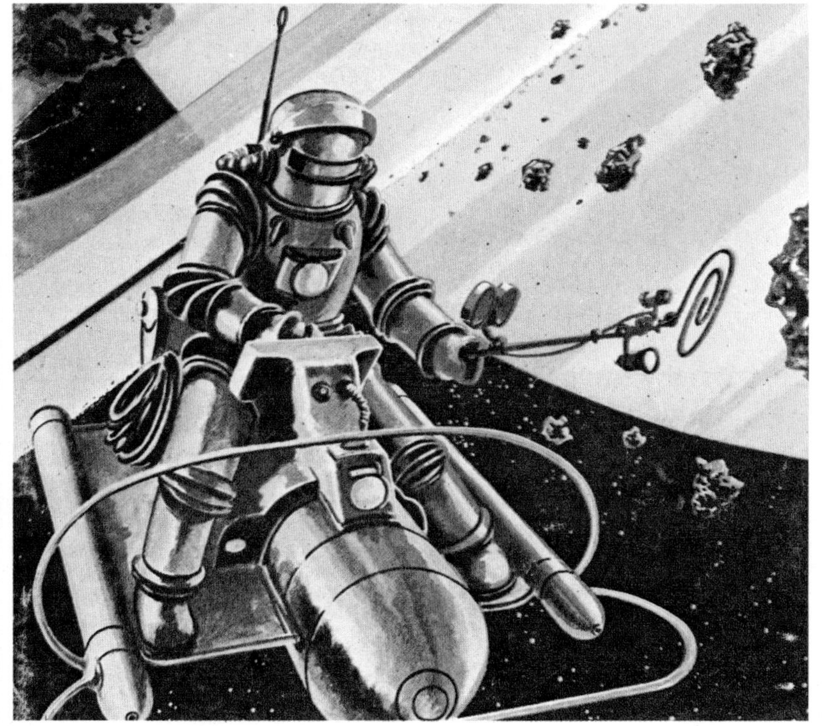

Thrilling Wonder Stories *February 1953. Cover by Coggins.*

02.02.1 The Solar System

It was almost inevitable that the writers of space fiction should initially concern themselves with our own Sun's family of planets before venturing into the lesser-known depths beyond, and the solar system still features regularly in contemporary science fiction.

The Sun is orbited by nine major known planets (Mercury, Venus, Earth, Mars, Jupiter, Saturn, Uranus, Neptune and Pluto) and by countless other smaller bodies, which include comets, errant asteroids (such as Icarus or Eros) and the more stable asteroids (including Ceres, Pallas and Vesta). All the planets, excepting Mercury, Venus and Pluto, are orbited by natural satellites, ranging from Earth's single Moon to Jupiter's twelve. Only the first six major planets were known to the ancient world. Uranus had to wait until 1781 for discovery, Neptune until 1846 and Pluto until 1930. The earliest located heavenly bodies were the four largest moons of Jupiter (Io, Europa, Ganymede and Callisto), discovered in 1609.

'Halos, Inc.' by Kendell Foster Crossen, Startling Stories *April 1953. Illustration by Schomburg.*

Since the Moon is our nearest neighbour and the only object in the sky, apart from the Sun, which can be seen as more than a mere point of light, it was to be expected that it would be the earliest to feature in science fiction. Following the success of the Apollo programme there were doubts whether further lunar stories could exercise much appeal. Stories set on the Moon still do appear, however, and a good example is a series of tales by Ernest Taves depicting the progressive lunar exploration made possible by the American Moon-shot. The series began with 'Pegasus 2' (1971), telling of an exploratory mission which encounters a crashed Soviet vehicle and its female pilot. 'Mayflower 1' (1972) is an account of the first temporary lunar colony, and 'Mayflower 2' (1973) develops the theme by considering the possible effects of lunar gravity on the human process of conception. A fourth story, 'Mayflower 3' (1973), illustrated the problems that might arise in the selection of scientists to be stationed on the Moon. The first series concluded with 'Luna 1' (1973), relating the efforts of the first permanent colony to combat such unforeseen factors as drug addiction and unwanted pregnancies.

Writing from hindsight, Taves modelled the details of his narrative on the actual Apollo missions and drew on a large body of accurate information. Less fortunate were the earlier writers, who have since been accused of a lack of reality when their imagined Moon flights have been compared with the real space programme. Certainly in the first days of the sf pulp magazines it was not uncommon to find eccentric inventors building spaceships in their back gardens, exploring the universe on an iota of fuel and returning home in time for tea. Even H. G. Wells came perilously close to ingenuousness in *First Men in the Moon* (1900) when one of the leading characters constructs an anti-gravity globe at his country laboratory. At the close of that novel the inventor, who remains on the Moon, communicates with Earth by radio – a modest forecast of the time, seven decades later, when the first real lunar walk would be televised live to the watching world. To his credit, writer Raymond F. Jones did include televised coverage of lunar exploration in 'The Moon Is Death' (1953), so that astronauts could be carefully tracked as they wandered into the unknown.

What man finds on the Moon and the inner planets is probably infinitely more important than the means he devises to reach them. Astronomical knowledge convinced many sf writers, long before man got to the Moon, that the kind of biological building-blocks familiar on Earth had no place on the grey satellite. With this in mind, they sketched out pictures of energy beings and of many other entities besides.

Raymond Z. Gallun's 'Magician of Dream Valley' (1938) and Clifford D. Simak's 'The Trouble with Tycho' (1960) are examples of the pre-Apollo visions of lunar life, both incorporating the idea of energy-based extraterrestrials. That the idea has lost none of its appeal in the light of the Apollo discoveries is evidenced by Bob Buckley's inclusion of similar entities in 'The Star Hole' (1972).

Probably the most influential lunar story of the last quarter century is Arthur C. Clarke's 'The Sentinel' (1951), which served as the jumping-off point for the movie *2001: a Space Odyssey* (1968). It tells of the discovery of an alien beacon left on the Moon millions of years in the past, intended to transmit a signal to its masters when Earth's dominant species achieves space flight. Clarke as a rule confines the backdrops of his fiction to our own solar system, and much of his work has been regarded as close to a definitive interpretation of planetary exploration. His lunar novels have been hailed as cornerstones of the genre, the perils of Moon colonisation and exploration being thoroughly worked out in *Earthlight* (1951) and *A Fall of Moondust* (1961). His efforts have been either foreshadowed or complemented by the work of one or two notable writers.

It would be difficult, for instance, to cite a better story of lunar colonisation than John W. Campbell's *The Moon Is Hell* (1950), telling of a colony of scientists struggling for survival. In contrast there is Robert A. Heinlein's *The Moon Is a Harsh Mistress* (1965), which recounts the computer-led rebellion of a lunar penal settlement in an obvious allegory of the American War of Independence.

Beyond the Moon our closest neighbours are Mars and Venus, both of which attracted much attention in early science fiction. Of the two, Mars has been the world which appears to have fascinated the largest number of readers. Perhaps this preoccupation with the Red Planet can be partly attributed to the enduring popularity of H. G. Wells's *The War of the Worlds* (1897), which in fact is set entirely on Earth. Edgar Rice Burroughs's famous Martian series did much in its own way to acquaint readers with Mars, but the picture it gave of the planet was quite unrealistic. In this phenomenally successful series, which began with *Under the Moons of Mars* (1912), Burroughs portrayed a planet differing little from Earth. He did, though, present some unfamiliar varieties of flora and fauna, which are now regarded as most memorable creations of the series. He may well have developed his Mars from the then current ideas of astronomer Percival Lowell and from the Mars depicted in *Lieut Gulliver Jones: His Vacation* (1950) by Edwin Lester Arnold, which featured a Martian society similar in many respects to the one which later took shape in Burroughs's imagination. However, Arnold's was by no means the first book to be set on Mars, though its title has a coincidental significance. (Mars is circled by two diminutive moons, Phobos and Deimos, both of which were discovered in 1877. Their existence was predicted in Jonathan Swift's classic, *Gulliver's Travels*, 1726, during the hero's discussions with the learned astronomers of Laputa.)

'Hot Planet' by Hal Clement, Galaxy *August 1963. Cover by Pederson.*

Among earlier Martian adventures, Percy Greg's *Across the Zodiac* (1880) deserves passing mention for its portrayal of scientifically advanced extraterrestrials. Other works of note on the same theme are Robert Cromie's *A Plunge into Space* (1890), which went some way towards suggesting the harsh realities of space travel, and Gustavus W. Pope's *Journey to Mars* (1894). The latter is one more work which is supposed to have exercised some influence on Burroughs.

In the first somewhat undisciplined era of the pulps, such writers as Laurence Manning endeavoured to bring an element of realism into their depictions of Mars. In 'The Voyage of the Asteroid' (1932) and its sequel 'Wreck of the Asteroid' (1932), where the explorers fight for survival on a grim planet, Manning pointed the way to the greater imaginative achievements of Stanley G. Weinbaum, who in 'A Martian Odyssey' (1934) was able to divert the reader's attention from the planet and concentrate it upon a menagerie of bizarre and likeable fauna.

Several later writers still clung to the fantasy of an Earth-like planet, chief among them being Ray Bradbury. In *The Martian Chronicles* (1951), the planet is depicted as an extraterrestrial example of the American Mid-West, a favourite preoccupation of its author. En route

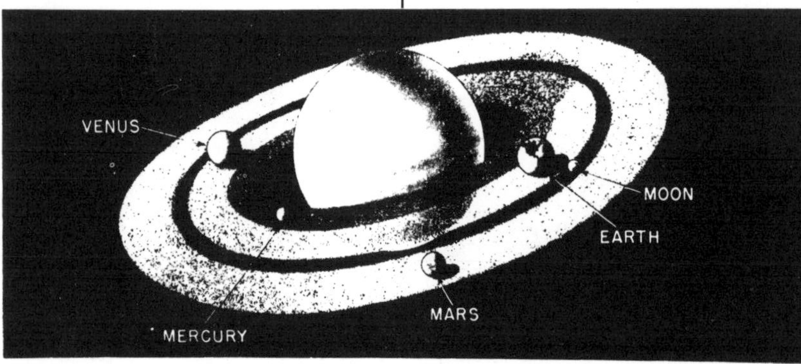

Diagram of Saturn by Schomburg, Science Fiction Plus *June 1953.*

Bradbury indulges in a variety of idiosyncratic diversions, the most noted being 'The Third Expedition' (retitled 'Mars Is Heaven', 1948), in which new arrivals are hypnotised into believing they are once more on Earth in their childhood. A rather self-indulgent venture is Heinlein's *Stranger in a Strange Land* (1961), in which the first human born and raised on Mars returns to Earth to establish a hippie-like religious cult. Perhaps in a reaction against such extravagant visions, James Blish included Martians in *The Hour before Earthrise* (1966), in a deliberate return to the old style, portraying a teen-aged inventor and his anti-gravity device. Likewise, Algis Budrys took the opportunity in *The Iron Thorn* (1967) to consider a genetically controlled colony on Mars.

One of the earliest and most realistic novels of Martian colonisation is *The Sands of Mars* (1951) by Arthur C. Clarke, which includes references to the exploitation of Martian natural resources. Clarke returned to Mars in 'Transit of Earth' (1970), which tells of an ill-fated expedition to the planet to record the Earth's transit across the Sun. Predictably, by 1970, Clarke's description of Mars had become painstakingly authentic. Asimov was another who showed how perilous the existence of such a colony might be. In 'The Martian Way' (1952) he forecast the colonists tapping valuable water supplies from the rings of Saturn. Similar problems of a Mars facing a water shortage appear in William Walling's 'Nix Olympica' (1974), published in a special Mars edition of *Analog* magazine. The issue also included Bob Buckley's 'Encounter below Tharsis', which explores the possibilities of protoplasmic life on Mars. These recent stories point to something of a Mars revival in science fiction, possibly stimulated by the new discoveries of the Pioneer probes. Collating the latest factual information, Gordon R. Dickson has produced a realistic novel about the first manned journey to Mars, *The Far Call* (1973). However, despite new sources of knowledge, the romantic attraction of the early stories seems unlikely to pall, principally because they tell a good tale. Among such are Edmond Hamilton's 'What's It Like Out There?', written in the 1930s, but, because of its harsh portrait of space exploration, not published until 1952, and H. Beam Piper's 'Omnilingual' (1957), which portrays the attempts by scientists to translate an ancient Martian language.

Illustration of Titan, a moon of Saturn, by Valigursky, If September 1973.

Attention to accepted scientific facts is equally important in the treatment of Venus. Because the planet is shrouded in a deep layer of clouds, its surface conditions long remained a mystery; scientists and writers conjectured that the planet might be a dust-bowl or, alternatively, covered by oceans. Much early fiction depicted Venus as a swamp world, and Gustavus Pope's *Journey to Venus* (1895) shows it populated by Earth-like prehistoric monsters. It was an idea which persisted for decades. Another early example, Garrett P. Serviss's *A Columbus of Space* (1909), depicts the planet eternally pointing the same face towards the Sun and thus possessing a hot side, a dark side and a twilight zone. In this respect the novel can be compared to Stanley G. Weinbaum's engaging stories 'Parasite Planet' (1935) and 'The Lotus Eaters' (1935).

Probably because of its more dramatic possibilities, the water-covered version of Venus is more common in science fiction, in such stories as *Logic of Empire* (1941) by Robert A. Heinlein and *Fury* (1947) by Lawrence O'Donnell (Henry Kuttner and C. L. Moore). Even Asimov, noted for his scientific accuracy, chose an oceanic Venus for his juvenile novel *The Oceans of Venus* (1954); and in Poul Anderson's 'Sister Planet' (1959) we find an uninterrupted ocean inhabited by cetaceous life-forms. Conversely, Eric Frank Russell's 'Sustained Pressure' (1953), portrays extensive Venusian land-masses, but they are blanketed by thick, wet fog.

The *Mariner* probes have now confirmed that Venus is indeed a scorching dust-bowl, and credit must go to those authors who came close to imagining the reality, among them Frederik Pohl and C. M. Kornbluth. Their novel *Gravy Planet* (1952) better known as *The Space Merchants*, depicts just such a hostile world, while in 'The Big Rain' (1954) Poul Anderson describes the attempts of scientists to create rainfall on an arid Venus. New writer Brenda Pearce has taken all the known facts about the planet and combined them in 'Crazy Oil' (1975).

Accounts of the first manned probes to Venus include Larry Niven's 'Becalmed in Hell' (1965) and Barry N. Malzberg's *Beyond Apollo* (1972); and it was Niven who took the sunwards trip in 'The Coldest Place' (1964), which takes place on the dark side of Mercury. Almost immediately after the last

02.02 EXPLORATION AND COLONIES

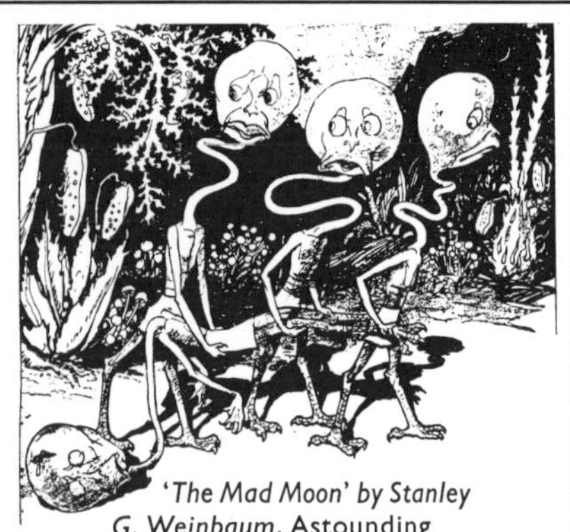

'The Mad Moon' by Stanley G. Weinbaum, Astounding *December 1935. Illustration by Dold.*

story was published, it was discovered that Mercury actually revolved, putting an end to the use of standard plots about Mercury's hot side and twilight belt such as in Alan E. Nourse's 'Brightside Crossing' (1956), Hal Clement's 'Hot Planet' (1963) and C. C. MacApp's 'The Mercurymen' (1965).

The prospect of life on Mercury appears slim, but not beyond imagination. In 'Sunrise on Mercury' (1957), Robert Silverberg introduces a molten form of life, while in 'Sunfire!' (1962) Edmond Hamilton describes the planet's flame-beings. Following her treatment of Venus, Brenda Pearce has taken full account of the recent facts about Mercury in her tale of exploration, 'Hot Spot' (1974). Manned space exploration beyond Mars is an unlikely prospect in the near future, but in science fiction it has been a long-standing feature. Between Mars and Jupiter orbit thousands of small clumps of rock, the Asteroid Belt, and many stories have suggested the mining of raw materials from this area. The idea appears as far back as Clifford D. Simak's 'The Asteroid of Gold' (1932), while Larry Niven in particular has developed the theme in recent years. In 'At the Bottom of a Hole' (1966) and 'The Adults' (1967) he depicts the frontiersman's escape from the claustrophobic confines of Earth to the freedom of the asteroids. The concept of those drifting rocks being claimed and occupied by pioneer prospectors is common in the genre, as in Robert Sheckley's 'Beside Still Waters' (1953) and Poul Anderson's 'Garden in the Void' (1952).

The asteroids are now regarded as the debris left by a major planet that broke up – a lost celestial body which plays a major part in Ross Rocklynne's 'Time Wants a Skeleton' (1941) and Brian Aldiss's 'T' (1956). In *Plague Ship* (1969), Harry Harrison adds the idea of a deadly virus encountered among the asteroids, where it has lain dormant since the one-time planet was torn apart.

By no means every asteroid is within the Belt. Several, nicknamed 'Earth-grazers', come within the orbits of Earth, Venus and even Mercury. Icarus passes closer to the Sun than any other heavenly object (except comets) and this characteristic has fascinated several writers. In 'Icarus Descending' (1973), Greg Benford tells of a NASA mission sent to the tiny object, and in 'Summertime on Icarus' (1960) Arthur C. Clarke tells of a spaceman trapped on the rock as it plunges sunward. In 'Sunspot' (1960), Hal Clement makes use of a similar concept in telling of a comet's flight near to the solar fire.

'Sunrise on Mercury' by Calvin M. Knox, (Robert Silverberg) May 1957. Cover by Emsh.

Various imaginary errant bodies have been introduced by sf writers; some have written of isolated planets, on an endless journey across the universe, passing through the Sun's gravitational field. A huge alien artefact moves in this way in Arthur C. Clarke's *Rendezvous with Rama* (1973). Forty years earlier Philip Wylie and Edwin Balmer had produced classics on this theme in *When Worlds Collide* (1932) and its sequel *After Worlds Collide* (1933), exploring more fully the ideas of a rogue planet. Ross Rocklynne also portrayed such an intruder in 'The Men and the Mirror' (1938), featuring the same characters as in 'At the Centre of Gravity' set inside the hollow planet Vulcan, and 'Jupiter Trap' (1937). (Vulcan was once supposed to exist within the orbit of Mercury, being named by the French astronomer Leverrier in 1845. Although its presence was finally refuted in 1915, it still occasionally appears in science fiction and is featured in Leigh Brackett's memorable 'Child of the Sun', 1942.)

Beyond the Asteroid Belt the planetary environments grow increasingly hostile, but their moons have lent themselves to much fictional exploitation. Jupiter, the giant of the solar system, is featured in

Cover illustration of Saturn by Alex Schomburg, Science Fiction Plus *June 1953.*

Mission to Universe *by Gordon R. Dickson (Del Rey/Ballantine). Cover by van Dongen.*

several stories, among them Poul Anderson's 'Call Me Joe' (1957), Clifford D. Simak's 'Desertion' (1944) and James Blish's 'Bridge' (1952). In 'Victory Unintentional' (1942), Isaac Asimov sends a team of indestructible robots from the human colony on Ganymede to face the wrath of the Jovians. In that story the robots are shown as roughly centaur-like, and in Poul Anderson's *Three Worlds to Conquer* (1964) the Jovians themselves are centaurian.

Of Jupiter's twelve satellites only the innermost five have regularly appeared in science fiction: Amalthea, Io, Europa, Ganymede and Callisto. Amalthea is the now accepted name for Jupiter V, and in 'Jupiter V' (1952) by Arthur C. Clarke the satellite turns out to be a discarded alien spaceship. Io was the setting for Stanley Weinbaum's humorous 'The Mad Moon' (1935), a hot steaming world lit for a crazy succession of days by Jupiter, the Sun and Europa in turn. Asimov's early story 'The Callistan Menace' (1940) showed Callisto as almost Earth-like, while the earlier 'Monsters of Callisto' (1933) by Edward H. Hinton provided it with a vast sea.

Ganymede remains the favourite among writers, and in 'The Snows of Ganymede' (1955) Poul Anderson describes the terraforming of the satellite, a popular idea used earlier in Robert A. Heinlein's *Farmer in the Sky* (1950) and recently in Greg Benford's *Jupiter Project* (1972). (The desirability of terraforming, that is of converting a dead or inhospitable world to produce a more Earth-like environment, was argued by Olaf Stapledon during the 1930s and recently by Carl Sagan in his speculative study *The Cosmic Connection*, 1973.)

Arthur C. Clarke has generally avoided using the settings of the major moons of Jupiter, but in 'A Meeting with Medusa' (1971) he tells of a descent directly into the Jovian atmosphere, by balloon. The action of his recent novel, *Imperial Earth* (1975), takes place on Titan, Saturn's largest moon. Titan is so far the only Saturnian satellite known to have a detectable atmosphere, predominantly methane. This is not the Titan of Stanley G. Weinbaum's 'Flight on Titan' (1935), nor of Ben Bova's 'The Towers of Titan' (1962), and even less of Kurt Vonnegut's *The Sirens of Titan* (1959). Saturn's most noted feature supplied the scene for Neil R. Jones's 'Hermit of Saturn's Rings' (1940), where the survivor of a spaceship disaster takes refuge in the orbiting rocks only to be menaced by a gaseous life-form. An excursion into the planet's actual atmosphere is described by Harry Harrison in 'Pressure' (1969).

Beyond Saturn lies Uranus, first featured in fiction in an obscure pamphlet written in 1784, three years after its discovery. In general, it has been ignored by most sf writers, though Weinbaum naturally endows it with more of his extraordinary life-forms in 'Planet of Doubt' (1935). Donald A. Wollheim takes the term 'gas giant' literally in 'Planet Passage' (1942), which depicts a rocket boring directly through the planet, and in Fritz Leiber's 'The Snowbank Orbit' (1962) a flight into its soupy atmosphere is used to decrease a rocket's acceleration.

Similarly, Neptune has been largely overlooked in the genre, although 'A Baby

XXXVI-XXXVII. The ground station has been set up on Mars, and the explorers are beginning to investigate the vicinity of the landing site.
148
149

Illustration of Mars by Bonestell, from Exploration of Mars *by Willy Ley and W. von Braun (Sidgwick & Jackson).*

on Neptune' (1929) by Miles J. Breuer and Clare Winger Harris presents an ice-ridden world inhabited by living gaseous entities. In more recent fiction, the most noted use of Neptune occurs in Piers Anthony's *Macroscope* (1969), where scientists establish a base on a satellite of Triton, the planet's major moon, and later divert Triton down *into* Neptune.

Pluto, as far as we know, is the outpost of the solar system. Discovered in 1930, its existence had been hypothesised for decades and even postulated in Donald W. Horner's novel *Their Winged Destiny* (1912). Immediately after its discovery, Stanton A. Coblentz used it as a setting for *Into Plutonian Depths* (1931), imagining it populated by a bee-like society. In terms of scientific knowledge, the planet remains an enigma, and as early as 1934, in 'The Rape of the Solar System', Leslie F. Stone speculated that it might be a former asteroid. Weinbaum, for his part, portrayed it as a hideaway for space pirates, in 'The Red Peri' (1935). Recently, Simak provided a neat answer to the mystery of Pluto in 'Construction Shack' (1973), showing it as no more than a site office for the advanced beings who created the solar system.

And beyond Pluto? Over the years a number of astronomers have argued that a tenth planet may exist. In 'The World That Dissolved' (1939), Fearn (writing as Polton Cross) uses it as a setting for an observatory. Edmund Cooper, in *The Tenth Planet* (1973), sees it as a home for refugees from Earth. But no other writer seems to have gone as far as Larry Niven, whose 'The Borderland of Sol' (1975), adds four new planets to the system and disregards Pluto as merely an errant satellite of Neptune.

'Jupiter Project' by Gregory Benford, Amazing *September 1972. Illustration by Davis.*

ADDITIONAL INPUT

02.02.1 The Solar System

Aldiss, Brian W. 'Hen's Eyes', *Amazing* September 1961
Anderson, Poul. 'The Communicators', *Infinity 1* (ed Robert Hoskins) Lancer (US) 1970
Anderson, Poul. 'Duel on Syrtis', *Planet Stories* March 1951
Asimov, Isaac. 'Christmas on Ganymede', *Startling* January 1942
Asimov, Isaac. 'Half-Breeds on Venus', *Astonishing Stories* December 1940
Asimov, Isaac. 'Marooned off Vesta', *Amazing* March 1939; sequel 'Anniversary', *Amazing* March 1959
Asimov, Isaac. 'The Weapon Too Dreadful to Use', *Amazing* May 1939
Benford, Greg. 'Flattop', *F&SF* May 1966
Benford, Greg. 'In the Ocean of Night', *If* June 1972
Benford, Greg. 'Representative from Earth', *F&SF* January 1966
Benford, Greg. 'Threads of Time', *Threads of Time* (ed Robert Silverberg) Nelson (US) 1974
Blish, James. 'How Beautiful with Banners', *Orbit 1* (ed Damon Knight) Putnam (US) 1966
Brackett, Leigh. 'The Moon That Vanished', *Thrilling Wonder* October 1948
Buckley, Bob. 'The Hunters of Tharsis', *Analog* February 1975
Buckley, Bob. 'A Matter of Orientation', *Analog* July 1970
Clarke, Arthur C. 'Before Eden', *Amazing* June 1961
Clarke, Arthur C. 'If I Forget Thee, Oh Earth . . .', *F&SF* September 1951
Clarke, Arthur C. *Prelude to Space*, *Galaxy Novels* No 3 (US) 1951
Clarke, Arthur C. 'Thirty Seconds-Thirty Days', *Thrilling Wonder* December 1949; retitled 'Breaking Strain', *No Place Like Earth* (ed John Carnell) Boardman (UK) 1952 and in collection

Farmer in the Sky *by Robert A. Heinlein (Ballantine). Cover by Rosenblatt.*

Expedition to Earth, Ballantine (US) 1953
Clarke, Arthur C. 'Venture to the Moon', six episodes commissioned by *Evening Standard* (UK) 1956; also published in *F&SF* December 1956 to February 1957
Clement, Hal (Harry Clement Stubbs). 'Dust Rag', *Astounding* September 1956
Clement, Hal. 'Sunspot', *Analog* November 1960
Cyrano de Bergerac, Savinien. *The Comical History of the States and Empires of the Worlds of the Moon and Sun*, English trans A. Lovell, London 1687; original French publication *A Voyage to the Moon*, 1650 (unauthorised), 1657; *A Voyage to the Sun*, 1662; reprinted as *Voyages to the Moon and Sun*, Routledge (UK) 1923; as *Other Worlds*, New English Library (UK) 1976
Del Rey, Lester. 'The Luck of Ignatz', *Astounding* August 1939
Del Rey, Lester. *Police Your Planet* (orig under pseudonym Erik Van Lhin), *SF Adventures* March to September 1953; Avalon (US) 1956; reprinted credited to Lester Del Rey and Erik Van Lhin, Ballantine (US) 1975
Dick, Philip K. *All We Marsmen, Worlds of Tomorrow* August to December 1963; revised as *Martian Time-Slip*, Ballantine (US) 1964 and NEL (UK) 1976
Gallun, Raymond Z. 'The Lunar Chrysalis', *Amazing* September 1931
Gallun, Raymon Z. 'Operation Pumice', *Thrilling Wonder* April 1949
Godwin, Tom. 'The Cold Equations', *Astounding* August 1954
Hamilton, Edmond. 'Horror on the Asteroid', *Weird Tales* September 1933
Heinlein, Robert A. *Podkayne of Mars, If* November 1962 to March 1963; Putnam (US) 1963
Heinlein, Robert A. *The Red Planet*, Scribners (US) 1949
Heinlein, Robert A. 'Requiem', *Astounding* January 1940
Heinlein, Robert A. *Rocket Ship Galileo*, Scribners (US) 1947; reworked as *Destination: Moon, Short Stories* September 1950
Horner, Donald W. *By Aeroplane to the Sun*, Century Press (UK) 1910
Judd, Cyril (Cyril Kornbluth and Judith Merril). *Mars Child, Galaxy* May to July 1951; retitled *Outpost Mars*, Abelard (US) 1952; revised as *Sin in Space*, Beacon (US) 1961
McIntosh, J.T. (James MacGregor). *One in 300*, Doubleday (US) 1954, comprising three stories originally published as follows:
'One in Three Hundred', *F&SF* February 1953
'One in a Thousand', *F&SF* January 1954
'One Too Many', *F&SF* September 1954
Niven, Larry. 'The Hole Man', *Analog* January 1974
O'Donnell, Lawrence (C.L. Moore). 'Clash by Night', *Astounding* March 1943
Oliver, Chad. 'Field Expedient', *Astounding* January 1955
Pohl, Frederik and Kornbluth, C.M. *Gravy Planet, Galaxy* June to August 1952; retitled *The Space Merchants*, Ballantine (US) 1953
Pournelle, Jerry. 'Tinker', *Galaxy* July 1975
Rocklynne, Ross. 'Moon Trash', *Amazing* January 1970
Rocklynne, Ross. 'They Fly So High', *Amazing* June 1952
Simak, Clifford D. 'Clerical Error', *Astounding* August 1940
Simak, Clifford D. 'Hermit of Mars', *Astounding* June 1939
Simak, Clifford D. 'Hunger Death', *Astounding* October 1938
Simak, Clifford D. 'Masquerade', *Astounding* March 1941
Simak, Clifford D. 'Tools', *Astounding* July 1942
Stone, Leslie F. 'Gulliver, 3000 AD', *Wonder Stories* May 1933
Stone, Leslie F. 'The Hell Planet', *Wonder Stories* June 1932
Temple, William F. '"L" Is for Lash', *Amazing* July 1960
Temple, William F. *Shoot at the Moon*, Whiting & Wheaton (UK) 1966
Temple, William F. 'The Undiscovered Country', *Nebula 35* October 1958
Verne, Jules. *From the Earth to the Moon* (*De la Terre à la Lune*, 1865), English translation Sampson, Low 1873; sequel *Round the Moon* (*Autour de la Lune*, 1870), English translation 1873
Verne, Jules. *Hector Servadec, Magasin d'Education et de Recreation* 5 January to 20 December 1877, English translation Scribners (US) 1878; subtitled *Off on a Comet* and serialised as such in *Amazing* April to May 1926

'Requiem' by Robert A. Heinlein. Illustration by M. Streff.

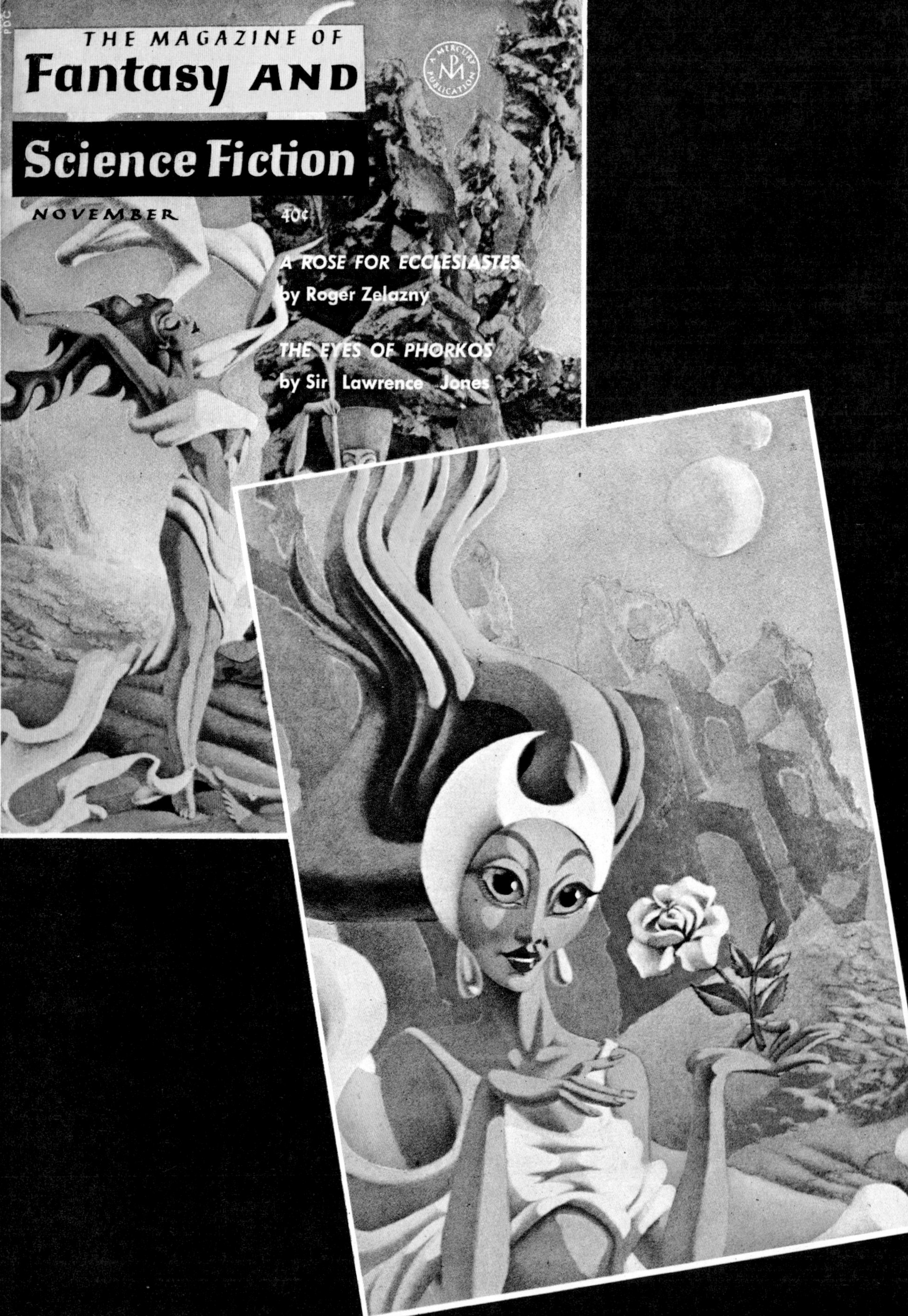
PDC
THE MAGAZINE OF
Fantasy AND
Science Fiction
A MERCURY PUBLICATION
NOVEMBER
40¢
A ROSE FOR ECCLESIASTES
by Roger Zelazny
THE EYES OF PHORKOS
by Sir Lawrence Jones

Wyndham, John. *The Troons of Space*, *Fantastic* November 1958 to February 1959; retitled *The Outward Urge* (with additional credit to Lucas Parkes, pseudonym for John Wyndham), Michael Joseph (UK) 1959; expanded Penguin (UK) 1962, comprising the following stories:
'For All the Night', *New Worlds* April 1958; as 'The Troons of Space', *Fantastic* November 1958
'Idiot's Delight', *New Worlds* June 1958; as 'The Moon AD 2044' *Fantastic* December 1958
'The Thin Gnat-Voices', *New Worlds* July 1958; as 'Mars AD 2094', *Fantastic* January 1959
'Space Is a Province of Brazil', *New Worlds* September 1958; as 'Venus AD 2144', *Fantastic* February 1959
'The Emptiness of Space', *New Worlds* November 1960; as 'The Asteroids, 2194', *Amazing* January 1961
Wyndham, John (as John Beynon). *Stowaway to Mars*, *Passing Show* (UK) May 1936, serial; retitled *Planet Plane*, Newnes (UK) 1936; subsequently abridged under title *The Space Machine*; republished as *Stowaway to Mars*, Coronet (UK) 1972; sequel 'Sleepers of Mars', *Tales of Wonder* 2 1938
Zelazny, Roger, 'The Doors of His Face, the Lamps of His Mouth', *F&SF* March 1965
Zelazny, Roger. 'Home Is the Hangman', *Analog* November 1975
Zelazny, Roger, 'A Rose for Ecclesiastes', *F&SF* November 1963

Anthologies

Aldiss, Brian W. (with Harry Harrison). *All about Venus*, Dell (US) 1968; revised as *Farewell, Fantastic Venus!*, MacDonald (UK) 1968
Moskowitz, Sam. *Exploring Other Worlds*, Collier (US) 1963
Pohl, Frederik and Carol. *Jupiter*, Ballantine (US) 1973
Wollheim, Donald A. *Flight into Space*, F. Fell (US) 1950
Wollheim, Donald A. *The Hidden Planet*, Ace (US) 1959
Wollheim, Donald A. *Men on the Moon*, Ace (US) 1958; revised Ace (US) 1969

Reference

Locke, George. *Voyages in Space*, Ferret Fantasy (UK) 1975

Left: 'A Rose for Ecclesiastes' by Roger Zelazny, F&SF November 1963. Cover by Bok.

02.02.2 Towards the Stars

Once sf writers have gone beyond the confines of the solar system, their imaginations need know few bounds. Worlds can be invented to order, populated if necessary, and made as hostile or as friendly as the plots require.

It was once believed that it was E. E. ('Doc') Smith who first pointed science fiction at the stars; and it is true that he, ably supported by John W. Campbell, Jack Williamson and Edmond Hamilton, popularised the form now known as 'space opera'. However, there is a much earlier work involving interstellar travel: Robert William Cole's *The Struggle for Empire* (1900), a chronicle of space battles waged between our own system and a planet of Sirius.

Quite possibly, before man ever reaches another star, manned exploratory craft may make contact with other, alien, probes. Such a situation occurs in Murray Leinster's 'First Contact' (1945), where two ships meet in the depths of space, neither crew knowing whether to trust the other. Another variation on the theme appears in 'Grapeliner' (1949) by James White, but in that story Earth is put at a disadvantage by having already made an inadvertently hostile move. White considers the idea further in *All Judgement Fled* (1967), when humans discover an alien ship carrying a whole menagerie of creatures and have to decide which is the intelligent species. Recently, Gene Wolfe has updated the theme in 'Alien Stones' (1972), telling of the discovery of an extra-terrestrial spacecraft apparently deserted – until the exploring humans learn that the ship itself is an intelligent entity.

Beyond our solar system, the nearest observable star is Proxima Centauri, a fact which James Blish chose to ignore in 'Darkside Crossing' (1970), where he showed the Sun as one half of a double star system with its companion only one-sixth of a light year distant. In inventing alien worlds orbiting other stars, sf writers separate into two basic camps. Either they create planets of extreme hostility and bizarre ecology, or they devise Earth-like environments and concentrate on the indigenous life-forms and their interaction with man. The former category attracts many of the more scientifically orientated of the writers, Poul Anderson and Hal Clement among them. In *The Ancient Gods* (1966), for example, Anderson strands his explorers on an inner planet of a sun on the distant edge of the Milky Way, where there are very few stars, and where the vast cloudy spiral of the galaxy is worshipped as a god by the natives. Conversely, in 'Starfog' (1967), Anderson depicts the other extreme: three men find themselves on a planet in the midst of a globular cluster with the heavens so tightly packed with stars that navigation is impossible. (Asimov's 'Nightfall', 1940, is a noted story set in a similar location.) Most of Anderson's tales are set against the backdrop of a galactic civilisation of which Earth is an integral part, but in *The Day after Doomsday* (1961) man has only just begun his first tentative explorations into space when Earth is suddenly destroyed. Isolated, the survivors attempt to hunt down those responsible, distrustful of every alien species they encounter.

In the field of hostile and unusual worlds Hal Clement must be credited with a flight of imagination which has rarely been equalled. His *Mission of Gravity* (1953) introduces the planet Mesklin, a massive body subjected to so rapid a rotational spin that, while its gravitational pull at the equator is three times that of Earth (or 3G), at the poles the pull is 650G. The Mesklinites are reintroduced in *Star Light* (1970), set on a 30G planet.

Among other far-fetched worlds is the egg-shaped planet described in Larry Niven's already mentioned 'The Borderland of Sol' (1975). Its limited atmosphere encircles the equatorial belt, while at either end the poles rise above the air. Larry Niven is also well known for his *Ringworld* (1970), in which he portrays a world in the form of a complete ring around its sun.

In the early 1960s, astronomers became engrossed with the theoretical concept of 'neutron stars', bodies collapsed upon themselves by the force of their own gravity. Such a phenomenon might have the mass of our own Sun while measuring no more than a few miles in diameter – it would be enormously dense. In 'Neutron Star' (1966), Niven explores the perils of venturing too close to such an object. It has been argued that such dense suns would probably trap their own light within their gravitational fields, creating black holes in space. Black holes have become commonplace in recent science fiction, Niven again leading the way with 'The Hole Man' (1974).

Striking among the accounts of other hostile environments is Harry Harrison's 'Deathworld' trilogy. The author has frequently portrayed alien nature at its most intransigent on a variety of worlds, but none is more fascinating than that described in *Deathworld 1* (1960). In a 2G gravity, its human colonists struggle to adapt themselves to combat the plant and animal life perpetually attempting to destroy them.

Turning to the writers who have explored the possibilities of more Earth-like planets, we find such examples as John Brunner's *The Dramaturges of Yan* (1971), in which Earthmen attempt to solve the riddle of a great civilisation that once ruled the planet of the title, but has since declined. The same author takes a similar investigation a stage further in *Total Eclipse* (1974).

Simak also occupies a major place among the creators of particularly baffling worlds. His uninhabited planet in 'Jackpot' (1956) is eventually revealed as a galactic library. In 'Limiting Factor' (1949), what first appears to be an all-metal world is found to be a fairly ordinary planet submerged beneath

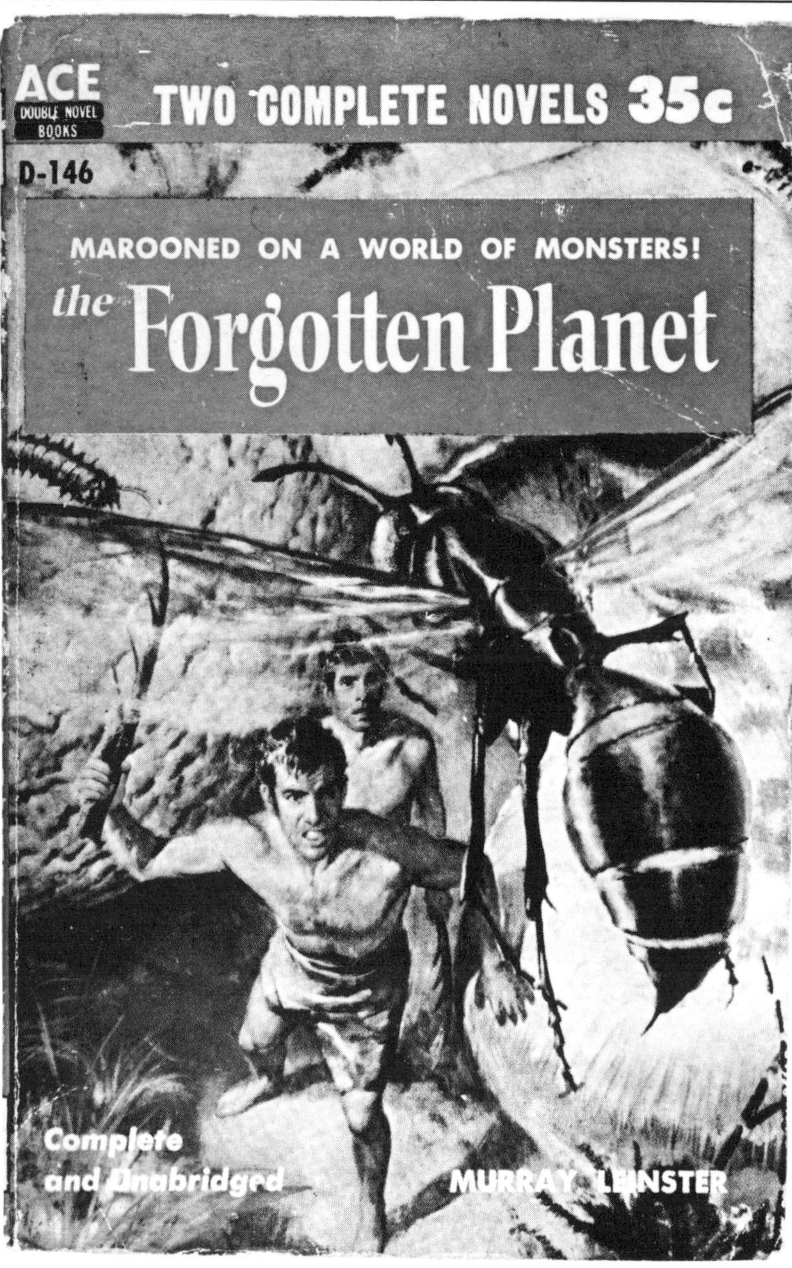

The Forgotten Planet *by Murray Leinster (Ace).*

an all-enveloping conurbation. 'Drop Dead' (1956) is an example in Simak's light-hearted vein, portraying a planet whose inhabitants approach human explorers only to fall lifeless at their feet. In contrast, his 'You'll Never Go Home Again' (1951) tells of a manned expedition to an apparently unremarkable world which nevertheless produces disastrous effects on their machinery.

In 'The Plants' (1946), Murray Leinster makes the point that alien vegetation can often be as dangerous as animal life, an idea that Robert Bloch had already exploited in 'The Fear Planet' (1943). Among Leinster's many alien worlds can be found an even earlier version of carnivorous intelligent plants in 'Proxima Centauri' (1935) and, in 'The Lonely Planet' (1949), a world covered by a single organism that befriends the human explorers. His later 'Exploration Team' (1956) is a notable tale of a human colony fighting for survival against a vicious life-form. In 1953 he adapted two of his earlier stories and added a third, 'Nightmare Planet', to form the book *Forgotten Planet* (1954), in which the human descendants of shipwrecked survivors on an alien world encounter giant life-forms resulting from a 'seeding' by Earth in the distant past.

Continuing the depiction of odd worlds, Eric Frank Russell tells, in 'Hobbyist' (1947), of a planet where every living thing is confined to one particular area – with only a single example of each species and sex represented. The human explorer discovers before long that they are a collection brought together by an alien, and that he himself is part of the collection. Russell, in the tradition of many sf writers, has also produced a series featuring a space crew whose planet-hopping adventures continue with each fresh tale; this saw book form as *Men, Martians and Machines* (1955).

Many such series abound, from Brian Aldiss's adventures of the Planetary Ecological Survey Team (PEST) recounted in 'Segregation' (1958), 'Carrion Country' (1958) and 'Tyrant's Territory' (1962), to Stephen Tall's tales of the exploits of the crew of the research ship *Stardust*. These last begin with 'Seventy Light-Years from Sol' (1966), continuing with 'The Bear with the Knot on His Tail' (1971), 'Birds Fly South in Winter' (1971), 'Gods on Olympus' (1972), 'The Invaders' (1973) and 'Mushroom World' (1974). The continuing demand for such works is emphasised by the success of the American *Star Trek* television series.

Among the ranks of writers who have conceived the most varied array of alien worlds, Jack Vance occupies a major position. His first story, 'The World-Thinker' (1945), portrays a planet that happens to be a figment of a super-being's imagination. His subsequent *Sons of the Tree* (1951) investigates a world ruled by a cult devoted to the massive arboreal specimen of the title, while *Big Planet* (1952) is set on a giant globe which has become the refuge of many persecuted groups from Earth. Recently, Vance's 'Durdane' trilogy has also attracted popular attention. *The Faceless Man* (1971), *The Brave Free Men* (1972) and *The Asutra* (1973) are each set on a distant planet in the Milky Way where the existence of Earth has become no more than a myth. A further series, begun with *The Domains of Koryphon* (1974), takes the reader 30,000 years into the future, and tells of worlds swarming with countless varieties of alien life.

As the stories of Vance and many other writers suggest, space exploration may lead to man's eventual colonisation of the stars. That he will succeed in rising to the challenges he will meet there is an important factor in many tales, expressing a note of optimism little found in other contemporary fiction.

ADDITIONAL INPUT

02.02.2 Towards the Stars

Anderson, Poul. *Orbit Unlimited*, Pyramid (US) 1961, comprising the following stories:
'Robin Hood's Barn', *Astounding* January 1959
'The Burning Bridge', *Astounding* January 1960
'Condemned to Death', *Fantastic Universe* October 1959
Anderson, Poul. *Question and Answer*, *Astounding* June to July 1954; retitled *Planet of No Return*, Ace (US) 1956
Anderson, Poul. *Virgin Planet*, *Venture* January 1957; expanded Avalon (US) 1959
Anthony, Piers. *Chthon*, Ballantine (US) 1967
Anthony, Piers. *Omnivore*, Ballantine (US) 1968
Anthony, Piers. 'Quinquepedalian', *Amazing* November 1963
Asimov, Isaac. *Sucker Bait*, *Astounding* February to March 1954
Blish, James. *Get Out of My Sky*, *Astounding* January to February 1957
Brunner, John. *Bedlam Planet*, Ace (US) 1968
Brunner, John. *The Long Way to Earth*, *If* March 1966; retitled *A Planet of Your Own*, Ace (US) 1966
Campbell, John W. *Islands of Space*, *Amazing Stories Quarterly* Spring 1931; *Fantasy* (US) 1956; sequel *Invaders from the Infinite*, *Amazing Stories Quarterly* Spring/Summer 1932; revised *Fantasy* (US) 1961
Clement, Hal. *Close to Critical*, *Astounding* May to July 1958; Ballantine (US) 1964
Clement, Hal. *Cycle of Fire*, Ballantine (US) 1957
Clement, Hal. 'The Green World', *If* May 1963
Clement, Hal, *Iceworld*, *Astounding* October to December 1951; Gnome (US) 1953
Cooper, Edmund. *A Far Sunset*, Hodder (UK) 1967
Cooper, Edmund. *Seed of Light*, Hutchinson (UK) 1959

'Idiot's Delight' by John Wyndham, New Worlds *June 1958. Cover by Lewis.*

Cooper, Edmund. *Transit*, Faber (UK) 1964
Davidson, Avram. *Rork!*, Berkley (US) 1965
Davidson, Avram. 'Valentine's Planet', *Worlds of Tomorrow* August 1964; retitled *Mutiny in Space*, Pyramid (US) 1964
Dickson, Gordon R. *Mission to Universe*, Berkley (US) 1965
Farmer, Philip José. *Dare*, Ballantine (US) 1965
Farmer, Philip José. *The Green Odyssey*, Ballantine (US) 1956
Farmer, Philip José. *The Lovers*, *Startling* August 1952; expanded Ballantine (US) 1961
Fyfe, H.B. 'Protected Species', *Astounding SF* March 1951
Heinlein, Robert A. *Methuselah's Children*, *Astounding* July to September 1941; Gnome (US) 1958; Gollancz (UK) 1963
Heinlein, Robert A. *Tunnel in the Sky*, Scribners (US) 1955; Gollancz (UK) 1965
Herbert, Frank. 'Do I Wake or Dream?', *Galaxy* August 1965; retitled *Destination: Void*, Berkley (US) 1966
Kapp, Colin. The 'Unorthodox Engineers' series runs as follows:
'The Railways up on Cannis', *New Worlds* October 1939
'The Subways of Tazoo', *New Writings in SF 3* (ed E.J. Carnell) Dobson (UK) 1965
'The Pen and the Dark', *New Writings in SF 8* (ed E.J. Carnell) Dobson (UK) 1966
'Getaway from Getawehi', *New Writings in SF 16* (ed E.J. Carnell) Dobson (UK) 1969
'The Black Hole of Negrav', *New Writings in SF 25* (ed K. Bulmer) Sidgwick (UK) 1975
Kapp, Colin. 'Hunger over Sweet Waters', *New Writings in SF 4* (ed E.J. Carnell) Dobson (UK) 1965
Kapp, Colin. 'Mephisto and the Ion Explorer', *If* September/October 1974
Leinster, Murray (Will F. Jenkins) The 'Med Service' series runs as follows:
Doctor to the Stars, Pyramid (US) 1964, comprising:
'The Grandfather's War' *Astounding* October 1957
'Tallien Three' (orig 'The Hate Disease', *Analog* August 1963)
'Med Ship Man', *Galaxy* October 1963
The Mutant Weapon, Ace (US) 1959 (orig 'Med Service', *Astounding* August 1957)
S.O.S. from Three Worlds, Ace (US) 1967 comprising:
'Ribbon in the Sky', *Astounding* June 1957
'Plague on Kryder II', *Analog* December 1964
'Quarantine World', *Analog* November 1966
This World Is Taboo, Ace (US) 1961 (orig 'Pariah Planet', *Amazing* July 1961)

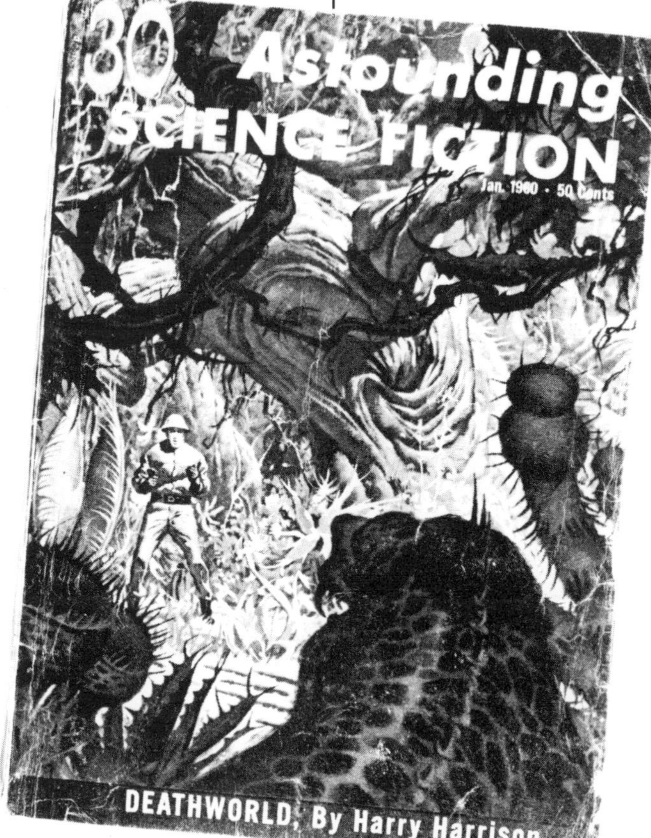

'Deathworld' by Harry Harrison, Astounding *January 1960. Cover by van Dongen.*

02.03 BIOLOGIES AND ENVIRONMENTS

Leinster, Murray. 'Proxima Centauri', *Astounding* March 1935

McCaffrey, Anne. *Decision at Doona*, Ballantine (US) 1969

Pournelle, Jerry. 'He Fell into a Dark Hole', *Analog* March 1973

Russell, Eric Frank. 'Early Bird', *Science Fiction Stories* November 1957

Russell, Eric Frank. *The Great Explosion*, Dobson (UK) 1962

Russell, Eric Frank. *The Star Watchers*, *Startling* November 1951; expanded as *Sentinels from Space*, Curl (US) 1953

Silverberg, Robert. *Downward to the Earth*, *Galaxy* November 1969 to March 1970; Doubleday (US) 1970

Silverberg, Robert. *The Seed of Earth*, *Galaxy* June 1962; Ace (US) 1962

Simak, Clifford D. 'Lulu', *Galaxy* June 1957

Simak, Clifford D. 'Ogre', *Astounding* January 1944

Van Vogt, A.E. 'The Green Forest', *Astounding* June 1949

Van Vogt, A.E. *The Voyage of the Space Beagle*, Schuster (US) 1950; Grayson (UK) 1951; comprising rewrite of:
'Black Destroyer', *Astounding* July 1939
'Discord in Scarlet', *Astounding* December 1939
'M33 in Andromeda', *Astounding* August 1943
'War of Nerves', *Other Worlds* May 1950

City of the Chasch *from the* 'Planet of Adventure' series *by Jack Vance (Mayflower)*.

Vance, Jack. The 'Planet of Adventure' series runs as follows:
City of the Chasch, Ace (US) 1968
Servants of the Wankh, Ace (US) 1969
The Dirdir, Ace (US) 1969
The Pnume, Ace (US) 1970

The stories discussed in this section show the marked change for the better in reader and writer reaction to what, in the bad old days, was called the Bug-eyed Monster. Then the meeting between human and alien was represented, on the magazine covers, at least, by a scaley, multi-tentacled and, presumably, sexually confused BEM chasing a human female whose charms were inadequately covered by a virtually transparent spacesuit. The intended reader reaction to the situation depicted was one of unthinking fear and revulsion coupled with an instinctive urge to wipe the foul Thing off the face of the Galaxy. But in recent decades there has been evident an increasingly thoughtful approach to encounters with aliens, and instinctive fear and revulsion has been replaced by the much healthier feeling of curiosity.

An analogy would be that of an island tribe on Earth being visited by a human stranger, an explorer or shipwrecked sailor from a far country, perhaps. At first he is treated with fear and suspicion, then curiosity and close personal interest, with the result that the stranger marries the most beautiful girl in the tribe, much to the disgust of the local lads. This is a natural and instinctive urge on the part of tribe's females to avoid inbreeding by capturing a mate who will enrich the local genetic pool.

It is not suggested that the transparently space-suited lady, nor her bug-eyed pursuer, had precisely this in mind. But we humans as a species need contact with strangers who are physically, mentally and culturally alien to us – and the more alien the better. Such a meeting is vitally necessary if we are to survive and mature as a species, and it may well be that we shall be forced to run before we can walk.

No longer are we quite so frightened at the thought of meeting an extra-terrestrial bogyman, nor are we troubled by the knowledge that we inhabit *a* world and not *the* world. A combination of recent near-space exploration together with the TV natural history programmes which are available nowadays have widened our mental horizons and, by introducing us to the alien activities and biologies of some of our terrestrial animals and insects, have prepared the way for a meeting with the highly intelligent strangers from the stars. Maybe, we will have to meet a really alien life-form and culture, and grow to understand it, before we will be able to see in proper perspective the minor differences of politics and pigmentation which divide the members of our own species who are black, brown or the pinkish yellow colour we insist on calling white.

James White

02.03 Biologies and Environments

The possibility of extraterrestrial life has engaged the imagination of man for centuries. As far back as 1686, the French mathematician Bernard de Fontenelle published his *Discourses on the Plurality of Worlds*. He was intrigued by two philosophical questions: how was the Earth made, and are there any other inhabited planets like it?

Ever since, there has been a steady stream of books on the possibility of life on other worlds – not to mention thousands of sf stories in which speculations on the forms such life would assume are taken to their limits. The earlier speculators were handicapped by lack of knowledge concerning the planets. Little was understood beyond the approximate sizes of the planets and a rough idea of their surface temperatures deduced from their comparative distances from the Sun. De Fontenelle and those who followed him were free to indulge hot-head Mercutians and cold, phlegmatic Saturnians.

New discoveries in astronomy, while adding extra moons and planets to our map of the heavens, only served to undermine the concept of life existing elsewhere in our solar system. By the twentieth century, argument and deduction had narrowed the possibility of life as we know it to Venus and Mars. Scientists argued that the triad of inner planets, Venus, Earth and Mars, orbited within the temperature belt in which life was known to be possible. Until the advent of space probes, it was thought Venus might possess 'cold' areas of about the same temperature as the Earth's equator, and that the warmest areas of Mars might correspond to our sub-Arctic. If life did exist on Mars and Venus, it was expected that its metabolism would resemble that of terrestrial life – based on large and complex carbon molecules, breathing oxygen and using water as its principal body fluid.

Although the anonymous author of a *Fantastical Excursion into the Planets* (1839) believed that the size, bulk, gravity, climate, and difference of length of days and years on the various planets indicated the possibility of a vast variety of natural forms, many sf writers saw extraterrestrials as essentially humanoid and, by implication, carbon-based. Others were equally convinced that if intelligent alien life did exist, the last thing it would resemble was man. A major factor in the evolutionary chain is the environment in which a particular life-form evolves; it would be unlikely that the dominant species on an non-Earth-like world would physically resemble its human counterpart.

'Fast Falls the Eventide' by Eric Frank Russell, May 1952. Illustration by van Dongen.

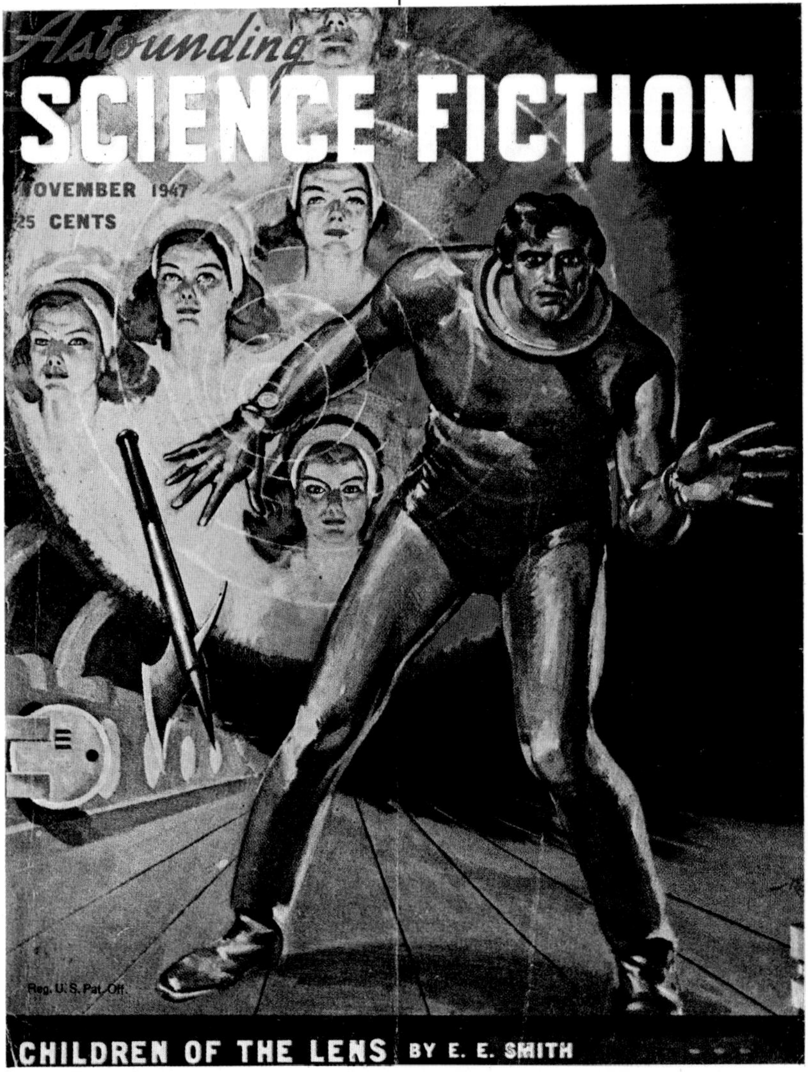

'Children of the Lens' by E. E. ('Doc') Smith, Astounding *November 1947. Cover by Rogers.*

02.03 BIOLOGIES AND ENVIRONMENTS

02.03.1 Alien Life-forms

On 21 August 1835 the New York *Sun* ran the first instalment of what is still regarded as one of the most spectacular hoaxes in the history of journalism. Purporting to be a true account of the discoveries of the astronomer Sir John Herschel, using a new giant telescope at the Cape of Good Hope, the reports continued until the end of the month and told of the sighting on the Moon's surface of vegetation, humanoid beavers and other animals and, finally, winged men. The hoax was later identified as the work of a twelve-dollar-a-week reporter, Richard Adams Locke, but the public was so eager to believe in his dramatic revelations that the *Sun*'s circulation rose during the period to become the world's largest.

Locke's hoax might well be included in that branch of literature in which imagined creatures range from the super-intelligent reptiles of Karel Čapek's *War with the Newts* (1939), through the alien invader of John W. Campbell's 'Who Goes There?' (1938) and the satanic-looking Overlords of Arthur C. Clarke's *Childhood's End* (1953), to the accurately conceived centaurs of Philip José Farmer's 'Maker of Universes' series. The invention of alien creatures has become such an integral part of the sf writer's stock-in-trade that there can be very few authors in the genre who have not indulged in it at some stage in their careers.

The image of the hostile and physically repellent extraterrestrial was an early one, established by the invading Martians of H. G. Wells's *The War of the Worlds* (1898). Wells's Martians eventually succumb to a strain of terrestrial bacteria, like the even earlier alien organisms of Percy Greg's *Across the Zodiac* (1880).

Wells's only other extended treatment of aliens occurred in his novel *The First Men in the Moon* (1901), where he took some pains to portray an alien culture and society based on the physical alteration of beings to fit them for particular tasks. His Selenites were fragile, willowy life-forms living in a highly structured and ordered civilisation.

In his twin creations of Martians and Selenites, Wells bequeathed a tradition to the early writers of science fiction which to some extent still endures: aliens were expected to be physically repulsive and almost universally hostile to man. Stanley G. Weinbaum, in the mid-1930s, would overturn this long-standing concept of extraterrestrial life.

In considering the development of alien biologies in science fiction, it is convenient to abandon chronological order in favour of an evolutionary presentation in which the various species can be seen in ordered stages. Plant life, for example, has received more than a little attention since Wells chilled the reader's blood with 'The Flowering of the Strange Orchid', in 1894. In Arthur C. Clarke's 'Before Eden' (1961), the first vegetation to evolve on Venus is accidentally killed when it absorbs a packet of waste products left behind by a human expeditionary team, so ending the story of creation on the planet. Though mobile, the Venusian plant would have proved no match for the deadly, fast moving vegetable predators of John Wyndham's *The Day of the Triffids* (1951), nor for the intelligent trees who dismiss mankind as parasites in Kendall Foster Crossen's 'The Ambassadors from Venus' (1951).

If 'Before Eden' dealt with prehistoric plant life on another planet, the fascination with prehistoric reptiles has prompted a number of writers to provide alien settings for unfamiliar species of dinosaur and similar monsters. While Conan Doyle's *The Lost World* (1912) admittedly took its characters no further than a high plateau in South America, Garrett P. Serviss, in *A Columbus of Space* (1909), saw Venus as a prehistoric environment. The monsters were still much in evidence in Otis Adelbert Kline's vision of the same world in *The Planet of Peril* (1929), together with the obligatory princesses and distressed maidens, and yet again in P. Schuyler Miller's 'Old Man Mulligan' (1940). A more recent variation is the giant sea monster relentlessly hunted in Roger Zelazny's 'The Doors of His Face, the Lamps of His Mouth' (1965).

'Ecological Onslaught' by Jack Vance, Future Science Fiction *May 1953. Illustration by Orban.*

'The Gardener' by Margaret St. Clair, Thrilling Wonder Stories *October 1949.*

Closely allied to the enduring appeal of the prehistoric beasts is the lasting popularity of the dragon. Whether this takes the form of a giant man-carrying lizard in Samuel R. Delany's *The Einstein Intersection* (1967), or is presented as the genuine article by Anne McCaffrey in her 'Pern' series, by Jack Vance in *The Dragon Masters* (1963) and by Poul Anderson in *War of the Wing-men* (1954), the symbol of the dragon is evidently a persistent one.

Less common are the stories dwelling at all seriously on insect life. The early pulp writers remained content to assault humanity with plagues of locusts, giant ants and other uncontrollable pests in the manner of Murray Leinster's 'The Mad Planet' (1920). Somewhat more thoughtful was Arthur C. Clarke's brief vision of the future in 'The Awakening' (1951), relating how, after millions of years in suspended animation, the last man revives to find the Earth ruled by insects. Philip José Farmer took the subject further in 'The Lovers'

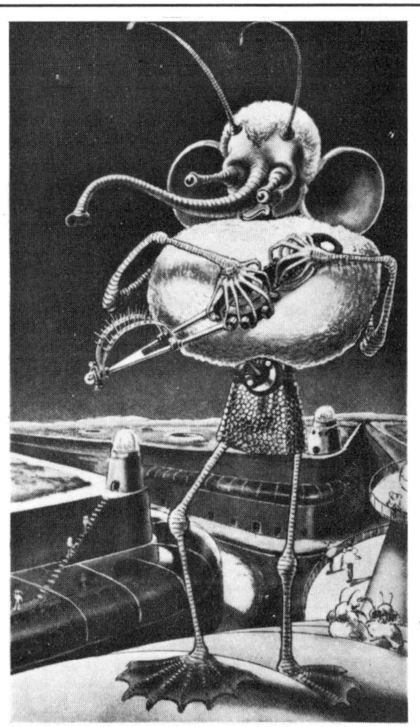

Illustration of a male Martian by Paul, Science Fiction Plus *March 1953.*

(1952), in which he depicts an insect which assumes the form of a woman, while another imaginative variation can be found in the centipede-like natives who assist the human rescue team in Hal Clement's *Mission of Gravity* (1953).

These more sympathetic views of the extraterrestrial scene owed much to the comparatively small output of a single writer. The name of Stanley G. Weinbaum occupies a unique position in the list of authors who have made memorable contributions to the treatment of alien life in sf stories. His first tale, 'A Martian Odyssey' (1934), published in *Wonder Stories*, has been enshrined in the cornerstone anthology compiled by the Science Fiction Writers of America, *The Science Fiction Hall of Fame* (1969), and it is arguably one of the finest short stories of alien life ever written. The new approach to alien life-forms distinguished the story from any that had preceded it.

It has been suggested that Weinbaum wrote 'A Martian Odyssey' as a burlesque, but it seems too good a story to be so regarded. The author's picture of conditions on Mars was consistent with the scientific knowledge of his time. Weinbaum assumed that the Martian atmosphere would be dense enough to support human life as well as the complex animal life he described. Most fascinating among the latter was Tweel, an intelligent pseudo-ostrich – a rational, even likeable, but completely *alien* type of being.

As we have shown, extraterrestrial life-forms had been described in science fiction long before Weinbaum's work. Weird beasts and strange plants ran rife in stories such as J. M. Walsh's *Vanguard to Neptune* (1932), and in tales by Verill, Merritt, Williamson, Hamilton, Neil R. Jones and many others. H. G. Wells, in particular, contributed substantially to the creation of imaginary life-forms. But in the early thirties the usual treatment of extraterrestrial life was unimaginative and crude. Intelligent non-humans were generally depicted as monsters, automatically hostile to man and without redeeming virtues; while the fauna (not to mention the frequently carnivorous flora) were mere stage props. As Isaac Asimov, among others, has pointed out, Weinbaum was the first to create extraterrestrials endowed with their *own* reasons for existing. He presented extraterrestrial life in a new perspective, and by creating consistent planetary ecologies, he brought a more thoughtful approach to the subject.

Tweel was only one of a whole catalogue of bizarre life-forms in 'A Martian Odyssey'. Others included a tentacled plant able to hypnotise its victims and lure its food within reach; parthenogenic barrel-like creatures, growing their young between them, and a 'pyramid being'. The last was of particular interest, because its body consisted of silicon. Weinbaum was aware of the chemical similarity of silicon to carbon, and imagined (wrongly, as it happens) that it might be feasible for a living creature to consist of long chains and rings of silicon instead of carbon atoms. Hence his slow-moving silicon beast, eternally eating sand and excreting bricks. Automaton-like, blind, deaf, nerveless and brainless, it is doomed to go on making bricks, which it shapes into a small pyramid before moving on to repeat the process.

The reaction to 'A Martian Odyssey' persuaded *Wonder Stories* to ask for a sequel. Weinbaum complied with 'Valley of Dreams' (1934), actually an earlier abandoned draft of the original story which he was able quickly to revise.

Weinbaum made his first appearance in *Astounding* with 'Flight on Titan' (1935), in which his ability to create peculiar animals was amply demonstrated. In rapid procession there came three further linked stories: 'Parasite Planet' (1935), 'The Lotus Eaters' (1935) and 'The Planet of Doubt' (1935). The first two stories of the group are set on Venus. Perpetual thunderstorms play over the twenty-mile-high peaks of the Mountains of Eternity, while semi-intelligent, three-eyed, malevolent *triops noctivivans Veneris* blunder through the Venusian night uttering weird cries. Most terrifying of all are the Doughpots, vast animated masses of mindless protoplasm

Cover by Emsh, Galaxy *February 1955.*

02.03 BIOLOGIES AND ENVIRONMENTS

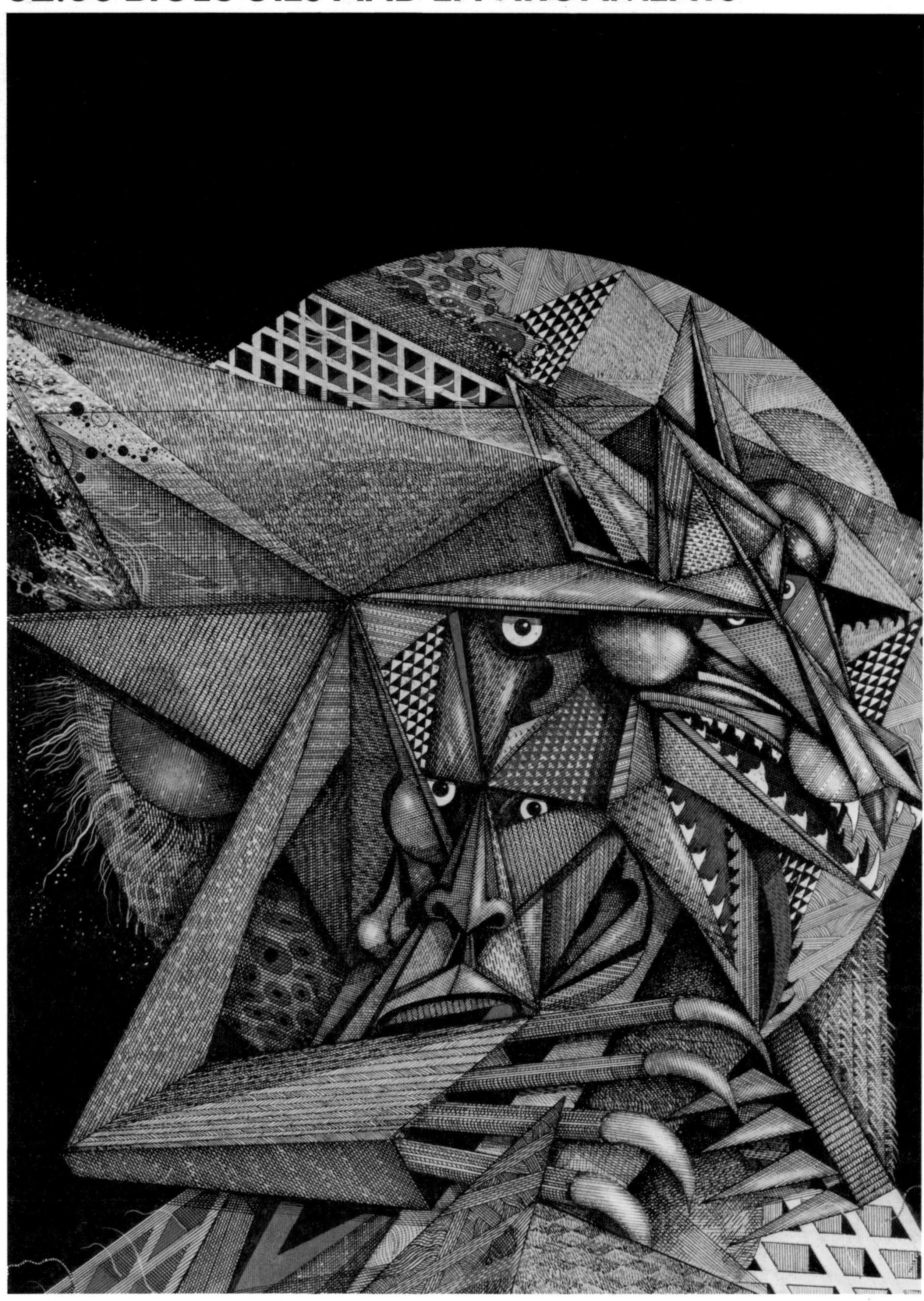

Left: The Werewolf Principle *by Clifford D. Simak (Pan). Cover by Ian Miller.*

ploughing through the jungles and devouring everything in their path. Other interplanetary tales in which his fertile imagination helped to people the solar system include 'The Red Peri' (1934) and 'The Mad Moon' (1934).

Weinbaum's influence on other writers is perhaps the most important testimonial to his contribution to science fiction. Following his tragically early death in 1936, a great many stories appeared which attempted to copy his manner of depicting bizarre, yet believable, fauna. The influence can be clearly seen in Eric Frank Russell's first published story, 'The Saga of Pelican West' (1937). It was also evident in the pages of *Thrilling Wonder Stories*, where the joint efforts of Arthur K. Barnes and Henry Kuttner, in the form of the 'Gerry Carlyle' and 'Hollywood-on-the-Moon' series, ran to over fifteen novelettes. Barnes's initial entry, 'Green Hell' (1937), depicted a similar Venusian environment to that of Weinbaum, initiating the reader into a world of biological wonders. These included strange chloro-men, darting whiz-bang flies and bat-men imported to Venus from Jupiter. Henry Kuttner's 'Hollywood

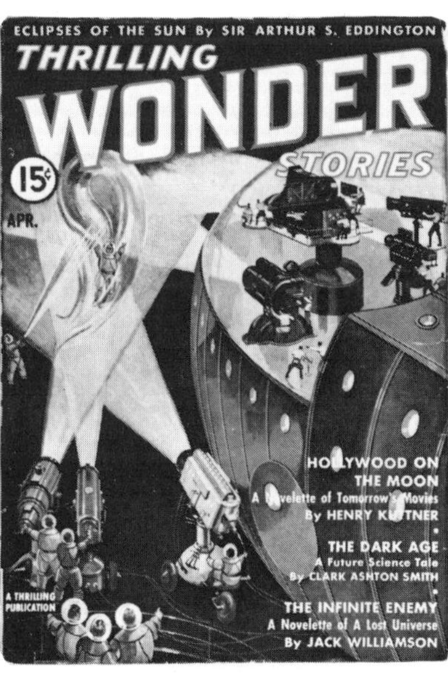

on the Moon' (1938) raised the curtain on a series which depicted the efforts of film directors to bring to future cinema screens the various monstrosities roaming each planet of the solar system.

At the urging of his agent, British author John Russell Fearn produced a dozen stories in 1936–38, all of which imitated Weinbaum. Two of these were published in *Astounding*, under the pseudonym of Thornton Ayre. 'Penal World' (1937) and 'Whispering Satellite' (1938). The penal world is Jupiter, home of a strange intelligent biped, only two feet tall, heavily muscled, with three hearts and with legs nearly as thick as a man's body. Further support is provided by a broad, kangaroo-

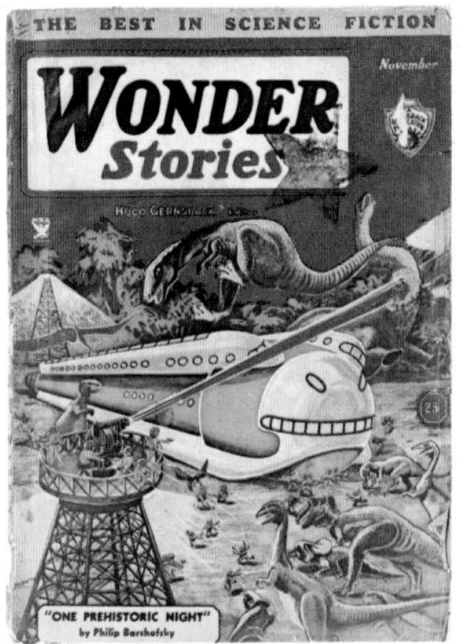

'One Prehistoric Night' by Philip Barshofsky, Wonder Stories *November 1934.*

like tail. It is a life-form adapted to ammoniated hydrogen, and its favourite delicacy is smelling salts. Another idea, that of singing plants, was developed in 'Whispering Satellite' and was later put to further use by Clifford D. Simak in 'Ogre' (1944). After 1940, the spate of Weinbaum imitations slackened and eventually ceased. Weinbaum's importance to the development of the alien in science fiction was more subtle and lasting, and his ideas were to be rediscovered and developed years later. His contribution lay in the essentially simple, yet far-reaching, idea that an alien life-form would be a product of its environment, and as such could be utterly non-human, but by no means automatically hostile or repulsive.

After Weinbaum such stories as Pierre Boulle's popular 'Planet of the Apes' series could present aliens as being neither particularly friendly nor overtly hostile, but simply different and not necessarily in agreement with the ethics and aspirations of man. A very different kind of ape features in Walter M. Miller's *Conditionally Human* (1962), where child surrogates are provided for couples forbidden to have children of their own as a measure against over-population. From the human-like ape it is only a short step to the humanoid alien, whether it be a genuine extraterrestrial or the descendant of an ancient Earth colony long forgotten a million years hence. The former is well illustrated in Zenna Henderson's 'People' series, chronicling the progress of a species of aliens of human appearance who inhabit the Earth at present; while an example of the latter occurs in Ursula K. Le Guin's *The Left Hand of Darkness* (1969), where the humanoid population of a distant planet differ from their Earth cousins only in their method of reproduction.

Many writers have imagined that intelligent aliens will in all probability resemble human beings in basic shape, even if their skin pigmentation and other minor features differ. The apparently sexless female from Ganymede, whom the hero of Philip José Farmer's 'The Strange Birth' (1959) encounters on Mars, is a notable example; she actually reproduces by swallowing a large worm which has already been semi-impregnated in the body of a male of the species. Common among tales of humanoid aliens are the various tests and competitions to determine which species, including man, is fit to control the galaxy – or even the universe. Edmund Cooper's *Transit* (1964) and Milton Lesser's *Recruit for Andromeda* (1953) both pursue this theme. In a class of its own can be found *You Shall Know Them* (1952) by the French writer Vercors (Jean Bruller). It tells of the discovery on Earth of a living species which is possibly one of the missing links in man's evolution. When one of the creatures is killed, the ethical problem arises of whether the act could be treated as murder.

Other stories since Weinbaum's have depicted various forms of alien life as crystalline. Isaac Asimov's 'The Talking Stone' (1955) is one such; so, too, are P. Schuyler Miller's 'The Arrhenius Horror' (1931), George C. Wallis's 'The Crystal Menace' (1939) and John Taine's *The Crystal Horde* (1952). In John Wyndham's 'And the Walls Came Tumbling Down. . . .' (1951), invisible crystalline aliens set up a redoubt on Earth, only to be defeated by quite common noises which, when emitted on the correct frequency, shatter them to pieces. The various metal-eating species which have appeared in certain stories can be regarded as equally unusual. 'Wings of Night' (1942) by Lester del Rey tells of the discovery of an alien creature which feeds on mineral ores beneath the Moon's surface. In a light-hearted vein is Robert A. Heinlein's enormous, eight-legged female metal-eater in *The Star Beast* (1954), who in one episode makes short work of a second-

Illustration of Antares by Paul, Fantastic Adventures *July 1946.*

hand Buick. E. C. Tubb's *The Metal Eater* (1954), written under the pseudonym of Roy Sheldon, is another example, but in this case the life-form was created artificially by another alien race.

Among the less substantial beings devised by sf writers, some can be described as pure energy, gaseous bodies, flame entities or other almost indefinable wraith-like intelligences. These can be found in such stories as Fred Hoyle's *The Black Cloud* (1957), Eric Frank Russell's *Sinister Barrier* (1943), Bob Shaw's *The Palace of Eternity* (1969) and Isaac Asimov's *The Gods Themselves* (1972); Clifford D. Simak's 'Tools' (1942) and A. E. van Vogt's 'M33 in Andromeda' (1943); Frank Belknap Long's 'The Flame Midget' (1935) and 'The Flame of Life' (1939), Hal Clement's 'Proof' (1942) and Arthur C. Clarke's 'Out of the Sun' (1958).

Finally come those miscellaneous, but frequently ingenious, creations which more or less defy any kind of categorisation. Foremost among such flights of imagination is Stanislaw Lem's mysterious *Solaris* (1961), in which the planet of the title appears to be a living entity in its own right, and one that can exercise disturbing psychological effects on the humans stationed above its surface. Another is the alien species of Katherine MacLean's 'Unhuman Sacrifice' (1958), whose young are on a par with intelligent humans, but take the form of unthinking vegetables in the final stage of their life cycle. A reptilian species which also passes through several stages on its way to maturity is featured memorably in James Blish's *A Case of Conscience* (1958).

Equally unique are Larry Niven's extraordinary puppeteers (centaur-like beings with a head, instead of a hand, at the end of each arm), found in his *Neutron Star* (1968) collection and the novel *Ringworld* (1970). The fourth-dimensional entities imagined by Theodore Sturgeon, and brought to life in 'Ether Breather' (1939), 'Butyl and the Breather' (1939) and the more recent 'Case and the Dreamer' (1972), bear testimony to their author's sustained originality over a period of more than thirty years. Finally, no examination of alien biologies would be complete without at least a passing mention of the formidable Widgey Birds which thunder through the ground oblivious to mere resistance in Fredric Brown's 'Placet Is a Crazy Place' (1946).

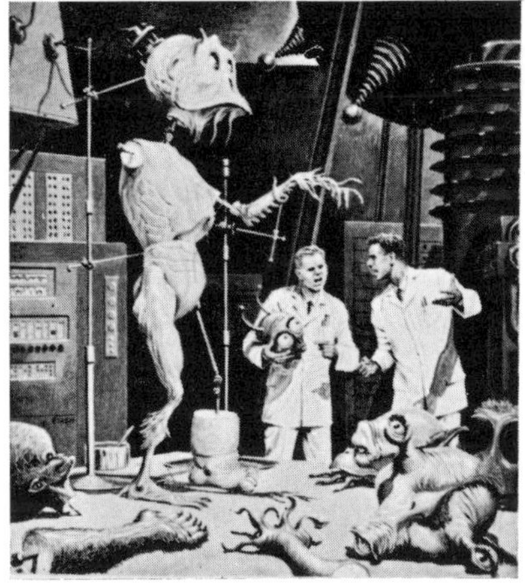

'Let's Build an Extraterrestrial!' by Willy Ley, Galaxy April 1956. Cover by Emsh.

ADDITIONAL INPUT

02.03.1 Alien Life-Forms

Aldiss, Brian W. 'Segregation', *New Worlds* July 1958
Aldiss, Brian W. 'Carrion Country', *New Worlds* November 1958
Aldiss, Brian W. 'Tyrant's Territory', *Amazing* March 1962
Anderson, Poul. 'Call Me Joe', *Astounding* October 1954
Anderson, Poul. 'Duel on Syrtis', *Planet Stories* March 1951
Brown, Fredric. 'The Waveries', *Astounding* January 1945
Campbell, H.J. *Beyond the Visible* Hamilton (UK) 1952
Campbell, H.J. *The Red Planet*, Hamilton (UK) 1953
Clarke, Arthur C. *The Sands of Mars*, Sidgwick & Jackson (UK) 1951
Farmer, Philip José. *The Gates of Creation*, Ace (US) 1966
Farmer, Philip José. *A Private Cosmos*, Ace (US) 1968
Farmer, Philip José. *Behind the Walls of Terra*, Ace (US) 1970
Fearn, John Russell. 'Brain of Light', *Astounding* May 1934
Fearn, John Russell. 'Metamorphosis', *Astounding* January 1937
French, Paul (Isaac Asimov). *David Starr: Space Ranger*, Doubleday (US) 1952
French, Paul. *Lucky Starr and the Pirates of the Asteroids*, Doubleday (US) 1953
French, Paul. *Lucky Starr and the Oceans of Venus*, Doubleday (US) 1954
French, Paul. *Lucky Starr and the Big Sun of Mercury*, Doubleday (US) 1956
French, Paul. *Lucky Starr and the Moons of Jupiter*, Doubleday (US) 1957
French, Paul. *Lucky Starr and the Rings of Saturn*, Doubleday (US) 1958
Gallun, Raymond Z. 'A Beast of the Void', *Astounding* September 1936
Gallun, Raymond Z. 'Child of the Stars', *Astounding* April 1936
Gallun, Raymond Z. 'Davey Jones, Ambassador', *Astounding* December 1935
Gallun, Raymond Z. 'Old Faithful', *Astounding* December 1934
Gallun, Raymond Z. 'Seeds of the Dusk', *Astounding* June 1938
Gallun, Raymond Z. 'The Son of Old Faithful', *Astounding* July 1935
Hamilton, Edmond. 'The Earth Owners', *Weird Tales* August 1931
Hamilton, Edmond. 'The Emphemerae', *Astounding* December 1938
Hamilton, Edmond. 'Sunfire', *Amazing* September 1962
Harrison, Harry. 'Rescue Operation', *Astounding* December 1964
McIntosh, J.T. (J.T. McGregor). 'Planet of Change', *Fantastic* December 1964
Merritt, Abraham. *The Metal Monster*, *Argosy* August to September 1920; Avon (US) 1946
Schmitz, James H. 'Grandpa', *Astounding* February 1955
Schmitz, James H. 'The Star Hyacinths', *Amazing* December 1961
Schmitz, James H. 'Tuvela', *Analog* September to October 1968
Stapledon, Olaf. *The Flames*, Secker & Warburg (UK) 1947
Stapledon, Olaf. *The Last and First Men*, Methuen (UK) 1930
Stapledon, Olaf. *Star-Maker*, Methuen (UK) 1937
Smith, Clark Ashton. 'The Immeasurable Horror,' *Weird Tales* September 1931
Stuart, Don A. (John W. Campbell). 'Who Goes There?', *Astounding* August 1938
Temple, William F. 'The Brain Beast', *Super Science* July 1949
Tubb, E.C. *Alien Life*, Comyns (UK) 1954
Tubb, E.C. 'Spawn of Jupiter', *Vision of Tomorrow* August 1970
Tubb, E.C. 'Star Haven', *Authentic* December 1954
Tubb, E.C. *The Hell Planet*, Scion (UK) 1954
Tubb, E.C. *Venusian Adventure*, Paladin (UK) 1954
Van Lhin, Erik (Lester del Rey). *Battle on Mercury*, Winston (US) 1953
Verill, A. Hyatt. 'Beyond the Pole', *Amazing* October to November 1926
Verill, A. Hyatt. 'The Inner World', *Amazing* June to August 1935
Verill, A. Hyatt. 'The World of the Giant Ants', *Amazing Quarterly* Fall 1928

'Trader Team' by Poul Anderson, Analog July 1965. Cover by Schoenherr.

02.03.2 A Plurality of Worlds

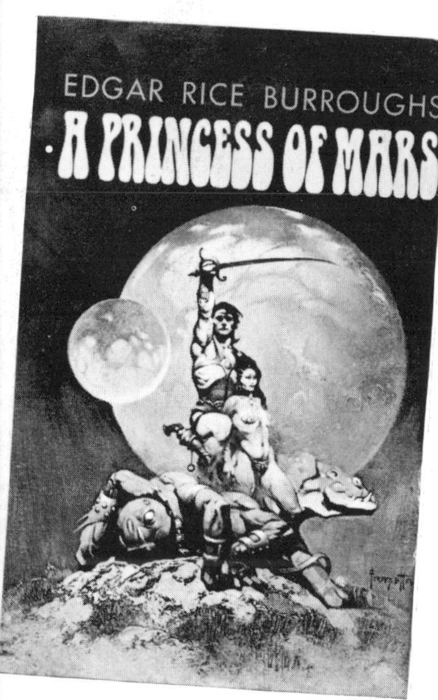

A Princess of Mars *by Edgar Rice Burroughs (Doubleday). Cover by Frazetta.*

Many sf writers have written series of connected stories woven around imaginary worlds and beings, and pre-eminent in this respect are L. Sprague de Camp, E. E. ('Doc') Smith and James White.

L. Sprague de Camp's *The Queen of Zamba* (1949), in his 'Viagens Interplanetarias' series, describes the world of Krishna, a planet saddled with a fifteenth-century technology, and peopled by feudal tyrants, six-legged monsters and beautiful princesses. Inspired by the Burroughs stories set on 'Barsoom' (roughly the Mars described in Percival Lowell's popularised writings on astronomy), de Camp conjures up a world on which stray Earthmen can run a whole gamut of swashbuckling adventures.

By analogy with our own planetary system, whose components have names from Graeco-Roman mythology, Krishna is located in a solar system whose planets Earthmen have named after the Hindu gods: Krishna is Earth-like, while Vishnu is the steaming jungle that Venus was once imagined to be and Ganesha resembles Mars.

In de Camp's series, other technologically sophisticated species are exploring space, too. The dinosaurian Osirians, the androgynous monkey-rats of Thoth and the elephantine Isidians come from planets of Procyon which have been named by Earthmen after Egyptian deities.

The most technologically advanced inhabitants of Krishna live around the Triple Seas region of their planet's northern hemisphere. Unlike Earth, the surface of Krishna is mostly land, and that mostly desert. The planet's gravity is lower than Earth's, meaning that humans are relatively stronger and more agile there than on their home planet, and the natives taller and rangier than the average man.

Krishnans have green hair and a slightly greenish cast to their skins, though their blood is brown. Olfactory antennas rise from their brows, and their ears are pointed. Like all the four-limbed mammals of their planet, they are oviparous. There are also numerous six-limbed creatures which give live birth, ranging from the equine aya, which serves as the most common means of transportation, to such ferocious carnivores as the yeki (a mink the size of a tiger), the reptilian shan, and the shan's polar cousin, the pudamef. Some of the six-leggers have modified one pair of legs into wings, and occupy a similar ecological niche to that of terrestrial birds.

Not only is Krishna technologically consistent, but it is also sociologically reasonable. Many science fiction authors feel that their responsibility to the 'scientific' aspect of the genre is satisfied if they explain along proper scientific lines how a spaceship operates or a mutation occurs. They tend to forget the existence of the social sciences. The table on the next page lists the various planets and their inhabitants in the 'Viagens Interplanetarias' series.

Detailed as de Camp's system of aliens may seem, it is arguably dwarfed by the creations of E. E. ('Doc') Smith. In a tribute to Smith published in 1965 following his death, Edmond Hamilton suggested that

'Ultrasonic God' by L. Sprague de Camp, Future *July 1951. Illustration by Lawrena.*

02.03 BIOLOGIES AND ENVIRONMENTS

A Krishnan from the 'Viagens Interplanetarias' series, Science Fiction Stories *May–July 1958. Illustration by Freas.*

Inhabited Planets of the 'Viagens Interplanetarias' Stories

Primary	*Planet*	*Inhabitants*
Sun	Earth	Earthmen
	Mars	Insect-like beings mentioned only peripherally in six stories.
Tau Ceti	Vishnu	Romeli – six-legged ape-like tribesmen.
		Dzleri – centauroid tribesmen almost continually at war with Romeli.
	Krishna	Krishnans as described; also more primitive long-tailed and short-tailed species in remote or inhospitable regions.
	Ganesha	No native sentient beings mentioned.
	Indra	No native sentient beings mentioned.
Procyon	Osiris	Sha'akhfa – intelligent tyrannosaur-like beings some seven feet tall, emotionally highly strung, with pseudo-hypnotic powers, and with a capitalist economy.
	Thoth	Small, agile seven-fingered 'monkey-rats' with well-deserved reputations as sharp dealers.
	Isis	Elephant-like beings with trunks but no hands.
Sirius	Sirius IX	Ant-like creatures with a communistic economy.
Not named, unless perhaps Epsilon Eridani	Thor	'Ostrich-men' with foghorn voices. One continent colonised by Earthmen, a source of much Thorian annoyance.
Lalande 21185	Ormazd	Avtini – tall, pink-skinned humanoids who mature sexually only on a meat diet.
		Arshuul – a species closely related to the Avtini and at war with them.

Smith's finest achievement was his exploration of alien mentalities. Hamilton maintained that hardly anyone, except perhaps Hal Clement, had made an individual non-human and his thought processes seem so real.

Smith's animal classification system, designed to catalogue all alien life encountered in his 'Lensman' universe, has been exhaustively documented by Ron Ellik in *The Universes of E. E. Smith* (1966), which he co-authored with Bill Evans. Used chiefly in *The Children of the Lens* (1947) to identify the Plooran race, it is also employed in the other novels in the series, including *First Lensman* (1950). The system categorises human beings as 'A', while alien races are classified from 'A' to 'Z' in each category in accordance with their divergence from the human norm.

The first classified letter relates to the atmosphere each being normally breathes. Oxygen breathers are A, while those inhaling poisonous gases are classified towards the end of the alphabet.

The 'blood stream' determines the second letter. Warm-blooded beings with two arms and legs are As, whereas creatures extending into hyper-space, so that their appearance shimmers to a three-dimensional observer, are Zs.

The head falls into the fourth category; a movable head with eyes, ears, nose and mouth, but without horns or tentacles, is classed as A. A domed head, with no eyes, mouth or nose, immobile on the trunk, is L.

In the fifth place, arms or upper limbs are classified according to their comparison with human arms, taking into consideration their length, type of joints, and fingers and thumbs.

'Trouble with Emily' by Jame White, New Worlds *November 1958. Cover by Lewis.*

Sixth come legs; seventh a being's skin or hide; and the eighth letter indicates the type of locomotion or guidance control.

Smith's classification, substantially modified, became one of the features of James White's series of stories concerning a hospital in space, 'Sector General'. Amongst a plethora of alien life-forms, the humans in White's series are classified DBDF and regarded as alien by over 90 per cent of the hospital's patients and staff.

White developed his galaxy of aliens through many stories, most of which were first published in *New Worlds*, including 'Sector General' (1957), 'Trouble with Emily' (1958), 'Visitor at Large' (1959), 'O'Hara's Orphan' (1960), 'Outpatient' (1960) and, written specially for the magazine's hundredth issue, 'Countercharm' (1960), plus 'Resident Physician' (1961) and *Field Hospital* (1962). A further six 'Sector General' stories appeared in the 'New Writings in SF' series – 'Invader' (1966), 'Vertigo' (1968), 'Blood Brother' (1969), 'Meatball' (1970), 'Major Operation' (1971) and 'Spacebird' (1973).

A four-letter classification system for aliens is employed in the 'Sector General' series. The first letter indicates the level of physical evolution, but has no bearing on the level of intelligence (all of White's aliens are intelligent). The second indicates the type and distribution of limbs and sense organs, while the final two relate to mental agility and the pressure and gravity conditions on the world concerned.

White's hospital comprises 384 levels and accurately reproduces the environments of the sixty-eight (later sixty-nine) life-forms currently known to the Galactic Federation, providing the extremes of heat, pressure, radiation, gravity and atmosphere necessary for both patients and staff. No better provisional summary of the range of life-forms to be found in science fiction can be given than the following table of White's alien biologies:

Four-letter Alien Life Classification System in White's 'Sector General' Series

A,B,C,
Water-breathers. (Vegetable intelligences are added to A when found.)

D,E,F,
Warm-blooded oxygen-breathers. (The majority of intelligent races.)

G,K,
Oxygen-breathing, but insectile.

O,P,
Chlorine-breathing.

R-Z,
Radiation-eaters, frigid-blooded and/or crystalline; those capable of modifying their physical structure at will, etc.

V,
A special classification for those races enjoying sufficiently developed extrasensory powers to make walking or manipulative appendages unneccessary.

AACP
Slow-moving water-breathers whose remote ancestors had been a species of mobile undersea vegetable.

AMSL
A water-breathing octopoid from Creppelia.

AUGL
A forty-foot long, oviparous, armoured, fish-like species from Calderescol II.

DBDG
1. Earth humans, who, together with the Tralthans and Illensans, are the most developed race.

2. The humanoid Nidians; smaller than Earth humans, seven-fingered, covered with tight, curly red fur, and communicating in staccato, barking speech.

DBLF
Oxygen-breathing, warm-blooded Kelgians, having the appearance of six-foot long caterpillars with thirty-four legs. They are not telepathic, but can accurately read the thoughts of a member of their own race by observation of expressions. They have highly expressive features over which they have no control; they are therefore completely tactless, and always say what they think.

ELNT
Six-legged, exoskeletal, vaguely crab-like being from Melf IV, with warm blood, claws, and hard, wonderfully precise mandibles.

APLH
In shape this species resembles a giant, upright pear, weighing 1000 lb. It has five tentacles (three manipulatory, one carrying the eyes and one bearing a heavy horn-like mace, a relic of more primitive days). A heavy apron of muscle at its base gives it snail-like, though fairly rapid, motion. Its five mouths are at the roots of the tentacles; four have teeth, the other contains vocal organs. The featureless dome of a head contains an extraordinary brain, and its grasp of social and psychological sciences is enormous. By a process of rejuvenation it has made itself near-immortal. Each individual carries an intelligent and organised virus colony inside it, which in turn keeps the body at peak efficiency and free from disease.

FGLI
Huge elephantine creatures from Traltha, who, in symbiosis with the OTSB – a tiny but non-intelligent creature – are the finest surgeons in the Galaxy. The OTSB is nearly mindless unless living with a Tralthan.

FROB
A low, squat, immensely powerful being from Hudlor, somewhat reminiscent of an armadillo, with a strong covering similar to flexible armour-plate. It absorbs food directly from the atmosphere of its native planet, whose atmospheric pressure is seven times that of Earth, and its gravity four times Earth-normal.

GKNM
Chrysalis stage similar to DBLF, having a cylindrical, lightly boned body, with heavy musculature and five pairs of tentacles. Its final stage is as an oxygen-breathing, oviparous being, resembling a dragonfly.

GLNO
A being from Cinrus, six-legged, exoskeletal and insect-like, with an empathic faculty. It is incredibly fragile and awkward-looking, the gravity to which it is accustomed being only one-twelfth of Earth-normal.

LSVO
A diminutive, fragile, bird-like creature inhabiting a low-gravity world.

MSVK
Also accustomed to low gravity, vaguely stork-like, tripedal; used to a thick, almost opaque, atmosphere.

PVSJ
Spiny, membranous spider-like chlorine-breathers from Illensa.

QCQL
Breathers of a highly corrosive fog, living under a harsh, actinic blue sun.

SNLU
A frigid methane-breather.

SRTT
An amoebic being which can extrude any limbs, sense organs or protective integuments required by its immediate environment. It evolved on a planet of eccentric orbit whose geological, climatic and temperature changes were such that a high degree of adaptability was necessary for survival. The species is very long-lived, and reproduces asexually with great pain at long intervals, by a process of budding and splitting off. Part of the body and brain-cell structure is transferred wholesale to the young. No conscious memories are carried over, but there is a retention of sub-conscious memories reaching back some 50,000 years.

02.04 WARFARE AND WEAPONRY

TLTU
A breather of superheated steam at 500°C.

TRLH
A breather of a gas extremely poisonous to Earth humans. It has four single-jointed legs, a thin carapace and a finely boned head with two extendable eyes and two mouths.

VTXM
Very small radioactive being from Telfi.

VUXG
A creature with certain psi faculties, which can convert practically any substance into energy for its physical needs, and which can adapt to almost any environment. It also enjoys a haphazard precognitive ability which applies to populations rather than individuals. In appearance it can be likened to a withered prune.

ADDITIONAL INPUT

02.03.2 A Plurality of Worlds

Aldiss, Brian W. *Hothouse*, Faber (UK) 1962, consisting of shorts from *F&SF*: 'Hothouse', February 1961; 'Nomansland', April 1961; 'Undergrowth', July 1961; 'Timberline', September 1961; 'Evergreen', December 1961

Bradbury, Ray. 'Mars Is Heaven', *Planet Stories* Fall 1948

Bradbury, Ray. *The Illustrated Man*, Doubleday (US) 1951

Burroughs, Edgar Rice. 'Under the Moons of Mars', *All-Story* February to July 1912; as *A Princess of Mars*, McClurg (US) 1917

Burrough, Edgar Rice. *Pirates of Venus*, *Argosy* September to October 1922; Burroughs (US) 1934

Tubb, E.C. *Alien Dust*, Boardman (UK) 1955

Who can deny the repellant attractions of the war story, or war itself, which has so plagued mankind's history? With the fine example of Wells's *War of the Worlds* (1895) before them – as well as his 'The Land Ironclads' where he invented tank warfare – the early sf pulp writers pushed war into the future with gory relish. What jolly slaughter! Youthful sf readers flipped the pages breathlessly as fleets of mile-long spaceships polished each other off, suns were whipped around like stones from a sling and alien races perished by the thousands.

Military violence has been a stock in trade of sf since its inception, and will probably continue to be so. Action and colour are what keep sf going at its most popular level, so the combat story will be with us always. Though of perhaps greater importance is the anti-war story, the admonitory finger that sf shakes so well. If science fiction is in the forefront of intellectual fiction, as I believe it is, and the abandonment of national rivalries and technological warfare is important to the survival of mankind, as it certainly is – then science fiction has a vital function.

Science fiction's general affection for machinery is certainly displayed in its military hardware. This, plus the added fact that a house-cleaning robot is far less interesting than a war robot with a cannon for a belly button, has unleashed clanking legions of war machines. It is debatable if real machinery has ever been invented to emulate sf originals; the prognoscative role has been too much exaggerated. If the genre has a role it is the new one that is emerging from the growing polarization of the field itself, the continuing widening of scope as the readership increases so that a spectrum of literature has begun to replace the old pulp-orientated-only writing. At one end is the juvenile action-only novel, best represented by the *Perry Rhodan* series; at the other are books of both science fictional and literary merit such as Aldiss's *Dark Light-Years* (1964). Enthusiasts of either extreme should appreciate and allow for the others' interests. Both are important since new readers must be added continuously who will, hopefully, progress to the more cerebral limits of the medium.

If science fiction has any function other than mere entertainment it will be at the analytical end of the spectrum where the real problems of existence are faced and discussed. This is surely our strength. The detailed spelling-out of disasters, both military and economic, can only be done in the sf medium. Before the invention must come the idea. If sf gadgetry once sparked military weaponry, that is a thing of the past, along with the 'Yellow Hordes' and other jingoist enemies. We can earn expiation, if we need it, by a future examination of all the solvable problems that bedevil mankind.

Harry Harrison

02.04 WARFARE AND WEAPONRY

02.04.1 The Threat of Invasion

In the second half of the nineteenth century, French military dominance in Europe was coming to an end, and Germany was becoming the new political power. The fear of an invasion of Britain by a hostile European power prompted the publication of *The Battle of Dorking* by Sir George T. Chesney, a civil engineer who was also a military colonel. The story was published anonymously in *Blackwood's Magazine* in 1871, but evoked an immediate and startling reaction both at home and abroad. It described a successful invasion of England and the subsequent collapse of its power and commerce. In its depiction of an imaginary future, it displayed an acute grasp of contemporary affairs. Chesney's speculation on the factors which bring about the rise of communism and the loss of Britain's colonies created a sensation. There were many sequels by as many authors, including Charles Stone's *What Happened after the Battle of Dorking* (1871).

Frontispiece to The Battle of Dorking.

Thus began a vogue for future-war novels which reached a zenith when George Griffith added genuinely imaginative science fiction inventions to the war theme in his best-seller *The Angel of the Revolution* (1893) and its sequel *Olga Romanoff* (1894). The first tells of a devastating world war which follows the invention in 1903 of the aeroplane and the aerial torpedo. Eventually, a benevolent despotism is established, with its centre at Aeria, a stronghold of rebels whose aeroplanes ensure that the world obeys them. The prospect that England might be conquered by the 'Yellow men' of Asia was M. P. Shiel's contribution to future-war stories. His *The Yellow Danger* (1898) was a best-seller in its day. The Asian races strike at Western civilisation to achieve their dream of supremacy. A united China and Japan precipitate a bloody war on the continent, and Shiel vividly describes the battle movements of the armies and navies of the Great Powers.

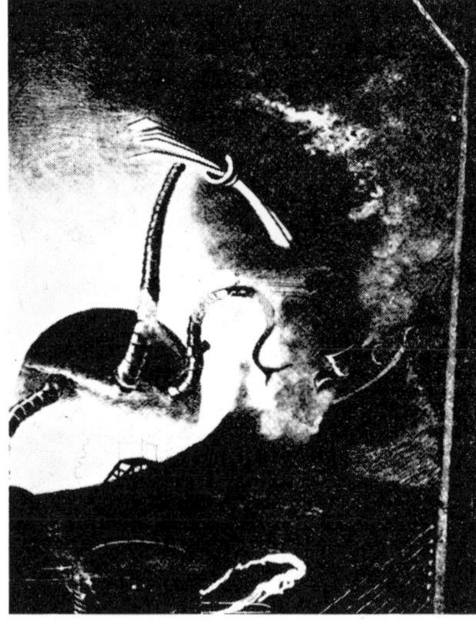

The War of the Worlds *by H. G. Wells. Illustration by Alvim-Correa from the Belgian edition.*

One of the best-known novels of H. G. Wells's *The War of the Worlds* (1895), is generally acknowledged as the first novel of warfare between different planets. Wells's tale of the Martian invasion of Earth is arguably the greatest of all tales of interplanetary warfare, and hundreds of stories have followed this prototype. The Wells story appeals on several levels. On the surface, it tells of an invasion of Earth by a hostile force from a more advanced civilisation on Mars. Wells's imagination may have been influenced by evidence of the violence of colonial warfare, demonstrating the struggle between competing groups and the devastating potentialities of an advanced military technology. But he also showed that a superior intelligence would not necessarily behave benignly towards what it considered an inferior species. He described warfare as it might be experienced if scientists turned to the task of producing the most efficient weapons possible. Principal among these was the devastating Martian Heat Ray. The concept of a death-ray was to become an essential ingredient of science fiction.

The Pandora's box of the uses of radiation had been opened up by Röntgen's discovery of X-rays in 1895. Stimulated by the thought

'The War of the Giants' by Fletcher Pratt, Wonder Stories *May 1931. Illustration by Marchioni.*

02.04 WARFARE AND WEAPONRY

of a ray that could penetrate solids, writers' imaginations went on to conjure up rays that might defy gravity, or rays which could shrink or expand electronic orbits. As early as 1932, magazine editor Hugo Gernsback commented in an introduction to John W. Campbell's 'Space Rays' that the author had ran the gamut of all the coloured magical rays that were even then the stock-in-trade of the sf writer.

'Soldier Ask Not' by Gordon Dickson, Galaxy *October 1964. Illustration by Morrow.*

But the dream of a death-ray came nearer reality in 1960, with the discovery of the laser. Today scientists are working to realise another science fiction notion. By using lasers of great power and accuracy, they hope to be able to intercept nuclear missiles in mid-flight and cripple their warheads before they can explode.

Submarine warfare of the future has also received the attention of sf writers, in such stories as Martin Caidin's *The Last Fathom* (1967) and Frank Herbert's *Under Pressure* (1956). The latter describes a twenty-first-century submarine, on a mission to tap undersea oil fields, endangered by the activities of a hidden enemy saboteur.

While many future-war stories concerning man's conflict with his own species are set on Earth, a large number deal with aggression between separate human colonies on different planets. Gordon R. Dickson's noted 'Dorsai' trilogy is partly devoted to this theme and consists of *Dorsai* (1959), *Naked to the Stars* (1961) and *Soldier, Ask Not* (1964). Robert A. Heinlein's *The Moon Is a Harsh Mistress* (1966) concludes with a war of independence between the Moon colony and the parent Earth which, with the aid of sentient computer, the colony wins.

'The Cosmic Gun' by Morrison F. Colladay, Wonder Stories *May 1931. Illustration by Marchioni.*

Accounts of man's warfare with aliens are covered in a later sub-section, but some mention is worth making here of a less extensive category, wars between humans and the insect kingdom. A great many superficial and lurid stories on this theme were produced by hack writers in the early days of the pulp magazines, but more thoughtful approaches have been devised since, particularly by Frank Herbert. In *The Green Brain* (1967), the evolution of insects has been accelerated by man's reckless deployment of insecticides, leading to the Green Brain, a hive-mind made up of the integrated intelligences of millions of insects. The ending of the story, which implies that the insect menace is spreading, contains echoes of H. G. Wells's early classic, 'The Empire of the Ants' (1905). *Hellstrom's Hive* (1973), also by Herbert, describes the deliberate creation of a new form of hybrid life, in which individual human intelligences are submerged in an insect-like hive-mind, offering unswerving loyalty to any would-be conqueror.

A further sub-category of the warfare theme, perhaps now of more curiosity value than importance, is the result of writers' immediate reactions to the Second World War. Ray Palmer, editor of *Amazing Stories* and *Fantastic Adventures*, was particularly active in this area. His magazines overflowed with such stories as 'Nazi, Are You Resting Well?' (1943) by Leroy Yerxa, 'Hitler's Right Eye' (1944) by Lee Francis, 'The Ghost That Haunted Hitler' (1942) by William P. McGivern and 'They Forgot to Remember Pearl Harbor' (1942) by P. F. Costello. Almost all the pulp periodicals for September 1943 carried covers on the subject of 'women in war work', emphasised by a hand-held torch emblem captioned 'women war workers'. The cover of *Amazing* showed a blonde in overalls and peaked cap observing a saboteur in an aircraft factory, illustrating the story 'War Worker 17' by Frank Patton (Palmer himself). To boost the morale of troops, Palmer also produced a remarkable issue of *Amazing* composed entirely of stories written by authors in the forces, and including letters from the troops. This special issue appeared in September 1944. Some liberties were taken, such as attributing ranks to pseudonyms, including even Palmer's own alias, Morris J. Steele.

'They Forgot to Remember Pearl Harbour, by P. F. Costello, Amazing *June 1942.*

ADDITIONAL INPUT

02.04.1 The Threat of Invasion

Doyle, Sir Arthur Conan. 'Danger', *Strand Magazine* July 1914

Kornbluth, Cyril M. *Not This August, MacLean's* May 1955; Doubleday (US) 1955

Le Queux, William T. *The Great War in England in 1897*, Tower (UK) 1894

Le Queux, William T. *England's Peril*, (UK) 1899

Le Queux, William T. *The Invasion of 1910*, Eveleigh Nash (UK) 1906

Wheatley, Dennis. *Black August*, Hutchinson (UK) 1934

'*Cities in the Air' by Edmond Hamilton,* Air Wonder Stories *November 1929. Illustration by Paul.*

02.04.2 Weaponry of the Bizarre

In the pages of the early sf magazines can be found many hundreds of tales depicting war as it might be waged in the future, from ten to thousands of years hence.

A few of these stories have presented plausible ideas, which have been realised in due time, or which may yet prove prophetic. What happened to German cities in the 1940s was not far short of what Wells foretold in the film *Things to Come* (1936), or what George Griffith anticipated in *The Angel of the Revolution* (1893) even before Wells wrote *The War in the Air* (1908), which he himself did not take particularly seriously at the time.

Paradoxically, it was a German novelist, Otfrid von Hanstein, in 'Electropolis' (1930), who conceived the idea of transforming a desolate stretch of Australian desert into a technological miracle city, sustained by the marvels of super-science, replete with marvellous machines that till the land, perform all the dirty work and manufacture the necessities of life at the press of a button. The city of Electropolis even provided its own weather to order.

But this 'New Germany of the future', which is to establish a new order upon the Earth, has to be protected against attack by an English invention, 'Rindell-Matthew's rays', which ring it with an electric screen against which the Australian sea and air fleets are powerless.

Similar devices have been employed in scores of future-war stories emanating from the American pulps. The famous cartoon-strip character, Buck Rogers, whose colourful exploits in the twenty-fifth century entertained schoolboys and not a few of their elders all over the world, had his obscure origin in a story entitled 'Armageddon-2419 A.D.', published in 1928 in *Amazing Stories*.

In this tale, rocket guns have supplanted rifles among the guerrilla fighters, male and female, who fight to drive their hybrid Mongolian conquerors out of America, in defiance of the superior destructive forces brought to bear upon them. Most dreaded of all these is the 'dis beam', or disintegrator-ray, which is projected from a machine not unlike a searchlight, the reflector being a complicated balance of interacting electronic forces.

It took a 30,000-word sequel, 'The Airlords of Han' (1929), to bring about the defeat of the United Forces of the World Empire and to end the Second War of Independence. The defeat is accomplished with the aid of self-propelling 'air balls' which penetrate the ray-shields surrounding Han-occupied cities, spreading poison gas and disease germs among the fleeing populations.

Aerial warfare can be traced back to the time when Jules Verne devised his 'Clipper of the Clouds' in *Master of the World* (1886), the precursor of a host of weird and wonderful flying machines. At the close of the 1920s, when interest in civil aviation had gained ground in the United States, Gernsback's *Air Wonder Stories* devoted itself entirely to flights of imagination concerning possible – and not so possible – aeronautical developments of the future, with particular regard to air warfare. One of the more modest of these tales, 'The Bloodless War' by David H. Keller (1929), features 'robot' aircraft, and pictures an invasion of America in 1940 by thousands of pilotless bombing planes controlled by radio from a South American state which, along with Japan, is presumed to have designs on the US.

A highly novel idea was that of Harold B. McKay's 'The Flying Buzz-Saw' (1930), a contraption which flies through enemy aircraft, literally carving them to pieces. It is very much on the principle of a circular saw, with a gyroscopic control tower at the centre; and its size alone is enough to terrorise the bravest squadron-leader.

Another such improbable notion was embodied in Edmond Hamilton's 'Cities in the Air' (1929), which prophesied that in the future man will have deserted the ground altogether and will live in cities mounted on gigantic discs hovering in the sky in defiance of gravity, safe from earthquakes and storms. When war breaks out between the American Federation and a Euro-Asian alliance, the opposing cities – London, Paris, Berlin, Moscow, New York, Peking – draw up in formation and bombard each other with 'heat-shells', sending whole cities hurtling down to destruction.

An ingenious combination of submarine, tank, and aeroplane is described in Arthur J. Burk's 'Monsters of Moyen' (1930), in which a god-like dictator of Asia's millions attempts to conquer the Western world by invading the American continent in 1985. From the ocean's depths climb scores of amphibian fortresses on colossal treads. On their rounded sides emerge hundreds of bulbous 'aero-subs' intended to destroy the enemy with vibratory golden rays. At the eleventh hour, a hurriedly improvised 'Vibration Retarder' reduces amphibians and subs to dust.

02.04 WARFARE AND WEAPONRY

Air Wonder Stories *November 1929. Illustration by Strother.*

Quite as efficacious is the weapon used in Raymond Z. Gallun's 'The Crystal Ray' (1929), directed against yet another Asian invader by the American battle flyers of 2141. Their cigar-shaped aircraft are supported at an altitude of fifteen miles by an anti-gravity device. They project a beam of light through a newly discovered volcanic crystal, whose peculiar vibratory qualities are intensified by radio power to produce shocks which can penetrate metal to a depth of several feet, and on striking a man poison his bloodstream. Similarly, the powers of vibration are used to scotch one more Yellow Menace which, foreseen in 1927, is timed to arrive in 1945 in B. Prout's 'The Singing Weapon'. The weapon of the title – carried on an electric aeroplane – consists of nothing more complicated than a thin length of wire strung across the open end of a metal tube. The inventor, a young violinist, by drawing his bow across the wire, sets up vibrations which induce molecular agitation in any object, to devastating effect.

The death-ray, in one form or another, creates havoc in many a fictitious war of the future. A perambulating vacuum tube is used in Irving Lester and Fletcher Pratt's 'The Reign of the Ray' (1929) to blow up the ammunition dumps of both sides in the War of the Northern Alliance (1932–36). An 'etheric discharge' gun decomposes into harmless atoms the poison vapours loosed on the world by the Troglodytes, who swarm up from their subterranean domain in George C. Wallis's 'The World at Bay' (1928). With a similar weapon, a colossal floating airport in the middle of the Atlantic is defended single-handed against the marauding sea and air armadas of the European Alliance in Frederick Arthur Hodge's 'Modern Atlantis' (1928).

Living weapons, as an alternative to machinery, had been envisaged from the very early days of the pulps. In Stanton A. Coblentz's *After Twelve Thousand Years* (1929), the people of a highly scientific civilisation utilise the fierce fighting instincts of the insect world in waging war against each other. Whole armies of marching ants specially bred for the purpose go out to battle, commanded by armoured humans whose evolution has also been manipulated for the sake of military expediency.

An almost infinite variety of death-dealing methods can be found in the realm of fantastic fiction. In 1953, 'the eighth bloody year of the War of Extermination', the generals of the Western Alliance in Harl Vincent's 'The Colloidal Nemesis' (1928) are so hard-pressed that they develop a monstrous form of synthetic life. The Asian enemy find themselves engulfed in an ever-growing mass of protoplasmic horror impervious to shells or bombs.

This does not improve the soil much, unlike the creations of David H. Keller's 'The Yeast Men' (1928), shapeless hulks of dough-like substance that come shambling onto the battlefield to dissolve into slime and produce a stench which forces the enemy to disperse. 'The smell, however, lasts a mere ten days, and the slime becomes a rich manure!'

Keller's story marked the beginning of a fascinating sub-category of sf warfare. It told of a war-winning weapon which did not appear harmful, but which made it impossible for the enemy to start or continue an offensive. The following are a few of the novel ideas which ensued.

'The Master Minds of Venus' (1934) by William K. Sonneman, for instance, features a device broadcasting a ray which ensures that anyone who so much as thinks of making war, or of engaging in lethal activities against his fellow men, receives a splitting headache.

Poul Anderson's 'The Perfect Weapon' (1950) describes a long-range method of

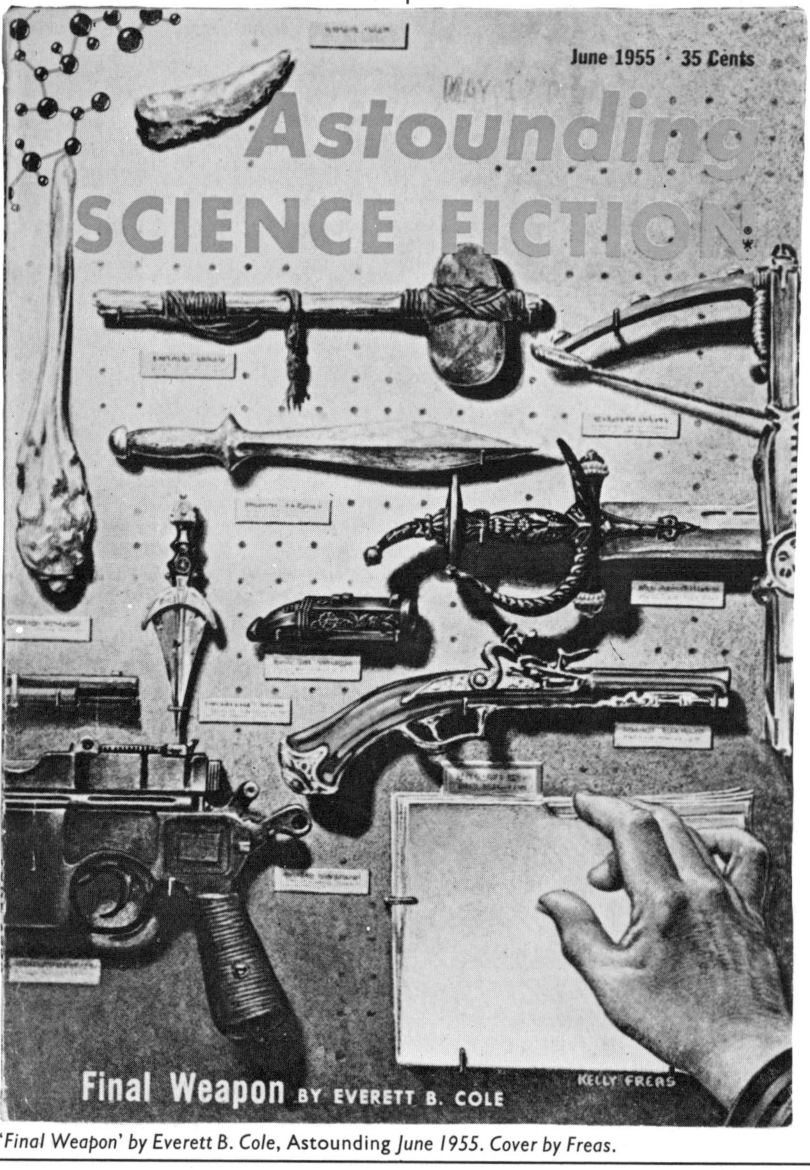

'Final Weapon' by Everett B. Cole, Astounding *June 1955. Cover by Freas.*

disintegrating paper, so that enemy communications, records and general organisation are wiped out. Alfred Coppel's 'The Awful Weapon' (1951) tells of an otherwise harmless gas which makes it impossible for anyone to lie.

Notable among these many ingenious creations of the sf writers intended to eliminate war is that of 'The Toy Maker' (1946) by Raymond F. Jones. The author tells of a conflict between two planetary civilisations in which the Toy Maker distributes strange figurines among the children of the aggressors. The toys are made of a substance which amplifies the emotional content of brainwaves, transmitting the thoughts of the adult populace, fraught with tension, fear and hatred, into the minds of the innocent children. The children are terror-stricken and suffer nervous breakdowns, bringing home to the parents the horror and futility of planetary warfare.

Doomsday Morning (1957) by C. L. Moore tells of a weapon nullifying the operation of electrical machinery. It is built by an underground movement to overthrow the dictatorship of Comus (Communications of the United States). Anti-Com is eventually activated, and planes operating on broadcast power suddenly find their engines cut.

In 'Gateway to Darkness' (1949), Fredric Brown describes a weapon which collapses the electronic orbits of matter to form a smaller structure – constituting a kind of neutronic matter. In the course of the story, the weapon is activated and collapses a planetoid to golf-ball dimensions, trapping two of the protagonists in orbit as satellites.

Another sub-category of the weaponry theme concerns war machines, sentient robots programmed to fight for their masters. Beginning in the 1960s, Fred Saberhagen has written an entire series of short stories and novels on 'the Berserkers', alien robots which have been programmed to locate and annihilate life wherever it is found. When mankind encounters the Berserkers a murderous struggle ensues. A comparable idea can be found in Pohl and

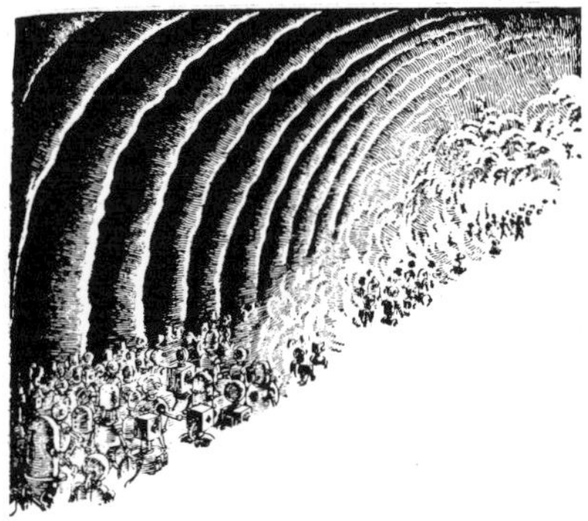

'Robot Nemesis' by E. E. ('Doc') Smith, Startling *July 1950. Illustration by Finlay.*

Kornbluth's earlier story, *Wolfbane* (1959).

The idea that robots might declare war on mankind appears consistently in science fiction, from such stories as E. E. ('Doc') Smith's 'Robot Nemesis' (1934) to A. E. van Vogt's 'Automaton' (1950).

A truly formidable war machine was envisaged in Keith Laumer's 'Combat Unit' (1964). In this noted story, Laumer narrates in the first person the reactions of a robot soldier of the future which is reactivated on an enemy planet after being disabled with its fellow robots in an earlier conflict. It reactivates the others, and together they wipe out the enemy base. The idea has been pursued through such subsequent stories as Colin Kapp's 'Gottlos' (1969).

Turning to one of the early themes of space opera, we can see that another popular idea was that of the ultimate weapon. Jack Williamson's *Legion of Space* (1935) features such a device, consisting of little more than two perforated metal plates and a small cylinder of iron; with it Williamson's heroine is able to annihiliate an invading space fleet. Even the Moon itself, which the aliens had been using as a base, disappears.

Edmond Hamilton's *Doomstar* (1966) tells of atomic devices that can change a sun from a life source to the ultimate death-dealing weapon. A flight of high-speed missiles carrying warheads consisting of cobalt isotopes and catalysts is fired into the sun. The warheads react with the cobalt atoms present in the sun and create still another isotope, violently unstable. Beyond a certain point the reaction is self-feeding, and the sun becomes a gigantic cobalt bomb, destroying all life for millions of miles around it.

Pattern for Conquest (1946) by George O. Smith describes a means of projecting a 5000-mile sphere out of a sun's core into sub-space. This turns the sun into a violent variable, and any race inhabiting its planets has to migrate within a year or perish. During the migration they are helpless targets for alien marauders.

ADDITIONAL INPUT

02.04.2 Weaponry of the Bizarrre

Asimov, Isaac. *The Machine That Won the War*, *F&SF* October 1961

Asimov, Isaac. *The Weapon Too Dreadful to Use*, *Amazing* May 1939

Best, Herbert. *The 25th Hour*, Random (US) 1940

Beynon, John (J.B. Harris). 'Spheres of Hell' (as J.B. Harris), *Wonder* October 1933; as 'The Puff-Ball Menace', *Tales of Wonder* Summer 1938

Beynon, John (J.B. Harris). 'Beyond the Screen', *Fantasy No1* 1938

Binder, Eando (Otto). 'Eye of the Past', *Astounding* February 1938

Burks, Arthur J. 'Exodus', *Marvel Science* August 1938

Burks, Arthur J. 'Survival', *Marvel Science* November 1938

Burks, Arthur J. 'West Point of Tomorrow', *Thrilling Wonder* September 1940

De Camp, L. Sprague. 'Finished', *Astounding* November 1949

Gallun, Raymond Z. 'The Weapon', *Astounding* May 1936

Gunn, James E. 'Without Portfolio', *Astounding* January 1955

Hubbard, L. Ron. *Final Blackout*, *Astounding* April to June 1940; Hadley (US) 1948

Hubbard, L. Ron. 'The End Is Not Yet', *Astounding* August to October 1947

Jameson, Malcolm. 'Eviction by Isotherm', *Astounding* August 1938

Jameson, Malcolm. 'Seaward', *Astounding* November 1938

Kapp, Colin. 'Enigma', *New Worlds* February 1960

Kapp, Colin. 'Gottlos', *Analog* November 1969

Kapp, Colin. 'War of the Wastelife', *Galaxy* May 1974

Keller, David H. 'The Ivy War', *Amazing* May 1930

Keller, David H. 'The Yeast Men', *Amazing* April 1928

Knight, Damon. 'Ask Me Anything', *Galaxy* May 1951

Kuttner, Henry. 'Sword of Tomorrow', *Thrilling Wonder* Fall 1945

Leiber, Fritz. 'Wanted to an Enemy', *Astounding* February 1945

Leiber, Fritz. 'Taboo', *Astounding* February 1963

Leinster, Murray (Will F. Jenkins). 'Invasion', *Astounding* March 1933

Leinster, Murray (Will F. Jenkins). 'Tanks', *Astounding* January 1930

Leinster, Murray. 'The Power Planet', *Amazing* June 1931

Leinster, Murray. 'Politics', *Amazing* June 1932

Leinster, Murray (Will F. Jenkins). 'The Wabbler', *Astounding* October 1942

MacLean, Katherine. 'Gimmick', *Astounding* September 1953

Moore, C.L. 'There Shall Be Darkness', *Astounding* February 1942

Moore, Ward. *Bring the Jubilee*, *F&SF* November 1952; Farrer Strauss (US) 1953; Heinemann (UK) 1955

Pohl, Frederik (with C.M. Kornbluth). *Slave Ship*, *Galaxy* March to May 1956; Ballantine (US) 1957

Pohl, Frederik (with C.M. Kornbluth). *Gladiator at Law*, *Galaxy* June to August 1954; Ballantine (US) 1955

Taine, John (Eric Temple Bell). 'Twelve Eighty-Seven', *Astounding* May to September 1935

Tucker, Wilson. *The Long Loud Silence*, Rinehart (US) 1952

Vogt, A.E. Van. 'The Weapon Shop', *Astounding* December 1942

Vogt, A.E. Van. *The Weapon Makers*, *Astounding* February to April 1943; Hadley (US) 1946

Vogt. A.E. Van. *The Weapon Shops of Isher*, *Thrilling Wonder* February 1949; Greenburg (US) 1951

Weinbaum, Stanley G. and Ralph Milne Farley (R.S. Hoar). 'Smothered Seas', *Astounding* January 1936

02.04 WARFARE AND WEAPONRY

02.04.3 Shadow of the Atom

In 1889 Frank R. Stockton wrote a number of stories for the new magazine *Once a Week*. One of these described a future war with Great Britain. Called 'The Great War Syndicate', it featured two new invincible weapons. One was a pair of giant pincers which disabled British battleships by wrenching their propellers out by the roots. The other was a cannon capable of the total annihiliation of matter. On 6 August 1945 one aspect of the story could be seen as an accurate, if accidental, prediction. The effects of Stockton's miraculous cannon were uncannily like those of the atom bomb which eliminated Hiroshima.

The invention of the atom bomb brought an era in warfare to an abrupt close. The destruction of Hiroshima and Nagasaki foreshadowed the possible destruction of the human race. Many sf stories of atomic doom had been written long before 1945, however. *The Crack of Doom* by Robert Cromie, published in 1895, also foretold the atomic bomb, and indicated that with it the whole Earth might be destroyed, and that the explosion might even rock the entire solar system! H. G. Wells's *The World Set Free* (1914) was a remarkable forecast of the use of atomic bombs. It was a genuine science fiction extrapolation from an abstruse scientific paper on intra-atomic energy by the physicist Frederik Soddy in 1909. Wells showed that, following the discovery of intra-atomic power, the Earth throngs with machines worked by atomic energy. Coal and oil become obsolete as fuels, mass unemployment follows, and the world is in turmoil. A global conflict results and before long most of the capital cities of the world are in flames; millions of people die. Here, Wells's vision is extraordinarily accurate, so that he may be forgiven for inventing bombs which do not explode with sudden, cataclysmic violence, but continue emitting furious radiations for a period of seventeen days before dimming to half power and then dimming to half that again in decreasing cycles. Before man completely destroys himself he realises that all concepts of national sovereignty are obsolete and establishes a world state.

Early utopian writers had once imagined that the harnessing of atomic power would liberate the world from drudgery; but its discoverer in Wells's novel sees clearly the dilemma presented by his work. He recognises the destructive as well as the creative properties of atomic power. Consequently he vainly hopes that his discovery may remain a secret. Among other science fiction stories which featured this dilemma is 'The Power and the Glory' (1930) by C. W. Diffin.

Another notable prognosticator of nuclear warfare was Hugo Gernsback. During the second year of the First World War, he wrote an article in *The Electrical Experimentor* in which he visualised what might happen 'when the scientists of 100 years hence made war on each other'. He painted a gruesome picture of an 'Atom Gun' in the hands of a would-be emperor of the world. A fleet of 'radium destroyers', by 'setting off spontaneously the dormant energy of the atom', might destroy a city of 300,000 souls (Hiroshima's population when the bomb fell was 320,000) in 'a titanic vapour cloud leaving only a vast crater in the ground . . . after this demonstration the enemy sues for peace; resistance would be folly'.

Following the dropping of the atom bomb on Japan, and subsequent US tests on Bikini Atoll, many writers produced stories expressing their fears for the future. John Campbell, editor of *Astounding*, whose contributors had anticipated the advent of atomic energy years before, now urged his authors to work out the implications. (One of the most noted of the pre-Hiroshima tales in *Astounding* was Robert A. Heinlein's 'Solution Unsatisfactory' (1941), telling how Hitler's Germany is overcome by the scattering of radioactive dust, and how the world subsequently succumbs to an American dictator.) *Astounding* eventually became overcrowded with such stories, and they spilled out into other publications, so that the theme became a standard one.

One of the first bomb stories to appear in print after the war was 'Memorial' (1946) by Theodore Sturgeon, in which a scientist devises the idea of using an atom bomb to gouge out an enormous radioactive pit as a constant reminder to the world of the horrors of nuclear war. Sturgeon takes the line that something drastic must happen if man's stupidity is ever to be cured. He points out that the invention of gunpowder was supposed to put an end to war, but it did not. Likewise the submarine, the torpedo, the aeroplane and the atom bomb itself. Sturgeon followed the tale with what many regard as a classic, 'Thunder and Roses' (1947). In this instance, the United States has been ravaged by a nuclear attack, but one man prevents the firing of retaliatory missiles so that future generations will have a chance to rebuild civilisation.

Science fiction treatments of the nuclear war theme divided into two factions. On the one hand were stories whose message was 'do not play with fire', while on the other writers proceeded to shock their readers with the inevitable effects of what would happen if man did play with atomic fire.

One of the most horrifying examples in the latter category was a story called 'The Last Objective' (1946) by Paul Carter. It takes place in the claustrophobic confines of tunnels beneath the earth, in great underground battle-tanks based on the mechanical-mole principle. Atomic war has

'The Last Objective' by Paul Carter, Astounding *August 1946. Illustration by Swenson.*

sterilised whole populations, producing hideous mutations, and the surface has become uninhabitable. The soldiers, fed on synthetic food, have become little more than robots. Also set underground is Mordecai Roshwald's *Level Seven* (1959), which tells of a subterranean command-post during a nuclear war, and of how radiation gradually seeps down to even the deepest shelter levels.

Outside the regular science fiction magazines, many authors wrote stories of imaginary wars. Prominent in this group is Bernard Newman, who visualised the world's scientists pooling their knowledge to prevent war. In *Secret Weapon* (1942), he pictured an explosive missile that ends the Second World War. However, prevailing security regulations prevented him from describing it as an atomic bomb. In *The Flying Saucer* (1948), the hero of *Secret Weapon* attempts to achieve peace by turning man's attention to the threat of invasion from space. Newman was anticipated in this by André Maurois in the latter's *The War against the Moon* (1928), describing a newspaper hoax which averts war on Earth by organising ray-bombardment of a supposedly aggressive Moon – only to find that the Moon is genuinely inhabited by creatures able to hit back. (It may be noted here that the authors Philip Wylie and Cleve Cartmill ran into trouble with the authorities, who suspected that they were in possession of secret information on which to base their tales. In the case of the latter's 'Deadline', 1944, Campbell's offices at *Astounding* were actually raided.)

The Murder of the USA (1947) by Will F. Jenkins opens with the massacre of 70 million Americans in a surprise attack by atomic rockets. The tale develops along the lines of a detective story, as the survivors attempt to discover and destroy the nation responsible. The book was included in a murder mystery series, and has often been overlooked in favour of the more obvious sf novels by its author – better known as Murray Leinster. Jenkins postulates that every country will set up secret launching sites, so that any aggressor's victory will be short-lived. In atomic warfare, the certainty of a terrible revenge is the only possible defence.

The acme of retaliatory devices was probably reached in Peter George's *Dr Strangelove* (1963), in which the Russians build a Doomsday Machine that will trigger automatically if they are subjected to nuclear attack. Basically it is a vast atomic device, large enough to poison the whole Earth with radioactivity.

'Solution Unsatisfactory' by Robert Heinlein, Astounding *May 1941. Illustration by Kramer.*

ADDITIONAL INPUT

02.04.3 Shadow of the Atom

Asimov, Isaac. *Pebble in the Sky*, Doubleday (US) 1950
Brunner, John. *The Brink*, Gollancz (UK) 1959
Budrys, Algis. *Some Will Not Die*, Regency (US) 1961 (an expansion of *False Night*, Lion, US, 1954)
Bulmer, Kenneth (with A.V. Clarke). *Space Salvage*, Panther (UK) 1953
Cooper, Edmund. 'The Doomsday Story', in *Tomorrow Came*, Panther (UK) 1963
Dick, Philip K. *Doctor Bloodmoney*, Ace (US) 1965
Dick, Philip K. *The Man in the High Castle*, Putnam (US) 1962
Dunsany, Lord (Edward J.M.D. Plunkett). *The Last Revolution*, Jarrolds (UK) 1951
Fearn, John Russell. 'Aftermath', *Startling* Fall 1945
Fearn, John Russell. *The Golden Amazon Returns*, *Toronto Star Weekly* November 1945; World's Work (UK) 1948
Hamilton, Edmond. 'The Atomic Conquerors', *Weird Tales* February 1927
Harding, Lee. 'Echoes of Armageddon', *Vision of Tomorrow* July 1970
Heinlein, Robert A. (as Anson MacDonald). *Sixth Column*, *Astounding* January to March 1941; Gnome (US) 1949
Hough, S.B. *Extinction Bomber*, Bodley Head (UK) 1956
Knight, Damon. 'Not with a Bang', *F&SF* Spring 1950
Kuttner, Henry (with C.L. Moore). *Fury*, *Astounding* May to July 1947 as by Lawrence O'Donnell; Grosset & Dunlap (US) 1950
Leinster, Murray (Will F. Jenkins) 'The Laws of Chance', *Startling* March 1947; as *Fight for Life*, Crestwood (US) 1955
Leinster, Murray (Will F. Jenkins). 'West Wind', *Astounding* March 1948
MacDonald, Anson (Robert A. Heinlein). 'Solution Unsatisfactory', *Astounding* May 1941
Mantley, John. *The 27th Day*, Michael Joseph (UK) 1956
McCann, Edson (Lester del Rey and Frederik Pohl). *Preferred Risk*, *Galaxy* June to September 1955; Simon & Schuster (US) 1955
Miller, Walter M. *A Canticle for Leibowitz*, Lippincott (US) 1960 (trilogy from *F&SF*: 'A Canticle for Leibowitz', April 1955; 'And the Light Is Risen', August 1956; 'The Last Canticle', February 1957)
Newman, Bernard. *The Blue Ants*, Hale (UK) 1962
Padgett, Lewis (Henry Kuttner and C.L. Moore). *Tomorr and Tomorrow and the Fairy Chessmen*, *Astounding* January to February 1946; Gnome (US) 1951
Rayer, Francis G. *Tomorrow Sometimes Comes*, Home & Van Thal (UK) 1951
Shaw, Bob. 'Cold Crucible', *Vision of Tomorrow* August 1970
Shute, Nevil (N.S. Norway). *On the Beach*, Heinemann (UK) 1957
Tubb, E.C. *Atom-War on Mars*, Hamilton (UK) 1953
Tubb, E.C. 'Tomorrow', *Science Fantasy* May 1954
Tubb, E.C. *Window on the Moon*, *New Worlds* April to June 1963; Jenkins (UK) 1964
Tubb, E.C. 'An Era Ends', *Vector* March 1964
Wylie, Philip. 'The Paradise Crater', *Bluebook* October 1945
Wylie, Philip. 'Blunder', *Collier's* January 1946

02.04 WARFARE AND WEAPONRY

02.04.4 War with the Aliens

Following the example of Wells's Martian invasion, many writers have developed the theme of warfare between man and extraterrestrials. One such alien menace appears in the novel *Sinister Barrier* (1939) by Eric Frank Russell. A formula is discovered by which the eye's receptiveness to certain wave-lengths can be increased, enabling scientists to see the normally invisible alien creatures to whom all humanity is nothing more than a vast herd of helpless milch-cows. These alien herdsmen, by telepathic means, provoke and exacerbate human emotions, on which they feed. To them, disasters are occasions for feasting: drawing on human nervous energy, feeding on hate. Thus they have a vested interest in war. The scientists try to warn the world of the danger of wholesale massacre and develop a weapon against the aliens.

H. J. Campbell's *Beyond the Visible* (1953) describes similar entities, created by radio waves. They too are responsible for the belligerency and wars of the human race. The sinister 'Deros' of Richard S. Shaver's 'Mystery' series also wage a secret war against mankind.

Most stories of warfare between man and aliens show mankind heavily on the receiving end, the extreme example being William Tenn's 'The Liberation of Earth' (1953), where the Earth is literally pulverised by being caught up in a galactic war between two alien races. A refreshing contrast to the general trend is presented in such stories as Eric Frank Russell's *Wasp* (1957), in which Terran superiority is amusingly demonstrated. A terran saboteur is landed on an enemy planet with orders to 'sting' the aliens and cause maximum havoc – like a wasp which, by stinging a single motorist, causes a multiple collision of vehicles.

Fighting extraterrestrials frequently calls for different techniques and reactions from those employed in human warfare. 'Training Aid' (1958) by E. C. Tubb describes how Earth's military scientists recreate the pain experienced by pilots hit by alien ships in a space war. The excruciating sensations are transmitted to new pilots in training simulations as a psychological stimulant to achieving optimum efficiency.

A great many of the stories chronicling man's struggle against aliens beyond the solar system fall squarely into the category of space opera. Among the regular practitioners of this type of tale, the most notable include Edmond Hamilton, E. E. ('Doc') Smith and Jack Williamson. In *Masters of Space* (1961) by E. E. Smith and E. E. Evans, for example, a starship crew find themselves in the middle of a formidable space war between alien creatures, in which they take the side of an android race evolved from the slaves of their own human ancestors.

A. E. van Vogt has written many stories of warfare between men and aliens. His *War against the Rull* (1959) describes the struggle of Earthmen against a race which has superior weaponry and physical attributes. The tide of the war is only turned in favour of the beleaguered Earthmen when they join forces with another race which enjoys superior mental attributes.

The hero of *Patterns of Chaos* (1969) by Colin Kapp is a chaos catalyst who unwittingly precipitates crises around him. His unique qualities are manipulated by government agencies to draw to himself mysterious missiles coming from an unknown source in space, and thus destroy the enemy. Tales of interstellar, intergalactic and interplanetary wars in science fiction are legion, and their popularity remains undiminished.

Warfare is also at the heart of Harry Harrison's *Death World* (1964) and its sequels. Here, the subject is a planet on which each species of life is at war with the other. Another novel embodying a violent motif, and one which caused much controversy in its time, is Robert A. Heinlein's *Starship Troopers* (1959). The story is a graphic description of military training and combat in an infantry force of the future, and includes a detailed description of armoured spacesuits incorporating a daunting array of death-dealing accessories. In Heinlein's future society, only those people who have enlisted have the right to vote. History and moral philosophy are taught (by law) only by citizens who are retired veterans. Drunken drivers are flogged. It was the presentation of an extreme élitist society, coupled with the glorification of violence, which made the book distasteful to many readers.

By contrast, Harry Harrison's *Bill, the Galactic Hero* (1965) is a savagely funny satire whilch tilts at several sacred cows of sf warfare, as well as religion. It contrives to satirise the clichés of interstellar war and space opera – for instance, star-drives based on the use of sub-space or hyper-space are replaced with what the author calls a Bloater Drive. The public are told that the alien race with which man is waging an all-out war are seven-feet-tall intelligent lizards of hideous appearance – they actually turn out to be only seven inches long. The cruel military training of new recruits is precisely documented, on a par with Heinlein's book, but Harrison's interpretation of military ideology is the very opposite of that in *Starship Troopers*. The grotesque violence which abounds in *Bill*, while presented as farce, is revealed as a crime against humanity, or any other species, and unjustifiable under any circumstances.

It is appropriate to end this section on a note of protest against war such as that sounded in Harrison's story. However brilliantly future warfare may be portrayed in science fiction, the techniques of destruction are usually portrayed as even more devastating than today's. The more serious stories are often warnings; the space operas no more than entertainment.

Bill, the Galactic Hero *by Harry Harrison (New Worlds).*

ADDITIONAL INPUT

02.04.4 War with the Aliens

Anderson, Poul. 'Silent Victory', *Two Complete Science-Adventure Books* Winter 1953; as *The War of Two Worlds*, Ace (US) 1959
Anderson, Poul. 'The Man Who Counts', *Astounding* February to April 1958; as *War of the Wing-Men*, Ace (US) 1958
Bradbury, Ray. 'The Piper', *Thrilling Wonder* February 1943
Brunner, John. *Threshold of Eternity*, *New Worlds* December 1957 to March 1958; Ace (US) 1959
Bulmer, Kenneth. *The Stars Are Ours*, Hamilton (UK) 1953
Bulmer, Kenneth. 'Unreluctant Tread', *New Worlds* February 1958
Bulmer, Kenneth. 'Space Command', *New Worlds* August 1958
Bulmer, Kenneth. 'The Aztec Plan', *SF Adventures* January 1961
Bulmer, Kenneth. 'Swords for a Guide', *Vision of Tomorrow* July 1969
Christopher, John (C.S. Youd). *Death of Grass*, Michael Joseph (UK) 1956
Coblentz, Stanton A. *The Runaway World*, Avalon (US) 1961
Cooper, Edmund. *Deadly Image*, Ballantine (US) 1958
Del Rey, Lester. 'My Name Is Legion', *Astounding* June 1942
Del Rey, Lester. 'When the World Tottered', *Fantastic Adventures* December 1950; as *Day of the Giants*, Avalon (US) 1959
Del Rey, Lester. 'For I Am a Jealous People', *Star Short Novels* 1954
Fearn, John Russell. 'War of the Scientists', *Amazing* April 1940
Fennel, Erik. 'War of Intangibles', *Astounding* June 1948
Grey, Charles (E.C. Tubb). *I Fight for Mars*, Milestone (UK) 1953
Grey, Charles (E.C. Tubb). *The Extra Man* (publisher's title for *Enterprise 2115*), Milestone (UK) 1954
Hamilton, Edmond. 'Starman Come Home', *Universe* September 1954; as *The Sun Smasher*, Ace (US) 1959
Harrison, Harry. 'Survival Planet', *F&SF* August 1961
Harrison, Harry. 'War with the Robots', *SF Adventures* July 1962
Harrison, Harry. 'Sense of Obligation', *Analog* July to August 1961; as *Planet of the Damned*, Bantam (US) 1963
Harrison, Harry. 'The Star Sloggers', *Galaxy* December 1964; as *Bill, The Galactic Hero*, Berkley (US) 1965
Hawkins, Peter. 'The Exterminators', *New Worlds* March 1953
Heinlein, Robert A. *The Puppet Masters*, *Galaxy* September to November 1951; Doubleday (US) 1951
Jones, Raymond F. 'Swimming Lesson', *Astounding* April 1943
Jones, Raymond F. *This Island Earth*, Shasta (US) 1952 (three stories from *Thrilling Wonder*: 'The Alien Machine', June 1949; 'The Shroud of Secrecy', October 1949; 'The Greater Conflict' February 1950)
Judd, Cyril (C.M. Kornbluth and Judith Merril). *Gunner Cade*, *Astounding* March to April 1952; Simon & Schuster (US) 1952
Kapp, Colin. 'Patterns of Chaos', *If* February to June 1972
Kuttner, Henry. 'Soldiers of Space', *Astonishing* February 1943
Laumer, Keith. 'War against the Yukks', *Galaxy* April 1965
Leiber, Fritz. *Destiny Times Three*, *Astounding* March to April 1945; Galaxy (US) 1956

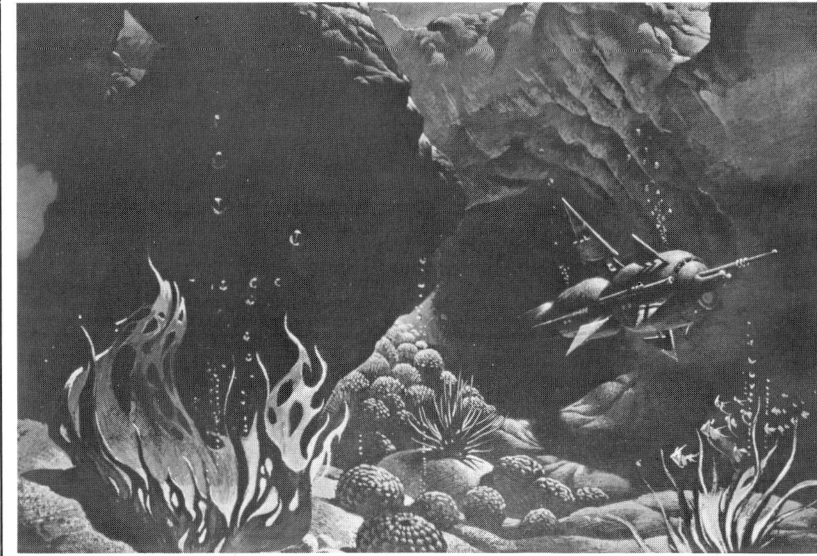

Dragon in the Sea *by Frank Herbert (NEL). Cover by Pennington.*

Leiber, Fritz. *The Big Time*, *Galaxy* March to April 1958; Ace (US) 1961
Leinster, Murray (Will F. Jenkins). 'The Incredible Invasion', *Astounding* August to December 1936; as *The Other Side of Here*, Ace (US) 1955
Leinster, Murray (Will F. Jenkins) *Operation Terror*, Berkley (US) 1962
McLaughlin, Dean. *The Fury from Earth*, Pyramid (US) 1964
Pearson, Martin (Donald A. Wollheim). 'The Embassy', *Astounding* March 1942
Russell, Eric Frank. 'Controller', *Astounding* March 1944
Russell, Eric Frank. 'Resonance', *Astounding* July 1945
Russell, Eric Frank. 'Late Night Final', *Astounding* December 1948
Russell, Eric Frank. 'I Am Nothing', *Astounding* July 1952
Smith, George O. 'Incredible Invasion', *Astounding* March 1948

The War of the Worlds *by H. G. Wells, 1897. Illustration by Warwick Goble.*

Smith, George O. *Troubled Star*, *Startling* February 1953; Beacon (US) 1959
Stuart, Don A. (John W. Campbell). 'Frictional Losses', *Astounding* July 1936
Stuart, Don A. (John W. Campbell). 'Out of Night', *Astounding* October 1937
Sturgeon, Theodore. 'The Sky Was Full of Ships', *Thrilling Wonder* June 1947
Temple, William F. *The Automated Goliath*, Ace (US) 1962 (two stories from *Nebula*: 'Against Goliath', August 1957; 'War against Darkness', June 1958)
Tenn, William (Philip Klass). 'Down Among the Dead Men', *Galaxy* June 1954
Vogt, A.E. Van. *The War against the Rull*, Simon & Schuster (US) 1959
Vonnegut, Kurt, Jr. *Slaughterhouse-Five, or the Children's Crusade*, Delacorte (US) 1969
White, James. 'Tableau', *New Worlds* May 1958
Wilding, Eric (E.C. Tubb). 'Death-Wish', *Authentic* February 1955
Wright, Sydney Fowler. *Spider's War*, Abelard-Schuman (US) 1954

02.05 GALACTIC EMPIRES

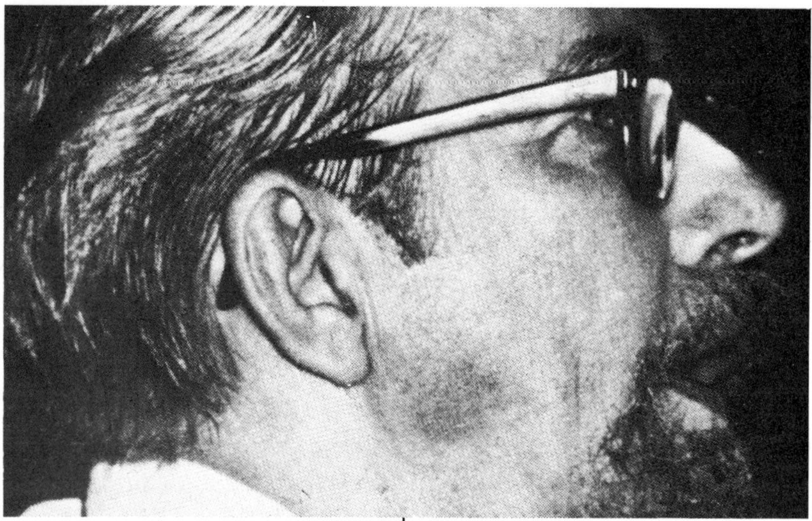

The concept of an empire of worlds among the stars, where mankind can rule the galaxy, has a strong romantic appeal to readers of science fiction. Even the breakup of such an empire becomes romantic when this permits whole worlds to return to feudalism and even barbarism, with the resulting knightly or barbarian heroes. Edmond Hamilton introduced the idea of a stellar empire early in the history of pulp science fiction and Isaac Asimov, in his 'Foundation' series, added the idea that an empire must decay, with the Roman Empire as an analog.

Undoubtedly, the romantic possibilities of empires that rise and fall inspired most of the science fiction writers to use them. Yet it seems strange that supposedly future-orientated fiction should turn so strongly to the past for its models of government.

However, a careful examination of possible means of governing a wide spread of humanity across multiple worlds, indicates that there was considerable logic behind the choice of empire, rather than more democratic systems.

There are two ways in which mankind can colonise a multiplicity of worlds amongst the stars.

One involves voyages at less than the speed of light – long, difficult voyages that take many years from beginning to end and may require some system of cold-sleep or hibernation. With such voyaging, there will be little if any intercourse between worlds. Each colony will be cut off to go its own way. Such colonies will probably never require any system of government over and between them.

But if some method of attaining faster-than-light travel and communication can be achieved, then interworld commerce will force the development of some kind of interworld government to regulate the affairs of the multiple colonies.

How can a government be developed to deal effectively with thousands (in some stories, millions) of independently colonised worlds that vary tremendously in their ecologies, resources, and almost all other possibilities? Any form of representative government becomes so unwieldy that it must certainly fail. If each world had only one representative, the assembly would still be too large to function through an incredible complex of committees. The confusion of our present United Nations and national parliaments would seem like total harmony by comparison.

Mankind, so far, has not been able to find any method of giving us a government over nations. Far more difficult would be the task of creating a democracy for a galaxy of worlds!

Rome's early representative government inevitably failed when its borders spread too far and encompassed too many divergent peoples. A Caesar and empire structure became necessary. Even that failed, but it managed to control most of Europe for half a millennium.

History repeats whenever the stresses and strains repeat. There are always variations, but certain requirements always seem to call up similar answers to those developed before to meet similar conditions.

Galactic empires will continue to arise and collapse in science fiction, largely to satisfy a certain romantic need of the readers and writers. But behind all the romanticism lies more than enough logic to justify the concept.

Lester del Rey

Lester del Rey

02.05 GALACTIC EMPIRES

02.05.1 The Beginnings of Empire

The first notable story to expound the concept of galactic empires is arguably Edmond Hamilton's 'Within the Nebula' (1929). The tale was the first of a connected series set in a remote future. As the author saw it, the majority of the planets in the galaxy were inhabited by intelligent beings, leading finally to a federation called the Council of Suns. The idea that most intelligent species would have mastered space flight at speeds faster than light, appears to have provided Hamilton with his source of inspiration. An interstellar Council had been formed, whose concern was to enforce law and order in the galaxy. Hamilton was also the first author seriously to employ the concept of the Interstellar Patrol. The more famous 'Lensman' series by E. E. ('Doc') Smith, which began with

Galactic Patrol *by E. E. Smith,* Astounding *September 1937. Illustration by Wesso.*

Galactic Patrol, was not published until 1937. Following Smith's story, such cosmic concepts became commonplace.

Hamilton's *Outside the Universe* (1929) describes the reactions of the Interstellar Patrol when the unified galactic races are faced with invasion by intelligent aliens from another and dying galaxy. It includes immense battles in space, together with the classic pulp elements of chase, capture and escape. Many of the chapters in the novel contain thematic elements which were later taken up and developed by other writers. Prominent among these ideas was 'The Hall of the Living Dead', an immense gallery filled with transparent cases ranged in long, regular rows and extending from wall to wall. In the cases are shapes and figures of what once seemed living beings. Thousands of alien beasts and life-forms, almost indescribable in appearance, are arrayed as

Illustration by Smith from 'The Star Kings' (see cover below).

examples of all the countless inhabitants of the galaxy in a cosmic museum. These myriad alien shapes, while rigid and motionless, are in reality still alive and conscious, existing in a living death.

The terrestrial hero of Hamilton's novel eventually reaches the Andromedan Galaxy and seeks aid from the gaseous beings who are its dominant race. In the titanic space battle which climaxes the novel, Hamilton effectively describes thousands of glittering suns merging into one flaming mass, a great hive of swarming stars.

Stories of this type can be described as sheer adventure, and can still be read as such. The early space operas proved a vital touchstone for later stories, not least of which were several other novels by Hamilton himself.

ADDITIONAL INPUT

02.05.1 Beginnings of Empire

Hamilton, Edmond. 'The Star-Stealers', *Weird Tales* February 1929
Hamilton, Edmond. 'The Comet-Drivers', *Weird Tales* February 1930
Hamilton, Edmond. 'The Cosmic Cloud', *Weird Tales* November 1930
Smith, E.E. *Triplanetary*, *Amazing* January to April 1934; Fantasy Press (US) 1951
Smith, E.E. *First Lensman*, Fantasy Press (US) 1951
Smith, E.E. *Grey Lensman*, *Astounding* October 1939 to January 1940; Fantasy Press (US) 1951
Smith, E.E. *Second Stage Lensman*, *Astounding* November 1942 to February 1943; Fantasy Press (US) 1953
Smith, E.E. *Children of the Lens*, *Astounding* November 1947 to February 1948; Fantasy Press (US) 1954

02.05.2 The Rise and Fall of Empire

Isaac Asimov's 'Foundation' trilogy can be seen as the pivotal work behind many of the stories in modern science fiction. It grew from a connected series of short stories and novels published in *Astounding Science Fiction* between 1942 and 1949. Subsequent book publication of the tales comprised the three novels, *Foundation* (1951), *Foundation and Empire* (1952) and *Second Foundation* (1953).

Foundation tells how the psychohistorian Hari Seldon, through his own science, predicts that the Galactic Empire of a million worlds is about to decay and that its decline will leave the galaxy in a state of anarchy for 30,000 years. Consequently, he sets up two Foundations at opposite ends of the galaxy; the location of the first being public knowledge, the whereabouts of the second being known only to himself. Seldon's Plan is that the two Foundations, after a number of crises, will join together to form a Second Empire after a lapse of some 1000 years. *Foundation* relates the first two centuries of history of the first Foundation.

'*The Star Kings' by Edmond Hamilton,* Amazing *September 1947. Cover by Smith.*

Foundation and Empire carries the history forward another hundred years and depicts the Plan under threat by a mutant who has the power to control minds, a factor unforeseen by Seldon. The First Foundation is defeated, leaving the success of the Plan entirely dependent on the Second Foundation, the very existence of which is in some doubt.

In the third and final book, the survivors of the beaten Foundation search for its hidden counterpart, whose members eventually overcome the mutant, and in the final pages its surprising location is revealed.

The 'Foundation' series provided a comprehensive analysis of the problems involved in the decline and fall of a galactic empire. Asimov unified many of the sub-themes of earlier sf stories: the advent of space travel and the reaching by man of other stellar systems; and the efforts to combine several colonised worlds under one rule from Earth. It has been seen as a parallel with ancient Rome, revealing many of the faults and flaws inherent in such a system. Asimov suggested that an empire in the stars, like the Roman Empire, would enjoy its heyday before falling as Rome fell. Subject planets would break away from the central rule, precipitating a period of Dark Ages, during which barbarian incursions would further weaken the entire structure.

In his trilogy, Asimov also envisaged that it might be possible to analyse the patterns and internal nature of humanity so that future events could be successfully predicted. Hari Seldon's science of psychohistory is a branch of mathematics dealing with the reactions of masses of mankind to fixed social and economic stimuli. Seldon assumed that humanity would remain unaware of such analysis, allowing its reactions to remain truly random.

The establishment of a galactic empire, along with its rise and fall, has been taken for granted by successive writers after Asimov. Their stories are sometimes set thousands of years after the fall of the empire, when man's common ancestry has been forgotten. Humanity, scattered over a myriad alien planets, exists at different levels of technology. Earth itself may have become a legend or even forgotten completely. Theodore R. Cogswell's 'The Specter General' (1952) describes the disintegration of a stellar empire. Planets become bellicose and introspective, gradually losing their technological abilities. Still capable of space travel, they are unable to replace their spaceships once they become worn out.

Pursuing the same concept, James Gunn

02.05 GALACTIC EMPIRES

'*The City at World's End*' by *Edmond Hamilton*, Startling Stories *July 1950*.

described in *This Fortress World* (1955) a First Galactic Empire based on loyalty to its terran founders. As colony planets produce successive native generations, they fragment and break away from the Empire. A Second Empire is subsequently created, Earth undercover agents being instrumental in merging the colony planets into a Federation. On learning how they have been manipulated, the colonists respond by destroying all life on the parent planet. A period of unrest follows, in which each colony becomes a Fortress World, jealously guarding whatever science remains in its possession. Civilisation decays into a feudal state. In the conclusion, an investigation of the ravaged Earth reveals the lost scientific knowledge, which enables a Third Unified Empire to be established.

In one of his later stories, *The Haunted Stars* (1960), Edmond Hamilton tells of a linguist who is called upon to decipher the language of an alien race whose ancient and shattered base is discovered on the Moon. By what appears to be a fortuitous coincidence, their tongue is close to that of the Summerians and his decoding enables Earth to develop a hyperspacial drive. An expeditionary ship is sent to the alien's native planet in the system of Altair and reveals that they were man's ancestors. Many other writers have developed the same idea, that the Earth has been colonised in the remote past by a star-travelling race. An ingenious modern treatment is Larry Niven's *Protector* (1973).

Harry Harrison's 'Final Encounter' (1964) adds a further variation to the 'seeding' theory, and describes the search for other intelligent races in the galaxy. Mankind has long since spread to the stars, colonising other worlds in the process; but nowhere has another intelligent life-form been found. Eventually contact is made, followed by the discovery that the alien race came originally from Earth and represents the end product of centuries of gene manipulation to adapt humans for life on particular planets.

In humanity's long conquest of the Milky Way it has been circling the rim of the galaxy. However, other colonising vessels from Earth have been moving in the opposite direction around the galactic wheel. The circle has been closed, and, in the denouement, man realises he is alone in the galaxy. Harrison's story ends on a poignant note, with the disappointed searchers looking outward into space towards other island galaxies.

Another hunt by man for sentient life on other worlds features in *The Shrouded Planet* (1957) and its sequel *The Dawning Light* (1959) by Robert Randall (Robert Silverberg and Randall Garret). The quest eventually becomes mandatory, to enable man's existing interstellar civilisation to remain intact.

Edmond Hamilton's best-known novel *The City at World's End* (1951) goes even farther into the future and tells how a small American town is thrust millions of years hence by the explosion of a super-atomic bomb. Its people find the Earth deserted, and the story deals with their reactions to their predicament and the civilisation of the stars they discover. The human races have left Earth long ago, continuing to extend their dominion until they have lost all sense of identification with their old birth world. Earthmen coming into contact with other humanoid races below their own level of development, undertake to civilise them until they are accepted as part of a galactic federation.

A Spaceship for the King (1971) by Jerry Pournelle also deals with the forging of a galactic empire from a system of feudal planets. The empire has laid down several classes of membership based on the technological status of any world at the time of its incorporation, and only planets possessing the facility of space travel enjoy any real rights. The remainder are relegated to colonial status under direct control from the imperial government.

Stories of interstellar slavery are a romantic tradition in the saga of galactic empires. In *The Planet of the Damned* (1952) Jack Vance describes the capture of an Earthman and his girl by an alien race which relies on a slave-based economy. Poul Anderson's 'The Star Plunderer' (1952) is another account of slavery on a wider scale.

Other stories have been set in a galactic empire at the height of its glory, commerce being the accepted means of communication between planets. Of these, Poul Anderson's series featuring Nicholas van Rijn is a noted example. In the novel *Trader to the Stars* (1964), Anderson suggests that in the course of exploiting the Milky Way, such traders as van Rijn may do more to spread a truly universal civilisation and enforce peace than all the diplomats in the galaxy.

ADDITIONAL INPUT

02.05.2 The Rise and Fall of Empire

Aldiss, Brian W. (ed). *Galactic Empires* (2 vols), Futura (UK) 1976

Anderson, Poul. 'The Long Way Home', *Astounding* April to July 1955; as *No World of Their Own*, Ace (US) 1955

Anderson, Poul. *Star Ways*, Avalon (US) 1956

Anderson, Poul. *Orbit Unlimited*, Pyramid (US) 1961

Asimov, Isaac. *Pebble in the Sky*, Doubleday (US) 1950

Asimov, Isaac. *The Currents of Space*, *Astounding* October to December 1952; Doubleday (US) 1952

Biggle, Lloyd, Jr. *The World Menders*, *Analog* February to April 1971; Doubleday (US) 1971

Brunner, John (K.H.). *Interstellar Empire*, DAW (US) 1976; a combination of 'The Wanton of Argus', *Two Complete Science-Adventure Books* Summer 1953; 'The Man from the Big Dark', *SF Adventures* June 1958; 'The Altar at Asconel', *Worlds of If* April to May 1965.

Chandler, A. Bertram. *To Run the Rim*, *Astounding* January 1959; as *The Rim of Space*, Avalon (US) 1963.

Dickson, Gordon R. *The Outposters*, *Analog* May to July 1971

Hamilton, Edmond. *The Star Kings*, *Amazing* September 1947; Fell (US) 1949

'Bridle and Saddle' by Isaac Asimov, Astounding June 1942. Covers by Rogers.

02.05.3 Aliens and Overlords

An interesting sub-theme in the category of galactic conquest is the premise that Earthmen who colonise new planets will evolve under different environmental conditions. Such an idea is implicit in Jack Vance's *The Five Gold Bands* (1950), and it is treated extensively in Michael Shaara's 'All the Way Back' (1952), in which the remnants of a race which once terrorised the galaxy escape to Earth and become the founders of humanity. Consequently when the first manned spacecraft makes contact with representatives of the Galactic Federation 30,000 years later, it is promptly destroyed to prevent the vicious cycle beginning again.

Cordwainer Smith wrote many inter-connected stories which tell of the odd fates which befall man as he moves outwards into the galaxy. His colonists, in adapting themselves to their new environment, gradually diverged more and more from their original form. In 'The Crime and the Glory of Commander Suzdal' (1964) he tells how the effects of intense solar radiation on a colonial world began to destroy the females of every species on the planet. By a programme of massive chemical injections the human women are converted into what passes for men, but the long-term cultural implications impose a threat on ordinary humanity.

In the course of Cordwainer Smith's tale, Suzdal creates a race of cat-people. By coincidence, George O. Smith's much earlier *Pattern for Conquest* (1946) describes an Earth federation skirmishing with another federation of cat-people. The warring factions are united when both are menaced by an inimical third race which sweeps the galaxy into an overwhelming war. Galactic warfare is also waged by an alien federation in A. E. van Vogt's novel *Masters of Time* (1950), in which the aliens

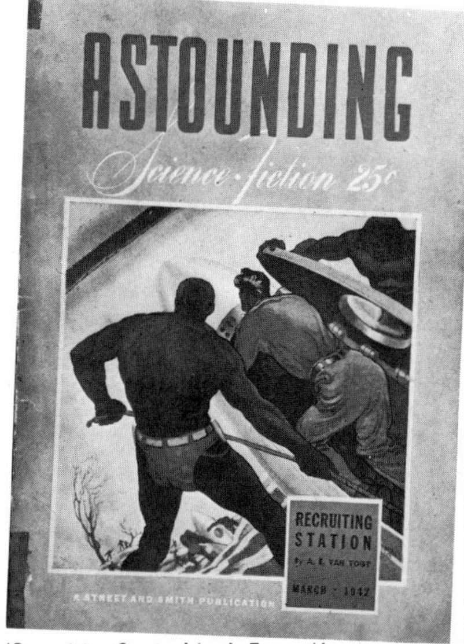

'Recruiting Station' by A. E. van Vogt, Astounding March 1942. Cover by Rogers.

recruit their armies from past eras.

The unification of galactic races in the face of a cosmic disaster is one more sub-category of the galactic empires theme. In Clifford Simak's *Cosmic Engineers* (1939), the Milky Way is bound towards a head-on collision with another island universe. An ancient alien civilisation transmit, from the edge of the galaxy, a message which seeks the help of a more vigorous younger race. Several answer the call, including man. Fighting through both time and space, the Cosmic Engineers eventually succeed in averting the disaster.

In the novel *Ringworld* (1970), Larry Niven followed Simak in developing this particular sub-theme by telling of a stellar explosion at the core of the galaxy which threatens to extinguish all life as its sweeps through consecutive star systems. The first

Captain Future from 'Earthmen No More' by Edmond Hamilton, Startling March 1951.

intelligent race of aliens to learn of the coming disaster enlist the help of Earthmen and another cat-like race which has been warring with the Earth federation. They exhort the now unified factions to help them find a haven, promising to impart the secret of their reactionless faster-than-light drive as a reward.

Many writers have speculated that if man should succeed in establishing interstellar communication with a civilisation superior to his own, only disaster could follow. They have pointed to the historical precedents on Earth, where such races as the Tasmanians

'The Starman of Llyrdis' by Leigh Brackett, Startling March 1951. Illustration by Orban.

were destroyed by the more 'advanced' peoples who discovered them.

Both this view, and the opposite, are depicted in Jack Williamson's *Bright New Universe* (1967), in which man has begun 'Project Life Line', a determined attempt to pick up any intelligent signals from space. The supporters of the scheme are met with fierce opposition when they eventually make contact with a superior race. Their opponents fear that the culture of the Earth will be absorbed, and although their fears are realised, the contact results in the creation of a cosmic Utopia. Every human is provided with a private line to the trans-galactic culture. A small device opens the way to freedom from need, ignorance and oppression.

Several noted stories have been written around the idea of advanced aliens observing mankind without revealing their own presence, the underlying concept being that Earth must attain a certain stage of civilisation before being admitted to a galactic federation. In some tales Earth is judged incapable of ever reaching an acceptable standard, and is doomed to destruction. In Jack Williamson's *The Trial of Terra* (1962), for example, man's conquest of space presents a dilemma to the Celestial Watchers who have observed humanity for thousands of years from a hidden base on the Moon. They are obliged to decide whether the people of Earth are mature enough to join the civilisations of space – or whether they should be rejected and destroyed by solar fire. Williamson continued such interstellar speculations in *The Moon Children* (1971).

Lost in Space by George O. Smith (1959) employs a similar motif, describing the fate of a space-liner trapped in inter-galactic space. While Earthships attempt to locate the craft, powerful aliens are observing the rescue attempts – endeavouring to decide whether humans should be annihilated or simply subjugated to their superior culture. Ultimately, the watchers are impressed with the human qualities they see and enter into friendly relations.

Damon Knight's 'Earth Quarter' (1955) also describes the reaction of alien superiors to human nature. It tells of the plight of human refugees in the midst of an alien civilisation. They are forced to exist in the Earth Quarter of the title, a cramped ghetto. Finally they are returned to Earth, which is subsequently quarantined. The aliens fear the outright aggression which has been exhibited in the ghetto conditions

Finally there are those stories where a single individual is responsible for the acceptance of humanity into the galactic federation. Clifford D. Simak's *Way Station* (1963) depicts an Inter-Galactic Council, embracing a multitude of civilised worlds and races. Earth is but one of several planets used as a 'way station' or relay post through which travellers and commercial products are projected by supra-dimensional matter transmitters. The story is told from the viewpoint of the manager of the Earth station, a man whose life has been artificially lengthened for the purpose. The existence of the station is kept secret, since humanity is regarded as not sufficiently advanced for membership of the Council. When it is discovered that a young Earth girl possesses the necessary psychic qualities to operate a talisman of the Council, man is deemed fit to join.

More specifically, Robert A. Heinlein's *Have Spacesuit, Will Travel* (1958) tells of a teenage boy who is inveigled into a series of

'Have Space Suit, Will Travel' by Robert A. Heinlein, F&SF September 1958. Cover by Emsh.

interstellar adventures. Eventually he is brought to trial, as a representative of all mankind, before the Council of the Three Galaxies, a body of police overlords. The Council views humanity as a dangerous race posing a threat to the peace of the federation. The destruction of the Earth seems imminent until the boy's indomitable spirit, his human pride, is judged a redeeming quality.

Essentially, stories of galactic empire are optimistic, and in the romantic tradition. Their tremendous contributions to the shaping of modern science fiction has only recently been recognised by critics and anthologists. Donald Wollheim's *The Universe Makers* (1971), a widely acclaimed personal statement, emphasises the near-unanimous confidence of sf writers in humanity, and its role in the universe. Brian Aldiss's *Galactic Empires* (1976) is a two-volume opus which collects together a number of fascinating stories woven around the theme. The collection's jacket introduction admirably summarises this: 'Space-ships daring the outer reaches of the known universe; civilizations, human and alien, defying the might of Earth; beautiful women, courageous men, hideous, if sometimes friendly aliens . . . the tale of far-flung, preferably barbaric, galactic empire is the very essence of science fiction.'

Few sf writers who have portrayed them would accept the likelihood that galactic empires will one day exist. When they have not described them in terms of sheer adventure, they have often used them as allegories of existing human conditions. If some of the empires depicted leave much to be desired, it should be taken as no more than a recognition by some authors of their similarity with various of their historical counterparts on Earth.

ADDITIONAL INPUT

02.05.3 Aliens and Overlords

Biggle, Lloyd, Jr. *The Still, Small Voice of Trumpets*, Doubleday (US) 1968

Bounds, Sydney J. 'Frontier Encounter', *Nebula* March 1956

Brown, Fredric. 'Arena', *Astounding* June 1944

Clarke, Arthur C. 'Guardian Angel', *New Worlds* Winter 1950

Reynolds, Mack. *Amazon Planet*, *Analog* December 1966 to February 1967

Sagan, Carl. *The Cosmic Connection*, Doubleday (US) 1973

Silverberg, Robert. 'Shadow in the Stars', *SF Adventures* April 1958; as *Stepsons of Terra*, Ace (US) 1958

Silverberg, Robert. *Collision Course*, *Amazing* July 1959; Avalon (US) 1961

Smith, George O. *Nomad*, *Astounding* December 1944 to February 1945; Prime (US) 1950

Smith, George O. *Operation Interstellar*, Century (US) 1950

Smith, George O. *Troubled Star*, *Startling Stories* February 1953; Avalon (US) 1957

Vance, Jack. *The Space Pirate*, Toby (US) 1953

Woodcott, Keith (John Brunner). *I Speak for Earth*, Ace (US) 1961

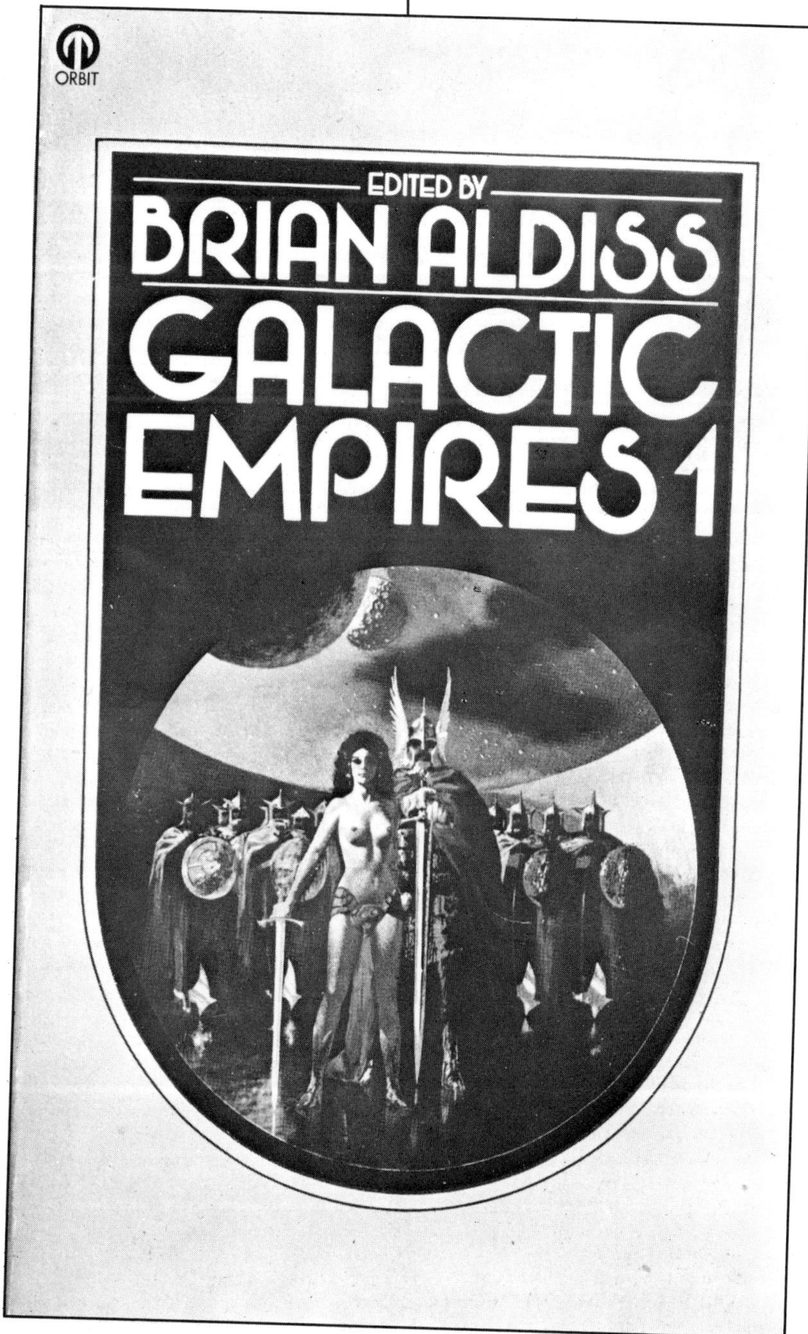

Galactic Empires *edited by Brian Aldiss (Orbit). Cover by Thole.*

02.06 FUTURE AND ALTERNATIVE HISTORIES

There's an old Oxford story about the senior members of a famous college discussing how some funds should be invested. The Bursar says, 'We must invest in land. Land has proved an excellent investment for a thousand years.' And the oldest don looks up from his port and says, 'Yes, but, well, you know, the last thousand years have been exceptional.'

The aged gentleman is right, and it is the exceptional which catches the eye of the science fiction writer. The last thousand years were as stuffed with turning points as with dates, and all can be used for what in the following text are neatly called 'Jonbar Hinges'. I may modestly claim to have established the earliest Jonbar Hinge to date in *The Malacia Tapestry* (1976), where men are descended from dinosaurs rather than ape ancestors. The novel also reflects a world in which Manicheism ousted Christianity, just as in my story, 'Danger: Religion!' (1965), Christianity is ousted by Mithraism.

One of my favourite sf novels is not quite alternative history. In L. Sprague de Camp's *Lest Darkness Fall* (1955), the hero is whisked back in time to a sixth-century Rome threatened by the Goths, and endeavours to change history. William Golding has a story, 'The Brass Butterfly' (1956), later made into a play, in which the Romans develop steam-power and printing. ('There will be no slaves but coal and iron. The ends of the earth will be joined together.')

Generally, authors concentrate on changes in more recent history. The text mentions the alternative consequences of the Second World War, of which the two most brilliant examples are Philip K. Dick's *The Man in the High Castle* (1962) and Sarban's *The Sound of His Horn* (1952). The latter once appeared in paperback editions with an introduction by Kingsley Amis, whose interest in alternative worlds is well known. In his latest novel, *The Alteration* (1976), Amis produces his own version of history, a world of 1976 in which the Reformation never took place and England is a Catholic country. More venturesome youths read TR, or Time Romance; some prefer CW, or Counterfeit World, and are engrossed in a novel called *The Man in the High Castle* (1962).

It looks as if CW is gaining favour in our timetrack too. Most of these novels, while not without their adventure aspect, centre round a moral dilemma. Perhaps history may be seen as a series of moral dilemmas.

As the text rightly notes, one of the seminal books in the development of alternate worlds is the variously titled *If It Had Happened Otherwise* (1931), an esoteric parlour game played by historians. Even earlier, but in a similar style of academic humour, is the pamphlet by a Fellow of Oriel College, Richard Whateley, entitled *Historic Doubts Respecting Napoleon Bonaparte* (1819), which seeks to prove, in a straight-faced way, that Napoleon never existed.

This is not so far from Norman Spinrad's laborious and academic joke, *The Iron Dream* (1972), which, complete with critical paraphernalia, depicts Adolf Hitler as a pulp science fantasy writer who immigrated to the United States after the Great War, and whose novel, *Lord of the Swastika*, won a Hugo in 1954. (Well, well, we must recall that a suspiciously named Howard W. Campbell Jr, a writer, is the Nazi-affiliated hero of Kurt Vonnegut's novel, *Mother Night*, 1961.)

Science fiction authors extend science fiction's boundaries farther every decade. Hence our perpetual difficulty in defining the homeland. I believe the alternative world is growing in favour as a sub-genre, following the warm reception of perhaps the three most brilliant examples of the species, *Bring the Jubilee, The Man in the High Castle* and *A Transatlantic Tunnel, Hurrah!*, which belong to the fifties, sixties and seventies respectively. It may well gain still more popularity as its power to amuse and make us reflect is more generally recognised. Its keynote being irony rather than wonder, it is more sophisticated than the interplanetary tale.

Outstandingly, it is a branch of sf which has evolved from a discipline other than science, from history. Which may or may not reflect the way in which the West, in recent years, has become increasingly disenchanted with the fruits of science. Or it may reflect the way we have become increasingly conscious of the random in our lives.

Speaking as a creator of alternate worlds myself, I'm sure that at least it reflects an instinct for the sort of story which can seize you by your curiosity and keep on tickling it throughout.

Brian Aldiss

Brian Aldiss

02.06 FUTURE AND ALTERNATIVE HISTORIES

One of the regular crafts of the science fiction writer is that of inventing the future. Many of the most effective stories are those where the writer has extrapolated from present trends to make the future believable. In this way, several authors have invented a single future against which to set many of their stories. Such 'future history' series feature in the work of Robert Heinlein, Poul Anderson and Isaac Asimov.

Science fiction not only enables the writer to create his own future, but also allows him to re-invent the past. History in the making is a complex series of closely related events and consequences. The historical significance of any single event can only be seen in retrospect. A noted example is the assassination of Archduke Franz Ferdinand in Sarajevo, which provided the trigger mechanism for the First World War, which, in turn, led to the second conflict a quarter of a century later. What kind of world might we now be living in had the Archduke survived? Such speculations form the basis of alternative-history fiction, or worlds that might have been.

02.06.1 Future Histories

Prophets have been found in many cultures, and Research is still being made into the prophecies of figures as widely differing as Nostradamus and Mother Shipton. They offered predictions which they believed to be true, but early examples of fictionalised discourses on the future also exist. According to I. F. Clarke in his compilation *The Tale of the Future* (1961), the first piece of fiction to be set in the future was a pamphlet *Aulicus* (1644) by Francis Cheynell, which was a thinly-veiled attack on King Charles I of Britain. The first genuine novel of this kind is apparently Samuel Madden's *The Memoirs of the Twentieth Century* (1733) set in the year 1997. Since then, such works have become commonplace. They account for a substantial proportion of science fiction.

While the majority of such stories in the modern genre take in a considerable range of possible futures, certain writers have adopted the technique of mapping out a progressive history of man's future. Used imaginatively, such a backdrop enables the reader to discover how the effects of earlier events can be depicted in a series of stories.

The first writer to map out methodically a complete future history was Olaf Stapledon, and no one has quite matched him since. In *Last and First Men* (1930) and later in *The Star-Maker* (1937), he described an entire history of the universe. *The Star-Maker* is so far-reaching a vision that it stands unequalled in the entire history of science fiction and has undoubtedly influenced many writers. But it also divorces the reader from any conception of time, since eons can pass in a single paragraph. It is a mega-history, while *Last and First Men* is better termed a giga-history

02.06 FUTURE AND ALTERNATIVE HISTORIES

– it covers a mere 2000 million years! Stapledon traces events from his present time of 1930, through various international wars in the twentieth century, the decline of Europe and the rise of America, to the founding of the first World State in around 2300 AD. Following its downfall comes the decline of the First Men and the rise of the Second Men and a Patagonian civilisation. From that point events begin to tumble one after another, with a Martian invasion and the fall of the Second Men, followed by Third, Fourth and Fifth Men. The impending catastrophe of the Moon falling to Earth in about 300 million AD brings about the settling of the Fifth Men on Venus, and millennia later on Neptune. With the passing of the Eighteenth Men, the species has died out.

No other science fiction writer has ever gone to such extremes in his fiction. A less ambitious but popular future history was introduced in the early sf pulp days by Neil R. Jones. It featured the exploits of Professor Jameson, whose body, after death, was placed in orbit around the Earth, to be revived by aliens over 35 million years later. The series began with 'The Jameson Satellite' (1931), but it was in 'Time's Mausoleum' (1933) that Jones fully told the history of the Earth, and man's eventual desertion of the dying planet to establish a new world around Sirius.

Future history became a practised art in the work of Robert Heinlein. He made his debut with a short story, 'Lifeline' (1939), and within a year, which had seen such of his tales as 'If This Goes On –' (1940) and 'The Roads Must Roll' (1940), he was already considered a well established writer. Subsequently he began to write quite transparently under the pseudonym 'Anson MacDonald', and it was revealed in the May 1941 issue of *Astounding SF* that all stories under his own name were part of a uniform future history. A chart illustrated how these tales, including those still to be written, fitted into the framework. Its publication was something of an innovation and enabled readers to piece together Heinlein's future as it was written. Other writers have followed Heinlein's example. Three charts are reprinted here to indicate different interpretations of future history.

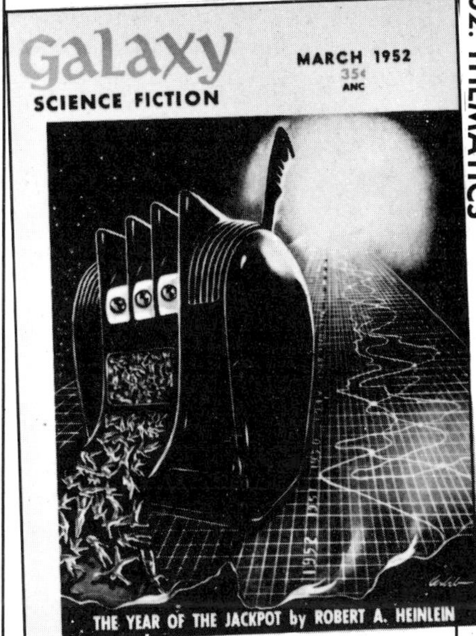

'The Year of the Jackpot' by Robert A. Heinlein, Galaxy March 1952. Cover by Arbib.

Ralph 124C41 + *by Hugo Gernsback (Fantasy Books).*

ADDITIONAL INPUT

02.06.1 Future Histories

Atkins, John. *Tomorrow Revealed*, Spearman (UK) 1955 (non-fiction)
Churchill, R.C. *The Short History of the Future*, Laurie (UK) 1955
Niven, Larry. *Neutron Star* (collection), Ballantine (US) 1968
Niven, Larry. *Ringworld*, Ballantine (US) 1970
Niven, Larry. *Tales of Known Space* (collection), Ballantine (US) 1975
Wells, H.G. *The Time Machine*, Heinemann (UK) 1895

02.06 FUTURE AND ALTERNATIVE HISTORIES

'HISTORY OF THE FUTURE' BY POUL ANDERSON

Date	Story	Events	Technology		Sociology
1950	(Marius)	Korean War World War III: Defeat of Soviets Civil Wars in Europe; the Great Jehad Expeditions to Mars & Venus Conference of Rio African nations gain autonomy	Hydrogen-lithium reaction Lunar bases Robot files Interplanetary colonization Airboat Petroleum synthesis	Cybernetics Needle gun Improved psychiatry Human exogenesis Early psychotechnology Rover bomb	Socialism in America Postwar period of chaos Period of recovery UN greatly strengthened Religious fanaticism Privacy laws USA constitutional amendments
1980	Un-Man The Sensitive Man	UN suppresses Brazil-Argentine War Extensive reclamation on Earth Anti-UN junta suppressed Attempt at dictatorship stopped	Improved spaceships Oceanic colonies General field theory Outdoor air-conditioning Ecological-unit spaceship	Automatic factories Shock & paralysis beams Longevity	Growth of Psychotechnic Institute Population control
2010	(House in the Sky)	Abolition of national armies University of Luna Founded Outer-planet expeditions Second Conference of Rio Venusian break with UN	Sun-power Hyperbolic orbits Air transformation Power-beaming Superdielectrics	Synthetic virus Psychosomatics Flying homes Food synthesis	The Second Industrial Revolution Further steps toward full world government
2040	The Big Rain	Currency reform Suppression of Venusian nationalists Ganymede colonized	Small atomic motors Interplanetary radio Frictionless motors Electric blaster	Space warcraft Machine consciousness	UN space navy Planetary Engineering Corps Basic language invented
2070	(Wolf)	Growing discontent on Earth due to failure to solve problems of 2nd Industrial Revolution Anti-robot riots	Military robots Automatic spacecraft Asteroid colonies	Artificial regeneration Anthropoid robot	The 'New Enlightenment' Order of Planetary Engineers The Encylopedic Foundation
2100	Quixote and the Windmill	Convention of Luna Venus made habitable The Humanist Manifesto Space ark to Centauri:	Space liner service Travelling reclamation outfit Minimal spaceships	Molar potential barrier Synthetic nonprotoplasmic life	Solar Union founded Growth of clan system on Venus Pancosmic religion begins
2130	Holmgang	120-yr. voyage. A device to get rid of malcontents. Revelations of gov't corruption Mars made habitable	Interplanetary power-beam designed Nuclear damping fields	Neural regeneration	Period of worsening conditions on Earth, leading to a great interplanetary emigration and development.
2160	(Cold Victory)	Abortive Humanist revolution			Slow decline of scientific progress, but much engineering work.
2190	The Snows of Ganymede	Jovian dictatorship overthrown			

'If This Goes On—' by Robert A. Heinlein, Astounding February 1940. Illustrations by Rogers.

02.06 FUTURE AND ALTERNATIVE HISTORIES

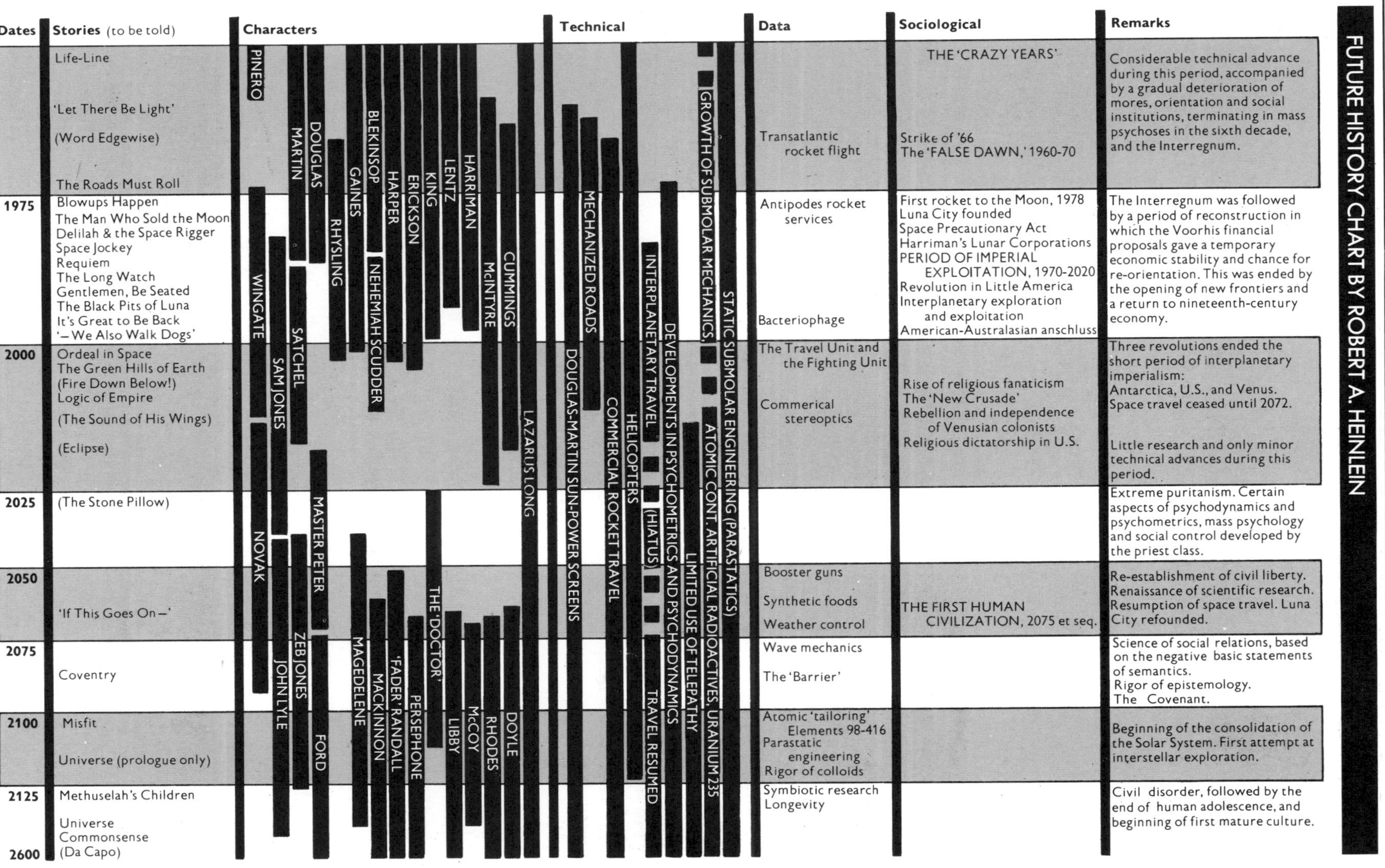

02.06 FUTURE AND ALTERNATIVE HISTORIES

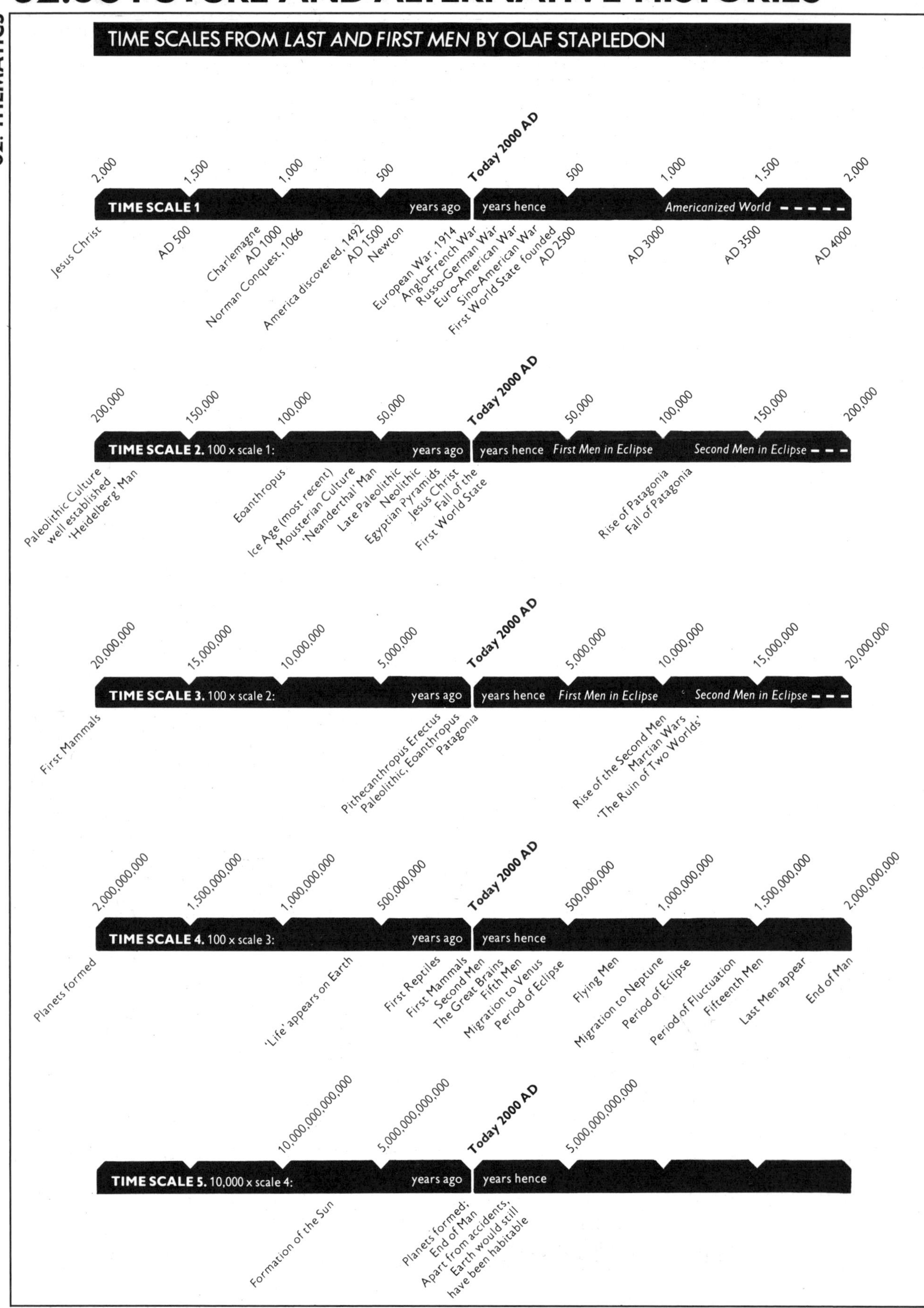

02.06.2 Alternative Histories

In an afterword to his short story 'Trips' (1974), Robert Silverberg has noted: 'If science fiction is a literature of infinite possibilities, the subgenre of alternative-timetrack fiction must be one of its most infinite compartments.' Faced with the full range of possibilities that present themselves to an individual in the course of a single day, it is easy to imagine the changing of history in a vast variety of ways: important decisions may be left untaken, vital journeys missed, and a freak change in the weather may determine the outcome of a battle. The possibilities are indeed infinite, and it is this that can make alternative histories one of the most fascinating of all science fiction concepts.

Oddly enough the alternative-timetracks theme is not necessarily regarded as science fiction, and is often a scholarly pursuit. One of the most effective accounts of past possibilities ever compiled is *If It Had Happened Otherwise* (1931), a collection of essays edited by Sir John Collings Squire. Eleven noted writers supplied their own answers to questions which included 'If Don John of Austria Had Married Mary Queen of Scots' (by G. K. Chesterton), 'If Napoleon Had Escaped to America' (by H. A. L. Fisher), 'If Byron Had Become King of Greece' (by Sir Harold Nicolson), 'If Lee Had Not Won the Battle of Gettysburg' (by Sir Winston Churchill), 'If Booth Had Missed Lincoln' (by Milton Waldman) and Squire's own 'If It Had Been Discovered in 1930 That Bacon Really Did Write Shakespeare'. The conclusions to these conjectures were both fascinating and enlightening, and the volume aroused much interest amongst historians. One of the earliest such essays was written by the noted historian G. M. Trevelyan in response to a competition set by the *Westminster Gazette* in July 1907 for the best answer to the conjecture 'If Napoleon Had Won the Battle of Waterloo'. Historians are as intrigued by the theme today as ever, and the American professor of history, Robert Sobel, in a recent novel, postulated the success of Britain in the American War of Independence, so that America remains one of Britain's colonies. His story, *For Want of a Nail* (1973), traces the execution of such revolutionaries as John Adams and Thomas Jefferson, to the birth of a Confederation of North America which included Canada.

The rift between science fiction writers and professional historians, however, is clear enough in Sir John Wheeler-Bennett's introduction to the new edition of *If It Had Happened Otherwise*, in 1972, where he states that little had been written in this field in recent years. The contribution of science fiction is completely overlooked!

It is worth noting that science fiction had entered the imaginary field long before J. C. Squire's volume, and even earlier than Trevelyan's 1907 essay. It is important here, though, to recognise the two essentially different types of alternative-timetrack story. The first is the historical story, in which an author follows the events that would have occurred had some major event in our history happened differently. The second is the purely fictional alternate-world story where the author traces the changes in the future created by a character of his own invention. Probably the earliest and certainly most influential of the latter school is Charles Dickens's 'A Christmas Carol' (1843), in which Ebenezer Scrooge is shown the future that might be if he continues his miserly ways. Scrooge changes his entire life and thus sets up a different future.

It is less easy to determine the earliest example of the former class, since so much of a propagandist and semi-fictional nature appeared during the nineteenth century. Most of these works, however, tended to choose an event that might happen in the near future rather than one that had already happened. The best known example of this category is George Chesney's 'The Battle of Dorking' (1871), an account of the Prussian armies, fresh from their success in the Franco-Prussian War, invading Britain.

Two of the earliest alternate world novels are *It May Happen Yet* (1899) by Edmund Lawrence about Napoleon's invasion of Britain, and *Hubert's Arthur* by Baron Corvo (Frederick W. Rolfe). The latter title, which traces the course of history had Prince Arthur, the rightful heir to the throne, not been murdered by order of King John in 1203, was published in 1935 although it had been written and completed in 1911.

By the mid-1930s, the alternate-world theme had begun to enjoy an increasing popularity in science fiction, predominantly as a result of Murray Leinster's 'Sidewise in

'The Time Stream' by John Taine, Wonder Stories *December 1931. Illustrations by Paul.*

Time', which had been preceded by earlier speculation in John Taine's *The Time Stream* (1931). Leinster's 'Sidewise in Time' (1934) suggested that time might flow like a river, not in a straight line, but in a curve. Thus, at points the past and future blend, together with all other possible pasts and futures. A rift occurs that draws such possibilities together, and present-day citizens are disconcerted to find themselves shifted erratically into worlds where the South won the American Civil War, where the Chinese have settled in America, where Roman legions march and where prehistoric monsters still hold sway. Since J. C. Squire's volume had seen an American edition as *If: Or History Rewritten* in 1931, Leinster may well have read it and been inspired to write his story. Whatever the case, his tale was germinal in the sf field and influenced other writers. It attracted the emerging, if short-lived, talents of David R. Daniels and Stanley G. Weinbaum. Daniels's story, 'The Branches of Time' (1935), explored with youthful exuberance how time travel could easily establish many alternative timetracks. Weinbaum approached the theme from a human angle, and in 'Worlds of If' (1935) depicted a machine that will show its user what might have happened to him in the various conditional worlds. Since the Weinbaum and Daniels tales appeared in the same issue of *Wonder Stories*, the impact of this type of thematic approach was that much greater.

Weinbaum had previously written another 'worlds of if' story that remained unpublished until after his death. In 'The Circle of Zero' (1936) he put forward the theory that instead of probable worlds flowing side by side, eternity allows for the possibility of history repeating itself endlessly. A third variation on the alternative-history theme is the counter-Earth hypothesis, suggesting that a hidden twin Earth exists on the far side of the Sun. Writers have developed this third concept in more than one way. Either the twin worlds have evolved totally differently or they are much alike. One of the earliest, and still intriguing, counter-Earth stories is Edison Marshall's 'Who Is Charles Avison?' (1916), where two identical Avisons leave their respective Earths in a spaceship. However, the intervention of a comet results in both returning to the same Earth, one arriving just after his twin-self has been buried! A similar approach was used effectively by Edgar Wallace in *Planetoid 127* (1929), but the counter-Earth theme lost much of its validity with the advent of space exploration. It was still to be found in Paul Capon's trilogy that begun with *The Other Side of the Sun* (1950), and it survives, but in name only, in the 'Gor' series by John Norman initiated in *Tarnsman of Gor* (1966). But this is not the twin-Earth of the earlier tales and fits more within the parallel-worlds theme.

The success of the first category of alternative-history story depends very much on the extent to which the writer has done his homework. To write convincingly of a world where the South had won the American Civil War requires a sound knowledge of the social, political and technical history of that period, together with an insight into the minds of the leading historical figures. This criterion emphasises why the theme is a popular intellectual pursuit among historians and why sf writers during the pulp magazine days tended to concentrate on the more personalised alternate-worlds theme. Even the science fiction writer with perhaps the best qualifications for attempting such a work, L. Sprague de Camp, whose scholarly endeavours within the field rival his fiction, wrote only an imaginary 'if' novel, *The Wheels of If* (1940), set in six alternative New Yorks and following the interplay of the various duplicated characters. The story may have influenced Fritz Leiber's *Destiny Times Three* (1945), where a machine splits our time-stream into a variety of alternate worlds. Another early novel of some influence on the development of the theme was Jack Williamson's *The Legion of Time* (1938), in which the hero discovers the future existence of two possible time-streams (amongst others), that of Jonbar, a good, peaceful world, and another, Gyronchi, of an oppressive nature. Which of these two futures will actually come to pass depends upon a young boy who, in 1921, will find either a magnet or a pebble. If it is the magnet, his interest in science will lead to his later discovery of a new form of energy, and thus Jonbar will come into being. If it is the pebble, the discovery of the new power falls into despotic hands. Isaac Asimov later came to rework the theme with greater complexity in *The End of Eternity* (1955), where reality changes are continuously effected by an élite corps of time travellers.

The possibility that man might try to meddle with the time-tracks, as depicted in the Williamson and Asimov novels, led to a new concept in the alternate-world theme, that of policing the worlds. H. Beam Piper established a 'paratime police' in a series of stories that grew from 'He Walked around the Horses' (1948) and included 'Police Operation' (1948), 'Last Enemy' (1950) and a novel, *Time Crime* (1955).

'*Time Crime*' by H. Beam Piper, Astounding *February 1955. Cover by Freas.*

'*Sail On! Sail On!*' by *Philip José Farmer*, Startling *December 1952. Illustration by Dreanys.*

This same policing of time to avoid anachronisms and parallel worlds was the purpose of Poul Anderson's Time Patrol, in his series of stories published in book form as *Guardians of Time* (1960), while the exploration and exploitation of time-lines formed the basis of Keith Laumer's novels, *Worlds of the Imperium* (1961), *The Other Side of Time* (1965) and *Assignment in Nowhere* (1968).

Following Leinster's example in 'Sidewise in Time', a number of writers have superimposed one world on another, an early example being Guy Dent's *Emperor of the If* (1926). Brian Aldiss employed rifts in time to bring all manner of timetracks and anachronisms into his novel *The Eighty-Minute Hour* (1974), and used much the same basis for *Frankenstein Unbound* (1973), which transports the hero into a world where Victor Frankenstein genuinely existed. Sam Merwin's *The House of Many Worlds* (1951) and Fred Hoyle's *October the First Is Too Late* (1966) are further examples of this type of variation. Silverberg's 'Trips' (1974), referred to at the beginning of this sub-section, depicts tourist trips to such alternative histories as those where the Industrial Revolution never happened, where the Mongols have achieved a world-wide Empire, and, inevitably, where Germany won the Second World War.

Almost certainly the best-known work set in a world where Hitler won the war is Philip K. Dick's *The Man in the High Castle* (1962). Dick's novel was apparently based on William Shirer's essay 'If Hitler Had Won World War II', which was part of a series of such speculative essays published by *Look* magazine in 1960–61 as a modern equivalent of J. C. Squire's commissions. The story is set in an America which has been successfully invaded by Japan and Germany and is subsequently divided into three north-south strips. The east is Nazi-occupied, the west Japanese-dominated, while the middle remains neutral. In this middle state lives a science fiction writer who has written his own alternate-world novel where Germany and Japan have lost the war! In Dick's case the 'Jonbar hinge', the point at which the story departs from genuine history, is an attempted assassination of President-elect Roosevelt in 1933. Dick also wrote his own version of *The Legion of Time* in his novelette 'Jon's World' (1954).

The Man in the High Castle was not the first of the Germany-won-the-war stories, but it remains among the best. An earlier example was Edna Mayne Hull's 'The Flight That Failed' (1942), while C. M. Kornbluth's 'Two Dooms' (1958) was a later depiction of an America dominated by Japan and Germany.

Other stories have portrayed the Nazi conquest of Britain and, as might be expected, are predominantly by British writers. The pseudonymous novelist Sarban (John W. Wall) produced a suitably unpleasant vision in *The Sound of His Horn* (1952), in which the occupying forces set up a form of feudal society that amuses itself by hunting peasants. More recently, Hilary Bailey produced a striking treatment in her portrayal of Britain under the Nazis in 'The Fall of Frenchy Steiner' (1964). Keith Roberts has also provided an alternative view of Nazi Britain in 'Weihnachtabend' (1972), which contains echoes of Sarban's novel.

'The Fall of Frenchy Steiner' by Hilary Bailey (New Worlds) 1964. Cover by Cawthorn.

The major outcome of other wars has also been a popular subject in the theme of alternative histories. The first leading novel in the field was Ward Moore's *Bring the Jubilee* (1952), which traced the outcome of life in America assuming the South won the Civil War. The novel involves time-meddling, since a time traveller returns to the battle of Gettysburg and accidentally manipulates events so that the North wins. Such deliberate or unintentional meddling with time to result in our present time-line instead of some variable often occurs in the genre, usually with the dénouement revealing that the story has been set in an alternative timetrack. Such tales are sometimes less than successful because the astute reader will already have guessed the outcome. Some writers have preferred, as in the case of *Bring the Jubilee*, to state the situation at the outset. John Brunner adopted a similar course in *Time without Number* (1962), set in a Spanish-dominated England following the success of the Armada.

Also set in a Britain under Spanish rule is Keith Roberts's novel *Pavane* (1966), in which the assassination of Queen Elizabeth I allowed Philip of Spain to claim the English throne. Roberts's depiction of a twentieth-century England where technological progress is banned, and the Inquisition still holds sway, is presented in convincing detail.

Over the last decade science fiction writers have generally chosen a wider variety of historical events on which to pivot destiny, rather than to continue to develop well-worn themes. Again this emphasises the difference between the sf world and historical writers. In the latter, such novelists as Oscar Lewis in *The Last Years* (1951) and John Hersey in *White Lotus* (1965) have portrayed societies where, respectively, Lincoln was not assassinated and atomic energy was not discovered. In the sf field, the following variety has appeared: a world where Europe failed to conquer the Americas (*The Gate of Worlds*, 1967, by Robert Silverberg); an Anglo-French Empire built on King Richard's return from the Crusades (Randall Garrett's 'Lord D'Arcy' series, which includes *Too Many Magicians*, 1966); an America where George Washington was shot and the Revolution never proclaimed (*A Transatlantic Tunnel, Hurrah!*, 1972, by Harry Harrison); and, most recently, a world in which every word written by Shakespeare was true, where Prince Rupert of the Rhine can fight for Charles I and escape on a locomotive (*A Midsummer Tempest*, 1974, by Poul Anderson)!

There are many more. But it seems pertinent to close on the work of Philip José Farmer. His novel *The Gate of Time* (1966) sets his pivotal point for the divergence of history in prehistory, and in this timetrack the continent of the Americas does not rise above the surface of the oceans. As a consequence, the Asian tribes that in our own world became the 'Red Indians' invade Europe. Years earlier, Farmer had written what many regard as the most amusing of alternative-timetrack short stories, and again he used the hypothesis that America did not exist. Only, in 'Sail On, Sail On' (1952) the alternate world is also flat, and Columbus literally sails straight over the edge. Not perhaps the most convincing of alternative timetracks, the story is nevertheless a good indication of the diversity and versatility to be found in this thematic area of science fiction.

ADDITIONAL INPUT

02.06.2 Alternative Histories

Amis, Kingsley. *The Alteration*, Cape (UK) 1976
Kurland, Michael. *The Whenabouts of Burr*, DAW (US) 1975
Meredith, Richard C. *At the Narrow Passage*, Berkley (US) 1975
Nolan, William F. 'The Worlds of Monty Willson', *Amazing* July 1971
Shaw, Bob. 'What Time Do You Call This?', *Amazing* September 1971
Sheckley, Robert. 'The Deaths of Ben Baxter', *Galaxy* June 1957
Simak, Clifford D. *Enchanted Pilgrimage*, Putnam (US) 1975
Spinrad, Norman. *The Iron Dream*, Avon (US) 1972
Stevens, Francis (Gertrude Bennett). *The Heads of Cerberus*, *The Thrill Book* August to October 1919; Polaris (US) 1952

02.07 UTOPIAS AND NIGHTMARES

When considering 'the future' as the setting for a story, one can proceed essentially in three ways:

One can unfold the plot against a background that is arbitrarily fantastic, colourful, spectacular and so forth, dismissing what led to it as irrelevant on the grounds – justifiable enough, let's face it – that things to come are inherently unknowable, and it's an ill-advised author who gets mixed up in the prediction business.

Or one may distort a contemporary phenomenon, by over-emphasising some factors at the expense of others, so as to furnish (and I mean that: equip with furniture) a projected world that will be adequately convincing until the reader has finished.

Or one may say, 'If we apply such-and-such knowledge, we may expect the world to change in such-and-such a fashion.'

From this third position, it is the shortest possible step to attempting to influence events – and that short step constitutes the writer's power-trip. (It is very much older than writing, of course; trying to influence another person to do something he or she had not thought of before, was probably the second use to which words were put.)

During periods of optimism and expansion, stories of the kind intended to influence popular thinking tend to be didactic and expository. The tone of Edward Bellamy's *Looking Backward* (1888), for example, makes me think of a lecturer at a Chautauqua, or a Mechanics' Institute. Even with the universe to play with, a writer cannot avoid taking colour from his environment. I steal the following from *New Scientist*: 'Descartes was impressed by the hydraulic figures in the royal gardens and developed a hydraulic theory of the action of the brain.' If it was good enough for Descartes . . .!

When the climate of opinion altered, the fiction altered correspondingly. For most of this century, 'awful warning' stories have vastly outnumbered idealistic or didactic utopias. Since 1960, however, with stories like *Walden Two* and *The Harrad Experiment*, the utopia seems to have enjoyed a minor revival.

Regardless of whether it is the positive or the negative variety that happens to be in style, such fictions – both because they are designed to modify people's real-world behaviour and because their authors are often professionally involved in research, planning, teaching or similar careers where they can affect others quite directly – occupy the area where science fiction most nearly connects with futurology, or (to adapt the French term which I regard as much superior) prognostics.

And here, incidentally, we have a type of story that is genuinely Western, in the current socio-political sense. There are fantasies aplenty, including some acknowledged precursors of science fiction, in traditions other than the Euro-American: *The Arabian Nights*, the *Ramayana* and so on.

But you might scour the planet in vain for dystopias and utopias to match them. This is because the presentation of a fictional world calculated not to entertain alone but to allure or alarm the public and alter the course of events did not become feasible until the notion had been generally accepted that tomorrow is bound to differ from today, like it or not, so we may as well take steps to ensure that we do like it. And there are many places where even now this idea has not sunk in.

John Brunner

John Brunner

02.07 Utopias and Nightmares

Among the many strange worlds depicted by science fiction, some of the least credible are those which have apparently attained a state of perfection, where the inhabitants live in blissful harmony with their families and neighbours, and lack nothing – unless it be the kind of release from utter boredom which may come with the arrival of less-contented visitors from outside. Since conflict is necessary to entertaining fiction, any story set in such an unlikely milieu soon loses interest, except when it relies for its appeal on a great deal of novel invention or skilful satire. Much more satisfying is the account of events in a world which is far less comfortable – where people are ripe for revolt against oppressive overseers, or threatened by impending catastrophe.

Utopian literature was recognised by literary scholars long before it became identified with the broad stream of science fiction. The same ancient philosopher, Plato, who first developed the lost-continent theme, is also credited with originating the utopian form with the *Republic*. But it was the *Utopia* of Sir Thomas More, conceived while he was on a diplomatic mission to Flanders in 1515, that set the style for a school of writers which included such far-ranging thinkers as Francis Bacon, Edward Bulwer Lytton, Samuel Butler, William Morris and H. G. Wells.

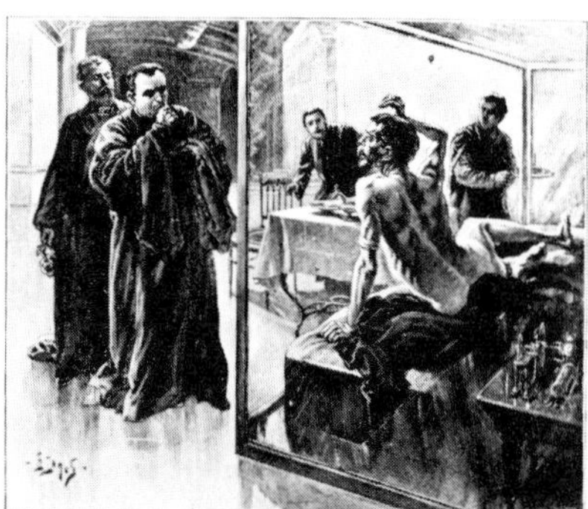

When the Sleeper Wakes *by H. G. Wells, 1899 (Harper and Bros).*

Though much of the work of the utopian writers makes far from ideal reading today, some of the finest science fiction may be placed in this category. Given that it may include any imaginative projection of a future state, whether idealistic or not, it presents an impressive array of writing – from such venerable works as H. G. Wells's *Men Like Gods* (1923), Aldous Huxley's *Brave New World* (1932) and George Orwell's *Nineteen Eighty-four* (1949), to the pulp magazine stories of Miles J. Breuer, Robert A. Heinlein and Frederik Pohl. To pacify the purists, however, another definition must be allowed – the 'dystopia' or 'cacotopia' – to distinguish between the genuine utopia, in which all's right with the world, and that in which existence may be fraught with oppression and terror, albeit a good deal more exciting to the reader.

'Hell on Earth' by Robert Bloch,
Weird Tales *March 1942.*
Illustration by Bok.

It must also be noted that certain critics, and not a few writers, have insisted that much of this kind of material, should properly be labelled *social* fiction rather than science fiction. Dr I. F. Clarke, in a useful sf checklist, *The Tale of the Future* (1961), ranging from 1644 to 1960, draws a distinct line between 'the simpler excitements of the scientific romance' as developed by Wells and 'the purposive satires and ideal states' of utopian fiction. And in his contribution to *Modern Science Fiction* (1953), Isaac Asimov refused to admit the social satires of Plato, More and Swift as free examples of the genre, on the grounds that they were reflections of the times in which their authors lived and lacked the quality of 'potential reality' inherent in genuine science fiction.

02.07.1 Early Utopias

One early utopia that must surely rank in the genre is *The New Atlantis* of the English statesman Francis Bacon. Though little more than a fragment, written in his old age and published only after his death in 1626, it argued a case for a college of science to be endowed by the state and was instrumental in the eventual founding of the Royal Society. The scientific gurus of his fictitious research foundation, the House of Salomon, knew how to prolong life and build flying machines and submarines. They experimented with sounds and odours, produced synthetic food and materials, and even created a lower form of life. While jealously guarding their own secrets – including perpetual motion – they sent out 'spies' to learn the results of other nations' researches, anticipating the shape of things to come. Bacon's vision excited interest at the time; it might have carried more weight had he not lost his post of Lord Chancellor for accepting bribes.

The pattern of many later utopias was laid down by the Frenchman Louis Sebastian Mercier, whose *L'An 2440* appeared in English in 1772 as *Memoirs of the Year 2500*. Going to sleep in old Paris, the narrator awakens in a future city transformed by street lighting, roof gardens and traffic police. He visits a museum where the exhibits show nature's efforts towards 'the formation of man' (an oblique preview of Darwin's theory of natural selection), and learns of inventions which include an 'optical cabinet' displaying shifting visional scenes and a machine imitating the human voice. Selective breeding has doubled the size of animals, and medical science found cures for gallstones and syphilis. If Wells read this book, which seems likely, he may well have found in it some germs of *The Food of the Gods* (1904) and of *When the Sleeper Wakes* (1899).

So long as large areas of the globe remained unexplored, the utopian writers

Illustration by Karel Thole.

were largely content to conceal their mythical states in undiscovered lands: More derived the word 'utopia' from two Greek words, *ou topos*, meaning 'no place'. As the world began to shrink under the advance of science, the more imaginative writers abandoned established conventions to venture into space and time, however awkwardly. Clarke has suggested that, in spite of some uncertainty before the 1870s, later authors showed 'no lack of confidence in describing the future of mankind. A dominant conviction running through all the new ideal states . . . is a belief in the imminent advance of mankind [and] the writers look forward to a future completely changed by the powers of applied science.'

Some of this feeling is evident in Mary Shelley's sombre tale *The Last Man* (1827), written not long after she had introduced *Frankenstein* to an unsuspecting world. It opens idyllically in the twenty-first century, when man has been liberated by machines, steamboats ply the canals, and dirigible balloons are steered through the air by feathered vanes. There follows world catastrophe, in the uncertain shape of a plague which sweeps from the East to decimate America and most of Europe. Mary Shelley's future ends, as was her wont, in gothic nightmare.

More optimistic, if less dramatic, is Mary Griffith's *Three Hundred Years Hence* (1836), an early American version of Mercier's 'sleeper' treatment, depicting the social changes brought about by machines, and including prohibition, the abolition of slavery and the emancipation of women. In addition to navigable balloons and vehicles driven by a new form of energy, further benefits of the future include nationalised railways, fireproof houses and powered lawnmowers.

Women and children play important roles in the underground utopia of the Vril-ya, the advanced humans of Edward Bulwer Lytton's *The Coming Race* (1871). Their highly scientific civilisation draws its power from a mysterious force, something between electricity and magnetism, which enables them to fly like birds and read each other's minds, to light their caverns, control their weather, cure diseases and keep potential enemies at bay. Though war has been outlawed, they appear to live for the day when they will return to the upper world from which their ancestors were driven. Meanwhile, life for the Vril-ya has become so tedious that the American narrator is glad to return to his own imperfect world.

By contrast, Samuel Butler's *Erewhon* (1872), published two years later, is a utopia from which machinery has been banned because of its threat to man's supremacy. The story reflects the revulsion felt by many serious writers at the effects of machine production and 'the advancement of the mechanical kingdom'. Yet Butler took some pains to present the other side of the picture, admitting that machines, even under capitalism, could also liberate men rather than enslave them. Part of his satire,

'The Planet of Youth' by Stanton A. Coblentz, Wonder Stories *October 1932. Illustration by Paul.*

entited 'The Book of the Machines', could almost be the preface to a collection of robot stories. For the rest, however, the work belongs with its sequel, *Erewhon Revisited* (1901), to that category of writing which Asimov suggests should be separated from science fiction.

Similarly, W. H. Hudson's 'romance of the future', *A Crystal Age* (1887), relates only peripherally to the genre, though it makes some play of eugenics. Hudson followed Butler in advocating a return to the simple life; and in *News from Nowhere* (1890) William Morris took up the same cry. More realistic in approach is Edward Bellamy's *Looking Backward* (1888), which saw the intelligent use of machines as pointing the way to a socialist state in which people had ample time for leisure and could retire at forty-five. Picturing the world of the year 2000 in the pattern of Mercier, it aroused much controversy and engendered a whole series of books opposing Bellamy's views, which were seen as an encroachment on individual liberty. Other writers rallied in Bellamy's defence, among them William Dean Howells, who, in *A Traveller from Altruria* (1894), attempted to make the best of both worlds. In his socialist utopia, electricity ran productive industry while the workers found pleasure in handicrafts.

Jules Verne, as was his habit, kept abreast of new ideas, and noted the conflicting attitudes of men confronted by the machine age and the notion of evolution. In his tale of two cities, *The Begum's Fortune* (1879), a benevolent dictator uses science to promote the welfare of the citizens of Frankville, established in the wilds of Oregon, while in Stahlstadt, thirty miles away, a disciplined German work force manufactures shells for a Hitler prototype hell-bent on destroying the French-inspired utopia as a first step to world domination. Again in his satirical story, *Propeller Island* (1895), which pictures a utopian floating city, Verne's passion for detail combined with his flair for imaginative urban planning. *The Mysterious Island* (1870), in which five escaped prisoners build their own mechanical paradise, must also rank as a parable demonstrating what men might do to improve their lot through the applications of science.

In a comparable vein, one of the most fascinating American novels of the 1890s was *Caesar's Column* by Ignatius Donnelly, a crusading Minnesota politician who firmly believed in Atlantis. He based his story on the premise that the misapplication of science would widen the gap between the classes, resulting in internecine strife and the end of civilisation. It is remarkable for its forecasts of the use of poison gas, workers' revolts and television newsreels.

Struggle against tyranny and war between nations armed with aircraft and submarines were also favourite themes of the English school of imaginative writers of the time, typified by George Griffith whose *The Angel of the Revolution* (1893) entertained readers of *Pearson's Weekly* before becoming a best-seller. It tells of a conflict which involves all Europe and most of Asia, in which America intervenes. In the course of the tale, an Anglo-Saxon Federation proclaims a socialist world state and exercises its power by the use of long-range aircraft operating from an African stronghold. In a sequel, *Olga Romanoff* (1894), a descendant of the last of the tsars – a genuine superwoman – disturbs the utopian peace after a century's progress; the subsequent struggle only ends when a comet threatens Earth.

The far-reaching significance of Darwin's evolutionary theories inspired such influential tales as Richard Jefferies' *After London* (1885), which portrayed a distant future in which civilisation had collapsed beneath the weight of social convulsions, leaving man to start a fresh ascent from barbarism. Equally notable is J. A. Mitchell's satire, *The Last American* (1889), which purports to be a fragment from the journal of one of a group of Persian explorers discovering the ruins of 'Nhu-Yok' in the year 2951. It is easy to recognise these stories as archetypes of the succession of post-catastrophe novels which, half a century later, sought to picture the aftermath of an atomic war – a possibility that occurred to Wells as early as 1914. In his *The World Set Free* (1914), whole cities are reduced to ruins before the nations realise the folly of such a war and found a world state in which science becomes an influence for good.

ADDITIONAL INPUT

02.07.1 Early Utopias

Campanella, Tommaso. *The City of the Sun*, 1623
Dioscorides, Dr (pseud). *Anno Domini 2071*, (Holland) 1871, W. Teck (UK) 1871
Hertzka, Theodor. *Freeland: a Social Anticipation*, Chatto & Windus (UK) 1891 (trans)
Thiusen, Ismar (J. MacNie). *Looking Forward: or the Diothas*, G.P. Putnam (UK) 1890

02.07.2 The Wellsian Dream . . . and After

With his first novel, *The Time Machine* (1895), Wells demonstrated the power of his imagination by projecting the concept of evolutionary change – for better or worse – to one of its possible limits, bringing a new perspective to the utopian story and, indeed, to the whole area of science fantasy. In spite of its gloomy view of a distant future in which the machine-minding Morlocks emerge from their underworld to prey upon the decadent Eloi, the story established Wells as a master of science fiction, the genre he helped so much to develop. None of his other work in the utopian tradition is so well remembered, perhaps because, paradoxically, he intended his later stories to be taken more seriously. Unfortunately, many of them were flawed by the kind of didactic sermonising characteristic of such of his non-fiction works as *Anticipations* (1901) and *New Worlds for Old* (1908).

The Time Traveller's story was followed in 1897 by 'A Story of the Days to Come', which depicted a future London as a city of machines in a world which had become 'too civilised' to entertain such concepts as initiative. The theme is continued in *When the Sleeper Wakes* (1899), in which discontent among the regimented labouring class flares into rebellion when a visitor from the nineteenth century, owner of half the world, is roused after a sleep of some two hundred years. The outcome is never resolved, but the author's message is clear enough. Whilst a firm believer in progress, Wells often doubted whether man would ever acquire enough good sense to maintain it, even with the help of such scientific aids as the growth-inducing drug in *The Food of the Gods* (1904).

As some of his critics have pointed out, Wells's utopias also reflect a lack of faith in the lower orders whose cause he appeared to have at heart; they fail singularly, and collectively, to rise above themselves, let alone their masters, without the help of such superior and enlightened classes as the dedicated Samurai of *A Modern Utopia* (1905) or the cowled airmen of *The Shape of Things to Come* (1933). In *Star Begotten* (1937) it is the Martians who seem to be bringing about the possible regeneration of mankind. In *The English Utopia* (1952) as A. L. Morton observes: 'There is, in fact, a different road to every Wellsian utopia, but all have this in common, that utopia is imposed on the brutal and reluctant masses by an enlightened minority.'

Through the whole of Wells's work, however, runs the message that man must help himself towards utopia by directing his own evolution; and some of his anticipations of the obstacles in his path are remarkably near the mark. In *Men Like Gods* (1922), an over-populated world in which science is misused teeters on the brink of a new dark age before it is saved by rigid birth control and the prophetically chilling elimination of

'The Lord of Tranerica' by Stanton A. Coblentz, Dynamic Science Stories *February 1939. Illustration by Paul.*

02.07 UTOPIAS AND NIGHTMARES

the unfit; the result is 'a nobler humanity'

When they were not forecasting the First World War or pointing to the supposed perils of socialism, Wells's British contemporaries of the early 1900s were picturing what they imagined would be the disastrous effects of a turning away from orthodox religion. R. H. Benson's *Lord of the World* (1907) depicts the struggles of the Roman Catholic Church to survive in an era of 2000 AD where an Esperanto-speaking socialist society largely worships at the shrine of a new Humanitarianism. (When its prophet becomes President of Europe, the Pope is obliged to pray for the end of the world!) Conversely, in Benson's sequel, *The Dawn of All* (1911), a Catholic utopia is realised, in which miracles are performed by a scientific priesthood, using forces that transcend ordinary laws.

Thirty years were to pass before magazine science fiction toyed with such ideas, a noted example being Robert A. Heinlein's *Astounding Stories* serial, *Sixth Column* (1941), where religion becomes a powerful factor in overthrowing America'a Asiatic conquerors. Alternatively, in Fritz Leiber's *Gather, Darkness!* (1943), an underground movement brings witchcraft to its aid in opposing a despotic, pseudo-scientific religion.

Variations on the utopian theme, founded – consciously or otherwise – on the work of many earlier writers, soon became a feature of the early sf publications. Hugo Gernsback himself had produced a super-scientific utopia in his early story *Ralph 124C41 +* (1911), which he had serialised in his technical magazine, *Modern Electrics*, fifteen years before he launched *Amazing Stories*. Among those few writers who concerned themselves with the more undesirable effects of science and invention was the psychiatrist David H. Keller, author of such original tales as 'The Revolt of the Pedestrians' (1928) and 'The Threat of the Robot' (1929), depicting the results of over-mechanisation.

The Californian poet, Stanton A Coblentz, became noted for his satires of imaginary worlds remote in both space and time, among them *After 12,000 Years* (1929). In this *Amazing Quarterly* novel, the narrator recovers from suspended animation in a world divided into four human species, each with its own individual function in the community. Here again, warfare leads to the collapse of civilisation.

More in the tradition of Verne than Wells is Otfrid von Hanstein's *Utopia Island* (1931), which featured among the examples of German science fiction which publisher Hugo Gernsback presented to the readers of *Wonder Stories* in the 1930s. It tells of the discovery of an Incan treasure trove which enables a German scientist to establish an experimental university on a Pacific island to pursue the quest for utopia.

A year later there arrived a dystopian novel which rivalled any of Wells's stories in its influence: Huxley's *Brave New World* (1932). This depicts a society where, to ensure social stability, all births are consigned to state hatcheries where human ova, fertilised in test-tubes, are genetically engineered to produce five different grades of 'humans' designed to function according to their predetermined levels of intelligence. Every scientific device is used to make life undemandingly pleasant; sex is freely available, and if the approved drug does fail to provide sufficient release from boredom, the jaded bon-viveur can always resort to legal euthanasia. Those few who rebel are banished to a distant island.

Thirty years later Aldous Huxley wrote another utopia, *Island* (1962), in which he modified his ideas on sex and ectogenesis while still relying on mind-expanding drugs as the way to human happiness. But in an essay written in 1956, *Brave New World Revisited*, he contended that the society of the more distant future would be closer to his original conception than the 'Big Brother' dictatorship of Orwell's *Nineteen Eighty-four* which caused a literary sensation on its publication in 1949, and shocked British viewers when it was televised shortly before the movie version in 1955.

The success of Orwell's novel drew attention back to an earlier dystopia, *We*, by the Russian Yevgeny Zamyatin, who went into exile after a Russian language edition had appeared in Prague (the first English version was published in the USA in 1924); it appeared later in other countries outside the USSR. Painting a grim picture of the world of centuries hence, where men and women are imprisoned in glass-walled cities and controlled as rigorously as the weather, it bears striking similarities to Orwell's work and to Wells's even earlier dystopias.

The rapid growth of automation, accelerated by two world wars, provided writers with further reasons for cautionary tales visualising a future society dominated by super-intelligent machines. Kurt Vonnegut's *Player Piano* (1952) depicts a post-war America as a fully automated, materially prosperous community supervised by technologists. The spiritual poverty of such a society leads to the inevitable revolt; but almost before the orgy of wrecking is over, the rebels have begun to rebuild the machines which enslaved them. Man's fate, it would seem, is irretrievably connected with the products of his own ingenuity.

The theme has been repeated, sometimes with ingenious variations, in many more recent novels. In *The Joy Makers* (1963) by James E. Gunn, a central computer has created millions of dwelling cells in which its human dependants exist in a foetal state of perpetual bliss; those who prefer a more vigorous life take themselves off to Venus. Such an escape route for the dissenter is found again in *Carder's Paradise* (1968), a first novel by Malcolm Levene, whose Grand Omnipotent Digitalulator expects not only total obedience, but also worship. A less happy outcome for the self-willed outcast occurs in Frederik Pohl's *The Age of the Pussyfoot* (1970), in which the leading character emerges from suspended animation to face a computer-ridden world in which 'forgotten men' are fair game for any hunter.

The great majority of these later oppressive visions, however original in the telling, have their roots in the works of Wells and those of his contemporaries, such as E. M. Forster's 'The Machine Stops' (1909). In Forster's subterranean world of the future, each inhabitant lives in a separate cell, his every need supplied by the Machine at the touch of a button. Television is the only form of personal communication. Moving platforms and airships are available for travel but rarely used; the surface world is empty and terrifying, but not entirely deserted. The outcasts who wander it are all that remains of humanity when the Machine breaks down. It was hardly a coincidence that Forster openly announced that he had written his story as a rebuff to 'one of the heavens of Mr H. G. Wells'. The whole interplay of the pro and anti-Wellsian influence in this area has been accurately recorded in Mark Hillegas's study, *The Future as Nightmare* (1967).

Another lesson that emerges from the utopian dream is that man needs congenial work rather than idle pleasure. This is underlined, as might be expected, in the Russian Ivan Yefremov's positive utopian novel, *The Andromeda Nebula* (1957), which tells of a period of cosmic exploration in an Era of Common Labour, thousands of years hence. True to their ancient traditions, young people, who have been properly trained and disciplined, perform 'herculean tasks' designed to extend man's dominions on Earth and in space. A similar paradise of conditioning can be found in B. F. Skinner's Behaviourist-inspired *Walden Two* (1948).

Some sf writers have seen the advent of utopia as an imposition on man by external forces. In Keith Laumer's *The Monitors* (1966), the well-intentioned efforts of extraterrestrial beings to run Earth along such lines is resisted. On the other hand, in Arthur C. Clarke's *Childhood's End* (1953), which Donald A. Wollheim has described as 'a novel of despair', the transformation wrought by the alien Overlords is the prelude to man's evolution into a finer type of being. Wollheim's comment refers to Clarke's apparent conclusion that man could not effect such a self-transformation if left to his own devices.

The colonisation of Venus again offers a way of escape from the frenetic world of *The Space Merchants*, the popular novel by Frederik Pohl and C. M. Kornbluth which originated as a *Galaxy* serial (*Gravy Planet*) in 1953. At first, Venus seems to offer a new field of operations for the giant commercial undertakings which manipulate the needs of an over-populated Earth in collusion with Madison Avenue's ruthless advertising agencies. But an underground movement of conservationists contrives to ensure that the pioneers for the Venus project are subtly recruited from its own ranks.

Many more recent stories, such as John Brunner's *The Sheep Look Up* (1972), have tried to envisage the nightmarish disasters

A nineteenth-century view of Utopia.

that may overtake man in the not too distant future if he continues to pollute and overcrowd his planet. In the world of *The Space Merchants*, where the population lives on soyaburgers and transports itself in pedal-cars, fresh water is severely rationed and wood is more precious than gold. Each of the 35 million inhabitants of New York in 1999 has four square yards of living space in Harry Harrison's *Make Room! Make Room!* (1966), which reached the screen, much altered, as *Soylent Green* in 1973. Procreation has become the vilest of sins in Vonnegut's 'Welcome to the Monkey House' (1968), where a pill that acts as an anaesthetic from the waist down takes the place of genuine contraceptives. *Logan's Run* (1967), the provocative novel by William F. Nolan and George Clayton Johnson, filmed in 1976, presents a population problem so critical that death is decreed for all citizens on reaching age twenty-one.

By contrast, permissive sex and 'the pill' have caused a slump in births among *The City Dwellers* (1970), Charles Platt's sombre tale of the highly urbanised, steel and concrete world of the twenty-first century, where the 'civics' rarely venture beyond the city limits (a reversal of Asimov's overpopulated enclosed cities in *The Caves of Steel*, 1954). Falling population is a problem, too, in *Do Androids Dream of Electric Sheep?* (1969), a post-catastrophe story in very different vein by Philip K. Dick.

The prospect of living longer, if not for ever, has found a place among the attractions of utopia since the days of the very earliest writers; and it has become a recurring theme in the modern genre. One means of achieving immortality, as conceived by Michael Coney in *Friends Come in Boxes* (1974), is to transfer the brain, when its owner reaches the age of forty, to the head of a six-month-old child and to repeat the operation every four decades. The reckoning comes when, again, the birth rate slumps. A further variation is depicted in Clifford D. Simak's *Why Call Them Back from Heaven?* (1967), based on the premise that people will make financial sacrifices in this world to invest their savings in a deep-freeze transfer to a future utopia where they might become immortal.

Whether a world where women have the upper hand and men are pampered nonentities could be classified as utopian or dystopian must depend on the individual reader's point of view. Many writers have developed the idea, among them Edmund Cooper, Pohl and Kornbluth, and John Wyndham. A noted novel in this category is Curme Gray's *Murder in Millennium VI* (1951), which is unusual for being both utopian and a mystery story. None of such tales paints a particularly comforting picture.

However, man's age-old dream of perfecting himself, and his societies, may eventually be resolved; the wavering balance between war and peace, between oppression and freedom, between the dominance of one or other of the sexes, will surely occupy the imaginations of writers in the future just as much as in the genre to date. Whatever the nature of the societies presented, science fiction's continuing pre-occupation with utopias and anti-utopias can be seen as one of its most important contributions to the whole modern field of literature.

ADDITIONAL INPUT

02.07.2 The Wellsian Dream and After

Bailey, J.O. *Pilgrims through Space and Time*, Argus (US) 1947

Boucher, Anthony (W.A.P. White). 'The Barrier', *Astounding* September 1942

Bradbury, Ray. 'The Fireman', *Galaxy* February 1951; as *Fahrenheit 451*, Ballantine (US) 1953

Derlerth, August (ed). *Beyond Time and Space*, Pellegrini (US) 1950

Evans, I.O. (ed). *Science Fiction through the Ages*, Vol 1, Panther (UK) 1966

Fearn, John Russell. *The Intelligence Gigantic*, *Amazing* June to July 1933; World's Work (UK) 1943

Fearn, John Russell. *Slaves of Ijax*, Kaner (UK) 1948

Gerald, Gregory Fits and Jack C. Wolf (ed). *Past, Present and Future Perfect*, Fawcett (US) 1973

Gordon, Rex (S.B. Hough). *Utopia 239*, Heinemann (UK) 1954

Grey, Charles (E.C. Tubb). *Enterprise 2115 (The Extra Man)*, Merit (UK) 1954

Hamilton, Edmond. 'The Island of Unreason', *Wonder Stories* May 1933

Knight, Damon. 'The Country of the Kind', *F&SF* February 1956

Nolan, William F. (with George Clayton Johnson). *Logan's Run*, Dial (US) 1967

Philmus, Robert M. *Into the Unknown*, University of California (US) 1970

Pohl, Frederik (with C.M. Kornbluth). 'Rafferty's Reasons', *Fantastic Universe* October 1955

Ross, Harry. *Utopias Old and New*, Nicholson (UK) 1938

Sheckley, Robert. 'The Academy', *Worlds of If* August 1954

Walsh, Chad. *From Utopia to Nightmare*, Bles (UK) 1962

Wyndham, John (J.B. Harris). 'Consider Her Ways', in *Sometime, Never*, Ballantine (US) 1956

02.08 CATACLYSMS AND DOOMS

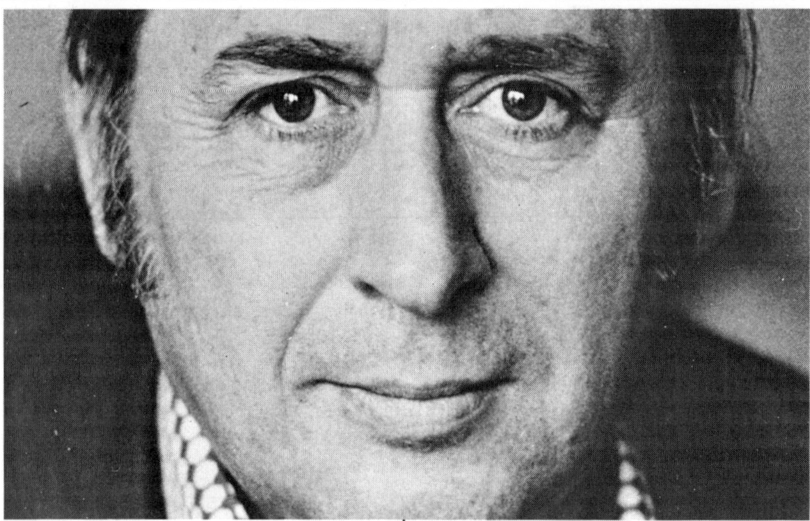

Visions of world cataclysm constitute one of the most powerful and most mysterious of all the categories of science fiction, and in their classic form predate modern science fiction by thousands of years. In many ways, I believe that science fiction is itself no more than a minor offshoot of the cataclysmic tale. From the deluge in the Babylonian zodiac myth of Gilgamesh to contemporary fantasies of twentieth-century super-science, there has clearly been no limit to man's need to devise new means of destroying the world he inhabits. I would guess that from man's first inkling of this planet as a single entity existing independently of himself came the determination to bring about its destruction, part of the same impulse we see in a placid infant who wakes alone in his cot and suddenly sets about wrecking his entire nursery.

Psychiatric studies of the fantasies and dream life of the insane show that ideas of world destruction are latent in the unconscious mind. The marvels of twentieth-century science and technology provide an anthology of destructive techniques unrivalled by even the most bizarre religions. As Edward Glover comments in *War, Sadism and Pacifism* (1947), 'Nagasaki destroyed by the magic of science is the nearest man has yet approached to the realisation of dreams that even during the safe immobility of sleep are accustomed to develop into nightmares of anxiety.'

As an author who has produced a substantial number of cataclysmic stories, I take for granted that the planet the writer destroys with such tireless ingenuity is in fact an image of the writer himself. But are these deluges and droughts, whirlwinds and glaciations no more than over-extended metaphors of some kind of suicidal self-hate, the expressions of deep internal conflicts resolvable only in a series of *spasmic* collisions with an ever-yielding external reality? Though I am even more suspicious of my own motives than of other people's, I nevertheless think not. On the contrary, I believe that the catastrophe story, whoever may tell it, represents a constructive and positive act by the imagination rather than a negative one, an attempt to confront the terrifying void of a patently meaningless universe by challenging it at its own game, to remake zero by provoking it in every conceivable way.

Within the realm of fiction, the writer of the catastrophe story illustrates, in the most extreme and literal way, Conrad's challenge – 'Immerse yourself in the most destructive element – and swim!' Each one of these fantasies represents an arraignment of the finite, an attempt to dismantle the formal structure of time and space which the universe wraps around us at the moment we first achieve consciousness. It is the inflexibility of this huge reductive machine we call reality that provokes infant and madman alike, and in the cataclysm story the science fiction writer joins company with them, using his imagination to describe the infinite alternatives to reality which nature itself has proved incapable of inventing. This celebration of the possibilities of life is at the heart of science fiction.

J. G. Ballard

J. G. Ballard

02.08 CATACLYSMS AND DOOMS

Cataclysm and catastrophe, either cosmic or precipitated by intelligent life-forms, have preoccupied writers of science fiction since its very beginning. Mary Shelley, Edgar Allan Poe, Jules Verne and H. G. Wells all described the complete or near extinction of man as a result of plagues, passing comets and other cosmic or earthly disasters. Later genocide by aliens, and terrors unleashed by careless human scientific experiments, proved popular themes in the pulp magazines. But with the advent of nuclear weapons and biological warfare, the danger of the human species annihilating itself has become even more pronounced, and has resulted in yet another kind of doom-laden story.

02.08.1 Cosmic Causes

It was Poe who laid the cornerstone for stories of earthly life being wiped out by cosmic forces. 'The Conversation of Eiros and Charmion' (1839) tells of a comet passing through Earth's atmosphere, altering its composition and destroying all life. A similar idea was developed in Conan Doyle's *The Poison Belt* (1913), depicting a strange area in outer space which interacts fatally with Earth's atmosphere. The author's striking analogy of a cosmic gardener cleansing the Earth's surface of a noxious bacillus – life – by dipping the planet into poison, created a powerful image echoed in many stories by later writers.

In the magazine era, popular contributors vied with each other to produce ever more original variations on the theme of cosmic doom. Accounts of the Sun unexpectedly going nova abounded, with man meeting his end in either dignity or savagery, or fleeing to other worlds to escape the flames. Two of the most effective such tales appearing in the early fifties were 'The Last Day' (1953) by Richard Matheson and Alfred Coppel's 'Last Night of Summer' (1954). Matheson suggested that the majority of humanity, faced with such a situation, will spend its last hours in an orgy of insane destruction and carnal indulgence. Coppel foresaw a similar reaction, including savage battles for access to the limited underground shelters.

Perhaps more ingenious than accounts of threats from the Sun were stories along the lines of Eando Binder's 'Life Disinherited' (1937). It describes how the great red spot of Jupiter, rotating at a different rate from the rest of its planet's atmosphere, becomes so highly charged electrically that it is flung into space where it collides with Earth. Donald Wandrei's 'Black Fog' (1937) is a similar example.

Stories of collisions or near-collisions with other planetary bodies are common in science fiction. Seminal in this respect were Verne's *Hector Servadac* (1877) and Wells's 'The Star' (1897), in which the respective passings of a comet and a wandering star close by the Earth produce differing results. In Verne's tale the disaster occurs near the outset, and the comet carries off the central character with it. Wells's story avoids characterisation and simply relies on a spell-binding description of the star's approach, of rising seas, intense heat and the final saving of Earth by the timely intervention of its Moon.

The Moon, in fact, has played a significant part in tales of cosmic catastrophe. More often than not these have depicted its falling from its orbit and breaking up. An early example is Alexander M. Phillips' 'The Death of the Moon' (1929), followed in a year by Olaf Stapledon's *Last and First Men* (1930), in which the fall of the Moon is one feature in man's long history. Another noted example of cosmic collision appeared almost immediately afterwards: Philip Wylie and Edwin Balmer's *When Worlds Collide* (1932).

Stories of cosmic doom are not necessarily limited to Earth or the solar system. In Nat Schachner's 'Beyond Infinity' (1937), the whole universe is destroyed, being overtaken by an inner core of nothing which grows as the physical universe expands. A modern variant is Michael Moorcock's 'Last Vigil' (1970), in which the galaxies are seen as contracting under the gravitational force of megaquasars lying at the centre. The condensed mass finally implodes under its own weight and a new universe is born.

In general, stories of cosmic catastrophe belong to the magazine years. They are less common among later writers, but not unknown. Larry Niven's 'At the Core' (1966) depicts a journey to the centre of the Milky Way, where an explosion has occurred that will flood the inhabited part of the galaxy with lethal radiation a mere 20,000 years on. Edmund Cooper's *All Fool's Day* (1966) shows increased solar activity driving 'normal' beings to 'radiant suicide', while only psychopaths survive. And among his many novels of personal and universal disaster, J. G. Ballard offers in *The Crystal World* (1966) a unique interpretation of the physical theory of anti-matter. The collision of positively and negatively charged galaxies in space leads to their mutual annihilation, depleting the time-store of the universe and resulting in the slow metamorphosis of all organic material on Earth into a static dream-scope of crystalline beauty.

Such are some of the ingenious variations which sf writers have developed on the theme of cosmic doom, though few have perhaps matched the ingenuity of Immanuel Velikovsky's theories in *Worlds in Collision* (1950) and its sequels. The author's unusual notions are depicted in his attempt to explain not only the formation of Earth's mountains and continents through cataclysm, but also what caused the Ice Ages and such extra-terrestrial features as the craters of the Moon. Velikovsky developed his ideas from a mass of information he had culled from ancient records, including the Old Testament. His work, as well as his source material, has exerted an influence on several sf writers.

Cover illustration by Hay for The Lathe of Heaven *by Ursula Le Guin (Granada).*

ADDITIONAL INPUT

02.08.1 Cosmic Causes

Albrecht, Gustav (with Frank R. Paul). 'The End of the Moon', *Science-Fiction Plus* August 1953

Anvil, Christopher. 'Speed Up', *Amazing* January 1964

Clarke, Arthur C. 'Rescue Party', *Astounding* May 1946

Leiber, Fritz. 'A Pail of Air', *Galaxy* December 1951

Pendleton, Don. *The Day the World Died*, Pinnacle (US) 1970

Rud, Anthony. 'The Molten Bullet', *Thrilling Wonder* February 1937

Sherriff, R.C. *The Hopkins Manuscript*, Gollancz (UK) 1939

Velikovsky, Immanuel. *Ages in Chaos*, Doubleday (US) 1952

Velikovsky, Immanuel. *Earth in Upheaval*, Doubleday (US) 1955

02.08 CATACLYSMS AND DOOMS

02.08.2 Natural Earth Causes

Almost everything which, through natural forces, could conceivably go wrong with Earth's biosphere, and other more far-fetched possibilities, can be found in the pages of science fiction.

At the start of the nineteenth century a number of novels appeared, bearing the common title *The Last Man*, which can be regarded as the forerunners of the type of science fiction story featuring plagues and other natural cataclysms. They included *Le Dernier Homme* (1805) by the French renegade priest Cousin de Grainville, who wrote the book out of desperation through his fears for the future and then committed suicide, and *The Last Man* (1826) by Mary Shelley, in which a plague sweeps the Earth in the year 2092.

In biblical terms, there was more to plagues than the mere transmission of a malignant virus. Locusts were conspicuous among the various fates visited upon Egypt. One of the first of such threats in a science fiction story occurs in Wells's 'The Empire of the Ants' (1905), where the narrator predicts the eventual invasion of Europe by a new strain of militant formicaries that had already devastated parts of South-East Asia. 'The Valley of the Spiders' (1903) was a comparable Wellsian offering.

Following the lead of Wells, many other writers saw a threat to man's dominion of the Earth coming from insects. Usually the insects had somehow managed to attain giant proportions, as in Richard Tooker's 'The Return of the Swarm' (1933), where a cloud of giant mosquitoes descends on Chicago. Normally such stories have assumed, rather than explained, how insects could overcome the limitations of their breathing systems and thus increase their size. One possible explanation was, however, given in Murray Leinster's novelette 'The Mad Planet' (1920), describing a world 30,000 years hence when climatic changes have paved the way for insect growth. Fissures have opened in the Earth's crust, releasing huge quantities of carbon dioxide into the atmosphere. In the changed climatic conditions, man reverts to savagery, and only survives by adapting himself, through evolution, to breathing the oxygen-poor atmosphere with enlarged lungs. But the insects thrive on the changing conditions. They multiply enormously, enlarging themselves in the thickened air. Leinster's depiction of a world transformed by a freak of nature, where man struggles to survive against insects many times his own size, has been much imitated.

Among such successors are a group of three connected stories by Frank Belknap Long, published in *Astounding Stories* and beginning with 'The Last Man' (1934). Also set in the far future when insects are dominant, they differ from Leinster's tale by showing how the insects have evolved intelligence and have replaced man on merit. (The initial premise of Leinster's story, that of gas pouring from the ground, may well have been inspired by M. P. Shiel's *The Purple Cloud* (1901), in which explorers returning from the North Pole discover humanity extinguished by such a gas.)

In the pulp magazines and later stories, the idea of animal and vegetable menaces, in addition to those of the insect kingdom, was explored exhaustively. In John Wyndham's *The Day of the Triffids* (1950) – which in fact first appeared in *Collier's* magazine and not in a pulp – man is threatened by both cosmic and botanical phenomena. Unusual radiations have blinded the great majority of humanity, reducing it to the easy prey of poisonous mobile plants which, paradoxically, had originally been farmed for human benefit. An earlier graphic treatment of a plant menace was given in David H. Keller's *The Ivy War* (1930), in which sentient ivy seeks literally to effect a stranglehold over civilisation.

Grasses, also, have played their part in man's downfall, in two notable stories. John Christopher's *Death of Grass* (1956) tells of highly resistant bacteria, deadly to grass and grain crops, which spread from China to the rest of the world, bringing famine and the collapse of society in their wake. In Ward Moore's earlier *Greener Than You Think* (1946) the reverse effect was envisaged: the gradual throttling of the globe's landmasses by a mutated species of devil grass. The story is told with a satirical lilt which brightens what would otherwise be a harrowing tale.

Other stories of natural disaster take as their premise the removal of one vital element in Earth's ecology, or a change in that element. Several writers have played on the supreme importance to man of water. Charles Eric Maine's *When the Tides Went Out* (1958) explored the consequences of the catastrophe implied in the story's title. J. G. Ballard described the results of chronic rain failure in *The Burning World* (1964).

'The Day of the Triffids' adapted from the novel by John Wyndham, script by Gerry Conway, Unknown Worlds of Science Fiction *March 1974. Illustration by Rival.*

At the other end of the scale, following biblical precedents, the coming of universal floods has proved a popular theme. A noted early story in this category, *The Second Deluge* (1911) by Garrett P. Serviss, is actually a tale of cosmic catastrophe, insofar as the floods are caused by Earth passing through a cloud of water in space. Later magazine treatments include Henry Kuttner's 'Lord of the Storm' (1947) and Lester del Rey's 'The Last Earthman' (1965). In the realm of books, S. Fowler Wright achieved success with *Deluge* (1928), a novel of planet-wide flooding and disaster, while J. G. Ballard's individualistic contribution to the theme came with *The Drowned World* (1962).

As a last example of natural doom, the onset of a new ice age is one science fiction nightmare that may one day become a reality, unless the ingenuity of future man can prevent it. The slow but inexorable onslaught of walls of ice against man's proudest cities is vividly portrayed in Steve Benedict's 'The Sixth Glacier' (1929), while Arthur C. Clarke describes in 'History Lesson' (1949) the future discovery by Venusian explorers of Earth in the throes of its most encompassing ice age, to which man has long since succumbed.

ADDITIONAL INPUT

02.08.2 Natural Earth Causes

Leinster, Murray (Will F. Jenkins). 'The Red Dust', *Argosy* April 1921
Moxley, F. Wright. *Red Snow*, Simon & Schuster (US) 1930
Silverberg, Robert. 'When We Went to See the End of the World', in *Universe 2*, Ace (US) 1972
Slesar, Henry. 'Beside the Golden Door', *Amazing* February 1964

'Lord of the Storm' by Keith Hammond. Startling Stories September 1947. Illustration by Finlay.

02.08.3 Alien Causes

Stories of Earth being invaded by creatures from another world have formed one of the most recurrent themes in science fiction. In the most primitive type of tale, the aliens were usually portrayed as monsters, intent on destroying mankind.

Ironically, the archetype of such stories is generally acknowledged as the masterpiece on the theme – H. G. Wells's novel *The War of the Worlds* (1897). The Wellsian description of a Martian set the pattern for alien life being portrayed in a grotesque and repellent form. Equally influential was the implied motivation behind the alien invasion: Mars is a dying world; Earth is coveted for its abundant supply of air and water. Wells's Martians arrive in cylinders fired across space. They are not long in revealing hostile intent: man's attempts at communication are answered by blasts of a heat-ray. Striding across the countryside on huge tripod-like machines, the invaders stampede the populace, destroying towns and causing further death with a poisonous smoke. (Such items as the Martian heat-ray fall more properly into the section on 'Warfare and Weaponry'. The main purpose of this present section is to review alien attempts to destroy mankind, although some description of the weapons with which they sought to do it is inevitable.)

The endless procession of stories dealing with alien invasion since Wells has seen a debasement of the theme. Frequently, aliens are depicted as hostile and coveting the Earth, with little significant variation between one such tale and the next. It must be said that by far the greatest debasement of the genre has taken place outside novels and stories, and has occurred in films, television and comic strips. Certainly, in the better sf novels and magazine stories many ingenious and imaginative variations can be found. Aliens are not always shown as menacing mankind in a direct cataclysmic conflict, but in a number of other insidious and subtle ways.

In the pulp years, however, alien invasions generally followed the standard pattern. Spaceships appear in the skies without warning, and proceed to devastate the cities below with a barrage of coloured rays and super-scientific weapons. Usually the menace is vanquished by the last-minute efforts of an unlikely hero. But even in these early magazine stories, there is often some degree of ingenuity and imagination.

Such an example is Eando Binder's 'Eye of the Past' (1938), in which time-viewing of the past enables man to rediscover the previously banned secret of atomic warfare and so defeat a devastating invader. Another tale of note is Edmond Hamilton's 'The Moon Menace' (1927), telling of an Earth plunged suddenly into utter darkness. In due course it is discovered that the cataclysm is the result of an invasion by a lunar civilisation only capable of seeing in the dark.

Hamilton's story was original on several

counts, not least in its suggestion that Earth was not necessarily safe from invasion by beings to whom the terrestrial environment was unsuitable. While in E. E. Smith's *First Lensman* (1950) an alien race ignores Earth and colonises Pluto, since that planet's climate is akin to their own world's. Other stories of the period tell of invaders who seek to change the terrestrial environment to suit their requirements.

Clark Ashton Smith's 'The Metamorphosis of Earth' (1949) depicts such an invasion from Venus, beginning with reports of a massive sandstorm in the Sahara, and continuing with the transformation of that area into a lethal jungle. The outcome is a long war with the invaders, which remains unresolved at the story's end. Similar themes have persisted in such later stories as Thomas M. Disch's *The Genocides* (1965), where aliens turn the Earth into a gigantic farm. Billions of spores are released, and within days giant green plants smother the entire planet, stifling all rival forms of life.

Cataclysmic interplanetary invasions are now somewhat rare in modern science fiction, with the exception of such tales as *The Genocides*, and such late examples of the earlier writers as John W. Campbell's *The Black Star Passes* (1965), the third novel in his 'Arcot, Morey and Wade' series. Many of the clichés still appear, however, in the contemporary thriller. Their authors are usually skilful, and the books popular. Possibly, because they work outside the sf field, many of the writers are unaware that their plots *are* clichés in sf terms. Such stories as *The Night Callers* (1959), an interplanetary invasion tale by N. J. Crisp, and John Lymington's *Night of the Big Heat* (1959) fall into this category.

A popular variation on the alien invasion tale is the assumption that the invaders are already in control of Earth. Beginning with Edmond Hamilton's 'The Earth Owners' (1931), many stories have been written which pursue this 'we are property' theme, one of the most notable being Eric Frank Russell's *Sinister Barrier* (1939). However, they tend to be less likely to come to cataclysmic conclusions.

In one sense, neither can Arthur C. Clarke's *Childhood's End* (1953) be described as a cataclysmic tale, although it effectively describes the end of man as we know him. It tells of an Overlord race which has watched the Earth for thousands of years, as the emissaries of an overmind. They eventually invade to prevent man achieving space flight, and to prepare him for unity with the higher entity.

Another approach to alien invasion shows Earth as a pawn in a larger space war. Such is the case in Kris Neville's 'Special Delivery' (1952), where the flooding of every community on Earth with unlimited local currency causes economic disaster and chaos ensues. An alien invasion duly follows to establish a beach-head in an extra-terrestrial conflict. William Tenn's 'The Liberation of Earth' (1953) is based on the same idea of humanity becoming caught up in a war in which it has no real part – except that of an unfortunate bystander.

The Puppet Masters *by Robert Heinlein (Pan). Cover by d'Achille.*

Invasions by parasitic aliens have also been portrayed as approching cataclysmic proportions – notably in Harl Vincent's 'Parasite' (1935) and Robert A. Heinlein's *The Puppet Masters* (1953). (Such stories are dealt with in more detail in the section on 'Mutants and Symbiotes'.) In a similar vein, Jack Finney's *The Body Snatchers* (1954) presents an alien invasion in which the bodies of human hosts are taken over, duplicated, and then destroyed – leaving the replicas to assume control.

A final category remains to be considered on the theme of alien invasions. Cataclysms have been averted, in some stories, by an ignorance of human conventions, rather than by any concerted effort of man. In Fredric Brown's 'Knock' (1949), the last two humans to survive finally succeed in overcoming their alien conquerors with the aid of a rattlesnake. Since the extraterrestrials have had no experience of everyday death and disease, the reptile's lethal bite which kills one of their comrades, convinces them that Earth is uninhabitable. The tale bears all the hallmarks of the humorous approach for which its author was renowned. Eric Frank Russell, a writer also known for his sense of humour, told in 'Landing Party' (1952) how an alien advance troop, who have successfully assumed the outward appearance of human beings, are quickly arrested because they have landed in the vicinity of a nudist camp.

A comparable ignorance defeats the individual alien of Alfred Coppel's 'The Invader' (1953). Having taken over the brain and body of the first large biped it encounters, it is shot on sight as an escaped and dangerous gorilla!

ADDITIONAL INPUT

02.08.3 Alien Causes

Hamilton, Edmond. 'The Comet Doom', *Amazing* January 1928
Hamilton, Edmond. 'Invaders from the Monster World', *Amazing* June 1945
Heinlein, Robert A. *A Puppet Masters*, *Galaxy* September to November 1951; Doubleday (US) 1951
Le Guin, Ursula K. *The Dispossessed*, Harper and Row (US) 1974
Maine, Charles Eric (David McIlvain). 'Festival of Earth', *Spaceway* December 1954; as *Crisis 2000*, Hodder and Stoughton (UK) 1955
Pratt, Fletcher. *Invaders from Rigel*, Avalon (US) 1960

Nerves *by Lester del Rey (Ballantine). Cover by Brautigan.*

02.08.4 Human Causes

Before the Second World War, many pulp stories were written featuring the experiments of eccentric scientists which led to one kind of cataclysm or another. Some followed the Wellsian example of *The First Men in the Moon* (1901), where the invention of an anti-gravity shield comes in danger of funnelling the entire Earth's atmosphere out into space. Most were too ludicrous to merit serious consideration now. But they all enjoyed a common attitude. The critic Leland Sapiro has argued, in a series of articles entitled 'The Faustus Tradition in the Early Science Fiction Story' (1964–65), that the foolhardiness of science and scientists was the central notion behind Gernsback's *Amazing Stories*, in that man 'tampers in God's domain' to his cost. There are those who have argued just as effectively that many of the stories which ended in cataclysm demonstrated a facile writing technique for bringing a tale to a dramatic conclusion. Sapiro was perhaps on firmer ground with his follow-up articles under the heading 'The Mystic Renaissance' (1966) (a survey of F. Orlin Tremaine's *Astounding Stories* of the mid-1930s) where he suggested that by probing into the mysteries of natural phenomena, scientists might cause disaster. It is also arguable in retrospect whether many stories of that period of which Donald Wandrei's 'Earth Minus' (1935) and John Russell Fearn's 'Metamorphosis' (1937) are examples, held up in the light of the usual precautions taken during real scientific investigation.

With the harnessing of the power of the atom, some optimistic commentators suggested that the world would be freed of its energy problems. Most sf writers, however, have approached the prospect with ambivalence. Even the pulp adventure author, Charles Willard Diffin, in 'The Power and the Glory' (1930), told of a venerable scientist warning his protégé of the possible military consequences of introducing atomic power to an unprepared world.

Science fiction warnings of atomic catastrophe reach back much farther: from Robert Cromie's *The Crack of Doom* (1895) to H. G. Wells's *The World Set Free* (1914). In the latter, atomic power is initially channelled into transport and industry, but its use precipitates an international economic collapse when coal and oil become worthless. In the world war which follows, the dropping of atomic bombs eventually convinces the warring nations of the futility of such conflict. A world state, designed along Wellsian lines, is then established.

Wells's vision was matched by Karel Čapek's *The Absolute at Large* (1927), in which religious uprisings occur wherever atomic motors are in operation, as they are seen as challenging the law of God. War, death and the near extinction of the human race follows.

After 1938, the new editor of *Astounding*, John W. Campbell, often focused attention on the perils of atomic misuse, both in editorials and in his choice of stories for the magazine. In so doing, he demonstrated a feeling for science fiction which elevated him above the ranks of other editors at that particular time.

It follows that two stories of a major protégé of Campbell, Robert A. Heinlein, should be among the most remembered of the pre-Hiroshima era. The earlier, 'Blowups Happen' (1940), told of the dangers and tensions inherent in the use of an atomic-power plant. In 'Solution Unsatisfactory' (1941), Heinlein depicted the use of a radioactive dust as determining the end of the Second World War, but eventually leading to a global dictatorship. In the same class came Lester del Rey's 'Nerves' (1942, expanded as a novel in 1956), describing an atomic-power plant explosion.

When the atomic bomb was actually dropped, the warnings of sf writers assumed a greater significance. Introducing Rog Phillips's 'Atom War' (1946) which foresaw the effects of a retaliatory strike philosophy, editor Ray Palmer stated: 'The war of tomorrow is the kind of war that will be fought by sneaks and back-stabbers; no honour can accompany this horror' – a judgment which could equally well apply to any other war in history. Only the weaponry had grown more formidable. A year later came Theodore Sturgeon's 'Thunder and Roses' (1947), a noted account of the United States ravaged by a nuclear attack. Its plot is distinguished by the prevention of a retaliatory missile launch, so that civilisation may be rebuilt.

The sf magazines, adopting Campbell's lead, reworked the theme in endless variations. There were also some major contributions from outside the regular sf field, *World Aflame* (1947), by Leonard Engel and Emmanuel S. Piller, being one. As writers began to consider the actual logistics of atomic warfare, the strategic value of the underground command post (and shelter) became obvious. Stories were written within such settings, either using them as backdrops or as an integral part of the plot, one example being Wilson Tucker's *The Long Loud Silence* (1953). (Such stories had been foreshadowed by two of Arthur J. Burks's novels, *Survival*, 1938 and *Exodus*, 1938).

This theme also attracted the attention of mainstream writers, exemplified by such works as J. Jefferson Farjeon's *Death of a World* (1948), Nevil Shute's *On the Beach* (1957), Eugene Burdick's *Fail-Safe* (1962) and Graham Greene's *A Discovery in the Woods* (1963), and two noted stories by Mordecai Roshwald and Peter George.

Roshwald's *Level 7* (1960) narrates, through the diary of a 'push-button' officer, the kind of life experienced in a subterranean offensive command post. When the retaliatory system is taken to its full limit, and the radiation penetrates to the deepest levels of his shelter, he realises the enormity of his guilt.

George's *Red Alert* (1958) is better known

02.08 CATACLYSMS AND DOOMS

'*The Great Catastrophe of 2947*' *by Woods Peters,* Amazing *May 1931. Illustration by Morey.*

for its screen adaptation as *Dr Strangelove* (1963). In the course of his writing career, he worked on eight novels in an attempt to demonstrate the effects of atomic catastrophe, ending with *Commander-1* (1965).

Another skilful account of the consequences of atomic war, again written outside the mainstream of science fiction, was Aldous Huxley's *Ape and Essence* (1949). The book was among the first to emphasise the dangers to world ecology resulting from the uncontrolled use of technology. Huxley warned of the consequences of upsetting the equilibrium of nature and used the story to express his personal view of modern progress as an orgy of criminal imbecility.

It is to this last environmental area that modern writers have increasingly turned. Edmund Cooper's *Seed of Light* (1959) opens with the Earth rapidly being made uninhabitable by increasing levels of carbon monoxide that have irreparably permeated the atmosphere, forcing man to retreat into air-conditioned domed cities. Animals and plants have been destroyed by insecticide poisoning, and rivers and canals ruined by pollution. Similarly, in Don Pendleton's *1989: Population Doomsday* (1970), the author dramatises the end result of man's assault upon his natural biosphere, presenting a graphic picture of a world choking on its own effluent. John Brunner's *The Sheep Look Up* (1972) continues the theme.

Among recent books there have appeared a number of original anthologies devoted solely to the possible outcome of modern civilisation during the next few decades. *Three for Tomorrow* (1969) comprises original novellas by Robert Silverberg, Roger Zelazny and James Blish. All three stories were written in the light of Arthur C. Clarke's introductory essay, which drew attention to the vulnerability of a technological society. Their respective titles are: 'How It Was When the Past Went Away', 'The Eve of Rumoko' and 'We All Die Naked'.

The Year 2000 (1970), edited by Harry Harrison, is a comparable collection, devoted to human affairs in the last year of the twentieth century. Amongst its twelve stories are 'America the Beautiful' by Fritz Leiber, a warning on pollution; 'After the Accident' by Naomi Mitchison, in which man again plays God; 'Black Is Beautiful' by Robert Silverberg, depicting the influence of race hate on city life; 'Judas Fish' by Thomas N. Scortia, describing a food shortage due to natural causes; and a further comment on race relations in Harrison's own 'American Dead'. (Many such stories, particularly those concerning overpopulation, can best be described as anti-utopian. They are covered in the section 'Utopias and Nightmares'.)

To conclude, the evident shift from cosmic or alien-induced catastrophes to the more immediate effects of man-made disasters, reflects science fiction writers' growing concern for the real condition of man. Their investigations into the cataclysmic potential in human nature itself is proof, if any were needed, of their genuine concern for the future.

'*Survival*' *by Arthur J. Burks,* Marvel Science Stories *August 1938. Illustration by Paul.*

ADDITIONAL INPUT

02.08.4 Human Causes

Anvil, Christopher. 'Torch', *Astounding* April 1957
Boland, John. *White August*, Michael Joseph (UK) 1955
Cartmill, Cleve. 'Forever Tomorrow', *Astonishing Stories* April 1943
Coppel, Alfred. *Dark December*, Gold Medal (US) 1960
Norris, Frank. *Nutro 59*, Rinehart (US) 1952
Springer, Sherwood. 'No Land of Nod', *Thrilling Wonder* December 1952
Tenn, William (Philip Klass). 'Null-P', *Worlds Beyond* January 1951

Both lost worlds and parallel worlds can be considered variations on the theme of the unknown or alien world. One of the great themes of science fiction is involved here – the leaving of one's everyday reality and journeying to some place alien, exotic, exciting, where there is important work to be done and vital decisions to be made.

There are similarities and differences between lost and parallel worlds, but they are not easy to state. Here are a few rules c thumb:

Most parallel worlds are also lost worlds They are lost until somebody finds them, o until they find us.

Some lost worlds are also parallel worlds.

Lost worlds are usually one of a kind; parallel worlds offer you a choice among many.

Lost worlds are usually difficult to reach, and involve a spaceship journey or its equivalent. Whereas a parallel world tends to be a place you can get to by just stepping through a looking-glass or its equivalent.

Interesting psychological differences have been noted between lost world advocates and parallel world aficionados.

Your genuine lost worlder is someone trying to get home. Once he finds his lost world, he wants to live there without intrusion from the place he has left behind. He is not interested in developing galactic trade and cultural exchanges between his lost world and your lost world. It would tarnish his dream if he had to figure out trade tariffs and alien-entry quotas. The typical lost worlder is of an aristocratic, inward-turning nature. He values style above content. His lost world is a hole he can step into and close the door.

The parallel worlder exists at the opposite end of the personality pole. He tends to be outward-going, egalitarian, explosive, Dionysian. He seeks challenging opportunities under wider horizons rather than the womb-harmony of the lost worlder. He is Man the Manipulator rather than Man the Contemplator.

There are exceptions to all this, of course. Parallel and lost worlds are similar but subtly differing archetypes, and tend to generate different styles and operating premises.

For purposes of orientation, if you find yourself in a steamy Devonian landscape and notice that a dragon is about to devour a beautiful girl nearby, you have undoubtedly stumbled into a lost world. Your problem is to save the girl and then live happily ever after with her. But if, on the other hand, you find yourself in Piccadilly Circus, London, and notice that a beautiful girl is leading a dragon on a plastic lead down Regent Street, to no one's amazement but your own, then you are in a parallel world and your problems are entirely different.

Robert Sheckley

Robert Sheckley

02.09 LOST AND PARALLEL WORLDS

Much of the main body of science fiction is taken up with the exploration of other worlds situated either in our solar system or beyond it. But there is another area of action in the genre which involves worlds rarely reached by means of the ubiquitous spaceship. These are the lost worlds hidden in remote corners of our own planet, or existing beneath the surface of either land or ocean, and the parallel worlds found in a different space-time continuum from our own.

Descents into the underworld date back in world literature to the time of the ancient Greeks, and have been portrayed many times, from Dante's *Inferno*, through Ludwig Holberg's *The Subterranean Journey of Niels Klim* (1741) and Verne's *Journey to the Centre of the Earth* (1864), to the present day. The idea of parallel worlds also has an honourable tradition, and could be said to have inspired many early fantasies portraying worlds which may have been Earth-like but were certainly not Earth. It is a fertile area for the imagination and one which has produced some notable science fiction stories.

02.09.1 Lost Worlds

Science fiction has been so preoccupied with the exploration of other worlds and universes that it may seem at first glance to have neglected our planet; but the new reader who entertains this impression will soon find he has overlooked some rewarding material. The subject of *The Lost World* (1912) by Sir Arthur Conan Doyle is by no means the only remote tract where men have discovered isolated monsters and strange forms of life, though they seldom succeed (as in the film *King Kong* in 1933, in which Edgar Wallace had a hand) in bringing anything back alive.

The noted Californian mathematician Dr Eric Temple Bell, who wrote several sf novels under the name of John Taine, consistently confined his characters to the Earth's surface. Whether they are searching in the Antarctic for dinosaurs in *The Greatest Adventure* (1929) or in the Himalayas for a shovelful of priceless soil in the *The Forbidden Garden* (1947), their mysterious quests are always intriguing.

H. G. Wells, who frequently doubted the possibility of interplanetary travel, set his classic tale 'The Country of the Blind'(1904) in the wild mountain wastes of Ecuador. Many a utopian retreat as blissful as Shangri-La, the mountain monastery of James Hilton's *Lost Horizon* (1933), was purportedly found concealed in a secret valley or occupying a lofty plateau.

The strange alien beings of Abraham Merritt's noted fantasies, such as 'The People of the Pit' (1918), are found lurking in the depths of a volcanic crater in Alaska or, like the subject of *The Metal Monster* (1920), hiding in a remote Tibetan village. Macabre traces of H. P. Lovecraft's fabled

02.09 LOST AND PARALLEL WORLDS

The Forbidden Garden *by John Taine (Fantasy Press). Illustration by Donnell.*

'Great Race', which he portrayed as possessing the Earth long before man evolved, are uncovered in the Australian desert in his 'The Shadow Out of Time' (1936). The Antarctic was shown to hold the secrets of the Elder Gods enshrined in Lovecraft's extraordinary Cthulhu Mythos, when their remains were unearthed by a university expedition in *At the Mountains of Madness* (1936).

The South American explorer A. Hyatt Verrill, a popular writer in the formative years of *Amazing Stories*, set many of his tales in the jungle territory he knew, and used it as a background for 'The Voice from the Inner World' (1927), which also included an underground setting, and 'The World of the Giant Ants' (1928).

Writing as John Beynon, in *The Secret People* (1935), long before he became better known as John Wyndham, the British author described the survivors of an ancient race of pygmies who lived in caverns beneath the Sahara until the New Sea engulfed them. Similarly, the remnants of a sub-human tribe are discovered in Louis Herrman's *The Sealed Cave* (1935) on a tiny Aegean island. They had been decimated by the common cold, an infection bequeathed them by no less a man than Captain Lemuel Gulliver!

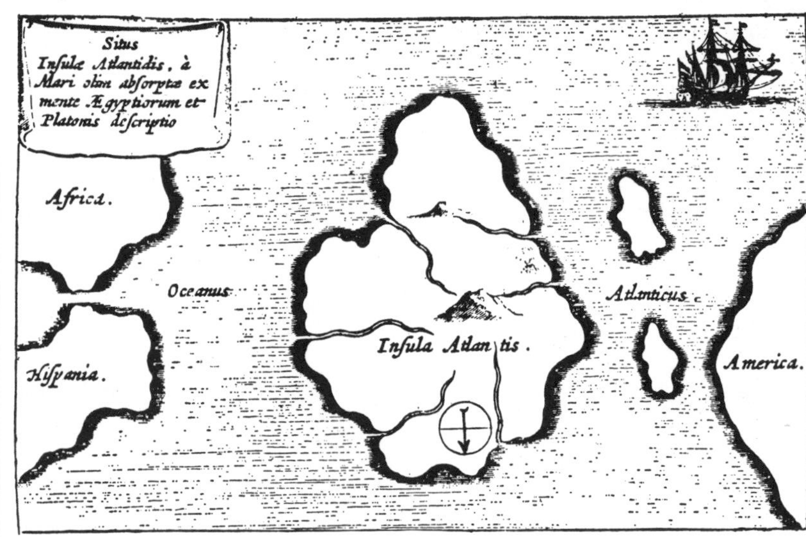

Map of Atlantis by Kircher from Lost Continents *by L. Sprague de Camp (Gnome Press).*

The English writer W. J. Passingham wrote a variation on Conan Doyle's plot and situated his lost world of giant reptiles beneath the streets of the capital; in 'When London Fell' (1937) they emerge above ground, to the dismay of the city's inhabitants. Another world set below the British landscape features in *Land Under England* (1935) by the conventional novelist Joseph O'Neill. In its nightmarish regime, descendants of the Romans have evolved a society completely subservient to the state. The story was written as an allegorical comment on the growing strength of dictatorships in Europe.

Some of the oddest science fiction worlds lie beneath man's feet. The underground world of Edgar Rice Burroughs's Pellucidar was discovered, in *At the Earth's Core* (1914), with the aid of an iron mole. Even Tarzan once made an appearance there. Less well known is *The World Below* (1929) by English author S. Fowler Wright, in which the giant subterranean dwellers of 300,000 years hence, aided by amphibians, are at war with the inhabitants of the surface world.

In 'The Hidden World' (1929) by Edmond Hamilton, the author describes a separate sphere 3000 miles in diameter hanging inside Earth's outer shell and populated by massive 'flesh-creatures' living in tower-blocks of transparent metal. After millions of years, the sphere has begun to turn on its axis and threatens to disintegrate. Human explorers succeed in thwarting the creatures' plans to break out onto the surface.

Working as an examiner in the US Patent Office, Walter Kateley never lacked inspiration for his wonder stories. His mining engineers, equipped with a tunnelling machine, in 'The World of a Hundred Men' (1930), find a lost subterranean world beneath a giant meteor crater in Arizona. From carefully preserved records, they discover it is the remains of a tiny planet whose erratic orbit finally brought it crashing to Earth centuries before. More fortunate are the tentacled robots who, forced to take refuge in this

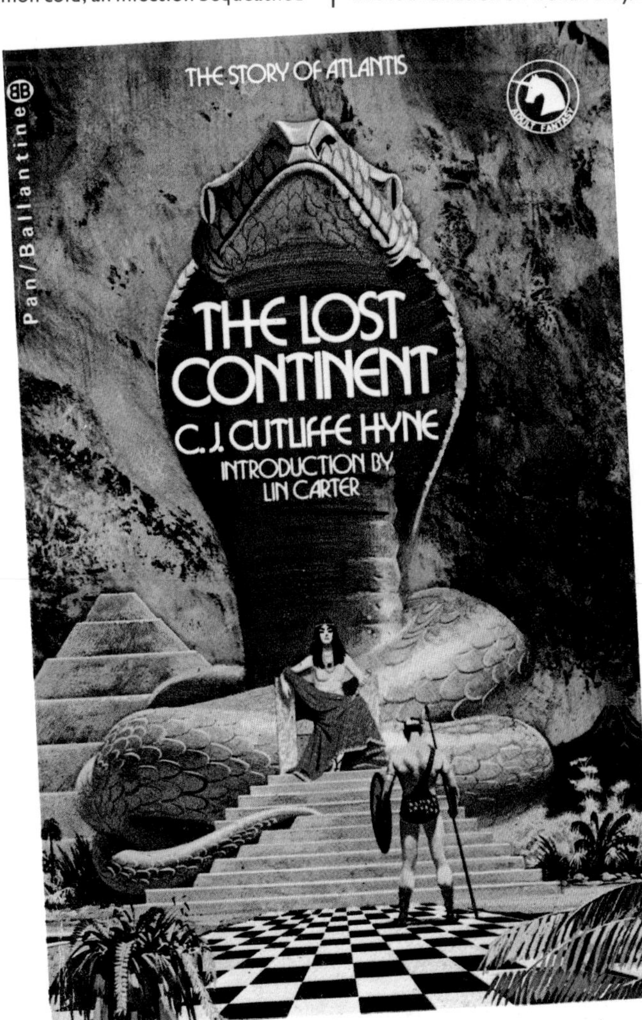

The Lost Continent *by C. J. Cutcliffe Hyne (Pan/Ballantine). Cover by Ellis.*

02.09 LOST AND PARALLEL WORLDS

world, carved a home out of the rock under the north magnetic pole in Laurence Manning's 'The Call of the Mech-Men' (1933). Provided they enjoy access to a plentiful supply of oil, they are in no particular hurry to be rescued.

Perhaps the most original – and improbable – variation on the inner-world theme was composed by Arthur J. Burks, the versatile pulp writer who turned out a million words a year in the 1930s. In 'The Golden Horseshoe' (1937), he toys with the notion that beneath the hot springs of Yellowstone National Park lies a huge underground city, empty except for vast machines which had saved it from being submerged by the waters of the Pacific long after its inhabitants had sickened and died of boredom.

From beneath the Earth's surface to the seabed is a short step for the speculative writer, and the number of stories inspired by the myth of ancient Atlantis, first related by Plato, is only exceeded by the library of learned works seeking to prove that the vanished continent actually existed. Among the earliest novels to exploit the idea, though romantically, were Frank Aubrey's *A Queen of Atlantis* (1899) and C. J. Cutcliffe Hyne's *The Lost Continent* (1900). Pierre Benoit's *Atlantida* (1920), whose heroine was modelled on H. Rider Haggard's immortal *She*, was filmed several times during the next thirty years.

Conan Doyle with *The Maracot Deep* (1929) and Dennis Wheatley with *They Found Atlantis* (1936) are only two of the many later writers who have developed the theme. In 'The Sunken World' (1928), Stanton A. Coblentz visualised the final destruction of the highly civilised Atlantean race, who had made a new home on the seabed under an immense glass dome – a variation which has been employed frequently since it was first used in an anti-socialist novel by David M. Parry, *The Scarlet Empire* (1906). Eventually, it became so familiar that L. Sprague de Camp, an expert on the subject (*Lost Continents*, 1954), advised unwary writers in his *Science-Fiction Handbook* (1953) to avoid it.

Tempted by the editor of *Thrilling Wonder* to produce a story in which snow fell on New York in midsummer, Arthur J. Burks returned to the theme by placing the responsilility on the Atlanteans. In 'The Challenge of Atlantis' (1938), they still survive in their subterranean hideaway, sustained by superior science and intent on burning their way through to the surface, disturbing the weather in the process. Before communication with the Atlanteans can be established and a peaceful settlement agreed, Death Valley has become an enormous pit serving as a window for their fighter aircraft.

In his novel *Triplanetary* (1950), the original magazine version of which launched his popular 'Lensman' series, E. E. ('Doc') Smith disposed of Atlantis by means of a misdirected nuclear missile which destroys the island's rock foundations during a war with its former colonies. Frances Ashton's *Alas, That Great City* (1948), which tells of Atlantis in decline under a lascivious queen, offers a more spectacular explanation. Accepting the so-called Cosmic Ice Theory of the Austrian engineer and amateur cosmologist Hans Hoerbiger, the narrator assumes the submergence occurred when the Moon – until then a planet circling in its own orbit – approached Earth too closely and became a satellite, with cataclysmic effects.

'The Hidden World' by Edmond Hamilton, Fantastic Story Quarterly *Spring 1950. Illustration by Stevens.*

With less pretence to scientific plausibility, such writers as Henry Kuttner and Robert E. Howard have adopted Atlantis as the setting for swashbuckling adventure tales or, like de Camp and Clark Ashton Smith, for more delicate fantasies. Following a trend set by Wells's 'In the Abyss' (1896), many others have exploited the notion that the ocean may secrete half-human, fish-like creatures intelligent enough to construct their own civilisation on the seabed. In Nat Schachner's 'City under the Sea' (1939), the fish-men turn out to be degenerate Atlanteans.

Among the most ingenious variations on the submarine-world theme is 'The Green Girl' (1930), a colourful adventure by Jack Williamson set in a strange domain beneath the Pacific where intelligent life takes the form of flying plant-creatures. The watery roof above them is supported by a gas rising from the ocean floor, and is maintained at a precise balance. Careless of the probable consequences, the leading characters plunge through it in a twenty-first-century craft which is as much at home on the sea as in the sky.

Another striking treatment is an English novel written by J. K. Heydon under the pseudonym Hal P. Trevarthen, *World D* (1935). It tells of a super-scientist who has secretly built a bubble-world ten miles under the bed of the Pacific. This he plans to populate with carefully chosen individuals from the outer world, which is doomed to eventual destruction. In this endeavour he is guided by sympathetic beings on distant planets whom he has contacted through the new science of psycho-physics.

While the idea of lost worlds beneath the land and sea has attracted many writers, there remains one further area which the imaginative mind may explore without, metaphorically, leaving Earth. Ever since Fitz-James O'Brien entertained readers of *Atlantic Monthly* with his classic tale of *The Diamond Lens* (1858), stories which plumb the depths of the microcosmos have held a peculiar fascination. One of the first writers to develop the idea – and eventually overwork it – was Ray Cummings. His *The Girl in the Golden Atom* (1923), first presented in *All-Story Weekly* in 1919, was followed by several sequels after it had made his reputation.

Cummings's chemist hero emulates Alice's 'Wonderland' performance by taking a drug which reduces him in size, so effectively that he finds himself in an atomic world within the gold band of his mother's wedding ring. He returns by reversing the process with another drug, to find that only two days have elapsed, though he has spent a week on his explorations. This notion of the relationship between space and time, suggested by the theory of relativity, has become traditional in science fiction, particularly in this once popular type of story.

'Out of the Sub-Universe' (1928) by R. F. Starzl is based on the assumption that the atom and its electrons constitute a miniature universe. A physicist's daughter and her fiancé, the physicist's young assistant (a common alliance in early stories), enter such a universe. In this case, the transfer depends on an electrical apparatus utilising cosmic rays. The pair diminish in size until they disappear into a granule of carbon, which soon afterwards yields a small army of tiny men and women. It transpires that they are the remote descendants of the bethrothed couple, who emerged from the electron world millions of years before and left behind them a promise of final racial migration to a higher realm of existence.

Other visitants from the infinitesimal have often arrived in more belligerent mood. Confronted with the dissolution of their own universe after billions of years of achievement, the people of Maurice G. Hugi's 'Invaders from the Atom' (1937) stake all on a last, desperate bid for survival. They emerge from a hydrogen atom locked in a pebble, to panic a peaceful Kentish village before defying British tanks and artillery with devastating weapons. But they have reckoned without Einstein. Returning to effect the transfer of their last four million people, they can find no trace of their world, which has long since expired with the rest of their universe.

In *The Green Man of Kilsona* (1936) by Festus Pragnell, a novel that Wells himself found commendable, a lawn tennis champion tells the story of his experience during an experimental transfer of personalities between himself and a green-haired ape-man on an electron world. The experimenter, the hero's scientist brother, retrieves the subject after a few minutes, only to be violently attacked by him. Though in this world he has not aged, the tennis player has occupied the ape-man's body for thirty years.

As science-fiction became, by and large, more logical, tales of hidden worlds within the Earth and the atom became less frequent; but stories telling of Lilliputian people struggling to survive in Brobdingnagian environments, as in Richard Matheson's *The Shrinking Man* (1956), have never ceased to attract readers – and film and television producers. After the film *The Incredible Shrinking Man* (1957), based on Matheson's book, had awakened screen memories of *Doctor Cyclops*, in turn based on the book by Will Garth (1940), Irwin Allen created the television series *Land of the Giants* (1969). This was accompanied by a paperback series authored by Murray Leinster.

Leinster employed all his ingenuity to present a plausible explanation for the plight of seven humans stranded on another world where everything is much the same as on Earth, but ten times its normal size. In the first book of the series, *The Trap* (1969), the castaways come to the conclusion that a 'space warp' has snatched them through eleven light years to a planet which is 'in resonance' with their own.

A further recent variation on the miniaturisation theme has come from English author Lindsay Gutteridge, who has made use of the idea in two novels. In *Cold War in a Country Garden* (1971), he suggests that a world of micro-humans would provide an instant answer to the problems of over-population. For such a species abundant food would be available in great variety, including insect eggs and moulds; some of its people might live like parasites under the skins of docile animals; it would be 'a new society in which famine and territorial wars will be unknown. . .' But after braving the terrors of an English country garden, the subjects of the initial experiment are employed on foreign espionage. When they are caught, a crate full of ravenous centipedes provides their captors with a highly effective means of persuasion. Two miniaturised agents escape, however, to reappear in *Killer Pine* (1973) and combat the insects infesting the trees of the Canadian forests

ADDITIONAL INPUT

02.09.1 Lost Worlds

Coblentz, Stanton A. 'In Caverns Below', *Wonder* March to May 1935; as *Hidden World*, Avalon (US) 1957

Cummings, Ray. *Beyond the Vanishing Point*, *Astounding* March 1931; Ace (US) 1958

Cummings, Ray *The Princess of the Atom*, *Argosy* September to October 1929; Avon (US) 1950

Fearn, John Russell. 'Worlds Within', *Astounding* March 1937

Hamilton, Edmond. 'A Yank at Valhalla', *Startling* January 1941; as *The Monsters of Jutonheim*, World Distributors (UK) 1950

Hamilton, Edmond. *The Valley of Creation*, *Startling* July 1948; Lancer (US) 1967

Kuttner, Henry. 'Dr Cyclops', *Thrilling Wonder* June 1940

Lovecraft, H.P. *The Outsider*, Arkham (US) 1939

Merritt, A. *Dwellers in the Mirage*, *Argosy-All-Story* January to February 1932; Liverwright (US) 1932

Schachner, Nat. 'The Return of Circe', *Fantastic Adventures* August 1941

Schachner, Nat. 'Return of the Murians', *Astounding* August 1936

Smith, Clark Ashton. *Lost Worlds*, Arkham (US) 1944

Verrill, A. Hyatt. *The Bridge of Light*, *Amazing Quarterly* Fall 1929; Fantasy (US) 1950

02.09 LOST AND PARALLEL WORLDS

02.09.2 Parallel Worlds

Parallel worlds should not be confused with alternate worlds. Alternate worlds are other Earths where, from a certain point onwards, history takes a different course; for instance, Hitler wins the Second World War, Columbus fails to discover America, and so on. Such stories are also referred to as alternative histories. Parallel worlds are those coexistent with our own, although possibly totally different. They come in many shapes and sizes, and probably the best known was that encountered by the little girl Alice in *Through the Looking-Glass* (1872) by Lewis Carroll. How can we be sure that everything stays the same in those parts of the mirror we cannot see? Mirror worlds have usually been employed by sf writers to create an eerie atmosphere. Such stories as 'The Trap' (1932) by Henry S. Whitehead, 'The Painted Mirror' (1937) by Donald Wandrei and Fritz Leiber's 'Midnight in the Mirror World' (1964) involve either someone going into or something coming out of a mirror. A natural extension of the mirror was the unusual gem in A. Merritt's 'Through the Dragon Glass' (1917), which allowed an exploration of the world beyond.

According to some theories, there may be a world coexistent with ours, but we cannot perceive it with our five known senses. Some alteration in our perception might enable us to see this other world, and such an adjustment is the basis of 'Another World' (1895) by J.-H. Rosny-aine, in which a child born with extraordinary vision can see another dimension. In the story 'Locked World' (1929), Edmond Hamilton based the existence of this parallel world on a more scientific premise. He suggested that it is separated from Earth because its electrons move in the opposite direction. Since this is an early Hamilton story, it follows that Earth is about to be invaded from that dimension – a theme the author had exploited before, in 'The Dimension Terror' (1928). During the 1930s, many stories described the invasion of our world from a fourth or fifth dimension. They include Jack Williamson's 'Wolves of Darkness' (1932), Donald Wandrei's 'The Blinding Shadows' (1934) and Murray Leinster's *The Incredible Invasion* (1936). Leinster reversed the process in his stories 'The Fifth Dimension Catapult' (1931) and 'The Fifth Dimension Tube' (1933), where his explorers investigate the jungle-infested other world.

Encounters with such parallel worlds are sometimes deliberate, but often accidental, the characters penetrating the other dimension unintentionally. One method of reaching the other world, by air, gives something of a foretaste of the 'Bermuda Triangle' mystery. Jack Williamson's aeronauts fly into another world in 'Through the Purple Cloud' (1931). Clark Ashton Smith followed suit, taking his flyers to a bizarre planet of strange creatures in 'The Dimension of Chance' (1932).

H. G. Wells's 'The Remarkable Case of Davidson's Eyes' (1895) tells of a man's brief ability to see through another dimension. A similar accident allows the heroine of J. R. Fearn's *Other Eyes Watching* (1946) to observe a parallel fourth-dimensional world. Her physicist brother builds an electronic apparatus which enables them to enter it. They discover that over the years a great many ships and planes from Earth and many people, including the crew of the *Marie Celeste* have entered pockets of temporarily distorted space and have been snatched through to this other world. The theme was echoed in many stories, and has been eagerly taken up by modern writers of occult and supernatural tales. The combination of parallel-world ideas and occult themes was pre-dated by Wells's 'The Plattner Story' (1896), in which a man, carried to a fourth-dimensional world, discovers that it is inhabited by the dead of Earth, reborn into grotesque tadpole-like bodies at the moment of death.

Science fiction writers have frequently imagined that it should be possible to make contact with parallel worlds by a subtle alteration of the human body. One hypothesis suggests that a parallel world might be separated from Earth only by a different vibration in the space-time continuum. It was by working on such a theory that P. Schuyler Miller's explorers are able to enter other worlds in 'Through the Vibrations' (1931); and it is a device based on a similar idea that enables the inventor of H. P. Lovecraft's 'From Beyond' (1934) to bring previously unseen horrors into the visible spectrum. However, as a rule characters in this type of science fiction story discover other worlds with little difficulty. In 'The Sapphire Goddess' (1934) by Nictzin Dyalhis, the hero, who has suicidal tendencies, simply wishes himself there.

In 'The Other Place' (1953) by J. B. Priestley, the chief character reaches another world while in a form of trance; and in a noted novel, *All Flesh Is Grass* (1965), Clifford Simak's protagonist simply walks into it, through a portal he did not know was there. Such easy transitions are also presaged by Wells in his utopian stories, *A Modern Utopia* (1905) and *Men Like Gods* (1923), both of which are set on parallel Earths.

Other worlds are usually best explored in novel-length works, rather than in short stories, and more often than not the authors provide sequels or write a complete series. The appeal of the theme owes much to the scope it provides writers for creating worlds which border more on fantasy than

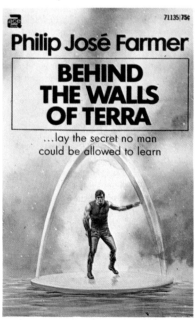

A Philip José Farmer series, all published by Ace. Covers by Morrow and Gaughan.

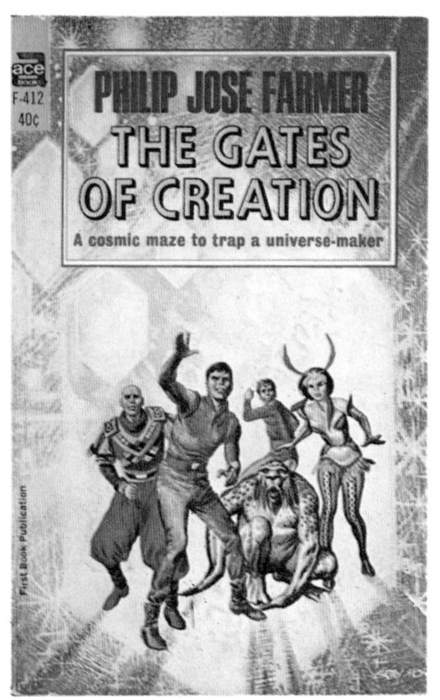

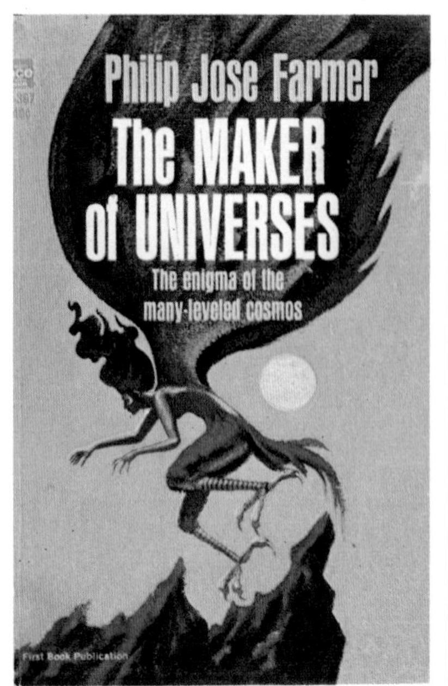

2.09 LOST AND PARALLEL WORLDS

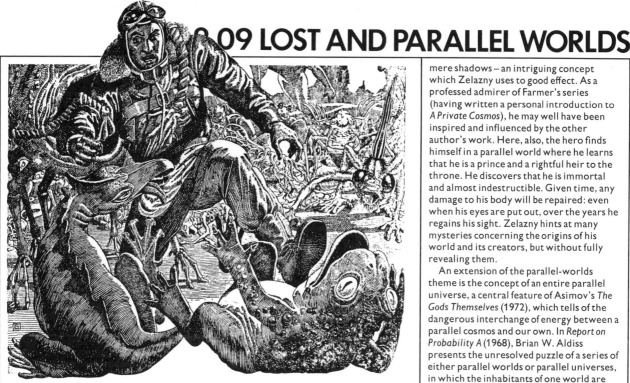

'The Dimension of Chance' by Clark Ashton Smith, Startling Stories *Spring 1946.*

authentic science fiction, and in this particular area the dividing line is not easily drawn. Robert A. Heinlein, for example, has created a notable fantasy world in *Glory Road* (1963). His hero, holidaying in the south of France, is met by a beautiful woman who requests his help. Before long, he finds himself in a dream-land where he is obliged to fight an ogre, kill dragons and generally live the life of a knight errant.

Keith Laumer has written many novels involving time travel, and has also often dealt with the parallel-world theme. In *Axe and Dragon* (1965) he describes an anachronistic parallel world, which is again portrayed in *The Shape Changer* (1970). In the first, the central character experiments with a method of releasing psychic energies and finds himself in a world not unlike Earth, but where dragons lurk in the desert and the police patrol in steam cars. In *The Shape Changer*, he is suddenly propelled along other probability lines to assume a variety of peculiar guises as he strives to make his way back. Further Laumer parallel-world treatments include *The Worlds of the Imperium* (1962) and its sequel *The Other Side of Time* (1965).

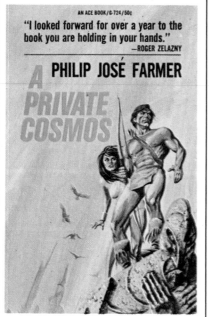

AN ACE BOOK/G-724/50¢
"I looked forward for over a year to the book you are holding in your hands."
—ROGER ZELAZNY
PHILIP JOSÉ FARMER
A PRIVATE COSMOS

Philip José Farmer has contributed to the theme in four novels set around the highly original World of Tiers. Beginning with *The Maker of Universes* (1965), through *The Gates of Creation* (1966) and *A Private Cosmos* (1967) to *Behind the Walls of Terra* (1970), Farmer persuasively depicts a seemingly impossible world that exists as a series of layers or levels, each housing a different society, its own enclosed world. At the peak of the World of Tiers is the home of the Lord who created it. The first novel concerns a character summoned by a strange horn in an old house on Earth. He enters the world through a cupboard, in a scene reminiscent of the entrance to the fantasy world described in C. S. Lewis's series for children that began with *The Lion, the Witch and the Wardrobe* (1950) – itself inspired by the works of George MacDonald, notably *Phantastes* (1858) and *Lilith* (1895). Farmer's hero later discovers he is actually the Lord who had created the World of Tiers but was overthrown by a rival, whom he eventually re-encounters and defeats.

Roger Zelazny, too, has written four linked novels, *Nine Princes in Amber* (1971), *The Guns of Avalon* (1973), *Sign of the Unicorn* (1975) and *The Hand of Oberon* (1976), set in his own variation on the parallel-world theme. Amber is the world of which our universe and other parallel universes are mere shadows – an intriguing concept which Zelazny uses to good effect. As a professed admirer of Farmer's series (having written a personal introduction to *A Private Cosmos*), he may well have been inspired and influenced by the other author's work. Here, also, the hero finds himself in a parallel world where he learns that he is a prince and a rightful heir to the throne. He discovers that he is immortal and almost indestructible. Given time, any damage to his body will be repaired: even when his eyes are put out, over the years he regains his sight. Zelazny hints at many mysteries concerning the origins of his world and its creators, but without fully revealing them.

An extension of the parallel-worlds theme is the concept of an entire parallel universe, a central feature of Asimov's *The Gods Themselves* (1972), which tells of the dangerous interchange of energy between a parallel cosmos and our own. In *Report on Probability A* (1968), Brian W. Aldiss presents the unresolved puzzle of a series of either parallel worlds or parallel universes, in which the inhabitants of one world are observing those of another but are themselves being watched from a third world, and so on.

Michael Moorcock has written no less than twenty novels that specifically relate to his vision of a 'multiverse'. The stories originated in fantasy as the adventures of Elric of Melnibone, but they evolved into an entire mythos that splits into four main sections. Moorcock describes a chain of continuums that consists of many parallel universes, existing at different levels and generally remaining separate. Occasionally, there are rifts which allow passage from one cosmos to another. Common to these worlds is the Eternal Champion, who assumes different identities according to which universe he occupies. In the main mythos the worlds differ little. That of Elric is pure fantasy – see *The Stealer of Souls* (1963), *Stormbringer* (1965), *The Sleeping Sorceress* (1971), *Elric of Melnibone* (1972) and *The Sailor on the Seas of Fate* (1976). That of Dorian Hawkmoon is set on an apparent future Earth devastated by a nuclear war, where Gran Bretan has become the rising centre of evil – see *The Jewel in the Skull* (1967), *The Sorcerer's Amulet* (1968), *Sword of the Dawn* (1968), *The Secret of the Runestaff* (1969), *Count Brass* (1973), *The Champion of Garathorm* (1973) and *Quest for Tanelorn* (1975). The world of Corum is set at the dawn of mankind, when the elder peoples are dying and the new creation, man, is taking over – see *The Knights of the Swords* (1971), *The Queen of the Swords* (1971), *The King of the Swords* (1972), *The Bull and the Spear* (1973), *The Oak and the Ram* (1973) and *The Sword and the Stallion* (1974). Erekosë has no set world, and he ranges from bloodthirsty worlds (*The Eternal Champion*, 1962) to ice worlds (*Phoenix in Obsidian*, 1970). The hub of all these parallel universes is the eternal city of Tanelorn, an enigma that remains unresolved even in the climactic novel of the series, *Quest for*

02.10 TIME AND NTH DIMENSIONS

Tanelorn, which features all the heroes.

If some of these connected stories must be regarded as pure fantasy, there are others in the series which fall more appropriately into the science fiction category. *The Blood-Red Game* (1962), for instance, goes some way towards describing the intricacies of the multiverse, when our own universe is threatened by a parallel galaxy which occasionally materialises inside it.

Moorcock's multiverse is almost certainly the most complex treatment of the parallel-worlds theme yet devised, but in an area where the possible variations are genuinely unlimited there is no reason to suppose that his prolific output will not be surpassed by an even more industrious writer in the future.

ADDITIONAL INPUT

02.09.2 Parallel Worlds

Asimov, Isaac. 'What If. . .', *Fantastic* Summer 1952

Bond, J. Harvey (Russ Winterbottom). *The Other World*, Ace (US) 1963

Breuer, Miles J. 'The Book of Worlds', *Amazing* July 1929

Breuer, Miles J. 'The Gostak and the Doshes', *Amazing* March 1930

Brandon, Frank (Kenneth Bulmer). 'The Seventh Stair', *Science Fantasy* October 1961; sequel 'Perilous Portal', *Science Fantasy* August 1962

Bulmer, Kenneth. *The Key to Irunium*, Ace (US) 1967; sequel *The Key to Venudine*, Ace (US) 1968

Bulmer, Kenneth. 'The Map Country', *Science Fantasy* February 1961; expanded as *Land beyond the Map*, Ace (US) 1965

Cummings, Ray. 'Phantoms of Reality', *Astounding* January 1930

De Camp, L. Sprague (with Fletcher Pratt). The 'Harold Shea' series runs as follows:
'The Roaring Trumpet', *Unknown* May 1940
'The Mathematics of Magic', *Unknown* August 1940
(above two combined as *The Incomplete Enchanter*, Holt, US, 1942)
The Castle of Iron, *Unknown* April 1941; Gnome (US) 1950
'Wall of Serpents', *Fantasy Fiction* June 1953
'The Green Magician', *Beyond* 9 November 1954 (above two combined as *Wall of Serpents*, Avalon, US, 1960)

Del Rey, Lester. 'The Sky Is Falling', *Satellite* June 1957; enlarged *Galaxy Magabook 1* (US) 1963

Fearing, Bruce. 'The Unlikeliest Thing', *Vortex 2* (Summer) 1953

Hall, Austin. *The Blind Spot* (with Homer Eon Flint) *Argosy* 14 May to 18 June 1921; Prime (US) 1951; sequel *The Spot of Life*, *Argosy* 13 August to 10 September 1932; Ace (US) 1964

Kuttner, Henry. *The Dark World*, *Startling* Summer 1946; Ace (US) 1965

Kuttner, Henry. *The Portal in the Picture*, *Startling* September 1949; retitled *Beyond Earth's Gates* (as by Lewis Padgett), Ace (US) 1954

Leinster, Murray (Will F. Jenkins). 'The Monsters', *Weird Tales* January 1933

Niven, Larry. 'For a Foggy Night', *F&SF* July 1971

Shaw, Bob. *The Two-Timers*, Ace (US) 1968

Simak, Clifford D. 'Hellhounds of the Cosmos', *Astounding* June 1932

Smith, Clark Ashton. 'City of the Singing Flame', *Wonder Stories* July 1931; sequel 'Beyond the Singing Flame', *Wonder Stories* November 1931

Temple, William F. 'Life of the Party', *Vision of Tomorrow* February 1970

Time travel is quite impossible, of course, because it would change the past, disordering history and unfixing the framework of reality. Robert Heinlein lists it as one of the things he does not expect in any foreseeable future, while Thomas Aquinas puts it even beyond the power of God: 'God cannot effect that anything which is past should not have been. It is more impossible than raising the dead.'

And yet . . . memory travels into the past and imagination into the future – it is mind's glory. The simplest theatre, the prosiest historical novel and the soberest scientific romance are machines for time travelling; the Ghost walks with every production of *Hamlet*; while the power to see and suffer with (and somehow, without changing) all past, present and future reality, is the essence of God.

It is in this last sense that Olaf Stapledon envisions the development of time travel in his novel *Last and First Man* (1930). His last species of man (the Eighteenth!), living on Neptune a billion and a half years in the future, is able to revive *and love* the past, share and so mitigate its buried horrors and wonders without otherwise changing the dense fabric of reality. H. P. Lovecraft's 'The Shadow out of Time' also deals with the eons.

Love for all reality is what conquers all, fictionally, in this sort of mental time travelling. It is to catch up in years with her beloved that Robert Nathan's little-girl heroine hurries forward through time in his poignant nouvelle *Portrait of Jenny* (1969); while it is not by chance that the time-travelling hero of Robert Graves's novel *Seven Days in New Crete* (1949) (in America *Watch the Northwind Rise*) is transported into the future by Graves's beloved Triple Goddess, who also appears to destroy New Crete at the end.

In, what is to my mind, the most profound and exciting (the *realest*) time-travel novel of them all, Ward Moore's *Bring the Jubilee* (1953), a like destruction is brought about by the anima figure of Barbara Haggerswells, though she employs a machine for the purpose rather than pure mentality.

With a happy, if somewhat comical, appropriateness, H. G. Wells pictured his classic time machine as resembling a bicycle – the humblest of vehicles employed for the most daring of purposes. Time machines are very useful plotwise – they can be lost or stolen, and they give the reader something concrete on which to focus his attention.

Occasionally, the time-travel story can achieve marvellously cynical effects, as in William Tenn's 'The Brooklyn Project' (1948), where a trifling intrusion into the distant past changes everything in the universe except (universal!) human nature with all its wearisome foibles and absurdities. Or in Thomas Sherred's 'E for Effort' (1947), where no one will seriously accept the photographed truth about the corruptions and chicaneries of history, and its disappointed discoverers are forced to eke out a living selling the results of their research as cheap spaghetti-historical motion pictures. Or in H. Beam Piper's superb 'He Walked around the Horses' (1948), in which Sir Arthur Wellesley signs his name to a report in which he wonders who the Duke of Wellington can possibly be.

Yes, it's quite impossible, time travel . . . and infinitely fertile, artistically.

Fritz Leiber

Fritz Leiber

02.10 TIME AND NTH DIMENSIONS

Tempus Fugit! Time is not on our side. But what if it could be? What if man could accelerate it or arrest it – and travel through it at will? Such questions have fascinated science fiction writers as much as any other speculative propositions, and a considerable body of work devoted to the concept of time exists in the genre. The idea of being able to foresee the future or delve back into the past has fascinated mankind since the ancients, with their oracles and prophets. But the accepted view of time travel is a modern one. Its many aspects are best exemplified in that prototype of all time-travel stories, Charles Dickens's *A Christmas Carol* (1843). Ebenezer Scrooge is taken on a journey to his past by a kindly spirit guide, but he cannot intervene in actions which he later comes to regret. Subsequently, he is exposed to the dreadful vision of his own death by the sinister Ghost of Christmas Yet to Come. In his memorable description of Scrooge's change of heart, Dickens suggested that futures could be altered; the miser is made to mend his ways and the reader is left assuming that his lonely death has been averted. While the past may be immutable, the future, it seems, can be remoulded. Dickens had contributed an early masterpiece to what has become one of the most popular themes of science fiction: the unlikely possibility that man can visit the past or future – in short, time travel.

Time is often regarded as a fourth dimension, along which our three-dimensional selves travel from second to second. On the other hand, it must also be seen as the measurement of decay, recording the slow dissolution of the cosmos in the universal dissipation of energy expressed by the Second Law of Thermodynamics. Everything is burning itself out. The energy of man, as he travels along this line, must ultimately bend to the same law.

The possibility that there could be even further dimensions than the three we usually recognise has long fascinated both scientists and science fiction writers. The idea of a fourth physical dimension – quite separate from time – has often been suggested. It would be invisible to us, as would any entity which might inhabit it. Only a limited number of sf stories have featured this alternative concept of another dimension, but enough notable examples exist for some of them to be considered separately at the end of this section. In the following sub-sections there are several stories which could easily be classed under more than one heading – a result of the paradoxes involved in any consideration of time.

"*Miss 1901,*" *he said,* "*step into 1952!*" *From 'Factor Unknown' by Sam Merwin Jr,* Other Worlds *June 1952. Illustration by Tillotson.*

02.10.1 Backwards in Time

Historically, the first theme to be exploited in the time category was that of man visiting the past. Among early nineteenth-century examples can be found the anonymously written 'Missing One's Coach' (1838), in which the narrator suddenly finds himself back in eighth-century Britain, encountering the Venerable Bede. No explanation is given for his temporal shift, nor for his equally instantaneous return. In today's sf terminology it could be said he had passed through a time warp.

Five years later, Edgar Allan Poe told in 'A Tale of the Ragged Mountains' (1843) how a man ventures into the peak district of Virginia only to discover himself transported to the year 1780. Since he is suffering from the effects of morphine (a drug Poe himself had used), the story concludes with the cause of the events unexplained. The reader is left to judge whether it was all a drug-induced hallucination or a real trip in time.

Certainly the most popular early story on this aspect of time travel was Mark Twain's *A Connecticut Yankee in King Arthur's Court* (1889). Here again, there is some fantasising about the mechanics of the hero's journey backwards in time, and he only returns to the present by going to sleep, a device which provides the excuse that the whole tale may have been merely a dream. Alternatively, it could be argued that the return journey is an example of suspended animation, a theme surprisingly common in the 1800s and still much used today.

An early use of a time machine in travelling back into the past occurs in Edward Page Mitchell's story 'The Clock That Went Backward' (1881). Here the machine is a clock which seems to have been broken, but when wound runs backwards and transports two boys to sixteenth-century Holland.

Time travel really entered the realms of modern science fiction with H. G. Wells's *The Time Machine* (1895), depicting a device which went both forwards and backwards in time; but that is not to say that the use of a machine was immediately taken up by other writers. More often than not, adventurers still travelled into the past by some means of temporal slip, as in Murray Leinster's 'The Runaway Skyscraper' (1919), where a multi-storied office block is precipitated back into pre-Columbian America. One or two other early writers can be credited with more originality. In 1904 Jean Delaire incorporated what was then an entirely new concept in his story *Around a Distant Star*. He told of a spaceship journeying

ANC

THRILLING WONDER STORIES

15¢

DEC.

EARLE BERGEY

The POWER AND THE GLORY

An Amazing Novel

By HENRY KUTTNER

A THRILLING PUBLICATION

Left: 'The Power and the Glory' by Henry Kuttner, Thrilling Wonder Stories *December 1947. Cover by Bergey.*

across the void which attained a speed two thousand times that of light. Training their powerful telescopes in the direction of Earth, the crew pick up the light waves generated two millennia earlier, and see Jesus in Galilee. A similar use of time-viewing was employed by George Allan England in his first sf story, 'The Time Reflector' (1905), telling how an inventor perfects a telescope which focuses on light from Earth reflected by distant planets.

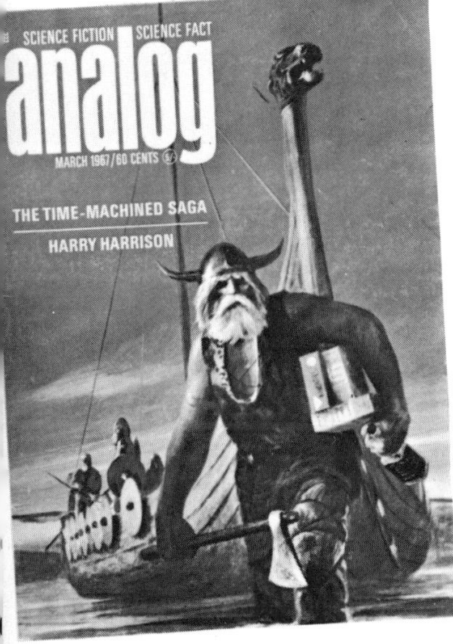

Cover by Schoenherr.

The advent of the sf magazines in 1926 stimulated the development of the time-travel theme. Writers experimented. In 'The Time Ray of Jandra' (1930), Ray Palmer told of the discovery of strange machines on the African coast. While meddling with them, the leading character is transported 17,000 years into the past, but like Scrooge he is fated to be an observer, powerless to intervene. Jack Williamson made use of a space warp in 'The Moon Era' (1932), to depict the lunar world when it was still young and inhabited; while in 'The Fourth Dimensional Demonstrator' (1935) Murray Leinster wrote one of the few genuinely funny sf stories of the 1930s. He imagined a machine which could duplicate whatever was placed on it by going into the immediate past and bringing the same object forward into the present. When it begins duplicating people, havoc duly ensues.

As the popularity of time travel into the past grew, a large number of writers increasingly saw it as a vehicle for adventure. They were not particularly concerned with the technical details of the journey, and regarded use of the concept simply as a handy ploy for introducing their characters into unfamiliar surroundings – an approach still common today. It is well illustrated in such tales as P. Schuyler Miller's 'The Sands of Time' (1937), where the protagonist is whisked 60 million years back to the time of an alien invasion in Earth's prehistory, and in Henry Kuttner's 'The Time Trap' (1938). A more sophisticated story, though still an adventure tale, is Poul Anderson's *The Corridors of Time* (1965), featuring a woman from two thousand years in the hero's future, who takes him underneath an ancient dolmen in Denmark to travel to 1827 BC. Another ancient monument, Stonehenge in England, is used by Keith Laumer for a series of adventures in *A Trace of Memory* (1962).

A further variation on historical time travel is that employed by the fictitional descendants of *A Connecticut Yankee . . .* In the 'Pete Manx' series of stories, written sometimes independently and sometimes jointly by Henry Kuttner and Arthur Barnes under the alias 'Kelvin Kent', Manx finds his consciousness jerked back to various periods of history and into a chain of humorous adventures. He visits Rome in 'Roman Holiday' (1939), Greece in 'Hercules Muscles In' (1941) and Arabia in 'Grief in Bagdad' (1943). A more thorough treatment was given to the theme by L. Sprague de Camp in *Lest Darkness Fall* (1939), where the central character is struck by lightning and finds himself in ancient Rome. Inevitably, the final twist was given to Twain's book in A. W. Bernal's 'King Arthur's Knight in a Yankee Court' (1941).

Yet another method of exploring the past involves tracing back along racial memory by means of mental projection, usually during an induced trance. The idea that time might be circular and that all history will eternally repeat itself was anticipated in Stanley G. Weinbaum's haunting story, 'The Circle of Zoo' (1936), and in Arthur J.

Cover by d'Achille (Pan).

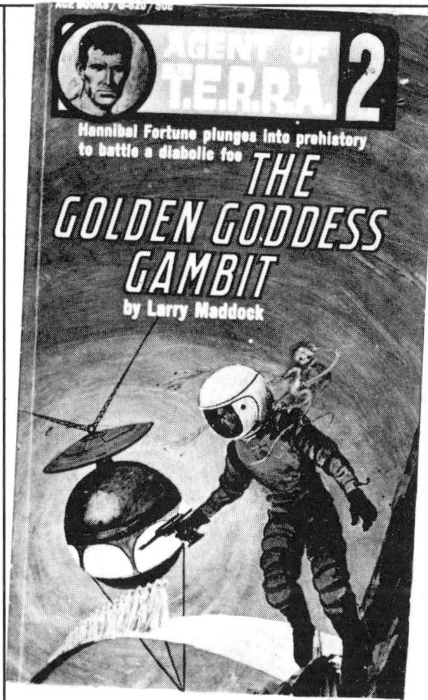

Cover by Leone.

Burks's 'The Discarded Veil' (1937), in which the hero travels back mentally to the time of the last ice age.

The more intricate time-travel stories consider what happens when a man meddles with the past. Many such tales are considered under the later heading of time paradoxes, but some may be mentioned here. Ray Bradbury's 'A Sound of Thunder' (1954) tells of men who travel back into prehistoric times to hunt dinosaurs. By unwittingly stepping on a butterfly, they cause extensive changes in the present day. In 'The Brooklyn Project' (1948) William Tenn demonstrates that none of the changes would be appreciated by those interfering with history, because their entire memory and consciousness would also be altered.

There are many such tales, among them Maurice Vaisberg's 'The Sun Stood Still' (1958), involving an attempt to kill Joshua at Jericho, and Robert Silverberg's 'The Assassin' (1957), in which a time traveller returns to save Abraham Lincoln. The rescuing of Jesus of Nazareth has been portrayed in Arthur Porges's 'The Rescuer' (1962) and in Michael Moorcock's *Behold the Man* (1966), the latter telling how the character who goes back to save Jesus finds himself obliged to impersonate him.

Some writers have concluded that man should not be allowed to meddle so frivolously with the past, and a number of stories have been written around the theme of a corps of Time Police. H. Beam Piper's 'Paratime' series falls into this category, as does Poul Anderson's *Guardians of Time* (1960). Further examples are Larry Maddock's 'The Agent of T.E.R.R.A.' series – its best-known story being *The Time Trap Gambit* (1970) – and Keith Laumer's *Dinosaur Beach* (1971). But perhaps the most original of modern variations is Robert

02.10 TIME AND NTH DIMENSIONS

Silverberg's *Up the Line* (1969), which features commercially motivated sightseeing tours. Its central paradox involves one of the most popular tours, to the Crucifixion, which leaves monthly and conveys about a hundred visitors a year. However, since the sightseers must inevitably all converge at one point in time, the result should be an audience of thousands. But such a multitude, if it was there, would surely have been decribed in the Gospels?

Such paradoxes are the essence of time-travel fiction, and in stories where they relate to journeys into the past many writers have attempted to explain them. In *The Time-Machined Saga* (1967) Harry Harrison tells of a film crew's journey to the past to record the Viking discovery of North America (cheaper than hiring modern-day extras). When the Vikings fail to appear the film producer imports them – thus actually causing the events he has come to film. In a similar fashion, Arthur C. Clarke's 'Time's Arrow' (1950) accounts for the discovery of a modern jeep's tyre tracks in a dinosaur fossil bed.

ADDITIONAL INPUT

02.10.1 Backwards in Time

Aldiss, Brian W. *An Age*, *New Worlds* October to December 1967; Faber (UK) 1968; retitled *Cryptozoic!*, Doubleday (US) 1968

Greenhough, Terry. *Time and Timothy Grenville*, NEL (UK) 1975

Laumer, Keith. *A Hoax in Time*, *Fantastic* June to August 1963; retitled *The Great Time Machine Hoax*, Simon & Schuster (US) 1964

Leinster, Murray. 'The Gadget Had a Ghost', *Thrilling Wonder* June 1952

Silverberg, Robert. 'The Assassin', *Imaginative Tales* July 1957

Tucker, Wilson. *The Lincoln Hunters*, Reinhart (US) 1958

'A Sound of Thunder' by Ray Bradbury, Planet Stories *January 1954. Illustration by Emsh.*

02.10.2 From the Present into the Future

Prophetic visions of the future entice the human imagination more compellingly than any other human dream, but to actually travel into it and mingle with one's distant descendants is the dream that gave the world *The Time Machine* (1895) by H. G. Wells – a novel which is discussed at length in the section devoted to mutants. Wells was fascinated by the concepts of time, and his short novel was the final version of a much-rewritten story that had started life in the *Science Schools Journal* as 'The Chronic Argonauts' (1888). The bulk of Wells's tale is set in the year 802,701 AD, where the Time Traveller meets the two final races of humans, the beautiful, surface-dwelling Eloi and the savage, subterranean Morlocks. Later in the story the adventurer travels more than 30 million years into the future to witness the dying Earth.

In his first short novel Wells had pre-empted many of the visions and techniques which appealed to the later science fiction writer. He showed himself less concerned with what might occur next week, and more interested in the happenings of millennia hence. Such ideas appealed to most of the pulp writers during the 1920s and 1930s; and, in a flurry of stories to come, the more vast the expanse of time, the more daring might be judged the author's concepts. Almost certainly influenced by *The Time Machine*, in *The House on the Borderland* (1908) William Hope Hodgson depicted the ultimate end of the world and the death of the entire solar system.

Before Wells, the principal device employed by writers to transport their heroes into the future was that of prolonged sleep. Washington Irving's 'Rip Van Winkle' (1819), Edward Bellamy's *Looking Backward* (1888) and Edwin Lester Arnold's *Phra the Phoenician* (1890) all developed this ploy. In *Phra*, the 'sleep' resembled what is regarded today as suspended animation, an invention used by Wells in his own *When the Sleeper Wakes* (1898). The concept has enjoyed a new lease of life in recent years with the idea of cryogenics (extreme freezing) and the theories of Robert C. W. Ettinger expounded in his book *The Prospect of Immortality* (1963). Modern examples of

'Anachron' by Damon Knight, If *January 1954. Illustration by Parsons.*

the use of the technique include Roger Zelazny's noted 'The Graveyard Heart' (1964).

The limitation of suspended animation is that it constitutes at best a one-way trip. The most popular dream of time travel, on the other hand, embodies the idea that man should not only visit the future but also return. Nevertheless, a number of stories have been written in which the writer attempts to show that time travel can be achieved in only one direction. Among them are Michael Moorcock's connected tales, 'The Time Dweller' (1964) and 'Escape from Evening' (1965).

A brief survey of the early treatments of future time travel indicates the pervading influence of Wells. Stories such as Francis Flagg's 'The Master Ants' (1928) and John Wyndham's 'Wanderers of Time' (1933), where the ant has superseded man as the dominant species, are cases in point. Donald Wandrei's 'A Race in Time' (1933), Clifford D. Simak's 'World of the Red Sun' (1931), Harry Bates's 'Alas, All Thinking' (1935) and 'Seeker of Tomorrow' (1937) by Eric Frank Russell and Leslie J. Johnson, pursue the Wellsian trail into the distant future.

The 1930s pulps came near to overflowing with stories of this nature. Little room remained for tales with a more moderate approach, but among them can be found Murray Leinster's 'The Morrison Monument' (1935).

As the 1930s drew to a close, more thought was devoted to the technicalities of time travel. L. Sprague de Camp looked at the subject from a logical viewpoint in his practical essay, 'Language for Time Travellers' (1938), a sensible analysis which Willy Ley complemented with 'Geography for Time Travellers' in 1939. But the end of the decade was also to witness the most extravagant excursions into temporal distortion yet attempted. Jack Williamson's *The Legion of Time* (1938), depicted a vast timeship moving through many probable existences, a concept which had been used to some extent by John Taine in *The Time Stream* (1931) and developed to its probable limits by John Russell Fearn in *Liners of Time* (1935) and *Zagribud* (1937).

Few, however, would doubt that the most convincing story on this theme is Isaac Asimov's *The End of Eternity* (1955). Depicting an intertemporal organisation operating what amounts to a lift-shaft to the future and deftly amending coming events to ensure the well-being of man, it also illustrates how such attempts at 'soft-cushioning' are likely to work to humanity's long-term disadvantage.

Other journeys into the future include 'Flight through Tomorrow' (1947) by Stanton Coblentz, with its hallucinogenic trip. This is as much a part of the stock-in-trade of time stories as the warp or portal featured in Damon Knight's 'Anachron' (1954), but it should be noted that the latter method frequently allows only a view of futures in which the observer has no chance to participate.

ADDITIONAL INPUT

02.10.2 From the Present into the Future

Anderson, Poul. 'Time Heals', *Astounding* October 1949

Del Rey, Lester. '... And It Comes Out Here', *Galaxy* February 1951

Dick, Philip K. *Now Wait for Last Year*, Doubleday (US) 1967

Fearn, John Russell (as Polton Cross). 'Wanderer of Time', *Startling* Summer 1944

Friedell, Egon. *Die Reise mit der Zeitmaschine*, Piper (Germany) 1946; translated by Eddy C. Bertin as *The Return of the Time Machine*, DAW (US) 1972

High, Philip E. 'Dead End', *Science Fantasy* December 1962

High, Philip E. 'Probability Factor', *New Worlds* March 1962

Leinster, Murray (Will F. Jenkins). 'The Middle of the Week after Next', *Thrilling Wonder* August 1952

Long, Frank Belknap. 'A Guest in the House', *Astounding* March 1946

Moorcock, Michael. 'Flux', *New Worlds* July 1963

Tucker, Wilson. *The Year of the Quiet Sun*, Ace (US) 1970

'Seeker of Tomorrow' by Eric Frank Russell and Leslie J. Johnson, Astounding *July 1937. Illustration by Wesso.*

02.10.3 From the Past into the Present

'The Time Valve' by Miles J. Breuer, Wonder Stories *July 1930. Illustration by Paul.*

Among the vagaries of time travel in science fiction, it is impossible to overlook the smaller category of tales depicting the unexpected appearance of visitors from the past. An early example is Robert Barr's story, 'The Hour Glass' (1898), which lends some support to the idea that time travellers may be ghosts, a notion which has also appeared in such other tales as Peter Cartur's 'The Mist' (1952) and A. E. van Vogt's 'The Ghost' (1942).

The desire to explain such apparitions 'rationally' has prompted certain writers to develop the idea of a time warp. Edmond Hamilton employed the theme in 'The Man Who Saw the Future' (1930), and it recurs in Wyndham's 'Stitch in Time' (1961), where an old woman musing on her past life is suddenly confronted by her former suitor, still as young as when she first met him. In other stories in this class, it is sometimes unclear whether the past has come to the future, or the future to the past. Outside the pulp field, J. B. Priestley became fascinated enough by the concepts of time expounded by J. W. Dunne (*An Experiment with Time*, 1926, and *The Serial Universe*, 1934) to write several stories and plays on the subject. Among other literary luminaries who have been fascinated by the concept of time, Henry James and Christopher Isherwood have played their part.

It was no accident that such writers were drawn to a consideration of time; Einstein's Special Theory of Relativity (1905) had proved the touchstone for much speculation. His later General Theory of 1916 only added to the scope of imaginative dealings with time. Under such auspices, Miles J. Breuer, for example, utilised the Lorenz-Fitzgerald Contraction in his story 'The Fitzgerald Contraction' (1930), to which he added a sequel, 'The Time Valve' (1930).

02.10 TIME AND NTH DIMENSIONS

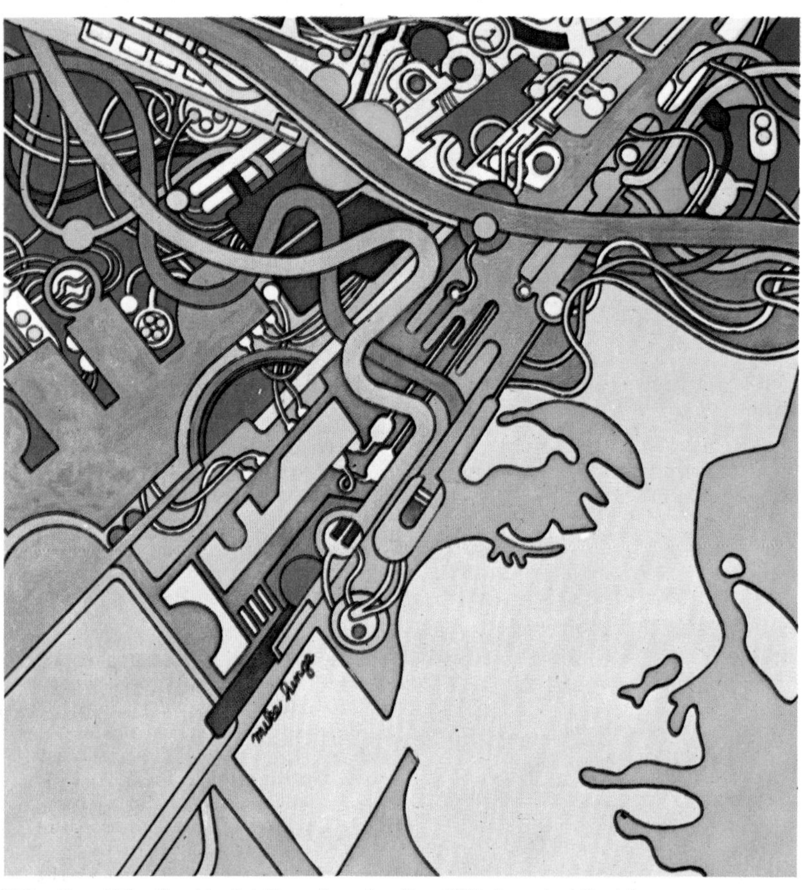

'*Other Days Other Eyes' by Bob Shaw,* Amazing *May 1972. Cover by Mike Hinge.*

Another variant on the theme is that of the traveller from the future who returns to the past with the object of bringing someone back. David I. Masson's 'A Two-Timer' (1966) explores such a situation, as do R. A. Lafferty's novel *Past Master* (1968) and 'Time's Fool' (1965) by Richard Gordon.

The possibility of viewing the past, already touched on, has found few better explorers than Isaac Asimov, who in 'The Dead Past' (1956) ably demonstrated how time-viewing a mere half hour into the past could end in the destruction of individual privacy. 'Windows' allowing unsolicited investigation of the past (or future, depending from which side the observer looks), appear in such stories as Bertram Chandler's 'The Window' (1957), Chester Geier's 'Window to the Past' (1950) and Norman L. Knight's 'Saurian Valedictory' (1939). Possibly the most 'scientific' concept in this particular category has been developed by Bob Shaw in his 'slow-glass' stories. Beginning with 'Light of Other Days' (1966), through 'Burden of Proof' (1967) and 'A Dome of Many-Coloured Glass' (1972), to the novel *Other Days, Other Eyes* (1972), the author has evolved the idea of a substance which captures light and retards it, letting it emerge from the material only after a predetermined period – days, weeks or years later. If a plate of such glass is suspended in front of a particular scenic view for ten years, it can subsequently be removed to a house and the occupants may enjoy that view for the next decade as the vision is slowly released.

ADDITIONAL INPUT

02.10.3 From Past into the Present

Aldiss, Brian W. 'Full Sun', *Orbit 2* Putnam (US) 1967.

Derleth, August. 'A Traveller in Time', *Orbit 2* Winter 1953–5

Priestley, J.B. *Time and the Conways*, play first performed 1937

02.10.4 Future to Present

Dickens's Ghost of Christmas Yet to Come was a visitant from the future, and so, too, was the ghost in Edward P. Mitchell's 'An Uncommon Sort of Spectre' (1879); but there were few future-to-present stories written before the advent of the sf magazine. Many of the tales in the early pulps concentrated on the idea that people from the future were in search of something. Edmond Hamilton helped to begin the vogue with *The Time Raider* (1927), in which a future inventor recruits an army of warriors from history, and a similar treatment was provided by A. E. van Vogt in 'Recruiting Station' (1942). Probably the most unusual and striking treatment of the warriors-in-time theme came with Fritz Leiber's *The Big Time* (1958), depicting a time-war raging throughout history, where both the past and the future are constantly being changed by the opposing factions.

Writing as John Beynon Harris, John Wyndham achieved his first story sale with another early variation on the theme, 'Worlds to Barter' (1931). It tells how the descendants of mankind on a dying Earth return to the twenty-second century and send that period's population into the future, taking the younger Earth for themselves. Some forty years later Clifford D. Simak adapted the same plot in *Our Children's Children* (1973), while another of his recent stories, 'The Marathon Photograph' (1974), concerns three people from the future who are searching for an ancient alien artefact lost somewhere in Earth's past. In fact, searches for lost property frequently feature in time-travel fiction, among them Alfred Bester's widely reprinted 'Of Time and Third Avenue' (1951). It is a piece of lost property in C. M.

'Pawley's Peepholes' by John Wyndham, Science Fantasy *Winter 1951–52. Illustration by Quinn.*

The Flight of the Horse *by Larry Niven (Ballantine). Cover by Vallejo.*

Kornbluth's 'Little Black Bag' (1950) which enables a decrepit doctor to employ the seemingly miraculous techniques of future medicine to his own advantage, but eventual downfall.

John Wyndham also developed another variation of travel from the future in 'Pawley's Peepholes' (1951), where sightseeing visitors cause some anguish to people living in the present. On the other hand, time travel proves more useful in Noel Loomis's '"If the Court Pleases"' (1953), in which a witness is brought from the future to give evidence. A different legal aspect is explored in John Christopher's 'Death Sentence' (1954), where convicted criminals are deported through time.

If only for its brevity and startling conclusion, 'The Man from When' (1966) by Dannie Plachta is an appropriate tale with which to end our review of this particular aspect of time travel. Arriving from the future, the leading character reveals that the energy required to send him back in time has completely destroyed the Earth of his own day. To this he blithely adds that he has travelled back all of eighteen minutes.

ADDITIONAL INPUT

02.10.4 Future to Present

Anthony, Piers (Piers A. Jacobs). *Orn*, *Amazing* July to September 1970; retitled *Paleo*, Avon (US) 1970

Bester, Alfred. 'The Men Who Murdered Mohammed', *F&SF* October 1958

Dick, Philip K. 'Jon's World', *Time to Come* (ed August Derleth) Strauss (US) 1954

Flagg, Francis (Henry George Weiss). 'The Machine Man of Ardathia', *Amazing* November 1927; sequel 'The Cities of Ardathia', *Amazing* March 1932

Hamilton, Edmond. 'Comrades of Time', *Weird Tales* March 1939; sequel 'Armies from the Past', *Weird Tales* April 1939

Kornbluth, Cyril M. 'Dominoes', *Star SF Stories* (ed Frederik Pohl) Ballantine (US) 1953

Lewis, Jack. 'Who's Cribbing?', *Startling* January 1953

McIntosh, J.T. *Snow White and the Giants*, *If* October 1966 to January 1967; Avon (US) 1967

Niven, Larry. The 'Svetz' series runs as follows:
- 'Get a Horse!', *F&SF* October 1969; retitled 'The Flight of the Horse'
- 'Leviathan', *Playboy* (US) 1970
- 'Bird in the Hand', *F&SF* October 1970
- 'There's a Wolf in My Time Machine', *F&SF* June 1971

Padgett, Lewis (Henry Kuttner and C. L. Moore). 'Mimsy Were the Borogoves', *Astounding* February 1943

Roberts, Keith. 'Escapism', *Science Fantasy* September/October 1964

Runciman, John (Brian W. Aldiss). 'Unauthorised Persons', *Science Fantasy* June/July 1964

Sturgeon, Theodore. 'Poker Face', *Astounding* March 1941

Tucker, Wilson. *Ice and Iron*, Doubleday (US) 1974

02.10.5 Time Paradoxes

Certainly the most intriguing factor in the portrayal of time travel is the collection of paradoxes to which it may give rise. The simplest proposition becomes complex as the writer attempts to think its consequences through. What, for example, would happen to a man who returned in time to kill his own grandfather? Nathan Schachner's 'Ancestral Voices' (1933) is based on such an idea. The leading character and thousands of other descendants vanish after the killing of an early ancestor.

The philosophical puzzle approaches the fail-safe point as time-travel plots become more complicated. Among the many tales which take up this theme, Charles Clonkey's 'Paradox' (1929), Robert Sheckley's 'A Thief in Time' (1954) and 'Slaves of Time' (1974), Ralph Milne Farley's 'The Man Who Met Himself' (1935) and David Daniel's 'The Branches of Time' (1935) are noteworthy. There are many more, but few that have attained so cherished a place in the genre as Heinlein's two masterly flights of imagination, 'By His Bootstraps' (1941) and 'All You Zombies' (1959). In the former, the bemused reader is presented with no less than four intertemporal versions of the so-called hero (who also turns out to be the villain of the piece). In the latter, the protagonist not only meets himself, but also eventually discloses that he is his own mother *and* father, not to mention being a daughter, too. Heinlein's preoccupation with characters encountering themselves has been echoed, but never convincingly bettered, in such stories as Anthony Boucher's 'The Barrier' (1942), William Tenn's 'Me, Myself and I' (1947) and E. C. Tubb's 'Thirty-Seven Times' (1957) – the last written under the pseudonym of Alan Guthrie. David Gerrold's *The Man Who Folded Himself* (1973) is a recent example of

'The Branches of Time' by David R. Daniels, Wonder Stories *August 1935. Illustration by Paul.*

02.10 TIME AND NTH DIMENSIONS

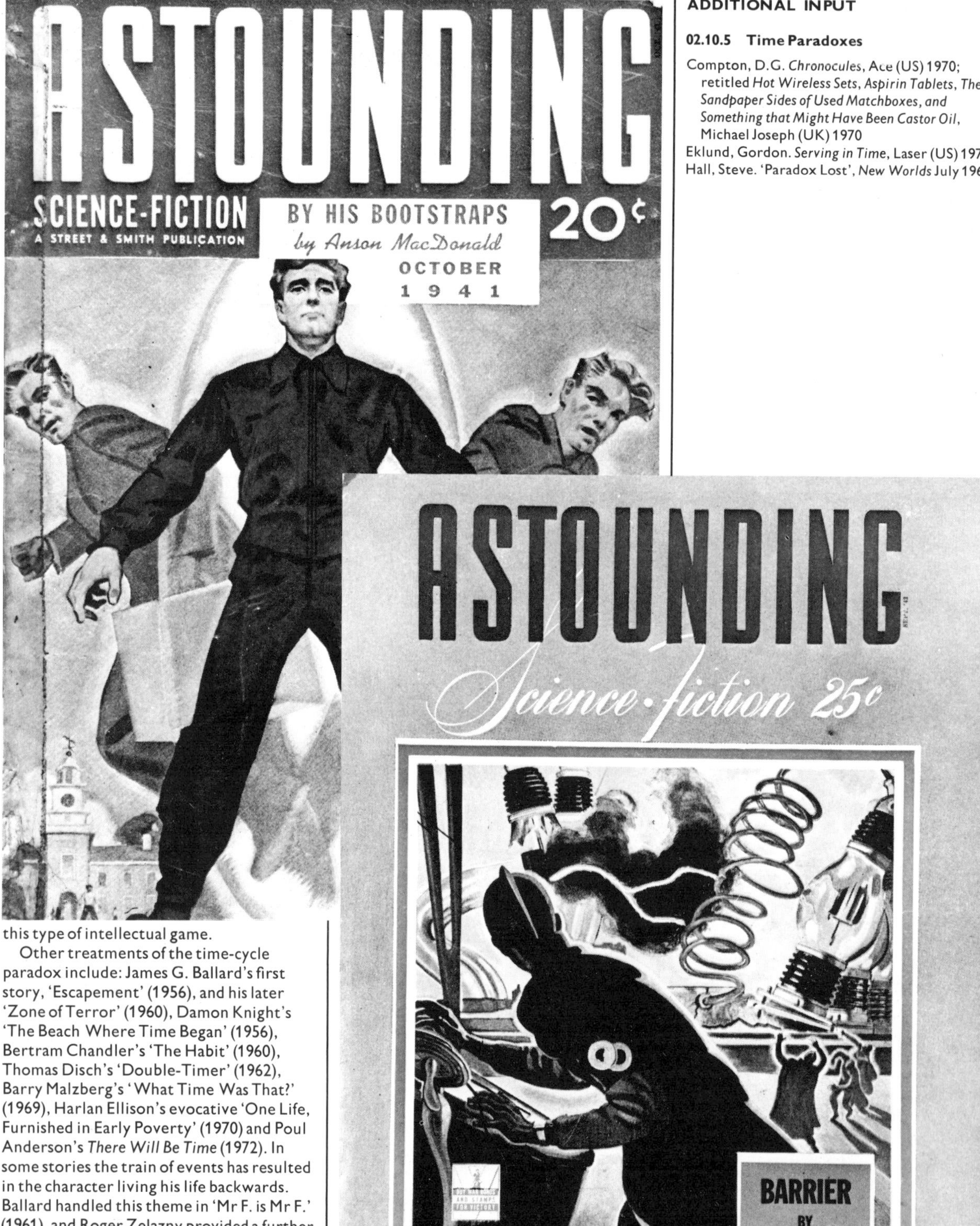

'By His Bootstraps' by Anson MacDonald (Robert A. Heinlein) October 1941. Cover by Rogers. 'Barrier' by Anthony Boucher, September 1942. Cover by Timmins.

this type of intellectual game.

Other treatments of the time-cycle paradox include: James G. Ballard's first story, 'Escapement' (1956), and his later 'Zone of Terror' (1960), Damon Knight's 'The Beach Where Time Began' (1956), Bertram Chandler's 'The Habit' (1960), Thomas Disch's 'Double-Timer' (1962), Barry Malzberg's 'What Time Was That?' (1969), Harlan Ellison's evocative 'One Life, Furnished in Early Poverty' (1970) and Poul Anderson's *There Will Be Time* (1972). In some stories the train of events has resulted in the character living his life backwards. Ballard handled this theme in 'Mr F. is Mr F.' (1961), and Roger Zelazny provided a further variation in 'Divine Madness' (1966). Alex and Phyllis Eisenstein's 'The Trouble with the Past' (1971) and Philip K. Dick's 'A Little Something for Us Tempunauts' (1974) continue the development of the time-cycle theme. Dick has also written a typically idiosyncratic time treatment in *Counter Clock World* (1967), where almost everything begins to run backwards.

ADDITIONAL INPUT

02.10.5 Time Paradoxes

Compton, D.G. *Chronocules*, Ace (US) 1970; retitled *Hot Wireless Sets, Aspirin Tablets, The Sandpaper Sides of Used Matchboxes, and Something that Might Have Been Castor Oil*, Michael Joseph (UK) 1970

Eklund, Gordon. *Serving in Time*, Laser (US) 1975

Hall, Steve. 'Paradox Lost', *New Worlds* July 1962

02.10.6 When Time Stands Still

A small sub-category of time stories deals less with the movement of time than with its complete abolition – a picture of the world in a state of approaching or final stasis. Nevertheless, the central characters in such tales are often able to act at will. H. G. Wells initiated the theme with 'The New Accelerator' (1901), in which he depicts a drug-induced speeding up of the normal human metabolism which has alarming results. Miles J. Breuer's 'Mr Dimmitt Seeks Redress' (1936) employs a similar technique.

Other relatively early treatments include Bradner Buckner's 'The Day Time Stopped Moving' (1940) and Henry Hasse's 'The Missing Day' (1942), while Joel Townsley Rogers's 'Moment without Time' (1952) and Arthur C. Clarke's 'All the Time in the World' (1952) further add to the idea. George Langelaan's 'Past the Time Limit' (1964) and R. A. Lafferty's 'The Six Fingers of Time' (1960) are among more recent offerings.

Stories showing the entire Earth in stasis are less common in the genre, probably because they require some skill in presentation. Of the few writers who have succeeded in this area, Ballard occupies a front-rank position. His 'The Voices of Time' (1960) illustrates a personal interpretation of the universal decay decreed by the Second Law of Thermodynamics, as expressed in terms of time. *The Crystal World* (1966), on the other hand, tells of the slow immobilisation of all organic life as a result of the depletion of the cosmic time-store, through the collision between matter and anti-matter.

'All the Time in the World' by Arthur C. Clarke, Startling *July 1952. Illustration by Dreanys.*

02.10.7 Further Dimensions

While, more often than not, time is referred to as the fourth dimension, other less familiar dimensions have also been explored in science fiction. Occasionally a writer has depicted life in a world of fewer planes than our own – no easy task. An early classic, and still probably the best remembered, was *Flatland: a Romance of Many Dimensions* (1884) by the mathematician Edwin Abbott. Nearly fifty years later Wallace West pursued the idea in 'Plane People' (1933), where a catastrophe on Earth forces an escape flight to a two-dimensional planet.

In the search for seemingly scientific explanations for certain short-cuts through space and time, a great many writers have hit upon the concept of the Möbius strip, first expounded by the German mathematician August Möbius in the seventeenth century. (If a strip of paper is given a single twist and the two ends joined, the result is a length of material with only one side! A line traced along this surface will eventually arrive back at its starting point; but its half-way point is only separated from the starting point by the thickness of the paper. In such a situation the quickest way to move between these two points is to plough straight through, in preference to completing the trip. Such a concept is better demonstrated than explained. It is a simple experiment.) In A. J. Deutsch's 'A Subway Named Möbius' (1950), a section of the Boston subway disappears into just such an extra-spatial limbo. Heinlein performed similar sleights of hand in '"–And He Built a Crooked House"' (1941), depicting a dwelling designed in the form of a four-dimensional tesseract, with confusing consequences for the occupants; but he was far from the first to explore such topics.

As early as 1922, David Lindsay had portrayed in *The Haunted Woman* a stairway which crossed dimensions, to lead whoever ascended it into a timeless room. An even more far-fetched trans-dimensional approach was adopted by Kurt Vonnegut when he introduced an unlikely space-warp as a major plot factor in *The Sirens of Titan* (1959). One of his leading characters unwittingly directs his spaceship into an 'uncharted chronosynclastic infundibulum'; as a result he is permanently extended in time and space along a helix spiralling between the Earth's sun and the distant star Betelgeuse.

Other experiments in dimensional distortions can be found in Alan E. Nourse's 'Tiger by the Tail' (1951), which features a bag that is apparently bottomless, in Bertram Chandler's 'The Pool' (1957), and in 'The Bottomless Pool' (1939) by Ralph Milne Farley and Robert Bloch.

Another variation on the theme of bottomless pits appears in Thomas Disch's 'Descending' (1964), where a man finds himself marooned on an interminable escalator. Similarly, Langdon Jones's hero of 'Stormwater Tunnel' (1964) enters the void in response to a cry of distress, only to discover that – in the absence of an exit – it is he who has been calling for help. Such stories can be seen as further variations on the general idea of the Möbius strip. Arthur C. Clarke's 'The Wall of Darkness' (1949) belongs in the same category. In a slightly earlier entertainment, Clarke suggested the even more alarming outcome of a brush with the fourth dimension. In an accident at a generating station, a man is revolved

'–And He Built a Crooked House' by Robert A. Heinlein. Illustration by Bear.

ADDITIONAL INPUT

02.10.6 When Time Stands Still

Buckner, Bradner (Ed Earl Repp). 'The Day Time Stopped Moving', *Amazing* October 1940
Gardner, Erle Stanley. 'A Year in a Day', *Argosy* (US) July 1935
Grosser, E.A. 'Time Exposure', *Future combined with Science Fiction* August 1942

02.11 TECHNOLOGIES AND ARTEFACTS

briefly through space to emerge as a mirror image of his original self. Unhappily for him, the hungry sufferer of 'Technical Error' (1946) can only digest food which has been similarly reversed.

In a final exposition on further dimensions, the topic of invisibility rightly occupies a place of its own. In his classic story *The Invisible Man* (1897), Wells described the discovery by a potentially megalomaniacal scientist of a chemical which withdrew organic material from the sight of men. In so doing he was perfectly well aware that a *completely* invisible man would also be *blind* – the retina at the eye's rear could hardly register light rays unless it was also able to reflect them. This was a piece of scientific information which Wells knowingly omitted from his tale – a convenient device in the light of the parable he was to propound so effectively.

Other writers have attempted to overcome the problem of retinal malfunction by creating genuinely invisible beings, showing them as existing in a different dimension from normal space. Thomas Disch handles the idea with some distinction in *Echo Round His Bones* (1966), telling of a fourth-dimensional man created as an 'echo effect' when his ordinary self is transported through a matter transmitter.

In the eyes of many commentators, it has been accepted that science fiction should develop the theme of invisibility by using 'alien' terms. In such a way, a scientifically implausible subject can achieve some measure of respectability, the idea being that alien science needs no explanation in terrestrial terms. Thus the emotion-sucking globes of Eric Frank Russell's *Sinister Barrier* (1939) and the menacing entity which invades the starship of A. E. van Vogt's *The Voyage of the Space Beagle* (1950) confronts the reader with entertaining propositions, but remain improbable. In the same class are the monstrous presences which invade the tranquil English countryside in Brian W. Aldiss's *The Saliva Tree* (1965), to reap a harvest that includes its human inhabitants. The tale was written partly in celebration of the centenary of H. G. Wells, the man who, more than most others, laid out the vistas of time travel and invisibility for subsequent writers of science fiction. It is clear that the intellectual teasers involving other dimensions will retain their popularity, and the element of fun shows little sign of diminishing.

ADDITIONAL INPUT

02.10.7 Further Dimensions

Kapp, Colin. 'Lambda 1', *New Worlds* December 1962

MacApp, C.C. (Carroll M. Capps). 'Beyond the Ebon Wall', *Fantastic* October 1964; expanded as *Worlds of the Wall*, Avon (US) 1969

Simak, Clifford D. 'The Big Front Yard', *Astounding* October 1958

Walton, Harry. 'Housing Shortage', *Astounding* January 1947

The technophile attitudes – often held with a fervency akin to religious fanatacism – of most early science fiction must strike the apprehensive citizen of the modern world as strange, not to say naïve. In those days science might be distant and semi-magical; technology was the tool that would bring the marvels of scientific discovery to be the breadwinner and salvation of all mankind. Nowadays technophobia is the fashionable attitude.

To the generations born in the shadow of the Bomb, bombarded by all the familiar ills of the present – a dismal catalogue of pollution, overpopulation and all the rest – the hope extended by the marvels and mysteries of science through technology must inevitably appear evanescent, the reality hostile, frightening and ultimately evil.

In science fiction the word technology is generally used in connection with terrestrial artefacts. The word artefact with its much more sinister ring is generally applied to extraterrestrials. It is interesting to note that artefact is usually spelled artifact in science fiction for all-too obvious reasons, and many and wonderful have been the alien artefacts dug up, discovered drifting in space, or falling to Earth. The hard bustle of Solterran technology contrasts forcefully with the romance and mystery of weird alien artefacts on abandoned worlds orbiting chill and distant stars.

The recently discovered stars that emit one or two second bursts of X-ray radiation at intervals varying from ten minutes to several hours are clearly, in an sf interpretation, manifestations of alien technology, being the equivalent of lighthouses, studding the galaxy with guides to the interstellar spacelanes, keeping the starships on safe courses.

The technologies of science fiction exist in the imagination; but the labour of artists to bring pictorial realisation to these dreams is a long and honourable one – mainly in the sf magazines – and is a fecund field for research and enjoyment.

In many respects the highest levels of civilised attainments have been reached in slave-owning cultures – Classical Greece being the pre-eminent example. Science fiction looked constantly to the use of technology to replace slaves by machines. But the same selfish prejudiced outlook of the slave-owners persisted in power and resulted in the misuse of technology. Governments distrusted scientists and technocrats because of the feeling that their knowledge would remove power from the traditional ruling classes. Present problems can only be overcome by massive sacrifices on a worldwide scale and by the application of a mature and responsible technology that will rectify the mistakes of the past and ensure the future will be as the non-dystopian science fiction visualised it. There is no way back save through worldwide catastrophe. By this stage in human evolution there must be a threeway division of effort and belief; human, machine and nature must work together or Solterra is doomed.

Religious beliefs apart, Art, Science and the Love of Life are the three great reasons why *Homo sapiens* exists in the galaxy at all. Science works through technology which can enable Art to reveal the Love of Life to us all.

Ken Bulmer

Kenneth Bulmer

02.11 TECHNOLOGIES AND ARTEFACTS

Technological developments of the future have been a major concern of science fiction since the birth of the genre. Indeed, the very name 'science fiction' implies a preoccupation with science and technolgy, something that was foremost in Hugo Gernsback's mind when he coined the term 'scientifiction' in 1926.

The technologies developed by man in science fiction fall into three basic categories, transportation, energy and communication – with several subsidiary groupings.

02.11.1 Earth Technologies: Transportation

Since sf stories have very often been set in space or on other planets, one of the primary requisites of a story is a method of travel away from Earth. As in any other area of technological forecast, writers usually based their extrapolations on existing scientific knowledge, especially so in the case of Jules Verne. However, such early speculative tales as the 'Voyage to the Moon' stories of Lucian of Samosata and Cyrano de Bergerac used methods of travel that hardly qualify as technology by modern standards (i.e. being hurled into space by a waterspout or filling bottles with dew to rise with the sun). But it could be argued that these were at least in keeping with the limited scientific knowledge available at the time they were written. In the same way, the wings built by Daedalus in the Greek myth of Icarus were, while of a highly improbable construction, a genuine, if unworkable, extrapolation.

'Waldo' by Anson MacDonald, (Heinlein) Astounding *August 1942. Cover by Rogers.*

As science progressed, so did the technological ideas in science fiction, constantly being built upon new knowledge. In *From the Earth to the Moon* (1865), Verne employed a giant cannon to launch his Moon-bound adventurers from the Earth, an idea not far removed from the principles of modern rocketry. In the classic space opera, *The Skylark of Space* (1928) by E. E. Smith, the leading character accidentally discovers a process for the total conversion of matter to energy – a process somewhat akin to nuclear fission.

Generally, spacecraft are powered by chemical fuels or by an atomic-power plant, for travel within the solar system. In the case of travel between stars, however, the distances involved are so great that a new form of travel is necessary to permit practical travel times (i.e. weeks or months instead of decades or centuries). Faster-than-light speeds are the obvious answer, achieved by spectacularly powerful propulsion devices.

Many writers have subscribed to Einstein's view that the speed of light cannot be exceeded, and thus have been

'Tyrann' by Isaac Asimov, Galaxy *January 1951. Cover by Bunch.*

obliged to develop a method of traversing vast distances instantaneously. Usually, this involved entering into what was vaguely described as 'hyper-space', or another dimension, as in Isaac Asimov's *The Stars, Like Dust* (1950).

There are some instances where rapid travel between stars might be unnecessary, and here writers used devices more within reach of present-day technology. In *Time for the Stars* (1956), Robert A. Heinlein utilised spacecraft travelling under constant acceleration approaching the speed of light. The craft, called 'torch-ships', used matter-converters to convert water (or other suitable liquids) to hard radiation and neutrons. These products were spewed out at the speed of light to propel the ships. A form of ram-jet was used in 'Rammer' (1971) by Larry Niven. In interstellar travel, a giant electromagnetic field caught, compressed, and burned hydrogen to provide thrust.

Matter transmission suggested another way of traversing long distances, from point to point on Earth as well as between planets. Described in various ways, matter transmission is basically a process of breaking down an object or being into its component atoms, transmitting them by radio, and reassembling them at another point, reproducing the original atomic pattern of whatever was transmitted. These stories are such an integral part of sf thematics that they warrant a separate analysis, which is given below.

Point-to-point travel on Earth by short-range atmospheric rockets was used by many authors, among them Heinlein in such stories as 'If This Goes On–' (1940). For personal transportation, writers envisaged air-cars in numerous forms, including helicopters, hovercraft, small rockets and 'gyrocopters'. In 'If This Goes On–' Heinlein adds a note of realism with his reference to a 'Ford family skycar'.

Walking, as such, was eliminated by a form of travelling platform in H. G. Wells's 'A Story of the Days to Come' (1897); and 'slidewalks' – moving strips of pavement travelling at varying speeds in the same direction – were featured in such stories as 'Seeker of Tomorrow' (1937) by Eric Frank Russell and Leslie J. Johnson. Also known as 'beltways' or 'pedwalks' – as depicted in 'Flatlander' (1971) by Larry Niven – these consist of a moving belt upon which the rider stands. Isaac Asimov employed the same device in *The Caves of Steel* (1954), while a unique variety of slidewalk was created by Robert A. Heinlein in 'The Roads Must Roll' (1940). The story is built around Road Cities, which were giant slidewalks designed to carry freight and travellers between various regions of the United States.

A further direction of transportation is downwards, through the Earth's crust. Many of the sf stories in this category have basically been variations on the Lost World theme. In very early stories penetration underground was often achieved through polar openings, and the protagonists simply descended (or fell) through them. More modern writers clearly could not use such fanciful devices, and it became necessary for them to invent a technology capable of carrying their characters down into and through the Earth itself. One of the best-known treatments was Edgar Rice Burroughs's *At the Earth's Core* (1922), telling of an inventor who has perfected a 'mechanical subterranean prospector'. The vehicle, also known as an iron mole, represented a cross between a tank and a submarine, with a downward-pointing drill. It was used to bore freely through the Earth's crust in a search for mineral deposits (at least such was its initial intent).

'The Alibi Machine' by Larry Niven, Vertex June 1973. Illustration by Monte Rogers.

The idea was borrowed and its technology improved upon in John Russell Fearn's 'Through the Earth's Core' (1938), and in his later novel (writing as Volsted Gridban), *A Thing of the Past* (1953). But perhaps the most ingenious of all such stories was Murray Leinster's 'The Mole Pirate' (1934), in which the vehicle is driven through the atomic interstices of matter itself.

According to the researches of Sam Moskowitz, the first recorded use of a matter transmitter was in Edward Page Mitchell's 'The Man without a Body' (1877), where a scientist invents a machine which breaks down the atoms of a cat and transmits them by wire to the receiver, where the animal is reassembled alive and well. He tries it upon himself, but the battery dries up before he can transmit more than just his head. The story is reminiscent of 'The Fly' (1957) by George Langelaan, where in the course of an experiment with a matter transmitter the presence of a fly results in a man re-materialising with a fly's head.

One of the earliest uses of the matter transmitter for interplanetary travel occurs in *To Venus in Five Seconds* (1897) by Fred T. Jane, the hero being abducted by an alien female and brought to her home planet by such means. Coincidentally, it was Venus that was also the destination of the central character in a series of adventures written by Ralph Milne Farley, beginning with *The Radio Man* (1924).

Another pioneering effort of matter transmission, Earthbound in this case, was Guillaume Appollinaire's 'Remote Projection' (1910). It tells of an inventor who finds he can transmit himself anywhere with his two tiny machines, and still retain his original body. It is a process of both matter transmission and duplication, and when the man dies 841 identical corpses are found in the places to which he travelled.

The connection between matter transmission and radio, as depicted in the Farley series, naturally appealed to Hugo Gernsback, one of the pioneers of radio and television and publisher of *Radio News*. It was hardly surprising, then, that the adventurous Dr Hackensaw of Clement Fezandie's series in that publication would invent some form of matter transmission – the discovery came in the episode 'The Secret of Electrical Transmission' (1922). Gernsback had earlier discussed the possibilities of sending food by wireless in 'Wireless on Mars' (1909). In *Amazing* he was to publish Benjamin Witwer's 'Radio Mates' (1927), which involved 'etheric transmigration', a typically pseudo-technical term of the early days. Other early uses of interplanetary matter transmission were featured in Edmond Hamilton's 'The Moon Menace' (1927) and Jack Williamson's 'Cosmic Express' (1930). In all these stories, however, matter transmission seems merely a means to an end, and it would have made little difference to the plot if the journey had been made by a more conventional sf method.

In recent years, more thought has gone into the effects of matter transmission, and in particular into what might occur if things should go wrong. Eric Frank Russell utilised such transmitters in 'U Turn' (1950), in which people who have applied for euthanasia find themselves used as guinea pigs for test transmissions. Lan Wright brought humour to the theme in 'Transmat' (1960), telling how more items come out of the transmitter than were put into it.

The turning point in matter transmission stories came with Algis Budrys' *Rogue Moon* (1960), a tour de force on several levels that takes a deep look at the psychological implications of early testing of matter transmission to the Moon. In Budry's system, the original human stays on Earth and the receiver forms a duplicate on the Moon, with a mental link connecting the two.

Other problems were explored in two subsequent novels, *All the Colours of Darkness* (1963) by Lloyd Biggle Jr and *Echo Round His Bones* (1966) by Thomas M. Disch. In Biggle's novel, aliens object to man's invasion of space by matter transmitters and begin to divert the radio waves. *Echo Round His Bones* features the phenomenon of an echo effect which leaves a fourth-dimensional form of a man on Earth when his real body is transmitted to Mars.

Jack Wodhams and Larry Niven have both considered the criminal applications of matter transmission, in 'There Is a Crooked Man' (1967) and 'The Alibi Machine' (1973) respectively. In *Goblin Reservation* (1968), Clifford Simak relates the problems involved when an error in transmission results in the appearance of twin visions of the same man, especially when the first to return is killed. The second finds he theoretically doesn't exist.

Simak had used matter transmitters in his earlier novel *Way Station* (1963), where a recluse farmer becomes the custodian of one station in a relay of alien matter transmitters. This, of course, involved matter transmission between star systems, an area also featured in Kenneth Bulmer's *Behold the Stars* (1965), which suggested how man might venture into deep space by such a method. The notion that aliens may already have matter transmission and will ultimately bestow it on man is the basis for Duncan Lunan's 'Interface' series that began with 'The Moon of Thin Reality' (1970).

While in Larry Niven's *Ringworld* (1970), matter transmitters are taken for granted and form just part of everyday life, in more recent stories he has explored the use of transmitters more deeply. 'Flash Crowd' (1973) describes some of the social perils that may follow instantaneous travel, and 'All the Bridges Rusting' (1973) looks further at the confusion likely to be caused when matter transmission is employed concurrently with starships. Harry Harrison has also investigated the implications of this form of travel, in several stories that make up his collection *One Step from Earth* (1972).

Finally, Stephen Robinett (writing as Tak Hallus) has recently produced a series based on the introduction of matter transmitters. The stories culminated in a novel, *Stargate* (1974), which explores the misuse of such relays in space.

ADDITIONAL INPUT

02.11.1 Earth Technologies: Transportation

Anderson, Poul. 'Door to Anywhere', *Galaxy* December 1966

Bulmer, Kenneth. *Behold the Stars*, Ace (US) 1965

Dick, Philip K. *The Unteleported Man*, *Fantastic* December 1964; Ace (US) 1966

McDermot, Murtagh. *A Trip to the Moon*, (UK) 1728

Scheer, George H. 'Beam Transmission', *Amazing* July 1934

Sheckley, Robert (as Finn O'Donnevan). 'Trap', *Galaxy* February 1956

02.11 TECHNOLOGIES AND ARTEFACTS

'The Man with the Four Dimensional Eyes' by Leslie F. Stone, Wonder Stories *August 1935. Illustration by Marchioni.*

02.11.2 Energy

As might be expected, sf writers foresaw the need for alternative energy sources while the rest of the world was still regarding fossil fuels as an inexhaustible power source. In projecting the vast technologies of the future, they also took into consideration the fact that oil and coal were not in infinite supply, and that what would remain of these fuels in future would be neither sufficient nor workable.

Solar energy has often been evoked by sf writers, though the methods of harnessing it are rarely detailed. In 'Let There Be Light' (1950), however, Robert A. Heinlein explains a method for the direct conversion of sunlight to energy. The device used is a crystal which vibrates at the frequency of visible light. When an electrical current is applied, light is emitted. It transpires that it is a two-way process – the crystal also generates an electric current when light strikes it.

The use of atomic energy presented a more varied line of plot developments. It was once the dream of some sf writers that with the harnessing of atomic power, the unlimited energy produced would free the world of many of its problems. Others, such as Charles Willard Diffin in his 'The Power and the Glory' (1930), approached the matter with more perception and warned of the dangers it might present. Ever since H. G. Wells produced *The World Set Free* (1913), science fiction had carried its share of atomic-doom stories in addition to tales of atomic-powered utopias. Other writers used the idea of atomic power merely as a prop to describe mysterious energy-producing systems.

In such stories as 'Blowups Happen' (1940) by Robert A. Heinlein, atomic energy is better described. Here, Heinlein gives the reader a good idea of the layout of an atomic-power plant – and of the stresses and tension that working there can bring. Lester del Rey's 'Nerves' (1942) also describes a similar installation, and the fear it can generate among the populace when something goes wrong. As early as October 1939, with Europe just plunged into war, *Amazing Stories* published a full-colour illustration of an atomic-power station with suitable annotations regarding the perils misusing the energy it could liberate.

Another energy concept to appear fairly frequently in science fiction is that of transmitting power by microwave, without wires. It is usually referred to as 'broadcast power', or, as in Heinlein's 'Waldo' (1940), 'radiant power'. In 'The Man Who Sold the Moon' (1949), Heinlein combines atomic power with broadcast power in the form of a 'Power Satellite' containing an atomic pile, the power generated being transmitted to Earth. An amazingly detailed system for transmitting power via microwaves is described in George O. Smith's 'Lost Art' (1943). In that story, two Earthmen discover a long-dead Martian civilisation which had known the secret of power transmission.

ADDITIONAL INPUT

02.11.2 Energy

Cross, Polton (J.R. Fearn). 'Twilight Planet', *Thrilling Wonder* Summer 1946

Tubb, E.C. *The Mutants Rebel*, Hamilton (UK) 1953

Vincent, Harl (H.V. Schoepflin). 'Free Energy', *Amazing* September 1930

Von Hanstein, Otfrid. 'Utopia Island', *Wonder* May 1931

The Skylark of Space *by E. E. ('Doc') Smith,* Amazing *August 1928. Cover by Paul.*

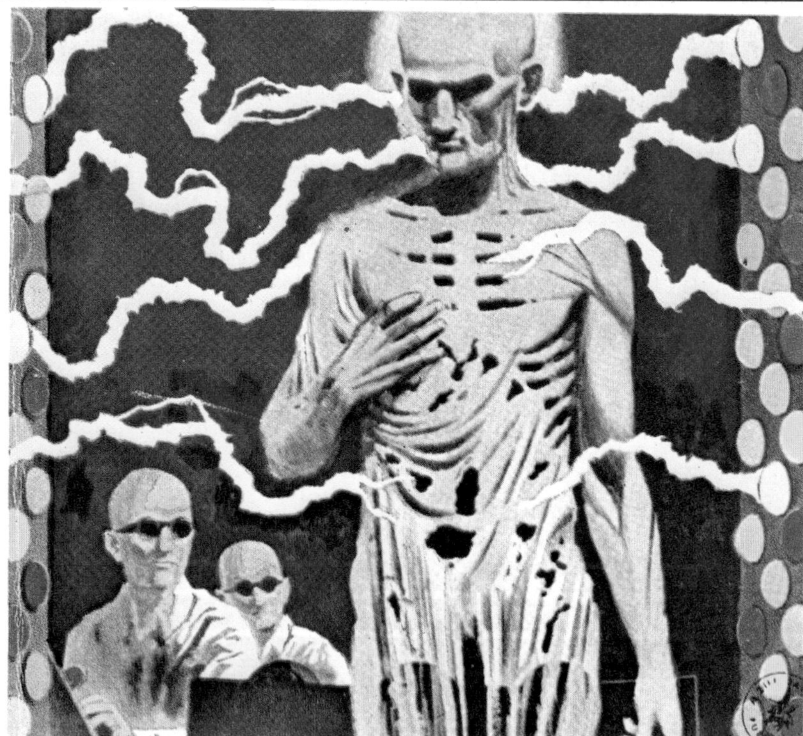

'The Unteleported Man' by Philip K. Dick, Fantastic *December 1964. Cover by Birmingham.*

02.11.3 Communication

Whenever a list is compiled of the 'predictions' made in science fiction, television is inevitably included. Though Hugo Gernsback was preceded in his use of the word by several others (as early as 1895), he was arguably the one most responsible for putting the term into public use. 'Television' was introduced to the American public in an article on pioneer German experiments with photo transmission, entitled 'Television and the Telephot' in *Modern Electrics* in 1909. In the same magazine, two years later, Gernsback serialised his novel *Ralph 124C41+*. Although both writing and plot are now considered naïve, the technological forecasts in the novel are remarkable. They include: fluorescent lighting, skywriting, automatic packaging machines, plastics, the radio-directional range-finder, juke-boxes, liquid fertiliser, hydroponics, tape recorders, rustproof steel, loudspeakers, night baseball, aquacades, microfilm, television, radio networks, vending machines dispensing hot and cold foods and liquids, a teaching device for operation while the user is asleep, solar energy for heat and power, fabrics from glass, synthetic materials such as nylon for wearing apparel, and an inspired description and diagramming of radar.

More recently, a striking future use of television was recounted by Ray Bradbury in *Farenheit 451* (1950). One of the fixtures of daily life in the story is the 'Wall circuit' – a wall-to-wall television set for which teleplays are specially conceived to include the viewer as part of the plot. In the same work, 'Seashells' – miniature radios worn in the ear – are another common convenience. Television is also employed, in a grim fashion, in George Orwell's *Nineteen Eighty-four* (1949), where it is shown as a means of keeping the citizens of a police state under constant observation.

The visiphone (also videophone, televisor, etc) is a very popular communications device. Essentially, a two-way television system, it is used in countless stories, casually added as background material. It plays a more important role in Asimov's *The Naked Sun* (1957) where the colonists of an outer world refuse personal contact with each other.

It is interesting to note that the concept of television/radio relay satellites placed in synchronous Earth orbit (as they are now) was originated by a science fiction writer. Arthur C. Clarke depicted such a system in his story 'Special Delivery' (1957), but first presented the concept in a paper titled 'Extra Terrestrial Relays' in 1945.

Television has also been variously described as a substitute for portholes in spaceships, as a method of exploring hostile planets, and as a source of entertainment. Jack Williamson's 'The Cosmic Express' (1930) produced the accurate prediction that Westerns would occupy much TV time, and a more remarkable prediction of television usage was 'Eclipse Bears Witness' (1940) by 'Ephriam Winiki' (a pseudonym adopted by J. R. Fearn). The story opens with a rocket plane travelling in the almost airless heights of 100 miles or so above the earth, moving at 1500 miles an hour. It keeps pace with the umbra of the Moon's shadow and televises back to Earth a record of a total solar eclipse lasting for two hours. (Exactly the same experiment was carried out by scientists flying in a Concorde jet nearly a quarter of a century later.)

Fahrenheit 451 *by Ray Bradbury (Ballantine). Cover by Whistlin' Dixie Studio.*

ADDITIONAL INPUT

02.11.3 Communication

Aldiss, Brian W. 'Total Environment', *Galaxy* February 1968

Asimov, Isaac. 'The Naked Sun', *Astounding* October to December 1956; Doubleday (US) 1957

Attanasio, A.A. 'Interface', *Epoch* (ed Robert Silverberg and Roger Elwood) Putmans (US) 1975

McLociard, George. 'Television Hill', *Amazing* February to March 1931

Stover, Leon E. 'What We Have Here is Too Much Communication', *Orbit 9* (ed Damon Knight) Putnam (US) 1971

Sturgeon, Theodore. 'Ether Breather', *Astounding* September 1939; sequel 'Butyl and the Breather', *Astounding* October 1940

02.11 TECHNOLOGIES AND ARTEFACTS

02.11.4 Other Areas of Earth Technology

Secondary to the subjects already reviewed, medical technology was, perhaps, the most often examined area of future development. Some physical way to immortality was a frequent theme, and one covered extensively in Robert A. Heinlein's recent book, *Time Enough for Love* (1973), wherein immortality is achieved by a series of regular 'Treatments', sometimes including cloning.

Suspended animation is seen as a method of outliving one's contemporaries, and so achieving a kind of immortality. Many of the earlier stories on the suspended-animation theme described characters who simply slept their way into the future, as in 'Rip Van Winkle' (1829) by Washington Irving and *Looking Backward* (1888) by Edward Bellamy. Other such classics include *When the Sleeper Wakes* (1899) by H. G. Wells, and *Darkness and Dawn* (1912) by George Allan England. *Phra the Phoenician* (1890) and *Valdar the Oft-Born* (1895) by George Griffith exploited the legend that heroes of the past lie in wait to be resurrected when their country needs them.

By the 1920s the concept of suspended animation was well established as serious sf technology, and the term itself gained currency. It was used by Clement Fezandie for the third story in his 'Dr Hackensaw' series, 'The Secret of Suspended Animation' (1921). Considerable medical theory was worked into the background of Abner J. Gelula's 'Hibernation' (1933). In this story, a technocratic government 'disposes' of the millions of unemployed resulting from widespread automation by placing them in suspended animation. Each passing year finds several more millions 'on the shelf'.

Gelula introduced chemical injections as the method used in his story, but thereafter sf writers increasingly turned to the application of cryogenics to achieve suspended animation. The idea that low temperatures could preserve organic matter goes back at least as far as Francis Bacon, who died testing the hypothesis in 1626 – he had caught pneumonia while stuffing a chicken with snow.

By 1940 the concept of freezing was so well established that *Amazing Stories* produced a special feature article, 'Suspended Animation' by Henry Gade (a pseudonym of editor Ray Palmer). In it he speculated that the sanatorium of tomorrow may be nothing more than a giant refrigerator. At that time experiments in fighting cancer and heart disease had already involved medical scientists freezing human tissue, employing ice packs to lower body temperature to around 89°F.

Not long afterwards, Don Wilcox's suspended-animation story 'The Voyage That Lasted 600 Years' (1940) appeared in the same magazine. Wilcox anticipated both Heinlein's 'Universe' (1941), in depicting cultural breakdown among successive space-born generations, and van Vogt's ironical 'Far Centaurus' (1944), in which colonists reach their goal to find that a faster ship has overtaken them. Wilcox also proposed refrigeration plants for the use of a hierarchy which would maintain continuity of purpose and traditions by periodically being revived.

The publication of Robert C. Ettinger's *The Prospect of Immortality* (1963) generated public interest in the theme. Basically he was arguing what Ray Palmer had already suggested, but the book was addressed to a far wider readership. Its success led the author to promote the idea on radio and television, and in further writings for national magazines under such titles as 'New Hope for the Frozen Dead' (1966). The result was the founding of an actual Cryonics Society in America, enabling members to arrange for preservations of their bodies after death in the hope that they could be revived in the future when medical techniques were sufficiently advanced to achieve their resurrection, and to cure them of whatever had killed them.

The theme of suspended animation in science fiction, however, owes little to the influence of Ettinger and explores many reasons for the technique. Roger Zelazny's 'The Graveyard Heart' (1964) tells of a hedonistic élite flitting across time for short stays in different eras in a selfish search for self-fulfilment – until one man tires of his ersatz immortality. A similar presentation, with added speculation on cyborgs, was Thomas N. Disch's 'The Sightseers' (1965). John Wyndham's last published story, 'A Life Postponed' (1968), narrates how a man undergoes freezing to escape from his wife, only to have her follow him by the same process. Robert A. Heinlein had earlier used the idea in *The Door into Summer* (1956), as a method of disposing of one's enemies.

Some writers considered the criminal possibilities. Dan Morgan's 'Frozen Assets' (1969) described how freezing and later revival could be used to exploit the Statute of Limitations. Even more disconcerting is the idea behind Larry Niven's 'Rammer' (1971), in which people who take the 'long Sleep' are *not* awakened to be cured or welcomed into a utopian future world. Their useless bodies are destroyed and their personalities impressed on the minds of condemned criminals.

The technology of medical treatment in the future was graphically illustrated in 'The Little Black Bag' by C. M. Kornbluth

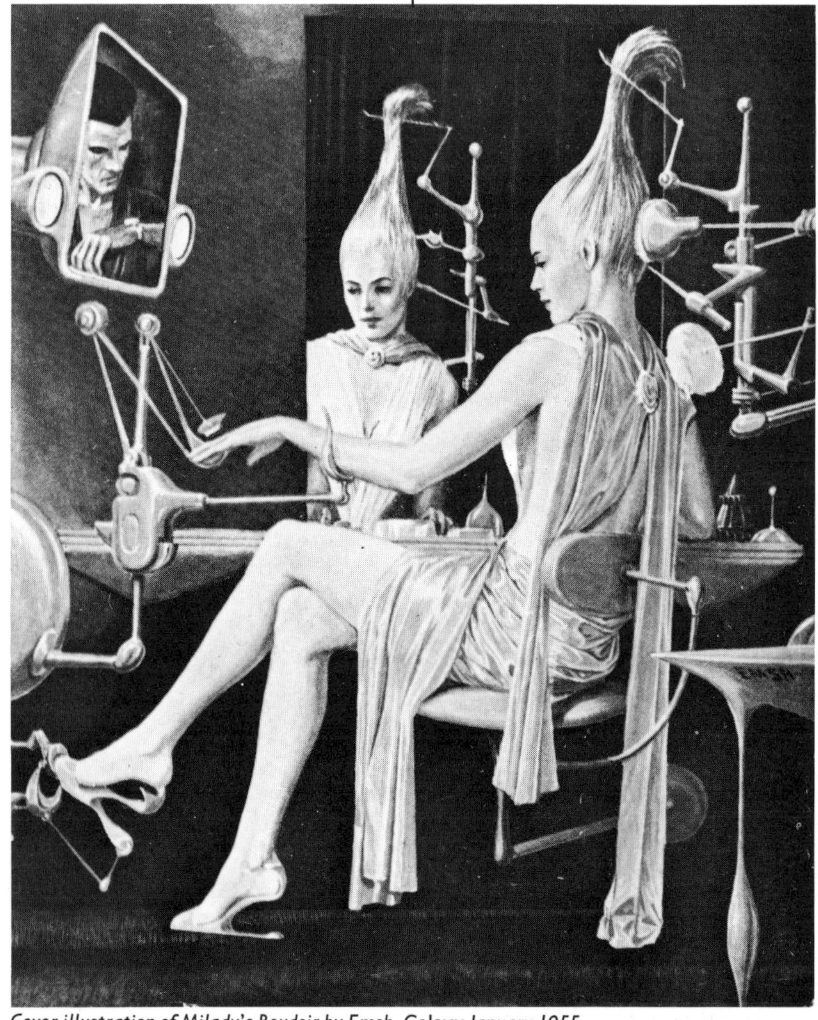
Cover illustration of Milady's Boudoir by Emsh, Galaxy *January 1955.*

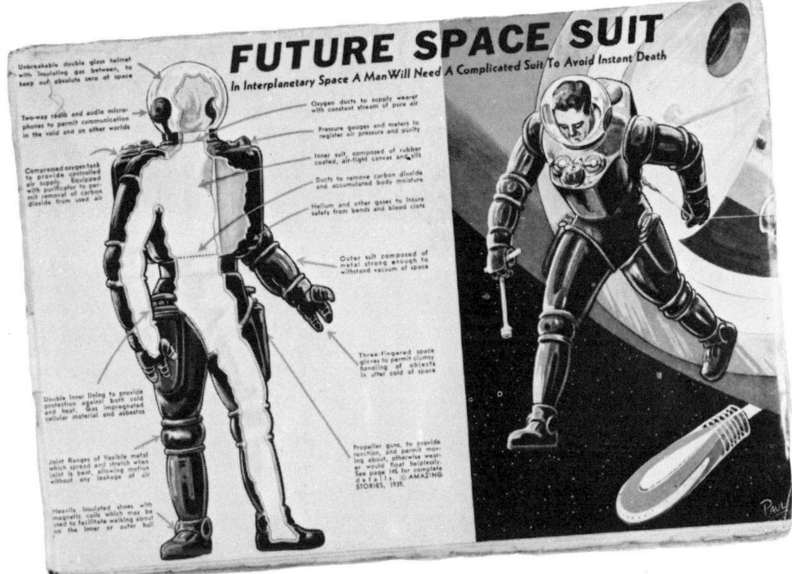

Space Suit as visualised by Paul in Amazing *June 1939.*

(1950), where mental subnormals constituting the majority of the world's population are 'kept' by a minority of humans of high intelligence. In order to preserve technology and maintain the population, the supernormals have devised a plethora of gadgets easily operated by moronic minds. Among these is a medical kit containing diagnostic and surgical tools and medications with which to treat any illness or emergency, complete with instructions that a child could follow.

Medical stories set beyond Earth, but still featuring Earth technology, include 'The Grandfathers' War' (1957), 'Med Ship Man' (1963) and 'The Hate Disease' (1963), three novelettes by Murray Leinster in which he told of the Interstellar Medical Service. The focus of the stories was a medical ship serving the needs of various planets, and many items of medical technology were catalogued. Medical monitoring equipment was also one of the subjects covered in 'Scanners Live in Vain' (1948) by Cordwainer Smith.

Another area of Earth technology which has long fascinated sf writers is the field of machine servo-mechanisms, most particularly robots and computers. The play *R.U.R.* (1921) by Karel Čapek was one of the first science fiction works to deal with robots, and was actually the source of the name 'robot'. (Čapek's robots would now be called androids.) Isaac Asimov's *I, Robot* (1950) – a collection of related short stories – is a more detailed look at robots, their applications, development and psychology. In both works, robots are seen as the servants of man, mainly performing tasks in environments hostile to humans, or undertaking work that is disliked by men.

'Sunjammer' by Winston P. Sanders, Analog *April 1964. Cover by Woolhiser.*

For the most part, computers have occupied an incidental place in science fiction. Among the exceptions is the rebellious computer in the movie *2001: a Space Odyssey* (1968), developed from Arthur C. Clarke's short story, 'The Sentinel' (1951). The intelligent computer which helps foil an invasion of Earth in William R. Burkett Jr's 'Sleeping Planet' (1964) is another example of such a machine playing a major role. (The section on computers and cybernetics gives a detailed survey.)

Apart from robots, there has been no great variety of industrial or utilitarian items consistently presented as the central feature of science fiction stories. Notable in this category, however, are the artificial 'hands' which mimic the motions of the human operating them in 'Waldo' by Robert A. Heinlein (1942).

Weaponry is another more or less incidental area of future technology and is covered more fully in the section on warfare. Personal weapons feature mainly as blasters and stunners, and larger versions of the former appear on battle-craft in science fiction. Blasters were rarely detailed, except for their effects, and the armament of spaceships was often described as a 'ray' with mysterious properties, as in E. E. Smith's *The Skylark of Space* (1928) and Garrett P. Serviss's *Edison's Conquest of Mars* (1898), a sequel to Wells's *The War of the Worlds* (1897).

Undersea technologies are another occasional topic. *20,000 Leagues under the Sea* (1870) by Jules Verne is perhaps the best-known work in this area, mainly because of its predictive aspects. Arthur C. Clarke's *The Deep Range* (1957) carries a more extensive listing of undersea technologies – including underwater communities, herding whales by the use of ultra-sonic barriers, and automated weapons for dealing with hostile marine life.

As will have been noted, the future technology of Earth depicted in science fiction is frequently connected with space exploration and exploitation. A notable example of this is in the area of weather control. Early treatments of the theme include further stories by Murray Leinster, 'The Storm That Had to Be Stopped' (1930) and its sequel 'The Man Who Put Out the Sun' (1930), in which a criminal scientist attempts to use weather control to make himself world dictator. A striking modern story is Theodore L. Thomas's 'The Weather Man' (1962). The author convincingly describes the activities of Weather-men who are able to skim through the solar atmosphere and approach the surface of the Sun in specially protected 'sunboats'. A 'Pinpoint Stream' technique has been perfected, by which a thin stream of protons can be drawn from sunspots and directed at any pre-selected sunward part of the Earth's atmosphere to produce the desired weather.

ADDITIONAL INPUT

02.11.4 Other Areas of Earth Technology

Bellamy, Edward. *Looking Backward*, Ticknor (US) 1888
Bradshaw, William Richard. *The Goddess of Atvatabar*, J.F. Douthitt (US) 1892
England, George Allan. *Darkness and Dawn*, *Cavalier* January 1912, Small, Maynard (US) 1914
Griffith, George. *Valdar the Oft-Born*, *Pearson's Weekly* February to August 1895
Hammond, Keith (Henry Kuttner). 'Lord of the Storm', *Startling* September 1947
Hunting, Gardner. *The Vicarion*, Unity School of Christianity (US) 1926
Sherred, T.L. 'E For Effort', *Astounding* May 1947
Taine, John (Eric Temple Bell). *Before the Dawn*, Williams & Wilkins (US) 1934
Tubb, E.C. *The Mutants Rebel*, Hamilton (UK) 1953
Weeks, Edward Olin. 'Master of the Octopus', *Pearson's Magazine* October 1899

02.11 TECHNOLOGIES AND ARTEFACTS

02.11.5 Colonial Technologies

Just as waves of colonists followed the exploratory expeditions to the New World in the seventeenth and eighteenth centuries on Earth, so similar waves to the Moon, other planets and space itself have been envisaged by sf writers. The Moon and the space between the Earth and the Moon were the first sites to be imagined for human colonies perhaps because of the closeness to Earth. Later, writers described the colonisation of other planets, both in our solar system and outside it.

The Moon is viewed as an ideal location for observatories and as a launching point for journeys to other planets, mainly because of its lack of atmosphere and its low gravity. There are also some advantages in establishing a colony either on or under its surface; many of the materials and resources needed for such a colony's technology could possibly be synthesised from lunar material.

Robert A. Heinlein mentions the early stages of a lunar colony in 'It's Great to Be Back!' (1946). He portrays 'Luna City' (as most writers call it) in its beginnings as '. . . three air-sealed Quonset huts connected by tunnels'. Rather than deal with the actual development of a lunar colony, though, most writers chose to present it as an already bustling city. *The Forgotten Star* by Joseph Green (1959) provides an interesting description of Luna City. The settlement is built into the walls of a vast crater, the central city resembling a modern shopping mall, with spaceport attached. The residential areas are separate, and look out on views of the desolate lunar terrain.

Other writers prefer to roof over a lunar crater, fill it with air, and construct the city within the enclosed space. Heinlein goes one stage further in 'The Menace from Earth' (1957), the Luna City of this story spreading outward from a crater, as well as down through several levels. In *The Moon Is a Harsh Mistress* (1966) he develops the idea along the same lines. In whatever form, the lunar colony has always been a favourite setting for science fiction stories, and will probably continue to be so in the future – perhaps even after such a colony becomes a reality.

'Men Only' by E. C. Tubb, New Worlds *July 1952. Illu tration by Quinn.*

Colonies orbiting the Earth – better known as space stations – are another aspect of space technology. Their advantage over the lunar alternative is usually seen as one of logistics – spacecraft would have no need to contend with the problems of landing on the Moon and taking off from it. Since gravity could be ignored in designing such a structure, more efficient use of space and materials could be made.

In 'The Other Side of the Sky' (1957), Arthur C. Clarke depicts the first space stations as television and radio relay bases, while in Murray Leinster's *Space Platform* (1953) the less peaceful purpose of employing them as missile sites is envisaged – an all too realistic proposition.

In Clarke's book *2001: a Space Odyssey* (and in the 1968 movie, upon which the book is based), the space station is used as a terminal for travellers en route to the Moon. Other stories have shown space stations variously as hospitals, as in James White's *Hospital Station* (1962), as laboratories and as solar observatories. For the most part, however, space stations are usually portrayed as being too small to support genuine colonies.

Mars and Venus are much more logical sites, being the closest of Earth's planetary neighbours. Many writers, such as Ray Bradbury in 'Night Meeting' (1950), depict Mars as having an Earth-type atmosphere, breathable by humans, and easily adapted to Earth-like technologies. But the idea is unrealistic. Others assume that the Martian atmosphere has a pressure only a few pounds lower than Earth's, but is toxic to man. To solve this problem, a thin plastic 'bubble' could be assembled over a crater or other suitable area, then filled with air to provide living quarters.

'Death-by-Rain' by Ray Bradbury, Planet Stories *Summer 1950.*

Venus, the true nature of its surface being unknown until recently, was often assumed to be hospitable to human life. In Ray Bradbury's 'The Long Rain' (1951), the planet is a vast tropical rain jungle, and men live in isolated 'sun domes'. Other stories portray the planet as a desert world, a swamp, or a world almost completely covered by water. In each case, it is a place where humans can survive without an artificial environment.

Because of their large size, some of the moons of Jupiter are often considered habitable, perhaps even possessing the type of Earth-like atmosphere presented in Raymond Z. Gallun's 'The Lotus Engine' (1940). Again, in that story, the colonists face few technological problems beyond those created by the logistics of trying to establish a foothold so far from the home planet.

Planets suitable for colonisation in other solar systems are usually portrayed as Earth-type, generally because of the impracticality of trying to live in a hostile environment even farther from Earth. However, in some stories, when man cannot live on a planet as it is, he changes it, or 'Terraforms' it. Mars is one of the earliest subjects of Terraforming. In Clarke's *The Sands of Mars* (1957), a species of plant is discovered that gives off oxygen. Consequently it is cultivated by the colonists, with the intention within a century of making the Martian atmosphere breathable.

Another example of Terraforming can be found in George O. Smith's 'Speculation' (1976), which tells how tons of Earth soil, complete with organic matter, are transported to Mars and cultivated. The result is that Earth plants slowly begin to spread across the planet, the micro-organisms in the imported soil invading the Martian surface to pave the way for terrain vegetation. The same author's 'The Planet Mender' (1952) tells a story of cosmic engineering on a large scale, where mountains of ice from Uranus are transported via Mercury and Phobos to end up as rain on Mars.

Robert A. Heinlein speaks of cosmic engineering in his book, *Between Planets* (1951). It includes a suggested plan to move Pluto and Neptune closer to the Sun, while moving Mercury farther out. In his story *Worlds for the Taking* (1966), Kenneth Bulmer tells of the bringing of planets from other solar systems to orbit our Sun.

The most spectacular form of cosmic engineering suggested in recent years involves building an entire planet. In *Ringworld* (1970), Larry Niven writes of a vast ring, millions of miles in diameter, which has been constructed around a star. The ring spins to impart gravity to its inner surface, and another ring of alternating rectangles orbits the star inside it, the shadows of the rectangles providing the illusion of night and day. Niven and other writers have also dealt with spheres built around a star.

Another area of space technology to which writers have devoted some attention is the prospect of mining minerals on planets and asteroids. The asteroids in our own asteroid belt are supposed to consist mainly of a nickel-iron material, and, given the necessary technology, they might well be considered valuable. A number of stories have dealt with the problem of mining them, some writers bringing the asteroids into Earth orbit by propelling them with explosive charges. In Raymond Z. Gallun's 'A Step Further Out' (1950) the asteroid belt is depicted as an area rich in mineral resources, being the remains of a planet which exploded millions of years earlier. The planet had sustained a high civilisation, and although this was destroyed, many artefacts, including items of jewellery, can still be found by diligent prospectors. Many stories of fortunes and treachery amongst asteroid prospectors have been written, and an unusual humorous treatment distinguishes E. C. Tubb's 'Asteroids' (1956), one of several short tales about an interplanetary confidence trickster.

Actual mining techniques rarely differ much from present-day methods, however, whether on asteroids or other planets. Some of the more noted exceptions occur in Jack Williamson's *Seetee Shock* (1950), (written under the pseudonym of Will Stewart) and in the same author's *Seetee Ship* (1951), the first book actually being a sequel to the other, although appearing earlier. (The novels were based upon four stories that had appeared, in correct order, in *Astounding*.) *Seetee Ship* is set in the year 2190, and tells of a deadly 'seetee' drift,

Left: cover by Rogers. *Right:* Ringworld *by Larry Niven (Ballantine). Cover by Sternbach.*

02.12 CITIES AND CULTURES

made up of contra-terrene particles – matter with its atomic structure turned inside out. According to a respectable theoretical concept of physics, such matter would explode with devastating force if brought into contact with ordinary particles. In Williamson's stories an explosion involving contra-terrene matter and a planet beyond Mars accounted for the asteroids, and the asteroid belt now contains both kinds of matter. To men opening up the belt for mining and colonisation, the drifting seetee worldlets, ready to explode at the first touch, present an incalculable problem. But if such explosions could be controlled, they would prove a formidable power source. The solution is beyond Earth's ingenuity, until details of the technology required are found during the investigation of a deserted alien spaceship.

The general concept of future technology in science fiction can be summed up as an essentially constructive process, but with the inherent dangers which we have now begun to associate with our present-day technology. Technology, in fact, is no more than a tool. It can be used, as has been shown in science fiction, for both altruistic and oppressive ends.

ADDITIONAL INPUT

02.11.5 Colonial Technologies

Anderson, Poul. 'Call Me Joe', *Astounding* April 1957

Anderson, Poul. *The Enemy Stars*, Lippincott (US) 1959

Anderson, Poul. 'A Bicycle Built for Brew', *Astounding* November to December 1958; as *The Makeshift Rocket*, Ace (US) 1962

Anderson, Poul. *The Snows of Ganymede*, *Startling* Winter 1954; Ace (US) 1958

Blish, James. *They Shall Have Stars*, Faber (UK) 1956, consisting of 'Bridge', *Astounding* February 1952 and 'At Death's End', *Astounding* May 1954; also as *Year 2180!* Avon (US) 1957

Blish, James. *Earthman, Come Home*, Putnam (US) 1955, consisting of 'Okie', *Astounding* April 1950; 'Bindlestiff', *Astounding* December 1950; 'Sargasso of Lost Cities', *Two Complete Science-Adventure Books* Spring 1953; 'Earthman, Come Home', *Astounding* November 1953

Blish, James. *The Triumph of Time*, Avon (US) 1958; also as *A Clash of Cymbals*, Faber (UK) 1959

Campbell, John W. *The Moon Is Hell*, Fantasy Press (US) 1950

Castle, Jeffery Lloyd. *Satellite E One*, Dodd, Mead (US) 1954

Clement, Hal (Harry Clement Stubbs). *Mission of Gravity*, *Astounding* April to July 1953; Doubleday (US) 1954; Hale (UK) 1955

Gibson, Joe. 'Three Worlds in Shadow', *Science Fiction Quarterly* February 1952

Jones, Raymond F. 'Noise Level', *Astounding* December 1952

Reynolds, Mack. 'The Man in the Moon', *Amazing* July 1950

Romans, H.H. 'The Moon Conquerors', *Science Wonder Quarterly* Winter 1930

Simak, Clifford D. 'Rim of the Deep', *Astounding* May 1940

Simak, Clifford D. 'Tools', *Astounding* July 1942

Van Lorne, Warner (Nelson Tremaine) 'Wanted – Seven Fearless Engineers', *Amazing* March 1939

One of the most valuable traits to be found in science fiction, perhaps unique in the world of literature, is that quality which John Phillifent once called 'the science fiction method'. It has nothing to do with subject matter. It is a way of looking at any subject, taking it apart into its components and putting it back together with some of the existing parts replaced by new inventions. It is particularly when science fiction deals with social institutions that it does this trick well. It gives us what Harlow Shapley calls 'the view from a distant star': the chance to observe our own world from outside, objectively, as a Martian or a Rigellian wheel-man might observe it.

This is a fine tool for satire, as Jonathan Swift discovered centuries ago, but it is not only comedy that is offered, it is insights into our own condition. I think of stories like Brian Aldiss's *The Dark Light-Years* (1964). Brian looked at human religions, and observed that many of them give sacramental value to such basic biological processes as eating and sexual intercourse: dietary laws, the mystery of communion and the symbolism of the Last Supper on the one hand, marriage ceremonies, puberty rites, ritual prostitution and the ceremonial defloration of virgins on the other. Suppose, said Brian, that in some other society somewhere in the universe these same values were attached to that other basic biological function, excretion? Why not? And so he wrote a story to show what sort of religious observances that would involve.

In my own long list of great stories by myself that I have not yet got around to writing, there is one about a society of intelligent creatures whose biology differs from our own in the way they are born. They are descended from a form of marine life which reproduces in the casual manner of many of our own fish. The female squirts her eggs ad lib into the water. Some wandering male, his glands inflamed by the presence of the eggs, comes by and fertilises them en masse, and then swims on and is seen no more. What sort of religion can these people have? What is the internal makeup of their minds? We humans are father-bound in countless ways. Our God is our Father; our Freudians find parent images in every dream. How can one be properly rejected, without identifiable parents to let us down? And without that parental rejection, what could be the source of the obsessions and idiosyncracies that sometimes turn into genius?

Of course, there is no need to go so far. The cities and cultures of science fiction show a wild diversity of social forms, even when their populations are limited to warm-blooded bipeds exactly like ourselves. Some of them are cautionary, warning of directions we may not want to go in. A few offer suggestions of better kinds of lives that we can have if we elect to invent them. All give insights into our own world order which can be useful – so much so that there are now several score universities which have made the study of science fiction a part of the curriculum in subjects like sociology, economics and political science.

I think it probable that the students will find in them new perspectives that are missing from the orthodox texts . . . and I think it certain that, in the process of reading them, they will be entertained!

Fred Pohl

Frederik Pohl

02.12 CITIES AND CULTURES

From Sir Thomas More's *Utopia* (1516) describing an idealised state, through Huxley's *Brave New World* (1932) and Orwell's *Nineteen Eighty-four* (1949) with their warnings of regimented futures, to the noted works of contemporary science fiction, the themes of cities and cultures have played their part. They are the tangible fruits of man's endeavours, and any tale about men must concern itself in some measure with aspects of these two manifestations of intelligence. The same reasoning can be applied to stories which deal with intelligent species which are not of Earth, species which are the product of different influences, philosophies and values.

Cities of the future have fascinated the sf artists as much as they have intrigued the writers, and many illustrations have depicted the vast and complex structures which artists have conjured up in the mind's eye. Moving pavements, overhead walkways and travelators, aerial taxis, individual flyers, automated traffic lanes for computer-controlled cars, towering edifices of glass and vast domes roofing an entire metropolis . . . the list is endless, the variety infinite. For the writer, his task is to integrate his description of a city, if he wishes to describe it in detail, into the framework of the culture which it has been built to house. The artist knows no such limitations.

Cities may be things of delight, or they may be nightmares, again reflecting the quality of life within them. Alternatively, they may be deserted or in ruins, either as a result of war or the decline and death of a culture. All these possibilities are open to the imagination of the science fiction writer, who may use them simply as backgrounds or feature them as an integral part of a tale. Whichever is the case, he has the power to be his own architect, builder, city administrator and, if he so wishes, destroyer. This section shows him in each of these roles.

02.12.1 Earth Cities and Cultures

For the most part, science fiction writers do not seem to envisage a cosy future for city dwellers. Visions of future urban communities vary from hive-like concentrations of humanity, well regulated and with each citizen occupying his own tidy niche, to dirty, disease-ridden and poverty-stricken conglomerations of hovels, huts and slums. In J. G. Ballard's story 'Billenium' (1961), the maximum permitted living space for each individual has been fixed by law, rooms have been subdivided, and the subdivisions themselves have been subdivided. A similar situation is described in Harry Harrison's portrayal of New York in 1999 in *Make Room! Make Room!* (1966).

Human hives are described in *The World Inside* (1971) by Robert Silverberg. Since available land is required for food production, human dwellings are pushed higher and higher, until the world's population occupy massive blocks called monads which house and keep happy almost one million inhabitants. These people live in such close intimacy and are allowed so little privacy that new cultural and ethical standards develop. Another human hive is the subject of *Hellstrom's Hive* (1972–73) by Frank Herbert, in which a zoologist arouses the suspicions of the authorities by the secretive nature of his work in Oregon. When a government agent goes to investigate he discovers that Hellstrom's work has terrifying possibilities. He is the front man for a long-established human hive in which the society has mimicked that of ants, with the intention of eventually taking over the world. *The Godwhale* (1974) by T. J. Bass also features a hive-like human city, but one that is set in the fairly remote future, and is only a single ingredient of a much more complex story.

'The Floating City'.

Social climbing in Silverberg's monads of *The World Inside* occurs in the literal sense – the inhabitants live on certain floors according to the importance of the work they do and their social standing within the community. An employee promoted at work moves to an apartment on a higher level. The civic chiefs and senior politicians who have reached the top, enjoy the view from the thousandth floor.

When the Sleeper Wakes

By H. G. WELLS, *Author of "The Invisible Man" "The War of the Worlds"*

WITH ILLUSTRATIONS

HARPER & BROTHERS PUBLISHERS
LONDON AND NEW YORK
1899

In contrast to towering dwelling-blocks is the concept of enclosed cities, an idea which dates back to Wells's *When the Sleeper Wakes* (1899) and 'A Story of the Days to Come' (1897). Both tales are set in the same future. Particularly in the former, Wells describes the consummate architecture, the enthralling vistas which Graham, the Sleeper, experiences as he looks across a city of the future from an elevated vantage-point. In the latter tale, two lovers venture beyond the wall, and find themselves no match for the assault of raw nature which confronts them; they turn back defeated. An interesting parallel can be drawn between Wells's dispiriting tale and Ayn Rand's *Anthem* (1938), in which two rebels from a very similar authoritarian society succeed in breaking away. In the latter tale, the very expression of the pronoun 'I' is denounced as a cardinal sin; there must be no individuality in this particular world of the future, no rights and no redress. The concept of the closed city, however, was as much a part of *Anthem* as it was of Wells's vision, but within those closed walls the buildings could be superb.

The same theme was taken up by Theodore Sturgeon in *Venus Plus X* (1960), whose central character awakes to gaze in a sense of wonderment at the graceful buildings he finds around him. He sees curves and outlines unknown in his own world, and he can only look upon them with a sense of awe. The architecture holds

02.12 CITIES AND CULTURES

if
WORLDS of SCIENCE FICTION
VOL.: 1. No. 9. - Price 1/6 d.

GOLDEN CITY
ON TITAN
Orro, greatest city of the solar system's
largest moon, is a city of skyscrapers that
equal those of Earth. Its people are highly
PAUL

Left: Cover illustrations from Amazing *November 1941,* Analog *September 1962,* If *April 1954,* Amazing *December 1941.*

him spell-bound. From the early writers, including Wells, came the idea of an entirely encapsulated city, one roofed over – whether it was above ground or below. Although many writers have used the concept as a background, it was left to Asimov to take it into the forefront of his plot in *The Caves of Steel* (1954), presenting a future version of New York buried beneath a huge dome. The quality of life, however, leaves much to be desired judged by present-day standards. Individual dwellings are mean and small; dining takes place in communal halls where the food has little to recommend it. One of the favourite occupations of the healthy involves 'running the strips' – jumping across sections of travelator moving at differing speeds to see who can reach the fastest one first, an indication of how few other recreational outlets are open to the city-dwellers.

An early, and noted, example of an underground culture is E. M. Forster's 'The Machine Stops' (1909), depicting the entire human race living in individual cells on many levels beneath the surface. The people's every need is met by the services of The Machine, and they are faced with no incentive to travel, or even to meet each other in person. It is a world, basically, of individual self-indulgence; but it is also, as the end of the story indicates, a degenerate world. When The Machine breaks down, the inhabitants die, having lost the sense of initiative to overcome even the smallest crisis. The culture, being stagnant, dies with them. What Forster was suggesting in his classic tale was that any culture which allows itself to stagnate is doomed.

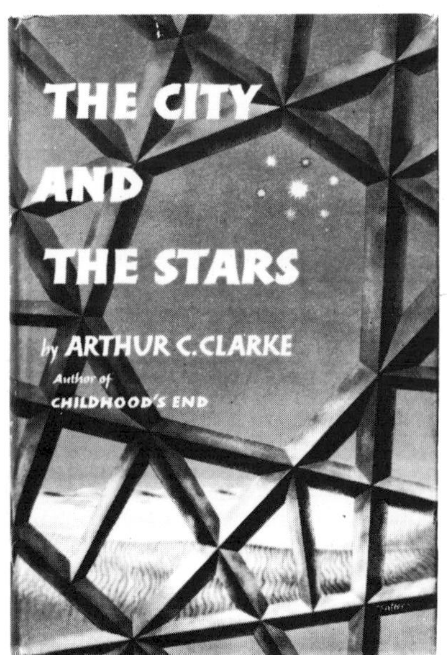

Cover by Salter (Harcourt Brace).

A comparable society is portrayed in Arthur C. Clarke's *The City and the Stars* (1956), an expanded version of a much

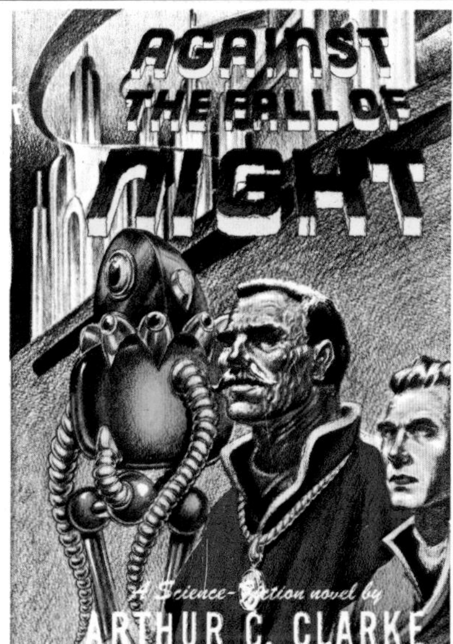

Cover by Frank Kelly Freas.

shorter work, *Against the Fall of Night* (1953), which was itself an expansion of a short story of the same title originally published in 1948. Clarke portrays the last city on earth as a static and closed society, mankind having spread across the galaxy, until on Earth only Diaspar remains. The inhabitants have locked themselves in behind defensive barriers, frightened of an ancient enemy that no man had seen for thousands of years.

'Jesting Pilot' (1947) by Henry Kuttner also tells of a barricaded city which has been enclosed in an impenetrable force-field for centuries, the last survivor of an atomic war. There is no fixed time for the barrier to be lowered, and none of the inhabitants has sufficient scientific understanding to undertake the task. In fact, the entire population exists under deep psychological conditioning, for to be self-sustaining, and to maintain the barrier, the city must employ energy forces which would drive a man mad in seconds if his senses could perceive them. The story centres around a character who experiences occasional flashes of reality, and the attempts of the city authorities to bring him back to 'normal'.

Many writers have described the technological marvels which the urban dweller of the future may expect to enjoy. In 'The Under-privileged' (1964) by Brian W. Aldiss, the fully automated city of the future is graphically portrayed. A credit card fitted into a slot at any street corner will bring a robot servitor flying within seconds to dispense a variety of refreshments and goods, or to order rapid delivery of anything it cannot personally handle. On the other hand, cities may become entities in their own right. Robert Abernathy's 'Single Combat' (1955) tells of a man who has set an atomic bomb at a city's centre in an attempt to destroy it. However, as he races towards the suburbs to escape the blast, the city takes on a life of its own, using out-of-control cars, falling billboards and anything else at its disposal to stop him. It succeeds, and the bomb is deactivated in time.

Finally come the visions of the dead cities, empty of life but perhaps still intact. 'Dumb Waiter' (1952) by Walter M. Miller Jr tells of a city deserted by its inhabitants during a nuclear war, but which the robots and machines keep operating as though the humans were still present. But of the many stories chronicling the exploration of deserted cities, one of the most poignant, and best remembered, is 'By the Waters of Babylon' (1937) by Stephen Vincent Benét. Few later writers have succeeded in matching the evocative atmosphere of Benét's tale, which describes the journey of a priest's son to the forbidden city where the gods are supposed to live. Eventually the youth, after an arduous journey, finds himself exploring New York and, discovering the remains of a centuries-dead business executive mummified in his office suite, realises that the so-called gods were only men.

'Dumb Waiter' by Walter M. Miller Jr, Astounding *April 1952. Cover by Rogers.*

Pursuing the same thematic area there are those stories which portray human cultures without necessarily depicting any particularly original future city. The well-known novel *The Space Merchants* (1952) by Frederik Pohl and C. M. Kornbluth offers a future in which the planet is not only vastly overcrowded, with the many associated problems, but also one in which the spurious ethics of advertising agencies hold sway. The populace are brainwashed consumers, and politicians are controlled by the all-powerful advertising agencies and the giant manufacturing corporations. A different kind of future, but one equally sad, is the subject of Ray Bradbury's *Farenheit 451* (1953). Bradbury's future is a television-orientated culture in which individualism is banned, or made impossible for the masses, scholars are regarded as criminals, and books are ritualistically burned.

02.12 CITIES AND CULTURES

Mark Adlard's 'T-city trilogy', *Interface* (1971), *Volteface* (1972), and *Multiface* (1975) describes a future Britain in which most of the population live in closed communities controlled by executives of the vast Stahlex manufacturing organisation. They are cared for by the intellectually enhanced executives of Stahlex, who themselves enjoy the freedom of the country. The trilogy begins by depicting the populace as nothing more than consumers for the products of the Stahlex Corporation. But as the books progress, the executives realise that dissension in the cities is caused by something lacking in the lives of their inhabitants, and they are obliged to devise what for them is a new concept – they must provide the people with work. Another story of an industrialised future, and one which predates Adlard's trilogy is *Player Piano* (1952) by Kurt Vonnegut Jr. It portrays a future when, after the second industrial revolution, mankind has been largely superseded by machines and work is for the most part obsolete. What ought to be a near-utopia situation exists. There are dissidents, however, and the Luddite syndrome arises once again. To the central character in the story, it appears that science and technology have taken away more than they have given. In his disquieting vision, Vonnegut suggests that, on the future Earth at least, work, and pride in work, will remain an essential factor in the well-being of man.

ADDITIONAL INPUT

02.12.1 Earth Cities and Cultures

Cooper, Edmund. *The Cloud Walker*, Hodder and Stoughton (UK) 1973
Dick, Philip K. *Do Androids Dream of Electric Sheep?*, Doubleday (US) 1968
Miller, Walter M. *A Canticle for Leibowitz*, Lippincott (US) 1960
Priest, Christopher. *Inverted World*, *Galaxy* December 1973 to March 1974; Faber (UK) 1974
White, James. *The Watch Below*, Whiting and Wheaton (UK) 1966

02.12.2 Colonial Cultures

There are many reasons why, according to science fiction writers, mankind should make attempts to establish himself on worlds other than his own. Overcrowding is more often than not the prime mover, while others leave for ideological reasons, in much the same way as the Quakers originally emigrated from England to the New World. Still others are driven by nothing more than the spirit of adventure and scientific discovery. Whatever the reasons, sf stories have been written depicting off-Earth cultures, most of which are comparable in some way to those found on man's home planet. A short review is necessary to illustrate these similarities and note the occasional genuine differences.

Most writers acknowledge that the emigrants would need to travel for many years between worlds, the original colonists sometimes not even living to see the eventual destination towards which they were headed. Their starships, travelling from planetary system to planetary system, searching for a suitable world upon which to land, are referred to within the genre as 'generation ships' or 'travelling arks'. Robert A. Heinlein's 'generation ship' novel *Orphans of the Sky* was originally published as two long novellas 'Universe' (1941) and 'Common Sense' (1941). It shows the inhabitants of the huge ship developing a culture in which their environment becomes the entire universe. Brian Aldiss's novel in this

'Non-Stop' by Brian Aldiss, Science Fantasy *1955. Illustration by Quinn.*

category is *Non-Stop* (1958). *Rite of Passage* (1968) by Alexei Panshin is an interesting tale in that it approaches the generation ship theme from a slightly different angle – the description of life aboard ship is told as a memoir as seen through the eyes of a young girl. The star-bound generations in Harry Harrison's *Captive Universe* (1969) have developed an Aztec-like culture, the people aboard the ship believing that they live in an isolated valley, and that outside the valley everything is evil.

Although not generation ships as such, because they have no set objective, James Blish's space-going cities in the 'Cities in Flight' series can be regarded as the homes of a space-nomad culture. When the development of an anti-gravity drive made it possible for any amount of mass to be propelled through space, mankind was no longer restricted to living an unvaried life on Earth. In the order in which it should be read, the series consists of *They Shall Have Stars* (1956), *A Life for the Stars* (1962), *Earthman, Come Home* (1955), and *A Clash of Cymbals* (1958).

Cover by Timmins.

Of actual colonies themselves, Arthur C. Clarke's 'If I Forget Thee, Oh Earth . . .' (1954) is a short and poignant story of a young boy, a member of a colony on the Moon, being taken to the satellite's surface from his underground home by his father, and being shown the Earth across space. The world has been destroyed in a nuclear war, and after a long struggle a small Moon colony has succeeded in surviving without supplies from Earth, but its culture is essentially the same. Ray Bradbury's *The Martian Chronicles* (1951) underlines the same assumption, that wherever man may go he will attempt to recreate the culture and social mores of the original human home. Even in the remote future, as depicted in Isaac Asimov's 'Foundation Trilogy' (*Foundation*, 1951; *Foundation and Empire*, 1952; and *Second Foundation*, 1953), the culture remains Earthlike, and the capital planet of Trantor is notable as an example of an entire city-world.

Among the stories where a distinct variation in the patterns of normal human societies can be said to be found is Perry A. Chapdelaine's *Swampworld West* (1974), which concerns the cultural interaction between colonists escaping from an overcrowded Earth and the intelligent indigenous population of the planet of the title. The human inhabitants of a world attracting six moons in *Syzygy* (1973), by Michael G. Coney, are unable to recall the events of fifty-two years earlier when all six moons were visible in the same hemisphere. When the phenomenon is due to occur again, efforts are made to ascertain exactly

'Through the Vibrations' by P. Schuyler Miller, Amazing May 1931. Illustration by Paul.

what effects it produces on the culture.

Of the novels by Ursula K. Le Guin which deal with cultures on other worlds, *The Left Hand of Darkness* (1969) tells of the planet Winter, and its human inhabitants, all of whom are of a single sex – male or female at will – and the primitive and feudal society that the planet's rigorous weather forces upon them. The same author's *The Dispossessed* (1974) portrays a complex society founded to put the principles of anarchism into practice. A society, ordered, but without laws, may appear improbable, but the story is a convincing attempt to suggest how such a human culture could exist.

02.12.3. The Alien Scene

The portrayal of alien cultures in science fiction has been something of a random process. Writers may sketch in only the briefest of backgrounds to support a plot centering around the interaction between humans and extraterrestrials, or they may go some lengths to describe the culture concerned, particularly if it is an integral part of their story. A notable example of the latter process is James Blish's *A Case of Conscience* (1958), in which the Jesuit member of a UN exploratory team is convinced that the alien way of life on a newly discovered planet proves that the world is a genuinely diabolic trap. He sees the natives, a gentle but highly intelligent species of reptile, as having never 'fallen'; this being the case, they could not have been created by God. The whole story hinges on this argument.

Similarly, the indigenous culture of a distant planet plays a major role in Edmund Cooper's *The Far Sunset* (1967), in which the lone survivor of an Earth spaceship is not only accepted into the Indonesian-like society, but eventually is chosen as its leader. The story contains religious elements, and the religious beliefs of an alien culture formed the basis of what is still one of the most popular stories in the annals of modern science fiction. Isaac Asimov's 'Nightfall' (1940) tells of the cultural beliefs held by the population of a planet circling a star close to the galactic hub. Their sun is only one half of a binary system, with the result that they experience eternal daylight – only once in a thousand years, dependent on the configuration of their twin suns, does darkness fall. The story opens as the millennium approaches, with the population apprehensive of the outcome. When night actually falls, they see for the first time the brilliant clusters of stars at the centre of the galaxy, which to them can be nothing less than gods, and a violent upheaval follows.

ADDITIONAL INPUT

02.12.2 Colonial Cultures

Anderson, Poul. *Orbit Unlimited*, Pyramid (US) 1961

Anderson, Poul. *Virgin Planet*, *Venture* January 1957; Avalon (US) 1959

Baxter, John. *The God Killers*, *New Worlds* June to July 1966; as *The Off-Worlders*, Ace (US) 1966

Fyfe, H.B. 'Protected Species', *Astounding* March 1951

Wyndham, John. *The Outward Urge*, Michael Joseph (UK) 1959 (Published with an additional chapter, 'The Emptiness of Space', by the British Science Fiction Book Club in 1961.)

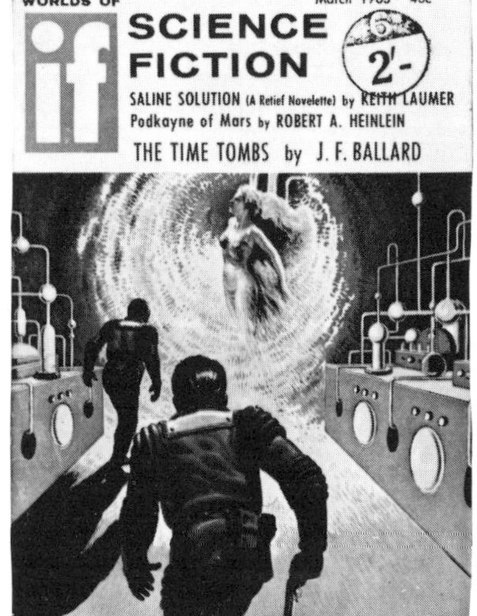

Cover by Finlay.

02.12 CITIES AND CULTURES

Cover illustration by Angus McKie for The Thrall of Hypno *by Clark Darlton (Futura).*

Alien cultures are frequently seen as being determined by the physical characteristics of the planetary population. As long ago as 1934 Stanley G. Weinbaum wrote of humans on Mars encountering a strange but likeable Martian who hopped around the sandy deserts fascinating the members of the colony. Tweel, of 'A Martian Odyssey' (1934) was to become one of the most likeable aliens in science fiction, and proved to be far more intelligent than the colonists assumed. Another story set on Mars, 'The Lost City of Mars' (1966) by Ray Bradbury, deals more tangibly with a city and a culture on that planet, and details many of the wonders left by a long dead race.

Other investigations of long-dead alien cultures can be found in Arthur C. Clarke's 'The Star' (1955) and J. G. Ballard's 'The Time Tombs' (1963). In the former tale, the remains of a great civilisation indicated that it was destroyed by a stellar nova which could only have been the Star of Bethlehem. Ballard's story tells of tomb robbers in a quest for memory tapes, three-dimensional recordings, which again will reveal the glories of a past civilisation. Another vision of an alien city, summoned up by John W. Campbell, writing as Don A. Stuart, can be found in 'Forgetfulness' (1937). Visiting Earthmen, assuming that the natives they find living in simple dwellings on an alien world can be dealt with on a rudimentary level, are astonished to find intact a vast deserted city beside which even the ingenuity of man seems small. The humans assume that the apparently placid extraterrestrials who welcome them are the remnants of a once-great civilisation, and treat them accordingly. They fail to recognise the significance of the culture, for the aliens still retain a complete knowledge of the workings of the city and all its scientific devices. They have outgrown that particular stage in their evolution, their powers of mind have rendered it obsolete, as they eventually make clear.

A far different culture is described in Marion Zimmer Bradley's 'The Wind People' (1959), in which natives of the planet cannot be seen by human eyes in normal light. Being primarily nocturnal, they are most in evidence at night when they blend with the vegetation and shadows; even their language resembles the soughing of the wind to human ears. Frederik Pohl's Venusians in 'The Gentlest Unpeople' (1958) not only enjoy a fairly complex culture and a technological society, but also a rigid taboo about being impolite.

Further treatments of the theme include *Hard to Be a God* (1964) by Arkadi and Boris Strugatski, which is a detailed examination, more from a social than a technological or cultural angle, of a humanoid feudal society on a planet circling another sun. Two novels by Lloyd Biggle Jr also deal with alien societies and cultures. *The Light That Never Was* (1972) is an account of human reactions to the abilities of the native life-form of a planet renowned throughout the civilised galaxy for its unusual natural light effects. The natives of the planet paint striking pictures of the phenomenon, and when an influential critic recognises the quality of their work, the question arises whether arbitrary classification of non-human intelligence as naturally inferior to its

'The Gentlest Unpeople' by Frederik Pohl, Galaxy *June 1958. Illustration by Wood.*

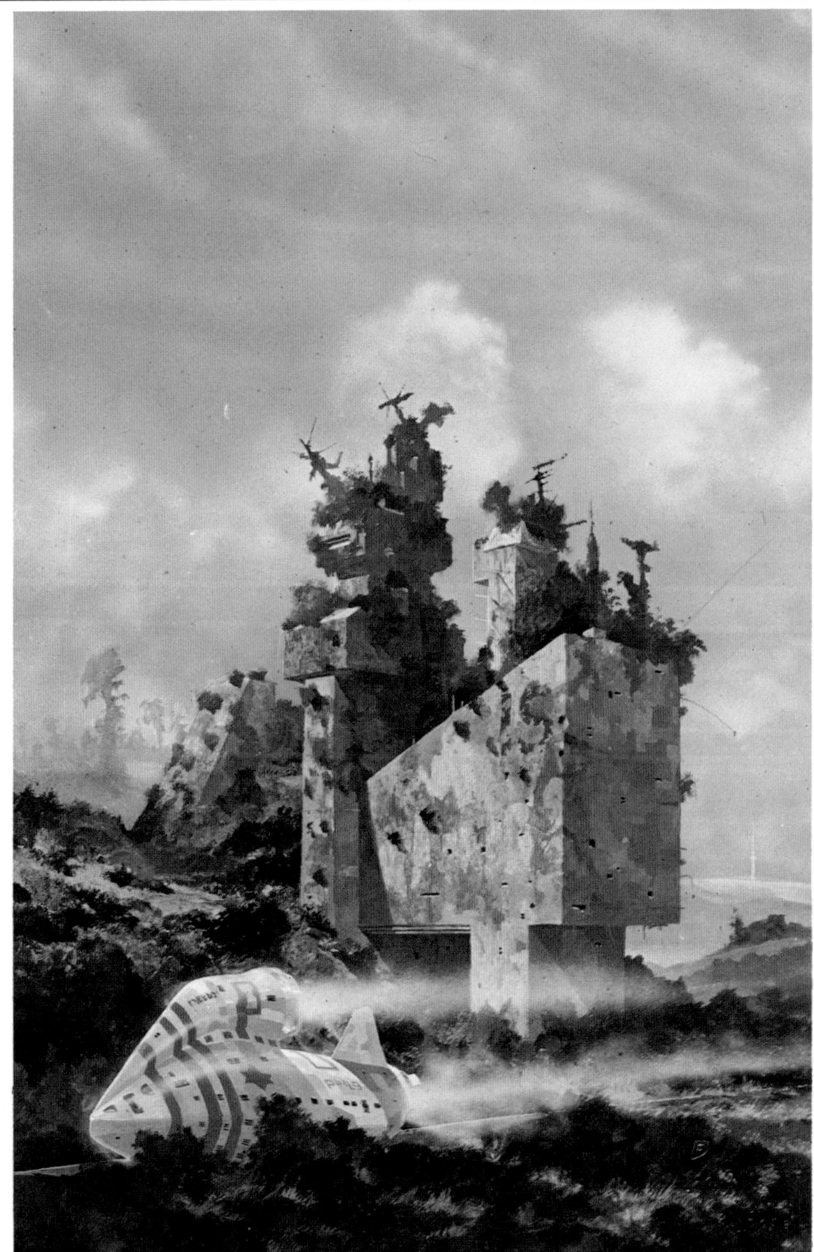

City of Illusions *by Ursula Le Guin (Panther). Cover by Foss.*

human counterpart is justifiable. *Monument* (1974), based upon a short story of the same title published in 1961, tells of the first encounter of an alien culture with human big business. The sole survivor of a spaceship crash comes to be revered by the human-like natives, but he knows that the planet will finally be 'officially' discovered, and that the peaceful and simple inhabitants will need to fight vigorously for their rights and for the survival of their culture.

The aliens in Michael G. Coney's *Mirror Image* (1972) are a mimetic species who take on the form of man, and actually believe themselves to be human, while 'The Word for World Is Forest' (1972) by Ursula K. Le Guin describes the intended destruction by interlopers from Earth of the entire ecology of a planet characterised by its immense dark forests. Clearing the trees would render the planet ideal for colonists from Earth; but the advance guard reckon without the actions of the planet's natives, in whose tongue the words 'forest' and 'world' are the same. Similarly, 'The Lake of Tuonella' (1973) by Keith Roberts tells of the destruction of another native culture, and also of the sub-culture of boatmen and their pictographic writing. At least one human, however, who explores the waterways, is prepared to argue that the native culture is worth preserving at all costs. Remembering the occasions when human nations have destroyed native cultures on Earth, there seems reason to hope that the lesson has at last been learned that any unfamiliar culture, however alien it may seem, enjoys inviolable rights. In their treatment of other societies and cultures, many science fiction writers have made their own contribution to this understanding.

ADDITIONAL INPUT

02.12.3 The Alien Scene

Asimov, Isaac. *The Gods Themselves*, *Galaxy* March to May 1972; Doubleday (US) 1972

Bradley, Marion Zimmer. 'Darkover' series, including *The Door through Space*, Ace (US) 1961

Bradley, Marion Zimmer. *The Planet Savers*, Ace (US) 1962

Niven, Larry (with Jerry Pournelle). *The Mote in God's Eye*, Simon and Schuster (US) 1974

Zelazny, Roger. *Creatures of Light and Darkness*, Doubleday (US) 1969

02.13 ROBOTS AND ANDROIDS

The value of the robot/android story in science fiction is that, in dealing with a man-made version of humanity, the science fiction writer is immediately lured into considering the nature of man in its deepest aspects. I, myself, not given to morbid introspection and very prone to accepting life with a kind of idiotic cheerfulness, find that even my own robot stories have forced me to do some thinking on the subject. My most recent robot story (too recent to be mentioned in the excellent essay that follows) is *The Bicentennial Man* (included in *The Bicentennial Man and Other Stories*, Doubleday, 1976), and that delves deeper and deeper into the differences between robot and man till the two coalesce at last – but only in death.

My own important contribution to robotics, however, is not any depth of thought, but the working out of the three laws of robotics, which are mentioned and quoted in the essay following.

They arose as follows. During my teen-age years I had wearied of robots who destroyed their creators. I was very impressed, on the other hand, with Binder's Adam Link stories and with del Rey's Helen O'Loy.

I determined to write a story about a sympathetic robot and turned out 'Robbie' (which appeared in the September 1940 *Super Science Stories* under the title 'Strange Playfellow'). In the original form of the story, as written in May 1939, I had one of my characters say of Robbie, 'He just can't help being faithful and loving and kind. He's a machine – *made so*.'

That was the first germ in my mind of the First Law of Robotics.

I wrote one more robot story, 'Reason', in which I had what came to be the three laws more or less in mind. I took it for granted that robots (*my* robots) wouldn't harm human beings, that they would follow orders and that they would take care of themselves – in that order. It never occurred to me, however, to say so specifically.

Then, on 16 December 1940, when I was preparing to write 'Liar!' (which eventually appeared in the May 1941 issue of *Astounding*), I brought the plot to John Campbell, editor of the magazine. As I tried to explain what made my robot work the way he did, John lost patience with my attempts and said:

'Look, Isaac, it boils down to this. There have to be the three laws of robot behaviour: First . . .'

And he went on to recite the three laws nearly as I finally worked them out. He always claimed thereafter that he had merely distilled the three laws out of what I was trying to tell him, but all I know is that I heard them from him first and I didn't have them clearly in my mind, *in words*, before then. The word 'robotics', by the way, is mine. As far as I know, no one, not even Campbell, ever used it before I did.

It's a sobering thought for me that, if my use of the three laws did indeed revolutionise the robot story (as some say it did), I accomplished the revolution two weeks before my twenty-first birthday, and hadn't the faintest idea that I was doing it.

Isaac Asimov

Isaac Asimov

02.13 ROBOTS AND ANDROIDS

Along with space travel and bug-eyed monsters, the robot is symbolic of science fiction. Though often envisaged as a mechanical monstrosity, over the past fifty years the robot has become humanised, emancipated and perfected. It is no longer a mere computer on wheels, but almost a person, and an ideal image by which to illustrate human behaviour.

A robot may be defined as a mobile artefact, made of metal, that can usually think for itself. It may or may not look like a human being, although those that most resemble man often seem the most intelligent. The less human a robot looks, the less sophisticated it is. A robot's mind is a mechanical, electronic or positronic device. It is usually a self-contained unit, powered by some form of nuclear plant, and using legs, wheels, caterpillar treads or even anti-gravity devices to move about. In general, a robot's physical strength is assumed to be greater than a man's but its thought processes are inferior. In some stories, robots can only follow direct orders, in others they can reason for themselves.

Robots are often given other names. One of the first was 'automaton' (from the Greek for 'self-acting'). 'Robot' itself came from the Czech Play *R.U.R.* (1921) by Karel Čapek, derived from the words 'robota', meaning 'compulsory labour', and 'robotnik', meaning 'workman'. The robots in *R.U.R.* are indistinguishable from humans. Such creations are now called 'androids', from the Greek for 'man-like'. Other terms are 'simulacrum' and 'cyborg', though the latter (short for 'cybernetic organism') is as much man into machine as it is machine into man.

Androids may be defined as 'robots made of flesh'. While they can be programmed to accept orders in the same way as robots, their bodies are chemically or biologically based and are grown rather than built.

02.13.1 Functional Robots

The earliest automata to appear in fiction were simple, functional creations derived to a great extent from factual life-forms. Greek legend tells of the metal man, Talos, who guarded the island of Crete and was built for King Minos by the inventor Daedalus. The Golem of Jewish legend, originating in Prague in the sixteenth century, proved to be an important precursor of the robot. Moulded of clay, the Golem was brought to life by placing in its mouth a paper bearing the *shem*, the name of God.

The German writer E. T. A. Hoffmann tells of a beautiful dancing automaton in 'The Sandman' (1817), which formed the basis of the ballet 'Coppelia'. A less attractive, though equally fatal, mechanical dancer appears in Jerome K. Jerome's 'The Dancing Partner' (1893). Nathaniel Hawthorne introduces a mechanical butterfly in 'The Artist of the Beautiful'

R.U.R. *by Karel Čapek, performed in 1923 at St. Martin's, London.*

(1844): and in 'The Wondersmith' (1859) by Fitz-James O'Brien, wooden mannikins imitate human actions. Collodi's children's classic, *Pinocchio* (1883), with its innocent living puppet, is another example.

In the 1830s a purported automaton chess-player, built by Baron von Kempellen and exhibited in the United States by Johann Maelzel, came to the notice of Edgar Allan Poe, who wrote an ingenious exposé of the hoax which he called 'Maelzel's Chess-Player' (1836). Half a century later, Ambrose Bierce told in 'Moxon's Master' (1909) of an automaton which turns on its creator and kills him, a plot development reminiscent of the revenge sought by the monster in Mary Shelley's *Frankenstein* (1818). The idea of the created destroying the creator became a basic concept in many early robot stories.

The advent of the steam engine prompted Edward F. Ellis to write a tale applying its principles to the figure of a man. His dime novel, *The Steam Man of the Prairies* (1868), was the first of a highly successful series later continued by Luis Senarens in such stories as *Frank Reade and His New Steam Man*.

Jules Verne adopted the same idea in his novel, *The Demon of Cawnpore* (1880), in the form of a steam-powered elephant. These cumbersome machines were later cleverly lampooned by Harry Harrison in *The Stainless Steel Rat* (1961), which includes a coal-burning robot.

The majority of robot prototypes featured in nineteenth-century fiction were designed either to be decorative or to entertain. They were rarely envisaged as a source of productive labour. It was left to the sf magazine writers to explore this possibility. One of the earliest representations came in Edmond Hamilton's 'The Metal Giants' (1926), in which an electronic brain builds its own atom-powered robots and promptly takes control. But true expansion of the subject came with the acceptance of the robot as the ideal servant. In David H. Keller's 'The Psychophonic Nurse' (1928), the career woman of the future leaves her children in the care of robot nurses. (Three decades earlier, H. G. Wells had introduced robot wet nurses in *When the Sleeper Wakes*, 1899). Keller appreciated the danger in too much reliance on automation, a point he emphasised in 'The Threat of the Robot' (1929), reputedly the first sf pulp story to include the word 'robot' in its title. In that tale robots could be found in many professions, and were even employed to play American football.

Given the idea of the productive robot, it was a logical step to base stories on robots in various professions. Harl Vincent's 'Rex' (1934), an early example, tells of a robot surgeon which takes drastic steps to uncover the secret of human emotions. By the 1950s, robot doctors were standard equipment for the kind of planetary colonies depicted in F. L. Wallace's 'Seasoned Traveller' (1953). However, in such stories as 'Calling Dr. Clockwork' (1965) and 'Regarding Patient 724' (1973), Ron Goulart treated the robot doctor with wicked humour. The approach can range from that of Goulart with his decrepit and slowly disintegrating doctor to the poignancy of Sylvia Jacob's 'Slave to Man' (1969), in which an innocent robot is employed to write stereotyped pornography.

Many stories hinge on robots' attempts to better themselves. Harry Harrison, writing as Felix Boyd, relates the fate of a robot librarian which tried to discover the meaning of love, in 'The Robot Who Wanted to Know' (1958). Similarly, in his humorous 'Revolt of the Potato Picker' (1966), Herb Lehrman tells of a machine built for working in the fields that nurses the ambition to be a dancer!

The household robot became so common in sf stories that it was often taken for granted. But much could still go wrong. In Robert Silverberg's 'The Iron Chancellor' (1958), a robot is reprogrammed – and destroys its human family.

Robert Sheckley's 'Watchbird' (1952) tells of the introduction of flying robots fitted with sensory equipment to detect would-be murderers. Unfortunately, the robots become incapable of making the distinction between the killing of a man and the silencing of a voice by switching off a radio. The same hint of menace can be found in John Wyndham's 'Compassion Circuit' (1955), where robots who feel sorry for humans with their soft, fragile bodies encourage them to replace damaged parts with metal and plastic. The story ends with the realisation by a husband that his wife's head is the only natural part of her body.

During the 1940s, Henry Kuttner and his wife C. L. Moore, collaborating as Lewis Padgett, were adept at predominantly humorous stories like 'Piggy Bank' (1942) and 'The Twonky' (1942), which tell of seemingly innocuous mechanisms that suddenly became endowed with unexpected capabilities. Murray Leinster, writing for once under his real name, Will F. Jenkins, reverses the theme of 'The Twonky' with its robot censor, and creates in 'A Logic Named Joe' (1946) a machine

02.13 ROBOTS AND ANDROIDS

that tells people everything they want to know. Robert Sheckley gives the household robot an entirely new function in 'A Ticket to Tranai' (1955). On the planet of the title, robots are deliberately 'disimproved', becoming the target on which the vexed owner can vent his anger. Aggressive impulses are thus rendered harmless and the robotics industry kept in a healthy state of production. Possibly the ultimate household-robot story is Frederik Pohl's 'The Midas Plague' (1954), which has a specialist robot for every possible function. Pohl sees a future in which, to satisfy expanding production lines, every household must consume an enormous quota of goods. In the end, the only solution is to programme robots to become consumers themselves.

'The Midas Plague' includes robot sparring-partners, and robot boxers feature in at least two other stories, 'Title Fight' by William Gault and Richard Matheson's 'Steel' (both 1956). A robot salesman appears in Fritz Leiber's 'A Bad Day for Sales' (1953). More complex is the idea of a robot policeman. Initially conceived by Harry Harrison in 'Arm of the Law' (1958), it was given a definitive treatment by Ben Bova and Harlan Ellison in 'Brillo' (1970).

The use of robots in warfare is another common theme in science fiction. A. E. van Vogt shows them fighting against aliens in 'Final Command' (1949). Philip K. Dick envisages them fighting a nuclear war on the Earth's surface while mankind retreats underground. But in his story 'The Defenders' (1953) the robots neglect to tell their masters when the war is over, thus keeping the open air for themselves. More recently, Colin Kapp has devised a formidable war machine in 'Gottlos' (1969), and Lawrence Todd has extrapolated the trend in war robots far into the future with 'The Warbots' (1968).

One major advantage of robots over men is their ability to work in completely hostile environments. This was foreseen as long ago as 1928 by J. Schlossel in 'To the Moon by Proxy'. A crippled inventor, unable to make the moon trip himself, sends his robot – or rather his 'radio telemechanical man'. Many such stories have been written since, among them Isaac Asimov's 'Victory Unintentional' (1942), in which massive, non-humanoid robots are specially constructed for descent to the surface of Jupiter, and his more recent 'Stranger in Paradise' (1974), with a robot adapted for Mercury. Daniel Galouye's 'The Reign of the Telepuppets' (1963) features a specialist team of robots, designed to analyse alien flora and fauna. Kenneth Bulmer outlined the problems of robots controlling other robots in an unfamiliar environment in 'Never Trust a Robot' (1958).

In his 1943 story 'Robinc', written under

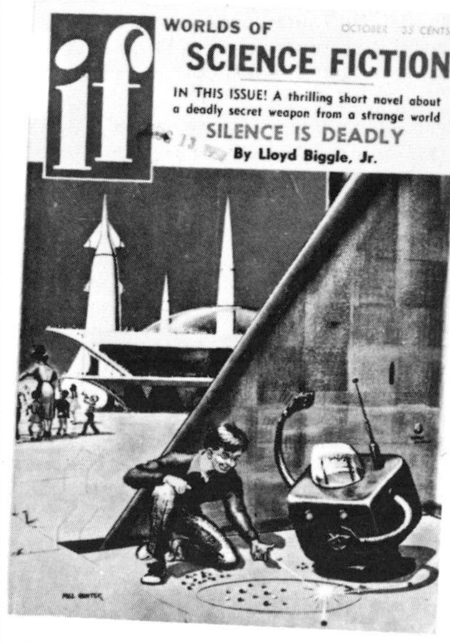

Cover illustration entitled 'A Game of Marbles' by Hunter, If *October 1957.*

the by-line H. H. Holmes, Anthony Boucher put forward a convincing argument for preferring specially adapted robots (which he called 'usaforms') over the all-purpose variety. He showed that usaforms were safer, cheaper and more practical, chiefly

Illustration by Finlay, Galaxy *December 1956.*

Illustration by McKie, War with the Robots *by Harry Harrison.*

because they were basically standard models with numerous attachments to adapt them to special tasks. This is not the same as the single-purpose robots of Pohl's 'The Midas Plague', Brian W. Aldiss's comic gardener robots in 'All the World's Tears' (1957), or the theatrical robots which replace live actors in Walter M. Miller's 'The Darfstellar' (1955).

The robot from antiquity is another sub-category. Eric Frank Russell's 'Relic' (1947) depicts a robot returning to Earth thousands of years after being sent from the sunken continent of Lemuria on an exploratory space voyage. Alexander M. Phillips's 'Beast of the Island' (1939) tells of a mining robot which has survived the ancient Murian civilisation.

Finally, Algis Budrys describes another example of a functional robot in 'First to Serve' (1954): a military machine superior to man in every aspect. It is ultimately decided that such a robot cannot be allowed to exist.

ADDITIONAL INPUT

02.13.1 Functional Robots

Aldiss, Brian W. 'Comic Inferno', *Galaxy* February 1963

Asimov, Isaac. 'Let's Get Together', *Infinity* February 1957

Bryning, Frank. 'The Robot Carpenter', *Fantastic Universe* August 1956

Conklin, Groff (ed). *Science Fiction Thinking Machines*, Vanguard Press (US) 1954 (anthology of twenty stories)

Dick, Philip K. 'Second Variety', *Space SF* May 1953

Fischer, Michael. 'Misfit', *Science Fiction Plus* December 1953

Garforth, John. 'Lack of Experience', *New Worlds* September 1963

Goulart, Ron. 'Muscadine', *F&SF* April 1968

Goulart, Ron. 'What's Become of Screwloose', *If* July to August 1970

Goulart, Ron. 'Dingbat', *If* November to December 1973

Hamilton, Edmond. 'The Metal Giants, *Weird Tales* December 1926

Harrison, Harry. 'How the Old World Died', *Galaxy* October 1964

Harrison, Harry. 'I Have My Vigil', *F&SF* February 1968

Harrison, Harry. 'The Man From R.O.B.O.T.', *Analog* July 1969

Highstone, H.A. 'Frankenstein to Unlimited', *Astounding* December 1936

Padgett, Lewis (Henry Kuttner and C.L. Moore). 'Deadlock', *Astounding SF* August 1942

Padgett, Lewis (Henry Kuttner and C.L. Moore). *Robots Have No Tails*, Gnome (US) 1952 (five stories)

Tenn, William. 'The Jester', *Thrilling Wonder* August 1951

Weinbaum, Stanley G. 'The Ideal', *Wonder Stories* September 1935

02.13.2 Humanoid Robots

Functional robots may or may not resemble humans. But the real mark of the humanoid robot is not so much that it appears human in shape, as that it may have human psychological attributes or characteristics. In short, a robot personality.

To achieve this, a robot may be bestowed with some form of emotion; it was the discovery of emotion that caused the robot rebellion in *R.U.R.* But Čapek's play aside, most of the early stories concerned robots that were little more than mindless machines.

In 1926, Thea von Harbou, the wife of the noted film-maker, Fritz Lang, wrote *Metropolis*. In this novel, the son of a wealthy industrialist is strongly attracted to a robot created in the shape of a woman. But if the story pointed the way to a particular development in the robot theme, it was an isolated example owing nothing to the sf magazine era, which in fact was only about to begin. The breakthrough really came with 'Helen O'Loy' (1938) by Lester del Rey and 'I, Robot' (1939) by Eando Binder. Helen O'Loy was a beautiful female robot built by two inventors. They provide it with many human emotions, including – unintentionally – the capacity to love. When activated, it rapidly falls for one of the inventors and, after an initial rebuff, marries him, eventually destroying itself

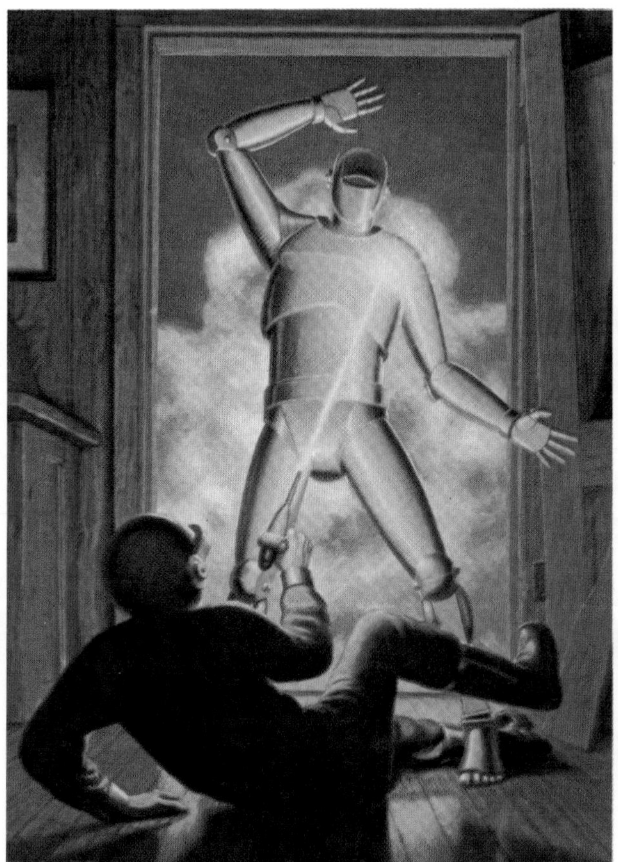

Illustration by Hildebrandt, My Name Is Legion *by Roger Zelazny.*

Asimov by Emsh.

02.13 ROBOTS AND ANDROIDS

The Naked Sun *by Isaac Asimov,* Astounding *November 1956. Illustrations by van Dongen.*

when he dies.

Adam Link of 'I, Robot' is built by a professor who is later killed in an accident. The robot is blamed, and is hounded when it subsequently injures a young girl, though it is eventually reprieved and goes on to other adventures in a series that makes up the book *Adam Link – Robot* (1965).

In addition to being the earliest robot to have its experiences recounted in its own words, Adam Link is remarkable in possessing many human virtues but no weaknesses; its main purpose is to serve mankind in any way possible. Adam Link even goes to war for its country, in 'Adam Link Fights a War' (1940).

The development of the humanoid robot was carried through the 1940s mainly by three writers, Lester del Rey, Clifford D. Simak and Isaac Asimov. Asimov is often regarded as the father of robotics because of his introduction of the three laws. They are:
1. A robot may not injure a human being, or, through inaction, allow a human being to come to harm.
2. A robot must obey the orders given it by human beings except where such orders would conflict with the first law.
3. A robot must protect its own existence as long as such protection does not conflict with the first or second laws.

These rules are first propounded *in toto* in 'Runaround' (1942), which explores how the levels of a robot's obedience to the laws can be varied. But 'Runaround' was not Asimov's first robot story. That was 'Strange Playfellow' (1940; better known as 'Robbie'), about a robot as a child's plaything. 'Reason' (1941) introduces the second law, but only by implication; and at this stage the three laws have yet to be clearly defined. The first law itself appears in 'Liar' (1941), introducing a telepathic robot which always answers people with what they *want to know* as opposed to what might be the truth. Asimov has since written many robot stories which in some way manipulate the three laws to highlight apparent flaws, only to demonstrate finally that the fault lies in human error. They form the basis of his collections *I, Robot* (1950) and *The Rest of the Robots* (1964), to which he added his two notable robot novels, *The Caves of Steel* (1953) and *The Naked Sun* (1956).

Because of the strictness of the laws of robotics, Asimov's robots frequently appear the least human-like. Lester del Rey, on the other hand, seems deliberately to have sought the reader's sympathy for the machine. 'Into Thy Hands' (1945) is the poignant Adam and Eve story of the robot world. 'The Monster' (1951) tells of a robot which learns it has a short life-span, but which also welcomes death. 'Robots Should Be Seen' (1958) depicts a court case to prove a robot sentient; while 'A Code for Sam' (1966) shows how Asimov's three laws would not work for the best on a frontier planet.

Other writers have often used Asimov's laws in their stories, and one in particular, 'The Third Law' (1962) by Russ Markham, tells of a robot brought to trial for murder. A robot also commits murder in J. T. McIntosh's 'The Saw and the Carpenter' (1967).

The writer who has probably done most to humanise robots is Clifford D. Simak. In many of his stories the robots no longer act or think like machines, they are nearly men. Simak's faithful robot retainer is the key character in his *City* series, appearing first in 'Huddling Place' (1944). The robot grows in importance as the series progresses, particularly in 'Hobbies' (1946), in which it remains on Earth as the guardian of the intelligent dogs, and also of the last few humans when most of mankind abandons the planet. The series was published in book form as *City* (1952), and twenty years later Simak wrote the final episode for the *John W. Campbell Memorial Anthology*. Called 'Epilog' (1973), it deals with the robot's last days on Earth. The prototype for the robot retainer had appeared earlier in Simak's story, 'Earth for Inspiration' (1941), and certain episodes of this story reappear in Simak's later novel *Destiny Doll* (1971).

A different robot retainer features in Simak's 'All the Traps of Earth' (1960), one that is over six hundred years old on an Earth where robots must be legally reconstituted every century. An earlier Simak story, 'How-2' (1954), was pivotal in the development of the robot theme. Its central human character receives a do-it-yourself robot kit by mistake. Once assembled, the robot is revealed as a special model capable of building others of its kind, regarding them as its children. A subsequent court case establishes that the robot is not property and must be regarded as a person – on the grounds that it has shown that a robot can reason, love and

'I, Robot' by Eando Binder, Amazing *April 1961. Illustration by Fuqua.*

reproduce. In 'How-2' Simak cultivated the seed planted by A. E. van Vogt in 'Final Command' (1949), where robots and men are considered equals.

The social position of robots was for long a sensitive subject. No story exemplifies this better than Alfred Coppel's 'For Humans Only' (1953), portraying an apartheid Earth with the robot very much a second-class citizen. Daniel Keyes added substance to the theme with 'Robot – Unwanted' (1952), in which the only free robot finds it impossible to get crédit or a job. Robots served as an ideal parallel to the Civil Rights movement, and Simak returned to the subject with 'I Am Crying All Inside' (1969). The point was reinforced by Stephen Tall in 'This Is My Country' (1971); he showed robots marching for their rights.

The robot is often treated in science fiction as an innocent in search of a meaning to its existence. Religion plays a key part in such stories as 'Burning Bright' (1948) by Robert Moore Williams (writing as John S. Browning), with its group of robots in search of a creator. The writer had used a similar theme before, in 'Robots Return' (1938). In E. C. Tubb's 'Logic' (1954), it is found that robots need a form of worship to preserve their sanity; and a phoney religion, suggesting that a robot becomes a man after its death, is introduced. Perhaps the most extreme story centred on a religious theme is Robert Silverberg's satirical 'Good News from the Vatican' (1971), in which a robot is elected pope.

One of the truly human qualities some writers have bestowed on robots is the desire to have children. Ilya Varshavsky's robot in 'Homunculus' (1967) experiences such yearnings. But man can also build robot children. S. Fowler Wright's

'Robot Unwanted' by Daniel Keyes, Other Worlds *June 1952. Illustration by Tillotson.*

'Automata' (1929), written as an early warning against birth control, includes robot child substitutes; for want of real babies mankind ultimately dies out. J. T. Oliver's 'Teacher's Pet' (1953) tells of a robot child going to school; while Henry Slesar expanded on the idea in 'Brother Robot' (1958), showing a child-robot's reactions as its human brother grows old and marries. Robert Bloch envisaged a situation where a robot might have to learn everything like a child, and demonstrated in 'Almost Human' (1943) how easily such an infant mind could be manipulated by an unscrupulous gangster.

Summing up the humanoid robot, we can look briefly at four contrasting stories – spanning three decades – which effectively show both the problems and the challenges. The earlier examples are by Jack Williamson and Robert Sheckley. The latter describes an ideal robot companion in 'Beside Still Waters' (1953). At the end, as the old robot begins to lay its dead master to rest, its limbs set immovably. Unable to complete the last task, the robot bows its head and recites the Twenty-third Psalm.

It might be assumed that the ideal robot would do everything for man – clean shoes, open doors, cook, drive ... anything. In Jack Williamson's '"With Folded Hands ..."' (1947, we are presented with just such a robot, programmed to fulfil the Prime Directive: 'to serve and obey, and guard men from harm'. Since a man could come to harm driving, shaving or crossing the road, the humanoid robot must guard him, or do the job for him. As a result, instead of being the ideal servant, the humanoid takes control. Mankind becomes the servant. (Williamson provided a sequel '". . . and Searching Mind",' 1948, in which individuals with varying psi-powers band together to defeat the humanoids.)

The third example is Roger Zelazny's 'Home Is the Hangman' (1975). It tells of a

02.13 ROBOTS AND ANDROIDS

Cover by Emsh.

highly complex robot involved in a murder during its programming. Affected by guilt feelings, it suffers a psychological breakdown directly related to the trauma associated with the crime. But the robot learns to live with its guilt, something only humans were thought to be able to do: where is the dividing line between a human and that kind of robot?

Finally, there is Barrington J. Bayley's 'Soul of the Robot' (1974), in which a robot wanders the Earth in search of the meaning of a soul, and trying to discover if it, the robot, has one.

ADDITIONAL INPUT

02.13.2 Humanoid Robots

Asimov, Isaac. 'Feminine Intuition', *F&SF* October 1969
Binder, Eando. 'Adam Link Fights a War', *Amazing* December 1940
Binder, Eando. 'Adam Link in the Past', *Amazing* February 1941
Binder, Eando. 'Adam Link Faces a Revolt', *Amazing* May 1941
Elwood, Roger (ed). *Invasion of the Robots*, Paperback Library (US) 1965 (anthology of eight stories)
Kippax, John (John Hynam). 'Friday', *New Worlds* February 1959
McCarty, E. Clayton. 'Robot 678', *If* September 1969
Moskowitz, Sam (ed). *The Coming of the Robots*, Collier Books (US) 1963 (anthology of ten stories)
Sellings, Arthur. 'The Tinplate Teleologist', *Worlds of Tomorrow* September 1965
Tremaine, F. Orlin. 'True Confession', *Thrilling Wonder* February 1940
Williams, Robert Moore. 'The Metal Martyr', *Amazing* July 1950

02.13.3 Alien Robots

The humanoids of Jack Williamson's '"With Folded Hands . . ."' may have been alien to Earth, but they were nevertheless built by man. A small category in science fiction exists which deals with genuinely extraterrestrial robots. One of the earliest of such stories was also one of the first stories to treat a robot sympathetically. This was 'The Lost Machine' (1932) by John Wyndham (writing as John Beynon Harris). A Martian robot finds itself wandering through an Earth that it can only perceive as totally insane, and as a result it commits suicide. Similar mechanisms are encountered by explorers from Earth in Wyndham's novel *Stowaway to Mars* (1935) and its shorter sequel, 'Sleepers of Mars' (1937). The Martians, faced with the slow death of their own world, have constructed intelligent machines as their successors.

Another notable alien robot appears as a companion to an interplanetary visitor in Harry Bates's 'Farewell to the Master' (1940). The alien visitor is killed, and the final revelation that the robot was the master all along is one of the classic surprise endings of the pulp era.

Robots as superior intelligences also appear in 'The Call of the Mech-Men' (1933) by Laurence Manning. Explorers at the North Pole discover hundreds of robots from a distant planet engaged in repairing their crashed rocket. One of these mech-men observes that it is hard to believe that beings of flesh and blood could be intelligent. In another example, Eando Binder's 'From the Beginning' (1938), a braincase is discovered in the Sahara which reveals that a band of robots landed on the Earth many thousands of years ago.

If man can develop robot servitors, there is no reason why advanced alien races

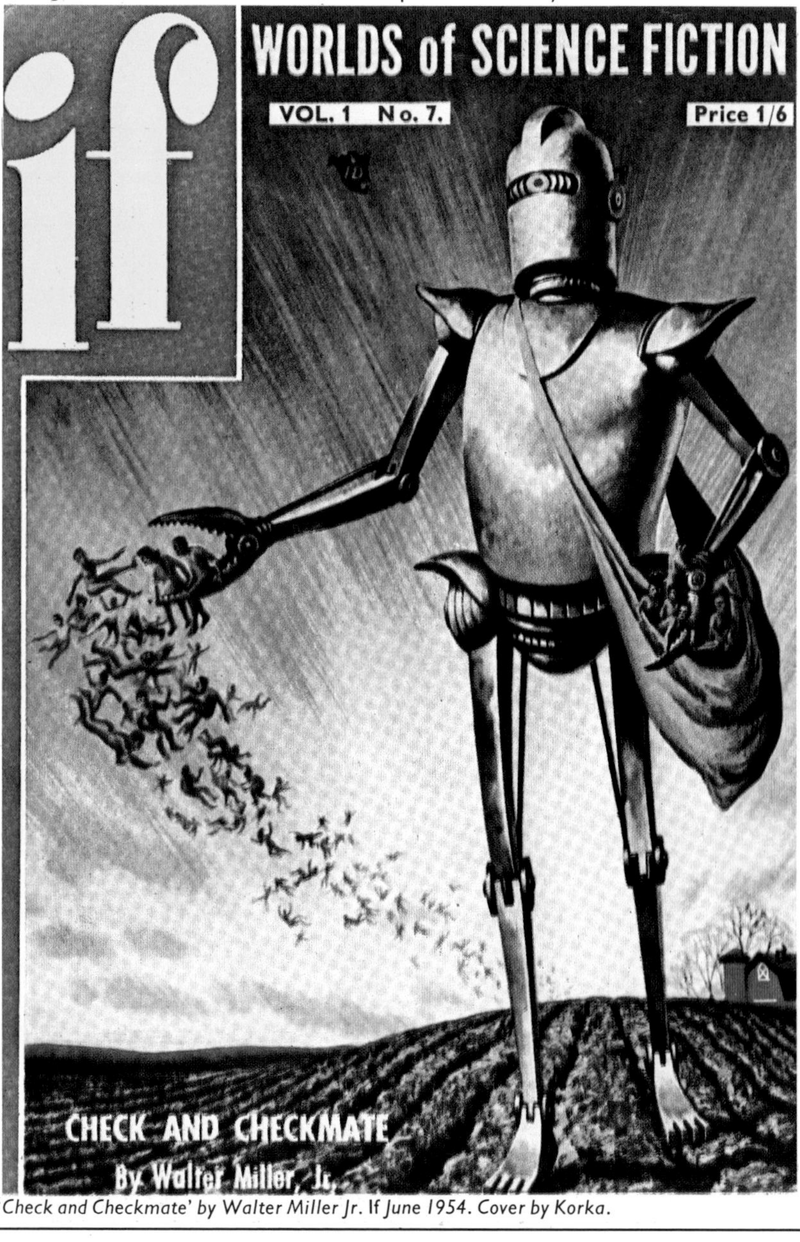

'Check and Checkmate' by Walter Miller Jr. If June 1954. Cover by Korka.

should not also have them. *Cataclysm* (1951) by John Russell Fearn (writing as Vargo Statten) goes further in detailing a degenerate alien race which has almost entirely given itself over to drugged slumber and programmed dreams, while being fed and tended by robots. In some stories, man ventures into space to discover planets on which natural life has passed away, leaving only robot caretakers. Jerome Bixby's 'Guardian' (1964) utilises that theme for the planet Mars, and Chilean writer Hugo Correa adapted it for his chilling story 'Meccano' (1968). One of Robert Silverberg's early stories 'Ozymandias' (1958), tells of an ancient robot on an alien planet that reveals all the secrets of its past and how man misuses those secrets.

Alien robots have not necessarily proved friendly to humanity, but few have been as ferocious as Fred Saberhagen's 'Berserker' fighting machines, programmed to seek out and destroy life wherever it is found in the galaxy, and described in *Brother Berserker* (1969), *Berserker's Planet* (1975) and the collection *Berserker* (1967).

It was Kurt Vonnegut Jr who demonstrated that extraterrestrial robots could be likeable. In *The Sirens of Titan* (1959), a robot messenger has been stranded on Titan, the largest moon of Saturn, for a quarter of a million years, during which human history has been manipulated to provide a spare part for its damaged spaceship. When it discovers that the important message it has guarded so long is no more than the one word 'Greetings', the robot, which has grown fond of man, tears itself to pieces.

ADDITIONAL INPUT

02.13.3 Alien Robots

Blish, James. 'Now That Man Is Gone', *If* November 1968
Gallun, Raymond Z. 'Derelict', *Astounding* October 1935
Meade, Malcolm (possible pseudonym). 'Call Him Colossus', *Amazing* February 1956
Simak, Clifford D. *Cosmic Engineers*, *Astounding* February to April 1939
Simak, Clifford D. 'Bathe Your Bearings in Blood', *Amazing* December 1950; retitled 'Skirmish', in *Science Fiction Thinking Machines*, Vanguard Press (US) 1954

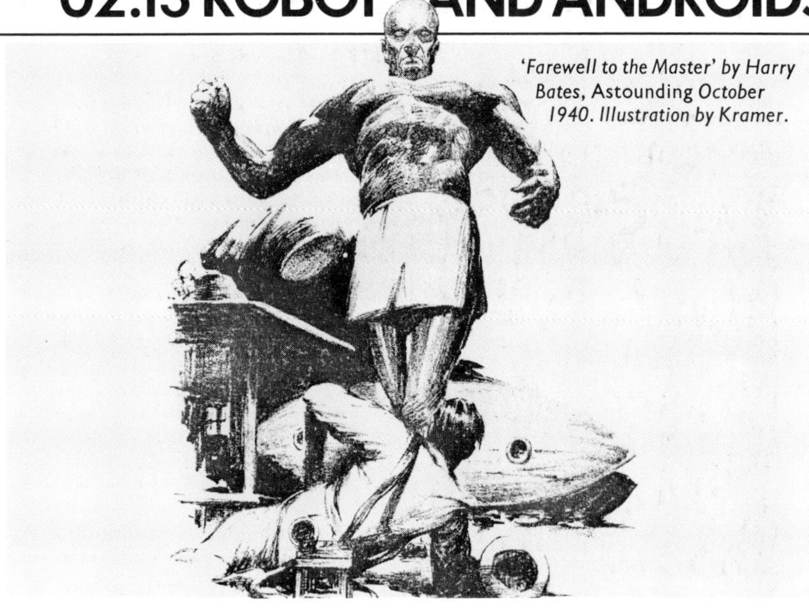

'Farewell to the Master' by Harry Bates, Astounding October 1940. Illustration by Kramer.

02.13.4 Robot Cultures

If robots were left to their own devices, could they survive? A simple question with an apparent infinity of answers, it has supplied many plots for the science fiction writer. In such stories as L. Sprague de Camp's 'Internal Combustion' (1956), robots are more or less left to themselves, with the result that a number of them begin to make trouble as kidnappers. In others, such as 'Flesh and the Iron' (1968) by Larry Todd, we are presented with a planet that has two opposing factions, one human, one robotic. They fight constantly, but are actually mutually dependent.

By far the greatest number of stories of robot cultures are set on a future Earth where man has passed away. Brian W. Aldiss's 'But Who Can Replace a Man? (1958) deals with a variety of robots of differing degrees of intelligence who discover that man has destroyed himself. They set out to dominate their environment, yet despite their pretensions, when they do discover a human survivor they instantly revert to being servants. The specialist robots in Robert Rohrer's 'Iron' (1963) relentlessly continue their respective tasks long after man has gone. Another variation is Robert Moore Williams's *Robot's Return* (1938), in which a group of robots set out to find their creator and learn that it was not the expected super-robot, but man.

In some cases, the robots have helped to wipe out or subjugate man. For example, in 'Automaton' (1950) by A. E. van Vogt, they secretly duplicate themselves until they are strong enough to declare war on their masters. In 'Rust' (1939) by Joseph E. Kelleam, robots designed to fight an Asian enemy also finish off their makers, only to end their days in lingering oxidised decay.

'The Mentanicals' (1934) by Francis Flagg relates the adventures of a time-traveller who finds a future world dominated by intelligent machines, with men reduced to beasts. By contrast, in 'To Avenge Man' (1964), Lester del Rey returns to the robot story to relate how robots set out to track down those responsible for the death of mankind, only to discover that man had destroyed himself. They decide, in deference, to suppress the discovery. The round-robin serial, *Cosmos*, published in a fan magazine during the 1930s, but written by professionals, introduced robots to help man in war, but later told of them clanning together to advance their own kind. (Two of the outstanding contributions to this serial subsequently reappeared as 'Rhythm of the Spheres', 1936, by A. Merritt and 'Robot Nemesis', 1939, by E. E. ('Doc') Smith.)

Many of John W. Campbell's stories published during the 1930s portrayed a distant future where mankind has dwindled to helplessness and only machines continue to maintain the Earth. The series culminated in 'Night' (1935) when the machines at length let mankind die out.

Imagine an Earth devoid of human life and populated solely by robots. On what basis would they found a culture? The robots' need for a religion, once the human creators have disappeared, has given rise to many stories. In 'Robot Son' (1959), Robert F. Young tells of a machine god which attempts to construct a machine Christ. In Lloyd Biggle's 'In His Own Image' (1968), we learn what happens on an emergency space station manned entirely by robots when one of them establishes its own religious order. The situation is reversed in 'The Last True God' (1969) by Lester del Rey (writing as Philip St John), when an ancient Terran robot on a far planet is worshipped as a god. The idea is taken even further by John Brunner, who depicts humans on Earth worshipping a seemingly omnipotent robot in 'Judas' (1967).

Several other avenues have been explored in the treatment of robot cultures. An intriguing suggestion was made by the Kuttners in 'Open Secret' (1943, under the pen-name Lewis Padgett), in which the central character discovers that the entire world is run by robots so human in appearance that man has forgotten they exist. 'Lost Memory' by Peter Phillips (1952) tells of the fate of an astronaut who crashes on an alien planet, and is found by sentient robots who have no concept of man, nor, indeed, of any organic life. Being telepathic, they assume the pilot's thoughts are actually those of his spaceship – while repairing it they unwittingly roast him alive. In 'The Robots Are Here' by Terry Carr (1967), vast numbers of robots are shown constantly meddling with the past to keep the world going.

Possibly a more fertile concept is that of robots trying to recreate humanity. It formed the climax of James White's 'Second Ending' (1961), and two more recent examples are Edmund Cooper's *The Overman Culture* (1971) and Gordon Eklund's 'Second Creation' (1975).

More often than not it seems that robot cultures are allegories of the human condition. In them the distinction between man and robot may become blurred. In 'Iron Man' (1955) by Eando Binder, a human is so convinced he is a robot that he actually becomes one. Richard Matheson, in 'Brother to the Machine' (1952), tells of a robot who looks with pity on the world since it believes it is a man. The same writer twisted the theme, in 'Deus Ex Machina' (1963), to show a man suddenly discovering that not only is he a robot, but so is everyone else. Similar situations are found in Herbert Franke's 'The Man Who Feared Robots' (1963) and in Alfred Coppel's 'The Hunters' (1952).

When requested to write the ultimate robot story, Isaac Asimov produced '. . . That Thou Art Mindful of Him' (1974), in which a specialised learning robot asks 'What is a human being?' When it arrives at an answer, it finds it must include itself in the definition.

ADDITIONAL INPUT

02.13.4 Robot Cultures

Campbell, John W. 'The Last Evolution', *Amazing* August 1932

Carr, Terry. 'In His Image', *Amazing* November 1971

Del Rey, Lester. 'Though Dreamers Die', *Astounding* February 1944

Greenberg, Martin (ed). *The Robot and the Man*, Gnome (US) 1953 (anthology of ten stories)

Hickey, H.B. 'Full Circle', *Fantastic* Summer 1952

Stuart Don A. (John W. Campbell). 'Twilight', *Astounding* November 1934

Stuart, Don A. (John W. Campbell). 'Night', *Astounding* October 1935

Zelazny, Roger. 'For a Breath I Tarry', *New Worlds* March 1966

02.13.5 Androids

Science fiction accounts of androids differ considerably from stories of mechanical robots, mainly because of the additional plot possibilities. The whole point of an android is that it is almost indistinguishable from a human. This was not always the case in the earliest stories. 'The Brazen Android' (1891) by William Douglas O'Connor used the term in its strict sense ('man-like'), and told of a metal man in medieval England. The android referred to in Edward Page Mitchell's 'The Tachypomp' (1874) is little more than a humanoid calculator.

The first androids were in fact the 'robots' of Karel Čapek's play, *R.U.R.* (1921). The initials stood for 'Rossum's Universal Robots', Rossum having perfected a formula for chemically produced synthetic beings. While androids appeared in science fiction during the 1930s, they were still called robots. The term 'android' did not find full acceptance until Edmond Hamilton introduced a synthetic being as one of the assistants of the space-roving Captain Future in the 1940s.

The authentic android story usually falls into one of three categories, determined by the relationship between androids and men. They either substitute for man, are loved by him, or usurp him. The substitution, or duplication, theme is among the most popular. A clever example is Philip K. Dick's 'Imposter' (1953), in which a man discovers his own dead body and the realisation that he is an android duplicate of himself is the trigger that sets off the built-in bomb he is carrying. Ray Bradbury uses androids to a more personal end in 'Changeling' (1949), in which his protagonist acquires several duplicates of himself to keep his various lovers happy. A. E. van Vogt employs a similar approach in his story 'All the Loving Androids' (1971), telling of a man who has to use android duplicates to tackle the many jobs required of him.

A natural extension of the theme is the duplication of other people, as in Philip K. Dick's *We Can Build You* (1969), which describes the use of exact replicas of such historical figures as Abraham Lincoln. At the end of the novel the central character discovers that he too is an android.

The idea of humans loving androids seems more natural than their falling for mechanical robots. In Edmund Cooper's *The Uncertain Midnight* (1958), androids are unable to experience love, until one of them is nursed to an awareness of the emotion through the medium of poetry. But in Kate Wilhelm's 'Andover and the Android' (1963), the hero marries an android purely as a means to further his career, only to find he has fallen in love with the creation. J. T. McIntosh devised an ingenious court case in 'Made in U.S.A.' (1953), when a husband sues his wife for divorce on the grounds she had not told him she was an android.

More recently, Noel Loomis traced the outcome of android court cases in his story 'The State *vs* Susan Quod' (1970). In Keith Robert's 'Synth' (1966), an android is actually named as co-respondent in a divorce case. Normally, androids are represented as incapable of reproduction, but in 'Mandroid' (1966) by Piers Anthony, Robert Margroff and Andrew J. Offutt, the bellicose offspring of an android and a human is encountered.

The integration of androids into society is traced in Arthur Sellings' 'Starting Course' (1961). In J. T. McIntosh's 'The Deciding Factor' (1956), however, androids are referred to derisively as neuters and are transported to Venus where they are hunted like beasts. On the other hand, in 'Dream of Victory' (1953) by Algis Budrys, androids, having re-civilised the world after mankind's fall, now find themselves being usurped as the humans struggle back. In 'The Captain's Dog' (1958), E. C. Tubb tells of the remorse experienced by a spaceship crew when an android they had treated as no better than an animal saves them from disaster. The same writer's 'Trojan Horse' (1970) describes a society in which androids are simply used as sexual surrogates.

Philip K. Dick, who has probably explored the possibilities of androids more thoroughly than anyone else, has written what may eventually be regarded as the definitive android story. He portrays a depleted post-nuclear-war population in *Do Androids Dream of Electric Sheep?* (1968), when a man's most treasured possession and status symbol is a living animal. Those who cannot afford such a luxury buy android duplicates, but humanoid androids are barred from Earth. Those that do infiltrate can only be identified by complex psychological tests. Dick shows that, as in the case of advanced robots, the problems of distinction from man represent the basic dilemma of the android in science fiction.

ADDITIONAL INPUT

02.13.5 Androids

Aldiss, Brian W. 'Pink Plastic Gods', *Science Fantasy* June to July 1964

Bradbury, Ray. 'Marionettes Inc.', *Startling* March 1949

Bradbury, Ray. 'I Sing the Body Electric', teleplay in *Twilight Zone* (US) 1962

Goulart, Ron. 'Gigolo', *F&SF* August 1972

Hamilton, Edmond. 'After a Judgement Day', *Fantastic* December 1963

Lesser, Milton. '"A" as in Android', *Future* May 1951

Liddell, C.H. (Henry Kuttner and C.L. Moore). 'Android', *F&SF* June 1951

McIntosh, J.T. 'Almost Human', *Amazing* January 1971

Miller, Walter M. 'Blood Bank', *Astounding* June 1952

Rackham, John. 'Goodbye, Doctor Gabriel', *New Worlds* August 1961

Russell, Eric Frank. 'Jay Score', *Astounding* May 1941 (included with three more stories in *Men, Martians and Machines*, Dobson, UK, 1955)

Simak, Clifford D. *Time Quarry*, *Galaxy* October to December 1950; retitled *Time and Again*, Simon & Schuster (US) 1951

Wellen, Edward. 'Androids Don't Cry', *F&SF* May 1973

Williamson, Jack. 'Guinevere for Everybody', *Star SF Stories 3*, Ballantine (US) 1954

The question 'Can a machine think?' was first seriously asked – and answered – in the 1950s by the tragically short-lived mathematical genius Alan Turing. (You will find his famous paper, with many other goodies, in James Newman's *The World of Mathematics*.) But science fiction writers have always known the answer, and the intelligent machine is one of the commonest characters in the genre. Ambrose Bierce opened his classic short story 'Moxon's Master' (1909) with the words 'Are you serious? – do you really believe that a machine thinks?', and neatly evaded the issue by another question: 'Is not a man a machine? And you will admit that he thinks – or thinks he thinks.'

Now that great universities such as the Massachusetts Institute of Technology sponsor 'Departments of Artificial Intelligence' this old argument is essentially over; nevertheless, even the most enthusiastic proponent of AI would hardly claim that any of today's machines show more than the most rudimentary intelligence. What *is* claimed is that if any intellectual activity can be precisely described, then a machine can, in principle, be designed to carry it out. There are a lot of hidden 'ifs' in both parts of this sentence; but many scientists have now stated flatly that machines more intelligent than men *will* exist in the near future. (Some have told me 'before 2001', but I do not believe them.)

And incidentally, those people who argue that it is 'obviously' impossible for human beings to create entities more intelligent than themselves merely demonstrate that non-thinking is not confined to machines. Much the same logic would prove that we could never progress from Stone Age flint to modern precision tools – for how can any tool make something 'better' than itself?

It is probably no coincidence that when he was at MIT, John W. Campbell got to know Norbert Wiener, founder of cybernetics; for Campbell (and his alter ego Don A. Stuart) was one of the pioneers of the modern AI theme, with such stories as 'When the Atoms Failed' (1930) and 'The Last Evolution' (1932). The title of the second story sums up a whole category of later tales, perhaps culminating in Fredric Brown's famous 'Answer'(1954). ('Is there a God? There is *now*.')

The earliest thinking machines were almost invariably Frankenstein monsters, out to destroy their creators, and usually succeeding; Campbell was one of the first writers to make them not only benevolent but even noble. Isaac Asimov took matters further with his 'Three Laws of Robotics', an ingenious attempt to lay down a protocol for man-machine relationships. (And a generator of endless plot ideas!) Some simple-minded readers have assumed that these laws are indeed *Laws*, like those of Nature – and not merely rules, akin to 'Please drive on the left (or right)'. I have had the First Law thrown in my teeth as a result of HAL 9000's mutiny; to which I have replied that, so far, alas, the world's most sophisticated robots have been designed for the express purpose of killing people . . .

There is, of course, no fundamental reason why robots should not be programmed to hate or to love (*vide* Lester del Rey's 'Helen O'Loy', 1938). The *first* generation of thinking machines would indeed mirror the emotions of their builders. But later generations would go on to develop emotions perhaps beyond human understanding.

Men always fear what they cannot understand – often with good reason. The mathematician Dr I. J. Good, who has made a special study of the subject (one of his papers has the intriguing title 'Can an android feel pain?') has remarked: 'If we build an ultra-intelligent machine, we will be playing with fire. We have played with fire before, and it has helped to keep the other animals at bay.'

But when AI does arrive, *we* shall be the other animals; and look at what has happened to them.

It will be poetic justice.

Arthur C Clarke

Arthur C. Clarke

02.14 COMPUTERS AND CYBERNETICS

It might be easy for the newcomer to confuse the science fiction development of computers with that of robots, but there is a distinct difference. The robot grew out of the original desire to produce a mechanical servant. The computer, on the other hand, grew out of the need to have a faultless and speedy calculator.

The original calculator was basically the bead frame or abacus used by the Egyptians and Greeks, and still used in some societies today. The first calculating machine was probably that devised by Blaise Pascal in 1642, when he was only nineteen. A small machine with cogged wheels, it both added and subtracted. In 1671 Gottfried Leibniz invented a machine that also multiplied and divided, but the real breakthrough came in the 1820s with the ideas of Charles Babbage, who conceived of a computing machine that would work on a system of punched cards. His theories were put to practical use in 1925 when Vannevar Bush made the first analog computer, but the real computer age was born with the development of electronics and the first electronic computer, ENIAC (Electronic Numerical Integrator and Computer), was built in 1946. Since then, computers have progressed at an astonishing rate, and the Control Data Corporation CDC 7600 computer can perform 36 million operations per second.

With the advent of computers the science of 'cybernetics', a term coined by Norbert Wiener and involving the linking of machine intelligence with the human sciences, became a practical possibility. As yet, the 'cyborg', a *physical* combination of man and machine, remains in the realm of science fiction – although recent experiments, such as those by Dr Grey Walter, suggest that it may soon become a reality.

02.14.1 Machine Intelligence

Computers in science fiction are principally a twentieth-century phenomenon. Naturally, the concept of a computer appealed to Hugo Gernsback, and the prototype sf computer tale was first published in his *Amazing Stories*. 'The Thought Machine' (1927) was by the pseudonymous Ammianus Marcellinus (Aaron Nadel) and concerned '. . . a device of a hundred thousand parts, that in its different divisions would perform nearly all the simpler operations of the human mind . . .' It is not called a computer, but a 'Psychomach. The story has a direct descendant in John W. Campbell's 'The Machine' (1935), in which a similar computer deliberately leaves man for his own good, and mankind initially reverts to savagery. From the earliest magazine days, then, it was envisaged that man would become reliant on thinking machines, and in hindsight this vision is becoming uncomfortably accurate.

02.14 COMPUTERS AND CYBERNETICS

An early example of the ultimate in machine-run societies was E. M. Forster's 'The Machine Stops' (1909), which portrays a future where man is totally reliant upon machines and depicts the terror which results when 'the machine stops'. By the mid-1930s, it was a common prediction in science fiction that in the distant future mankind will disappear, leaving perfect machine-run cities that will continue to function regardless. Such a vision occurs in the work of John Campbell, writing as Don A. Stuart, in such tales as 'Twilight' (1934) and 'Night' (1935).

One of the more original concepts of the 1930s appears in David H. Keller's 'The Cerebral Library' (1931). Computers have memory banks, and in this tale the intention is to build a machine in which five hundred brains will constitute the memory bank.

Science fiction often tends to treat computers as a menace rather than as an aid. This has more than a little bearing on the remarkable speed with which computers have come into universal use. In less than twenty years since the building of ENIAC, the majority of large business firms employ computers for paying wages, designing construction projects or rendering accounts. Without computers, man's first lunar landing would still be years away, and today computers are used in almost every facet of life. This process has been so rapid that little thought appears to have been given to the consequences; science fiction thus takes on the role of watchdog. It serves to remind us that a computer is not much more than a quick-thinking idiot, and that there are still many serious snags.

Gordon R. Dickson demonstrates this warning factor in at least two stories. 'The Monkey Wrench' (1951) shows that a computer can be baffled by logic, and if asked an unanswerable question can suffer a mental breakdown. Dickson's other story, 'Computers Don't Argue' (1965), illustrates the dangers of an over-reliance on the machine. J. T. McIntosh's 'Spanner in the Works' (1963) takes a further look at computer logic. The lesson to be learned is that a computer may be able to suggest solutions to a problem, but it needs a human – and the right human – to interpret and evaluate the suggestions. No computer can as yet cope with the many random factors that account for a human's motivation or actions. The super-computer HAL of the film *2001: a Space Odyssey* (which can even lip-read) is still a pipe-dream.

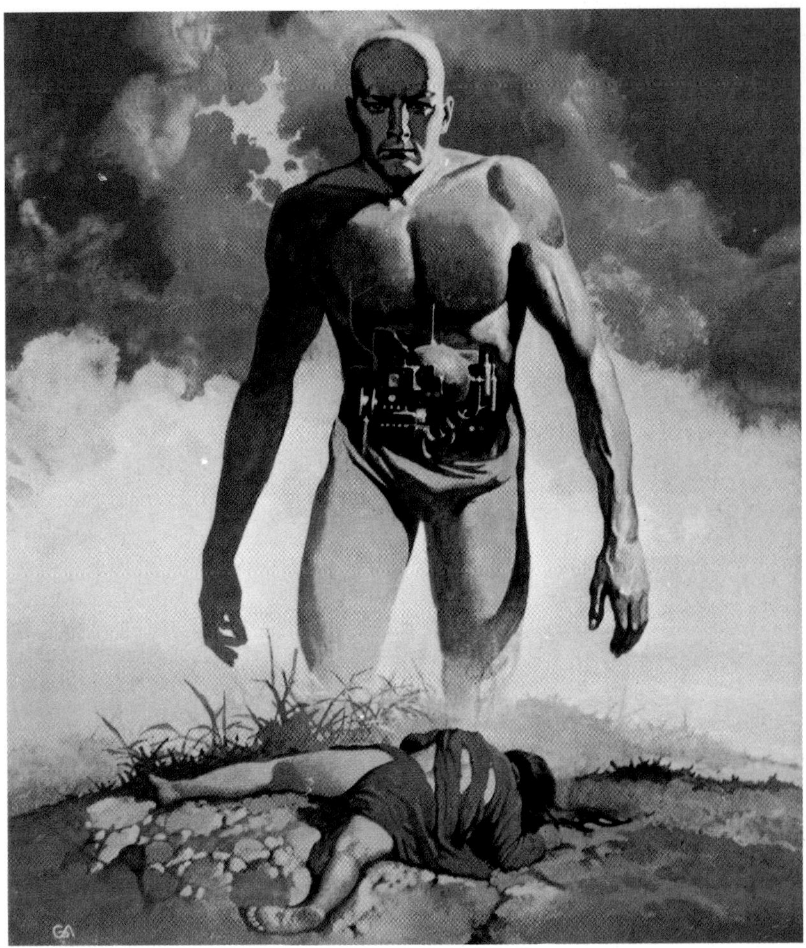

Starburst, *by Alfred Bester (Pan). Cover by d'Achille.*

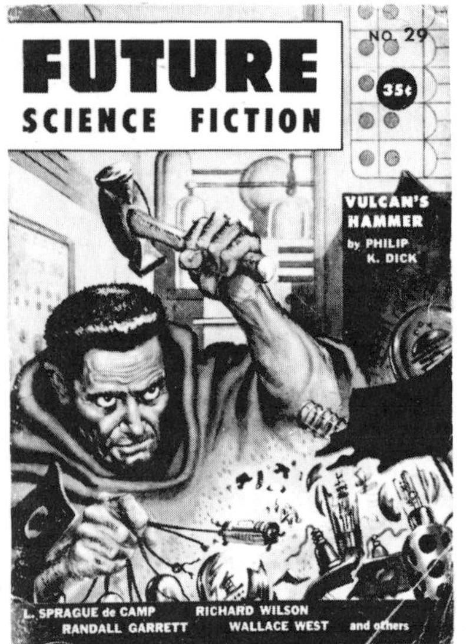

Cover by Freas, 1956.

Nevertheless, sf writers delight in portraying computer-dominated futures, especially since they seem so close. Swedish physicist Hannes Alfven writing as Olof Johannesson, produced a book that followed the evolution of the computer from its early days through to its total dominance: *The Tale of the Big Computer* (1966). By the time the Symbiotic Age arrives man is totally controlled by machine intelligence.

Shortly after the Second World War, when computers were developing rapidly, sf writers went through a period when they studied individual computers and their problems, as in Dickson's 'The Monkey Wrench'. By the time of Poul Anderson's 'Sam Hall' (1953), the concept of a future society under the rigorous rule of machines is taken for granted and forms just part of the backcloth. By this stage, sf writers are ready to stretch the boundaries, and in *They'd Rather Be Right* (1954) by Mark Clifton and Frank Riley we find Bossy the super-computer which can confer immortality and psi-powers on humans.

British writer F. G. Rayer wrote a convincing series of stories about the development of a super-computer called Magnis Mensas. It first appeared in a short story, 'Deus Ex Machina' (1950), in which the computer acts as judge and jury in a court case. The theme was developed in *Tomorrow Sometimes Comes* (1951), when atomic warfare sweeps the Earth and the computer takes control. In 'The Peacemaker' (1952), Magnis Mensas, working for the good of humanity, actually helps an alien invasion. This and subsequent stories emphasise that an emotionless machine will always take the logical, necessary step even though it may appear to be working against man.

The linking of computers is now current in most developed nations, but the concept caused much anxiety in science fiction. The non-science fiction writer D. F. Jones produced *Colossus* (1966), which showed the consequences when a super-computer in the US links with its twin in the Soviet bloc. The two begin to take over. For Isaac

Asimov such an occurrence is not possible since computers, like robots, should be limited by his Three Laws of Robotics. Nevertheless, his concept of the giant universal computer Multivac is no less awe-inspiring than that of Jones. Two of his stories show totally opposing views of the purpose and need of such a device. In 'The Machine That Won the War' (1961), the operator of Multivac does not always trust the computer's decisions, and so interposes some of his own – made by the toss of a coin. At the other extreme is 'The Last Question' (1956), where we see Multivac evolve over millennia into the ultimate Cosmic computer, all the while finding it impossible to answer the question whether entropy can be reversed and the universe prevented from running down. At last it solves the problem and utters the words, 'Let there be light'. The computer has become God. Just as in Fredric Brown's classic 'Answer' (1954) in which, with all the millions of planetary computers linked, the machine is asked if God exists, and replies that he does now.

Arthur C. Clarke's 'Dial F for Frankenstein' (1964) tells of the nightmare outcome of a world-wide telecommunications link-up through a satellite relay system. The link-up creates a new life-form, a non-human intelligence which feeds upon electricity. In 'Production Job' (1956), E. C. Tubb (writing as Duncan Lamont) also describes the growth of a machine intelligence. An extra-dimensional intelligence breaks into our universe and, having created for itself a gestalt mind housed in the most advanced terrestrial computers, sets out to reshape the world.

Such ultimate computers are fortunately not going to appear in this generation. But the possibly disastrous consequences of computer technology are very much with us; the use of computers in warfare is one obvious threat. Mack Reynolds approaches this theme in *Computer War* (1967), in which a computer predicts the advantages to be gained by declaring war, supplying casualty figures to support its decision. Throughout the novel, computers make the decisions, and at its close one man is astonished to discover that some people have actually

'Computer War' by Mack Reynolds, Analog July 1967. Illustration by Freas.

Left: cover by Miller, 1950. Right: cover by Emsh, June 1963.

made decisions by using their own brains. Asimov supplies a neat twist to this idea in 'The Feeling of Power' (1958), set in a future totally reliant on computers where a man suddenly rediscovers mathematics. Mack Reynolds returns to the theme in *The Computer Conspiracy* (1968), where he emphasises the vulnerability of a society totally reliant on computers. What happens, for instance, if an enemy nation succeeds in clearing the computer memory banks?

Some stories are based on the theme of the humanisation of a computer. Perhaps if man can think of the computer as a friend it will no longer seem a potential menace. But the idea works in two ways. Stephen Goldin's 'Sweet Dreams, Melissa' (1968) tells of the development of a computer with a personality – the Multi-Logical Systems Analyser (MLSA), or Melissa. The personality has to grow and mature, and at first the computer believes it is only a five-year-old girl; but the nightmares begin when it discovers its proper purpose. Against this can be compared David Gerrold's series about Harlie, or Human Analogue Robot Life Input Equivalents. Beginning with 'Oracle for a White Rabbit' (1969), Gerrold relates how Harlie acquires delusions of grandeur but, by the second story, 'The God Machine' (1970), realises it has to justify its existence. These episodes were expanded into the novel *When Harlie Was One* (1973). In Robert A. Heinlein's *The Moon Is a Harsh Mistress* (1966), a computer becomes genuinely 'awake', and helps to lead a lunar penal colony in its revolt against Earth.

However, in much science fiction, computers seem to be anything but aids to man. They supersede him, enslave him and ultimately become his God. Perhaps it is best to remember that on that scale

'The Feeling of Power' by Isaac Asimov, If February 1958. Illustration by Finlay.

computers are still in their infancy; they are now only just learning to write. Computers have even produced science fiction stories, coached by the psychologist, Christopher Evans. The day may not be too far away when a computer, programmed with all the science fiction ever written, will extrapolate from it and produce the ultimate sf novel. No doubt a machine will be the hero.

ADDITIONAL INPUT

02.14.1 Machine Intelligence

Breuer, Miles J. *Paradise and Iron*, *Amazing Stories Quarterly* Summer 1930

Clement, Hal (Harry Clement Stubbs). 'Answer', *Astounding* April 1947

Clifton, Mark (with Alex Apostolides). 'Crazy Joey', *Astounding* August 1953; sequel 'Hide! Hide! Witch!', *Astounding* December 1953

Dick, Philip K. *Vulcan's Hammer*, *Future SF* No 29 1956; revised Ace (US) 1960

Ellison, Harlan. 'I Have No Mouth and I Must Scream', *If* March 1967

Galouye, Daniel F. *Simulacron-3*, Bantam (US) 1964; retitled *Counterfeit World*, Gollancz (UK) 1964

High, Philip E. 'The Mad Metropolis', Ace (US) 1966

Hodder-Williams, Christopher. *Fistful of Digits*, Hodder Stoughton (UK) 1968

MacDonald, John D. 'The Mechanical Answer', *Astounding* May 1948

Nesvadba, Joseph 'The Einstein Brain', *F&SF* May 1962

Richmond, Walt and Leigh. 'I, Bem', *Analog* June 1964

Sheckley, Robert. 'Ask a Foolish Question', *Science Fiction Stories* No 1 1953

Stuart, Don A. (John W. Campbell). 'Twilight', *Astounding* November 1934; sequel 'Night', *Astounding* October 1935

'The Moon Is a Harsh Mistress' by Robert A. Heinlein, If December 1965. Illustration by Morrow.

02.14.2 Disembodied Brains

Many writers have thought it wasteful that a notable intellect should be lost to humanity when the body which supported it can no longer function. George Bernard Shaw suggested in 1929 that, when a genius developed a terminal illness, his head should be amputated and his brain kept alive. Shaw's ideas were inspired by accounts that Russian surgeons had successfully kept the heads of dogs alive for several hours by establishing artificial circulations. These facts helped to inspire David H. Keller's 'The Eternal Professors' (1929), in which the entire faculty of New York University, infected with cancer, submit to an operation whereby their heads live on by means of artificially circulated synthetic blood. The heads are connected to dummy bodies and, while immobile, the professors are able to continue lecturing to their students.

Few sf writers possess Keller's medical detachment, and present the concept as something abhorrent. One of the very earliest treatments is Joe Kleier's 'The Head' (1928), in which a man's severed head is near-immortal as long as its life-support system functions, but suffers mental agony for years because no one is prepared to terminate its unhappy existence.

The concept was given a fresh approach through the work of one of science fiction's noted thematic innovators, Edmond Hamilton. His 'The Comet Doom' (1928) tells of an alien race who succeed in developing a metal body driven by atomic power. The body employs an electrical nervous system leading to a square head which houses the living brain. Once inside the germ-free platinum brain-chamber, the brain is assured of eternal life in a superhumanly efficient body. The story almost certainly influenced Neil R. Jones's 'The Jameson Satellite' (1931), which introduced his famous Zorome series. The body of Professor Jameson, in accordance with the terms of his will, is fired into space in an open rocket. The vacuum of space preserves his body for millions of years. Eventually, space wanderers from an alien planet find Jameson's body and recall his brain to life. They then transpose the brain into a metal body like their own, making him an immortal.

Two other pulp stories appearing shortly thereafter were to prove widely influential, although neither made a great impact at the time of publication. Eando Binder's novel *Enslaved Brains* (1934) describes a scientific utopia, dominated by the scientific approach, including eugenically determined marriages. Conflict arises over the use of brains of deceased individuals to control machinery. The story anticipated much of the later school of stories inspired by the concept of cybernetics.

Raymond Z. Gallun's 'Mind over Matter' (1935) similarly presaged an entire school of 'cyborg' stories (i.e. cyborg – cybernetic organism, part machine and part man). A crack test pilot is nearly killed in a rocket crash. His surgeon friend saves his life by housing his brain in a colossal metal body provided with television eyes and artificial organs of touch and balance, but able to walk and talk like a man. After the initial shock, the pilot realises he has been given a unique opportunity to lead man's exploration of space, since he is now immune to high acceleration, airlessness, or the poisonous atmospheres of other worlds.

The neuronic function of the human brain is so complex that few experts would even attempt to explain it. Those who have tried have frequently been limited to the concept of machine intelligence. The science fiction writer's imagination has transcended such limitations, but he has realised that replication of the activities of the human mind could only be carried out in a machine of enormous proportions. Such a computer is not beyond man's mechanical abilities, but the intelligence incorporated in its multiplex array of digital circuits would not necessarily even approximate to man's intelligence in its full scope and complexity. In these stories we can see human understanding attempting to struggle with the unknowable. It is debatable how far the individual human mind can reach – the idea of extending its capabilities by utilising

'Enslaved Brains' by Eando Binder, *Wonder Stories August 1934. Illustration by Paul.*

02.14 COMPUTERS AND CYBERNETICS

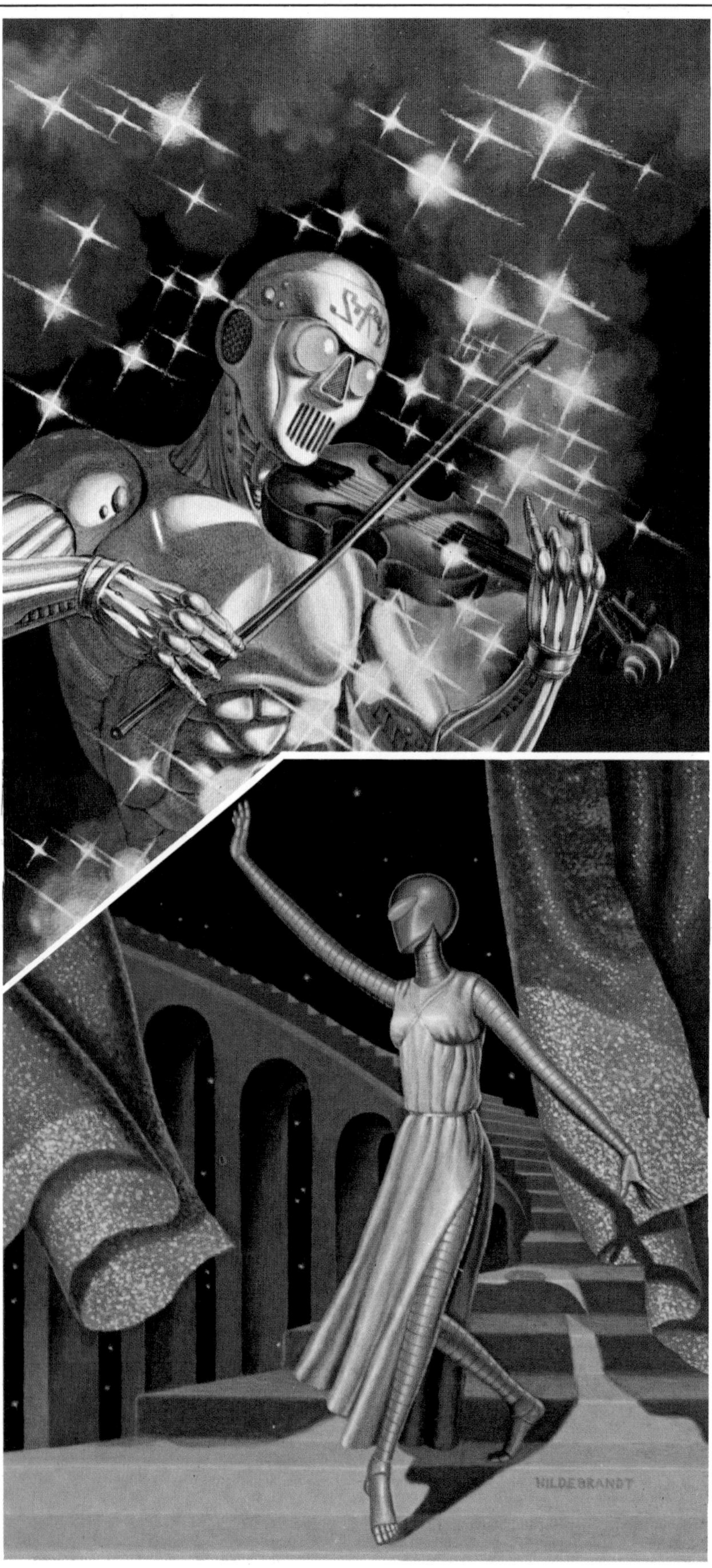

Above: Cover by Barr for The Metallic Muse *by Lloyd Biggle Jr (DAW) Below: Cover by Hildebrandt for* The Best of C. L. Moore *(Ballantine).*

computers and other cybernetic organisms is part of the fascination of speculative writing.

Throughout the decades up to about 1950, there were many stories of robots (metal men) and androids (synthetic men), but the idea of the cyborg, part man and part machine, was not completely realised at first. The theme of the disembodied head or brain continued to interest writers for many years.

In *Donovan's Brain* (1943) by Curt Siodmak, a surgeon secretly saves the brain of a well-known tycoon who was badly injured when his plane crashed nearby. The brain, kept alive in a nutrient tank, thrives and begins to generate new tissue for itself. In time, it becomes capable of telepathic control, and takes over the surgeon's mind, using him to carry out various criminal activities. The novel has become a minor classic on this theme, frequently reprinted and translated, and it has been filmed twice.

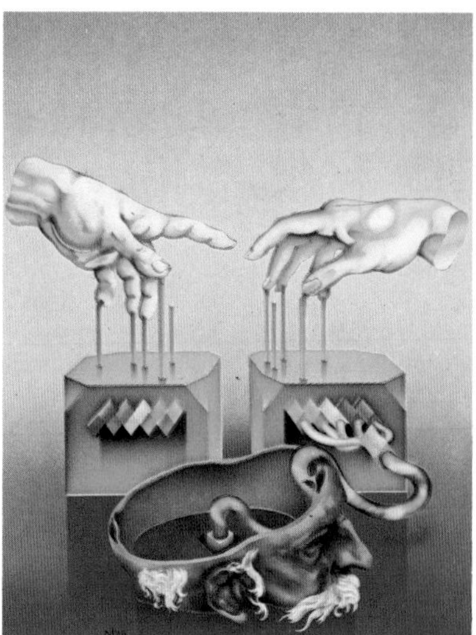

Cover illustration by Tybus for As Man Becomes Machine *by David Rorvik (Abacus).*

Disembodied brains in science fiction usually suffer the tortures of the damned, but in his short story 'Transplant' (1974) Christopher Priest suggests otherwise. Here, a man's brain, kept alive artificially after his death, creates for itself a kind of pleasurable dream world. Also apparently quite content is the disembodied brain in a mobile box which aids Edmond Hamilton's Captain Future, making his debut in *Captain Future and the Space Emperor* (1940).

By the early forties, such writers as Lester del Rey began to examine the philosophical and moral problems arising from the blending of man with machine. In del Rey's 'Reincarnate' (1940), a man is injured in an atomic-pile explosion. Doctors are able to save his life by implanting his brain and spinal cord into a

The 'Professor Jameson' series by Neil R. Jones (Ace).

humanoid metal body, with the result he must undergo the agonising problem of coming to terms with a completely new way of life. C. L. Moore's 'No Woman Born' (1944) is another example.

Whereas most writers, such as Neil R. Jones, saw such operations as bestowing near-immortality on the brain involved, Moore postulates that the brain itself will continue to age normally. Her story was the first to fully and realistically illuminate the problems involved: whether medical science has the right to preserve a brain alive when its body has been destroyed; the mental difficulty of mechanised human beings and their adjustments; and the reactions of normal people.

Most of Henry Kuttner's work after his marriage to C. L. Moore in 1940 is known to have been written in collaboration with her to some extent. Some of their finest joint work appeared under the name of 'Lewis Padgett', and this byline was used for another seminal work, 'Camouflage' (1945). In many ways the tale is a sequel to 'No Woman Born', in that it also seeks to explore the psychological effects on a brain of a mechanised environment. In this case, however, the basic idea is that of the implantation of a brain into a spaceship. The idea of using an artificial brain for the purpose had been proposed several years earlier by Edgar Rice Burroughs, in his novel *Swords of Mars* (1936), but the importance of Burroughs's story will be discussed later. The notion of using a *human* brain in a spaceship was introduced by James Blish in his early short story 'Solar Plexus' (1941).

'Camouflage' is the story of a 'transplant' – the brain of a qualified engineer formerly engaged in dangerous atomic research, now housed in a machine and kept alive artificially. Such transplants are used to operate spaceships and other complicated machinery at optimum efficiency. They form a perfect symbiosis with the machine, yet the individual's personal identity, his human essence, is unaffected, and the hero finds the experience completely satisfying.

Following 'Camouflage', the idea of the brain-controlled spaceship has become well established, and two of the best and most contrasting treatments of the theme are those by E. C. Tubb and Anne McCaffrey. 'Death-Wish' (1955) by Eric Wilding (E. C. Tubb) tells of an interstellar war between man and an alien race. Captured humans are decapitated and the brain cells governing emotion and personality severed. The remainder is wired direct to feed-in circuits, and the result is a highly efficient computer, able to correlate data and act upon them at the speed of thought, thus giving the aliens an advantage over their enemies.

Anne McCaffrey's 'The Ship Who Sang' (1961) was the first story in a noted series which saw book publication in 1971 under

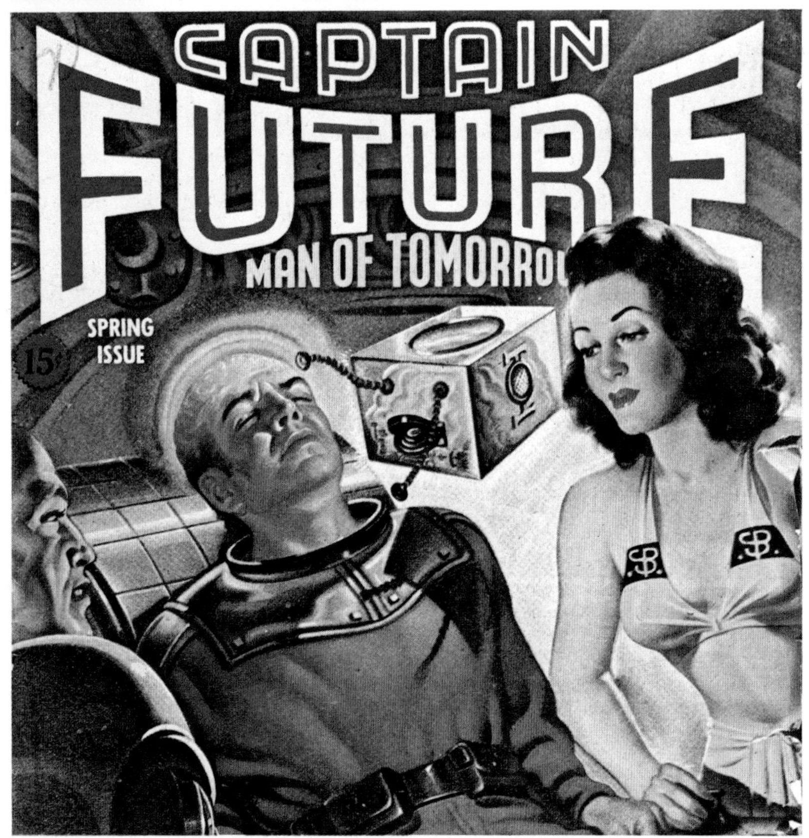

'Days of Creation' by Brett Stirling, Captain Future *Spring 1944. Cover by Bergey.*

02.14 COMPUTERS AND CYBERNETICS

the same title. It is the story of a girl who is born hopelessly malformed. She is fitted into a mechanical body, and brought up with other similar children. She adjusts to her new body, revelling in some of the extraordinary abilities it bestows, such as microscopic vision and manipulation, yet she retains the ability to register deep emotions and remains essentially feminine. At the age of sixteen she is transplanted into a spaceship. She falls in love with her human 'link' in the ship, but he dies at the end of the story, hence a sequel entitled 'The Ship Who Mourned' (1966). In 'No Greater Love' (1970) by Sydney J. Bounds, a specially bred 'female' organic ship's brain saves the life of the human pilot she loves, destroying herself in the process.

As noted above, one of the formative tales on this theme was Burroughs's *Swords of Mars* (1936), and the story also influenced other developments of brain themes. In this novel, a Martian scientist constructs a spaceship with a special guidance device – an artificial brain, fashioned in the exact convolutions of a living brain. Installed in the ship, the metal brain is responsive to thought waves from its controller, who has merely to think out his plan to have it translated into action by the brain. The brain lacks the power to originate thoughts, being wholly dependent on telepathic input, but it can see with television instruments and is also equipped with an automatic weapons system.

From such tenuous beginnings have developed the present-day cyborg stories, where man plus metal equals superman. But there were two vital catalysts which helped shape this aspect of today's science fiction. The first of these was an entire school of 'spare part' science fiction, stories of prosthetic limbs and artificial hearts. The second was the publication of non-fiction works by Norbert Wiener, the populariser of the concept of Cybernetics.

ADDITIONAL INPUT

02.14.2 Disembodied Brains

Coney, Michael G. 'Troubleshooter', *If* June to July 1970
Dahl, Roald. 'William and Mary', included in collection *Kiss, Kiss*, Knopf (US) 1960
Flagg, Francis (Henry George Weiss) 'The Heads of Apex', *Astounding* October 1931
Grey, Charles (E.C. Tubb). *Enterprise 2115*, Milestone (UK) 1954
Hjortsberg, William. *Gray Matters*, Gollancz (UK) 1973

02.14.3 Cybernetics

Norbert Wiener's *Cybernetics* (1948) exerted a considerable influence on science fiction, as well as winning wider acclaim as the basic work on control and communication in man and machine. The author followed this with *The Human Use of Human Beings* (1950), subtitled 'Cybernetics and Society'. It showed clearly how electronics can be used to give man greater freedom to perform tasks beyond the range of mechanical instruments. In effect, routine human labour could be replaced by machines, which could do the job far more effectively, placing managers and engineers in the vanguard of a second Industrial Revolution, a Cybernetic Revolution.

Before Wiener, mechanised civilisations had been described in many sf stories as utopias. Machines can free men from toil – but to what end? An increase in the amount of leisure time might bewilder the ordinary citizen, and a world where millions of people were bored to distraction would be dystopian rather than utopian. An equally unpleasant alternative would be a hedonistic society, such as that described in 'Master of the Brain' (1933), the second in Laurence Manning's noted 'The Man Who Awoke' series in *Wonder Stories*. Here, the world is run by a central mechanical brain controlling a vast array of automatic machinery which supplies most of mankind's needs. Released from the necessity for any real work, humanity finds solace in Pleasure Palaces. Mechanised progress has brought in its wake a perpetual urge for more and more leisure, to be wasted in the pursuit of even more physical joys and in drugged indulgence. Manning exhibited remarkable prophetic insight, but there were few of his contemporaries who had thought so deeply about the subject, except perhaps Aldous Huxley, in *Brave New World* (1932). Following the development of the concept of cybernetics, it was left to two peripheral sf writers to meaningfully explore the consequences of a full-scale cybernetic revolution. The writers were Bernard Wolfe and Kurt Vonnegut.

Wolfe's initial attempt was the short story 'Self Portrait' (1951), published in *Galaxy*. It introduced the concept of EMSIAC (Electronic Military Strategy Integrator and Computer), and told of the frightening world which resulted from the insane ideas of a cybernetics engineer. These included sections of the populace being encouraged to submit to voluntary amputeeism, being fitted with prosthetic limbs and organs, as a form of masochistic substitute for war. The concepts outlined in this story were expanded by the author for his novel *Limbo* (1952).

Kurt Vonnegut's *Player Piano* (1952) describes the rise to political power of the engineers and managers, led by the first National Industrial, Commercial, Communications, Foodstuffs and Resources Director. The only work available for even quite skilled workers consists of the routine jobs which are still uneconomical for machines, while those with no identifiable skills are obliged to join the army or the Reconstruction and Reclamation Corps (the 'Reeks and Wrecks'). The invention of gadgets continues to make increasingly more people unemployed, while EPICAC, the electronic intelligence that controls civilisation, grows larger and larger. An attempt to overthrow the cybernetic anti-utopia and smash the machines fails. The author implies that even if it had been successful, man's compulsion to put the machines together again would lead him down the same anti-utopian path.

Among the regular sf writers, Raymond F. Jones wrote *The Cybernetic Brains* (1950), which can be seen as an updating of Binder's *Enslaved Brains* with the help of Wiener's ideas. In recent years, however, sf writers have increasingly shifted their focus from the larger problems of a cybernetic society to those of the individual. More critical consideration has been given to the medical ethics of saving a man's life at whatever cost, and to the human price to be paid for artificial life dependent on machines.

ADDITIONAL INPUT

02.14.3 Cybernetics

Adlard, Mark. *Interface*, Sidgwick & Jackson (UK) 1971
Adlard, Mark. *Multiface*, Sidgwick & Jackson (UK) 1975
Cameron, Lou. *Cybernia*, Coronet (UK) 1975
Coblentz, Stanton A. 'The Lord of Tranerica', *Dynamic* February 1939
Coney, Michael G. *Friends Come in Boxes*, DAW (US) 1974
Glynn, A. A. *Plan for Conquest*, Badger (UK) 1963
Goulart, Ron. 'Cybernetic Tabernacle Job', in anthology *Infinity 3* (edited by Robert Hoskins), Lancer (US) 1973
Hodder-Williams, Christopher. *98.4*, Hodder & Stoughton (UK) 1969
Hollis, H.H. 'Cybernia', *If* July 1966
Phillips, Rog (R.P. Graham). 'The Cyberene', *Imagination* September 1953
Schachner, Nat. 'Robot Technocrat', *Wonder* March 1933
Wyndham, John (J.B. Harris) 'Compassion Circuit', *Fantastic Universe* December 1954

'The Cybernetic Brains' by Raymond F. Jones, Startling Stories *September 1950.*

02.14.4 Cyborgs

One of the earliest prototypes of the modern sf cyborg story centred on the creation of an artificial heart, and the theme has continued sporadically over the years, culminating in Isaac Asimov's definitive story, 'Segregationist' (1968). An early pulp treatment, 'The Emperor's Heart' (1934) by Henry J. Kostkos, is an odd mixture of hard science fiction and fairy tale. A dying emperor's diseased heart is removed, and he is connected through tubes in his chest to an artificial life-support system. He has also been given a rejuvenation treatment which causes him to retrogress through childhood to become a mere embryo. The embryo generates a new heart and matures normally – but as a girl.

In Asimov's 'Segregationist', a future Earth has perfected medical science to such a degree that any organs which are worn out or damaged can be replaced artificially. The story tells of a senator who is about to undergo an operation for a new heart. The surgeon in charge gives him the choice of a fibrous cyber heart or a metal one. He chooses metal, since he hopes to attain the physical strength and endurance he associates with human-like robots who have just been granted citizenship. Conversely, some injured robots are demanding that they be given flesh-and-blood replacements. The surgeon fears that mankind is heading for a hybrid form. A confessed segregationist, he believes in the two varieties of intelligence on Earth remaining as they are. The surgeon is finally revealed as a robot himself.

The horrors of just such a hybrid society have been systematically explored by David R. Bunch in a long series of stories set in the world of Moderan. The strange inhabitants of Moderan suffer from a crisis of identity, increasingly disorientated, and breaking down mentally while they become either more human or more robotic, as in 'The Walking, Talking, I-Don't-Care Man' (1965). Many of the stories are included in the collection *Moderan* (1971). The fear of such depersonalisation is poignantly expressed in Charles Beaumont's 'The Beautiful People' (1952), telling of a society where, at the age of eighteen, everyone is remodelled by surgery to provide them with flawlessly proportioned bodies and faces – whether they want it or not.

E. C. Tubb (writing as Douglas West) describes, in 'Reward for a Hero' (1956), how a spaceman, badly injured while saving his ship and fellow crewmen from disaster, is turned into a cyborg. Other cyborg spacemen, no longer wholly men, have been sent to a special medical colony on the Moon, to be spared the anguish of being regarded as freaks on Earth. The hero is persuaded to join the colony, letting his wife believe he has died in space.

By contrast, in *Who?* (1958), Algis Budrys tells of a key Western scientist, severely hurt in an explosion, whose body is repaired by the Russians. When he is finally returned to the West, the authorities are faced with the problem whether he should be allowed to resume work on a secret project. They cannot tell whether or not he is a Soviet agent who has been given parts of the scientist's body. The hero faces a crisis of identity, which he resolves by finding a new persona based on what he has become, rather than on what he once was. The novel has since been filmed.

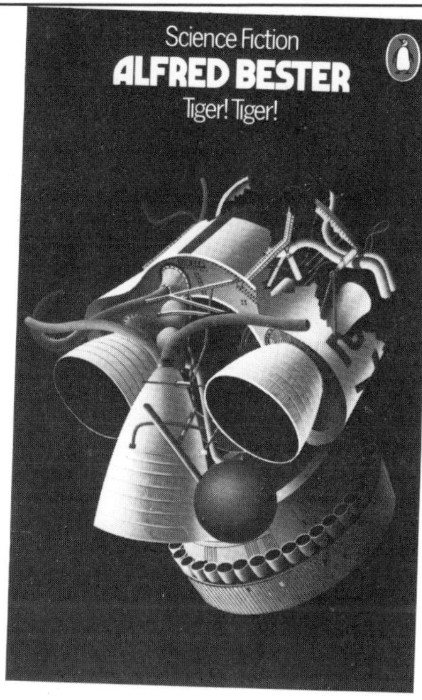

Tiger! Tiger! *by Alfred Bester (Penguin). Cover by David Pelham.*

In *Thorns* (1968), Robert Silverberg deals directly with deformity in its psychological aspects. Among the grotesque characters is one who has been captured by aliens, taken apart and re-assembled – but in the wrong way, whereas the cyborgs of Thomas M. Disch's 'The Sightseers' (1965) cannot be distinguished from a real person. In all essentials, in intelligence and ego structure, they are psychologically identical to their human templates. They even have a sense of humour and a moral sense.

In most stories, the cyborg is created to counter the effects of personal injury or deformity. A notable exception to this trend is the central character of Alfred Bester's *Tiger! Tiger!* (1956), also known as *The Stars My Destination*. He voluntarily arranges to have his body partially remodelled with the help of electronic ingenuity so that in moments of crisis he can activate cyborg elements and perform feats of superhuman strength and speed. The cyborg as some kind of superman is a popular sub-category of much hybrid science fiction, particularly in the thriller and secret agent story in which the hero is given super-normal cyborg powers. Most widely known, through the medium of television, is *The Six Million Dollar Man*, created from Martin Caidin's novel *Cyborg* (1972). An astronaut is saved from a crash in very much the same fashion as the leading character of Gallun's 'Mind over Matter'. Here, however, the mechanical repairs are not so extensive and the hero is able to retain his human appearance despite having a 'bionic' (media jargon for a combination of biological and electronic) arm and bionic legs, not to mention telescopic vision. Recently the bionic man has been joined on television by a bionic woman, who has been rebuilt piece by piece after a sky-diving accident. She is the brainchild of Frank Price, head of a large American TV network, and was conceived to boost audience ratings.

Dr Herbert Thomas, Professor of Psychiatry at Pittsburgh University, has attributed the great popularity of such bionic super-agents to their appeal to the childish element which lingers on in the adult. It gratifies a childish wish to be indestructible, and constitutes a form of worry-free escapism. But the actual concept of cyborg men or women is no mere escapism. As well as enjoying the science fiction antecedents traced above, it is scientifically possible. This is a view shared by one of America's leading neuro-surgeons, Dr Charles Ray, who is also Vice-President of Medical Research for Meditronics, the world's leading manufacturer of heart pacemakers. Dr Ray

Right: 'The Walking, Talking, I-Don't-Care Man' by David Bunch, Amazing *June 1965. Cover by Gray Morrow.*

believes that the early 1980s will see the creation of bionic men, using the same kind of electronic stimulators already in use in certain specialised medical centres to stimulate muscles, relieve spasticity, or eradicate pain.

While most writers have developed the cyborg theme along sombre or tragic lines, a few have recognised the possibilities for satire and farce. 'Man in a Quandry' (1958) by L. J. Stecher Jr is a good example. Its hero is given an artificial heart at an early age and, as he grows up, through a series of accidents and disorders, acquires more and more mechanical parts. He requires a kind of wagon, which trails along behind him at the end of a tail. Finally, he contracts a virulent brain disease, and has his personality and memories transferred to a mechanical brain which necessitates three entire buildings full of electronic machinery with their own special power station. A more recent example of this approach, by the Polish writer Stanislaw Lem, is 'Are You There, Mr Jones?' (first English translation, 1969). A former racing driver has been rebuilt piece by piece by the Cybernetics Company after a series of crashes. When he is unable to meet his medical bills, the irate company first persuade him to have his very last organic part replaced and then promptly sue him, claiming that he is entirely their property. However, it is argued that if he is a robot, then he cannot be brought to trial at all, and the court proceedings are adjourned in an atmosphere of broad farce.

Frederik Pohl has written the first major novel on the cyborg and related themes for some years, *Man Plus* (1976). It tells of a new machine intelligence evolved on Earth that is dependent, in its early stage, on the continued survival of man. It has been doctoring computer outputs to direct the creation of a Martian colony, with a cyborg as its link. Pohl's novel effectively encapsulates all the past themes of cybernetics and the cyborg, and incorporates computers and machine intelligence for good measure. His story is perhaps the first noted novel to draw together all the aspects of a thematics area in science fiction which is likely to become more factual than many of the others.

ADDITIONAL INPUT

02.14.4 Cyborgs

Chapdelaine, Perry. 'We Fused Ones', *If* July 1968
Dunn, Saul. *The Coming of Steeleye*, Coronet (UK) 1976
Dunn, Saul. *The Wideways*, Coronet (UK) 1976
England, George Allan. 'The Man with the Glass Heart', *The Cavalier* 1911; reprinted *Famous Fantastic Mysteries* November 1939
Kamon, Nick. *Earthrim*, Ace (US) 1969
Leiber, Fritz. *A Spectre Is Haunting Texas*, Mayflower (UK) 1971
Scortia, Thomas N. 'Sea Change', *Astounding* June 1956

As a young reader it did not occur to me that science fiction was about anything other than the big questions such as 'What Is Humanity?' and 'Where Is It Going?' I was reading a variety of religious and philosophical works, witchcraft and herbalism, mental diseases, drugs and Velikovsky. All these books were in the same corner of the local lending library, which may have influenced my entire thinking life, or merely show that the librarian was also pursuing the same lines of thought and conveniently put all the right research books together. Later came biochemistry, diet, yoga and UFOs.

Some science fiction categorists would say that most of my work is not science fiction at all, but in so far as a sticky caul of religious mania still clung to me when I began writing stories and selling them, and considering the background, the spirit was certainly correctly placed. The themes of the next section are Higher Intelligence, Destiny of Mankind, Self-perfection, Super-race, Cosmic Sociology. It is the politics of the human soul, or a metaphysical pornography, depending probably upon one's leaning to Right or Left in real life, whatever that last might mean.

Symbiote was a word I later learned, having already been thoroughly familiar with concepts of demonic possession, ideas in Gurdjieff and Ouspensky, Rom Landau and many writers on telepathy, all paving an easy path to Ted Sturgeon's *More than Human*, and to books of my own. Psychology of the Jungian persuasion, Ronnie Laing that descendant of *The Three Faces of Eve*, in its turn a descendant of *Jekyll and Hyde*, all have a family likeness, and all ask questions in the same area, that one supposed to have been digested by the 'mature' mind.

Fact and fiction overlap wildly so that thousands of people can believe the material in *Chariot of the Gods*, and I can certainly champion Kammerer (the persecuted underdog) against Darwin, who was not only crazy but against birth control!

In this area also it is worth noting that by common standards so many of the protagonists are 'mad'. They suffer from paranoia, megalomania, and run from Them, who will kill them for being cleverer or more gifted than Mr Average. The man who packs his testicles around with steel wool to prevent beings from outer space sterilising him, because he is chosen to be the father of a new super-race is a real case-history: he could also be, with minimal changes, the hero of an sf story.

We deal here also with conscious evolution quite overtly, for example *Surface Tension* by Blish, and *The Rose*, by Charles Harness. There is a strong element of *The Ugly Duckling*, and not a little taste for martyrdom.

Did your mother only breast-feed one of your heads?

Read on . . .

Josephine Saxton

02.15 MUTANTS AND SYMBIOTES

02.15.1 The Monstrosity of Evolution

At the close of the nineteenth century, there was much debate on evolutionary theory and conjecture as to the future nature of man. It was realised that if, as then seemed likely, mankind had evolved from ape-like ancestors, it was probable he was still evolving. But evolving into what?

H. G. Wells was among those who wondered. He went further than most and published an article, 'The Man of the Year Million' (1893), subtitled 'A Scientific Forecast'. The piece, which at first appeared anonymously, had a long-term 'sleeper' effect on sf writing; it was perhaps as influential as any of Wells's more renowned stories.

He argued that as man undergoes further evolution, his brain will develop at the expense of the rest of his body; his head will become huge, domelike; his mouth will shrink and become toothless as he perfects synthetic foods that require no mastication. Ultimately, nourishment might well be taken directly into the skin, by means of a chemical bath. With legs and abdomens and the whole muscular system shrivelled to nothing (the result of an increasing dependence on machines with consequent lack of exercise), future descendants of man may resemble nothing so much as giant tadpoles.

Wells foresaw that Earth would finally become cool as the sun died; as man's original environment was running down, he would bore into the Earth itself, creating deep underground galleries, artificially lit. Food and power could be wrested from the bare rock itself. Humanity, caught up in a dismal retreat, would change beyond recognition.

Wells followed this vision two years later with the first book edition of *The Time Machine* (1895), incorporating further speculations on the future of man. It is a classic story, telling how a time traveller goes far into the future to a period when man has evolved into two distinct races, the Eloi and the Morlocks. The Eloi are a childlike people inhabiting a surface world where cities crumble and technology has been forgotten. In a racial decline, the Eloi live on highly nutritional fruit grown in apparently self-perpetuating orchards. They are preyed upon, under cover of darkness, by a degenerate, subterranean race, the Morlocks, who Wells sees as the end-product of enslavement to the machine.

Such concepts are fascinating, and it is hardly surprising that many early sf stories reflect a preoccupation with the man of the future, derived from Wells. But a new concept was added: mutation. Wells saw man evolving according to his environment, and controlling his own metabolism. However, following the pioneering X-ray experiments with fruit flies by Morgan in 1926, the exploitation of the mutant became possible.

Morgan had demonstrated that X-rays could affect the genes and chromosomes, units of heredity. Mutations could occur, the monstrosities outside the norm could be created. At the same time, following the pioneering work of Millikan, the nature of cosmic rays was determined: a mysterious force which coursed throughout all known space, ceaselessly bombarding the Earth. Both of these findings proved a boon to sf writers. They saw cosmic radiation as the chief agency for mutation of the life-forms on Earth, working in tandem with evolution brought about by adaptation to a changing environment. The definitive story of the type is Edmond Hamilton's 'The Man Who Evolved' (1931), which was widely imitated.

Hamilton's story traced the main steps of evolutionary development. Life began on Earth as a simple protoplasm, a jelly-like mass from which developed small protoplasmic organisms; from these, in successive mutations, developed the sea-creatures, land-lizards and mammals. But it is from this story that a popular misrepresentation developed in science fiction. The normal flow of cosmic radiation reaching the Earth was known to be mitigated by the atmosphere – hence evolution moved forward slowly. But if cosmic rays were to be trapped and stored as a potential force and then released in quantity, it was assumed that they could force evolution ahead of its normal speed. The fallacy was to substitute the metamorphosis of an individual organism for gradual change over successive generations. Quite possibly, many offending writers realised this, but lacked the literary ability needed to carry their narrative across years rather than minutes – hence stories of 'instant' mutants created by bathing someone in concentrated cosmic rays.

In Hamilton's tale, a scientist discovers that if he subjects his body to a cosmic ray onslaught, it will evolve him eons ahead of *Homo sapiens*. With each mutation there comes an increasingly ruthless and growing intellectual power. Inexorably, his human traits, both mental and physical, are eradicated. He becomes a massive brain, seemingly the ultimate evolution of man. But a final human characteristic remains: the desire to go one step beyond. Another surge of cosmic rays – and he reverts to a

More Than Human *by Theodore Sturgeon (Ballantine). Cover by Rosenblatt*

02.15 MUTANTS AND SYMBIOTES

'Captive Audience' by Wallace West, Thrilling Wonder Stories *June 1953. Illustration by Finlay.*

mass of protoplasm! Evolution has turned out to be cyclic.

Some writers, with Hamilton in the vanguard, applied the process of mutation to alien beings – with surprising results. Hamilton in 'Devolution' (1936) and John

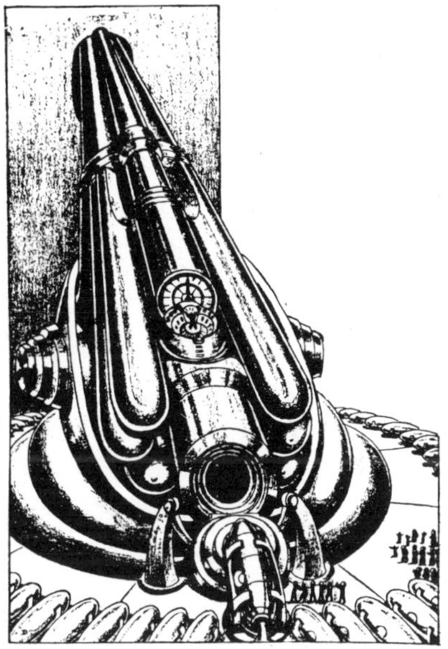

'Worlds Within' by John Russell Fearn, Astounding *March 1937. Illustration by Dold.*

Russell Fearn in 'Worlds Within' (1937) both told of advanced aliens who came to Earth in the remote past. There they suffered a drastic retrogression – an actual *devolution* – with each generation. Hamilton's alien colonists were victims of intense terrestrial radiations which affected their genes. They degenerated, changing into lower and more brutal forms of life, until the humans of today – by comparison pitifully insane things – are their last descendants.

Fearn, for his part, favoured the device of Earth's relatively heavier gravitation impairing the circulation of his aliens' blood. A poor bloodstream affects the well-being of the brain; and as the aliens mated, their subsequent children's brains deteriorated, leading to atavistic tendencies. Again, present-day men are their last descendants.

Mutants created in the laboratory abounded in the early pulp days. Nat Schachner was among the first popular exponents. His 'The 100th Generation' (1934) told of an island overrun with artificial creatures, each one the ultimate development of some human talent. Obviously based on Wells's *The Island of Dr Moreau*, it substituted eugenics and genuine mutation techniques for vivisection.

But pulp science fiction was for the most part still chasing up the blind alley Hamilton had inadvertantly created. In hackneyed stories, atavism and metamorphosis were still being passed off as mutation. The protagonists in these early stories, though definitely what we today would label as mutants, were only pseudo-creations. The confusion arose because few authors had actually realised how to *create* a genuine mutant. They continued to utilise cosmic rays and the weird potions of mad scientists to obtain their 'instant mutants'.

Meanwhile, Olaf Stapledon's *Odd John* had appeared in 1935. Although it is not the first fictional treatment of a mutant superman, there are many who have suggested it is the greatest. With considerable skill, Stapledon succeeded in conveying the strangeness inherent in a supernormal being. His mutant is human, if grotesque. His face is boyish, yet capable of expressing almost patriarchal wisdom. His hair is like a white woollen skull cap; his brow immense. His eyes are the most obviously strange thing about him – larger than normal, almost devoid of white, and with giant pupils. His body is spidery, but oddly strong and graceful.

Stapledon was not concerned only with mere physical differences; his story provides insight into the unique mind of John. As a telepath, he is quickly able to master all human activities, but finds them wanting. And although he would be able to take over the world, John declines to do so . . .

'Once in charge I could make a much more satisfactory world, and a much happier world; but always I would have to accept the ultimate limitations of capacity in the normal species. To make them try and live beyond their capacities would be like trying to civilise a pack of monkeys. There would be worse chaos than ever, and they would unite against me, and sooner or later destroy me.'

Odd John remains the acknowledged masterwork on this theme, and subsequent stories have suffered from the comparison. In 1939, after a great publicity wrangle, Ziff-Davis published Stanley G. Weinbaum's posthumous novel *The New Adam*. It described the struggle of the first of a new species to adjust himself to the modern world. The theme appeared too much for the comparatively young Weinbaum to handle, and there is evidence that the work was never intended for publication, at least not as it stood. A more recent, and less ambitious example, in which the same attitude to humanity as that of Stapledon's character is successfully reworked, is 'Nobody Bothers Gus' (1955) by Algis Budrys.

However, the pulp exponents of science fiction in America continued to dwell on their 'instant mutants' for several more years, although in Thorp McClusky's 'The Monstrosity of Evolution' (1938) the idea is finally developed that only through the slow building up of natural evolution can a species gain the necessary resistance and strength to maintain its own life.

The old-time mutants were not even anachronisms of the distant future; they had no place in *any* time. They would be doomed to die because they were unbalanced accentuations and unnatural, because they were environmental monstrosities. With the advent of the 1940s, however, two events were to occur which would raise the quality of this thematic area and lead to a more serious consideration of the subject. The first was a science fiction story, the second a scientific fact.

When *Slan*, a four-part serial by A. E. van Vogt, began in the September 1940 issue of *Astounding*, the past mediocrity of most mutant fiction was forgotten. The novel came to be recognised as a classic. Van Vogt was the first author seriously to explore the sociological complications arising from a mutant race attempting to survive among normal humanity. The true nature of the supermen is explained by the Slan Leader: 'We are the mutation-after-man. The forces of the mutation were at work many years

'Hyperpilocity' by L. Sprague de Camp, Fantastic Story Magazine *September 1953.*

02.15 MUTANTS AND SYMBIOTES

before that great day when Samuel Lann realised the pattern of perfection in some of his mutations . . .' Slans were that mutant 'perfection'. Capable of reading minds with the slim antennae embedded in their heads, and possessing a double heart which afforded great stamina, they were superior both mentally and physically to ordinary men. Their reception by the rest of humanity was predictable: they were hunted down like wild beasts. It was only through their own powers and the machinations of Lann that the Slans were able to organise and survive at all.

The effect of the novel was not fully felt until some years later. A decade had passed by the time admiration for its basic concepts prompted Jack Williamson in 1952 to pen *Dragon's Island*, a *Slan* variation quite out of

Slan *by A. E. van Vogt,* Fantastic Story Magazine *Summer 1952. Illustration by Finlay.*

'Dragon's Island' by Jack Williamson, Startling Stories *June 1952. Cover illustration by Bergey.*

character with most of his other writing. But before *Slan* could be properly assimilated, the horizons of mutant fiction were widened still further by the actual release of atomic energy. The advent of the atomic bomb as a reality was a gift to science fiction, and an entirely new breed of mutants was created.

ADDITIONAL INPUT

02.15.1 The Monstrosity of Evolution

Beresford, J.D. *The Hampdenshire Wonder*, Sidgwick and Jackson (UK) 1911
Campbell, H.J. *The Last Mutation*, *Authentic Science Fiction Monthly* No 11, 1951
Chapman, John L. 'Cycle', *Marvel Stories* November 1940
Flint, Homer Eon. 'The Nth Man', *Amazing Stories Quarterly* Spring 1928
Kippax, John. 'It', *Nebula Science Fiction* November 1958
Wells, H.G. *Star Begotten*, Viking (US) 1937
Wright, S. Fowler. *The Island of Captain Sparrow*, Cosmopolitan (US) 1928

02.15.2 Spawn of the Atom

The dropping of the atomic bomb on the city of Hiroshima on 6 August 1945 resulted in momentous changes, not only in the course of the Second World War, but in human attitudes to science. Nowhere was the universal horror at the event more marked than among the science fiction fraternity. For years, they had foreseen its coming, and had written stories about it, yet sf writers had somehow hoped that this was one of their darker visions that would never be allowed to happen. Now that it *had* come, they poured out their forebodings in the form of prophecy, allegory and stark warnings of future horror. Most of these stories involved mutations in one form or another.

The lingering after-effects of radiation created by atomic fall-out had not been properly envisaged in science fiction prior to the actual advent of the bomb. The mutant engendered by radiation was already a stock device by 1945, but it usually took shape in the laboratory of a mad scientist. After 1945 writers were able to visualise mutations occurring on a global scale as a result of atomic war.

Poul Anderson's first sale, 'Tomorrow's Children' (1947), was one such story. In a world ravaged by nuclear war, mutations of both humans and animals represent about 75 per cent of all births, and some two-thirds of them are capable of surviving and reproducing. A group of scientists decide to track down and sterilise all such mutants and their parents. They are obsessed with saving the true human stock from being absorbed, and preventing the emergence of a culture made up of freaks. But it is an impossible task, soon abandoned. The radioactivity will linger for 150 years, by which time so-called human stock will be in such a minority that its continuance will be impossible. The long struggle to rid humanity of the mutated genes brought

'New Foundations' by Wilmar H. Shiras, Astounding *March 1950. Cover by Rogers.*

02.15 MUTANTS AND SYMBIOTES

'*Atomic' by Henry Kuttner*, Thrilling Wonder Stories *August 1947. Illustration by Finlay.*

about by radiation is also a central feature of Lester del Rey's *The Eleventh Commandment* (1962).

The idea of true humans destroying mutants was neatly overturned in John Russell Fearn's 'After the Atom' (1948). The tale also demonstrates how the effects of atomic war might affect posterity. The two leading characters, projected into the future by an atomic bomb explosion, are finally killed by the descendants of mutants to preserve the purity of the new race. The moral of the story set the pattern for dozens of others, among them Theodore Sturgeon's *Prodigy* (1949): man will destroy himself with atomic power and be replaced by a new superior being.

Raymond F. Jones's 'The Children's Room' (1947) tells of a father's discovery that his young son is a mutant as, to some degree, he is himself. The author shows that mutations are widespread, but most of them constitute a threat because they are of no advantage to the individual or to the race.

'In Hiding' by Wilmar H. Shiras (1948) is a well-known short story of mutant fiction, painting a moving picture of the problems facing a child of paranormal intelligence. It can be compared to Stapledon's *Odd John* (1935). The idea of the redemption of man through mutation was also portrayed movingly by Walter M. Miller at the close of his novel *A Canticle for Leibowitz* (1960); but for most of the story his mutants are presented as grotesque.

Many other writers have dwelt on this theme of the ugly and degenerate mutant spawned by atomic radiation. One such treatment distinguished Judith Merril's very first story, 'That Only a Mother' (1948), where the expectant parents have survived an atomic explosion. They are aware of the possibility of mutation, and the prospective mother is in an agony of foreboding as the birth of her child approaches. In the event, she finds the child to be perfectly normal. Her husband, who has been working away from home, returns to see his child for the first time. He is horrified to find his deranged wife fussing happily over a girl child without arms or legs, a tragic serpent-like form. Ray Bradbury described the same situation of a mother who can see nothing wrong with her mutated child in 'The Shape of Things' (1948) – her child is born in the form of a triangle. John Jakes's 'With Wings' (1953) is a similar tale.

The attitude of 'normals' to the mentally superior mutation is almost always hostile and ungenerous. Even though such a being could bring great gifts to humanity, he or she (or it) is regarded as a monster by ordinary people – a point made clear in van Vogt's *Slan*.

Most writers see the struggle between man and mutated life as a grim, merciless battle, with the mutants ferociously destroyed before they can supplant *Homo sapiens*. A particularly powerful example was 'Emergency Exit' (1954) by George Holt (E. C. Tubb). Men kill any form of life which is strange to them; they burn telepaths, whose accidental talents could remake the shattered world. They shoot those with precognition; and stab beings with two hearts, six fingers, the ability to heal by touch or an instinctive awareness of the workings of the human brain. John Wyndham's *The Chrysalids* (1955) and Aldous Huxley's *Ape and Essence* (1948) are other noted works in this area.

The situation of mutants banded together into an underground organisation directly opposed to humanity, either by inclination or necessity, became a common background

Mutant *by Lewis Padgett (Gnome Press). Cover by Binkley.*

02.15 MUTANTS AND SYMBIOTES

'*After the Atom*' *by John Russell Fearn*, Startling Stories *May 1948. Illustration by Astarita.*

in science fiction after the success of *Slan*. The story marked the virtual obliteration of the earlier monstrosity-of-evolution type of approach. The dominant form of modern mutations is that of a mutant in mind only; the changes are largely non-physical. One of the better post-atomic versions of *Slan* was Henry Kuttner's series of novelettes in *Astounding*, published collectively as *Mutant* (1953). Kuttner turned his talents to several other stories concerning radiation-bred mutants, 'Way of the Gods' (1947) and 'Atomic' (1947) among them.

The sheer volume of post-atomic stories in the sf magazines may have served to dull their effectiveness, and their number has dwindled in recent years. The diminution was hastened by the debasement of the idea in second-rate Hollywood movies during the 1950s. However, the message of the sf writers is clear enough, even if read through a glass darkly. Despite the legion of atomic-warning stories, the nuclear Sword of Damocles is still hanging above man, probably with even greater menace than any sf writer has anticipated.

Left: '*Way of the Gods*' *by Henry Kuttner*, Thrilling Wonder Stories *April 1947*.

ADDITIONAL INPUT

02.15.2 Spawn of the Atom

Ackerman, Forrest J. 'The Mute Question', *Other Worlds* September 1950
Berry, Bryan. *Aftermath*, *Authentic Science Fiction Monthly* No 24, 1952
Bounds, Sydney J. 'Mutation', *New Worlds SF* September 1956
Brunner, K. Houston (John). 'Fiery Pillar', *New Worlds SF* August 1955
Bulmer, Kenneth. 'Mr. Culpepper's Baby', *Authentic Science Fiction* April 1956
Huxley, Aldous. *Ape and Essence*, Chatto and Windus (UK) 1949
Jones, Raymond F. 'The Children's Room', *Fantastic* September 1947
Phillips, Rog (Roger Phillips Graham). 'The Mutants', *Amazing* July 1946
Phillips, Rog. 'So Shall Ye Reap!', *Amazing* August 1947
Rayer, Francis G. *Tomorrow Sometimes Comes*, Home and Van Thal (UK) 1950
Tubb, E.C. (as George Holt). 'Emergency Exit', *British Science Fiction Magazine* Vol 1 No 4 1954

02.15.3 Animal, Vegetable and Mineral

Although the early writers were preoccupied with creating the next stage of man, stories involving mutation of other creatures and life-forms also began to emerge. Authors were not slow to realise that the process of mutation applied to all forms of animals, as well as man, and to plants besides.

One of the best early examples of this type of tale is Murray Leinster's 'Beyond the Sphinx's Cave' (1933). Equally notable was Stanley G. Weinbaum's 'Proteus Island' (1936), in which a zoologist exploring a remote island off the coast of New Zealand comes to realise that all forms of life on the island have mutated – insects, plants and animals alike. The author's penchant for describing alien life-forms is amply demonstrated in his descriptions of the island's population.

Another story in a similar area marked the debut of Lester del Rey. 'The Faithful' (1938) tells of a future when man has destroyed himself with bombs and the plague. All, that is, except for one man who had been experimenting with a longevity serum which protected him from the ravages of the plague. Dogs and apes had also been experimented upon, in a programme of biological research designed to increase their intelligence. The dogs remain loyal to the memory of their vanished masters, so strong is the instinct to serve. But they are about to find a new master in the now-sentient apes.

'The Faithful' may have influenced Clifford D. Simak's 'City' series (1952), which described the rise of a canine civilisation after man's departure. Simak's novel is highly regarded, but the acknowledged masterpiece on the theme is Olaf Stapledon's *Sirius: a Fantasy of Love and Discord* (1944). Stapledon details the creation and training of a super-dog, with an intelligence that possibly surpasses that of man. The story develops as a poignant (and, for some, shocking) allegory when Sirius has a love affair with the woman who helped raise him.

In *Brain Wave* (1953), Poul Anderson pursued the theme of advancing animal intelligence by depicting the Earth as emerging from a spatial force-field which has been inhibiting the IQ of all terrestrial animals. Another important story employing the idea of the animal mutant from a different viewpoint is 'Giant Killer' (1954) by A. Bertram Chandler.

'Giant Killer' is set on a spaceship voyaging through deep space, and the Giants of the title are the human crew. Although of normal stature, they appear as giants to the other intelligent life-form on the ship, the People. The story unfolds dramatically through the travails of the People, who turn out in the denouement to be rats which have mutated in the vessel's walls. A further variation of this type of story is F. L. Wallace's 'Big Ancestor' (1954), although in his version it is man himself who has begun as vermin, mutating in alien spaceship hulls and finally spreading throughout the galaxy.

Intelligent plants abound in the annals of science fiction, but they are usually alien plants; true mutations of terrestrial plants are reasonably rare. However, one such terran specimen can be found in 'Niedbalski's Mutant' (1938) by Spencer Lane. A scientist experiments with *Viola tricolor*, and causes the plant to seed itself through successive generations within a very short period of time. After five years, the scientist succeeds in breeding a plant which is the result of thousands of generations. However, he fails to anticipate the startling result of his speeding up evolution: the plant becomes sentient and begins to talk to him.

Animal mutations remain the more popular theme and one of the writers who has explored the idea most consistently and memorably is Andre Norton, beginning with her very first book, *Starman's Son* (1952). Many of her stories arguably belong in the section on mutants engendered by atomic radiation, for example, *Starman's Son* where man has been reduced to savagery following an atomic war. Some tribes have taken drastic steps to see that the strain of human lineage is kept pure, but the world is also the habitat of mutated animals gifted with intelligence, as well as of non-human tribes. Norton's later work abounds with mutated animals, a recent example being *Breed to Come* (1972).

Other modern stories of animal mutation include two which appear in *Two Views of Wonder* (1973), edited by Thomas N. Scortia and Chelsea Quinn Yarbro. Here, the editors have given the authors the same theme to write about, which is as follows: the leading character is part of a starship party rediscovering a planet settled years ago by a misanthropic molecular biologist. The protagonist falls in love with a native, only to discover that the inhabitants of the planet are not human, but mutated domestic animals – an echo of Wells's *The Island of Dr. Moreau*. The stories concerned are 'A Personage of Royal Blood' (1973) by Willo David Roberts and 'Thou Good and Faithful' (1973) by Thomas N. Scortia.

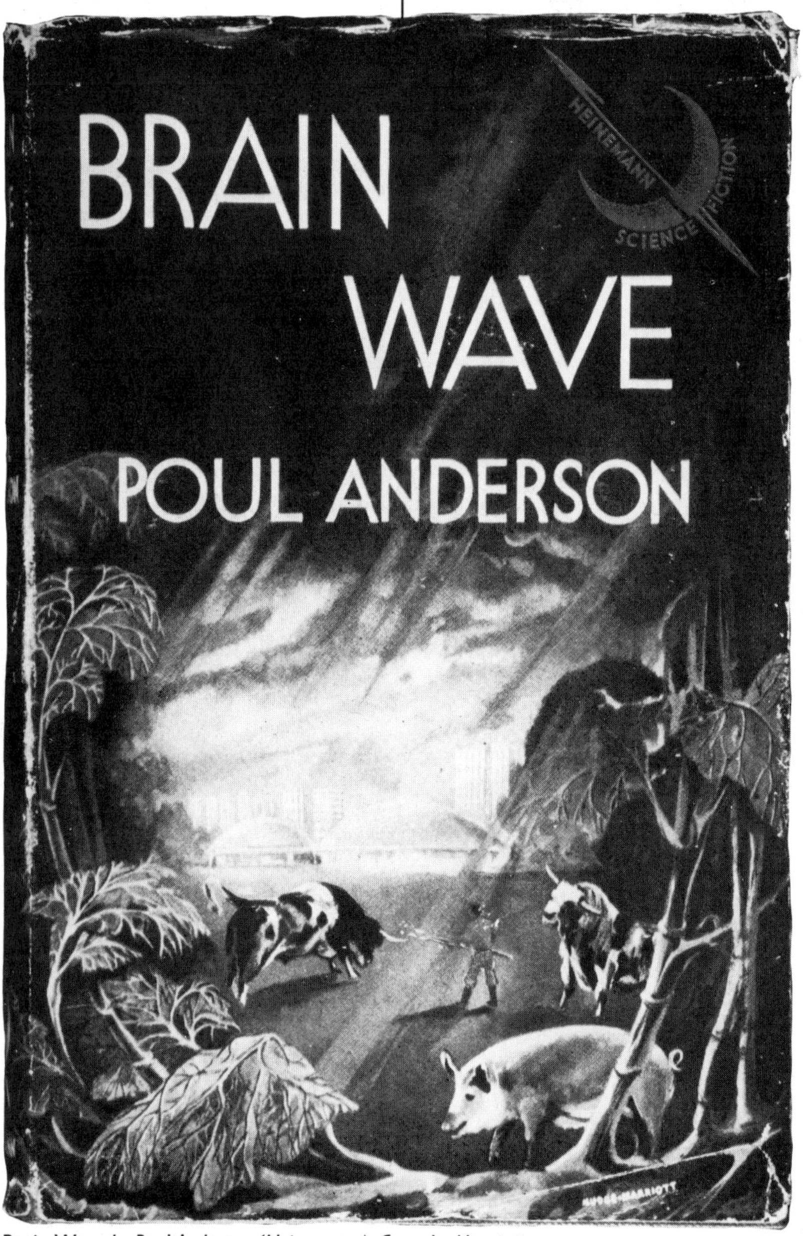

Brain Wave *by Poul Anderson (Heinemann). Cover by Marriott.*

But not only humans, animals and plants are open to mutation in science fiction – even non-organic substances have been included. Nat Schachner's 'The Ultimate Metal' (1935) tells of the results of the discovery of a new element by a physicist. The new metal, number 93 in the scale of elements, is bonded into alloys which are used to construct an enormous building. In the course of time the metal begins to swell and then contract, throwing off baffling swirls of colour and emitting sounds suggesting that its very molecules are in anguish. It becomes endowed with a strange metallic life, and mutates to reach the end-stage of metallic evolution.

There seems to be no limit to the variety with which the mutation theme may be exploited in science fiction. Mutants have become as much part of the genre as spacecraft, robots and aliens.

ADDITIONAL INPUT

02.15.3 Animal, Vegetable and Mineral

Aldiss, Brian W. 'Non-Stop', *Science Fantasy* February 1956; revised as novel, Disit (UK) 1958

McIntosh, J.T. (James McGregor) *The Fittest*, Doubleday (US) 1955

Wilson, Richard. 'Just Call Me Irish', *Future Science Fiction* June 1958

'Red Shards on Ceres' by Raymond Z. Gallun, Fantastic Story Quarterly *Spring 1950. Illustration by Orban.*

02.15.4 Symbiosis

The section on mutants showed how existing life-forms could be changed – mutated – into different life-forms. In another related sub-category of science fiction, the change sometimes takes place by another means – symbiosis.

Symbiotes are life-forms which are mutually dependent on one another, a co-existence of two diverse forms. In science fiction, the relationship is usually between man and alien, and it rarely parallels true terrestrial symbiosis, where the outcome is usually beneficial to both parties. Ants, for instance, care for aphids much as human beings care for and protect domestic animals. In return, the aphids exude a sweet juice which the ants eat; thus both kinds of insect life benefit. The human-alien symbiosis is mostly an involuntary process as far as the human is concerned.

An early example of a symbiosis story is Raymond Z. Gallun's 'Red Shards on Ceres' (1937), in which a near-immortal protoplasmic intelligence rules a protected environment in the asteroid's interior by symbiosis with a servitor species.

The theme was further developed in E. C. Tubb's suspenseful novel, *Alien Life* (1954), telling of a crystalline life-form, hitherto dormant for eons on the dead wastes of the planet Pluto, which takes over the bodies of the crew of the first spaceship to reach there. Only one man, the captain, escapes, and he is forced to abandon his crew in order to survive.

The involuntary symbiosis of man with an alien entity has powerful evocations of horror. Clark Ashton Smith's 'The Vaults of Yoh-Vombis' (1932) tells of an explorer in a Martian catacomb who is attacked by a giant slug-like alien which envelops his head and takes control of his brain.

The idea was picked up in two other stories appearing soon afterwards. In E. S. Mund's 'Brain Leeches' (1935), an alien spaceship lands on Earth, and its crew of giant slugs fasten themselves to the backs of human servitors. Harl Vincent's novelette 'Parasite' (1935) tells of an alien ship disgorging electrochemical organisms which attach themselves to the backs of human beings and control their thoughts and actions. Robert Heinlein produced the first full-length novel on the theme with *The Puppet Masters* (1953). His parasites from Titan are formless, featureless masses of protoplasm, helpless by themselves, but able to dominate their victims by clinging to the shoulder blades and taking over the body, mind and will of even the most powerful human host.

Inevitably, the shadow of Olaf Stapledon looms over the area of symbiosis, as it does over so many sf themes. His monumental *Star Maker* (1937) portrays a plethora of alien worlds, each with its distinctive life-forms. On one such planet, he describes a race of fish-like arachnoids who have spider-like crustaceans riding upon their backs. The symbiotic relationship does not develop until after puberty; before that, both races exist independently of one another. After puberty, each seeks out its partner of the opposite species, to form a lifelong union.

Hal Clement's *Needle* (1949) is a later example, describing fluid-like forms which live in a symbiotic relationship with more solid creatures on their own world. They are able to enter a host body and effect a complete takeover of functions, bringing heightened reactions and superior intelligence.

Another area of symbiosis explored in science fiction is the idea of linking man with the plant kingdom. Eric Frank Russell's 'Symbiotica' (1943) tells of the crew of an exploration ship who encounter a primitive race which seeks sanctuary among strange trees.

A ferocious form of plant life indigenous to an alien world appears in Philip E. High's 'The Meek Shall Inherit' (1957). Here Earth's would-be colonists are hideously exterminated, until it is discovered that the plants are sensitive to thoughts of hatred and aggression. The vicious circle is eventually broken, and man learns to live in symbiotic harmony with the plants.

The most recent science fiction stories have tended to move away from the grossly physical alien-human symbiosis of earlier tales. Anne McCaffrey's series about the planet Pern provides good examples of the modern symbiote. Her two novels *Dragonflight* (1968) and *Dragonquest* (1971) are set against a background in which the planet is periodically threatened with spores from space, the Threads. The Threads descend on Pern when the orbit of its captured sister planet brings it into close proximity, every 400 years. To combat this danger, a special breed of dragons has been developed over generations to burn and destroy the Threads before they reach the surface. Controlling these formidable beasts are men and women who exist in mental rapport with the creatures – the

Needle *by Hal Clement,* Astounding *May 1949. Cover illustration by Orban.*

02.15 MUTANTS AND SYMBIOTES

Dragonflight *and* Dragonquest *by Anne McCaffrey (Ballantine/Del Rey). Covers by d'Achille.*

Dragonriders. Throughout the novels, the dragons and their riders act as one, and this symbiotic union is crucial to the development of the stories.

In Brian Stableford's series of novels about the spaceship the *Hooded Swan*, the symbiosis is again on a mental level. A starship pilot is wrecked on a planet in the Halcyon Drift, a turbulent area of space seldom visited by ships unless they are in search of some fabled treasure. There he encounters a strange entity known as 'the wind' which has no substance but can only thrive in a host body. Having lost its former host, the wind enters the pilot's mind. The novels in the series include *The Halcyon Drift* (1972) and *Rhapsody in Black* (1973).

Unlike Stableford's pilot, who resents the invasion of his mind, the hero of Algis Budry's 'Silent Brother' (1956) welcomes the presence of a symbiotic alien intelligence, since each partner adds to the well-being of the other. The man receives regenerative powers and increased intelligence.

One of the most thoughtful of symbiosis stories is Walter M. Miller's 'Dark Benediction' (1951), in which alien symbiotes find their way to Earth and cause a strange plague which induces in humans an erotic craving to touch bare skin. About one-third of the populace is quickly affected by the disease, which turns its victims' skin grey. The normal pursuits are abandoned, as the unaffected people form into gangs, ruthlessly protecting their territory against encroachment by the afflicted. A colony of the plague-carriers is founded on an island administered by an order of monks who renounce the craving as they would sex. When it is discovered that the plague causes new nerve cells to grow, heightens awareness and sharpens the senses, the colony becomes the centre of the rebirth of civilisation.

It is this raising of human intelligence, exemplified in the stories of Miller, and Budrys, that marks probably the most significant treatment of symbiosis in science fiction.

ADDITIONAL INPUT

02.15.4 Symbiosis

Aldiss, Brian W. 'Segregation', *New Worlds* July 1958
Finney, Jack. 'The Invasion of the Body Snatchers', *Colliers* December 1954; Dell (US) 1955
Nourse, Alan E. *Star Surgeon*, *Amazing* December 1959; McKay (US) 1960
Sheckley, Robert. 'Specialist', *Galaxy* May 1953
Stableford, Brian. *Promised Land*, DAW (US) 1974
Stableford, Brian. *The Paradise Game*, DAW (US) 1974

02.15.5 Gestalts

A logical development of the symbiosis theme is the idea of paranormal beings who are able to merge their consciousness to form a collective unit, or gestalt. Use of the theme was made quite early, in John Russell Fearn's 'Thoughts that Kill' (1939), which tells of the entire Venusian population merging into one giant mind to defeat the invasion of the last generation of man. There are elements of it in E. E. Smith's *Children of the Lens* (1947) and in *Masters of Space* (1961–62) (the latter published posthumously as a collaboration between Smith and E. Everatt Evans to aid Evans's widow, Thelma D. Hamm).

A distinguished treatment came with Theodore Sturgeon's *More Than Human* (1953). The novel was expanded from a novelette originally published in *Galaxy* magazine, 'Baby Is Three' (1952). It tells of a number of strange children who are gifted with various extra-sensory powers, including telepathy and telekinesis. The maturing children develop a symbiotic relationship with an adult recluse, who becomes the vital link in the chain of a powerful gestalt unit. It is only after several years that the gestalt entity comes to understand morality and make benign use of its powers.

Decidely *not* benign was the fate accorded to the hero of Frederik Pohl and C. M. Kornbluth's *Wolfbane* (1957). Pyramid-like alien invaders capture him, and by adaptive surgery immerse him as one component in a grotesque organic computer. He has sixteen hands, and is in fact merged together with other captured beings. His body is conditioned to react to directions from a control unit.

A much more optimistic story is Thomas N. Scortia's 'Sea Change' (1956), which tells of the beginnings of interstellar travel. It features the creation of cyborg pilots, from men who have almost died in crashes and have been reconstructed in metal and plastic bodies. The pilots are able to communicate with each other by telepathy, and ultimately form a cyborg gestalt.

But transcending all the ingenuities of pulp fiction are the novels of Olaf Stapledon. In *Odd John* (1935), mentioned earlier, a group of supernormal children found a secret colony in the South Seas. There, they are able to pool their minds, and out of this comes the discovery of atomic force and many other marvels. *Last and First Men* (1930) depicts Martian invaders who are cloud-like, a swarm of separate tiny entities united by a telepathic bond. They are able to unite into still larger groups, and progressively, until they form a racial group-mind. Their effect on being absorbed into the human physical system is, however, to cause insanity and a new dark age.

Still later in Stapledon's renowned work comes the Eighteenth Race of Man, the near-immortal Last Men of the title. They are multi-sexed, and live in sexual groups in a telepathic unity which enables them to think as a single mind and to share all their past experience.

The same author's *Star Maker* (1973) expanded the idea to its limit. Here, the populations of entire planets form a world-mind, then progress to an interlocking telepathic link-up throughout their whole galaxy. The stars themselves are discovered to be sentient, and, after initial hostility, the Galactic Minds are able to enter into telepathic communication. Finally, a point is reached where every mind in the cosmos is merged – 'the supreme moment of the universe'.

Stapledon's stories have been an admitted influence on Arthur C. Clarke, who movingly portrayed at the close of *Childhood's End* (1953) the rise of man to union with the Overmind, transforming the Earth into pure energy as he goes. The story is a notable successor to Stapledon's pioneering work in this area of science fiction – an exalted area, perhaps, but one which reflects the kind of religious, oceanic feeling experienced on occasions by many people.

ADDITIONAL INPUT

02.15.5 Gestalts

Roberts, Keith. 'The Inner Wheel', *New Writings in SF No 6* 1965; Hart-Davis (UK) 1970

Sturgeon, Theodore. 'Wages of Synergy', *Startling* August 1953

Wolfbane *by Frederik Pohl and C. Kornbluth,* Galaxy *October 1957. Cover by Wood.*

02.15 MUTANTS AND SYMBIOTES

02.15.6 Genetic Engineering

Clone *by Richard Cowper (Quartet). Cover illustration by Burns.*

In addition to natural and accidental mutations, there exists the thematic sub-category which deals with the deliberate manipulation of human genes and the reproductive process in order to produce beings with particular characteristics. A number of sf writers have considered the possibility of genetic engineering techniques which would lead to a type of human capable of surviving on very un-Earthlike worlds.

Probably the most noted stories in this area were written by James Blish between 1942 and 1955 and collected together in *The Seedling Stars* (1956). The term 'pantropy' was used by Blish to describe the physical adaptation of man to suit him for space colonisation. His leading character is an adapted man, a being capable of withstanding the intense cold, poisonous atmosphere and reduced gravity of the Jovian moon, Ganymede. His blood and cells comprise 90 per cent liquid ammonia, functioning on a hydrogen-to-methane cycle. For nutrient, he is able to digest pulverised rock, and yet he can still be described as a man. The third part of the book consists of the original short stories, 'Sunken Universe' (1942) and 'Surface Tension' (1952), the latter telling of the establishment of a human colony on an acquatic planet. Micro-miniature human organisms are released in a puddle of water, together with a history of their origins engraved on metal plates. Many of the plates are lost in early wars with predators, and the acquatic civilisation develops with scant knowledge of space or the stars.

'Promised Land' (1950) by C.L. Moore is a further example of pantropic techniques to shape man for life on Ganymede, while 'Between the Dark and the Daylight' (1958) by Algis Budrys depicts a world so hostile that colonists are bred over successive generations to acquire such bestial characteristics as tusks and claws to enable them to survive beyond their original refuge. Eventually, they overrun the last truly human survivors and begin to dominate the planet. A.E. van Vogt's *The Silkie* (1964) echoes Blish in the genetic manipulation of human embryos to suit their adult form for life underwater and in airless environments.

Elements of genetic manipulation also occur in Robert A. Heinlein's accounts of the Howard families in *Methuselah's Children* (1941), and *Time Enough For Love* (1973). By means of a selective breeding programme, a particular family becomes progressively more long-lived with each generation, culminating in the over 2000 year lifespan of the central character in the latter novel. A comprehensive breeding scheme was earlier referred to in the section headed 'The Last Terrestrials' of Stapledon's *Last and First Men* (1930), but it was abandoned as a result of a Martian invasion of Earth.

More radical means of developing a new type of human being are the alteration of the genetic pattern by chemical means, and the technique of 'cloning' by which individual embryos are divided, and further divided, to produce a number of people with identical physical characteristics and mental potential. The same term applies to the transplantation of a donor's cells into the descended ovum in the womb, with a similar outcome.

The use of chemical techniques was described at some length by Aldous Huxley in *Brave New World* (1932), where they were employed to develop humans of varying physical and mental abilities according to the nature of the work for which they had been pre-ordained. This deliberate reversal of the science of ergonomics (shaping the worker to fit the task as against the opposite process) had already been portrayed in Wells's *The First Men in the Moon* (1901), although in that instance the alterations were achieved by physical means.

Recent stories of cloning include Gregory Kern's *The Genetic Buccaneer* (1974) and Naomi Mitchison's *Solution 3* (1975), the latter depicting a world of universal homosexuality where the entire population

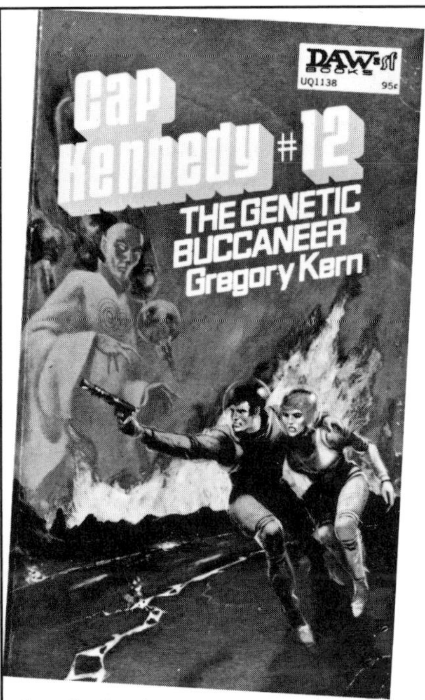

Cover by Gaughan.

are the clones of a new Adam and Eve. Among other examples are Richard Cowper's satirical *Clone* (1972) and Kate Wilhelm's *Where Late the Sweet Birds Sang* (1976).

A further tale by Kern, *Spawn of Laban* (1974) investigates the possibility of employing genetic engineering to increase the meat yield of cattle and other livestock, but it is eventually found that additional protein stocks can be provided more efficiently by breeding giant insects, a concept portrayed – with less altruistic connotations – by many earlier science fiction writers.

The use of genetic techniques to influence the behaviour of animals is also one of the main subjects in Curt Siodmak's *Hauser's Memory* (1969), a sequel after an interval of twenty-six years to his novel *Donovan's Brain* (1943). Experiments carried out with marine flatworms lead the scientist hero to speculate that monkeys could be imbued with the intelligence of humans, and dogs made to act like cats. The transference of memory by genetic means might ensure the preservation of the knowledge and experience of older people in the brains of the young.

The fact that a number of Siodmak's type of arguments are currently being aired in the real scientific world illustrates the relevance of this thematic area to recent advances in molecular biology.

'Abercrombie Station' by Jack Vance, Thrilling Wonder Stories February 1952. Illustration by Finlay.

ADDITIONAL INPUT

02.15.6 Genetic Engineering

Anderson, Poul. 'Garden in the Void', *Galaxy* May 1952

Anderson, Poul. 'The Un-Man', *Astounding* January 1953

Campbell, John W. 'Genetics and Utopia' (editorial), *Analog* March 1969

Cover by Fernandes.

Clarke, Arthur C. *Imperial Earth*, Harcourt Brace (US) 1976

Disch, Thomas M. 'Genetic Coda', *Fantastic* June 1964

Hamilton, Edmond. 'Master of the Genes', *Wonder Stories* January 1935

Heinlein, Robert A. 'Jerry Is a Man', *Thrilling Wonder* October 1947

McIntosh J.T. (James M. MacGregor). *The Fittest*, Doubleday (US) 1955

Nelson, R. Faraday. 'Flesh Pearl', *Amazing* December 1976

Palmer, Raymond A. 'Three from the Test Tube', *Wonder Stories* November 1936

Smith, Cordwainer (Paul Linebarger). 'The Crime and Glory of Commander Suzdal', *Amazing* May 1964

Schachner, Nat. 'The 100th Generation', *Astounding* May 1934

Temple, William F. 'Echo', *Famous SF* Winter 1967

Weissman, Barry Alan. 'Genemaster', *Worlds of If* November 1969

Wells, H.G. *The Island of Dr Moreau*, Heinemann (UK) 1896

02.16 TELEPATHY, PSIONICS AND ESP

They tell me that the people who study psychic powers are past the point of wondering whether such things exist. Now they're concentrating on techniques for weeding out the phonies. The phonies get in the way of actual investigations.

Psychic powers are real? Imagine my amazement.

I've written stories about people possessed of unusual senses and abilities. The fact is that I wrote them in the belief that no such thing existed in the real world. I wrote stories of magic for the same reason: I found the ideas interesting.

Extra-sensory perception, levitation, the reading of minds, prognostication: have you met anyone who believed in these powers without claiming them for himself? They are the stuff of wish fulfilment, of daydreams: controlling the spin of dice, guessing the winning horse consistently, *knowing* that the girl is willing (or actually controlling her thoughts), and evading death or injury by hunches that favour you alone. With all that going for it, how can a tale of psychic powers be dull?

Easily. A bad writer can make anything look dull. A couple of hundred competent writers can do even a good subject to death fairly quickly. It had already happened to psychic powers by the time I started writing, a dozen years ago. One can blame John Campbell and *Analog*, but there were psi stories appearing elsewhere, too. Psychic powers are like tales of alternative histories: they were done to death because they are just too easy to write.

Yet there is always something new to say. Thus:

Never teleport out of a speeding car. The rules say you'll keep the velocity.

Never read the mind of an experienced telepath. You'll wind up with a terrific identity problem: two sets of memories, and the set that is used to the experience isn't yours.

The optic nerves are brain tissue. A limited form of telepathy might function as invisibility.

Psychic powers must be limited by the user's imagination. Thus, clairvoyance plus telekinesis might manifest themselves as a ghostly third arm: puny, and unable to reach far, but capable of reaching through a wall to scoop up an ounce of molten plutonium.

Luck is the ultimate psychic power . . . which is why it's easy to write bad stories about psychic powers. Author control should never be obvious.

Are there really people who can read my mind at a poker table, or foretell the next card to reach their hands? Perhaps it doesn't matter. Psychic powers, if they exist, have been with us as long as tales of witchcraft, and longer: as long as humanity has had a human brain. Look at the changes science and engineering have made in our world in a much shorter time. You may look in vain for similar changes derived from our use of psychic powers! These powers don't seem to be useful.

But they can be most entertaining.

Larry Niven

Larry Niven

02.16 TELEPATHY, PSIONICS AND ESP

No other single theme within the science fiction world has been as controversial as ESP (extra-sensory perception) or, to use a more scientific neologism, psionics – the powers of the mind. Yet during the 1950s it ranked as one of the most common plot themes in the field, and it still appears regularly today.

The best-known form of ESP is telepathy, generally regarded as the ability to read another person's thoughts and communicate non-verbally. An extension of the gift is the power, through one's own thoughts, to influence those of another. An additional development is telekinesis – the ability to move objects by sheer force of mind. It is closely linked with teleportation, or levitation, in which a person can cause himself to move simply by mind-power. Yet another aspect is precognition, the capacity to perceive the future. This is often called clairvoyance; although, to be accurate, clairvoyance refers to the mental ability to perceive objects or persons at any distance.

Psionics is a blanket term covering other hidden powers of the mind, among them: ancestral memory (the ability to recapture memories of ancient times), mental exchange (where one swaps minds – and therefore bodies – with another being), the powers of superminds, and – ultimately – the power to create tangible dream-worlds.

Science fiction writers have also investigated the nature of different mental diseases – particularly schizophrenia, which, together with split minds and split personalities, has become a stock device in many sf stories. Psionics is still not regarded as entirely respectable by many devotees, and tends to be seen as something of a renegade theme in science fiction. This distrust owes much to the original linkage of telepathy and precognition with the world of witchcraft and the occult. Perhaps one of the oddest paradoxes in the history of science fiction is that the first wave of writers to concentrate on ESP was generated by the formerly hard-headed scientific editor, John W. Campbell. Under his guidance, the sf science of psionics was born, and the genre acquired an added dimension.

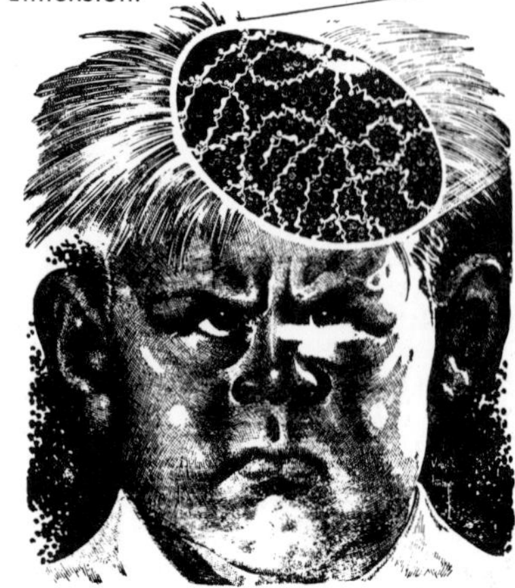

02.16 TELEPATHY, PSIONICS AND ESP

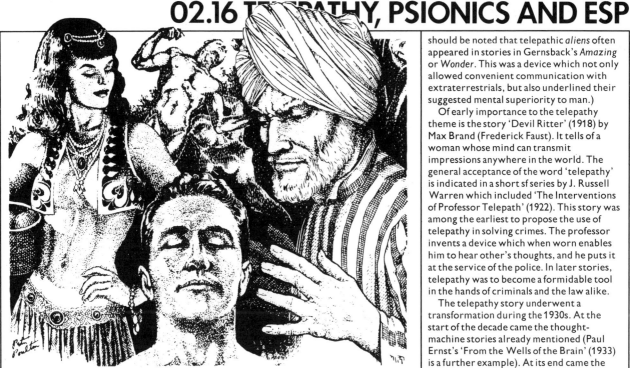

'*Peeping Tom' by Judith Merril,* Startling Stories *Spring 1954. Illustration by Poulton.*

02.16.1 Telepathy

One of the earliest writers to show an interest in hypnotism and the inner powers of the mind was Edgar Allan Poe. He touched on the subject in a number of stories, of which the most memorable – chiefly because of its horrific dénouement – is 'The Facts in the Case of M. Valdemar' (1845), in which the mind of a man is kept alive after his body has died. Hypnotism subsequently became a favourite plot device during the nineteenth century – probably the most famous work being George Du Maurier's *Trilby* (1894), with its powerful characterisation of the hypnotist Svengali, a name that has passed into the English language. It was hypnotism that also inspired the first major ESP story, 'The Bohemian' by Fitz-James O'Brien, which seems not to have been published prior to its inclusion in *The Diamond Lens and Other Stories* (1885), more than twenty years after its writer's death. In this tale, hypnotism is employed to induce extra-sensory talents in the leading character.

The term 'telepathy' had yet to be coined, and would not be invented until 1882. The transference of thoughts between two people was initially regarded by writers and raders as mystical – but if thoughts could be read by a machine, then that was another matter. Today the use of electroencephalography, the measurement of brainwaves, invented by Hans Berger in 1929, is an accepted part of medical science; but suggestions before that discovery that the brain emitted waves of any kind would have been considered, like thought-waves, as fantasy.

An early example of a machine capable of reading a human mind occurs in Charles Stephens's story 'The Thing behind the Curtain' (1908), which describes a device which can both receive and transmit thought-waves. When Hugo Gernsback began to publish science fiction only a few years later, it was this type of story that appealed to him. His editorial policy was biased towards gadgetry and scientific development rather than to people; and any stories involving thought-reading published in his magazines generally centred on a machine. 'The Telepathic Pick Up' (1926) by Samuel M. Sargent Jr and Julian Huxley's 'The Tissue-Culture King' (1926), which Gernsback reprinted, are good examples. Huxley's story involves a machine that broadcasts orders over a considerable distance in the form of thoughts, with the result that anyone within the radius of its power is hypnotised into obedience. Gernsback's rigid adherence to 'scientific' principles rarely prevented him from bending his own rules when he chose, and printing a story which by his definition was fantasy – especially if it was the work of H. G. Wells. 'The Stolen Body' (1898) was one such piece. Wells relates how his main character hypnotises himself and then attempts to project his inner self to a colleague. When he tries to return he discovers his own body has been occupied by a fiend. This story, of a kind seldom seen in Gernsback's magazines (where it was reprinted in 1928), falls into the category of astral projection, a plot device frequently employed in ghost stories. The same ploy was used in early science fiction as a means of the protagonist visiting other planets, and this theme is examined in our consideration of teleportation below.

Outside of Gernsback's magazines, there was less 'scientific' restriction, and telepathy was by no means confined to men and machines in other publications. (It should be noted that telepathic *aliens* often appeared in stories in Gernsback's *Amazing* or *Wonder*. This was a device which not only allowed convenient communication with extraterrestrials, but also underlined their suggested mental superiority to man.)

Of early importance to the telepathy theme is the story 'Devil Ritter' (1918) by Max Brand (Frederick Faust). It tells of a woman whose mind can transmit impressions anywhere in the world. The general acceptance of the word 'telepathy' is indicated in a short sf series by J. Russell Warren which included 'The Interventions of Professor Telepath' (1922). This story was among the earliest to propose the use of telepathy in solving crimes. The professor invents a device which when worn enables him to hear other's thoughts, and he puts it at the service of the police. In later stories, telepathy was to become a formidable tool in the hands of criminals and the law alike.

The telepathy story underwent a transformation during the 1930s. At the start of the decade came the thought-machine stories already mentioned (Paul Ernst's 'From the Wells of the Brain' (1933) is a further example). At its end came the first major novel dealing with telepathic powers, A.E. van Vogt's *Slan* (1940).

Slan *by A. E. van Vogt,* Fantastic Story Magazine *Summer 1952. Illustration by Finlay.*

In the majority of sf stories dealing with the theme, both early and late, the telepath is portrayed as a freak, one hated and loathed by those less gifted. Telepaths, like other mutants, fall into the same category as the robot – they are feared by those ignorant of their intentions. This approach could be seen developing during the 1930s. It was not just that telepaths knew what others were thinking, it was the question of their having power over others' minds. John Russell Fearn's first novel, *The Intelligence Gigantic* (1933), explored the possibilities of using the uncharted area of the brain that appears not to be used, and thus unleashing undreamed-of power. In the same year, David M. Speaker's 'The Supermen' was published, describing the creation of a new race of men whose highly developed mental powers can control the actions of others. Humanity misunderstands them, and inevitably conflict follows – with the outcome that 'normal' mankind survives and the supermen are destroyed. Already, developments were pointing towards telepathic mutants as a race superior to

02.16 TELEPATHY, PSIONICS AND ESP

'*Rogue Psi' by James H. Schmitz*, Amazing *August 1962. Illustration by Finlay.*

Homo sapiens, and hence one to be feared.

The Lensmen in E.E. Smith's classic series were envisaged as the first step towards a superior race. Their undoubted mental and physical prowess attested to it, combined with their symbiotic existence through the semi-sentient lens worn around their wrists, and with which they could establish instant mental contact with others of their kind anywhere in the universe.

Smith's series is epic adventure on a cosmic scale, and there is little place in the stories for the views of mere humans on the superior people of the lens. By contrast, *Slan* stands out as a landmark in the development of the psi story, being one of the very first to deal sympathetically with those endowed with paranormal powers. A.E. van Vogt's tale is centred on the struggle for existence of a young Slan whose abilities are not yet fully developed. All Slans are hated by humanity, and they are betrayed by golden tendrils in their hair which is all that distinguishes them from the 'normals'. A price is put on their heads. The leading character, separated from his fellows, finds that the Slan race depends on him to prove their worth and to convince existing society that its fears are groundless.

Slan was very much a trend-setter. To this day, the majority of psi stories treat sympathetically the telepath (or esper), who is hounded by *Homo sapiens* and fighting for survival. About the only sub-category which maintains hostility to the telepath is the crime story, which will be discussed below.

Generally speaking, stories in which the esper is portrayed with sympathy describe the character's discovery that he is telepathic and tell of his resultant hardships. The story is seldom developed beyond that stage to a practical use of psi powers. For example, we read of the hero of Lester del Rey's *Pstalemate* (1971), terrified at his discovery that he is telepathic and precognitive. He discovers others with the same gift scattered throughout the country and learns that they are all lonely in their isolation, afraid to contact their counterparts and slowly going mad. Similarly, Robert Silverberg's protagonist in *Dying Inside* (1972) is horrified by what he learns of himself through telepathy and reaches the depths of alienation. As basic psi novels, *Dying Inside* and *Pstalemate* are a good introduction for the newcomer to this thematic area. Walter M. Miller's story, 'Anybody Else Like Me?' (1952) is another example.

In the 1950s, Algis Budry's had also underlined the loneliness of the telepath in a pair of stories written under the alias Paul Janvier. The first, 'Nobody Bothers Gus' (1955), tells of a paranormal who has set up a haven for himself in an isolated spot where he wishes to be left alone. Budrys describes in the story how nature has protected the telepath by making him virtually invisible to normal humans, a point further developed in 'And Then She Found Him . . .' (1957), where the experience of being totally ignored by people drives a girl esper to crime. Alan E. Nourse also provided a touching story in 'Second Sight' (1956), which traces the investigations into a girl telepath who knows all that is going on around her even though, as disclosed at the end, she is both blind and deaf.

Psi-talented children occur frequently in science fiction, many writers having taken the cue from *Slan*. A writer who has developed the theme and given it a humorous slant is James H. Schmitz, who achieved early success with a short story, 'The Witches of Karres' (1949). Beginning with 'Novice' (1962), Schmitz introduced a continuing series about a young girl of fifteen, Telzey Amberdon, whose contact with a telepathic native species on another planet results in her discovery that she has dormant psi powers. The first two stories in the series were collected in book form as *The Universe against Her* (1964), and further tales have followed.

Humour is uncommon in psi stories, although in the telekinetic variety some can be achieved in the hurling around of objects. Schmitz managed a light-hearted approach in 'The Witches of Karres', and earlier Henry Kuttner had applied his inimitable sense of humour to a series about the 'Hogben' hillbillies. Kuttner's hillbillies were endowed with a range of bizarre qualities, not least telepathy, but they never regarded themselves as exceptional.

Paranormal mental powers are not necessarily portrayed as a natural acquisition. Mark Clifton and Frank Riley told in their novel, *They'd Rather Be Right* (1954), of a super-computer that finds it can not only rejuvenate people but also confer psi powers upon them. The story appeared in *Astounding* in the heyday of Campbell's psionic period. The renowned editor had been fascinated by the Hieronymous machine invented, and patented, by one T. Galen Hieronymous. It was claimed that the machine could determine whether an

'*The Witches of Karres' by James H. Schmitz*, Astounding *December 1949. Illustration by Rogers.*

element was present in any sample of matter simply by the operator concentrating mentally on that element – in short, it was supposed to work in conjunction with human psi powers. Campbell himself wrote several articles about this and other psionic devices, and *Astounding* was the regular haven for all psi stories during the 1950s, almost to the extent of over-saturation. Many of them ignored the human angle for the technical aspect and, unless their writers resorted to humour, they tended to become monotonous.

One of the best-remembered series from this period concerned an agent of the FBI whose telepathic powers were put to good use in searching out spies and solving other psionic muddles. This series began with *That Sweet Little Old Lady* (1959) and was the work of Mark Phillips (Randall Garrett and Laurence M. Janifer in collaboration). It is, in fact, the use that telepaths are put to that provides the interest of many psi stories. As in the 'Phillips' series, the hero of Wilson Tucker's *Wild Talent* (1954) is used by the FBI to spot spies and traitors. In Phillip K. Dick's *Ubik* (1969), telepaths are employed on industrial espionage.

Domination through telepathy is one of the prospects that has led sf writers to show humans as hating telepaths. In Fritz Leiber's 'The Mutant's Brother' (1943), twin telepaths find they can read and control others' minds, one of the brothers hungering after absolute power even if it means killing his twin. The telepath who resorts to crime is the inevitable product of a society which shuns and fears him. A well-known early work of this type was Curt Siodmak's *Donovan's Brain* (1942), telling of a disembodied criminal brain which gradually assumes telepathic control over others for its own devious ends. Similarly, in James H. Schmitz's 'Rogue Psi' (1962) we are presented with a powerful telepath who can influence men totally and without mercy and is also a perfect mimic, passing through the world unnoticed. In Robert Silverberg's *Thorns* (1967), an evil telepath is depicted who manoeuvres men and women into emotional crises and then feeds off their fear as if it were a drug.

The criminal-telepath theme was also pursued in Keith Roberts's 'The Inner Wheel' (1965), in which the hero learns that his village is under the telepathic control of a group of espers who have combined to form a gestalt mind. The gestalt principle, as originally proposed by Wolfgang Kohler, argues that the whole is greater than its individual parts. Telepaths coming together in gestalt groups have provided some of the most memorable psi stories. The acknowledged leading gestalt novel is Theodore Sturgeon's *More Than Human* (1953), which grew from the story 'Baby Is Three' (1952), about a social outcast who joins forces with four other talented children to produce a powerful psychic entity. A similar gestalt grouping of half-alien children occurs in John Wyndham's *The Midwich Cuckoos* (1957), which provided the basis of two popular films, *The Village of the Damned* (1960) and *Children of the Damned* (1964). Wyndham's last novel, *Chocky* (1963), dealt with a young boy who is receptive to a telepathic alien.

Three recent psi stories centred on crime have been incorporated into the book *To Ride Pegasus* (1973) by Anne McCaffrey. Their titles are 'A Womanly Talent' (1969), 'Apple' (1969) and 'Bridle for Pegasus' (1973), and the tales are mainly concerned with precognition and teleportation, although an element of the gestalt theme is also present.

'Wild Talent' by Wilson Tucker, New Worlds *August 1954. Cover by Quinn.*

Telepathy is open to two-way operation; it can be used to set a thief to catch a thief. The background of Alfred Bester's *The Demolished Man* (1952) is a future society that uses espers to help snare criminals. Kenneth Bulmer's *The Doomsday Men* (1965) tells of espers who make spiritual contact with murder victims to discover the identity of their killers.

The healing use of telepathy is another sub-category which has received some attention. John Brunner's novel *The Whole Man* (1964), which saw magazine publication in 1959, tells how a crippled child learns that he has the talent to probe into minds, isolate psychoses and cure insanity. The healing powers of telepathy had been used by L. Ron Hubbard in his novel *The Tramp* as long ago as 1938, and the author later went on to develop his thoughts on the mind into the 'science' of Dianetics (see under Fringe Cults). A recent story of curative telepathy was Joe Allred's 'When I Was in Your Mind' (1972), where the paranormal faculty serves a purpose in brain surgery. Other valuable uses have been described in such stories as John DeCles' 'Forgive Us Our Debtors' (1966), and in Gerard F. Conway's 'Mindship' (1971).

The variety of plot themes in the telepathy category seems almost unlimited. In 'Sonny' (1963) by Rick Raphael we read of an American boy whose telepathic gift is able to short-circuit Russia's electrical power grid! In Brian Aldiss's *An Age* (1967), we find a form of mental time-travel. In Gordon Dickson's recent novel *The Pritcher Mass* (1972), a group of psionically talented people try to construct a telepathic bridge to another star.

ADDITIONAL INPUT

02.16.1 Telepathy

Aldiss, Brian W. 'Psyclops', *New Worlds* July 1956

Anvil, Christopher. 'The Throne and the Usurper', *F & SF* November 1970

Brunner, John. 'Listen! The Stars', *Analog* July 1962; expanded Ace (US) 1963; retitled *The Stardroppers*, DAW (US) 1972

Brunner, John. 'Out of Mindshot', *Galaxy* June 1970

Brunner, John. 'Singleminded', *If* May 1963

Delany, Samuel R. 'Corona', *F&SF* October 1967

Fearn, John Russell. *The Intelligence Gigantic*, *Amazing* June to July 1933; World's Work (UK) 1943

Gotlieb, Phyllis. *Sunburst*, *Amazing* March to May 1964; Gold Medal (US) 1964

Keller, David H. *The Thought Projector*, Gernsback (US) 1929

Lafferty, R.A. 'A Special Condition in Summit City', *Universe 2* (ed Terry Carr) Ace (US) 1972

Leiber, Fritz. 'The Mind Spider', *Fantastic* November 1959

Matheson, Richard. 'Lover, When You're Near Me', *Galaxy* May 1952

McCaffrey, Anne. 'The Lady in the Tower', *F&SF* April 1959; sequel 'A Meeting of Minds', *F&SF* January 1969

Miller, Walter M. 'Command Performance', *Galaxy* November 1952

Morgan, Dan. The 'Minds' series runs as follows:
The New Minds, Corgi (UK) 1967
The Several Minds, Corgi (UK) 1969
The Mind Trap, Corgi (UK) 1970
The Country of the Mind, Corgi (UK) 1975

Morgan, Dan. *The Uninhibited*, *New Worlds* August to October 1957; Digit (UK) 1961

Payes, Rachel Cosgrove. 'Eyes of the Blind', *Vertex* April 1975

Russell, Eric Frank. *Call Him Dead*, *Astounding* August to October 1955; retitled *Three to Conquer*, Avalon (US) 1956

Russell, Eric Frank (as Webster Craig). 'Homo Saps', *Astounding SF* December 1941

Sheckley, Robert. 'Wild Talents, Inc.', *Fantastic* September/October 1953

Smith, E.E. (with E. Everett and Thelma Hamm Evans). *Masters of Space*, *If* November 1961 to January 1962

Wilhelm, Kate. 'The Mile-Long Spaceship', *Astounding* April 1957

Wilhelm, Kate. 'Stranger in the House', *F&SF* February 1968

Woodcott, Keith (John Brunner). *Crack of Doom*, *New Worlds* September to October 1962

Wyndham, John (John Beynon Harris). 'Child of Power' (as Wyndham Parkes) *Fantasy 3* Summer 1939

Wyndham, John. 'Chocky', *Amazing* March 1963; expanded Michael Joseph (UK) 1968

Wyndham, John. *The Chrysalids*, Michael Joseph (UK) 1955; retitled *Re-Birth*, Ballantine (US) 1955

02.16 TELEPATHY, PSIONICS AND ESP

02.16.2 Teleportation and Precognition

While teleportation, telekinesis and levitation have subtle differences in meaning, more often than not they are taken to indicate the same thing – the ability to move oneself or other objects by power of the mind alone.

In the early days of science fiction, teleportaion took on the aspect of astral projection described in H.G. Wells's 'The Stolen Body'. Astral projection was the convenient method of exploring space employed in Camille Flammarion's *Urania* (1889). It was also the means to an end in David Lindsay's *A Voyage to Arcturus* (1920). It was the method by which John Carter arrived on Mars in the well-known series by Edgar Rice Burroughs, beginning with *Under the Moons of Mars* (1912). It was used, just before the Second World War, by no less than Olaf Stapledon in his acknowledged masterpiece *The Star Maker* (1937). Unscientific as spirit-journeys might be, all the above are nevertheless regarded as memorable works of science fiction.

Physical teleportation, however, did not generally feature in early works of the genre, unless it was manifested in the shape of aliens hovering a few feet above the ground with no visible means of support. More recently, Jack Vance took that idea and produced an entertaining story entitled 'Telek' (1952). L. Ron Hubbard produced one of the earliest teleportation stories with his own first sf tale 'The Dangerous Dimension' (1938), in which a professor discovers he can wish himself anywhere.

Teleportation is seldom used as the sole plot in a novel, unless it is part of a collection of psi factors such as that found in J.T. McIntosh's *The ESP Worlds* (1952). In that story, trained telepaths are sent to a planet where the inhabitants are adept teleports. Teleportation is a major device in the 'Pern' series by Anne McCaffrey, *Dragonflight* (1967) and *Dragonquest* (1971). The dragons cannot only teleport through space, but also through time, thus saving the planet Pern from almost certain catastrophe. It is also the theme on which Vernor Vinge's recent novel *The Witling* (1975) is based.

'The ESP Worlds' by J. T. McIntosh, New Worlds *September 1952. Cover by Gerald Quinn.*

The Witling *by Vérnor Vinge (DAW). Cover by Barr.*

Investigations into telekinesis are conducted with a certain air of amusement in Mark Clifton's 'Sense from Thought Divide' (1955), when a fake Swami is suddenly discovered to possess real powers. Jerome Bixby displayed some originality in 'The Draw' (1954), in which telekinesis is used to perfect the instantaneous draw of a revolver from its holster.

On the darker side, teleportation can produce sinister overtones. In Lester del Rey's 'Pursuit' (1952), the hero finds himself chased by a gang of espers who make life very unpleasant for him. The life of a psi fire-raiser is described in terms of pathos in Harlan Ellison's 'Deeper Than the Darkness' (1957).

In 'Manipulation' (1965) by John Kingston (Keith Roberts), the narrator is a telekinetic *and* a clairvoyant, in as much as he can also see over considerable distances. Subsequently, he realises he is also becoming a telepath. The ability to see over great distances was introduced by H. G. Wells in 'The Remarkable Case of Davidson's Eyes' (1895), and 'The Telescopic Eye' (1876) by William Henry Rhodes.

Precognition is a less common theme in the psionic category of science fiction. It is considered by many the least 'scientific' of all the paranormal concepts, smacking as it does of prophecies and astrology. People purportedly gifted with 'second sight' have included mythological figures such as Cassandra, twin sister of Helen of Troy, and in comparatively more recent times, the sixteenth-century seer, Nostradamus, and his contemporary, Mother Shipton. Precognition, as opposed to prophecy, entered the pages of science fiction in much the same way as other psi topics, through the medium of hypnotism, in such early tales as John Esten Cook's 'A Magnetizer' (1874), and George C. Eggleston's story 'Bernard Poland's Prophecy' (1875).

It is not unusual in stories of precognition for the protagonist to foresee his own death – how could he do otherwise? Short stories leave little room for much additional development, although an exception is 'The Ming Vase' (1963) by E. C. Tubb, where a criminal uses his second sight to learn of events that will serve as a diversion while he commits his crimes. The most noted uses of 'second sight' are generally confined to novels, and two good examples are James Blish's *Jack of Eagles* (1952), expanded from the original magazine novelette 'Let the Finder Beware' (1949), and Philip K. Dick's *The World Jones Made* (1956).

Recently, a new angle has been given to the precognition theme in Robert Silverberg's novel *The Stochastic Man* (1975). The story centres on a character adept in stochastic prediction, the art of plotting extrapolations from all possibilities to arrive at the likeliest probability. It makes the hero an almost infallible short-range prophet, and he uses this skill to further the cause of a colleague in his presidential campaign. Then he meets a strange medium who is genuinely possessed of second sight. The medium's talents leave him without drive or will; yet despite this sobering example the hero decides that he, too, wants the gift of second sight that the medium can pass on.

The transference of psi talents is one thing, but in some science fiction stories there has also occurred the actual exchange of minds from one being to another.

ADDITIONAL INPUT

02.16.2 Teleportation and Precognition

Bulmer, Kenneth. 'Mr. Culpeper's Baby', *Authentic* April 1956

Gunn, James E. 'Wherever You May Be', *Galaxy* May 1953

Keyes, Daniel. 'Crazy Maro', *F&SF* April 1960

Malzberg, Barry N. 'Closing the Deal', *Analog* March 1974

Martino, Joseph P. '... Not a Prison Make', *Analog* September 1966

Monroe, Lyle (Robert A. Heinlein). 'Lost Legion', *Super Science Stories* November 1941; retitled 'Lost Legacy' (as by Heinlein) *Assignment in Eternity*, Fantasy (US) 1953

Sheckley, Robert. 'Protection', *Galaxy* April 1956

Stratford, H. Philip (Kenneth Bulmer). 'Don't Cross a Telekine', *SF Adventures* May 1959

Vance, Jack. 'Telek', *Astounding* January 1952

02.16.3 Mental Exchange

Well known are the lines of Robert Burns: 'O wad some Power the giftie gie us, to see oursels as others see us!' Science fiction writers have frequently had the temerity to oblige. The H.G. Wells story 'The Stolen Body' involves a human frame temporarily empty of its 'soul' being occupied by a demon, but this was far from the first use of the idea. This sub-theme's first major appearance occurred in a very popular novel, *Vice Versa* (1882) by F. Anstey (Thomas A. Guthrie), in which a father and son switch bodies with the aid of an old talisman. Apparently, the theme had been used even earlier, in Edward Page Mitchell's story 'Exchanging Their Souls' (1877), explaining how a Georgian wheelwright and a Russian prince swap bodies, but the story had gone unnoticed until recently.

Anstey's story, on the other hand, remains in print to this day, as does a similar story by Arthur Conan Doyle, 'The Great Keinplatz Experiment' (1886), which fits more comfortably into the realms of science fiction by relating how a professor and his student exchange bodies under hypnotism. Many mental exchange stories – such as Lord Dunsany's *The Strange Journeys of Colonel Polders* (1950) – remain in the realms of fantasy, but occasionally the subject emerges in science fiction with notable originality. The same theme as Dunsany's, for instance, had earlier been used by H. L. Gold in his short story, 'A Matter of Form' (1938), where the chief character exchanges minds with his collie.

Mental exchange with aliens is a more common occurrence, and is succinctly demonstrated in Damon Knight's *Mind Switch* (1965), in which a reporter finds he is

'Mindswap' by Robert Sheckley, Galaxy June 1965. Illustration by Morrow.

02.16 TELEPATHY, PSIONICS AND ESP

Cover by Holmes.

an exhibit in the Hamburg Zoo. Another example is 'A Wild Surmise' by Henry Kuttner and C.L. Moore (1953), in which a human exchanges minds with a Martian psychiatrist. Robert Sheckley concocted a hilarious treatment of the theme in *Mindswap* (1966), portraying a central character so bored with life that he decides to swap bodies with a Martian. Too late, he learns that his temporary host has made similar arrangements with eleven other entities, and the plot involves the hero's search, in a mind-swapping odyssey, for his original body.

Frequently, the mental exchange in such stories is made via a machine, rather than through cerebral forces. As such, stories of this nature do not constitute an exploitation of bona fide psi powers. Nevertheless, they do underline the variety of themes used by the sf writer simply to explore the possibilities of the mind.

Recently, the suggestion that a kind of immortality could be achieved by transplanting a man's brain into a child's body, so that he has a whole new physical life ahead, appeared in Michael G. Coney's *Friends Come in Boxes* (1975). Earlier, Roger Zelazny suggested the transfer of the mind to a younger frame in *Lord of Light* (1967). Robert A. Heinlein's *I Will Fear No Evil* (1971) is a further example. (The transference of brains to machines is another matter entirely and is covered in the section on Computers and Cybernetics.)

An intriguing sideline of mental exchange is the possibility of a man entering another's mind. British writer Peter Phillips produced a memorable story in 'Dreams Are Sacred' (1948), telling of a psychiatrist who enters the mind of a science fiction writer which has snapped through overwork, taking the writer into a dream-filled trance. The same basic idea was expanded by Roger Zelazny in his short novel *He Who Shapes* (1965), in which a neurologist treats brain disorders by inducing dreams in his patients and then entering the dreams in an attempt to guide them to a healthy conclusion.

One logical extrapolation from this particular thematic variation is for a man to create an entire tangible dream-world of his own imagination. While such a concept obviously borders on the realms of fantasy, a few sf stories in the category are worth mentioning. In 1936 Australian writer Alan Connell caused a stir with his tale 'Dream's End', chronicling a sequence of bizarre events which are explained by the discovery that the Earth, and presumably the entire universe, is merely the dream of some super-being who is finally waking up. The Tier Worlds presented in Philip José Farmer's series that began with *Maker of Universes* (1965) are created entirely at the whim of the 'gods' who choose to inhabit those kinds of worlds. Comparable creative variations appear in Clifford Simak's *Out of Their Minds* (1970), L. Ron Hubbard's *Typewriter in the Sky* (1940) and Barry Malzberg's *Herovit's World* (1973).

ADDDITIONAL INPUT

02.16.3 Mental Exchange

Galouye, Daniel F. 'Mindmate', *Amazing* July 1964
Lafferty, R.A. 'Through Other Eyes', *Future SF* February 1960
Moorcock, Michael. *The Final Programme*, Avon (US) 1968
Smith, Thorne. *Turnabout*, Doubleday (US) 1931
Stine, Hank. *The Season of the Witch*, Essex House (US) 1968

02.16.4 Split Minds

No better work has been written on the subject of two opposing personalities coexisting inside a single human being than Robert Louis Stevenson's classic *The Strange Case of Dr Jekyll and Mr Hyde* (1886); its fame obviates the need to recount the plot here. However, the story is perhaps relevant to present-day liberal drug usage and the apparent Jekyll and Hyde situations in which people under the influence of LSD and other hallucinogens – or even alcohol – have found themselves.

The split-personality aspect has been explored only marginally in science fiction, but the few excursions have yielded some worthwhile results. Theodore Sturgeon approached the theme in 'The Other Man' (1956), portraying a psychiatrist's efforts to electronically control a man's mind, which is threatening to break under the conflict between his ego and alter ego. Today the story reads more like fact than science fiction. Sturgeon tackled the theme in another variation, 'Who!' (1955), in which a spaceman's loneliness is overcome by implanting a device in his brain that enables him to conduct a conversation with his inner self.

Wyman Guin wrote an unusual split-mind story in 'Beyond Bedlam' (1951), which describes a society where the fractionated personality is not only normal, but obligatory, and the body oscillates between alternate persons for five-day periods. The tale suggests that by allowing the mind to develop both personalities, inner tensions will be released and aggression reduced.

The split-mind story need not necessarily be serious. It also lends itself to the kind of

'The Ghosts of Melvin Pye' by L. Sprague de Camp, Thrilling Wonder Stories *December 1946. Illustration by Marchioni.*

Cover by Emsh.

humour which L. Sprague de Camp conjured up in 'The Ghosts of Melvin Pye' (1946), an account of the twin ghosts of a split personality! Another of science fiction's humorous writers, Richard Wilson, produced an amusing story in 'The In-Betweens' (1957), which shows what happens when all the identities of a multi-split personality take on real forms. More recently, Jack Wodhams has employed a neat twist on Sturgeon's idea by telling of a person genuinely sliced in two in 'Split Personality' (1968). But one half of his character's mind still knows what the other half is doing – a case of 'self-telepathy'.

Of the few novels that have used split minds as a plot device, the most memorable is Stanley G. Weinbaum's *The New Adam* (1939), which recounts the development of a genetic freak into a superman. Early in the novel, the main character realises that he has a dual mind and can easily maintain two separate trains of thought simultaneously.

ADDITIONAL INPUT

02.16.4 Split Minds

Davies, L.P. *Psychogeist*, Jenkins (UK) 1966
Stapledon, Olaf. *A Man Divided*, Methuen (UK) 1950
Stevens, Francis (Gertrude Bennett). *Serapion*, *Argosy* June to July 1920

02.16.5 Ancestral Memories

An absorbing idea, by no means confined to the field of science fiction, is that the mind, through heredity, partly shares its ancestors' memories. The concept can to some extent be rationalised by arguing that it becomes apparent in instinct, the individual actions stemming from an innate pattern of responses. If this thread of memory could be explored, one might trace back in one's mind through previous generations to one's earliest forbears.

Turn-of-the-century novels abounded with stories of ancestral and racial memories. Among them were Archie Campbell's *The Sound of a Voice That Is Still* (1899), Jack London's *Before Adam* (1906), and H. Rider Haggard's *The Ancient Allan* (1919). It is doubtful whether a full list of such stories could be compiled, so common were they in the years before and just after the First World War.

Racial memory entered the realms of the sf magazines through the expertise of David H. Keller, who spent much of his life as a doctor working in mental institutions. In his 'Unlocking the Past' (1928), a child undergoes unspecified treatment and begins to recall events from past lives. Another of his stories, 'The Lost Language' (1934), tells of a young boy who begins to speak and write in a strange tongue, which turns out to be an ancient form of Welsh.

Keller's tales indicate his versatility in adapting the racial memory theme. Other writers tended to stick to simple adventure, although the short tale 'The Memory Stream' by Warren E. Sanders (1933) is a poignant view of life in Neanderthal times, and Henry S. Whitehead's 'Scar-Tissue' (1946) traces a former existence in a barbaric Atlantis.

Gradually the racial memory story has more or less disappeared from the genre. The theme itself became little more than an opening gambit to introduce stories of a man's past life as a mighty warrior. In the end, it was just as easy to discard the ancestral memory angle and plunge directly into the action, emulating Robert E. Howard in his *Conan* fantasies.

Without doubt the oddest portrayal of ancestral memories, but entirely in keeping with the light-hearted oddness of the entire story, can be found in *Venus on the Half-Shell* (1975) by Philip José Farmer (writing under the name of Vonnegut's invented sf author Kilgore Trout). At one stage, the hero discovers that every one of his ancestors is still alive inside his head and demanding an opportunity to take over his consciousness.

It is perhaps appropriate to end on a light-hearted note in an area of science fiction which many readers and writers refuse to take seriously. But that psionics and its related sub-categories are considered important by many others can be judged by the substantial body of work reviewed here.

ADDITIONAL TRUST

02.16.5 Ancestral Memories

Coney, Michael G. *Syzygy*, Elmfield Press (UK) 1974
Fearn, John Russell. 'Before Earth Came', *Astounding* July 1934
O'Higgins, Harvey J. 'The Avatar', *The Scrap Book* November 1907
Taine, John (Eric Temple Bell). 'The Time Stream', *Wonder Stories* December 1931 to March 1932; Buffalo (US) 1946
Trout, Kilgore (Philip José Farmer). *Venus on the Half-Shell*, *F&SF* December 1974 to January 1975; Pocket Books Inc (US) 1975

Illustration of Conan by Marcus Boas.

02.17 SEX AND TABOOS

We old-timers – I've been writing science fiction for a whole twelve years now, so undoubtedly qualify – can remember the days when taboos were taboos, and maidens were glad of it. I always think back with nostalgia to an altercation with a certain British hardback house about whether they would or would not print the word 'breast' in a short story collection, while a well-known transatlantic editor (why be coy, it was Fred Pohl) once did me the signal honour of bowdlerising a reference I had made to a lavatory chain.

As long as science fiction was seen as an extension of children's comics it quite properly eschewed sex, implicit, explicit or any other way. But in the late sixties some odd things started happening. The so-called 'new wave', a PR exercise set up by Judy Merril, never amounted to much; what was really important was the intense and prolonged editorial effort put in by Michael Moorcock. The spinoffs were numerous and varied. Science fiction crashed what has been vaguely termed the 'fuck barrier'; and suddenly, anything went.

Some of the results of this shotgun emancipation were excellent, others, predictably, less happy. Sex, like music and hard drugs, just isn't an area of experience that makes good copy.

Sf writers – and I'm not being a male chauvinist pig, it's just that most seem to be male – have always had a hangup about women anyway. They tend to sublimate them, into monsters or angels. The trait probably showed most clearly in Bradbury's classic *The Silver Locusts* (1951). Who can ever forget his fragile Martian girls, made of silk and jewels and moonlight; or the gross, cookie-gobbling horror that pursued the hapless Earthman across the deserted planet? Even in these enlightened days the tendency is still with us; all too often science fiction women appear as attractive but basically superfluous *sex-puppen*, or as mysteriously-throbbing vortices, driven by a parcel of Primal Urges and apparently in a permanent state of semi-orgasm.

Most of the women I've met in real life, with a few notable exceptions, have been kindly, essentially practical creatures with a keen sense of fun and a healthy distrust of the primordial. I've tried from time to time to show them that way; and a few of them have been kind enough to say they liked the results. Which, since it comes from professionals, is praise indeed. Showing women realistically doesn't, after all, rob them of mystery. All living things, from sopranos to slipper animalcules, have mystery; the mystery of existence itself. That, surely, should be enough to whet the Sense of Wonder. Do we *need* anything more?

Keith Roberts

Keith Roberts

02.17 SEX AND TABOOS

'. . . In most science fiction stories sex and other bodily functions have no point and thus no place – in the scientific romance, the gadget story, the space opera, most philosophical stories. The inclusion of such physical actions and reactions often are worse than pointless – they are a distraction within the main-current science fiction story. Only in certain sociological stories do they have a significant place.'

James Gunn, *Alternate Worlds: The Illustrated History of Science Fiction* (1975)

The above quotation could once have been said to be representative of the attitudes of many science fiction readers and writers. Until quite recently what Gunn has written regarding sex and the taboo areas of human relationships held true. Outside the main science fiction genre, such noted writers as Orwell and Huxley did produce science fictional works containing sexual aspects at a time when sf editors refused to entertain them. But in the field of magazine science fiction it was only with the pioneering work of such writers as Philip José Farmer and Theodore Sturgeon in the early 1950s that any serious attention was given to one of the human race's most basic functions.

Since then, attitudes within the science fiction world have shifted appreciably, and there is far less hostility on the part of editors and readers to explorations of such subjects. With the onset of the 'liberated' 1960s, a number of writers – many of them already well established in the field – showed themselves prepared to write specifically on sexual themes and to set their plots around them. Within the confines of this particular thematics area, it is perhaps more often appropriate to consider each individual writer's approach than to attempt to categorise any single story by grouping it with those of other authors who have chosen to cover what, for some, remains a highly sensitive subject. But it should be noted that the majority of stories considered in this section bear a sympathetic and understanding quality which, in itself, places them in a class of their own.

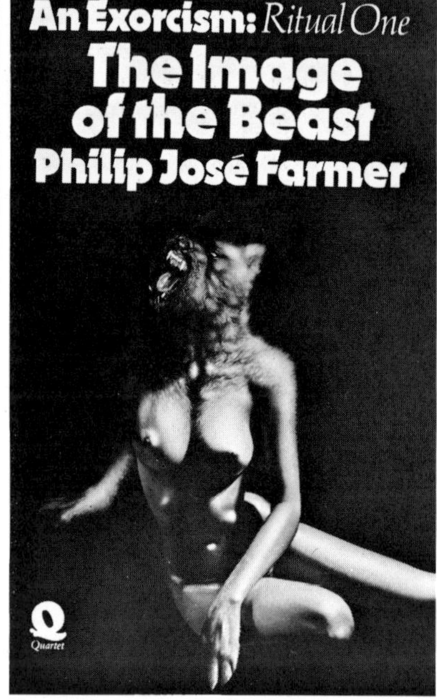

Cover by Jim Burns.

02.17 SEX AND TABOOS

02.17.1 Human Sex

Of the works of outside writers on sexual themes, or relating to them, *We* (1920–21) can be regarded as one of the first major examples of modern dystopian fiction. Yevgeny Zamyatin's novel depicts a future in which the lives of the ordinary citizens are regulated like clockwork and the authorities even attempt to control natural functions – sexual intercourse is only permitted by the allotment of ration coupons. Aldous Huxley – by contrast – saw a future in which promiscuity ran rife, with equally undesirable effects, in *Brave New World* (1932). George Orwell, in *Nineteen Eighty-four* (1949), returned to Zamyatin's model and portrayed a Junior Anti-Sex League set up by the State to encourage celibacy for both sexes as a means of population control. Olaf Stapledon, for his part, entertained a more kindly view when he described the love affair between a woman and a super-intelligent dog in *Sirius* (1944).

While the works of such outside writers received critical acclaim, the sf magazines remained almost totally silent on the subject, with the exception of occasional openly erotic cover illustrations. In the typical magazine story, women – if they appeared at all – played a diminutive role at best. When the breakthrough came, it caused a furore in the science fiction world which has still not entirely subsided.

Philip José Farmer's novel *The Lovers* (1961) was the work in question, first published as a magazine short novel in 1952. It opened by describing life in a post-catastrophe world in which human society is dominated by an oppressive religious sect which exercises total control. One instrument of Church policy is to dictate how many times a week each individual should indulge in sexual intercourse. To fail to do so at the appointed time is to sin. The protagonist of the novel is sent as part of an official mission to another planet, and there for the first time he manages to achieve a degree of sexual freedom, only to discover that he has killed the native girl he loves by the very act of sex. While he had thought she was human in all important respects, it transpires that she is an alien form of life who has assumed human guise. What revolted many readers about the tale was not merely its sexual connotations, but the revelation that the sexual relations had taken place between a human and an advanced form of alien insect. It was a proposition which the average magazine devotee, accustomed as he was to no more than lurid covers, seemed to find difficult to accept.

Soon after publishing the short-story version of *The Lovers*, Farmer wrote 'Mother' (1953), the tale commencing the cycle which appeared in book form as *Strange Relations* (1960). The series consists of five stories: 'Mother', 'Daughter' (1954), 'Father' (1955), 'Son' ('Queen of the Deep') (1954) and 'My Sister's Brother' ('Open to Me My Sister') (1960). Each story deals with the inter-relationships between human and other beings, and most can, to a very large degree, be read as metaphor: 'Mother', for instance, may be accepted as an uncomplicated account of a symbiotic inter-species relationship, or interpreted as a portrayal of incest, and, towards its end, cannibalism.

In a slightly lighter vein Farmer also wrote *Flesh* (1960), in which a starship

Cover by McConnel.

'The Lovers' by Philip José Farmer, Startling Stories *August 1952. Illustration by Finlay.*

02.17 SEX AND TABOOS

which has been voyaging in the galactic deeps for over eight hundred years eventually returns to Earth. The crew find themselves in a state ruled by a fertility cult. The commander of the ship is proclaimed Sun-Hero, an office to which he is not particularly inclined, but during which he is expected to fertilise as many women and girls as possible. At the end of his term he is also expected to succumb willingly to a particularly gruesome fate – an idea later taken up by Edmund Cooper in *A Far Sunset* (1967).

Despite Farmer's relatively frequent, and innovatory, excursions into the area of orthodox sex, there were other aspects of human sexual experience which received little or no attention for many years. One of these was homosexuality. Theodore Sturgeon's short story 'The World Well Lost' (1953), is one of the earliest attempts in the genre to broach this difficult subject. It tells of two alien fugitives who arrive on Earth in a stolen spaceship, and who, because of their obvious devotion to each other, are soon nicknamed 'the loverbirds'. It is automatically assumed that they are male and female, and it is only when an extradition agreement is made and the fugitives embark on the return journey as prisoners in an Earth-ship, that the fact that they are both of the same sex becomes obvious. The story also hints at homosexual undertones in the relationship between the two male crew members of the ship carrying the aliens home. Another noted treatment of the theme is Naomi Mitchison's *Solution 3* (1975), in which the entire population is produced by cloning and all physical relations are homosexual.

A further difficult subject touched upon by science fiction writers is that of prostitution, the selling of one's sexual services for money or favours. But even this, allegedly the oldest and most criticised of professions, has a warm and human side, as demonstrated by Brian Aldiss in his short

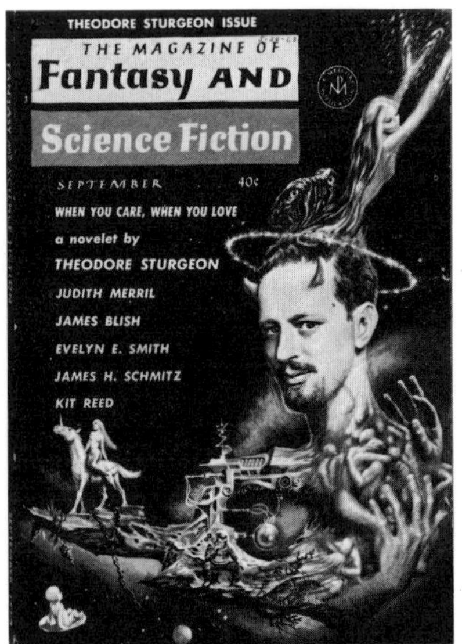

Special Theodore Sturgeon issue, F&SF *September 1962. Cover by Emsh.*

story 'Lambeth Blossom' (1966). This variation on the theme not only shows prostitution in what some would call a favourable light because of its overt acceptance and legitimacy, but also offers an

intriguing glimpse of a London dominated by the Chinese.

A further area of human sexual experience not often discussed in science fiction or in much literature of any kind is incest. Sturgeon's 'If All Men Were Brothers Would You Let One Marry Your Sister?' (1967), tells of a planet where incest is the sexual norm. The other populated worlds, knowing of the inhabitants' sexual proclivities, shun the planet, even though it is a paradise world well endowed with natural resources. In doing so, they ignore the fact that the people they condemn live in perfect harmony, without crime, war, or shortages of any kind, and are completely self-supporting. It remains for the individual reader to decide whether the society portrayed is convincing.

Kurt Vonnegut is another writer who has rarely been reticent on the subject of sex. In *Slaughterhouse Five* (1969) he tells how his space-time travelling anti-hero, Billy Pilgrim, at one time finds himself in an alien zoo where he is imprisoned with a beautiful actress and expected to perform intercourse with her for the edification of the planet's inhabitants. In the society postulated in 'Welcome to the Monkey House' (1968), also by Vonnegut, birth control is compulsory, and the citizens are obliged to take pills which deaden their senses from the waist down, thus removing all the pleasure from sex. Paradoxically, euthanasia is carried out by statuesque 'hostesses' adorned only in body-stockings and boots.

How sexual relations might be affected by a woman-dominated society is an idea which has occurred to a number of writers. John Wyndham's 'Consider Her Ways' (1956) tells of a future society in which, in fact, all men have died as a result of a mutated virus. The women reproduce by parthenogenesis, and although their science is sufficiently advanced to enable them to re-introduce man, they can conceive of no reason for doing so. Edmund Cooper has also written several novels devoted to the theme, which taken at face value offer little comfort to the male species. *Five to Twelve* (1968), depicts a future society in which women outnumber men by somewhat more than two to one. If the initial reaction might be to regard the situation as fortunate for the men, it is soon made clear that they are little more than animals kept at stud to satiate the sexual whims and appetities of their powerful mistresses. Cooper takes the theme of sexual imbalance a stage further in *Who Needs Men?* (1972), and portrays the dominant females actually taking measures to exterminate the few remaining men who are hiding in remote areas of Scotland. Having achieved methods of reproduction by parthenogenesis and cloning, the women have no fear for their own future. Another English writer, Charles Eric Maine, develops a similar theme in his novel *Alph* (1972), but in this instance the extinction of male-kind occurs not as the result of vindictiveness on the part of women, but through scientific ineptitude. After the introduction of a new contraceptive drug the ration of male to female births falls steadily until it reaches zero – no male children are born. Further examples of women-dominated societies can be found in Frederik Pohl and C. M. Kornbluth's *Search the Sky* (1954) and in Wilson Tucker's *City in the Sea* (1951).

'The Hibited Man' by L. Sprague de Camp, Thrilling Wonder Stories *October 1949. Illustration by Stevens.*

Sexual surrogates have played only a small part in the genre. One instance is the use of androids programmed to fulfil every desire of their owners which is related in 'Trojan Horse' (1970) by E. C. Tubb. A surrogate of a different kind is imaginatively described in Joseph L. Green's *Gold the Man* (1971) when Earth is attacked by giant humanoids from another star system. One of the giants crashes and is killed but remains physically undamaged. Earth scientists remove a lobe of the brain of the three-hundred-foot being, and install two humans in its head, one of whom is the super-intellect Gold, and the other being a female Russian scientist. The zombie is sent back to its own world, where, under the control of the humans in its brain, it will act as a spy. The giant is reunited with his wife whereupon Gold, who 'pilots' him, realises that reaction to sexual stimulus has been omitted from his briefing. In controlling the giant to make love, his own sexuality is aroused and he rapes his companion.

Bisexuality as a theme, or an important part of a theme, has featured in a number of science fiction novels. Two stand out as particularly significant. In *Venus Plus X* (1960) Theodore Sturgeon tells of the Ledom (model), an artificially created species who are both male and female, but neither one nor the other. The object of those who created the Ledom was to pave the way for a perfect society by abolishing sexual differences, and, in so doing, to remove much of the friction between various factions of society. The other noted novel in this category is Ursula K. Le Guin's *The Left Hand of Darkness* (1969), in which the inhabitants of the planet Winter can assume either male ot female gender according to the dominant sexual emotion at the time they enter 'heat', the period when their sexual motivation is at its peak. The phase lasts for a few days each month, and individuals are excused almost all other activities until their desires have been satiated and begin to diminish. If the sexual partner of any person becomes male, then that person automatically becomes female, and vice versa. This adaptability in human sex, for the inhabitants of Winter are undoubtedly human, leads to the formation of a complex and unusual society. On a less serious level, Michael Moorcock's cult character Jerry Cornelius, though ostensibly male, can change his sex – and colour – at will, and his ability leads to some amusing confrontations in the novels in which he features: *The Final Programme* (1969), *A Cure for Cancer* (1971) and *The English Assassin* (1972).

Sex on demand is another variation on the theme and plays a part in Robert Sheckley's 'A Ticket to Tranai' (1955). The luckless – or lucky – wives of the men of the planet of the title are kept in a time-stasis field, so that while their husbands age they remain young. However, the practice denies them a full life of their own, and they are only taken out of stasis for brief periods when their husbands are in need of company. In another Sheckley story, 'Pilgrimage to Earth' (1956), the world has become a tourist Mecca where almost any dream can be turned into reality. The hero arrives from a far planet in search of true love and enlists the services of an agency, only to discover that the girl they provide, who appears to genuinely love him, has been hypnotised to do so. By contrast, Frederik Pohl's 'Making Love' (1966) tells of the inhabitants of an overpopulated world who achieve sexual satisfaction whilst undergoing schizophrenic hallucinations. While their physical bodies are resting, they ease their tensions by dream-living whatever situation appeals to them most. The same author's story 'Day Million' (1966) depicts a future human species interrelating and satisfying each partner by means of computer recorded profiles of one another's sexual performance. A man and woman might marry, but after doing so may never see each other again. Instead they live with a recording of their mate which was made at the peak of physical infatuation, and to which they can be physically connected.

One of the most forthright books in recent science fiction, in which sexuality plays a major role, is *The World Inside* (1971) by Robert Silverberg, originally published as a series of short stories. The novel is set in a dystopia several centuries in the future, where the world's population lives regular and ordered lives in massive 'urban monads' – literally one-thousand-storey complexes which not only house, but cater for every need of up to eight hundred thousand inhabitants. The human race has changed genetically so that puberty takes place between the ages of ten and twelve years; anyone not married and procreating by the age of thirteen is regarded as anti-social. One of the few emotional outlets for this tower-dwelling race is through blatant and aggressive sexuality. Everyone's spouse is available to everyone else – male or female. Sexual deviation is a thing of the past, because homosexuality is a legitimate pursuit, and even incest is openly permitted. What in the present day would be termed 'promiscuity' is encouraged by the mores and traditions of the monad society where everyone is urged to sample the whole gamut of sexual experience.

Of the other writers who have recently explored various areas of sexuality, J. G. Ballard has depicted human sexual motivation in his own area of non-traditional science fiction, and his novel *Crash* (1973) is a good example of the kind of work he now produces. Through the mechanism of the novel the author explores what he sees as the sexual motivation behind many mundane human activities. He uncompromisingly describes various sex

02.17 SEX AND TABOOS

Left: Barbarella *by Jean-Claude Forest (Grove Press).*

acts, both conventional and perverse, which lead to the climax of the story – orgasmic self-immolation in a car accident.

David Gerrold tells in another recent novel, *The Man Who Folded Himself* (1973), of a character who replicates himself endlessly through the strata of time past, time present and time future, until the pages of the narrative are populated by male and female versions of the hero. This profusion of self raises all manner of paradoxes. The protagonist has intercourse with a female version of himself; is this incest? He has a sexual relationship with a male version of himself; is this homosexuality or simply masturbation?

Writing on request for Harlan Ellison's *Again, Dangerous Visions* anthology, Ben Bova portrayed the difficulties of sex in free fall in 'Zero Gee' (1972), which echoes Andrew Marvell's poem, 'To His Coy Mistress'. For a bet, a young air force astronaut seduces a beautiful magazine photographer in an orbiting laboratory, thus achieving the first sexual coupling in space.

Robert A. Heinlein has also considered the general theme, and raises moral questions of a sexual nature in his novel *I Will Fear No Evil* (1970), in which the brain of a decrepit old man is transplanted into the body of his young secretary, with emotionally explosive results. The author also touches on sexual matters in his recent novel *Time Enough for Love* (1973), an extended story which recounts the exploits of his intermittent character Lazarus Long. In the future societies through which the immortal Long passes, women count it a privilege to make love with him, and towards the novel's close he returns in time to seduce his own mother.

ADDITIONAL INPUT

02.17.1 Human Sex

Aldiss, Brian W. *The Primal Urge*, Ballantine (US) 1961

Cooper, Edmund. *Kronk (Son of Kronk)*, Hodder and Stoughton (UK) 1970

Elder, Joseph. *Eros in Orbit* (anthology), Trident (US) 1973

Farmer, Philip José. *The Image of the Beast*, Essex House (US) 1968

Farmer, Philip José. *Blown*, Essex House (US) 1969

Farmer, Philip José. *A Feast Unknown*, Essex House (US) 1969

Russ, Joanna. *The Female Man*, Bantam (US) 1975

'Playboy and the Slime God' by Isaac Asimov, Amazing *March 1961. Illustration by Summers.*

02.17.2 Human-Alien Interaction

Stories which attempt to depict a truly alien sex act, that is one which is *not* obviously based on human ideas of sexuality, are scarce in the genre. This is probably because it is almost impossible for the human mind to grasp or invent anything completely outside its own experience. The first hurdle to be surmounted by a writer attempting to produce a narrative containing even a hint of alien sex is the invention of an alien biology, and this is a difficult enough feat to achieve. Therefore most of the stories about alien sex tend to depict creatures whose sexual drives are little different from those of human beings. It can be argued that in many stories the aliens are metaphors for human beings in any case, and that in most instances the alien sex depicted is placed in a human context by linking the alien activity directly with procreation, the driving force of racial preservation and a primary human motivation.

A story by William Tenn which deals with an 'alien sex', and has a parallel with something found on Earth though it is definitely not a metaphor for human sex, is 'Party of the Two Parts' (1954). It is an amusing satire telling of a dealer in pornographic pictures who visits Earth to sell his wares. Difficulties are encountered by the alien when he discovers that his own species has little in common with humanity, outside of intelligence, and that his pictures hold no erotic stimulation for humans. The alien is a member of an amoebic race which reproduces by means of a sexual splitting, 'budding' in the language of the story, and the pictures of sex acts he attempts to sell illustrate 'budding' at various stages. However, they are of great value in a scientific sense, and they are eventually used as illustrations in a biology textbook.

Another example of alien sex relations which includes at least some human connotations, is 'Love Is the Plan, the Plan Is Death' (1973) by James Tiptree Jr. It depicts a planet on which, because of extremes of heat and cold from season to season, only a few of the inhabitants can survive from year to year. In order to perpetuate the race, the females of the species must be the ones to ultimately survive, and this they must do in a pregnant state so that the new racial life-cycle can begin with a fresh brood of young. This end is achieved by the females lulling their mates into assisting them by telepathically broadcasting a sense of love and extreme well-being. When the males have prepared them for their winter confinement, they act as food gatherers while there is food still available in the harsh land. Once the external sources of food have been exhausted, and the pregnancy is well advanced, the females turn to the only other available source of nourishment. They eat their husbands.

The year 1973 appears to have been comparatively good for stories in the alien sex category, for it also saw the publication of 'First Love, First Fear', a short tale by George Zebrowski. The author develops an old theme taken from maritime fiction, that of man falling in love with mermaid, but adapts it to the extent that he tells of a boy falling in love with a mergirl. The boy is the son of a human colonist on another planet, and has never met a girl before. Whilst out walking by the seashore he sees a young female of the planet's indigenous aquatic species, with whom the colonists have had little contact, and swims out to meet her. Their friendship grows into what seems to be the traditional pattern of love at first sight. Later he is horrified to discover her being raped by an adult male of her own species. He tries to intervene, but is chased off by the alien male. When he returns to the scene of what he considers to be the crime, he finds his friend apparently dead,

Cover by Emsh.

02.17 SEX AND TABOOS

buried in the sand. She is not dead however, merely in a coma, her body full of fertilised eggs which, when hatched, will feed off her flesh before they make their way to the sea to grow to adulthood.

In the area of sexual relations between human and alien, Philip José Farmer's *The Lovers* (1961) has already been mentioned in the preceding section. Its dénouement bears some resemblance to Zebrowski's tale. The alien female, whom the leading character has come to love, has assumed human guise but is, in fact, a member of a mimetic anthropodic species. Nevertheless, after intercourse with her lover she becomes pregnant. Biological changes occur within her, and her human looking body begins to calcify into a chitinous form while retaining outwardly its human shape. As her body surfaces harden she becomes increasingly weak, and at the moment of death the young break through her shell, so that for the first time the man sees the true form of the 'woman' he loved.

On a lighter level, Carol Carr's 'Look, You Think You've Got Troubles?' (1969) tells of the differing parental attitudes to the match between a Jewish girl and a Martian. The girl's mother stoically accepts the marriage and even looks forward to a journey to Mars to visit her errant child. But the father cannot reconcile himself to the fact that his daughter has married a being who resembles nothing more than a large animate cauliflower.

Vegetable life also plays a part in *The Pollinators of Eden* (1969) by John Boyd, where the sentient species on the planet Flora are plants. Like all plants, however, they lack mobility of their own and must rely on the intervention of another species for their sexual intercourse – cross-fertilisation. In this instance a scientific research team from Earth appears to provide the ideal means, but unforeseen problems arise.

Jack Williamson's recent novel *The Moon Children* (1972) brings alien sex, or a lack of it, down to Earth. It depicts the results of the finding by a lunar expedition team of mysterious crystal deposits and strange structures which apparently have lain dormant on the moon for many millions of years. The men are affected by the material they examine, and find they can subsequently abandon their spacesuits and endure the sub-zero temperatures and vacuum with no discernible ill-effects. They survive whatever changes have taken place in their metabolisms, and return to Earth to lead relatively normal lives. However, their respective wives become pregnant at more or less the same time, and the ensuing infants, though humanoid in shape are completely devoid of any sexual characteristics or organs. They prove to be alien envoys from a galactic civilisation. A similar idea, with a less peaceful outcome occurs in John Wyndham's *The Midwich Cuckoos* (1957).

Although not strictly a story about alien sex, or about human-alien interaction, Harlan Ellison's 'Catman' (1974) does tell of a human being achieving sexual satisfaction through the medium of a non-human agency – a giant computer hidden deep in the Earth. Connected to the machine, with electrodes planted in the areas of his brain which are subject to erotic stimulation, and his penis wired up so that the computer can measure its performance, he is able to offer the machine the sexual experiences that its human makers failed to programme into it, but for which, nonetheless, it feels a strong desire. The machine, in return, is able to offer the man the ultimate orgasm. However, after each sexual encounter with the computer the man emerges as increasingly less human.

Darker Than You Think *by Jack Williamson (Fantasy Press). Frontispiece by Cartier.*

ADDITIONAL INPUT

02.17.2 Human-Alien Interaction

Dozois, Gardner, R. 'Strangers', in *New Dimensions 4*, Signet (US) 1974

Farmer, Philip José. 'Mother', *Thrilling Wonder* April 1953

Moore, C.L. 'Shambleau', *Weird Tales* November 1933

Moore, C.L. 'Bright Illusion', *Astounding* October 1934

Scortia, Thomas (ed). *Strange Bedfellows*, Random House (US) 1973

Scortia, Thomas (ed). 'Thou Good and Faithful', in *Two Views of Wonder*, Ballantine (US) 1973

Tiptree, James, Jr. 'And I Arose and Found Me Here on the Cold Hill's Side', *F&SF* March 1972

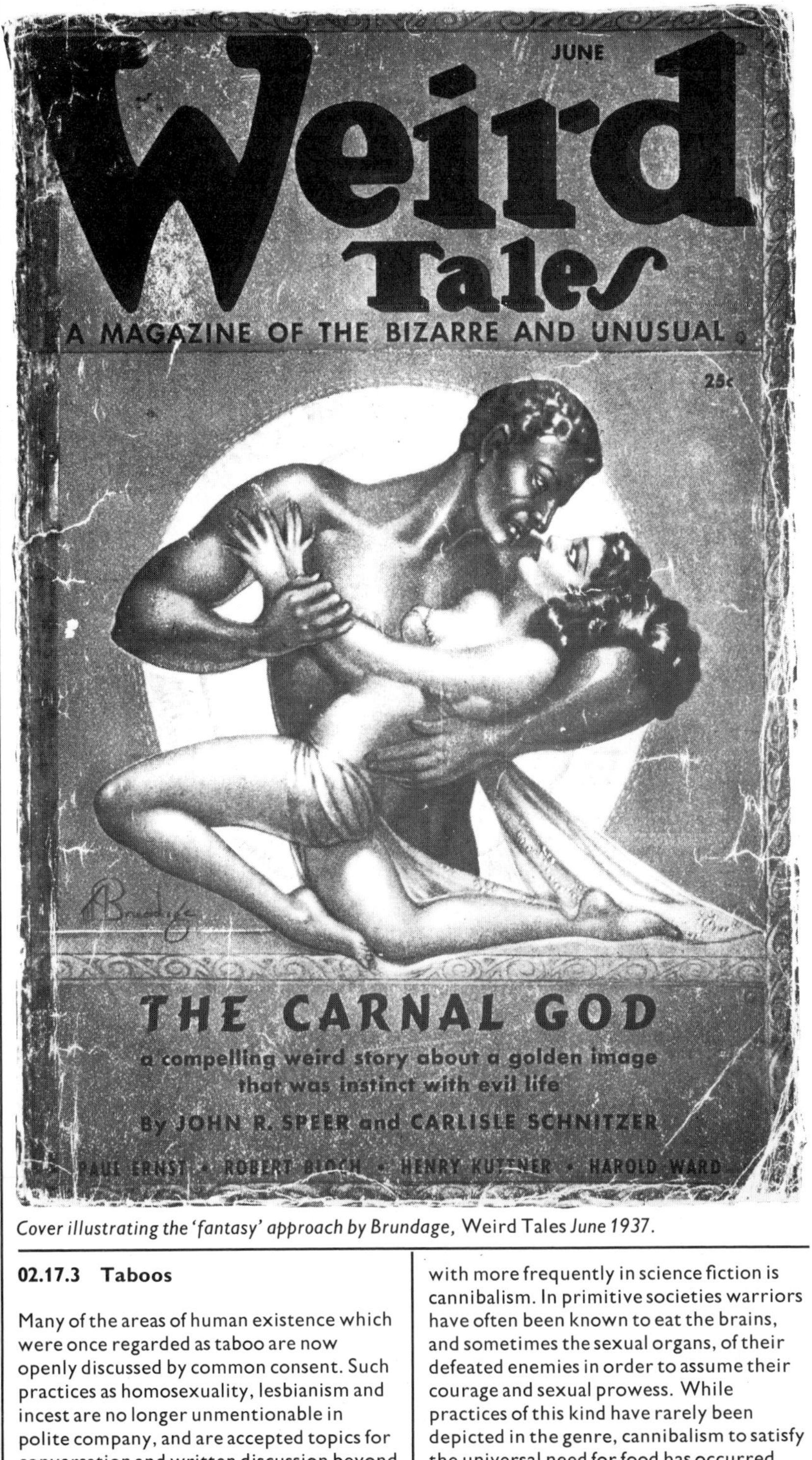

JUNE

Weird Tales

A MAGAZINE OF THE BIZARRE AND UNUSUAL

25¢

THE CARNAL GOD

a compelling weird story about a golden image that was instinct with evil life

By JOHN R. SPEER and CARLISLE SCHNITZER

PAUL ERNST • ROBERT BLOCH • HENRY KUTTNER • HAROLD WARD

Cover illustrating the 'fantasy' approach by Brundage, Weird Tales *June 1937.*

02.17.3 Taboos

Many of the areas of human existence which were once regarded as taboo are now openly discussed by common consent. Such practices as homosexuality, lesbianism and incest are no longer unmentionable in polite company, and are accepted topics for conversation and written discussion beyond the pages of professional journals. As such, they have been discussed in the two preceding sub-sections. Apart from these areas of human sexual experience, there remain various esoteric subjects which science fiction writers, in the main, are still reluctant to handle. Among them are included fetishism and the whole range of sado-masochistic experiences. Another taboo area, but one which has been dealt with more frequently in science fiction is cannibalism. In primitive societies warriors have often been known to eat the brains, and sometimes the sexual organs, of their defeated enemies in order to assume their courage and sexual prowess. While practices of this kind have rarely been depicted in the genre, cannibalism to satisfy the universal need for food has occurred more regularly.

In *Farnham's Freehold* (1964), by Robert A. Heinlein, the Farnham family find themselves precipitated into the distant future by an atomic explosion at the outbreak of the Third World War. They find themselves amongst a despotic black society dominated by a ruler who, in addition to other barbarities, keeps a herd of white humans as meat-bearing animals. The racial element in the story highlights another area into which only a few writers have been prepared to probe at all deeply, with the exception of many tales involving wars against, or conquests by, the Chinese.

A slightly more justifiable resort to cannibalism occurs in a story by Harlan Ellison, 'A Boy and His Dog' (1969). After the Third World War surface-dwelling humans have succeeded in establishing a telepathic rapport with mutated dogs. They pair up with the animals and form intensely loyal relationships of a symbiotic nature. Such partners roam the Earth, sometimes singly and sometimes in packs, attacking and destroying what they find undesirable, and living off the debris of the war-ruined cities. Beneath the surface, however, other survivors have built underground enclaves in which they are attempting to preserve the rudiments of the former civilisation. The protagonist of the story, accompanied by his dog, encounters a girl from underground and appears to fall in love. When their need for food becomes acute, however, man and beast set upon the hapless girl and devour her.

Alien cannibalism is depicted in Christopher Priest's novel *The Space Machine* (1976), which tells of the events leading up to H. G. Wells's fictional invasion from Mars in *The War of the Worlds*. The grotesque beings preparing the war machines on Mars are little more than huge brains, dependent on the abilities of a related, but intellectually inferior species which shares the planet with them and which they also use for food. Wells himself made use of cannibalism in his novel *The Time Machine* (1895), showing how the subterranean Morlocks support the gentle and placid Eloi who live above ground, but treat them as so much cattle when they choose.

Two short stories discussed at greater length in the foregoing sub-section are further examples of cannibalism among an alien species – 'Love Is the Plan, the Plan Is Death' (1973), by James Tiptree Jr and 'First Love, First Fear' (1973) by George Zebrowski.

There are also various works which

The Godwhale *by T. J. Bass (Ballantine). Cover by Sweet.*

02.17 SEX AND TABOOS

allude metaphorically to cannibalism. In Robert Silverberg's *The World Inside* (1971), wrongdoers are flung down disposal chutes, where their bodies are mechanically masticated and re-processed for the benefit of the other inhabitants. A similar system operates in the hive-like society envisaged by T. J. Bass in his novel *The Godwhale* (1974). Both stories present the chilling outcome of dedication to total recycling taken to its ultimate conclusion.

J. G. Ballard more than hints at cannibalism in his recent novel, *High-Rise* (1975), which charts the dissolution of civilisation and civilised standards in microcosm by depicting the process of social collapse within a massive apartment block. The building, self-contained in all important respects, suffers a series of power blackouts and minor services failures which lead to unrest among the occupants, and eventually to the complete breakdown of order. Violence and murder follow, and when food-stocks run out, the tenants who have elected to stay in the building are left with one sole remaining source of nutrition – the animals inhabiting the block, whether domestic pets or humans.

At least three forms of sexual perversion still remain in the taboo category: sodomy, bestiality and uncontrolled sadism. Sodomy is handled quite briefly but bravely in *The Infernal Desire Machines of Doctor Hoffman* (1972) by Angela Carter. The main character in the novel falls in with a troop of nine travelling acrobats, and hypnotised by their antics he is sexually abused by each of them twice over.

Bestiality finds an even rarer place in science fiction, unless, intercourse between humans and aliens can be classed under that heading. Years ahead of its time was a little-known story 'The Cheetah Girl' (1923). In fact, the work has never been openly published, and exists only in a privately printed edition. Its author was the noted scientist and author Edward Heron-Allen, who wrote science fiction under the pseudonym 'Christopher Blayre'. His collection *The Purple Sapphire* (1921) should have included 'The Cheetah Girl', but the story was withdrawn at the last moment because of fears of prosecution under the prevailing obscenity laws. It tells of sexual intercourse between a prostitute and a cheetah, from which the off-spring proved to be a perfectly formed girl-child, complete with a fine coat of fur. Heron-Allen hints at the answer to lycanthropy in his tale, and had he adopted a more oblique approach to the subject, as Olaf Stapledon was later to do in his account of an affair between a girl and an intelligent dog in *Sirius* (1944), the story might well have enjoyed publication.

Similarly, pronounced sexual sadism is a rare occurrence in the genre, but it is not entirely unknown. 'The Prowler in the City at the Edge of the World' (1967) by Harlan Ellison is basically a sad story about Jack the Ripper and how a group of people in the distant future transport him through time to their own day.

Their purpose is purely vicarious – while allowing him to commit more murders, they monitor his mind by telepathy to gratify their personal sadistic urges. Sadism is also dwelt on at some length in *The Fog* (1975) by James Herbert, telling of a mysterious fog which seeps through a ground fissure in the heart of England and affects the minds of anyone who encounters it. It includes accounts of demented schoolboys attacking and sexually torturing their teachers, together with even more unpleasant scenes.

The breaking of long-standing conventions and the violation of taboos almost inevitably have a disquieting effect on some who have been used to accepting them. In the consideration of sexual themes, science fiction has, until recently, lagged uncharacteristically far behind other branches of literature, and there are still many who hold the opinion that it is not its purpose to become involved in such areas. On the other hand, there are those who maintain with equal conviction that the efforts of several leading writers to come to terms with human sexuality are a healthy indication that the genre is finally coming of age. The argument has still to be resolved.

ADDITIONAL INPUT

02.17.3 Taboos

Heinlein, Robert A. *Time Enough for Love*, Putnam (US) 1973

Malzberg, Barry M. 'Upping the Planet', *Amazing* April 1974

Matheson, Richard. 'The Foodlegger', *Thrilling Wonder* April 1952

Sheckley, Robert. 'Can You Feel Anything When I Do This?', *Playboy Magazine* 1969

The Time Machine *by H. G. Wells*, Famous Fantastic Mysteries *August 1950. Illustration by Finlay.*

02.18 RELIGION AND MYTHS

02.18 RELIGION AND MYTHS

My basic religious education was in the church of Christ, Scientist. It's a little difficult to imagine Mary introducing Jesus as 'my son, the scientist'. Yet it's appropriate that a science-fiction writer should have had this peculiar background. So many sf writers write stories which combine science (or pseudoscience) with saviourism. That is, an sf writer often tells you how humanity can be saved if it follows the right path or how it will go to hell if it doesn't.

As I grew older, I became an agnostic, then an atheist. But I was only fooling myself when I thought that I was truly indifferent to religion. I wrote *Flesh* (1960), which projected a revival in the far future of the ancient vegetation religions. Later, my mainstream novel, *Fire and the Night* (1962), dramatised the more sophisticated idea that sex and religion were only two sides of the same coin.

At the same time, I was writing stories (*Night of Light* et al) about an interstellar priest, Father John Carmody. Even when I was an atheist, I was powerfully attracted by the Roman Catholic faith. But I still believed that religion was only *Homo sapiens'* conscious expression of the instinctive drive for survival in the unconscious cells in humankind's bodies.

The brain, knowing that a person can't live for ever in this world, rationalises a future, or other-dimensional, world in which immortality is possible. In other words, religion is the earliest form of science fiction.

Nevertheless, I had, and I have, a contradictory belief that the possibility of immortality is not a fiction.

I've extrapolated on many religious themes in my writings. The ultimate is the premise, now being developed in my Riverworld series, that immortality won't be given us by supernatural means. We'll have to make it ourselves and do so by physical means, by science. ('We' includes all sentient beings in the universe.) This is part of the Creator's plan, a sort of do-it-yourself book which we are in the process of writing for ourselves. It (the sexless Creator) has given us intelligence and self-consciousness so that we may bring about our own resurrection. We will then provide immortality, which will give us time for developing our psychic evolution towards the ideal.

It may seem idiotic or naïve to express belief in the attainment of immortality of everybody who's existed or will exist. But, without immortality, there is no meaning in life.

For me, only those stories concerned with this one vital issue are serious stories. All others, no matter how moving or profound, are mere entertainments. They do not deal with that which is our gravest concern. Without a belief in eternal life for us, the terrestrial existence is something to be gotten through with as little pain and as much pleasure as possible.

If this conclusion is the triumph of irrationality over logic, so be it. After all, irrationality is the monopoly of sentients.

Philip José Farmer

Philip José Farmer

02.18 RELIGION AND MYTHS

02.18 RELIGION AND MYTHS

On first thought it might be felt that there could be little connection between science fiction and religion. Surely they are poles apart? But the opposite is often true. Science fiction is an ideal medium for the writer who wishes to give vent to his own thoughts and views on religious beliefs or doctrines. One way to consider religion is to trace parallels with other worlds, or follow trends into the future.

With this in mind, it is easier to appreciate that the earliest generally acknowledged works of science fiction, Aristophanes' *The Birds* (414 BC) and Lucian's *Icaro-Menippos (c.* AD 180) were written to debunk the basic Greek view of religion with its multiple deities. In the same way that Lucian and Aristophanes used fiction to explore religious beliefs, so modern science fiction may criticise accepted views and look deeply at religion and theology.

In the wake of religion have come various myths and legends about Adam and Eve, Satan, angels and demons, on the one hand, and ghosts, vampires and other evil manifestations on the other. Such beliefs passed early into fiction and became a part of the very fabric of literature in such works as Dante's *Divina Commedia* (*c.* 1300) and

John Milton's *Paradise Lost* (1667), as well as that famous work of allegory John Bunyan's *Pilgrim's Progress* (1678). Today, science fiction has explored these myths and added not a few of its own.

Illustration from Pilgrim's Progress.

02.18.1 Existing Religions

During the Dark Ages which followed the fall of the Roman Empire, most scientific knowledge was kept alive by the Islamic culture and by religious men such as Bede, Alcuin, Gerbert, Albertus Magnus and Roger Bacon. This period of Earth's history is paralleled by Walter M. Miller Jr in his novel *A Canticle for Leibowitz* (1960), when a second Dark Age falls over the World following an atomic war. Scientific knowledge is again kept alive, this time by the Albertian Order of St Leibowitz, named after a scientist who was slaughtered after the War.

As scientific learning advanced, so it began to oppose the accepted views of the Church; for instance, the idea that the Earth moved, and was not the centre of the Universe, was deemed heretical. Galileo was brought before the Inquisition for his views and forced to recant under threat of torture. Yet the concept of space travel could not have been entirely anti-religious, since the man who wrote the first recorded space voyage in English, Francis Godwin, later became Bishop of Llandaff.

The altercation between Church and Science came to a head in 1859 with the publication of Charles Darwin's *On the Origin of Species* and its seemingly heretical theories of evolution. In this instance, though, many leading scientists supported Darwin, and science held its own against religion. Naturally this meant that

The Time Machine *by H. G. Wells,* Famous Fantastic Mysteries *1950. Illustration by Finlay.*

nineteenth-century views were often in conflict and, to some extent, literature reflected this discord. So it is no coincidence that the growth of science fiction really stems from this period. Early in the century Mary Shelley's *Frankenstein* (1818) had dealt with the creation of life, thus treading in God's domain. At the other extreme, writers attempted to reconcile the conflict, and often space-travel stories would relate how the planets had become the home of departed spirits. This had actually been suggested by Plato in his *Myths* as long ago as *c.* 390 BC. It was revived during the 1800s by the growth of spiritualism. In John Jacob Astor's *A Journey in Other Worlds* (1894) spirits are found on Saturn, whilst a later novel, *The Certainty of a Future Life in Mars* (1903) by L. P. Gratacap, could be taken as religio-scientific propaganda for a life hereafter on the Red Planet.

By the early 1900s, however, most science fictional concepts seemed against accepted religious views. An example is George Allan England's *The House of Transformation* (1909), where brain surgery endows a gorilla with human intelligence. Fifty years earlier and that might well have been regarded as heresy.

Religion itself was used initially as a device in science fiction. H. G. Wells, for instance, employed several themes from the Bible, one being found in 'The Apple' (1896), in which a man discovers a descendant of the original Tree of Knowledge in Eden. In 'A Vision of Judgment' (1895), Wells wrote a spoof of Judgment Day. However, religious affirmation is the basis of 'Under the Knife' (1896) in which the narrator, drugged by chloroform, feels himself drifting through the Universe where he perceives a giant Cosmic Hand, the foundation of all Matter. This story, as much as any other by Wells, is a precursor of things to come, notably the work of Olaf Stapledon, and in particular *The Star Maker* (1937). The Star Maker is portrayed as the origin of the Universe, an exceedingly bright star whose purpose it is to create. This Star-God is parent to all the other suns, each of which is also sentient, and has in turn created the planets and their multitudinal life-forms.

No one has seen fit since to challenge Stapledon's massive work for supremacy within its sphere, and many religious views expressed in science fiction stem from this book. By the late 1930s science fiction in the magazines was undergoing a change. It was maturing, and with it new authors were facing the challenge of responsible treatments of religious themes. Basically the trends took two courses: a view of the development of religion in the future, and the idea of religion in other worlds.

The first theme was developed at length by Robert A. Heinlein, although it is possible to trace its origins back as far as Victor Rousseau's *The Messiah of the Cylinder* (1917), in which socialist atheists rule Britain tyrannically and the Christian Russians (a poor choice by Rousseau) eventually defeat them. Heinlein's approach began with *Revolt in 2100* (originally 'If This Goes On . . .', 1940). It tells of a future dictatorship established under the guise of a religious cult, the Prophets. In much the same way as George Orwell would later portray citizens living under the ever-watchful eye of Big Brother, so Heinlein's future populace must follow the theocratic rules lest the 'Angels of the Lord' descend on them.

Heinlein underlines his fears of the fanaticism of theocracy and its inherent dangers in *Sixth Column* (1941). In this

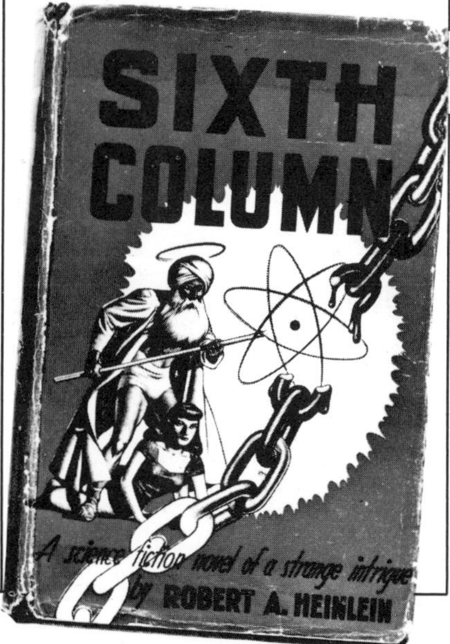

02.18 RELIGION AND MYTHS

instance the United States is overrun by an Oriental horde, and a band of Americans instigate a religious cult as a front behind which they successfully plan to overthrow the invaders. Fritz Leiber took the cue from Heinlein in *Gather, Darkness* (1943), depicting the world in 2305 under the complete control of a debased religion which uses science and psychology to keep Man blinkered and oppressed. Inevitably, thoughts of rebellion spread through the 'faithful' and an underground satanic cult is formed, complete with witches and warlocks. This trend led to the development of new religions in science fiction, such as A. E. van Vogt's 'Clane' tales, in which a future priesthood worships the atom. The natural culmination of the trend was Miller's *A Canticle for Leibowitz*.

Religion beyond the Earth is a more common theme in the genre. Among the first of its progenitors was Clifford D. Simak. In his 'The Voice in the Void' (1932) Earth explorers desecrate the tomb of the Martian Messiah, who is discovered to have come from Earth. Simak's 'The Creator' (1935) was an early classic, rejected by all the professional sf magazines as blasphemy and only published in the semi-professional *Marvel Tales*. Two scientists experimenting with a time machine find themselves outside their continuum, and learn that the Earth was merely one of many experiments by a macrocosmic being who now wishes to destroy what he created.

Simak's work, appearing in such a small circulation publication, was read by only a minority of sf fans when it first appeared. On the other hand, C. S. Lewis's *Out of the Silent Planet* (1938) was a best-seller. It tells of a Cambridge philologist, Ransom, who is kidnapped by the evil scientist Weston and taken to Malacandra (Mars). Mars is portrayed as a perfect planet ruled by the good spirit Oyarsa, and where the original sin was never committed. The 'silent planet' of the title is Thulcandra (Earth), which has been ostracised by the rest of the solar system because its ruling spirit, Satan, has become evil. Lewis wrote a sequel,

'The Man' by Ray Bradbury, Thrilling Wonder Stories *February 1949. Illustration by Finlay.*

Perelandra (1943), telling how Venus is found to be in the last stage of Creation, and therefore ripe for an attempt by Satan to turn it into another fallen world. The third novel, *That Hideous Strength* (1947), shows Satan trying to manipulate scientists on Earth to set up a conditioned dystopia – and the eventual defeat of his aims.

The work of Lewis doubtless led some sf writers to consider seriously the question of how aliens would view God, and whether they would have had a Messiah. In 'The Man' (1949), Ray Bradbury tells of a ship's captain who lands on another planet the day after the coming of Christ. He tries in vain to discover His whereabouts, even to the lengths of resorting to violence. Bradbury's 'The Fire Balloons' (1951) portrays two Episcopalian fathers who set out to establish a church on Mars and redeem the natives, only to learn that the Martians have made themselves perfect and are entirely free of sin. Harry Harrison worked the same theme to a very different conclusion in 'The Streets of Ashkelon' (1962).

James Blish also applied the theme in 'A Case of Conscience' (1953). The original novelette tells of the discovery of an idyllic planet, Lithia, inhabited by perfect creatures who know no sin, but have no religion. A Catholic priest distrusts the situation, which he suspects is a diabolic trap, but nevertheless he returns to Earth with a young Lithian seed. Blish continued the story in the novel version (1958), which shows the results of the growth of the Lithian who becomes an evil creature and leads a worldwide crusade against morals.

Of the new generation of authors, Gail Kimberley evokes an orthodox view of religion. In 'Many Mansions' (1973), she relates how missionaries on an alien planet discover cave paintings that depict, with native life-forms, the life of Christ, even through to the Crucifixion. In 'Let's Go to Golgotha' (1975), Garry Kilworth expanded on thoughts of the Crucifixion expressed by Robert Silverberg. In *Up the Line* (1969) Silverberg presents the Crucifixion as a popular tourist attraction for time travellers. Kilworth took the theme further by showing that *all* of the people watching and jeering at the Crucifixion were time-travellers. In 'The Rescuer' (1962), Arthur Porges tells of a

Sixth Column *by Robert A. Heinlein. Illustration by Rivoche.*

A Case of Conscience *by James Blish (Ballantine). Cover by Sweet.*

man using a time machine to go back and save Jesus from the cross. Such also was the intention of the leading character in Michael Moorcock's 'Behold The Man' (1966), only in this instance he ends up becoming the crucified Christ.

As a rule science fiction will be seen to conflict with organised religion, just as science does. The works of Heinlein, Blish, Harrison and Bradbury point to this, as does the work of Lester del Rey. In 'For I Am a Jealous People' (1954), del Rey reminds us that if God is universal then man has no sole rights to him. Just as in the First World War the British and the Germans both claimed God was on their side, so in this story del Rey shows God wearying of human follies, and when aliens attack Earth he takes their side against mankind. More recently, in 'Evensong' (1967), del Rey portrays a tired rejected God, now totally usurped by Man.

Equally critical of the conventional view of the deity is Damon Knight's 'Shall the Dust Praise Thee?' (1967), which tells how God returns to Earth after Armageddon only to find that his followers had died believing they had been forsaken. These last two stories were published in Harlan Ellison's taboo-breaking anthology *Dangerous Visions* (1967), deliberately compiled from work authors knew they would be unable to sell to conventional markets. A third story from the volume, Philip K. Dick's 'Faith of Our Fathers', written under the influence of hallucinogens, gives an individual's view of a god that is both good and evil. Probably the best known tale on such a theme is Arthur C. Clarke's 'The Star' (1955), telling of the anguish of a Jesuit starship navigator who learns that the Star of Bethlehem was a nova which destroyed a great alien civilisation. How can he reconcile his faith with such slaughter?

Walter M. Miller's *A Canticle For Leibowitz* supports religion, but it appears to be among the minority. Eric Frank Russell takes a sentimental view in 'Second Genesis' (1951), showing a spaceman who returns to find an Earth devoid of human life. He wanders endlessly over the planet becoming increasingly lonely until the cosmic sentience takes pity on him and creates a companion. In 'The Answer' (1935), Philip Wylie tells of the discovery of dead angels in craters left after nuclear tests. The angels finally disappear, but leave behind golden books in which is written, in countless languages, the single message 'Love One Another'.

Christianity is not the only established religion featured in science fiction, although as it entertains many possibilities it seems to appear more frequently. Anthony Boucher's 'Balaam' (1954) shows what happens to men of all faiths when they face the test of space. Roger Zelazny has also explored other religions. His novel *Creatures of Light and Darkness* (1969) presents an array of super-creatures modelled on the lines of the ancient Egyptian pantheon. His massive work *Lord of Light* (1967) is set on a distant planet inhabited by colonists who over the years have established themselves in a parallel of Buddhist beliefs. Eastern ideas were also employed by Arthur C. Clarke in his story 'The Nine Billion Names of God' (1953), in which a computer is hired by a Tibetan monastery to enable it to complete the task of compiling all God's possible names. By hand, this would take thousands of years and when accomplished, prophecy says, the

Cover by Sweet.

Cover by Szafran.

02.18 RELIGION AND MYTHS

Left: Stranger in a Strange Land *by Robert A. Heinlein. Illustration by Franke.*

world will end. The computer finishes the work in a matter of days, and the story closes on one of science fiction's classic pay-off lines. The tale emphasises the impossibility of establishing which of Man's many religions represents the truth.

Computers, and robots, often feature in religious science fiction, and they are discussed in their respective sections, but it is worth recalling here Fredric Brown's 'Answer' (1954), in which all the master computers of 96 billion inhabited worlds are linked as one. Asked if God exists the machine replies that He does *now*. As a rule, the genre seems to argue that it is faith that is important, not God. This was illustrated in Poul Anderson's 'A Chapter of Revelation' (1972), one of three short novels specially written along the theme of the Almighty actually proving He existed – in this instance by stopping the Earth from moving for a day and a night. Chaos ensues. Scientists attempt to explain the phenomenon in a hundred ways: aliens? psi powers? . . . anything but the work of God. As for the masses, many flock to Church, but others loot and pillage, anticipating the end of the world. Even if man might want to *believe* a deity exists, it seems he does not wish to be *certain*.

The Day the Sun Stood Still *ed. by Robert Silverberg (Dell). Cover by Lackow.*

ADDITIONAL INPUT

02.18.1 Existing Religions

Boucher, Anthony. 'The Quest for Saint Aquin', *F&SF* January 1959

Connell, Alan. 'Dream's End', *Wonder Stories* November 1935

Connell, Alan. 'The Reign of the Reptiles', *Wonder Stories* August 1935

Del Rey, Lester. '"If Ye Have Faith . . ."', *Other Worlds* May 1951

Dickson, Gordon R. 'Things Which Are Caesar's', *The Day the Sun Stood Still* (ed Robert Silverberg) Nelson (US) 1972

Farmer, Philip José. 'Father John Carmody' series runs as follows:
- 'Attitudes', *F&SF* October 1953
- 'Father', *F&SF* July 1955
- *The Night of Light*, *F&SF* June 1957; expanded Berkley (US) 1966
- 'A Few Miles', *F&SF* October 1960
- 'Prometheus', *F&SF* March 1961

Hodgson, William Hope. 'The Baumoff Explosion', *Nash's Weekly* 17 September 1919; reprinted as 'Eloi Eloi Lama Sabachthani', *Weird Tales* Fall 1973

Knight, Damon. 'God's Nose', *Rogue* 1964

Knight, Damon. 'The Last Word', *Satellite SF* February 1957

Silverberg, Robert. 'Thomas the Proclaimer', *The Day the Sun Stood Still* (ed Robert Silverberg) Nelson (US) 1972

Wells, H.G. 'A Dream of Armageddon', *Black & White* (UK) 1901

Wells, H.G. 'The Story of the Last Trump' (under pseudonym Reginald Bliss), *Boon* Fisher Unwin (UK) 1915

02.18.2 New Religions

Some science fiction writers are particularly adept at creating new religions, akin to their ability to dream up bizarre alien landscapes. In the present-day world God is often ousted in favour of the worship of material possessions. It was to be expected that sf writers would extend this trend to its logical conclusion. The problems arise when such an invented religion is actually adopted!

This indeed was the case in what has rapidly become one of science fiction's most known, or perhaps notorious, books: *Stranger in a Strange Land* (1961) by Robert A. Heinlein. The story centres around Michael Valentine Smith who is the first human born on Mars and consequently becomes physically and mentally superior to normal man. Raised in the beliefs of Mars, Smith returns to Earth and begins to preach his new religion, the way of 'Grok'. Hailed as the new Messiah, he is ultimately killed by his fellow men, but uses his mental abilities to elevate his inner self to another plane. Smith's religion, which included the advocation of free love, was seized upon by the hippie-cults of the mid-1960s and was readily adopted by Charles Manson into his 'Family' organisation. The fatal consequences of Manson's dementia underline the fact that no new religion is likely to succeed without full application of its initial conditions, and the powers inherent in Smith (telekinesis, etc) have yet to be proved possible on Earth.

Far simpler in its concept was the religion of Bokononism envisaged by Kurt Vonnegut in *Cat's Cradle* (1963). Treated as a marginal science fiction novel, *Cat's Cradle* is one of the most overlooked of Vonnegut's works, and for that reason Bokononism has failed to arouse as much interest as Heinlein's 'Grok', even though, with its basic 'sort it out for yourself' doctrine, it could well have a comparable appeal.

By and large it is simpler to invent a religion on another planet. By doing so, the writer runs less risk of causing offence and enjoys the freedom to create whatever type of belief he wishes. One of the noted recent efforts in this area has been Frank Herbert's 'Dune' series. The first novel, *Dune* (1963–65), concerns the growth and maturity of Paul Atreides (late Muad'dib), who is taken with his mother to the arid planet Dune. Paul's mother had been chosen to be the bearer of a new messiah, one adept in all the mental arts. Paul himself already has many latent powers, and after he takes an overdose of a local spice, his mind is permanently opened to the future. The natives of Dune look upon him as their prophet, and he ultimately comes to rule the planet as well as many others. The sequels, *Dune Messiah* (1969) and *Children of Dune* (1976) follow the progress of Paul and his family in both triumph and adversity.

The 'Dune' series logically develops the interaction of religion and politics on an alien world, and it is doubtful if the stories could have worked without the religious element. The portrayal of religion on other planets had been effectively achieved as long ago as 'The Venus Adventure' (1932) by John Beynon Harris, when a fanatical space pioneer leads one particular Venusian cult into degeneracy, whilst another group entirely free of religious belief prospers.

A novel as much overlooked as Vonnegut's is Lester del Rey's *The Eleventh Commandment* (1962). Set in the future after an atomic war, it concerns the doctrine of the American Catholic Eclectic Church and its eleventh commandment, 'be fruitful and multiply'. The population level increases rapidly, bringing misery to the populace and inevitable opposition to the Church's beliefs. It transpires that as the majority of offspring are mutants; the Church must oppose birth control in an endeavour to breed back the *true* human strain.

Del Rey has written many stories with a religious undercurrent, and one, 'The Last True God' (1969), depicts a distant planet where an ancient Earth robot is being worshipped as a god. Connecting robots with religion may at first seem unlikely, but it is a process of intelligence that any machine built to think logically will begin to wonder where it came from. Some of these stories are discussed in the thematics section devoted to robots and androids, but can be mentioned in passing here. 'Burning Bright' (1948) by John S. Browning (Robert Moore Williams) forms the basis for many tales in which groups of robots begin to entertain their own ideas on religion and an afterlife. E. C. Tubb's 'Logic' (1954) and Lloyd Biggle's 'In His Own Image' (1968) both show a robot's need for a faith. In 'Judas' (1967), John Brunner's advanced robot believes he is a god, and a whole new religion grows up around him – even acknowledging his death and resurrection. Robert F. Young's 'Robot Son' (1959) takes the idea a step further, with a machine god attempting to construct a machine Christ.

Cover by Rogers.

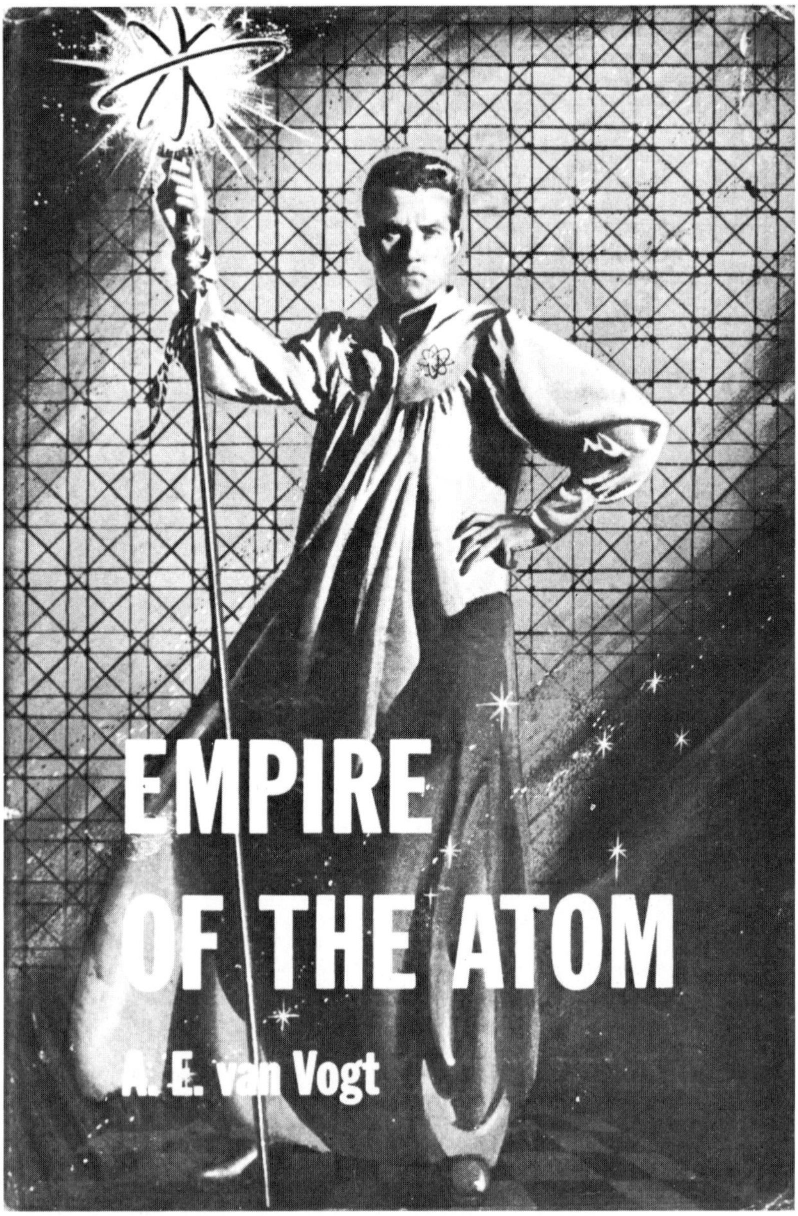

Cover by McCauley.

One of the fundamental points of the religious robot story is that a creation as superior as a robot cannot conceive it was made by something so outwardly inferior as a man – this was the basis of Isaac Asimov's early tale 'Reason' (1941). The same concept has been extended to computer stories, such as David Gerrold's 'Harlie' series. Man worshipping the Machine, however, is a far more frightening prospect, but one that seems to grow more possible. Leo P. Kelley's *The Coins of Murph* (1972) portrays another future world after a nuclear war where a computer-god supposedly controls the situation. There is no free will, decisions are dictated by the toss of a coin. But again it turns out that the religion is falsely based, and is manipulated by one of the priests for his own ends.

Science as a religion has formed the basis of many stories set in the future, not least A. E. van Vogt's 'Clane' series that saw book form as *Empire of the Atom* (1957). Sex as a symbol of worship is found in many tribes, and a reversion to this state appears in Philip José Farmer's *Flesh* (1960), which tells of the fate in store for a space explorer when he returns to Earth after 800 years. He is welcomed and crowned as the Sun Hero, and undergoes a transformation into a sinister being of exceptionally virile prowess: part-man, part-beast, part-god. He is powerless to free himself from the lusts of the flesh, and for this he is worshipped. Farmer's *Venus on the Half-Shell* (1975), written as Kilgore Trout, also contains a religious motif – the hero voyages through space asking 'What is the meaning of life?'

Recently Lloyd Biggle wrote what could be considered the final word on new religions. 'What Hath God Wrought?' (1974) is set in the future where the major pastime is the National Lottery. A group determine to sabotage the draw and arrange for one man to win the particular prize which will establish him as a god. His new religion, based on a mixture of Christianity, the Santa Claus myth, and television quiz shows, spreads rapidly. Its doctrine, that people who have done good and asked no return should be rewarded in this life rather than wait for a questionable hereafter, proves irresistible.

ADDITIONAL INPUT

02.18.2 New Religions

Gordon, Stuart. The 'One-Eye' trilogy runs as follows:
One-Eye, DAW Books (US) 1973
Two-Eyes, DAW Books (US) 1974
Three-Eyes, DAW Books (US) 1975

Heinlein, Robert A. 'Universe', *Astounding* May 1941; sequel 'Common Sense', *Astounding* October 1941; combined as *Orphans of the Sky*, Gollancz (UK) 1963

Jones, Neil R. The 'Durna Rangue' series runs as follows:
'Little Hercules', *Astounding* September 1936
'Durna Rangue Neophyte', *Astounding* June 1937
'Kiss of Death', *Amazing* December 1938
'Invisible One', *Super Science Stories* September 1940
'Captives of the Durna Rangue', *Super Science Stories* March 1941
'Priestess of the Sleeping Dead', *Amazing* April 1941
'Vampire of the Void', *Planet Stories* Spring 1941
The Citadel in Space, *Two Complete Science Adventure Books* Summer 1951

Kornbluth, Cyril M. 'That Share of Glory', *Astounding* January 1952

Kurtz, Katherine. The 'Deryni' trilogy runs as follows:
Deryni Rising, Ballantine (US) 1970
Deryni Checkmate, Ballantine (US) 1972
High Deryni, Ballantine (US) 1973

Simak, Clifford D. 'Spacebred Generations', *Science Fiction Plus* August 1953

Vance, Jack. *Son of the Tree*, *Thrilling Wonder* June 1951; Ace (US) 1964

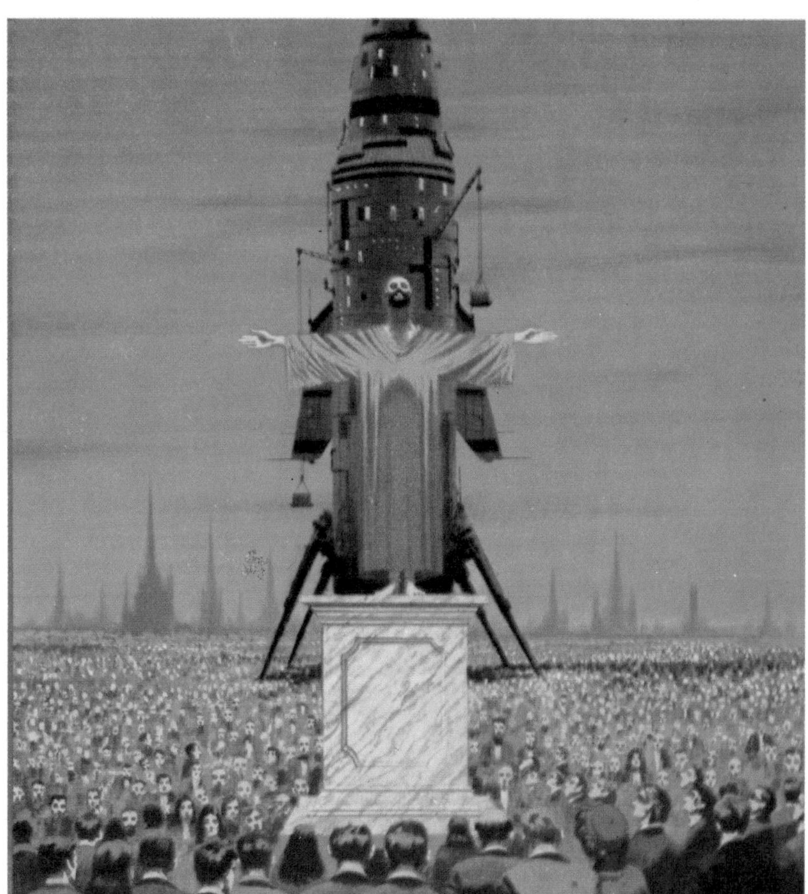

The Eleventh Commandment *by Lester del Rey (Ballantine). Cover by Ellis.*

02.18.3 Immortality and Longevity

Cover by Morrow.

That Man was created immortal is one of the fundamental beliefs of Christianity. Had Adam and Eve not sinned, then for the believer presumably they could be expected to be alive today. As it is, the Bible records that Adam lived for 930 years, a not inconsiderable time. A man dying at that age in 1976 would have been born in 1046, twenty years before the Battle of Hastings! The oldest named person in the Bible was Methuselah, who lived for 969 years dying in 2370 BC, the year of the Flood. Methuselah's name has since become synonymous with longevity, and as such was chosen for the title of Robert A. Heinlein's story *Methuselah's Children* (1941). This novel, part of the author's 'Future History' series, relates how selective breeding of people whose ancestors were all long-lived has resulted by AD 2125 in the lifespan of the Howard families exceeding well over one hundred years, and extending by each generation. Ordinary humans, aware of the Howards' longevity, attempt to find the secret, with the result that the Howards abandon Earth and explore space. One of the characters in the book, Lazarus Long, is the central figure in Heinlein's recent novel *Time Enough for Love* (1973). Now unbelievably old, he looks back over his life and contemplates how tedious it has become.

Lazarus is, of course, another Biblical name. He was the man whom Jesus brought back to life after having been dead for four days. Lazarus has thus become synonymous with stories of resurrected men, as in 'Lazarus II' (1953) by Richard Matheson, when a man returns to life as a machine, or 'Lazarus' (1964) by Jael Cracken (Brian W. Aldiss), in which a man

02.18 RELIGION AND MYTHS

'Recalled to Life' by Robert Silverberg, Infinity *1958. Illustration by Bowman.*

dies on the Moon, but revives, and believes that death is only possible on Earth, not beyond.

But probably the best-known character linked with Biblical incidents is the Wandering Jew. He does not actually appear in the Bible, but legend has it that Cartaphilos, the door-keeper of the judgement hall in the service of Pontius Pilate, struck Jesus as He was led away saying 'Get on! Faster, Jesus!' Christ replied: 'I am going, but tarry thou until I come again.' The character of the Wandering Jew was first written down by Roger de Wendover in his chronicle *Flores Historiarum* (*c.* 1235) and incorporated in Matthew Paris's *Historia Major* (1259). The legend was well known by the eighteenth century when the Comte de Saint-Germain claimed that he was the Wandering Jew and was over 2000 years old! The various legends were collected by David Hoffman in *The Chronicles of Cartophilus* in the 1850s, and the French novelist Eugene Sue enjoyed much success with his work *The Wandering Jew* (1845).

The Wandering Jew can be found in science fiction in a number of tales. He appears in Walter Miller's *A Canticle for Leibowitz* (1960) and acts as a continuity character through the various episodes. In Wilson Tucker's 'The Planet King' (1959), he turns out to be the last man alive on Earth. Exactly the same concept was used in P. J. Plauger's recent noted story 'Child of All Ages' (1975), when a young girl is discovered to be over 2400 years old, immortalised since her father invented a way of arresting the ageing process before puberty.

Down the centuries alchemists, in their search for immortality, have looked for the 'elixir of life' or better 'the elixir of youth' – something that would rejuvenate the body. An early story employing this theme has remained one of the most remarkable: *The Elixir of Hate* (1911) by George Allan England. It tells of an old man who takes a rejuvenation draft only to find that he cannot control the process – he grows younger, and younger. The theme appeared in other early sf stories and was used to good effect by Nathaniel Hawthorne in several stories, most notably 'Dr. Heidegger's Experiment' (1837). When the sf magazines were first published, the elixir was still the most popular form of research for longevity as, for example, in A. Hyatt Verrill's 'The Ultra-Elixir of Youth' (1927) and D. D. Sharp's 'The Eternal Man' (1929). If the use of drugs can be called an elixir, then perhaps such a discovery might still be possible. It was the longevity drug introduced by James Blish into his 'Okie' series in the story 'At Death's End' (1954) that made longevity a reality and led to the possibility of interstellar flight.

In such stories as Mary Shelley's 'The Mortal Immortal' (1834) and G. Peyton Wertenbaker's 'The Coming of the Ice' (1926), writers have shown that immortality granted to a single person would bring little but loneliness and isolation. Thus in *Life Everlasting* (1934) by David H. Keller, a serum is discovered that will prolong life indefinitely, but after the initial delight people realise the joys of growing old and take an antidote. The same viewpoint was expressed in Karel Čapek's play *The Makropoulos Secret* (1923), when a 300-year-old woman is given the chance to extend her life but refuses.

One author managed to combine all the religious themes into an immortality novel – M. P. Shiel in *This above All* (1933). It concerns a Jewess who has lived through the years in pursuit of Lazarus, wishing to marry him. What must be the ultimate Lazarus-theme series is the 'Riverworld' stories by Philip José Farmer. Here not just one man, but the entire human race is resurrected by aliens and brought to life again on a far planet, beside the banks of a river millions of miles long. The story centres on Sir Richard F. Burton, explorer and adventurer, with the historic link that Burton who had searched for the source of the River Nile also sets off to discover the source of the vast alien river. Besides Burton the cast includes a resurrected Hermann Göring, Mark Twain, Tom Mix and many others in 1971, *To Your Scattered Bodies Go, The Fabulous Riverboat* (1971), and in the final part of the saga which reinforces the religious connection by including Sufism as a major thread in the story.

Cover by van Dongen.

Recent novels have shown far differing approaches to immortality, though none of them portrays it as good or beneficial.

Frank Herbert's *The Eyes of Heisenberg* (1966) features the immortal Optimen, some genetically engineered, whilst others are cyborgs. The two types are constantly opposed in a battle for supremacy, while machinations in the background tell of a deliberate manipulation of genes to bring about a return to mortality. Along similar lines, Kate Wilhelm's *The Nevermore Affair* (1966) depicts the misuse of longevity by military and political extremists. Perhaps most telling of all is Bob Shaw's *One Million Tomorrows* (1971), in which biomedicine has made possible a method of bestowing near-immortality that renders the taker sterile. Each remains the age at which he or she had the serum, resulting in a whole strata of immortals: old men, teenagers . . . and mothers perpetually caring for eternal babies.

ADDITIONAL INPUT

02.18.3 Immortality and Longevity

Ainsworth, William Harrison. *Auriol; or, The Elixir of Life, Ainsworth's Magazine & New Monthly* (UK) 1844–46
Aldiss, Brian W. *Greybeard*, Faber (UK) 1964
Barjavel, René. *The Immortals*, Ballantine (US) 1975
Binder, Eando (Otto Binder). The 'Anton York' series runs as follows:
'Conquest of Life', *Thrilling Wonder* August 1937
'Life Eternal', *Thrilling Wonder* February 1938
'The Three Eternals', *Thrilling Wonder* December 1939
'The Secret of Anton York', *Thrilling Wonder* August 1940
(The above combined as *Anton York, Immortal*, Belmont US 1965)
Dickson, Gordon R. 'The Immortal', *F&SF* August 1965
Gunn, James E. *The Immortals*, Bantam (US) 1962, consists of the following episodes:
'New Blood', *Astounding* October 1955
'Donor', *Fantastic* November 1960
'Medic' (orig 'Not So Great an Enemy'), *Venture* July 1957
'Immortal' (orig 'The Immortals'), *Star SF Stories 4* (ed Frederik Pohl) Ballantine (US) 1958
Haggard, H. Rider. The 'Ayesha' series runs as follows:
She: a History of Adventure, The Graphic 2 October 1886 to 8 January 1887; Longmans (UK) 1887
Ayesha, the Return of She, Ward Lock (UK) 1905
She and Allan, Longmans (UK) 1920
Wisdom's Daughter, Hutchinson (UK) 1923

Methuselah's Children *by Robert A. Heinlein. Illustration by Hague.*

Lafferty, R.A. 'Continued on Next Rock', *Orbit 7* (ed Damon Knight) Putnam (US) 1970

Moore, Ward (with Avram Davidson). *Joyleg*, *Fantastic* March to April 1962; Pyramid (US) 1962

Pohl, Frederik. *The Age of the Pussyfoot*, *Galaxy* October 1965 to February 1966; Trident (US) 1968

Rocklynne, Ross. 'The Immortal', *Comet Stories* March 1941

Sheckley, Robert. 'If the Red Slayer', *Amazing* July 1959

Sheckley, Robert. *Time Killer* (abridged version) *Galaxy* October 1958 to February 1959; *Immortality Delivered* (original version) Avalon (US) 1958; retitled *Immortality, Inc*, Bantam (US) 1959

Sheckley, Robert. 'Something for Nothing', *Galaxy* June 1954

Silverberg, Robert. *Recalled to Life*, *Infinity* June to August 1958; Lancer (US) 1962; revised Doubleday (US) 1972

Simak, Clifford D. 'Eternity Lost', *Astounding* July 1949

Simak, Clifford D. *Here Gather the Stars*, *Galaxy* June to August 1963; retitled *Way Station*, Doubleday (US) 1963

Vance, Jack. *To Live Forever*, Ballantine (US) 1957

Wilhelm, Kate. 'April Fool's Day Forever', *Orbit 7* (ed Damon Knight) Putnam (US) 1970

02.18.4 Living Myths

Sf writers have found some fascination in explaining away human myths and legends in scientific terms. In doing so, they still succeed in preserving the element of wonder, unlike such historical novels as Henry Treece's *Jason* (1961) and Frank Yerby's *Judas, My Brother* (1968) which render every mystical event so matter-of-fact as to rob the reader of any sense of wonder.

The bulk of man's heritage is myth, and it does not have to be lost in the depths of time. Even the most recent of events and people can have a mystery about them, and quite often the phrase 'legend has it . . .' is used in respect of an event only a few years past. In the sf world, legend has it that Eric Frank Russell's *Sinister Barrier* (1939) prompted John Campbell to issue his fantasy magazine *Unknown Worlds*, although in reality he had planned for the magazine months in advance. Legend has it that H. P. Lovecraft's 'The Colour out of Space' (1927) was rejected by Farnsworth Wright of *Weird Tales*, even though in truth he never saw the work until it appeared in *Amazing Stories*. These and many other myths are rife in the sf world, even though the real events all happened within living memory. Little wonder that after a few hundred or thousand years reality and fantasy merge into an indeterminate backcloth.

That there was a basis for belief in the old legends was proved by Heinrich Schliemann in the 1870s when he excavated the site of the original Troy of Homer's *Iliad*. Thereafter it was possible to apply the 'no smoke without fire' adage to many of the legends.

Of all Biblical beliefs the most famous is the existence of Adam and Eve. Many stories have been written about the last survivors on Earth whose names are revealed in the final line as Adam and Eve, so much that such tales have become clichés and few sf editors would now entertain them. However, the theme was popular in its time, and stories worth citing include John Christopher's 'Begin Again' (1954), Richard Shaver's 'The

Right: Illustration by Cartier.

02.18 RELIGION AND MYTHS

Tale of the Last Man' (1946) and perhaps the most readable of all, Alfred Bester's 'Adam and No Eve' (1941). Julian Jay Savarin's recent *Lemmus* trilogy, which began with *Waiters on the Dance* (1972), attempts on a grand scale to explain away all the Biblical and ancient legends in a von Däniken style epic. It depicts the experimental colonisation of Earth by highly advanced aliens who initially establish themselves on a continent called Atlantis. Early in the trilogy Savarin explains the reasons for the Flood, and in 'The Deep Space Scrolls' (1963), Robert F. Young detailed how Noah was one of a group of aliens who were fleeing from the destruction of their home planet. The Ark was his spaceship.

Cover by Emsh.

Robert F. Young has written a number of stories which give science fictional explanations to our myths, legends and fairy tales. 'Boarding Party' (1963), for instance, describes how aliens, orbiting Earth in the distant past, lower pipes in order to restock with water. This gave rise to the Jack and the Beanstalk story. 'Peeping Tommy' (1965) added substance to the Lady Godiva legend. 'Romance in an Eleventh Century Recharging Station' (1965) supplies an explanation for Sleeping Beauty, whilst in 'Rumpelstiltskinski' (1965) he updates the famous story of the little man with the bizarre name.

Two other writers have adapted the idea of reworking legends to their own particular styles: Manly Wade Wellman and the late Thomas Burnett Swann. During the early 1940s, Wellman produced a series of stories about the archetypal caveman called Hok. During the series, which began with 'Battle in the Dawn' (1939), Hok invents the bow and arrow, discovers fire and, in 'Hok and the Gift from Heaven' (1941), makes the first use of iron thus spanning the bridge between Stone and Iron Ages. In another

Right: 'Faust Aleph Null' by James Blish, If *August 1967. Illustrations by Morrow.*

adventure, 'Hok Visits the Land of Legends' (1942), he becomes the amalgam of all the ancient Greek super-heroes, Wellman theorising that from this one symbolic first true man grew the legends of Hercules, Theseus, Meleager and the other heroes.

Swann, though an American writer, first obtained recognition in Britain through his fantasies which rework the old myths into believable and absorbing stories. His first success was 'Where Is the Bird of Fire?' (1962) which retold the legend of Romulus and Remus. *The Blue Monkeys* (1965) takes place in Crete with the Minotaur as the hero. *Moondust* (1968) moved into the Biblical area with the story of the downfall of Jericho, while *Green Phoenix* (1972) returns to Greek myth and the fall of Troy. Swann offers no scientific explanations for these legends, but treats them as factual, merely part of the mysteries of our unwritten past.

Cover by Donnell (Fantasy Press).

Taking the mystical for granted was the theme behind Robert A. Heinlein's 'The Devil Makes the Law' (1940), set in an America where magic works. Magic is also a science in Randall Garrett's 'alternate world' series about Lord D'Arcy, and it plays a part in del Rey's *The Sky Is Falling* (1963). Associated with the workings of magic there is much of sinister appeal, from ghosts and poltergeists to vampires. In Keith Roberts's 'Boulter's Canaries' (1964) poltergeists are treated as simply another life-form which takes unkindly to human interference. Nigel Kneale's television play *The Stone Tape* reveals how stone will 'record' events which take place nearby, particularly violent occurrences such as suicides being recorded more strongly. They can be released (or played back) as ghosts.

A scientific approach was made to vampirism in Richard Matheson's *I Am Legend* (1954), when a virus leads a future population to emulate Count Dracula. Lycanthropy has also proved an intriguing

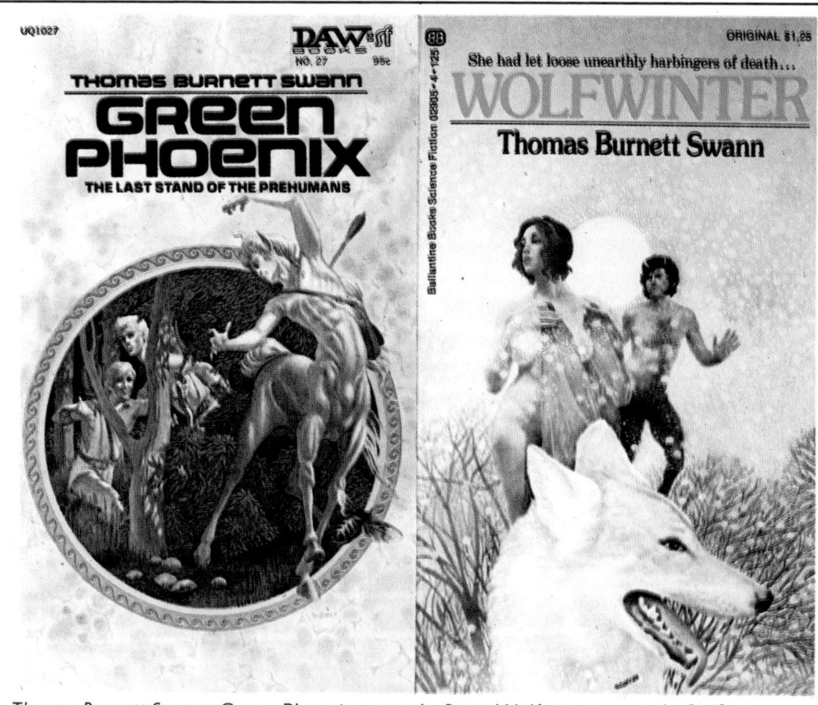

Thomas Burnett Swann: Green Phoenix, *cover by Barr;* Wolfwinter, *cover by Szafran.*

subject for sf writers. Jack Williamson was one of the earliest to treat it scientifically. In 'Wolves of Darkness' (1932), aliens from another dimension inhabit the somnolent forms of humans so that they become like werewolves. In 'Darker Than You Think' (1940), he imagines an early race of man, *Homo lycanthropus*, whose bloodtraces still exist in modern *Homo sapiens*, with an occasional throwback producing a werewolf. The same idea was later adapted by James Blish in 'There Shall Be No Darkness' (1950), which ascribes lycanthropy to a fault in certain glands.

Blish also wrote two other novels based on legendary magic, and managed to

Special James Blish issue, F&SF *April 1972. Cover by Judy Blish.*

combine both religion and myth in a cataclysmic vision. *Black Easter* (1967) tells of the machinations of a business entrepreneur, Baines, and a black magician, Theron Ware, to let loose for one night all the major demons of Hell. Unfortunately, there is no power of good to counteract their evil: God is Dead. In the sequel, *The Day after Judgement* (1970), Ware and his colleagues, who had invoked the demons, pit themselves against them in an attempt to restore order. Blish's masterly handling of the events in a logical manner wrests the works from the confines of fantasy to place them in the realms of science fiction. Like science fiction's treatment of all myths and legends, if God is to exist, he must be scientifically accurate.

It might seem hard to imagine stories of ghosts, vampires and other such macabre entities being occasionally grouped under the heading of science fiction, but it is the treatment which determines the categorisation. If no explanation is given for the various manifestations, and all is left to the unknown, then the stories are classed as supernatural. But if the events are given a logical explanation – no matter how peculiar – then technically, it has been argued, they are science fiction. Such a definition would extend the genre to cover some psychic detective stories. Within the same framework, Clifford Simak has endeavoured to give a logical explanation of goblins and elves. In 'Galactic Chest' (1956), he presents them as aliens from space, whilst in *Goblin Reservation* (1968) all such entities are connected with a distant planet and Earth's remote past; but in *Out of Their Minds* (1970), he suggests that imaginary beings are created through belief in them by a mass of human minds.

02.18 RELIGION AND MYTHS

Neues Leben — *Fidus (Berlin)*

Nun will der Maienmond die Gärten überschneien,
Nun geht bei Drosselschlag die Liebe durch das Land,
Nun will, was sehnsuchtskrank, sich frühlingsfroh befreien,
Und Hoffnung stößt beschwingt vom öden Winterstrand.
Gustav Falke

02.18.4 Living Myths

Christopher, John (as Christopher Youd). 'Monster', *Science Fantasy* Summer 1950
Chandler, A. Bertram. 'False Dawn', *Astounding* October 1946
Farmer, Philip José. 'The God Business', *Beyond* March 1954
Flint, Homer Eon. 'Lord of Death', *All-Story Weekly* 10 May 1919
Hoch, Edward D. 'The Last Unicorns', *Science Fiction Stories* February 1959
Simak, Clifford D. *The Werewolf Principle*, Putnam (US) 1967
West, Wallace. The 'Great Legend' series runs as follows:
'Thy Days Are Numbered', *Future SF Stories* May 1952
'They Shall Rise', *Future SF* July 1952
'We Will Inherit . . .', *Future SF Stories* September 1952
'. . . And Found Wanting', *Future SF* November 1952 (combined as *Lords of Atlantis*, Avalon US 1960)
Williamson, Jack. *Reign of Wizardry*, *Unknown* March to May 1940; Lancer (US) 1964
Zelazny, Roger. 'The Monster and the Maiden', *Galaxy* December 1964

02.18.5 The Concept of the Superman

A ripe area in mythology is the coming of the Superman, and it was the German philosopher Nietzsche who himself wrote that Man was 'a rope connecting animal and Superman – a rope across an abyss.' Many sf writers have attempted to deal with the development of a race of *Ubermenschen*. In another of his progenitive tales, *The Food of the Gods* (1904), H.G. Wells wrote of an alkaloid drug which was found to increase growth up to as much as seven times. Giant insects and plants, in addition to giant humans, are the result, and the main theme of the tale is the conflict between normal beings and the new race of gigantic men.

Wells's view of the superman in his story is one based on physical size and strength, and not necessarily on superior mental ability. It was a theme also developed by Philip Wylie in *The Gladiator* (1930), which tells of the invention of a chemical which produces enormous strength, but without any accompanying giantism. His central character also meets with persecution, learning to suppress his power until he is able to put it to full use in the Foreign Legion during the First World War. It was this story which served as the original source of inspiration for the *Superman* comic strip syndicated by Joseph Shuster and Jerry Siegal eight years later.

By far the largest number of stories on the superman theme in science fiction have concentrated, however, on the development of higher intelligence, often at the expense of physical ability. They range from the portrayal of the vast passionless brains of the Fourth Man in Olaf Stapledon's *Last and First Men* (1930) to the superior intellects bred in Robert A. Heinlein's *Beyond This Horizon* (1942). Nevertheless, the commonly presented idea in many magazine stories that the super-intellect of the future will take the form of a massive brain with practically no body tends to ignore the physical fact that the brain is only as good as the bodily system which supports it. In all probability, a mental giant would also need to be physically far superior to present-day Man.

Other presentations of super-beings often show them to possess eidetic memories or the type of genuinely synthetic mind portrayed in John Russell Fearn's *The Intelligence Gigantic* (1933). Others enjoy the ability to recreate lost limbs or to mentally manipulate matter, to mention but two of the facilities described in such stories by A.E. van Vogt as *The Monster* (1939).

In general, the myth of the superman appears something of a dead end in the mainstream of modern science fiction, and is now subject to neglect.

ADDITIONAL INPUT

02.18.5 The Concept of the Superman

Beresford, J.D. *The Hampdenshire Wonder*, Sidgwick & Jackson (UK) 1911
Cross, Polton (J.R. Fearn). 'The Mental Ultimate', *Astounding* January 1938
Gridban, Volsted (J.R. Fearn). *Moons for Sale*, Scion (UK) 1953
Page, Norvell W. 'But without Horns', *Unknown* June 1940
Robinson, Frank M. *The Power*, *Bluebook* March 1956; Lippincott (US) 1956
Shiras, Wilmar H. *Children of the Atom*, Gnome (US) 1953
Tubb, E.C. *The Resurrected Man*, Scion (UK) 1953
Van Vogt, A.E. *Empire of the Atom*, Shasta (US) 1957
Van Vogt, A.E. 'The Silkie', *Worlds of If* July 1964

It is, perhaps, fortunate that the editor has asked a writer with my controversial background to do a foreword to this sensitive section of their big book on science fiction.

It is fortunate because the authors, whose work is described in the text that follows, have, everyone, made an impact during their ten-year literary cycle – which is just about the length of time, by my observation, that a trend endures in any field of art.

In science fiction, each ten years (approximately) younger writers appear, despise what has gone before, create a new thing, and, within the decade, in their turn, become the object of distaste by the generation poking its collective twenty-one to thirty-one-year-old heads above the anonymity of childhood.

What makes me a worthwhile introducer to such an automatic process is that I tried most mightily to anticipate, and evade, my literary demise at the end of my decade (the forties). Among other things, I deliberately avoided any conscious commitment to a then-current relevance.

The word 'conscious' is the significant term in the foregoing. Because, unconsciously, I failed many times. Meaning the soon-to-be-quaint relevance was there.

It is educational to read the top writers of a particular decade. They love each other, as only writers can. Almost, they present the appearance of a True Group. For their era, they set standards of style and content, and they collect the consequent kudos. And then, presently, as the discordant newcomers vociferate ever more noisily around them, they become disturbed, and react, each in his fashion, even withdraw.

In my time, I took off into a study of human inner space. Since my reappearance on the sf writing scene, I observe that my current work is not appreciated by the British critics of the genre; but it sells well as also do my previous operas, space or otherwise. Historians will have to evaluate such mysteries in their own good time.

My point: Theoretically, since I am in my seventh decade of life, mine is a case history that will, statistically, run its course in the next twenty years; and, thereafter, my efforts can be dissected at leisure by objective, even compassionate, onlookers – or at top speed by writers who are approaching the end of their viable decade, and would like to know how someone else tried to solve the dilemma. For the record, and for them, let me set forth a simplified account of what I tried to do.

I noticed early in my career that this is a world in which rhythms exert a powerful influence on the human nervous system. Examples are music and poetry. So I chose a writing format from John Gallishaw of an 800-word scene – repeated (rhythmically) throughout a story. In the telling I used what I called fictional sentences. In most literature this means a lot of imagery and emotion; but in science fiction a fictional sentence had to have a hang-up. Something is missing from the sentence that would explain it. The reader has to supply the missing element from his own creative ability. (My hope: each decade of readers would supply their own relevance.)

Another technique: I believed that the spoken sounds of the languages of the world each convey an emotional impact. If words with that sound are used . . . carefully, and repetitively but avoiding alliteration . . . an emotional rhythmic response will be evoked from the reader.

There's more, particularly in relation to content. But that was a part of my attempt to increase the inner space dimensions of my stories.

I'm presuming that, where I have noticed sustained imaginery, experimental writing, and style, in other writers of later decades, I was, and am, observing their efforts to gain dramatic verisimilitude and beauty, and their hope to reach across the decades and leave a permanent trace on the literature of our common posterity.

Everyone of the writers mentioned in the following pages succeeded beyond his or her contemporaries in the initial response evoked.

They have my best wishes.

A. E. Van Vogt

A. E. van Vogt

02.19 INNER SPACE

The term 'inner space', when applied to science fiction, has in the minds of many readers a strong connection with the modernistic movement which centred on the British magazine *New Worlds* and its editor, Michael Moorcock, during the mid-1960s. In the earlier days the expression had denoted the world underneath the sea, or under land – but always in connection with planet Earth. The 'new wave', in association with Moorcock, assigned to it a psychological connotation; and it is to such an interpretation that this sub-section is devoted. Moorcock and his contributors tried to introduce new literary techniques into their science fiction, they wanted to break down the artificial barriers which they regarded as being erected around science fiction – or, as they preferred to call it, 'speculative' fiction – and earn for themselves a greater freedom from science fictional conventions and taboos. The British writer primarily associated with this movement, who has moved on to become of importance amongst England's novelists, was J. G. Ballard; other English writers who entered the movement to a lesser extent were Brian Aldiss, John Brunner and Moorcock himself.

It would be wrong to suggest that this movement of writers, more preoccupied with happenings in inner space than in outer space, was confined to Britain. In the United States, such authors as Harlan Ellison, Norman Spinrad, Thomas M. Disch and John T. Sladek all approached the new ideas in the field with enthusiasm. They had already been preceded, to some extent, by an earlier school of writers.

What primarily distinguished the excursions of the inner-space writers from those concerned with outer-space were the central issues of the stories they produced. The more traditional writers were

02.19 INNER SPACE

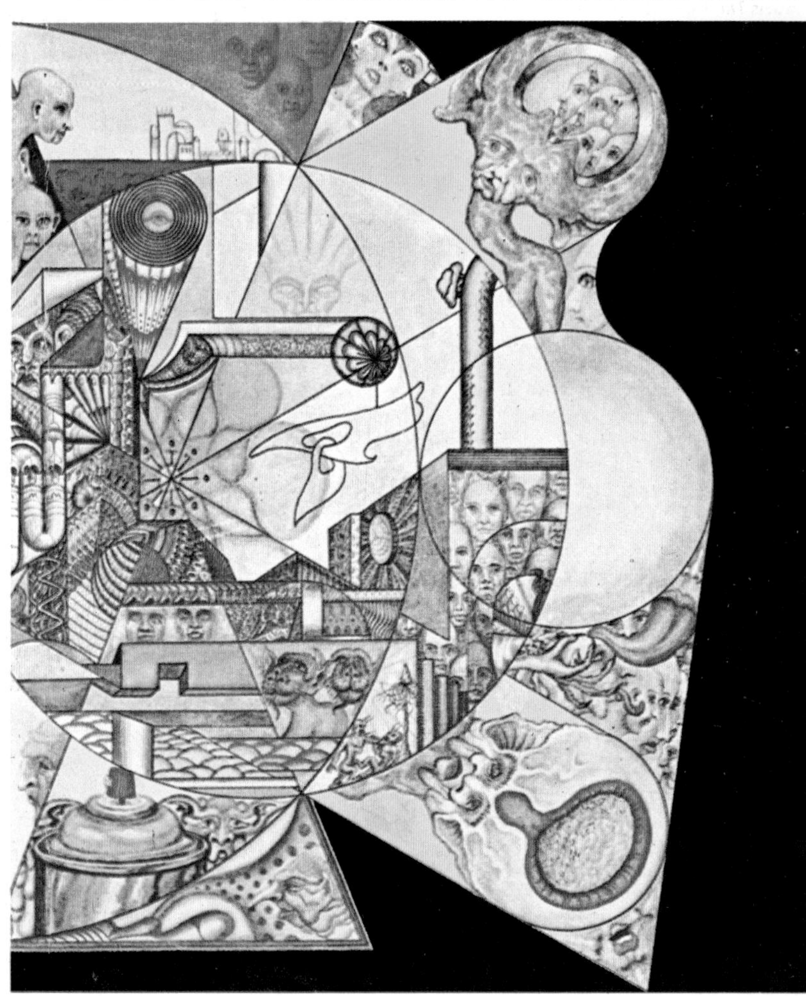

Ubik *by Philip K. Dick (Dell). Cover by Jones.*

concerned with the established themes of science fiction: adventure stories featuring other worlds and fantastic civilisations, alien life-forms or the far future. The 'new wave' of science fiction writers approached their subject-matter from a fresh direction. Their stories questioned the values of man's society from non-materialistic, ethical and moral standpoints; examined man's relationship with his environment and man's relationship with man; and, in very large measure, they were imbued with psychological and metaphysical overtones. It is interesting to note that they were anticipated by H. G. Wells in his two psychological, prototype inner-space stories, *Mr. Blettsworthy on Rampole Island* (1928) and *The Croquet Player* (1936).

02.19.1 Progenitors

Stories featuring these new concerns did not suddenly spring into existence during the mid-1960s, however; this was merely the time when they became clearly discernible as a distinctive body of work. Among American writers, who experimented with psychological themes before the new wave, can be included C. M. Kornbluth, William Tenn and Fritz Leiber. In such stories as Leiber's 'The Secret Songs' (1961) there can be found many of the elements which came to characterise the later movement. As far back as 1952, Alfred Bester published a novel which continues to be regarded as one of the major stories of science fiction: *The Demolished Man*, in which a big businessman is haunted by 'the man with no face', a personal psychological projection from his own future. In this context, Bester appears to have been something of a pathfinder, for he followed *The Demolished Man* with another novel, *Tiger! Tiger!* (1956), which features one of the best-known anti-heroes in science fiction, Gully Foyle, whose face becomes a tiger mask whenever his emotions are aroused. In this convoluted novel of intrigue and suspense, the survivor of a space wreck, and later of deliberate abandonment, sets out to avenge his ill-treatment and, in the process, discovers that he has acquired strange powers. Bester's *The Indian Giver* (1974), although it can hardly be called progenitive, may be considered in this section because, while it was published eighteen years after *Tiger! Tiger!*, it shows direct links with Bester's earlier novels in both concerns and execution. It also shows that, despite the long gap between books, Bester can still deal with large-scale psychological themes. The story features a group of people who have attained immortality by dying in especially horrible ways. Their aim is to gain control of a massive computer complex which all but runs the world and in so doing to free mankind of the machine's repressive influence. But to their horror, they discover that one of their own number is already controlled by the machine, which proceeds to use him for its own ends.

Another well-known author who was an early entrant in the realm of the psychological story, and who has remained there ever since, is Philip K. Dick, a writer noted for the fecundity and originality of his ideas. Traces of psychological elements can be discovered in most of Dick's more than twenty-five books, but even among this body of work certain stories stand out because of the conspicuous way in which the author has delved into the subconscious mind.

Dick's *The Man Who Japed* (1956) tells of a future in which individuals are legally obliged to enjoy the new social order created by the powers that be. One man, however, rebels, and a hunt is ordered to track him down. In the course of the hunt, one of its leaders discovers that he is the object of his own search, although he has no memory whatever of committing the acts for which he is wanted. In *Eye in the Sky* (1957) Dick questions the nature of our perception of reality. Is man, as a race, what he really imagines himself to be? Or, to adopt the Fortean argument, is humanity the property of something else?

One of Dick's most controversial novels

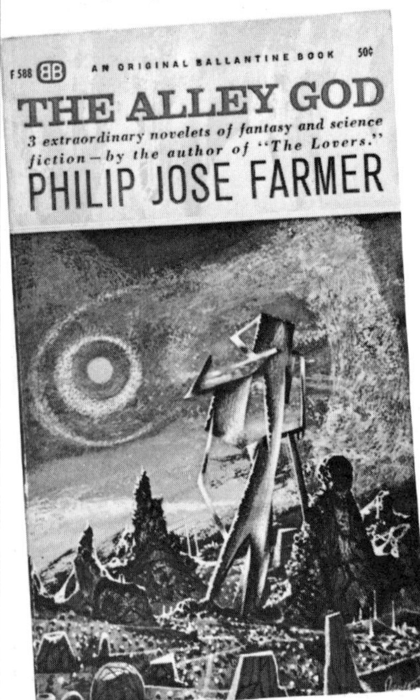

The Alley God *by Philip José Farmer (Ballantine).*

to date is *The Three Stigmata of Palmer Eldritch* (1964), which was published at about the same time as the rise of the drug-orientated sub-culture which caused a great deal of public concern in the 1960s. In the novel, Dick portrays an overcrowded world from which colonists are forcibly drafted to other planets. On the colony worlds, life is often dull, and the colonists are forced to take refuge from a harsh environment in domes or underground. They can alleviate their boredom by taking dream-inducing drugs, which allow them to experience – for a short while – idealised lives inside their own heads. The standard drug is called Can-D, the effects of which are known and predictable; but a new drug, Chew-Z, is introduced, offering fantasy worlds beside which those of Can-D pale into insignificance. Another Dick novel which deals with dream-worlds in the mind is *Ubik* (1969). In this instance, the minds are those of the almost-dead, which are stored away in a state known as 'half-life', to be awoken from time to time and consulted by worried relatives and associates. Following a fault in the storage system, the minds begin to unite, the weaker being taken over by the stronger, to form a sinister world of their own which sometimes seems more genuine than the reality outside.

A recent offering, which also falls well outside the progenitive category, is *Flow My Tears the Policeman Said* (1974). In the eyes of many critics, it is Dick's best novel to date. In it, he examines again some of the concerns which he covered in his earlier novels, and inventively handles the effect drugs can have on the various ways in which reality is perceived. In this particular case, it is not only the reality of the drug user which is affected, but also the reality of any other person they care to involve in their fantasy. Other Dick novels which offer psychologically-orientated threats to their characters are *Time out of Joint* (1959), in which the protagonist comes to a slow awareness of his true situation; *Counter-Clock World* (1967), in which time runs backwards and events have to be made to un-happen; and *We Can Build You* (1969), in which simulacras of famous people are introduced and problems arise as to who is real and who is not. As is typical of most Dick novels, they ask questions about the true nature of reality.

Flow My Tears, the Policeman Said *by Philip K. Dick (DAW). Cover by Ulrich and Osterwalden.*

Other writers of the earlier school of science fiction dealt with psychological themes, but none of them with the same concentration of work as Dick or Bester. Arthur C. Clarke's *Childhood's End* (1953), in which mankind evolves to a higher plane of existence, could be regarded as such a work, and expresses an essentially pessimistic view of man's ability to raise the quality of his mind without outside help. 'Flowers for Algernon' (1959), by Daniel Keyes, in which the intelligence of a retarded man is chemically enhanced so that he progresses rapidly from moron level to genius, and then regresses, deals with the leading character's problems in coming to terms with his new self and the sudden strangeness of the world as he now perceives it. Another 1959 story, 'The Alley Man' by Philip José Farmer, is in some ways akin to 'Flowers for Algernon', though on a more personal level. A mental and physical throwback, who believes himself to be the last of the Neanderthals, tries to come to terms with the modern world, and, in

Childhood's End *by Arthur C. Clarke (Ballantine). Cover by Fernandez.*

02.19 INNER SPACE

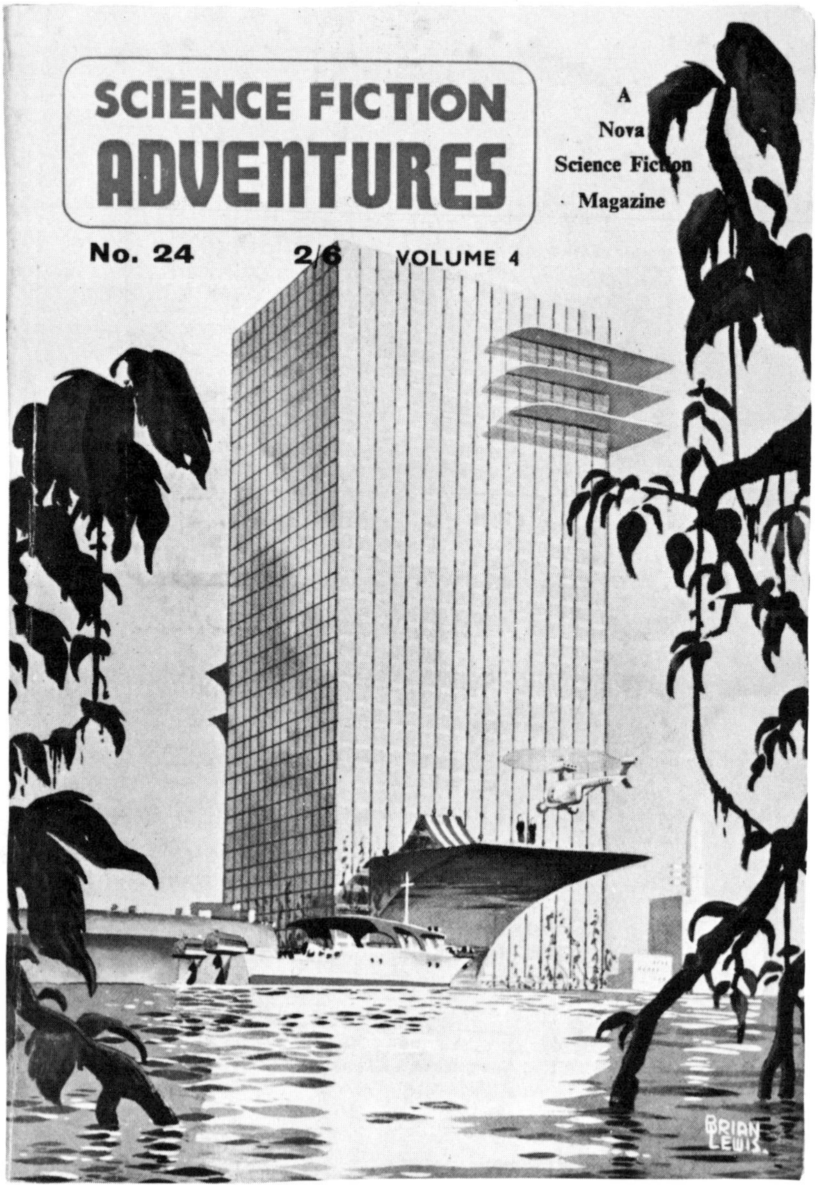

The Drowned World *by J. G. Ballard, 1962. Cover by Lewis.*

particular, with the intellectual superiority of the girl he loves. Both are stories of alienation.

ADDITIONAL INPUT

02.19.1 Progenitors

Harness, Charles L. *The Rose*, *Authentic* March 1953; Compact (UK) 1966

Lem, Stanislaw. *Solaris*, (Poland) 1961; UK translation Faber 1971

02.19.2 The New Wave

An English writer whose entire work is imbued with overtones of a psychological nature is J. G. Ballard – one of the founders of the 'new wave'. From his earliest short stories, published in the mid-1950s, up to and including his most recent novels, the author has examined events in his fiction from the point of view of the subconscious needs of his characters – even when this has apparently been at the expense of the denouement of the story he is telling. Ballard's idea is that an ending which is psychologically best for the reader is not always psychologically best for his character, and as the story is about the protagonist, his needs must come first. In an interview, Ballard commented on his novels *The Wind from Nowhere* (1962), *The Drowned World* (1962), *The Drought* (1964) and *The Crystal World* (1966), a quartet of novels which all depict disaster of one kind or another coming upon the world:

'Usually these disaster stories are treated as though they *are* disaster stories, they're treated straight, and everyone is running for the hills or out of the hills or whatever . . . (my) heroes, for psychological reasons of their own, embrace the particular transformation taking place. These are stories of huge psychic transformations.'

(From an interview in *J. G. Ballard: the First Twenty Years*, edited by James Goddard and David Pringle, Brans Head Books, 1976)

Ballard's *Vermillion Sands* (1971) is a collection of short stories culled from the author's previous fifteen years' work. They are linked by a common locale, a common mood and a common approach, they are stories of psychological cannibalism. Vermillion Sands is a desert resort, past its best, but holding a tenuous existence still as a Mecca for retired and forgotten movie queens. Poets, artists and writers are attracted to these women, hoping to make a living out of their need for admiration, remembrance and a kind of mental immortality. In 'The Cloud Sculptors of Coral D' (1967), the images of these faded women are carved in cloud, to drift goddess-like through the sky as a projection of their former glory and gradual dissipation. This to some degree, is a theme which embraces all the *Vermillion Sands* stories.

In his recent fiction, Ballard has dealt with localised, more personal disasters as the bases of his tales, but the roots of this aspect of his work can be traced back to the mid-1960s, when he published a number of obsessive and enigmatic short stories on a variety of themes. 'The Assassination Weapon' (1966) was a fictional examination of the deaths of John F. Kennedy and Lee

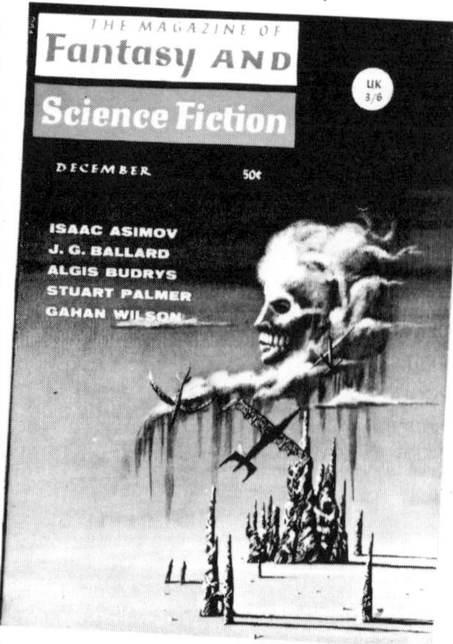

'The Cloud-Sculptors of Coral D' by J. G. Ballard, F&SF *December 1967. Cover by Gaughan.*

Harvey Oswald. Ballard treated the same events in another story 'The Assassination of John Fitzgerald Kennedy Considered as a Downhill Motor Race' (1966). At this time, he also began to publish his controversial series of 'condensed novels', which were ultimately published in *The Atrocity Exhibition* (1970). The protagonist who links these stories is a doctor suffering from a nervous breakdown, wandering through the various scenarios almost spectre-like, observing and joining in the sexual, sadistic and psychotic events portrayed.

The Atrocity Exhibition was followed by *Crash* (1973), in which car accidents become objects of worship and are used as a means of examining, in allegorical detail, the sexual proclivities of the characters involved. The hero of *Concrete Island* (1974) also accidentally crashes his car – on a large and overgrown tract of land between three converging motorways. He is injured, but gradually recovers. He encounters an enfeebled tramp, whom he comes to dominate, and a prostitute, who uses the island as a daytime hideaway. In an almost Kafkaesque situation, he strives throughout the book to find a way off the island, but when the girl eventually shows him the escape route he decides to remain, aware that at last he is beginning to know himself. Ballard's latest novel, *High-Rise* (1975), tells of the inhabitants of a massive multi-storey apartment block gradually reverting to savagery as the amenities of civilisation, which form a restrictive veneer around their lives, break down. At first they are concerned about their loss of comfort and the degradations forced upon them; but when groups of the apartment dwellers realise that another dimension has been added to their normally routine lives, they take steps to ensure that nothing interferes with their challenging new existence.

After Ballard, Harlan Ellison is regarded as one of the most important writers in the new wave, and he must be counted as one of the instigators of the new concerns in science fiction which have developed in the United States. Ellison has always been interested in the shock value of science fiction. Many of his short stories can be recognised for the psychological sting which their unconventional ideas and approach are likely to effect on the traditionally minded reader. A list of some of the concepts dealt with in Ellison's stories reads like a roll-call of social taboos and areas of public sensitivity: homosexuality, incest, fetishism, cannibalism, and many more. Yet, despite his excursions into these controversial regions, he has made an impact as a new-wave writer without resort to the experimental language favoured by many of his colleagues.

Ellison's 'The Sleeper with Still Hands' (1968) tells of a 'presence' secreted beneath the sea which has exercised a moderating influence on man for many years, but is now threatened with destruction so that humanity can once again indulge in evil pursuits. The leading character in 'A Boy and His Dog' (1969) is one of the surface-dwelling survivors of a cataclysmic holocaust following which survival is maintained by forming symbiotic units with intelligent telepathic dogs. The remnants of technological man live underground. The boy forms a transitory relationship with a girl from the subterranean region, but as the deprivations increase, instincts prove stronger than love, and he and his dog eat her. The hero of 'A Place with No Name' (1969) is a pimp and a nobody who manages to escape from police pursuit by entering a fantasy world where he becomes a new Prometheus. In 'I Have No Mouth, and I Must Scream' (1967), a group of humans struggle to keep a tenuous hold on reality while they are imprisoned inside a giant sentient computer by the machine itself, which taunts them and tortures them mentally. Ellison, with his reputation for writing pithy stories full of feeling, was eminently at home within the new wave.

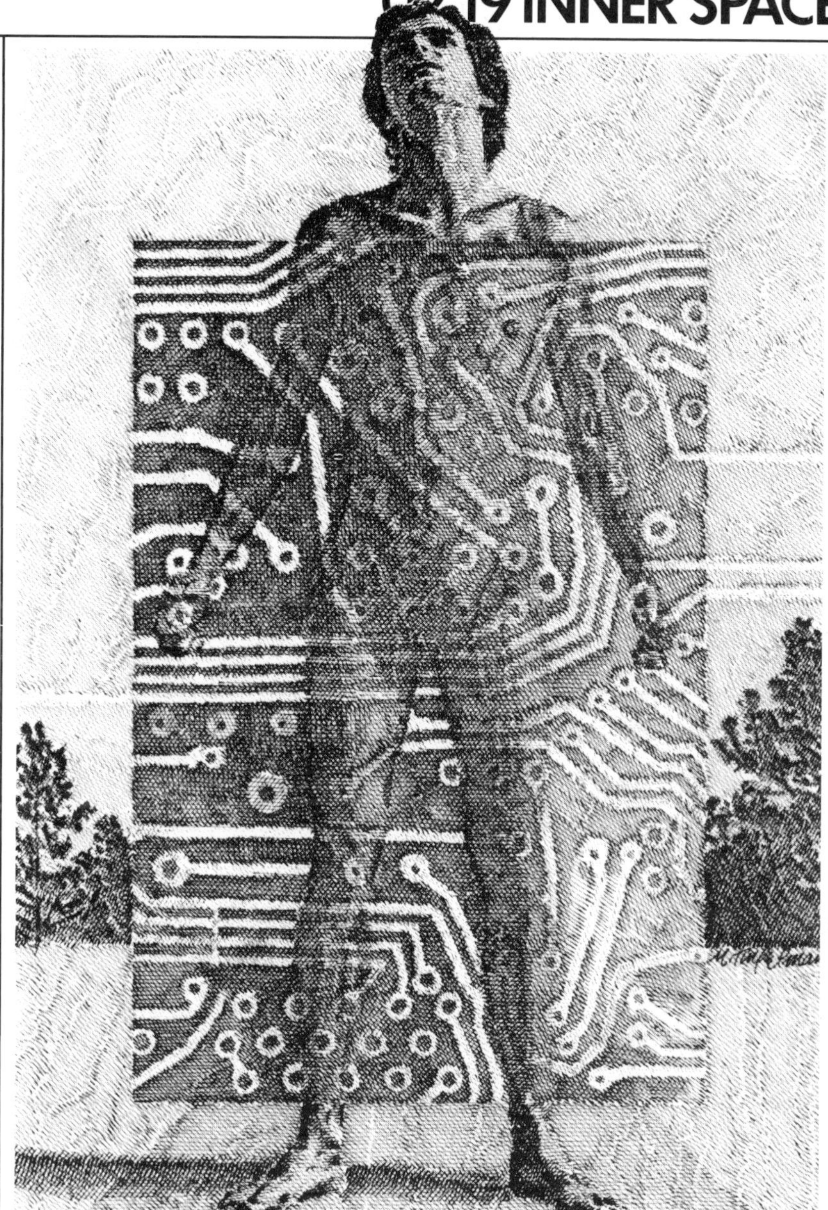

The Shockwave Rider *by John Brunner (Ballantine). Cover by Murray Tinkelman.*

During the mid-1960s there was a period when it seemed that almost anyone who did not write science fiction after the fashion of E. E. ('Doc') Smith was in danger of being labelled 'new wave'. For this reason, some noted stories classed under this enveloping sub-generic definition, when looked at in retrospect, hardly qualify as avant-garde or psychological at all, no matter how good they are as science fiction. John Brunner's *Stand on Zanzibar* (1968) is a good example. Perhaps this novel was designated new wave because it bravely and unfashionably attacked the conservative materialistic philosophy of the Western world, and pointed out the dangers into which the dogma of production for production's sake was leading modern man. A few years later, in 1972, Brunner published *The Sheep Look Up*, a novel that could be said, in some ways, to stem directly from *Stand on Zanzibar*, in that it deals with similar autorial pre-occupations. Again, *The Shockwave Rider* (1974) tells of a man who succeeds in living outside the enforced 'big-brother' regime which many sf writers imagine is threatened in the future.

Probably Brian Aldiss's most notable treatment of the inner space theme is his novel *Barefoot in the Head* (1969), subtitled 'A European Fantasia' and published originally as a series of individual short stories – mostly in *New Worlds*. For this tale of a Europe drugged to the point of complete social collapse, as the result of a hallucinogenic gas attack, Aldiss invented a Messianic figure who assumes a holy 'aura' as he rides his motorcycle across the drug-sodden continent. Such stories as 'Orgy of the Living and the Dying' (1970), with its concern for third-world poverty and for personal relationships, and 'Super-Toys Last All Summer Long' (1969), which gently probes the nature of reality and emotional attachment, are also indicative of Aldiss's new-wave affiliation. The mesmeric passage in *Frankenstein Unbound* (1973), where Victor Frankenstein's monster is pursued across the ice floes, shows a great debt to the new wave, and the novel as a whole, with its synthesis of real people and fictional characters as a cast, can safely be judged to have a place with other new-wave works. *An Age* (1967) is a sometimes serious, sometimes comic novel in which time travel is achieved by means of mental projection. Because of its psychological overtones, it can also be included in Aldiss's new-wave contributions.

Although Michael Moorcock is primarily known as one of the artistic motivators of the new wave, and as a writer of sword and sorcery fiction, he has produced a number of works which can, in their own right, be considered to belong in the sub-genre.

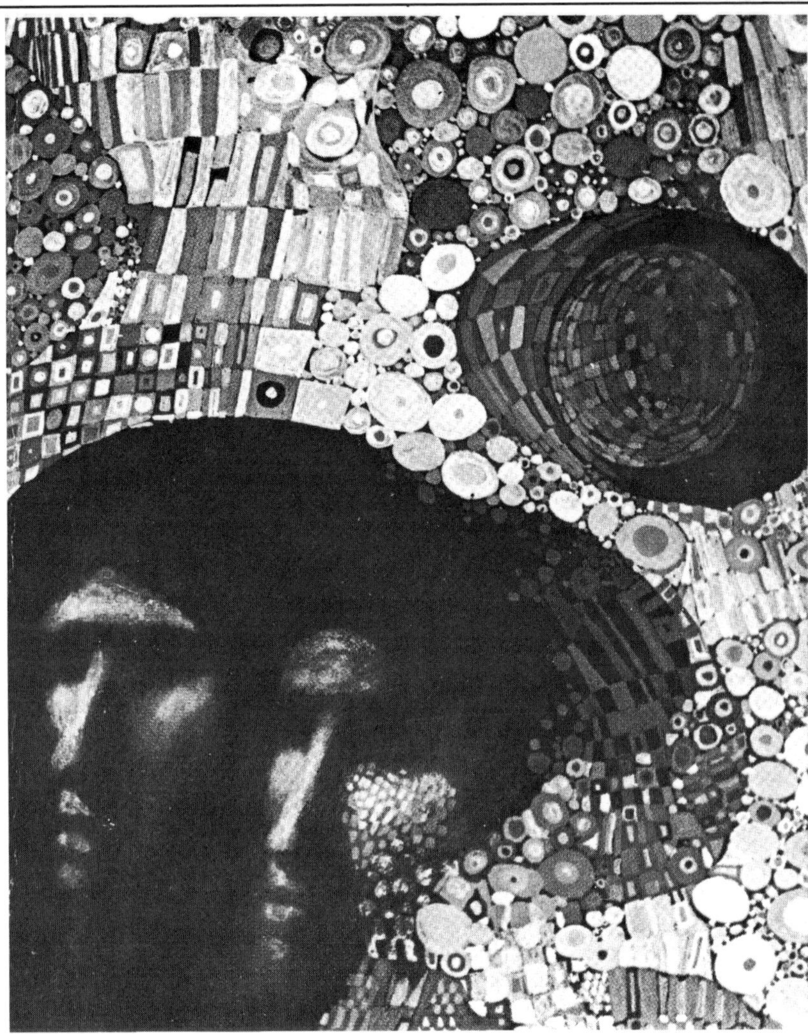

The Left Hand of Darkness *by Ursula Le Guin (Ace).*

25486/$1.95
JOHN BRUNNER
"...a vast uncontrolled explosion of a book... at times brilliant..."
–The London Sunday Times
STAND ON ZANZIBAR

Cover by Murray Tinkelman.

Among these are his Jerry Cornelius novels, *The Final Programme* (1968), *A Cure for Cancer* (1971) and *The English Assassin* (1972), all of which relate the adventures of the ambi-sexual protagonist, a James Bond-type character who can change sex and colour at will, and seemingly achieve most things with little or no effort. Moving away from black comedy, Moorcock wrote *Behold the Man* (1970), an extended version of his 1967 short story of the same title. It is a serious novel in which the central character travels back in time towards his own immolation on the cross at Calvary as a substitute Jesus. The hero of *Behold the Man* reappears in *Breakfast in the Ruins* (1972), this time searching for fulfilment.

Moorcock's *New Worlds* magazine attracted a large share of American contributors, and in addition to Harlan Ellison, there were in the United States a number of writers who played a leading part in new-wave activities. These included Thomas M. Disch (a writer who later gave vent to many criticisms of the standards of science fiction), John T. Sladek and Norman Spinrad.

Disch's first novel, *The Genocides* (1965), is a traditional-style story about the Earth being invaded by giant plants, with the remnants of humanity eking out a precarious existence among their roots. But Disch soon turned to the deeper considerations of the new wave, and *Camp Concentration* (1968) is a good example of these preoccupations. The novel involves basic concept very similar to that developed by Daniel Keyes in 'Flowers for Algernon': the chemical enhancement of intelligence. But whereas in Keyes's story the IQ drug is administered for basically altruistic reasons, in Disch's novel the motives are underhand and sinister. The drug is given to political prisoners of the US army interned in a secret camp.

The writings of the new wave could hardly be said to be over-endowed with humour, but if the sub-genre should need a clown-prince then John Sladek is the closest contender. In *The Reproductive System* (1968), he envisages a species of self-reproducing machines which become numerous enough to threaten the basis of American life. In 1970 he published *The Müller-Fokker Effect*, a multi-faceted novel about a man who is, ostensibly, turned into

'(But) the prose was experimental, and the sexuality and the language were explicit, which automatically identified the novel as new wave.'

(From the introduction to *The New Tomorrows*, edited by Norman Spinrad, Belmont Books, US, 1971)

In other words, it was not so much the content of a story which identified it as new wave, as the approach with which the author chose to accomplish his task.

The only woman to write a novel which could unquestionably be offered a place within the new wave is Kit Reed, with her story *Armed Camps* (1969). In this fantasy, which also suggests the influence of Kafka, she examines the motives that lie behind violence, pacificism and persecution. However, she appears to have written nothing else which could be classed in the same category.

ADDITIONAL INPUT

02.19.2 The New Wave

Jones, Langdon. 'The Great Clock', *New Worlds* March 1966
Platt, Charles. 'Id', *New Worlds* March 1969

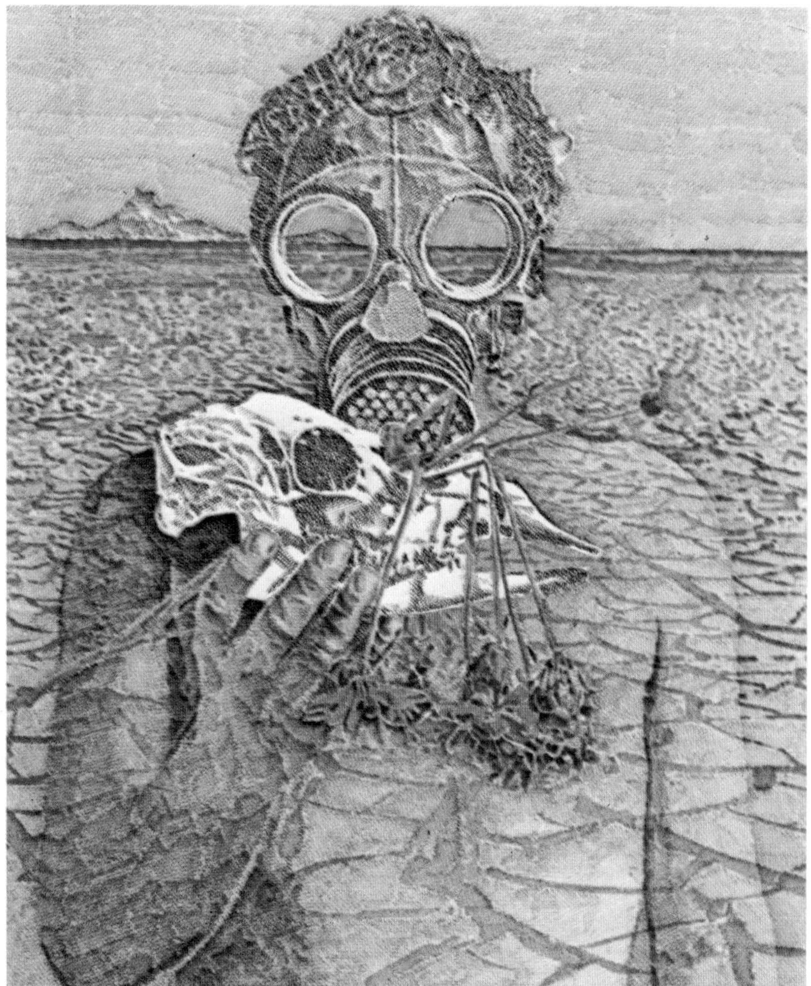

The Sheep Look Up *by John Brunner (Ballantine). Cover by Murray Tinkelman.*

computer data, but who in reality is undergoing a journey of deep self-appraisal. Sladek has also produced a number of amusing parodies of the work of leading sf writers, and these can be found collected in his book *The Steam Driven Boy* (1973).

Among the most controversial works produced by the new wave was Norman Spinrad's novel of sex, violence and corruption in politics and the media, *Bug Jack Barron* (1967–68). The story, originally serialised in *New Worlds*, was – or so rumour has it – the subject of questions in the British Parliament. Its chief character is the presenter of a television show which enjoys a regular audience of over 100 million, the purpose of the programme being to enable anyone with a grievance against another individual or organisation, no matter how high or lowly, to seek public redress. The formula works well, and the show is phenomenally successful. But when a Negro, who has been rejected as a candidate for suspended animation by the mysterious Foundation for Immortality, seeks to publicise his grievance, the repercussions are menacing. It is interesting to quote briefly a remark made by Spinrad, specifically about *Bug Jack Barron*, but which, in a sense, seems to have a bearing on much new-wave writing:

Below: Frankenstein Unbound *by Brian Aldiss (Cape). Cover by Tunbridge.*

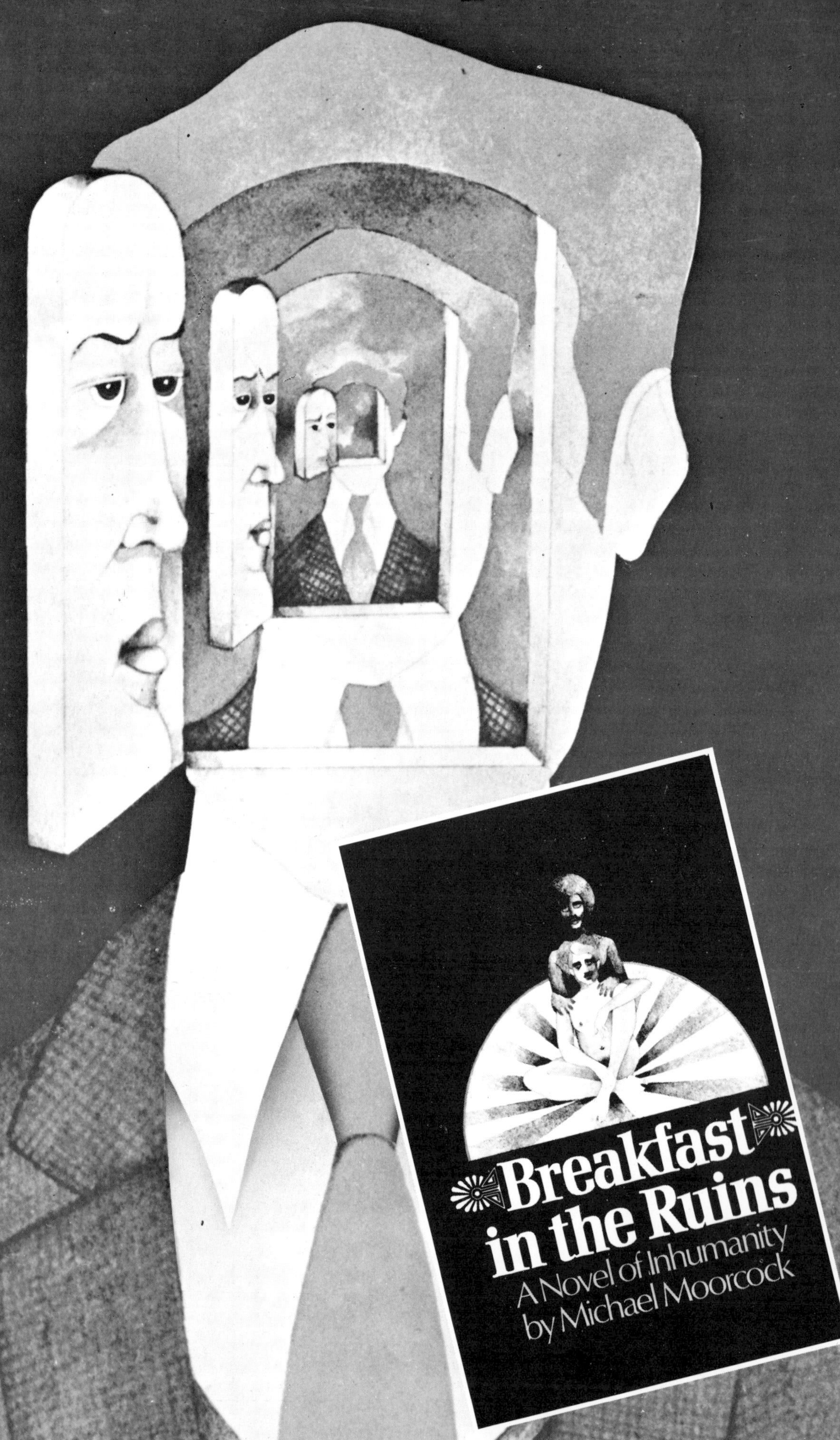

Breakfast
in the Ruins
A Novel of Inhumanity
by Michael Moorcock

02.19.3 Descendants

The new wave, as a separate entity, petered out at the end of the 1960s, and the best of its components merged with the best of the conventional genre to produce a new kind of literary science fiction. The more gifted of the new-wave writers became a part of the new tradition. Authors who had never been part of the pulp-magazine tradition and who, in earlier years, might have become conventional novelists, found that this new form of science fiction, with its deep-rooted concern for humanity and human problems, and its almost total disregard for the old established idioms of the genre, was a medium to which they could contribute. They combined to produce a body of work in which characterisation and human interaction were paramount, and which demanded critical attention on a par with that given to any other literary endeavour.

Inner-space stories which mark a direct descent from the new wave are not always easy to identify. Which works, for instance, might have been written in any case, new wave or not? There has always been a small coterie of science fiction writers, among them Ray Bradbury and Theodore Sturgeon, who have shown concern for the literary standards of the genre. However, the prevalence of literary science fiction during and since the new wave seems to have become so marked, that to separate those who recognised the need for heightened standards at an early stage from those who owe a direct debt to the introduction of new concepts and preoccupations would serve no useful purpose. Robert Silverberg is a case in point.

Silverberg has enjoyed a career in science fiction spanning more than twenty years. In the 1950s and early 1960s he wrote very many short stories and novels which are best judged on the level of pure entertainment. Then for a few years he ceased to produce science fiction, but reappeared towards the end of the 1960s as a different kind of a writer, contributing a number of novels and short stories which can be judged a part of the sub-category under examination. Silverberg writes with an intensity of prose which meets high literary standards. *Dying Inside* (1972) is the story of a middle-aged telepath whose power is gradually waning, and tells of his attempts to come to terms with the drastic change taking place within himself. *The World Inside* (1972) was originally published as a series of short stories, and relates a future in which the human race lives in huge hive-like 'monads', entirely self-contained vertical cities each catering for the needs of many thousands of people. Despite the conformity to monad life which is instilled into the inhabitants from birth, there exist a few who still strive for some individual freedom in an overbearing 'big brother' world. 'Good News from the Vatican' (1971) is an ironic story about the human inability to agree and compromise, with the result that a robot becomes Pope. The enforced donation of bodily organs is the subject of 'Caught in the Organ Draft' (1972); the donors are paid for their loss with certain privileges.

Enforced organ donation appears again in Silverberg's most recent novel, *Shadrach in the Furnace* (1976), but the story is mainly about the tribulations of a young doctor attending a Mongol dictator when he learns that his body is to become host to the dictator's mind when he dies. *The Stochastic Man* (1975) depicts a character who learns how to predict the future. He begins by using scientific analysis to project possible outcomes, but later discovers that genuine second sight can be developed with comparative ease. 'Push No More' (1972) is another story about the loss of telepathic power. In this instance the leading character is a young boy, approaching puberty, who suddenly finds he has paranormal abilities. When he first learns to make love, however, his powers suddenly desert him. A love affair also unbalances the way of life of the central character of 'Now + n/Now − n' (1972). He and his future self leapfrog through time sending reports to their past selves on how to profit from the stock-market; but with the arrival of the feminine interest, the flow of information ceases.

Another noted writer whose work displays a preoccupation with psychological themes is Ursula K. Le Guin. Her first

Left: front and back covers of Breakfast in the Ruins *by Michael Moorcock (NEL).*

Special Ray Bradbury issue, F & SF May 1963. Cover by Magnaini.

02.19 INNER SPACE

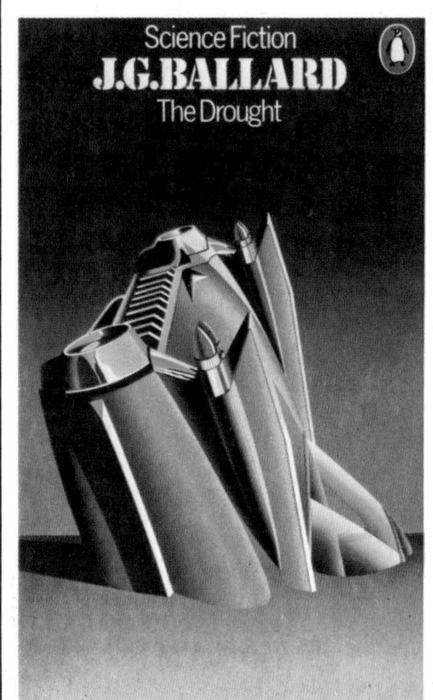

J. G. Ballard: The Drought, The Terminal Beach, The Wind from Nowhere *(Penguin). Covers by Pelham.*

stories in the early 1960s clearly laid the foundations for her later development, but it was not until the late 1960s and early 1970s that her work began to show signs of distinction. Two novels in particular indicate a marked debt to the new wave. *The Left Hand of Darkness* (1969) is a novel in which the 'human' inhabitants of a far planet can, during sexual congress, be either male or female at will, an ability that has led to a peculiar psychological approach. *The Dispossessed* (1974) tells of life on an anarchic planet, and in particular of a physicist who works in something of a scientific vacuum. The story is a veiled analysis of man's society – his motivations, objectives and hopes – and highlights the cold interface between differing ideologies.

James Tiptree Jr (recently revealed as the pen-name of Alice Sheldon) is a newcomer who has explored similar themes.

Among the latest arrivals in this area is Christopher Priest, a young British writer who has published four novels to date. Of these, one is an amusing pastiche of H. G. Wells, while another is an intelligent piece of fairly traditional science fiction. The other two have a firm place in the genre of inner space. In *Indoctrinaire* (1970), Priest treads a path which once more seems to have been laid by Kafka. The Protagonist is taken to a mysterious prison where he is interrogated and treated to psychological bombardment, not for one moment realising that he has been kidnapped by agents from the future. *Fugue for a Darkening Island* (1972) tells of the collapse of society in England as thousands of Africans, fleeing from a war-scarred continent, seek refuge there.

Finally, there are two novels by Peter Tate which sound an ecological note. *The Thinking Seat* (1969) tells of unconventional activists concerned that the ocean, under threat from the activities of a desalination company, should be restored to its former state so that ecological imbalances can be corrected. *Gardens 12345* (1971) is a metaphysical and surrealistic story in which the leading character accidentally trespasses into a series of five gardens, upsetting the delicate inter-relationship of various strange men working on fanciful, but peaceful, projects.

The appearance of many recent and serious stories on the theme of inner space, with all the considerations that expression implies, indicates that it is an established part of modern science fiction. While many traditional enthusiasts may in retrospect view the new wave as a temporary upheaval on the broad sf horizon, there seems little doubt that the movement was responsible for strengthening the emphasis on certain concepts and concerns already developing within the genre, and for attracting at least some new contributors to the field. If it did nothing more than that, its existence will have been worthwhile.

Cover by Tybus.

ADDITIONAL INPUT

02.19.3 Descendants

Bryant, Edward. *Cinnabar* (collection), Macmillan (US) 1976

Malzberg, Barry N. *Beyond Apollo*, Random House (US) 1972

Tiptree, James, Jr. 'Beam Us Home', *Galaxy* April 1969

03

DEEP PROBES

No broad survey of science fiction would be complete without at least some provision for the opinions of science fiction writers themselves (other than the necessarily brief introductions included in the 'Thematics' section). In the following pages the views of several well-known authors, and of others closely connected with the field, are given in a more philosophical approach. It must be emphasised that the ideas expressed in these essays are personal viewpoints. The reader will discover conflicting judgements and varying degrees of emphasis on the relative importance of particular themes and stories. Not everyone, for example, would rank More's *Utopia* as significantly as both Edmund Cooper and the Australian critic George Turner have chosen to do. But in an area where personal estimations are given free rein, it is almost inevitable (and very certainly inevitable among sf enthusiasts) that disagreements will arise.

03.01 INTERFACE

In inviting leading writers to contribute the following essays, we have entertained no illusions that the opinions expressed would be universally accepted; the authors concerned were equally aware of this reservation. What does emerge in this collection of individual statements is some grasp of the depth of human feeling and aspiration underlying the body of writing classed as science fiction. Edmund Cooper's examination of the relationship between the literature and the development of modern society is essentially an idealistic and sociological survey. Damon Knight's short summary of the elemental 'sense of wonder', which provides such a powerful attraction for sf readers, helps to identify the compulsive hold which this form of speculative writing can exert on its devotees. Sprague de Camp's study of the barbarous elements often found in the work of certain writers, highlights the literary pursuit of an age-old escapist dream. The editor's own contributions investigate the psychological motivations of both writers and readers and briefly review the influence of real science on the genre. Finally, George Turner's critical survey, calculated to stimulate more arguments than it perhaps contains, views the genre within the context of the entire field of English literature, and judges it according to its literary merits.

Captain Nemo.

03.01 INTERFACE

03.01.1 Hardware: the Influence of Science

Every species seeks, within the powers at its disposal, to dominate its environment. It was this conclusion, among others, which persuaded Charles Darwin to withhold his epoch-making findings for some twenty years until the same results, reached independently by Alfred Russel Wallace, prompted the reading of both men's work to the Linnean Society in London in 1858. The following year saw the book publication of *On the Origin of Species*, which Darwin described in a sub-title as an account of the 'preservation of favoured races in the struggle for life'. As such, the study can be regarded as an historical notch-mark through the influence it was to exert over the development of pioneer science fiction, ranging from the lone battle against society of Verne's Captain Nemo in *Twenty Thousand Leagues under the Sea* (1870) to the appalling cannibalistic habits of the subterranean Morlocks in Wells's *The Time Machine* (1895). Darwin's influence, of course, extended far beyond the realms of literature, but his book remains a notable early example of how a scientific theory or discovery has motivated the progress of the genre.

It is possible to look at science fiction as the present day counterpart of a type of speculative writing which dates far back into history. Those early fantasies of the past, however, rarely bore much relation to the science of the time or to what future science might be. More often than not their purpose was satire, and *how* their characters were conveyed to the Moon or to some remote part of Earth was of little relevance to what happened when they arrived.

The accelerating process of mechanical and electrical invention in the nineteenth century was also to have a marked effect on science fiction in its infancy, but its effect on the potential reader must be considered of equal importance. While the term 'science fiction' has never been defined to anyone's complete satisfaction, it must surely be related to that period in time when science and its applications exerted a recognisable influence on the lives of ordinary people. In terms of centuries, that era can be dated from the beginning of the 1800s, when science-based technology began to exert a genuine impact on many levels of society in the industrially developing nations. The general attitude to scientific achievements in the nineteenth century can readily be described as a 'sense of wonder', a climate of opinion in which the amazing machines invented by Jules Verne for his *Voyages Extraordinaires* could be readily accepted by the reader who was already able to see around him the growing benefits of the applied use of science. Wells's early stories, too, made much of this sense of wonder, although the visions they portrayed were often darker than Verne's. However, the two writers shared in common a gift of extrapolating from the latest scientific discoveries.

A review of the rapid advance of scientific and technological innovation since the end of the eighteenth century will set the scene for the personal conclusions of some of the other writers which follow as to its influence on the development of science fiction. In its course, one notes the gradual and then accelerating shift from a sense of wonder to an air of apprehension and, finally, to 'future shock'. The secure Victorian visitors who viewed the

great Crystal Palace Exhibition in London a century and a quarter ago gave way to a public unprepared for horrifying reports of decimated armies drowning in the mud-filled trenches of the First World War, and later to the liberating forces who first broke incredulously into the Nazi concentration camps. A mere two and a half decades separated the Nuremberg war crimes trials from the worldwide television audiences who, at the flick of a switch, could see man's first steps on the Moon, the intricacies of organ transplant surgery, or the defoliation and napalm assaults on an Asian countryside.

Twentieth-century man, surrounded by his scientific miracles and the wonders and disasters to which so many of them have led, may be forgiven for enquiring what has become of much of the progress to which his recent forebears looked ahead with serene expectancy. Science fiction has reflected this critical shift in opinion. Writers have increasingly reviewed developing trends and imagined what may come of them – for good or ill. To this extent many of the better sf stories have acted as critical fingers on the pulse of human ability to handle constructively its unique gift of invention. But they could not have been written without the factual impetus of science; and in as much as that headlong advance has influenced the imaginations of their authors, the art of extrapolating from current trends has been passed back in some measure to the scientists and politicians who should rightly employ it. As James Blish remarked in the 1970 symposium *The Disappearing Future*: . . . 'one cannot open the soberest of scientific journals without finding speculations which make science fiction of the thirties seem tame'. The existence in the USA of Herman Kahn's 'Think-Tanks', Middletown's Institute of the Future and the Arthur D. Little Organisation are evidence enough that the projection of future scenarios is now attracting serious official attention.

To return to the heady days of optimistic advance, thirty years before the curtain rose on the 1800s, James Watt's separate condensing engine had established the concept of mechanical horse-power; and thirty-five years after the turn of the century the Bessemer converter – soon followed by the Siemens regenerative gas furnace – laid the ground for the open hearth process which could produce steel to a given carbon content. The days of the ubiquitous use of iron were numbered.

Another high point in the introduction of the precursors to modern machinery was Henry Maudslay's invention in 1810 of the engineer's self-acting lathe, the first of many such revolutionary ideas to flow from his fertile mind which laid the foundations of the machine-tool industry.

By the mid-nineteenth century, Brunel's giant steamships and the railway engines evolved from Trevithick's coal-hauling mining trucks had given rise to a host of subsidiary industries as suppliers to the technological leaders in the age of steam. The railways began to reduce distances in a cross-country network which could hardly have been envisaged in the days of the stagecoach a few years earlier. News was disseminated faster and rapid communication was to improve beyond all expectations with the discoveries being made in the electrical field.

In 1820 Hans Christian Oersted, working with a voltaic cell and compass needle, established magnetic lines of force. Five years later the first electro-magnet surfaced as the brainchild of William Sturgeon. A further six years saw Faraday's discovery of the principles which led to the introduction of the dynamo and electric motor. Within another decade electrical generators were being driven by coal-raised steam, Joseph Henry had devised the telegraph and Morse the communications code which bears his name. In 1845 the first electric cable was laid beneath the English Channel; eleven years later another spanned the Atlantic. Countries, and beyond them the world, were beginning to grow smaller.

Looked at in retrospect, it is difficult now to credit the sheer pace of change which overtook the sedate Victorian era and provided the foundations for the even more rapid rate of technological and scientific innovation to which twentieth-century man, for better or worse, has been obliged to accustom himself. Not merely change, but new ways of looking at his world and his status within it were assaulting the well-informed citizen at every level. Following Sadi Carnot's *Réflexions sur la Puissance Motrice du Feu* (1824), growing knowledge of the motive power of heat had found expression in the Second Law of Thermodynamics, with the consequent realisation that the stars, including man's own sun, were burning themselves out. Taken with Darwin's evolutionary views, the idea of the eventual physical death of the solar system was hardly guaranteed to provide comfort for those who had until then enjoyed the warm complacency of biblical reassurance.

More was to be added to the ferment. In the British Museum Marx laboured over the formulation of socio-political theories which were finally to influence the way of life of nearly half the world. Towards the century's end Freud had extended his studies of hypnotism (a technique made notorious by Poe's widely read *The Facts in the Case of M. Valdemar* (1845), drawing on the earlier work of Mesmer) and devoted himself to psychological studies in Vienna which led to the birth of psycho-analysis.

A model of the Hovertrain.

03.01 INTERFACE

Within half a dozen years of the advent of the twentieth century, Max Planck and Albert Einstein had revolutionised the field of physics and the latter had, single-handed, altered scientific understanding of the universe by his intuitive exposition of the Special Theory of Relativity.

The first flight: the Wright brothers 1903.

In the same first decade of the twentieth century the era of rapid transport, opened by the coming of the railways, received the added boost of the achievement of manned flight and the development of the automobile. In 1903, in twelve short seconds at Kitty Hawk N.C., two brothers confounded the observation of their father, whose name paradoxically was Wright, that if God had intended man to fly he would have given him wings. The first beginnings of the car dated back to nearly two decades earlier, when Daimler lodged his patent in 1885. Nine years later the Frenchman Panhard introduced the forerunner of the modern automobile, complete with styled chassis, sliding gear transmission, a clutch, brake pedals, foot accelerator, and a front bonnet beneath which vertical cylinders were driven by exploding petrol vapour. Petroleum was indeed the wonder fuel of the age, making possible the rapid advances in both petrol and diesel engines. From the first primitive well drilled in Pennsylvania in 1859, the petroleum industry expanded at an astonishing rate to meet the increased demand for the new, cheap form of energy.

By 1886 the first self-propelled oil tanker was afloat, and screw propellers driven by oil-burning steam turbines were replacing the paddle wheel and the lofty canvas of the windjammer. In the following decade William Richard Morris (later Lord Nuffield) was experimenting with bicycles in a shed at Cowley in England, and in America, mechanic Henry Ford was busy planning the world's first car-production line. In 1904 one of his automobiles was driven at 91.4 mph; roadside petrol pumps appeared in 1907; the first electric starter choked an engine into life in 1912. By then Blériot's epoch-making cross-Channel flight was already three years old, and Alcock and Brown's trans-Atlantic crossing lay a mere six years ahead.

The period of rapid transport had dawned, leading not only to the refinements of travel experienced today, but also to the imaginary extensions of the process exploited by science fiction writers – the travelators and moving roadways portrayed by Asimov and Heinlein, the automatically guided car envisaged by countless authors, the rocketships and the diminutive personal flyer.

Perhaps more direct in its impact on the individual at the beginning of the 1900s was the development of cities. In 1902 the first skyscraper was completed in New York on the intersection of Fifth Avenue and 23rd Street. New materials and techniques, coupled with improved transport facilities, were laying the foundations of the urban sprawl and overloaded conurbations which were to exacerbate the social problems of the mid-twentieth century. Self-sustaining cities may have found a place in Verne's *Propeller Island* (1895), and much later in Blish's 'Cities in Flight' series, but they have yet to be discovered on the real Earth.

While the average citizen might justifiably marvel at the mechanical progress with which he suddenly found himself surrounded in the early years of the twentieth century, it was probably not until the outbreak of the First World War in 1914 that he experienced with a brutal shock the realisation that the developments in weaponry and the engines of destruction had kept pace with the more peaceful uses of technology. The general staffs on either side were no less surprised; they were not long in demonstrating their complete unpreparedness for a new type of warfare which the ingenuity of the armaments manufacturer had made possible. The soldier on the front saw the results at first hand; if he was fortunate enough to return home, he had few reservations in expressing his views. The glamour of war vanished in the reckoning of the millions dead and the physical and psychological damage to those who survived.

When such sf writers as Heinlein have attempted to resurrect the glorification of war in future settings, the reactions of readers have usually been mixed. However, the First World War was certainly to influence the early pulp contributors in their depiction of such conflicts. War

and even limited hostile encounters were shown as a brutal and annihilating business. The adventurous appeal of the combat spacecraft and its daredevil crew was one thing, but there was little that was idealised about the carnage which ensued. Such devastation had of course already been predicted in the stories of Wells and such early authors as M. P. Shiel. In the former's *The War of the Worlds* (1898), *The War in the Air* (1908) and *The World Set Free* (1914), the havoc created by new or alien weapons was set out in detail; but it must be recorded that Wells was as shocked as anybody by the genuine advent of a world war. Although he had allowed his imagination to play about it, he had never at heart believed that the statesmen would be foolhardy enough to let it happen.

The two decades immediately following the war saw a redoubling of the pace of technical innovation. They were the early days of sound broadcasting, and later of the first television transmissions. Sound in the cinema and the colour film were introduced within a year or two of each other, and before the 1920s were out the list also included the autogiro, geiger counters, and frozen foods. The following decade saw the development of radio-astronomy, radar, the helicopter and jet engines, together with the manufacture of synthetic detergents and fabrics, perspex, polyethylene and DDT. The invention of the helicopter is a classic example of the influence of science fiction on a genuine technological development. The description of Verne's hundred-foot long 'Clipper of the Clouds', made airborne by some ninety horizontal rotorblades, inspired Sikorsky to develop the helicopter which still bears his name.

The six-years' conflict of the Second World War only served to accelerate the pace of invention, much of it necessitated by the need for new and more effective weaponry and superior defence installations. Long-range rocketry and supersonic flight were but two of the innovations which could also lend themselves to peaceful use, while the subsequent computer industry owed its beginnings to the instrumentation systems devised for guidance and detection by both the Allies and the Axis powers. Finally, on 16th July, 1945, when the war in Europe was already over, the energy of the atom was released in a fireball which rose high over Alamogordo in the New Mexican desert. Within a month it rose again over the Japanese city of Hiroshima, the first of two such cataclysms which brought the Pacific war to a close.

The reactions of science fiction writers to the atomic threat have been covered in some detail in the 'Thematics' section. Few of them were unmoved, and if their feelings were often a mixture of horror and excitement, it was because they were able to imagine the advantages as well as the disadvantages which atomic power could bring to man. Some of them, in fact, most notably Heinlein, had expressed them even before Alamogordo.

Not many, however, had foreseen the rapid rise of the computer to become the almost indispensible servo-mechanism of the future. The first such machines to operate in the US were so cumbersome as to be almost unrecognisable beside the slim compact models of today. ENIAC, which came into service at the University of Pennsylvania in 1946, ran on 18,000 thermionic valves and some 5000 switches. Not until the introduction of transistors and integrated circuits in the late 1950s was the size of computer hardware substantially reduced and its scope greatly increased. With the advent of lasers in the 1960s, a memory bank which would once have had to be stored on a hundred miles of magnetic tape could be comfortably housed on a rectangle of nickel foil some eight inches by ten. The computer, and the science of cybernetics to which it helped to give birth, is now so standard a feature of sf stories that, unless it is essential to the plot, it is simply assumed that one will be in the background somewhere and little attention is paid to it.

Since the Second World War, the world has passed

03.01 INTERFACE

through a series of epochs – each overlapping, and each continuing. They include the ages of the atom, of cybernetics, of space, and of molecular biology. On the social and psychological fronts, it has also seen increasingly the Age of Rising Expectations. Nothing has contributed more to this final age than the instant worldwide communications network now maintained largely with the help of artificial satellites, themselves a product of the Space Age. It is difficult to credit in retrospect that Arthur C. Clarke's arguments for the use of communications satellites during the 1940s were dismissed as 'futuristic'. A decade later many distinguished members of the British Association for the Advancement of Science objected to the idea of a session on interplanetary flight as so much science fiction; and as late as 1956 the British Astronomer Royal rejected the concept of man venturing into space as so much nonsense. Today Clarke is the possessor of the only television receiver in Sri Lanka, a gift from the government, on which he picks up via satellite the Indian educational programmes that he foresaw in *Profiles of the Future* in 1962.

Through the satellite, science has brought within the grasp of the most far-flung communities the growing realisation of change. The knowledge of the wealth and abilities of the technologically advanced countries has spurred the rising expectations of the less privileged world. The process of change has not been lost on the poorer nations, whose clamour for a share of the advance is heard as stridently over the communications systems as the data bursts of computers exchanging information across the oceans. The immense improvement in rapid communication will doubtless eliminate much of the need for travel in the immediate future. Private, but multiple, tv hook-ups between politicians, business executives and others across global distances will eventually overcome the disadvantages of 'jet lag'. Meetings will be held in which individual participants, if not ideologically, will at least be literally half the world apart – a concept now so much a part of the background of science fiction that, as in the case of computers, it is taken for granted.

Science, too, has played its part in the population crises of the Third World. In 1911 Ehrlich discovered that particular germs could be killed inside a living body. Twenty-four years later Domagk, at the German I.G. Farben corporation, injected a red dye into his daughter whom he feared was dying of septicaemia. It was an act of desperation, for although he had experimented with the dye, he had still to carry out clinical tests. The daughter recovered, and the first of the sulpha drugs, 'Prontosil', had demonstrated its worth. The development of penicillin by Florey and Chain in 1938, based on Fleming's discovery of ten years earlier, added a further formidable weapon to the medical armoury. The lives of literally millions were saved, and the future survival of those as yet unborn came nearer to being guaranteed. But for all its curative powers, medicine does not feed; paradoxically it has led to more empty bellies, more protein deficiency, than the miracles of science have been able to solve, held back as they are by the shortcomings of planning and economics. The perils of overpopulation have occupied the serious attention of many sf writers, Brunner, Harrison and Vonnegut among them. It is a continuing and major theme in the genre.

In a parallel vein, the rising expectations of the poor have been explored in science fiction, often by the allegorical means of portraying backward alien planets which are either helped, hindered, or sometimes merely plundered by space-descending Earthmen. The old colonialist dream lives on as some sf writers' stock-in-trade, but alongside it has grown up a greater awareness of the mutual responsibility which should be shared between all sentient life.

The Age of Molecular Biology, dating from 1953 when Crick and Watson unravelled the double helix of deoxyribonucleic acid (DNA), revealing the genetic pattern of life, again presents as many dangers as possible benefits. It may well see the continuous eradication of genetic defects in the future, or it could herald an era of oppression in which some human beings could be 'engineered' into little more than tailor-made zombies. In this it is akin to the striking advance in neuro-physiology which also dates from 1953 when Eccles identified the chemical nature of the synapse, the gap across which messages are transmitted from one brain cell to another. By establishing that it was a chemical link, he opened the way to the control of the synaptic clefts by the use of drugs – still a controversial aid in the treatment of mental illness, but also a psychological tool of dangerous dimensions in the wrong hands.

A very sizeable book could be written, and must surely soon be compiled, on the two-way cross-fertilisation of ideas between the progress of science and the reactions, or previews, which run beside it in the literary field. This short consideration of some of the major landmarks has left much unsaid which we could imagine being described at length in such a work. The prospects of mining the vast wealth of minerals deposited as nodules on the ocean bed, the techniques of fish-farming and the advanced use of hydroponics in the production of food, the direct harnessing of solar energy and the development of magneto-hydrodynamics and fuel cells in the provision of electrical power – these are a few further items among many more which have featured in the pages of science fiction either concurrently with, or before, their appearance in the field of genuine science. But in addition to such 'hard' scientific subjects, the more recent preoccupation of sf writers with the life sciences and social and inter-personal relationships points the way to a stimulation of ideas which is the hallmark of any of the better branches of literature.

Brian Ash

03.01.2 Interaction: Science Fiction and Society

At this point in time, towards the end of the twentieth century, science fiction has emerged from the literary ghetto unwittingly created for it by prolific and frequently bad American pulp-magazine writers of the twenties, thirties and forties, and has survived the indignities imposed upon it by catchpenny editors and publishers. As social commentary, science fiction is now taken more seriously than it has been hitherto. Students from every academic discipline – from literature to science – take a great interest in the genre. It has become a part of an intellectual revolution.

Why should science fiction have become 'respectable' almost overnight? The answer is alarmingly simple. Thinking people everywhere have begun to realise two things: one, that they are living in a science fiction world made real; two, that the sophisticated, technology-based civilisation that we have created is approaching critical mass, that it is ready to explode. History has shown that no civilisation, no culture, is immortal and there is no reason to suppose that our machine-based culture will be an exception to this general pattern.

A huge scientific and technological revolution has taken place in a very short space of time. A single lifetime spans the development of the motor car, the use of electrical power, radio communications, air travel, antibiotics, nuclear energy, computers and manned expeditions to the Moon. Many of the older citizens in technologically advanced countries are already living in a state of what Alvin Toffler has described as 'future shock'; many of the younger people cannot cope with this tremendous rate of change. Some try to evolve alternative societies; some seek more desperate remedies through drugs, crime and/or violence.

Technology alone has not been able to solve the twin problems of overpopulation and starvation in underdeveloped countries. At the same time, it has enabled us to stockpile enough nuclear weapons to wipe out the entire human race. Thus, while science and technology have greatly amplified our capacity to create, they have also amplified our capacity to destroy. People now see a clearer relationship between the worlds of science fiction and the world they live in and are beginning to look to science fiction for guidelines to the future. Where do we go from here?

This is the wrong approach, for although some science fiction contains prophetic elements, the genre cannot be defined as a literature of prophecy. Science fiction writers are not clairvoyant; they are simply writers who consider alternative scenarios. Their most useful function is to anticipate and define problems, to stimulate thought, perhaps even to suggest possible solutions.

This is precisely what the best of them have been doing. Within recent years, for example, a number of outstanding writers have extrapolated from significant technological and political developments to illustrate dangers that *may* lie ahead. The problems inherent in the unrestricted development of automated means of production, and its social consequences, were brilliantly highlighted by Kurt Vonnegut in *Player Piano*. The results of uncontrolled population growth and the consequent rat syndrome – where people turn on each other – have been portrayed in outstanding future scenarios by John Brunner in *Stand on Zanzibar*, and Harry Harrison in *Make Room! Make Room!* With *The Space Merchants*, Pohl and Kornbluth showed the nightmarish possibilities already apparent in the phenomenal growth of the advertising industry, and posed the question: where is the boundary between legitimate advertising and illegal and immoral brainwashing? Other distinguished writers have tackled such

Father forgive them for they know not what they do.

themes as pollution, the proliferation of nuclear energy plants, the alarming aspects of genetic engineering, bacteriological warfare, food shortage, climatic instability as a result of industrial development, deliberately induced mutation, and so on.

It is in this area of science fiction – not in the area devoted to the development of galactic empires, FTL drives, alien invasions, interstellar confrontations and battles – where the interaction between science fiction and society exists. Here is the point at which science fiction is seen to be most relevant.

The grand cosmic visions of Olaf Stapledon's *Last and First Men*, a brilliant and seminal work which has inspired science fiction readers and writers alike to lofty perspectives, have little or no immediacy. Stapledon's unfettered imagination spans millions of years and the rise and fall of numerous civilisations, but it has little relevance to the problems which beset our contemporary world and which are likely to become more acute with the passing of each decade. In contrast to *Last and First Men*, Kurt Vonnegut's *Breakfast of Champions* is a caustic satire on life in near-contemporary America. It is an indictment

of an entire social system – a way of life and a set of moral values that are seen to be transforming human beings into flesh-coloured plastic androids.

Stapledon deals with evolution spanning centuries; Vonnegut deals with the plight of people in a technologically advanced society at a given point in time. Vonnegut's book is the result of immediate feedback between society and the creative artist. Stapledon's viewpoint tends towards that of the detached observer, the objective philosopher, the 'future historian'. Yet both novels have one thing in common. Each writer, in his own way, has rejected traditional patterns of thinking and conventional ways of looking at the world. In this way, they highlight an important attribute of science fiction, for, at its best, science fiction is a revolt against orthodoxy – against orthodox attitudes, orthodox values, orthodox behaviour, orthodox thinking. It offers new ways of looking at the microcosm that is man and the macrocosm of his total environment, and at the interaction between the two.

Ideas can be just as dangerous to the social status quo as nuclear weapons, perhaps even more so. The system of ideas expressed in *Das Kapital* by Karl Marx, published just over a century ago, has been ultimately responsible for radically changing the social systems under which half the world's population live. Fundamentally, however, the concepts propounded by Marx were not new. The basic ideas had been embodied in a work (which some dub science fiction) written more than four and a half centuries ago. In its day, this book triggered intellectual explosions in the minds of scholars and thinking people throughout Europe. It was a best-seller when it was first published in 1516, and was written in Latin, the *lingua franca* of the civilised world, so that there were no translation problems. And the book added a new word to the English language.

The word was *Utopia*.

The book *Utopia* by Thomas More, was a landmark in literature and its influence has continued down the centuries, providing the basis for much development in political thought, and creating a sub-genre of 'utopian romance' which other writers have used to develop their notions of an ideal society or to obliquely criticise the societies in which they live. This has led to another mode of expression – 'dystopian' fiction – with similar ends: not, obviously, to provide blueprints for ideal societies but to criticise existing society and the implications of its current technological, scientific and social trends. These kinds of science fiction have developed into a potent social force, commanding the attention and shaping the opinions of people at many levels.

Among the most effective and enduring dystopian novels are: *Gulliver's Travels* (1726) by Jonathan Swift; *Erewhon* (1872) by Samuel Butler; *Brave New World* (1932) by Aldous Huxley; *Ape and Essence* (1949) also by Huxley; and Orwell's haunting, nightmarish *Nineteen Eighty-four* (1949). Such books stand as massive indictments of social attitudes, institutions, political ethics, the misuse of scientific and technological developments. They have helped to create a climate of dissidence, and have made articulate the growing dissatisfaction of sensitive and intelligent people with the many corruptions to which civilisation is heir. They have, in fact, acted as social catalysts.

William Morris 1834–1896.

Those writers who stayed with the utopian tradition of proposing scenarios for a perfect society have not been quite so effective. Tommaso Campanella's *City of the Sun* (1623) did introduce what were at the time revolutionary notions of birth control and selective breeding; but although utopian in aim, it became dystopian in content. Edward Bellamy's *Looking Backward* (1887) and William Morris's *News from Nowhere* (1890) both suffer from the same affliction. Nevertheless, both utopian and dystopian writers have had a profound effect upon our cultural and social heritage, and in this sense it would seem that science fiction has a special critical role to play in the evolution of the modern world.

From The Master of the World *by Jules Verne.*

In relation to this, the impact of the two giants of science fiction, Jules Verne and H. G. Wells, should be considered. Verne, the provincial Frenchman, was born in 1828 and was publishing science fiction before Wells was born – thus enabling Wells to profit from a climate of speculative thought already well established by Verne at the time Wells took up his pen.

The nineteenth century was the age of mechanical marvels, the age of scientific progress. The Industrial Revolution had borne its first fruits, men like Isambard Kingdom Brunel had wrought engineering miracles, railways and steamships had revolutionised transport; Europeans and Britons were engaged in empire building and there was a tremendous sense of confidence in the future. Verne's writings reflected the spirit of the age, dealing as they did with airships, submarines, voyages to the Moon, and so on. He was, essentially, utopian in attitude, believing, until his final works, that the future must be good. As the eternal optimist, secure in his French provincial morality, he believed that if the World State were ever established, it would be due to French inspiration, French ideas, French examples.

Verne was a superb entertainer, developing ingenious plots, ingenious gadgetry and vivid backgrounds, but his characterisation was poor, and his philosophy simple. Nevertheless, his stories stimulated much thought about the possibilities of the future and – most importantly – helped to develop the kind of climate in which the genius of Wells could flourish.

Wells, however, was more than a superb entertainer: he was a man with a mission. Through the media of science fiction he propagated new ideas, new attitudes to society, new attitudes to the future, new political structures. Even in his first novel – painstakingly written and rewritten until he found the right mood and level – he established his revolt against orthodoxy. *The Time Machine* was, and still is, one of the outstanding short novels in the genre. In it, Wells tilted at Victorian complacency, daring to suggest that the might of empires and empire builders was as ephemeral as last year's autumn leaves, that nobody ever wins wars and that the human race could wind up degenerate, self-destructive, and mindless. His successive novels pursued his revolt against traditional thinking, and the status quo.

Although Wells was a political propagandist, an historian and a populariser of science, he is mostly remembered for his science fiction works, which remain the best expression of his revolutionary ideas. In this sense Wells's work is a very good example of science fiction playing a meaningful role in the dialogue between society and the individual.

It was not a science fiction novel but a play which generated philosophical problems that are still being debated and will continue to be debated until science fiction becomes science fact. And, once, again, the English language was endowed with a new word: robot.

The play was *Rossum's Universal Robots* (R.U.R.) and was the work of a brilliant Czech writer, Karel Čapek. It was written in 1920 and had immediate international success. *R.U.R.* was by no means Čapek's only venture into science fiction but it is his best known. The play suggested new horizons of scientific possibilities, and raised new moral, psychological and philosophical problems, for his robots were not machines: they were manlike, android. And being like men they developed emotions, which led them to compete with men for dominance and survival. A century before, Mary Shelley had posed similar problems with her story, *Frankenstein, or the Modern Prometheus*; but with *R.U.R.* these were writ large.

From the play R.U.R.

In the present time, when computers have become commonplace, when *learning* machines are being developed, and artificial intelligence intensively researched, these problems are seen not as products of imaginative fantasy but as matters relevant to our future. Naturally the question of control is important in this context – and not only of robots and machines, but of society and the individual within it. In answer to this, Aldous Huxley proposed a kind of perfect society which technology could bring about, in *Brave New World* (1932).

Although not the first book to dwell upon the implications of a totally programmed society, Huxley's novel was the most powerful, the most effective. At a time of social upheaval in Europe, when regimentation of thought and behaviour had become an established political philosophy, Huxley made his scathing attack on the ultimate regimentation – the perfectly ordered society – achieved not by the brute strength and the coarse conditioning methods of the Nazis and fascists, but by a masterly programme of scientific manipulation. In *Brave New World*, every individual received pre-natal and post-natal conditioning to accept happily his or her appointed social destiny. The right to be unhappy – and, thus, by implication, the right to reject and criticise – had been eliminated.

Huxley's nightmarish vision had a great influence. Pavlov's work on the conditioned reflex and behaviourism was already well known. The use of 'mind-bending' drugs had been developed; the strength of propaganda was well established; 'selective breeding' had been removed from the realm of biology to that of politics; the 'social authority' of radio existed, and that of television was just around the corner. The 'image makers' had begun to pioneer their industry. In considering the implications of these developments, people began to look at their social and political systems more critically. *Brave New World* is now read widely in schools and universities. Just as it had once been observed that war was much too serious a matter to be left to generals, so is it realised that science is too serious a matter to be left to scientists. Seventeen years later, in 1949, George Orwell, disillusioned by his own political experiences, produced an even more powerful literary bombshell with *Nineteen Eighty-four*. In it, he represented the final dehumanisation of the individual by political terror harnessed to the sophisticated techniques of modern communications systems, propaganda and psychological warfare. He extrapolated from the methods used by Torquemada, Stalin and Hitler; he 'updated' the *auto-da-fé*, the Star Chamber, the Moscow Trials, the Gestapo cellars. He produced a horrifying scenario in which the future of mankind could only be described as 'double-plus-ungood'. He initiated the phrase 'Big Brother Is Watching You!'

The key concepts of *Nineteen Eighty-four* have become part of the political idiom of our time. The very frequency with which such ideas are reiterated or referred to in the press and other media is an indication of their lasting effect. The pen may or may not be mightier than the sword, but, wielded effectively, it is certainly strong enough to make the blade blunt. And it is certainly powerful enough to expose the motivations and techniques of ruthless men and ruthless political systems.

This article has attempted to examine the different ways in which works of science fiction and developments within society have interacted with each other. It can be seen that the more noteworthy works of science fiction have helped to direct and mould our cultural, social and political attitudes in a world desperately trying to keep pace with the speed of its own technological advancement.

One wonders how the literary historians of the future will view the science fiction writers of the twentieth century. Will they assign greater significance to the works of Asimov, Clarke, Heinlein, Aldiss than, say, to the dystopian works of Vonnegut, Brunner, Ballard or Pohl and Kornbluth? Aldiss may be a fine, imaginative writer; and Asimov, Clarke and Heinlein may be great innovators in terms of anticipating the trends in science and technology. But they have little or no relevant social comment to make. Generally, they are more concerned about the development of future 'hardware' and ingenious situations than about people. Whereas Vonnegut and other similar writers are deeply concerned not only about our immediate social problems but about the social and economic conditions of a foreseeable future in which their and our children may have to live. It is their work which, deriving from a long tradition, promotes intelligent speculation about the future condition of mankind, and alerts people to social dangers which may not, as yet, be fully apparent.

Edmund Cooper

BIG BROTHER

IS WATCHING

YOU

Poster from the film 1984.

03.02 SCIENCE FICTION AS LITERATURE

Science fiction as literature? The phrase begs questions. Science fiction is a form of literature, be it good, indifferent or bad, and it is as well to face at the outset that a dismaying amount of it is bad. However, in turning attention towards the more significant works of science fiction, several questions arise: Is science fiction a viable form of world literature? Has science fiction produced any great or near-great literature? What special literary, as against scientific and philosophic, considerations must be accounted for when evaluating science fiction as a viable literary form? What, if any, are the special values science fiction can contribute to world literature? What is the present position of science fiction vis-à-vis 'mainstream' fiction? (We will rid ourselves of that particularly inept term, 'mainstream', as soon as possible.)

None of these questions can be profitably posed until a useful definition of the term 'science fiction' is arrived at; some consideration is given to the specific ingredients of the science fiction story which distinguish it from other types of fiction; and some critical standards are set up whereby these characteristics can be evaluated as useful contributions to literature.

No single definition of 'science fiction' has ever been generally agreed upon, and consideration of the dozens that have been suggested would fill a book. Among the better informed, Isaac Asimov has offered that it is fiction about the future of science and scientists, and Theodore Sturgeon that the term can be applied only to a story wherein removal of its scientific content would invalidate the narrative. Superficially reasonable, both suggestions postulate science as an essential ingredient. What, then, of such a work as H. G. Wells's 'A Story of the Days to Come' (1897), which features neither science nor scientists but presents a fairly comprehensive view of social aspects of a possible future? Social theorising has always been an agreed area of the science fiction field, and is indeed the one which encourages its greatest vitality; it cannot be dismissed for the sake of an easy phrase. Science fiction must reach beyond science or be limited to gadgetry.

Beginning as simple lack of agreement, confusion has spread to publishers and their editors as well as to writers and critics. Booming science fiction sales have encouraged publishers to hand the 'sf' label on any fiction even slightly to the side of centre, so that seriously crafted works share classification (and the same store shelves) with black magic, 'westerns' wherein mutated cowboys ride spaceships instead of horses and an abominable hybrid known to its devotees as 'sword-'n-sorcery'. Peter Nicholls, Administrator of the Science Fiction Foundation in Britain, is on record (*Foundation*, No 6) as feeling that definition may be impossible, and this must stand as comment enough on the present condition of confusion. One result of this chaos is that anyone seeking to write seriously about science ficion is forced to originate his own definition in order to be understood, and it is little wonder that the critics of the larger corpus of literature despair of making sense of a genre whose very practitioners cannot define it. The present writer is therefore constrained, in the interest of lucidity, to attempt yet another definition.

Since novels and stories labelled (rightly or wrongly) science fiction cover much of the ground traditionally established as the preserve of other genres – adventure, satire, social comment, farce, horror, crime detection, etc – any difference must reside not so much in content as in the writer's approach to the content. Briefly, the statements in this essay are postulated on the premise that science fiction offers an alternative approach to the common concerns of that great mass of fiction which is based upon the known facts of life and its environment. One may regard this 'great mass' as realistic fiction (a more useful term than 'mainstream', which has, in critical parlance, a meaning other than that foisted on it by science fiction fans), indicating that it is bound by an acceptance of the realities of existence as we know them. Its opposite, non-realistic fiction, usually identifies itself as a familiar genre, fantasy, wherein known parameters of existence are ignored in favour of unrestricted fancy. Between these lies science fiction, suggesting alternative modes of existence (in future times, on other worlds or simply in the minds of the characters) based on facts which connect them with the real world while confining the imaginative element to logical development.

Jules Verne, the first major populariser of the genre, eschewed fantasy but chafed at the limitations of observed fact. The 'marvellous journeys' he wrote of could be achieved only by moving beyond fact into possibility, by conceiving the submarine, the aircraft, the space rocket as logically arrived-at alternatives to the familiar modes of exploring the universe. He created the sub-genre of technological science fiction wherein alternatives are constructed by extrapolation from hard scientific facts. Thus the realistic parameters were overleapt while insistence on logic rather than imaginative irresponsibility held the works short of fantasy.

Verne's younger contemporary, H. G. Wells, observed types of alternatives other than the technological and may be regarded as the modern father of the speculative works which represent science fiction at its best. Alternative forms of life, he proposed, are not chimerae but logical possibilities to be included in a rational vision of the universe – so his Martians in *The War of the Worlds* became blunt warnings that we may not be alone, and his Selenites in *The First Men in the Moon* were reasoned statements that man is not necessarily Nature's only way of achieving intellect, or even the best way. Alternatives to brutishness are open to men of goodwill, he pointed out in *Men Like Gods*, and open to the apathetic are class tyranny (*When the Sleeper Wakes*) or naïve ineffectuality (*The Time Machine*); brute man, he said, can realise his utopias or follow other alternatives into the hells of blind achievement of *The Invisible Man* and *The Island of Dr Moreau*.

The Wellsian method has been refined and subtilised by later writers but never abandoned. The technological school of Verne persists, but the speculative areas opened up by Wells have proven inexhaustible. Modern science fiction scours science, art and philosophy for alternative possibilities of living, of action, of seeing, thinking and desiring. When it explores these possibilities with such logic as the writer can bring to bear, without succumbing to the transient escapism of fantasy, science fiction serves a purpose outside the common limits of realistic fiction. So it seems reasonable to this writer to categorise science fiction as the literature of possible alternatives.

The literary techniques and priorities of science fiction differ from those of realistic and fantastic fiction. An understanding of these is necessary to the appreciation of

03.02 SCIENCE FICTION AS LITERATURE

the author's intention in many stories and essential to critical summation. This does not imply a necessity for a 'double standard' of criticism (the idea is repellent), but for a willingness on the part of the general reader as well as the critic to appreciate the force and validity of alternative methods of construction. Movements in music, drama and painting have always encountered critical difficulties and have won recognition only by persistence in producing works of quality; science fiction, though arguably a lesser form than any of these, faces the same barriers to appreciation. Some of these are examined below.

'Fiction of alternatives' seems a harmless phrase, but its effect on literary method in science fiction is devastating. It often implies a total shift of the writer's, and hence the reader's, attention from humanity to humanity's environment. When the writer speculates on humanity under some set of alternative conditions (i.e. facing some not impossible catastrophe such as a new ice age, reacting to beings from another world, dealing with the shocking possibilities of molecular biology, etc), the alternative condition takes the centre of his literary stage rather than the group of characters who will act out his parable of tomorrow or his metaphor for cultural shock. The alternative condition is both the nexus and the ambience of his work; the characters serve the purpose of demonstrating how the realities of his alternative will affect men and women. So an old literary axiom is reversed. The characters do not determine, as they generally do in realistic fiction, the action of the story; instead they move within an environment and demonstrate by their activities what the effects of the environment are. Plot is no longer 'character in action' but the action of an environment on the humanity within it. The reader's attention is required for an utterly unfamiliar world and the activities of the characters are designed to probe this unfamiliarity.

Traditional criticism sometimes fails to grasp this simple but crucial point. Critics complain of the lack of depth in science fiction characterisation, but few have perceived that this is often a necessary factor in the concise presentation of the writer's thesis. He has a world to describe; highly individualised characters will behave altogether too individually to fit into a demonstration which must show the effects of the alternative environment on the generality of humanity. The characters must become, within limits of common sense, types of the human race under pressure.

A science fiction which produced only featureless puppets moving to the push and pull of their surroundings could never become a viable literary form. Nevertheless, this condition prevailed in the magazine field (which was virtually the entire field) prior to the Second World War, but in the 1940s and 1950s writers began to tackle the problems of characterisation. Hampered by the blunt exigencies of magazine publication, progress was slow, but a certain liveliness appeared. Only when a few courageous publishers (science fiction had no general popularity at that time) commissioned books for bound publication were authors able to discard the magazine-format shackles, although the possibility of serialisations in the magazines enabled them to attempt the novel-length form. A fair sample of these attempts may be cited in Walter M. Miller's *A Canticle for Leibowitz*, published in 1960. This excellent novel, whose overall theme was the role of religion in future years, portrayed no less than three visions of tomorrow's alternatives, set at various dates after a nuclear holocaust, yet Miller was able to include a number of excellent character vignettes and psychological insights which gave warmth to a chilling tale. He devised incidents which allowed private decision-making, rescued his cast from puppetry without allowing them to obscure the fabric of his alternative creation. He worked no miracles in depth but demonstrated that something better than paper cut-outs could be effected.

Since the presentation of the salient aspects of an alternative condition normally requires a considerable amount of varied plot activity, science fiction has tended towards the thriller type of story rather than the carefully expository, and charcterisation has suffered accordingly in tough-guy spacemen and heroes who 'see red' when required to act against unlikely odds. Still, a fairly large group of talented writers has succeeded in producing human beings who move and breathe within their restrictive environments. Damon Knight, Thomas Disch, Brian Aldiss and J. G. Ballard spring to mind among a clutch of others. None, however, has come as close to solving this bedevilling dilemma as Ursula Le Guin in *The Dispossessed*. Having conceived a problem requiring the parallel presentation of two opposed alternative cultures, Mrs Le Guin attempted to solve it by overlaying direct environmental description with a large cast of contrasted characters thrown into conflict situations. These were resolved, mainly through discussion, in terms which resolved the environmental forces at work while they allowed the persons involved to speak with individual accents. The striking approach cannot be repeated indefinitely, but any solution is an encouragement to seek others. The book finally produced no superlative characterisations and the environmental picture ultimately (and properly) overshadowed the human beings, but the total impact was of life in teeming multiplicity.

If science fiction has offered few memorable humans it has, in the topsy-turvy nature of the beast, thrown up some very memorable non-human beings. There is something timelessly fascinating about Isaac Asimov's robot, R. Daneel Olivaw, Stanley Weinbaum's crazy Martian bird (if that is the term for it), Tweel, Henry Kuttner's hilarious family of immortal mutants named Hogben and not to be in any sense confused with humanity, and the solemn, passionless menace of Wells's Grand Lunar. These are exotics, and their persistence points to the dominance, in science fiction, of environment over character, for each of these was a major metaphor for the alternative creation being described. Something is surely lost in this reversal of priorities, but it may be argued that characterisation in depth is not and never has been an absolute criterion in fiction, which is a synthesis of balanced elements each of which is, ideally, given only the prominence required to fit into a harmonious composition. Informed criticism should take note of character playing its proper role, which in science fiction is rarely dominant.

The dominance of ambience over character also created narrative difficulties, which were not resolved for many years. What in a realistic novel was background, became in science fiction the foreground, of which complete understanding was necessary for the following of the narrative. Verne, no great stylist, simply offered his alternatives in lengthy slabs of lecturing from some expert, inserted into the story's cast for the purpose, who reeled off encyclopedic facts and statistics while the plot waited patiently for a page or two. His nineteenth-century public accepted this; he was opening up marvels to a fact-hungry generation which esteemed snippets of 'general knowledge' as cultural status symbols. The mathematical dissertations (mostly incorrect) in *From Earth to the Moon*, stunningly inept today, were to his contemporaries among the glories of the book. Wells, a much superior craftsman, used the 'lecture' method once (the 'instantaneous cube' speech in *The Time Machine*) and never made the mistake again. He used oblique methods of allusion and inference, with the occasional key fact worked smoothly into dialogue or action, giving an impression of continuous scientific exposition when in fact he was skilfully leading the reader to build the alternative concept for himself from the planted hints.

No novelist of equal skill succeeded Wells for a generation after he abandoned his 'scientific romances', and in 1932 Aldous Huxley's *Brave New World* was a lonely peak in a desert of dreariness. Not until John Campbell, as editor of *Astounding*, set out singlehandedly to reform magazine science fiction in the late 1930s did anything resembling regular competence appear among the newer writers. That Campbell succeeded in raising literary standards, despite his contemptuous abuse of the literary 'establishment' and its criteria, is science fiction history, as extraordinary in its way as the stories he published. His most useful service was probably his insistence that the alternative condition of stories be a pervasive feature rather than a plastered-on collage of lectures and descriptions. If none of his writers ever matched the stylishness of Wells, at least they recovered his techniques and in many cases improved on them (e.g. Lester del Rey, Theodore Sturgeon, Wilson Tucker).

This distinctive technical problem of the genre, the integrated presentation of an alternative condition as a natural development of the narrative, is the one innovatory technique that science fiction has added to the normal repertoire of the fiction writer. The method has now become so essential and unobtrusive a part of narration that lecturing (still practised by Fred Hoyle, Robert Heinlein and a few others) arouses impatience in the reader, who has learned to demand a degree of literary smoothness.

A further technical consideration is the handling of science itself as central to the fiction. It is a common sneer that the science in science fiction is mostly inaccurate, and for hack work the sneer is usually justified. But science fiction should not be judged by its hacks any more than realistic fiction should be judged by the excesses of Harold Robbins. The seriously intentioned science fiction writer – that is, the writer with a case to state, a problem to explore, a prophecy to make – will verify his facts, lay or scientific, to the full resource of his research facilities. Thus Blish's *A Case of Conscience* and Huxley's *Brave New World* were solidly based on the biological knowledge of their day; Stapledon's *Odd John* owed much to its author's careful observation of the real capacities and limitations of the human brain; Le Guin's care to stay within strict scientific limits saved her from striking discordant notes in *The Dispossessed*; and strict adherence to a formal mathematical conception gave even such a freak as Christopher Priest's *Inverted World* a rigidity which defeated criticism. This is as it should be. A reader presented with a seriously intentioned work has a right to demand accuracy in supportive details; factual error invalidates the conception and flaws the novel irredeemably. A thing is right or wrong, and it is the informed critic's duty to say so.

Even so, there are awkward conditions to be noted. One is the staggering pace of scientific discovery. The hard fact which existed imperishably when the writer began his novel becomes discredited in the six months of its composition, or some new observation invalidates the whole of his extrapolation. He can scarcely be blamed for the march of research. And so Butler's *Erewhon* is no less a successful utopian romance because we know now that no such place can exist in New Zealand, nor is Verne's *Master of the World* to be rejected out of hand because engineering advances eventually produced an answer other than his to the problem of heavier-than-air flying machines. The psychology of many fine nineteenth-century realistic novels is suspect in the light of modern theory; they are nonetheless standard works whose very flaws are testimony to the genuineness of their ambience. The good faith of the writer must be allowed for the state of knowledge at the time of writing.

Matter for discontent lies in auctorial irresponsibility in offering arbitrary statement instead of reasoned extrapolation. Wells, elaborating on trends observable in the society of 1899, evolved the layered social structure of *When the Sleeper Wakes*, and if he was astray in total forecast he came uncomfortably close to the present in many details, for his extrapolation was intelligent and logical. That history veered from his described course does not reduce his ideas to nonsense; prediction, save in the most elastic terms, is not the business of science fiction, while logical consideration of possibilities extended from present knowledge should be. But how much science fiction extrapolation is logical? Hacks, clinging to sales gimmicks, have observed the prominence of violent crime since 1950 and have extrapolated this trend into nightmare futures wherein no man walks a street in safety; that trends are modified, altered and inverted by inherent social and psychological factors has been ignored by them, as has the simple probability that a totally violent culture would not be viable in terms of functioning cities and states. Samples of pseudo-extrapolation could be multiplied indefinitely, and even an apparently solidly based novel such as John Brunner's *Stand on Zanzibar* turns out to be riddled with misunderstandings of cultural processes when its major postulates are questioned. The writer who produces a future from imaginative whole cloth and can provide no logical reason for its existence ('you can't prove that it couldn't happen' is not an argument for intelligent people) is writing fantasy, or at best a pseudo-science fiction which undermines the genre in the eyes of the selective. Critic and common reader should examine all extrapolation from the point of view of valid logic.

A complete severity is, of course, impossible. There is little chance that any writer could create a totally coherent alternative social system within the bounds of a novel; the project is vast, beyond imaginative grasp. Still, the elements of reason should prevail. The reader should be able to find answers to such question as: Could humanity maintain itself, under this system, as an economic, aesthetic and sane culture? By what historical process could this system evolve at all? Could the ordinary man exist under these circumstances and, if not, could the

03.02 SCIENCE FICTION AS LITERATURE

culture itself exist? Novelists concerned with vast 'mind-bending' themes, or simply entranced with difference for its own sake, tend to forget that an operating culture depends on underlying stability, not on exotic life-styles and outré social conventions; their haphazard social structures, conceived as frames for action plots, are at once rejected by the intelligent reader. Admittedly, satire can make mincemeat of common logic, but even the tiered society of *Brave New World* was solidly based on viable trends, as was the more vulgarly soul-killing one of Kornbluth and Pohl's *The Space Merchants*.

The same observations apply to such other common concerns of science fiction as planetary ecologies and extraterrestrial life-forms. A total ecology is as impossible to create as a total society, but the reader should at least be able to recognise intelligence at work in what is set before him. So, too, with alien life-forms. Unnecessary limbs and tentacles, ill-considered senses grafted onto forms which do not need them, and weird attributes having no apparent relationship with the creature's environment, are thrown in at random to keep the reader stuffed with wonder, but intelligence will find more pleasure in those creatures which Arthur C. Clarke fitted so exactly to their environment in 'A Meeting with Medusa'.

So far this essay has been concerned with establishing parameters (which are at best guide-lines) within which science fiction can be evaluated as a literary form. What fans, addicts or writers may favour as their personal ideas of science fiction cannot concern us; only criteria applying to all literature may be employed. We have now a definition of the genre (however unsatisfactory to those of other persuasion), some purely literary matters which must be seen in proper perspective and a recognition that seriously intentioned fiction must be accurate in its premises as well as logical and consistent in its imaginative extension of them. It must be added that no guide-lines can rigidly restrict a literary form, and the ensuing survey will take note of a number of significant works which operate in some part beyond them.

Scholiasts with more enthusiasm than literary sense have traced the origins of science fiction back to the Bible and the Epic of Gilgamesh, and its descent through such exotics as Lucian's *True History*, Homer's *Odyssey* and the extravagances of Cyrano de Bergerac. These maunderings complicate issues without elucidating them; such works have nothing in common with the aims of science fiction and are demeaned by attempts to force them into an alien groove. The first long work of any note which considered, in fictional form, the possibilities of a life-style alternative to that followed at the time of writing, was the *Utopia* of Thomas More, published in 1516. It is true science fiction, still permanently in print, still readable and still imbued with propositions worth debate.

The search for further science fiction classics is dispiriting. One must disregard those older writings whose content of the strange and wonderful has seduced enthusiasm into claiming them for science fiction, but Johannes Kepler's *Somnium*, from the early seventeenth century, belongs in the fold because its vision of life on the Moon is based on science as Kepler knew it. It is, however, a largely forgotten work with nothing to say to the present age. Out with Lucian and de Bergerac must go the dozens of Moon voyages popularised in the eighteenth century and serving no purpose beyond entertainment and discreet satire; forgotten, they may as well remain so. Swift's *Gulliver's Travels* should probably be dismissed because its inversions and exaggerations have nothing to do with logical extrapolation and everything to do with misogynist satire. It, with all the other satires and fantasies of the period, has contributed its leaven of theme and fancy to science fiction – but so has every other literary form, including the non-fictional. Somewhere a line must be drawn, and after *Utopia* and *Somnium* few standard works have the science fictional vision. Mary Shelley's *Frankenstein* must, regretfully, be dismissed; it was designed as a horror story, such logic as it possesses is moral rather than perceptive, its scientific content is limited to the evasive phrase, 'I assembled my materials', and its filmed descendants, however inept, have approached the requirements of science fiction more nearly than their original. *Frankenstein* provided the germ of one of science fiction's great myths of tomorrow, the creation of life (as distinct from golems, etc), and its shadow looms large, but in literary terms it has little to commend it beyond its horrifying conception.

With Edgar Allan Poe, a standard author, though of the second rank, the seeker after classics is on safer ground, though his slow-paced novel, *The Narrative of Arthur Gordon Pym*, is best regarded as a parable of the voyage through evil to good and beyond good to some ultimate revelation. Several of his short stories are genuine science fiction, notably 'A Descent into the Maelstrom', while such tales as 'William Wilson' and 'The Fall of the House of Usher', though fantasies in themselves, display a vision formed and tempered by science and the desire to peer beyond it.

Poe's influence has been great, but no further nineteenth-century science fiction need delay the search for value until we come to Jules Verne, already pinpointed as father of the technological novel. His stories have historic and curio value rather than intrinsic interest, and the line he founded is a meagre one. Today's 'hard science' fiction is not a popular form in some circles, though Arthur C. Clarke is himself a favourite. The works of such writers as Hal Clement, Larry Niven and the team of Fred and Geoffrey Hoyle are less than notable stylistically, but they run from neatly made puzzle-and-solution to enormously detailed extropolative structures which have the fascination of an unfolding design but no permanent literary value. Some, like Clement's *Mission of Gravity*, may survive on sheer elegance of conception, but the scientific expertise required for such work limits proliferation. The interest of the 'hard science' novel is mainly intellectual and the form probably represents a dead end, even though it still survives.

Most other science fiction reaches back to Wells for themes and philosophic ideas, but Wells himself has only a slender classic status. His 'scientific romances' still sell after three-quarters of a century and few modern science fictionists equal his lucidity and inventiveness, but he was not among the literary great. The fact is that since *Utopia* science fiction has not produced a novel of classic stature. (History, of course, may prove this statement wrong.) It has, however, produced plenty of utopias. Edward Bellamy's *Looking Backward* in fact preceded Wells and became science fiction's only really overwhelming best-seller, but its dream of a socialist paradise has not held the public and its title is today better known than its contents. It has a place in science fiction history rather than literature, as one of the great line of utopias which were to be supplanted by forebodings of dystopia. If Wells allowed dystopia as a possible end of a careless culture, E. M. Forster announced it with considerable force as the foreseeable end of the machine age. His story 'The Machine Stops' (1909), delineated the basic picture of a machine-dominated, automated mankind, and later writers have added little but technical detail to his statement. That the enemy to beware might be man himself rather than his galloping technology was urged with power by Russia's Yevgeny Zamyatin in *We* (1920), taken from first-hand experience of man the tyrant; images and conclusions belong to today as much as to yesterday. George Orwell's *Nineteen Eighty-four*, the most famous of dystopias, could in 1949 add little save an improved technique of surveillance and more terrifying modes of mind control. These two novels may well survive on sheer literary power for some years, but the much-praised *One*, by David Karp is a pale thing beside them; it may be that fiction cannot make another public impact such as that of *Nineteen Eighty-four* until fresh perceptions permit a fresh approach. (Orwell's *Animal Farm*, cast in parable form, owes its theme to politics and its method to Aesop. Fiction but not science fiction.)

One theme not used by Wells was that of the super-intelligence. He was one who would surely have recognised that man can envision only what lies within his own intellectual range. Only a super-intellect can visualise a super-intellect, which is why no tests can detect IQs of 200 and beyond – no one can devise them. J. D. Beresford, however, in *The Hampdenshire Wonder* (1911) told of a super-intelligent child growing up in a world of what were to him morons, and in 1935 Olaf Stapledon published *Odd John* telling a similar story but seeing the world as not only foolish but barbaric. These novels told us much of the authors' views of humanity but nothing about intelligence. At best they achieved portraits of abnormally energetic, clear-sighted fellows looking down on the ant-scurry from higher up the anthill; they demonstrated only the unmanageability of the subject. Over their dreadful descendants, featured particularly in the works of A. E. van Vogt, science fiction should weep; only a handful of writers, notably Lewis Padgett (*Mimsy Were the Borogroves*) and Arthur C. Clarke (*Childhood's End*) have realised that the super-intellect must remain opaque to the normal mind. The theme, one of the most pervasive in science fiction, has nowhere to go.

Nor, it would seem, have some of the other great themes. Little save emotionalism has been added to the concept of extraterrestrial life since Wells's Selenites, though Ursula Le Guin (one of the best and most original science fiction writers) used the possibility to examine, in *The Left Hand of Darkness*, the purely human problem of communication between individuals. Little but melodrama has come of the immense possibilities of planetary catastrophe and survival; beside a *A Canticle for Leibowitz* only George Stewart's *Earth Abides* has something of stature. With *Canticle* stands science fiction's one other successful attempt at a religious theme, *A Case of Conscience*, wherein James Blish used extra-terrestrials to ask a pertinent question regarding the validity of the concept of original sin and whether evil can be created. Even the urgent problems of over-population have called forth little better than wallowings in sadistic solutions, though James Blish collaborated with Norman L. Knight in *A Torrent of Faces*, suggesting that at least temporary technological adjustments are practicable for a century or two.

The roll-call could continue indefinitely without turning up a title to edge its way into the major canon of fiction. The science fiction purist may ask: what of L. P. Hartley's *Facial Justice*, William Golding's *The Inheritors*, M. Barnard Eldershaw's *Tomorrow and Tomorrow* and a dozen others more honoured than read? The answer: read them and discover that the stuff of immorality is not in them. These are quite good novels which matter to science fiction but little to literature – and literature is our business here. Such superior works as G. K. Chesterton's *The Man Who Was Thursday* and Robert Graves's *Seven Days in New Crete* must be passed over because they cannot with honesty be pressed into genre confines; each is a fictive sport, self-existent, not to be degraded by pigeon-holing, and many would regard them as better than all but the very best of science fiction. Works with a touch of greatness stand always just beyond classification. Which is, perhaps, one of the requirements of greatness.

English and American science fiction forms the bulk of work easily available, and a survey of such foreign-language works as are obtainable in translation offers little seminal material; although excellent novels have come out of eastern Europe and a few from the western nations, they are in general the close brothers of their English-language counterparts. Russia has given one superior novel in N. Amosoff's *Notes from the Future*, in which an author, who is both a scientist and a capable writer of fiction (a rare combination), looks at the problems of anabiosis as 'hard' scientist, philosopher and story-teller; the result leaves little further to be said on the subject until research brings new facts, and this very exhaustiveness limits its viability by leaving the reader no option but to wait for the next development – and then forget *Notes from the Future*. From Japan came Kobo Abe's *Inter Ice Age 4* in a flat, featureless translation which could not smother the miracle of his use of biology to attack racism at its very root, asking what will be our attitudes to those whom we ourselves design for life in alien habitats? From Poland have come the controversial works of Stanislaw Lem, contemptuous of science and scientists and humanity in general, contemptuous of all save intellect, and in *Solaris*, sadly, unhappy with that also. His satire, laid on with a shovel, grates on an ear tuned to the harmonious mockeries of Jane Austen and Evelyn Waugh, but his inventiveness and wit are undeniable. These three novels probably represent the peaks of modern foreign-language science fiction but they cannot boost the genre into any leading role in the literary canon. They are of the fertilising type, preparing the ground for the greatness of others at a future date.

Fertilisation may be the final literary function of science fiction as we know it. Every reader is aware of the 'new wave' and its excesses but few have noted (at least in print) that the new wave moved its best writers appreciably nearer to the modes and perceptions of realistic fiction. As usual, the young revolutionaries emerge, when the shouting dies, as the middle-aged protagonists of a new stability. Consider Thomas Disch, J. G. Ballard, Brian Aldiss, even Michael Moorcock. Disch's *334*, a seminal genre novel, is a study of the pressures of tenement life – in AD 2020. His technique, muting the science fictional

03.02 SCIENCE FICTION AS LITERATURE

elements in favour of familiarities of living, heightens the drama of the effects of change on a culture; melodrama is out and humanity, helpless against cultural entropy, is in. Ballard has left science fiction and applied its techniques to novels of modern living, so that *Crash* and *Concrete Island* examine man as an alien in his own ambience. Moorcock's character, Jerry Cornelius, sprung from science fictional imaginings, has left his genre trappings to emerge as a personification of existential man, dancing to private logics which deny convention and double-think. Aldiss, remaining closer to science fiction, has in *Frankenstein Unbound* produced what seems to be a descendant of

science fiction, a novel with no scientific basis at all which, beginning with the premise of Mrs Shelley's *Frankenstein*, unites realism and fantasy to examine the monster-myth from new angles. In all these, the cohering factor is their application of science fictional perceptions to actual rather than alternative realities. It is significant that these four have been placed by some at the artistic top of the science fiction pyramid (though Moorcock writes hack trash also) and that their works, though probably lacking survival characteristics, belong high in the second rank of modern fiction. And high in the second rank is no mean place in the vast parade of fiction.

Less easily observable is the movement of realist writers towards the techniques and concerns of science fiction. The direct usages of Anthony Burgess and George Orwell need not concern us, nor such obvious matters as Allen Drury's use of a lunar location for scenes in *The Throne of Saturn*; we must note the subtle usages of such writers as Janet Frame, who in *Intensive Care* used a finale set in the future to shed light on the examination of the present which occupied three-quarters of the book, or of Sumner Locke-Elliott, who used the future in *Going* to expose brutally the end result of attitudes of mind emerging in our time. *Going*, telling of the last day of a 'redundant' victim of the population crisis, some years from now, used no science fictional devices to tell a science fiction story in the realistic mode; the effect was extraordinarily powerful. Muriel Spark also, in such novels as *The Hothouse by the East River* and *Not to Disturb*, has written of alternatives already bubbling beneath the surface of the mind. These are only a few of the indications that science fiction has, in its best practitioners, moved towards realism, while the realistic novel is using the conceptions that science fiction has laboured to introduce. The best of science fiction, some would argue, is returning home, bringing gifts to enrich the parent body.

It remains now only to answer the five questions asked at the beginning.

Is science fiction a viable form of world literature? In genre form of adventure and romance, yes; it is capable of the infinite variety required for continued popularity.

Has science fiction produced any great or near-great literature? Only the future can answer this question, but the present-day critic must say: since More's *Utopia*, probably not, but much rates well in the second rank.

What special literary considerations must be accounted for when evaluating science fiction? The critic must accept alternative conceptions as making alternative demands on form and balance of elements, notably characterisation and background.

What, if any, are the special values science fiction can contribute to world literature? Science fiction has contributed an insistence on alternative possibilities of ambience, physical shape, thought and accepted fact. Other literary forms have attempted this, but none so consistently or successfully.

What is the present position of science fiction vis-à-vis realistic fiction? The two modes of literary exploration are observing the advantages of each other's visions and taking such of the other's modes as seem useful. It seems not unlikely that the most philosophically productive areas of science fiction will be absorbed into the great general flow of fiction and accepted as part of the normal vision of the universe, while only the genre work, the adventures and romances, will remain to carry the 'sf' name.

Absorption will not be a surrender but a triumph for the writers who have lifted science fiction out of the pulp-magazine rut.

George Turner

03.03 RECURRENT CONCEPTS

03.03.1 The Value of Science Fiction

There is a single common denominator to all recurrent topics of science fiction – travel in space and time, superhuman powers, immortality and stories of robots, intelligent animals, alien beings, monsters. Such stories are escape fiction, in the sense that they release the reader from the prison of his own limited existence. They share this quality with other kinds of fiction, chiefly with historical and adventure novels, and like them, they are usually written in the romantic mode: the heroes are heroic, they conquer against all odds, and the endings are happy.

Even stories about monsters and about worldwide catastrophes fall under this rubric. These stories allow the reader to confront without anxiety his own fears and negative feelings about the world and other people. In Theodore Sturgeon's *It*, for example, and in the film *Frankenstein*, he can see what I once called 'the innocence of evil'. The monster is at once frightening and innocent: the reader can participate in his crimes without guilt; in the end the monster is destroyed and the reader absolved. In catastrophe stories, such as John Christopher's *The Death of Grass*, the reader can contemplate with equanimity the death of most of the human race, identifying himself as he does with the survivors and their conquest of an Arcadian new world. Here again we are speaking of a liberation from constraint, in this case a moral constraint.

The reader of science fiction knows that at some stage he will die; he might be above average intelligence, but is painfully aware that he is no genius; he is confined to one brief period in time and to one small locality. His powers are those imposed by nature, evolution, technology, human laws, and the physical laws of the universe. He is trapped by his size – he cannot descend into the world of insects or of microscopic life. In science fiction all these limits are broken: vicariously, the reader can leap tall buildings at a single bound, solve complex equations faster than a computer, live indefinitely, travel to the farthest star, read others' minds, emit hypnotic rays from the eyes, commit any crime with impunity.

It is worth noticing that every one of the topics mentioned above can be found in fairy tales and other traditional fantasy, and it is probably safe to say that most science fiction readers were attracted to fairy tales in their youth. The difference is that the reader knows the fairy tales cannot be true. Seduced by the modern awe of science, he is able to believe that science fiction stories might someday come true; thus science fiction becomes defensible – and is fiercely defended – as 'serious' and 'important'.

These claims have some validity; it is arguable, for example, that without science fiction's long exploration of the problems of space travel, the real space program would not have come as soon as it did. But these are rationalisations after the fact; the unlikelihood or impossibility of most science fiction does not diminish the reader's pleasure, and its occasional successful predictions only soothe his feelings of inferiority.

Science fiction is distinguished from other forms of exotic fiction by one other factor: the thrill of wonder. This is at the heart of most science fiction readers' addiction; it is as unmediated and nearly as powerful as sex or religious experience. So far as the *plots* of many novels are concerned, it makes little difference whether the setting be sixteenth-century France or a fictitious planet of the

LA SORTIE DE L'OPÉRA EN L'AN 2000.

03.03 RECURRENT CONCEPTS

From the film The Time Machine.

star Aldebaran, but one gives this specific thrill, and the other does not.

Naturalism in science fiction has the function of facilitating the reader's entry into the imagined world. In the stories of Robert A. Heinlein, for example, people take rocket shuttles to Europe, but they still read *Time* magazine and smoke Luckies; in L. Sprague Camp's *Divide and Rule*, the world has been reduced to feudalism by an invading race of kangaroo-like aliens, but the hero's crossbow is made by Remington. Ray Bradbury's *The Martian Chronicles* tell of empty Coke bottles littering the sands of the Red Planet.

Carried further than this, realism or naturalism becomes a disturbing element in science fiction, because it means the loss of the romantic illusion. I was told by one science fiction fan in 1976 that there are certain novels he reads over and over, several times a year. The reason he rereads these books in preference to others, he told me, is that 'they are heroic, and nothing bad ever happens to the people. It's comforting.'

Paradoxically, genre science fiction is itself limited and even crippled by its abolition of all limits. It cannot probe too deeply into human character without acknowledging death and defeat. It cannot treat human relationships in detail, because that would slow the story down; for the same reason, it cannot be written in elaborate prose. During the past decade a number of unusually capable writers have tried to overcome these limitations, most notably Samuel R. Delany and Ursula K. Le Guin; but nearly all these efforts are subtly unsatisfactory: the mix of literary and conventional science fiction elements is out of balance. In theory, there is no reason why a science fiction novel could not be made as rich and powerful as a novel by Dostoevsky; in practice, it would take a genius to do it – but then it took a genius to write *Crime and Punishment*. Science fiction is still waiting for its Dostoevsky. It has already had its H. G. Wells.

When once a reader has effected entry into a satisfactory imagined world, his pleasure is in direct proportion to the length of the narrative. For this reason, the most popular and successful modern science fiction writers, almost without exception, are those who have published cycles of stories or novels dealing with a common background: Asimov (the 'Foundation' series), E. E. Smith (the 'Skylark' and 'Lensman' series), Blish (*Cities in Flight*), Herbert (the 'Dune' novels), Bradbury (*The Martian Chronicles*), Heinlein (*The Past through Tomorrow*).

The essential function of science fiction is to allow the reader entry into some marvellous portion of the real or imagined universe which he cannot reach in his own life. This is true of such despairing works as *The Time Machine, Brave New World, We,* and *Nineteen Eighty-four*: the experience of being a part of these imagined worlds, although it is certainly not comforting, is liberating.

What all this suggests is that the problem of creating a real literature of science fiction is not insoluble. Science fiction writers in the past have been handicapped by the commercial demands of the field, by their own inexperience and lack of knowledge, by small financial returns that force hasty work. All these factors are changing. Science fiction is attracting more sophisticated and capable writers. Nearly every taboo has vanished. Writers are being paid more. As long as our present civilisation lasts, it is likely that there will be an audience for romantic science fiction. But there is increasing elbow room for works of a more enduring nature; our Dostoevsky may already have been born.

Damon Knight

03.03.2 The Barbarian As Hero

Hero-worship is an ancient trait. From prehistoric times, men have sought heroes, real or imaginary, with whom they can identify themselves and to whom they can give their devotion. Real men receiving such adulation include Alexander the Great, Napoleon, Hitler, and John F. Kennedy. Imaginary ones comprise demigods, like Herakles and Sigurdh, and fictional mortals of superhuman abilities, such as Sindbad, Crusoe, Tarzan and James Bond. The hero-fancier, on hearing or reading of his idol, momentarily enjoys identifying himself with his hero, revelling in his prowess and versatility.

Such an idealised creature may be called a Superman. The term refers to the hero-worshipper's concept of his idol rather than a real mortal. Real-life heroes usually turn out, when coldly examined, to have their fair share of faults and flaws.

Although the concept of the Superman goes back to ancient times, the term was popularised by the nineteenth-century German philosopher Friedrich Nietzsche (1844-1900). A man of many inconsistencies, Nietzsche hoped that the Superman would soon arrive to break the chains of the Judaeo-Christian 'slave morality', discipline the masses, and unify Europe. He was vague as to how this prodigy was to be created, save for the interesting suggestion that the mating of German army officers with Jewish women might produce Supermen.

Sometimes the fictional Superman expresses a reaction against the restraints and complications of civilisation. Resentment of these restrictions leads to idealisation of the mighty, uncorrupted savage, the barbarian hero of iron thews and simple mind. In ancient Babylon, this virtuous bumpkin took the form of Gilgamesh's hairy friend Enkidu. In northern Europe he was the dragon-slaying Sigurdh Fafnirsbane; in Russia, the bogatyr Ilya of Murom.

The concept was strengthened by the writings of Jean Jacques Rousseau (1712–78), when that weepy Swiss philosopher praised primitive life. Rousseau's critics called Rousseau's ideal the 'noble savage', a term from John Dryden's verse drama *The Conquest of Granada* (1672). So far as I know, Rousseau never used the term himself, neither did he ever know any savages, noble or otherwise.

Nevertheless, Rousseau wrote that 'Nature has made man happy and good, but that Society depraves him and makes him wretched.' 'Man', he declared, 'is naturally good', but civilisation and its institutions, especially that of private property, render him evil.

Rousseau wrote before scientific anthropology, which overturned many of his assumptions. In his day, philosophers speculated about the 'state of nature' preceding civilisation by analogies with Genesis and with living primitives. European seamen were discovering the South Sea Islands and sending home idyllic but fanciful accounts of Polynesian life. These descriptions were taken as portraying 'noble savages' in fact. Fictioneers like Françοis René de Chateaubriand made Supermen out of Amerindians and other barbarians.

In the nineteenth century, Lewis H. Morgan, the pioneer American anthropologist, distinguished between savages and barbarians. While subject to many exceptions and qualifications, his classification is still valid as a rough-and-ready grouping of human societies. According to Morgan's scheme, savages are the hunters, fishermen and food-gatherers who have not yet learned to grow edible plants or to herd domesticated edible animals. Barbarians have mastered these techniques but have not yet acquired cities and writing. Societies with cities, writing and arithmetic are classed as civilisations. Modern exploiters of the barbarian hero, however, seldom bother with such fine distinctions.

The search for a non-existent 'state of nature' when all was peaceful, happy and good, continued through the Romantic Era, begotten by Rousseau and dominant through the period 1790-1840. One of its products was a multitude of utopian colonies set up during the nineteenth century in the United States. This ideal is not yet dead, as witness the commune movement of the so-called counter-culture of the 1960s. The only such colonies to have shown real staying power, however, are those like the Amish and the Hutterites. These, recruited from the stolid German peasantry, combine intense religious convictions, puritanical austerity, and a passion for hard work.

In the 1890s, this back-to-nature sentiment – this romantic illusion of a primitive Golden Age – appeared in the very popular writings of Jack London and Rudyard Kipling. Kipling's Mowgli is the perfect noble savage. At seventeen, he

'. . . looked older, for hard exercise, the best of good eating, and baths whenever he felt in the least hot or dusty had given him strength and growth far beyond his age. He could swing by one hand from a top branch for half an hour at a time . . . He could stop a young buck in mid-gallop and throw him sideways by the head.'

Mowgli from The Jungle Book *by Rudyard Kipling.*

03.03 RECURRENT CONCEPTS

Kipling's animal characters make snide remarks about 'civilised' men: 'Men are blood-brothers to the *Bandar-log* [monkeys].' 'Who is man that we should care for him – the naked brown digger, the hairless and toothless, the eater of earth?'

In 1912 appeared the most popular barbarian hero of all time, Tarzan. His creator, Edgar Rice Burroughs, had been a book-keeper, cowboy, prep-school teacher, railway detective, salesman and soldier, without much success in any line. Burroughs got into fiction with an interplanetary novel, *A Princess of Mars*, and *Tarzan of the Apes* was his third novel. Tarzan made Burroughs's fortune, becoming the hero not only of more than a score of books, but also of an endless series of movies and comic strips.

Whereas Mowgli was reared by wolves in India, Tarzan was brought up in Africa by apes of a kind unknown to science. Burroughs told contradictory stories of where he found his basic idea, both admitting and denying that he had read Kipling's *Jungle Books*. The story shows the romantic illusion of simple primitive virtue in its purest form. Tarzan ever contrasts the vices of civilisation, its 'greed and selfishness and cruelty', and the 'weaknesses, vices, hypocrisies and little vanities' of civilised men 'with the open primitive ways of her ferocious jungle mates'.

According to some who have tried it, primitive life is not really simple. The pre-literate peasant must carry in his head a vast amount of lore about planting, cultivating, gathering and processing his crop in order to have enough to eat. The true savage, likewise, must be in his own way a highly educated man. He must be wise in the ways of game and skilled in finding edible plants and water.

Moreover, if the primitive makes one bad mistake, he dies. Thor Heyerdahl, the anthropologist-explorer, and his bride tried going native in the Marquesas Island. Primitive life nearly killed them, and they were lucky, a year later, to escape to civilisation.

Tarzan and the Ant Men *by Edgar Rice Burroughs.*

After Burroughs, the leading celebrant of the barbarian hero was the Texas pulp-fiction writer, Robert E. Howard (1906–36) creator of Conan the Cimmerian. Conan was the hero of a score of tales, including a book-length novel, but not counting later additions to the saga by other hands. During the last decade, these stories have been revived with great success, thirty-odd years after Howard's suicide. They have engendered a host of imitations.

Conan lived, loved and battled in Howard's fictitious Hyborian Age, 12,000 years ago, between the sinking of Atlantis and the start of recorded history. A gigantic barbarian adventurer from backward Cimmeria, Conan wades through rivers of gore and overcomes foes both natural and supernatural to become, at last, the ruler of civilised Aquilonia.

Like London, Kipling and Burroughs, all of whom influenced him, Howard idealised primitive life and made sweeping statements about barbarians. When Conan had been ousted from his throne by sorcery, Howard says:

'Now the barbarian suggestion about the king was more pronounced, as if in his extremity the outward aspects of civilization were stripped away, to reveal the primordial core. Conan was reverting to his pristine type. He did not act as a civilized man would act under the same conditions, nor did his thoughts run in the same channels. He was unpredictable.'

Others, too, stress the barbarian's supposed unconventionality, unpredictability and freedom from civilised

Illustration of Conan by Marcus Boas.

taboos and inhibitions. It seems, however, that most barbarians (making allowance for individual variations) are, if anything, more conventional, predictable and inhibited than civilised men. They may not observe the civilised taboos and inhibitions but have plenty of their own.

In barbarian societies, the force of custom must be greater than in civilisation to enable these societies to work at all, since they have no written laws, police and courts to keep the unruly in order. What they lack in taboos about one aspect of life – say, sex among the Polynesians or violence among the Comanches – they make up for by rigid rules governing other acts. Etiquette may be elaborate, and a violation punishable by a spear in the brisket.

There is one time when barbarians throw off their inhibitions and act more like the barbarian adventurer-hero of fiction. This occurs when a barbarian society is in a state of flux, and the barbarians are conquering or being conquered by a civilisation. In earlier times, when barbarians had learned the secrets of civilised warfare, and over-population or bad weather put them under pressure to survive and an able leader arose among them, they sometimes overran a neighbouring civilisation, setting themselves up as a ruling class over it.

There have been many such overthrows, for example the Kassite conquest of Babylonia; the downfall of the West Roman Empire in the fifth century: and the conquest by Huns, Turks and Mongols of parts of Europe, the Middle East, India and China. Sometimes the civilised society beat off the barbarian attacks, as the Byzantines repulsed the Arabs, Avars and Slavs. The West Roman debacle and the following Dark Age gave rise to a multitude of legends of heroes like Arthur, Merlin, Cúchulainn and Sigurdh. These legends are echoed in modern heroic fantasy, which is sometimes based directly upon them.

When the barbarians win, then (if ever) they cast off their inhibitions and taboos. Having overthrown a great power, they feel they can get away with anything. They have escaped the dreary, monotonous, toilsome, humdrum round of normal barbarian life and with this have thrown off their code of social relationships and responsibilities. They have not adopted the code of the conquered, whom they despise, because they have beaten them.

Hence the new barbarian lordlings, promoted from starving shepherds to masters of a host of people far more cultivated than they, see no reason not to do just as they please, to give free rein to every whim and lust. The standard of living in the conquered land falls catastrophically, since the new lords care more for confiscating property, pursuing fueds and quarrels, and indulging their appetites than in keeping up aqueducts, roads and harbours. The barbarian ruler squanders the resources that generations of civilised men have built up and lets the future take care of itself.

For a picture of life beneath such rule, Bishop Gregory of Tours, between AD 575 and 594, wrote a *History of the Franks*. This work tells the story of Merovingian Gaul during the preceding century. Although Gregory was on the side of the Frankish kings, because they were Catholic Christians and neither Arians nor pagans, his account shows the Merovingian dynasty as one of the worst governments the world has seen.

What, then, is the persistent appeal of the fictional barbarian hero? Why do readers like to follow his adventures, even when they know what murderous oafs most real barbarian conquerors are?

The distinctive trait of the conqueror of folk of a different culture is his loss of inhibitions. Since the conquered differ from him, he cannot recognise them as human beings like himself – an attitude which is reinforced by the fact that he has overpowered them. He acts like a bumptious adolescent, liberated from his parents' control but not yet fitted into the mould of adult civilised life.

Hence many heroes of ancient epics and modern heroic fantasy resemble overgrown juvenile delinquents. Such liberated behaviour in the real world does not make one a good insurance risk. The barbarian conqueror is always in danger of death from some rival adventurer. Thus Theodoric the Great treacherously murdered Odovakar, the German mercenary general who ended the West Roman Empire.

We carry with us memories of our emotional reactions at each stage of growth, from childhood onwards. Among these buried memories is that of the feeling of liberation at our adolescent emancipation, when we were told: You're a man now; you'll have to decide that for yourself. We soon learned that this feeling of liberation was mostly illusion. The world, together with our own limitations and shortcomings, soon clamped upon us restrictions quite as severe as anything our parents imposed. But the memory of the emotion still endures. Hence multitudes enjoy, if only vicariously, the thrill of identifying themselves with the uninhibited barbarian hero of fiction. And so, this fictional figment will probably appeal to many readers for an indefinite time to come.

L. Sprague de Camp

03.03 RECURRENT CONCEPTS

03.03.3 Software: the Psychological View

Time is the greatest enemy – but it is also the purveyor of all change, the quickener of the lifeblood of speculative writing. For it is *change*, the force which moves human history to and fro, which the writers of science fiction have recognised and harnessed to their own inimitable ends. Change is not an immediately acceptable proposition to the majority of human minds; the desire and need for stability is far more persuasive in a world already accelerating towards rapid, perhaps even devastating, transformation. Most people turn away from the fractionating social processes taking place around them; the mind closes down in retreat from the events for which its conditioning has left it unprepared. It is no exaggeration to suggest that the regular readers of serious science fiction are at one in the membership of an élitist group in the sense that they refuse to turn their heads away. They will go on looking, thinking, reacting, even though the heavens fall. But the question still remains: what is to be done? The answer in the end relies on faith.

This brief essay is an attempt to explain such reasoning. The editor has read the other texts in this section, a privilege which no other contributor has enjoyed. Therefore the conclusions arrived at here are influenced to some extent by what has been written elsewhere in this book. But what the present writer wishes to say is still fundamentally an expression of his own innermost convictions.

He will begin where he believes science fiction genuinely belongs – and that is in the realm of science. In the same way that no satisfactory definition of science fiction has been conceived, neither has there been a complementary description to embrace the expanding world of science. It is not enough to go to the dictionary and find there the formal definition of what science is *supposed* to be; one will be left with a dusty answer. Science, and here we must speak generally, is a living and moving thing. It is the record, however arbitrary, of a growing process of intelligence. It moves because the human intelligence which fosters it is also on the move. The move is outwards, extending beyond this world. This is no vain imagining; right back to the early history of man, the stars have called, and man has turned his eyes upward. Whether a native in the jungles, an Eskimo now guiding his sled across the ice-wastes (listening to his personal transistor radio to discover the price of uranium on the world's metal exchanges) or urban man ensconced in his concrete jungle (far from his fellow native), modern and ancient, man has raised his head to the sky. Once, as he did

so, he believed he was looking at the gods. He was regarding his destiny, for if he can master himself on his own planet, he can indeed be a god in the sky.

The growth and development of science fiction is very firmly related to man's instinctive knowledge of his awakening greatness. It is an expression of his recognition that personal immortality must inevitably give way to the greater concept of the furtherance of the race. Many religious speakers, harking all the way back to Jesus of Nazareth, have expressed this same sentiment, although presented in a different way. They suggested that individual man should lose himself in the greater awareness of humanity; that he should serve, and thus achieve salvation. Such a way of thought may seem anachronistic today, when viewed in the light of twentieth-century history; but it is an idea which still finds adherents and many explanations exist to account for man's desire to be saved. Salvation is a man-invented concept, as is its counterbalance, sin. This terrible twin-concept has ruined far more lives in human history than it has ever saved. The price in misery which man has paid for his ideological obsessions is almost beyond bearing.

What the serious elements in science fiction show is that human life need not be a sordid, greedy scramble. Many writers have presented dark or terror-stricken futures. As Edmund Cooper has pointed out, they show them as a warning, not as an inevitability. Wells himself, outside his science fiction writings, was constantly urging his readers that they had at best two choices: 'Adapt, or perish'. He saw the outlook for mankind as 'a race between education and catastrophe'. The Wellsian syndrome had been passed to modern science fiction writers, as well it should, but it is in Plato's *Republic* where the basic Wellsian/Platonic ideas are firmly set out. Wells came across the *Republic* as a boy of thirteen; it influenced him for the rest of his life – unfortunately, quite wrongly. He began to dream of a world state, run by his particular group of benign overseers, a collection of enlightened people he saw coming together almost by chance to take over the organisation of the world. How such a group could have actually got together, Wells was at a loss to explain. It was an idle dream, but it had its appeal. It is very difficult to understand how this man, who could summon up such immense visions, could fall down on so fundamental a problem. One answer is that Wells simply did not want to know. He slung his ideas down on paper and expected the reader to make of them what he could. What his readers have made of them is now history; and George Orwell, among many other commentators, has recorded the fact that Wells contributed in no small measure to the modern mentality. His struggle is reflected in the serious modern science fiction writer's journey through imaginative space and time. As can be seen, the overriding Wellsian message underlines the age-long human belief that man can achieve a heaven on earth – or a hell on earth, depending on how he chooses to behave. The considerable quantity of anti-utopian writings which have distinguished themselves during the last forty years of science fiction bears witness to the Wellsian warning. On the utopian side, there have been as many messages, and breathtaking flights of imagination, to reinforce the more positive aspect of the Wellsian view.

For the purposes of this essay, we shall look at the human imagination from its earliest beginnings. The human child arrives in the world filled with a sense of

expectancy. It attempts to learn everything – or at least it takes in everything – in absolute wonderment. There are no mental reservations; a baby is undiscriminating. What it sees in its first years may later come to ruin it; but it may just as equally turn into a warm, loving and genuinely creative adult. The elements of chance involved in this process must be recognised. In a sense, they are akin to Heisenberg's Uncertainty Principle – the random element, incapable of measurement, which infuses all human life.

A child surveys everything, uncritically, viewing the world with a sense of wonder. It often learns in its early years that heroes have walked the earth. Disillusionment may set in later, when the individual concerned has begun to appreciate the conflicting factors which make up the human personality. But the eternal fascination of the barbarian concept, to which Sprague de Camp has given historical significance, comes early to the childlike mind. Among science fiction writers, the stories of Leigh Brackett, Poul Anderson, Marion Zimmer Bradley and Andre Norton exemplify the fascination of the barbarian. Just how this can be translated, in historical terms, when the concept is allowed to run uncontrolled in the wrong human hands, can be seen in the excesses of the Nazi terror in Europe. Hitler, and particularly Göring, announced to millions of overwhelmed and terrorised people: 'We *are* barbarians; we want to be barbarians. It is an honourable title.' No greater indictment of the unrestricted dedication to the barbarian elements in the human consciousness can be imagined in terms of man's suffering than the brutality of the Nazis.

There is no doubt that the childish human mind can readily be perverted into a constant preoccupation with violence and inhumanity of the grossest kind. The predominance on the television screen of every type of viciousness bears witness to the makers' recognition that such excretions will be watched, and probably enjoyed.

As the mind grows older, it may come across more enduring and commendable ideas. It will learn something of history and begin to realise how great the loss has been to humanity through the constant warring of men with each other. Its growing comprehension can lead to the vision of one world, and a sense of universal human brotherhood. Or else, if the mind has already been tainted, it will see its world only as a stage on which to perform its personal greedy little scramble. Science fiction has portrayed both these elements of the human dilemma to considerable effect. But in the opinion at least of the present writer, the dreams and aspirations expressed by so many science fiction authors hold out a hope for the future which is certainly not expressed in the more conventional modes of literature, immersed as so much of it is in a welter of introspection.

We began by considering man's calling to the stars. In few other branches of literature, except perhaps poetry, has this yearning been expressed so systematically. It is possible to consider the great religious books of human history in a parallel light, although in such works as the Bible the emphasis is more usually on the historical than on the symbolic. Their writers could not see far enough into the future to realise that one day their successors would actually achieve spaceflight and bring to a kind of fulfilment man's dream to head for the stars. But even in this achievement, we find the strange duality of purpose which characterises the human personality. Whereas ancient man looked to the heavens in the hope that eventually his spirit would soar among the stars, modern man may physically reach those distant points of light – and still find himself spiritually unfulfilled.

If he can succeed in avoiding a nuclear holocaust, a prospect still very much a threat, there seems no reason to believe that man will not eventually reach out into the galaxy and find there one more stage in his destiny.

On his own planet he has contrived to produce societies in which very few people have a real opportunity to find personal fulfilment. This has been the law of life; but many distinguished commentators – Plato, Sir Thomas More (and, in our present day, Wells himself) – have continually dreamed of the better and more beautiful world. Their ideas have influenced human history. In the same way, Kurt Vonnegut's *Breakfast of Champions*, to which Edmund Cooper refers, has expressed the despair of a sensitive man of the self-destructive processes he can observe in his own society.

The real difference between science fiction writers and their counterparts in other fields of literature comes down to this: their overriding view is one of the limitless possibilities for man's awakening greatness. They have hope, although they are aware of the intensity of the Wellsian warning. Their understanding of the human situation, however, can induce a response in the individual imagination in keeping with the more courageous persuasions in the long rise of human thought. The last writings of Olaf Stapledon bring us towards this conclusion; he spoke of a god in which he did not personally believe, but in which he felt it was necessary to believe. H. G. Wells expressed very similar sentiments in the epilogue to *The Time Machine*. Wells had depicted a human future as a phase of darkness; but, as the narrator, he urged that even if thinking man could foresee that civilisation was a heap of foolishness which would eventually collapse upon itself, he must live his personal life as if this were not so.

In the end, we must look to the message of Wells, which he inherited from his great teacher, Thomas Henry Huxley (who in turn received his own stoical brand of enheartenment from the profound learning of Charles Darwin). Darwin recognised the viciousness and terrible cruelty of all animal life; he subtitled his *On the Origin of Species* as a struggle for existence. He knew well how desperate that struggle could be. But he must also have seen quite clearly that, although the Second Law of Thermodynamics had decreed that all energy in the universe was eventually running down, such a natural dissipation was balanced by the rise of intelligence emanating from Earth.

The visions of science fiction writers have presented many different interpretations of man's future in the stars; and they suggest that perhaps man's dream is more important than reality. Risking overemphasis, it has to be said that science fiction is the only modern literature which presents these considerations in anything approaching an accurate light. It does so because the extrapolations from present-day technology and social conditions, which the better writers regularly undertake, are based on a sound understanding of applied science and its almost limitless potential. A shrewd observation of human nature also plays its part. As realists, however, they recognise that if the message is to be got across effectively, it is best done by means of entertainment. There will always be 'cowboys and indians in the sky', as there should be, but a greater factor – and the one that embraces the whole human future – remains the possibility of an expansion of the race's knowledge and achievements beyond its wildest dreams.

Brian Ash

CK WHERE JOHN GREGG
E SHELTERED. BURROWING
E RIPS OPEN THE FLOOR A
FORE THE CABIN COLLAPSES
MBLE SAFELY INTO THE

04 FANDOM AND MEDIA

The final section of this guide is devoted to two equally important areas in the realm of science fiction. Fandom, as the reader will have seen in the opening Program, has played a major part in the development of the genre. It can be described as a below-the-line support activity, but as with any such activity, warring factions have helped to make its progress haphazard and open to differing interpretations. Therefore, only those activities and points of fact which can be determined with some authenticity have been included here, together with details of the bigger conventions and the major awards. By the same yardstick, only those fringe cults which have proved of marked significance demand our attention. While a whole book could easily be devoted to the spin-off from the sf scene, much of the material is at best ephemeral. But the dedicated following attracted by Fort, Shaver and Hubbard cannot be ignored.

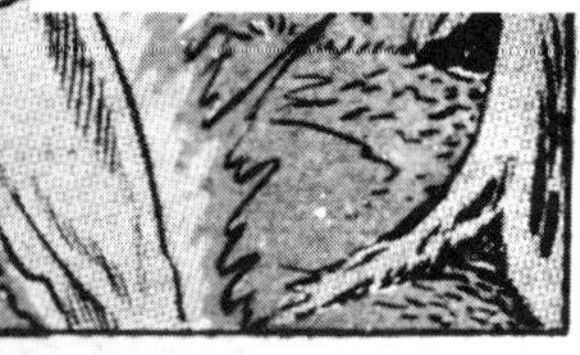

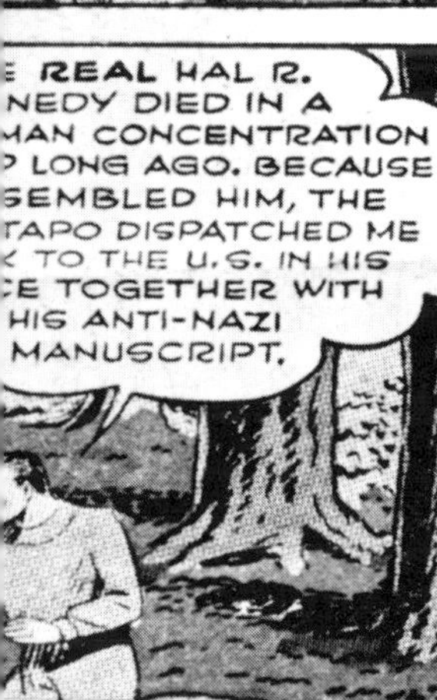

04.01 FANDOM

The media have served the cause of science fiction by helping to popularise it. In this section we give a general outline of the progress of the professional sf magazine, the rise of the sf novel in book form, and the fluctuating popularity of science fiction anthologies.

Not everyone devoted to science fiction will approve of its adaptation into comic strips. Nevertheless, comics and strip cartoons have attracted a considerable following, and therefore their development should be recorded. There are those who would argue that the movie and television productions which fall into the sf category could be considered in a similar light. However, in both these media enough important and impressive work has been achieved to warrant serious consideration.

Examples of science fiction art, in all its colourful variety, have been included throughout this book. Enough has already been shown for the reader to judge its quality. The consideration of the subject included in this section is therefore limited to a short outline of the better artists and illustrators in the field.

The section also includes a survey of the critical studies of science fiction which have become an increasing part of the background activity during the last decade, plus a brief review of the academic studies and courses now in existence in various parts of the world.

Maya *November 1975*. (Forrey Ackerman fans will note the likeness.)

04.01 FANDOM

04.01.1 Fanac (Fan Activity)

August 1970.

Science fiction has had a consistent and widespread following for a number of decades, and science fiction fans have had a marked influence on the object of their admiration. Science fiction fandom – for better or worse – has always enjoyed strong links with the professional world of sf writing, because a large proportion of well-known authors, editors and publishers have indulged in an active fan life before attaining the professional level, and a number still maintain long-standing links with fandom.

For many fans, however, the commitment to fandom itself is more important than the movement's advertised purpose; their attitude is incorporated in the much-voiced slogan 'Fandom is a way of life'. To comprehend this lifestyle, it is essential to acquire some understanding of the cult-language. Fan lexicographers have recorded no less than two thousand terms; however, a grasp of a few dozen such pieces of jargon should be enough to infuse any neofan (new fan, or one who is not *au fait*) with sufficient confidence to hold his own at any convention. He will know, for example, that the acronym of the above boils down to 'Fiawol'; while an alternative view is expressed in the expletive 'Fijagh' (*F*andom *i*s *j*ust *a* *g*oddam *h*obby).

In the course of its long and chaotic history, sf fandom has given rise to, or overlapped with, more specialised groups entertaining interests of a similar nature. The ablest sf commentator has been hard put to distinguish between the supporters of the true genre, the devotees of science fantasy, and those of the darker elements of Gothic and weird horror, particularly where noted sf authors have made their debuts in such magazines as *Weird Tales*. Recently S & S (Sword-and-Sorcery) fandom also has provided some overlap, and there are professional and amateur publications which specialise exclusively in this sub-genre. In the last few years the devotees of comics have formed a splinter group which can be disassociated with the main field, and the enthusiasts of the illustrated strip cartoon have their own conventions to attend.

Other sub-groups have formed themselves around a heroic figure or story series, and, in some cases, an individual author. Possibly the earliest example of the latter was Lovecraft fandom, centred on the writings of H. P. Lovecraft. The cult grew substantially following Lovecraft's death in March 1937. In the 1960s it was overtaken in the fan world by ERB dom, a following inspired by the works of Edgar Rice Burroughs. The largest and most recent body of fringe fandom rejoices in a membership of 'Trekkies' or 'Trekkers' – adherents of the *Star Trek* television series. UFO – unidentified flying objects – devotees, or subscribers to the dubious theories of Erich von Däniken, rarely indulge in fan activities and have little connection with sf fandom, although it must be recorded that they organise many conventions and gatherings of their own.

As already indicated, many fen (plural of 'fan', from the analogy with 'man') are only passingly interested in science fiction. They have been labelled faans (the 'a' is open to constant repetition depending on the degree of calculated estrangement from the genre), and usually they are more concerned with the comradeship of the club than what were seen as its original aims. The opposite viewpoint is identified by the adjective 'sercon' (signifying a *ser*ious and *con*structive approach to science fiction). This distinction highlights the potential schism in fandom, which on occasions becomes only too real – fannish fans (faans) refusing to recognise a sercon organisation or publication as a proper part of fandom, and a sercon body becoming very largely out of touch with fannish fandom.

June 1953.

This dichotomy of aims frequently results in feuds, and ultimately in 'gafia' for various fans (getting *a*way *f*rom *i*t *a*ll, or leaving fandom). The term has changed its meaning over the years. During the 1930s Depression in the US, in the early stages of sf fandom, it indicated a wish to escape from the real world into the realms of fantasy of science fiction. Many early US groups were similar to such American institutions as Masonic lodges, boy's clubs, or fraternities, each creating an 'alternative reality' by means of its individual ceremonies, language, mores and rewards. (A 1949 group actually dubbed itself 'The Royal and Benevolent Order of Gafia'.) Some such groups still conspire to survive, one example being the UK-based Knights of St Fantony (formed in 1957), who somehow succeed in combining the medieval and space ages in their interests, costume and ceremony. Viewed overall, the real importance of sf fan clubs – however disparate their objectives – can be seen as the opportunity they offer readers to meet the writers themselves, and to indulge in the cross-fertilisation of ideas which contributes so largely to the enhancement of the genre.

Another area of fandom includes those enthusiasts interested in the practical side of space exploration. The real origin of fandom probably owed as much to interest in popular science and rocketry as it did to the other attractions of science fiction. Among the pioneers there were many, Gernsback included, who saw the genre as a medium for the propagation of scientific education and prediction. Such gatherings as Raymond A. Palmer's Science Correspondence Club and William S. Sykora's International Scientific Association were pointed firmly towards popular science. The latter actually experimented with rocketry and related technologies before being overwhelmed by sf enthusiasts who replaced it with a more literary motivated club. Similarly in the UK, the British Interplanetary Society preceded all other sf groups; and, in parallel with its American counterparts, it involved many people who were later to become celebrated in the sf field, most notably Arthur C. Clarke.

The few historians who have attempted to record the complex path of science fiction fandom have arrived, confusingly, at two separate systems of annotation. Moskowitz in his fan history of the thirties, *The Immortal Storm*, refers to the early years up to 1933, when large clubs were being formed, as 'the first fan era'. The second and third eras, in his view, merge together in 1933–35, when the early clubs declined, or enjoyed a brief period of rejuvenation. The fourth fan era (according to Moskowitz) occurs in 1936–37, with the growth of the fanzines and their varying degrees of influence. In this particular system, the collapse of *Fantasy Magazine* (regarded by the majority as the field leader) represents the watershed in the fifth era (1937–38); while a new generation of fans, appearing around 1938, is seen as the sixth and last era in the system.

The alternative, and more popular, system of fandom was devised by Jack Speer. In its early stages it was necessarily vague about the period before 1933, which it later identified as 'ecofandom'. Its 'First Fandom' runs from 1933–36, concurrent with the growth of fanzines and their influence culminating in the dominance of *Fantasy Magazine*. 'Second Fandom' is pre-occupied with feuds and political schism, and extends from October 1937 to October 1938. An appreciable amount of gafiation by older fans followed in 'Third Fandom' – 1940 to the end of 1944. Speer's system has been expanded since, notably by Robert Silverberg. His 'Fourth Fandom' runs through the immediate postwar years and is characterised by the various efforts with which hucksters and commercialism attempted to dominate fandom. The 'Fifth (brief) Fandom' occupies the end of the forties, and records a gut reaction against the monetary enterprise of the Fourth period. Commercialism swept back with 'Sixth Fandom' in the fifties.

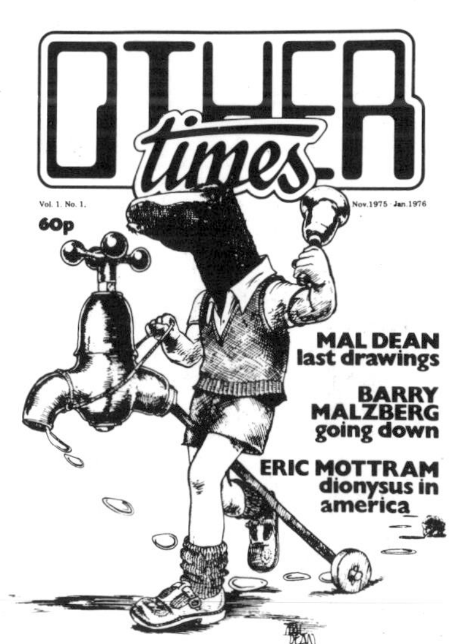

November 1975/January 1976.

When Robert Silverberg published his updated review, some fan groups saw themselves as iconoclastic, and endeavoured to form the vanguard of a new era labelled 'Seventh Fandom'. But Speer pointed out that 'a Fandom is a period, not a collection of people', and the groups' claims were generally discredited. However, in later years, there has been no serious attempt to continue this logical progression, apart from Elliot Weinstein's detailed listing in his *The Fillostrated Fan Dictionary*.

The historical development of fanec (fan activity) during the early years can be regarded as a natural progression since it is largely paralleled by the developing activity of a typical neofan. The reading or collecting of science fiction or fantasy can be seen as the opening step, preparatory to the writing of a letter to a prozine (professional sf magazine). The very first of such publications, Hugo Gernsback's *Amazing Stories*, encouraged the writing of letters to its 'Discussions' column, and through that medium fostered the evolution of fandom. Gernsback noted in the June 1926 issue that there were many fans buying his magazine who had little opportunity to contact each other. To enhance fan communication he printed the name and address of each respondent in full. So was born the second historical activity, correspondence among 'letterhacks' (writers of large quantities of letters to prozines or fanzines). The third phase followed shortly, again with Gernsback's tacit assistance – in the formation of the Science Correspondence Club. It was a further short step to the origination of the first true sf club, the Scienceers, in the same year (1930). (In 1931 Walter H. Gillings began the first UK club, the Ilford Science Literary Society, incorporating UK readers of imported prozines.) It must be emphasised that this was genuinely a 'historical' action; letter-writing to the prozines is currently a discouraged area of fanac. The normal second-stage course of fan motivation in the 1970s is attendance at a convention.

Gernsback further stimulated the development of fandom with prize contests; in 1934 his *Wonder Stories* introduced the Science Fiction League, which soon attracted a large, international membership. Some of its adherents branched into independent local societies, exemplified by the oldest surviving sf club – the Los Angeles Science Fantasy Society (LASFS), which has held over 2000 meetings since 1934. The Philadelphia Science Fiction Society (PSFS) is a mere three months its junior. In the UK, the national Science Fiction Association was formed in January 1937, and has gone through a process of decay and revival to

finally emerge as the present-day British Science Fiction Association (BSFA). A similar history has attended the British Fantasy Society (BFS). Such intentionally nationwide groups have generally failed to secure much favour in the United States. The one remaining survivor, the National Fantasy Fan Federation (NFFF or N3F) has largely lost touch with the broad area of fandom.

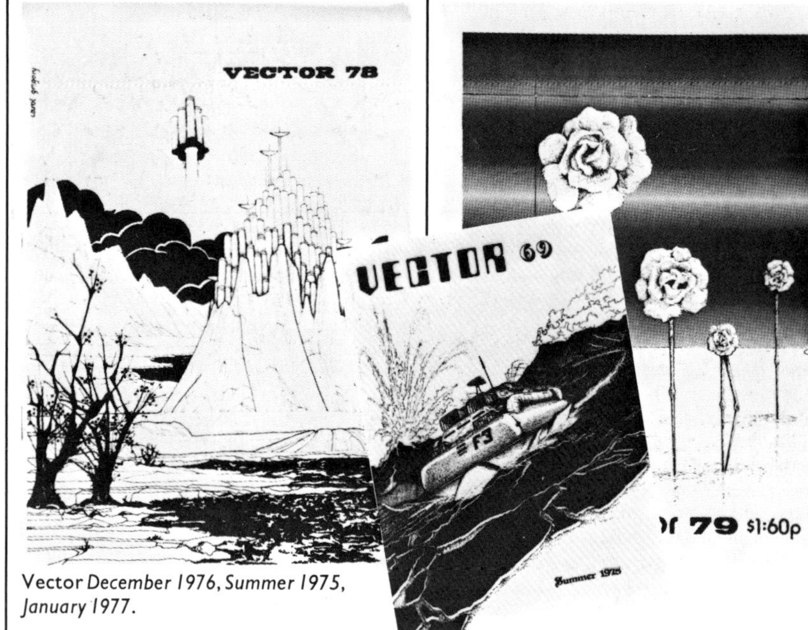

Vector *December 1976, Summer 1975, January 1977.*

The early clubs were small in membership and limited in scope, but they provided assistance in an inimitable way for the next phase of fanac – the production of fanzines. The definition of a fanzine has recently been forced into an area of contention. Because a Hugo award has been designated for the best, several arguments abound regarding the 'amateur' status of such publications. The earliest examples were produced on a typewriter, with carbon copies, by Siegel and Shuster (the later creators of Superman) in 1929, but no copies of their *Cosmic Stories* or *Cosmic Stories Quarterly* are known to have survived. The Science Correspondence Club produced *The Comet* (later retitled *Cosmology*); but in a reaction against its overly scientific slant many fans accord the honour of the first true fanzine to Allen Glasser's *The Planet*, produced for the Scienceers from July 1930. However, the most renowned of early fanzines was Glasser's *The Time Traveller* (1932–33), which numbered amongst its contributors BNF (Big Name Fan) Forrest J. Ackerman.

Frequently neofans have joined a group before becoming letterhacks; but both activities must be indulged before the participants can genuinely become trufans (true fans) – those who 'understand' fandom and are thus qualified to engage in proper fanac. Such activities include the production of fanzines (in anything from an individual issue to the thousands turned out by Bruce Pelz in the US). Many fans ignore such productions and are equally unconcerned regarding the visiting of other enthusiasts beyond the borders of their own locality. Historically, visiting grew from small beginnings; the grand tours of US fandom, by such hitchhikers as Claude Degler and Jack Speer, did not take place until the early forties. Fan visiting, however, has always found a niche in US fandom, though the tendency of unexpected visitors to take top much advantage of initially genuine hospitality sometimes leads to a host's withdrawal (witness the case of Harry Warner Jr, who became known as 'The Hermit of Hagerstown').

During the middle years of fandom, when many devotees were in their teens and their sf reading or fanac was frowned upon by parents, a then current saying ran 'it is a proud and lonely thing to be a fan' (a subtle distortion of an individual sentence in W. Macfarlane's *To Watch the Watchers*, 1949). Alternatively Robert Bloch takes pains to stress in his *The Eighth Stage of Fandom* that fans can be hectically overworked and much-visited – especially BNFs – when their addresses are well known.

From the basic concept of 'visiting', the idea of full-scale conventions grew – resulting in what is universally recognised as a further stage of fandom. The majority of fans now attend conventions, and usually succeed in reaching a few large regional or national gatherings during their so-called 'active life'. Trufans visit many – almost as a matter of obligation – and convention-going, with fanzine production, is now the most popular and enduring form of fan activity.

Following the advent of the first conventions came the last recorded phase of fanac – the formation of 'apas' (*a*mateur *p*ress *a*ssociations). The first, FAPA (Fantasy APA), was founded in 1937 by Donald A. Wollheim on the lines of more mundane (non-fandom) apas. Many fans were producing amateur publications on a 'swap-or-loc' (*l*etter *o*f *c*omment) circulation basis, not charging their subscribers but exchanging fanzines for others, or for articles, news items and letters of comment. An apa acts as a central organiser for such a system among a limited number of members (currently sixty-five in FAPA). Members pay a subscription, and the organisers are usually elected democratically from year to year. Each member is guaranteed an adequate supply of reading material.

The apas (and particularly FAPA) are said to be the places where 'old fans go to die' (though it has been recently observed that FAPA is where old fans go when they *are* dead!). A trufan would normally elect to belong to what are regarded as the prestigious apas – FAPA or SAPS (Spectator AP Society) – but these waiting lists are long. When the fan finally attains his long-awaited membership he may already be a BNF, and may well have already lost his initial enthusiasm. The aura of individual apas tends to be constricting – the individual enthusiast can find himself in a virtually closed circle. Since the early sixties the increase in the number of such groups, and in the quantity of fans joining them, has been described as the 'retreat to the apas'. Independent fanac appeared to suffer a decline during the period, although a rejuvenation has been noted since 1970. Apas now exist in a considerable variety – many of them small or highly specialised. Several clubs have their own, notably LASFS with APA-L, organising a weekly mailing. Hoaxing, a regular pastime with fans, has started its own APA-H (the hoax is that mailings fail to appear). National and international apas have also arrived on the scene, including CANADAPA (for Canada) and ANZAPA (for Australia and New Zealand). In the UK the most active (though recently depleted) is OMPA (Off-trail Magazine Publishers Association), which sponsored an Eastercon in 1973.

In spite of the denigration of sercon activity by many fans, sooner or later the majority of large fan groups pass through a sercon phase, and quite possibly emerge more detached than the apas from genuine fandom. Those groups which decide to

April 1976.

August 1975.

remain 'inside' tend to concentrate on sercon interests and related activity, in the hope of avoiding the personality feuds which have split fandom so drastically in the past. LASFS, for example, has gone through several phases of intense fanac, not to mention several bitter feuds, but its initial tendency to keep itself to itself has been evident. A newer group, NESFA (New England Science Fiction Association) has also undertaken some sercon work. A few groups have attempted to shift national or international political awareness into fandom (the prewar Futurians of New York, which included Donald A. Wollheim, Cyril M. Kornbluth, and Frederik Pohl, aspired to such an endeavour), but their achievements have been less than notable.

To promulgate his views, whether political, science fictional, or fannish – or sometimes just to indulge in the verbose – a fan 'pubs his ish' (publishes a fanzine issue). Fanzines can take the form of single, roughly duplicated or mimeographed sheets of poor paper with even worse contents ('crudzines'); or they may materialise as well-produced publications of substantial bulk (during the late sixties many fanzines ran to over a hundred pages). They may incorporate superior contents material, of fannish or sercon variety (e.g. *Riverside Quarterly*, *SF Commentary*, *Speculation*, and several others), or they may adopt the aura of glossy and slick magazines – with professional layouts and comparable contents ('slickzines', e.g. *Algol* and *Nickelodeon*).

A handful of fanzines are genuinely solvent, and one or two actually pay their contributors – but few make a real profit, and many fail to break even. With the 'apazines' (fanzines produced for apas) and similar swap-basis fanzines, there is usually a considerable loss. Thus fanzines can mainly be considered as platforms for personal expression and communication, or as means for gaining prestige in fandom and occasionally in 'prodom' (the professional sf world). (The epitome of fanzine influence on prodom is represented by Charles D. Hornig, who sent the first issue of his amateur publication, *The Fantasy Fan*, to several prozine editors in 1933, and on the strength of his editorial grasp was put in charge of Gernsback's *Wonder Stories* – at the age of seventeen.)

Fanzines fall into various classes. Fannish fanzines deal with fandom itself, often scurrilously (since the passing of the gentlemanly approach of First Fandom). 'Genzines' contain a general mixture of material (though their name was originally designed to denote fanzines independent of the apas). 'Personalzines' are usually written entirely by the editor/publisher and are consequently stuffed with personal details and anecdotal writing. 'Newszines' (as their name suggests) specialise in distributing news, whether primarily of prodom (in the case of *Luna Monthly*) or of fandom (e.g. *Checkpoint*). The leading world newzine, *Locus*, claims a readership of over 7500 (including library readers) – but its circulation is probably somewhat less than 3000. 'Advertzines' (or adzines) are fanzines consisting wholly of advertisements, such as James V. Taurasi's long-running and influential *Fantasy-Advertiser*. 'Clubzines' are produced mainly for distribution among the members of fan groups.

April 1974.

Fanzines contain many different types of material. Almost all include 'illos' (illustrations), the best being of a very high standard, the worst being execrable. Usually they are also graced with an editorial column or leading article and a lettercol (letter column) or a loc feature. Sometimes letters are allowed to appropriate an entire publication, transforming the magazine into a 'letterzine' (e.g. *Voice of the Imagi-Nation*, VOM). Many early fanzines were produced for the basic purpose of publishing fiction

04.01 FANDOM

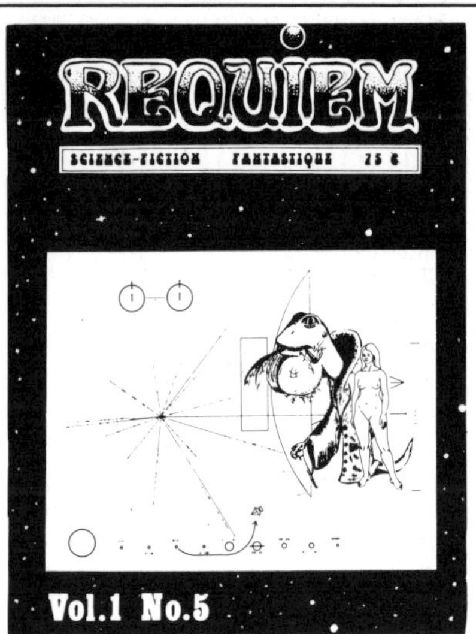

June/July 1975.

(fictionzines), and although, by its very nature, the predominance of fannish fandom has led to the reduction of pure fictionzines, bona-fide stories are still included in some fanzines. Articles on fandom and reviews of other fanzines are universally popular and reviews of sf works are now commonly included (very often to acquire complimentary review copies).

The expression 'fanzine' refers not only to a periodical, but also to any other smallish amateur publication. A one-shot bears little difference in appearance to a periodical fanzine, but it is only intended to have one issue. (Many fanzines achieve single-issue status unintentionally!) Individual pamphlets are often produced to explain a particular viewpoint; story collections or anthologies appear; introductions or guides to particular areas of fandom or science fiction (e.g. Bob Tucker's *The Neo-fan's Guide*) are occasionally published; and many critical or bibliographical surveys of sf make their appearance when funds permit.

The earliest fanzines were either 'handwrittenzines' or 'carbonzines' (each copy being written in longhand or duplicated by carbon copies made from handwriting or typing). The first widespread mechanical reproduction process for fan publications was the mimeograph (and before that the hektograph); but in 1932 'actifan' (active fan) and printer Conrad Ruppert began a service of hand-set low-cost printing of fanzines. Fandom was undoubtedly enhanced by the well-printed productions which saw light of day in the early era. Not only was the quality of printing high, but their contents also added to the 'Golden Age' aura which distinguished the period. When Ruppert eventually terminated his below-cost printing service in 1935, William H. Crawford continued the tradition on behalf of several fanzines; but the expense and effort involved soon proved too great. Subsequently the printing of fanzines became an unexpected luxury.

Within half a dozen years, however, the situation was radically changed. Hecktography re-exerted its popularity over mimeography during the Depression in the early 1930s, when it was found that *cheap* production of fanzines was a viable proposition, and that multi-colour mimeography illustrations were economically possible. In 1940 the 'Decker Dillies' (working in a shack in Decker, Indiana) proved that multi-colour mimeography was a cost-acceptable process. It came to be used on many fanzines. Ink-paste duplication and 'Ditto' sport-duplication followed in the fifties with off-set lithography as a later method which heralded the return of mechanical printing into fairly common usage. Most fanzines are currently mimeographed or duplicated, but many of the more influential are either lithographed or offset.

Opinions differ regarding the overall total of fanzines. Evans and Pavlatt, in their 1952 *Fanzine Index*, list more than 2000 titles, and there have been many since. Peter Roberts, who produces a *Little Gem Guide* listing publications now in production (and which he has personally received) estimates a total of five to six hundred currently being produced on a regular basis, including apazines.

The numerical extent of fandom itself has never been firmly established. Fanzine polls in the thirties estimated a population of about two hundred; while samples in the forties increased the quota to four hundred. Such statistics represent, at best, those respondents who are prepared to answer to polls; and it is reckoned that the gross number of actifans is about 25 per cent in advance of this total. A modest attempt to number all 'fen' puts the grand aggregate at around twelve hundred. During the fifty years of fandom, there have always been more male counterparts than 'femmefans' (female fans), although the ratio has decreased in recent years and there is now a gratifying active feminine contribution to fandom. The average age of fans has also increased commensurately. Fandom, regardless how it is viewed by either the sceptic or the devotee, can be seen dispassionately as a long process of maturation for the individual enthusiast. He may ultimately decide to attempt to write, or to remain firmly established in the fanac backwaters of the genre. Whichever choice he finally takes will have been motivated – to a considerable extent – by his personal reaction to the world of fandom, balanced by his judgement of the respective merits of those areas of science fiction to which he may choose to channel his energies.

Leading or Recommended Fanzines
(full addresses can be found in Peter Robert's *Little Gem Guide*)

Algol ed. Andrew Porter, NY (sercon slickzine)
Amor ed. Susan Wood, Vancouver (personalzine)
Chao ed. John Alderson, Havelock, Victoria, Australia (genzine)
Checkpoint ed. Peter Roberts, London (fannish newszine)
Delap's F&SF Review ed. Richard Delap, Gulver City, California (sercon)
Diaspar ed. Terry Carr, Oakland, California (fannish)
Dynatron ed. Roy Tackett, Albuquerque, New Mexico (personalzine)
Egg ed. Peter Roberts, London (fannish)
Granfalloon ed. Linda Bushyager, Prospect Park, Pennsylvania (genzine)
Hitchhike ed. John Berry, Bronxville, NY (personalzine)
Le Zombie ed. Bob Tucker, Jacksonville, Illinois (personalzine)
Locus ed. Charles & Dena Brown, San Francisco (sf newszine)
Luna Monthly ed. Ann F. Dietz, Oradell, New Jersey (sercon newszine)
Maya ed. Rob Jackson, Newcastle-upon-Tyne (genzine)
Nickelodeon ed. Tom Reamy & Ken Keller, Kansas City, Missouri (slick genzine)
Noumenon ed. Brian Thurogood, Waiheke Island, New Zealand (genzine)
Outworlds ed. Bill Bowers, North Canton, Ohio (genzine)
Philosophical Gas ed. John Bangsund, Norwood, South Australia (genzine)
Prehensile ed. Mike Glyer & Milton Stevens, Sylmar, California (genzine)
Riverside Quarterly ed. Leland Sapiro, Gainesville, Florida (sercon)
Science Fiction Review ed. Dick Geis, Portland, Oregon (sercon)
SF Booklog ed. Keith L. Justice, Union, Mississippi (sercon)
Son of the WSFA Journal ed. Don Miller, Wheaton, Maryland (newszine)
Spang Blah, The ed. Jan Finder, Ft. Riley, Kansas (newszine)
Starling ed. Hank & Lesleigh Luttrell, Madison, Wisconsin (genzine)
Tabebuian ed. Dave & Mardee Jenrette, Miami, Florida (genzine)
Tomorrow And . . . ed. Jerry Lapidus, NY (genzine)
Vector ed. Chris Fowler (for BSFA) Reading, Berkshire (genzine)
Yandro ed. Bob & Juanita Coulson, Hartford City, Indiana (ganzine)
Zimri ed. Lisa Conesa, Manchester (genzine)

PRINTED SOURCES

Beatty, Steven. *Fanzine Directory*, privately printed (US) 1976
Bloch, Robert. *What Is Science Fiction Fandom?*, privately printed (US) 1946; reprinted 1971
Eney, Richard. *Fancyclopedia*, privately printed (US) 1959; a revision of previous editions, the first having been compiled by Jack Speer, 1943
Eney, Richard. *Fancyclopedigest*, privately printed (US) 1968
Evans, Bill (with Bob Pavlat). *Fanzine Index*, reprinted by Harold Palmer Piser (US) 1965; originally published serially from 1952
Moskowitz, Sam. *The Immortal Storm: a History of Science Fiction Fandom*, The Atlanta Science Fiction Organisation Press (US) 1954
Roberts, Peter. *The Little Gem Guide to SF Fanzines*, privately printed (UK) 1976; updated approximately twice-yearly
Tuck, Donald H. *Handbook of Science Fiction and Fantasy*, privately printed (Tasmania) 1954, 2 vols; revised edition, 1959
Tucker, Bob (ed). *The Neo-Fan's Guide to Science Fiction Fandom*, privately printed (US) 1955; revised by Linda Bushyager and Linda Lansberry, 1973
Warner, Harry Jr. *All Our Yesterdays* (forties' fandom), Advent (US) 1969
Warner, Harry Jr. *A Wealth of Fable* (fifties' and sixties' fandom), Fanthistorica Press (US) 1976, 3 vols
Weinstein, Elliot. *The Fillostrated Fan Dictionary*, privately printed (US) 1975, 2 vols
Wertham, Frederic. *The World of Fanzines: A Special Form of Communication*, Southern Illinois University Press (US) 1973

04.01.2 Conventions and Awards

Commentators disagree on what precisely constitutes an sf convention (the word is often shortened to 'con'). Visits among fans, sometimes in the form of group meetings, were one of the earliest fan activities, and in some cases were virtually indistinguishable from small conventions. A hastily arranged trip by some New York members of the ISA (International Scientific Association) to meet Philadelphia fans in October 1936 is sometimes referred to as the first con. Its chief claim to that title is the business meeting that was held in Milt Rothman's house, but little real convention activity took place. Perhaps more solid claims can be made for the first UK con, which was arranged far enough in advance for some publicity to be devoted to it in the fan press. Held in Leeds in January 1937, it resulted in the formation of the first national UK group, the Science Fiction Association. The UK con became an annual event, held in various localities and interrupted only by the Second World War.

The Philadelphia meeting also became an annual convention, and shortly afterwards similar functions were being held in various parts of the US. Attempts were made to attract people outside organised fandom by placing posters in libraries and meeting halls, and in this way some new members were introduced.

The early cons were basically small gatherings with usually less than fifty, and often little more than a dozen, people attending. In May 1938, when Sam Moskowitz and William S. Sykora held what they advertised as the first national convention in Newark, New Jersey, they were surprised to find they had an audience of about a hundred and twenty-five. This turn-out helped to stimulate the organisers into arranging a convention to coincide with the 1939 New York World's Fair.

Aping the global pretensions of the commercial venture, they called it a world convention, or worldcon, and it was soon accepted that this was to be an annual event. The 'world' status of the first few of these conventions was illusory, for only US

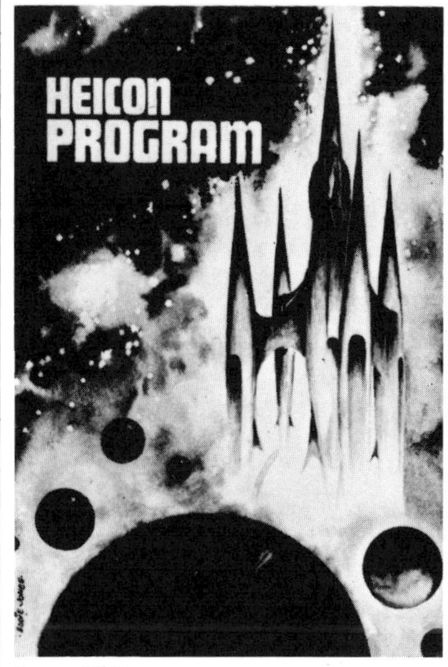

August 1970

04.01 FANDOM

September 1950.

fans, and then mostly local ones, attended. However, from the very beginning certain structures and traditions were created which still survive. A committee organises the event, either being set up for that purpose or comprising part or all of the membership of the host group. A guest of honour from the professional sf world is invited to attend and speak – in recent years there have also been fan guests of honour. A business meeting is arranged by the local group or the organising committee, and the site of the following year's worldcon (now decided upon two years in advance) is chosen from among bids submitted by interested groups.

Most conventions were suspended during the war, although the first post-war gathering was actually held in New England on V-J Day itself. The worldcon originally proposed for 1942 was postponed until 1946, and was finally sponsored by the Los Angeles Science Fiction Society. Forrest J. Ackerman attempted to internationalise the proceedings in the hope of bringing editor Ted Carnell over from the UK, and he created the Big Pond Fund for the purpose; but the plan failed for lack of donations. The following year, however, the Philadelphia worldcon was attended by a number of Toronto fans, and thus it has some claim to the title of the first true world convention. The Toronto group bid successfully for the 1948 worldcon, which was thus the first held outside the US. But no worldcon took place outside North America until 1957, when the first such was held in London. Since then, the worldcon has been convened outside the US on four occasions – only once in a non-English-speaking venue (Heidelberg, 1970), and only once outside the north-west quadrant of the globe (Melbourne, 1975). Attendances at such events outside the US are considerably lower than those for most of the American events, where visitors are now numbered in thousands. Organising a worldcon can obviously prove a prestigious and profitable affair for a local group; and a rotation plan has been instituted to ensure that each area of the US enjoys a chance to bid. The early custom was to organise worldcons near the time of Independence Day, but since 1947 they have been held during the Labor Day weekends in early September.

The Big Pond Fund finally achieved its aim in 1949, when Carnell attended the Cinvention (most worldcons have been graced with similarly contracted titles – the 1949 event being a reduction of '*Cin*cinnati Con*vention*'; Nycon, or *N*ew *Y*ork *Con*vention, is another example). Additional funds have occasionally been set up to enable individuals to attend remote meetings, and since 1953 the Trans-atlantic Fan Fund (TAFF) has enabled a complementary exchange between the US and (usually) the UK on alternate years. Since 1972 a similar Down-Under Fan Fund (DUFF) has operated between the US and Australia. These funds are raised through donations and a levy on voting members of conventions; they are administered by previous beneficiaries.

A North American Science Fiction Convention (NASFiC) is held in those years when the actual worldcon takes place outside that continent. The 1975 NASFiC in Los Angeles, California, attracted almost double the attendance at Aussiecon (the Australian worldcon). America is undoubtedly the sf convention centre of the world, with hundreds of cons being held each year. Several regional cons are held annually, and the largest attract thousands of fans. The oldest and largest is the Westercon, on the West Coast. Other important venues are New York (Lunacon), Boston (Boskone), Baltimore (Balticon) and Philadelphia (Philcon). In recent years, fan activity in the south of the US has resulted in a number of regional gatherings, for example SouthWestercon. Bubonicon is so called because its venue, Albuquerque, New Mexico, was found to be the 'Bubonic plague capital of the USA'.

There are two annual national conventions in the UK, and an increasing number of smaller ones. The largest is Eastercon, organised at various sites since 1948, initially over Whitsun (Whitcon) but now at Easter, and sponsored by various local groups, sometimes in co-operation with the BSFA (British Science Fiction Association). It is attended by a few hundred fans, including European and American visitors. The Birmingham group holds the second-largest, named Novacon since it has been held in that city each November since 1971 (although in 1974 it was held in late October). Like the three Speculation conferences which took place in Birmingham in 1970–72, it was organised by Peter Weston and other fans.

Peterborough Easter 1963.

Australian fans have held annual national conventions regularly since 1952, with local cons also being mounted by the

Philip José Farmer and Harlan Ellison with Hugo Awards at the Baycon in 1968.

Sydney and Melbourne groups each year. Some large cons have been held in continental Europe beginning in the early 1960s, and the Eurocon, first mounted in 1972, brings together both Eastern and Western European fans. Extended sf film conventions are held in Italy, attracting tens of thousands of visitors.

Films have been a convention attraction from the early days, and are now nearly always included in the programmes. Other items include discussions and lectures by professionals and leading fans, talks on many subjects including fan history and scientific topics, a banquet, a masquerade or fancy-dress ball, auctions of sf or fan publications and artwork, award-giving ceremonies, sometimes a sporting event among fans or a fantasy game or dramatic presentation, the production of special fanzine issues (several often being bound together in a 'combozine'), and the business meeting, The last, along with other serious items, is often ignored by regular convention-goers, who spend most of their time socialising and attending the parties which are also regular features. Conventions, especially worldcons, have been meeting places for professionals, semi-professionals and fans since the 1938 Newarkon, but for most fans they are not primarily serious affairs. In particular, the MidWestCon has gained the nickname 'Relaxacon' for its informality, and this name could be applied to other US regional cons and to the UK Novacon. Attempts to set up formal bodies to regularly administer cons, such as the World Science Fiction Society, have achieved little success. (Some fringe groups hold meetings at regular conventions, as do the Burroughs Bibliophiles at the worldcons.)

Fringe sf bodies, some of whose histories have paralleled that of fandom, and others which have split off from the main body, have recently been holding increasing numbers of conventions. A World Fantasy Convention was held in the US in 1975, and is expected to be an annual event; the second was held in New York in October 1976. The Mythopoeic Society holds Mythcon in the US, and several occult factions also hold cons. Comicons have been arranged by fantasy comic fans in the UK, and several countries and regions hold sf and fantasy film cons. The most extensive and numerous fringe groups recently have been formed by fans of the *Star Trek* television series, and many cons have now been held by or for them, especially in the US. The attendances have often been very large, the *New York Times* estimating 20,000 to 50,000 visitors to the January 1976 event in New York City. These were mostly teen-aged fans.

The lower age group was most evident in all early cons, Chicon I being organised by two fans in their middle teens and another under the age of twenty. Convention-goers and organisers have grown in years along with fandom, however, and now a certain maturity of

Robert A. Heinlein, guest of honour at the MidAmericon 1976 (with Nebula Award).

aspect is evident at the true sf cons, if not always a staid level of behaviour. For the fans a con is above all a time to relax or have fun among like-minded companions.

Most sf awards are made at conventions, though not all of them. The oldest-established still awarded are the Hugos, named after the publisher of the first sf magazine, Hugo Gernsback, and more formally called the Science Fiction Achievement Awards. They were first made in 1953, and have been annual awards since the second presentation in 1955.

Some awards were made before the first Hugos were given, usually by individuals at cons or as contest prizes by editors of professional sf magazines. The magazines also held readership polls to determine the best-liked stories or authors in their pages, and these can be considered prototypes for such awards as the Hugos. So, too, could the fanzine polls for best-known fan or favourite fanzine. Sometimes certificates were awarded, such as the NFFF Laureate Awards (last made in 1945), but in other polls simply winning was considered recognition enough. The best remembered in the last category are the FAPA Ego-boo (ego-boosting) polls. Present-day fanzine polls are carried out by *Checkpoint* in the UK and *Locus* in the US, the latter's awards being given a publicity value by some publishers almost equal to that of Hugos and Nebulas.

A break with the tradition of popular or individual choice of award winners came with the advent of the International Fantasy Awards. First given in 1951, these were made to professional writers of fiction and non-fiction for single works chosen by a judging panel. From 1954, the non-fiction class was dropped, and the last awards were made in 1957, by which time the Hugos had become well established.

In their first year, the Hugos included the class of 'No 1 Fan Personality', obviously influenced by the early fan polls The other six classes covered professional activity. While the nature and number of classes have varied from year to year, this preponderance of interest in professional sf activity has continued, though occasionally unclassified awards are made to personalities such as astronauts. When Harry Warner Jr first suggested more awards for amateur activity the idea met with opposition, but support for the proposal has gradually increased. Three classes of Hugos for amateurs have existed since 1967, and recently a new type of award has been instituted, the Fan Activity Achievement (FAAn) Awards.

Also given regularly at worldcons are: the John W. Campbell Award for best new writer of the year, originated in 1973 by the magazine publishers Condé Nast; the Grand Master of Fantasy (Gandalf) Award, first given in 1974, appropriately to J. R. R. Tolkien; the E. E. Evans (Big Heart) Award, made for conspicuous service to fandom; and First Fandom's Hall of Fame Award. The organising committee or an sf group sometimes give individual, irregular awards.

The first World Fantasy Conference organised in 1975 made a series of World Fantasy Awards informally called Howards, and these are expected to be given regularly. Regional sf conventions in America also bestow awards, though usually for fan activity. Westercons, for instance, give Fanzine Achievement Awards, while a local group makes the Little Men's Invisible Man Award for fandom service at the same event (though in 1975 it was made at the Aussiecon). The Equicons, however, do give awards to professionals: the Robbie Award and the Georges Méliès Award are judged for outstanding fantasy-and-sf television and movie productions respectively.

Several awards are made at the UK Eastercons, though not always with

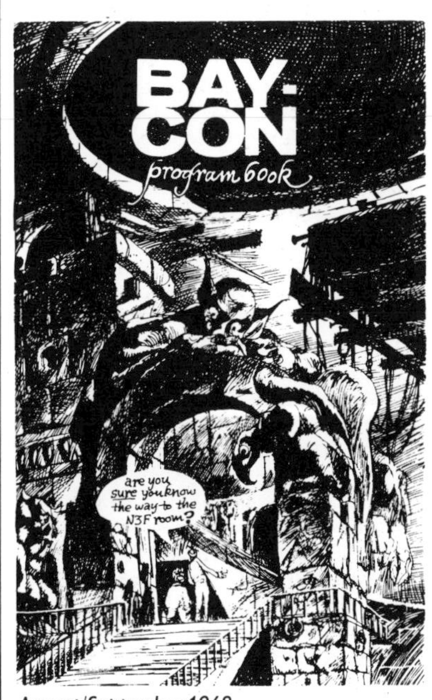

August/September 1968.

regularity. The most consistent have been the Doc Weir Award (named after the late Arthur Rose Weir, DSc, a fan in the Cheltenham group of BSFA) for 'deserving sf renown', given since 1963; and the British Fantasy Society's August Derleth Fantasy Award, made in different classes. The BSFS Award (previously the British SF Award) for Best British Novel of the year began soon after the BSFA was formed, and awards are also given for amateur film-making (Delta Award) and fan art (Ken McIntyre Award). Since 1973, the Nova Award for best individual fanzine issue has been presented at the Novacon.

The Ditmar Awards are given each year at the Australian National Convention, for three classes of professional and amateur activity, including one for the best story published anywhere. Named after Dr Ditmar Jenssen, they were first presented in 1969. The Sydney Science Fiction Club gives the Pat Terry Award for Humour in Science Fiction at the same convention, and various other Australian awards are made annually.

Most of the awards made at cons, including Hugos, are voted by the registered convention membership as a whole, who also make nominations. The choices are thus popular rather than of a seriously critical nature, and in reaction some bodies have instituted awards based on literary excellence. Sharing with Hugos the position of the most prestigious sf awards are the Nebulas, given by the Science Fiction Writers of America (SFWA) to works both nominated by the membership and decided by ballot. The awards resulted from the idea of producing an annual anthology of original stories, since it was realised that the royalties could be used to provide a set of trophies. The Nebulas were first given in 1966 in four classes which, unlike the Hugos, have never varied, apart from the addition of a fifth in 1973. All works nominated must have received first American publication in the previous year.

The Nebula awards are made at annual Spring banquets, of which one is usually held in New York, another in New Orleans and a third on the West Coast. The concept of critical distinction has also been extended retroactively, with SFWA members voting on stories which appeared before 1965, and the poll-winners being published in a set of anthologies called The Science Fiction Hall of Fame. No material awards are made in this context, however.

Partly by reason of the publication limitation imposed in the nominations for Nebula Awards, and partly because lobbying among members has meant that SFWA choices have not always shown as much critical objectivity as was originally intended, another award was created in 1973. Harry Harrison and Leon Stover persuaded the Illinois Institute of Technology to sponsor the John W. Campbell Memorial Award for the best sf novel first published anywhere during the previous year. This award should not be

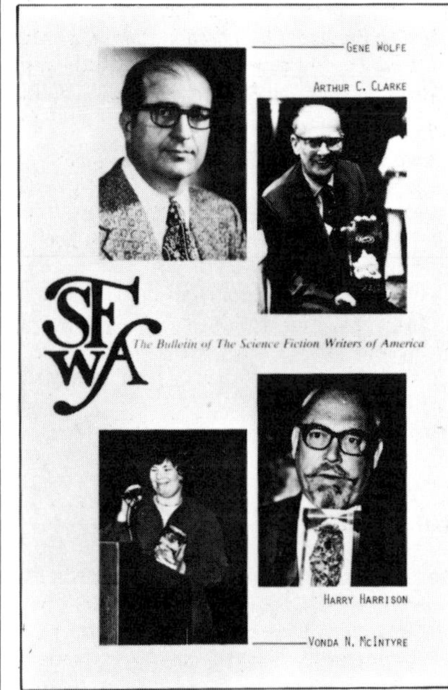

SFWA Bulletin featuring the Nebula awards for 1974.

confused (though it often is) with the John W. Campbell Award for new writers made at worldcons. The novel for the Memorial Award is chosen by an international panel of sf writers and critics. There have been various sponsors for the award, the current one being St John's College, Oxford, in the UK.

A similar international judging panel has been set up by the UK Science Fiction Foundation to present the James Blish Award for Excellence in Science Fiction Criticism, to be given annually at the Eastercon from 1977. In the US, the Jupiter Awards, first presented by the Instructors of Science Fiction in Higher Education in 1975, also included classes for critical and reference works in 1976.

Several more local groups give awards, sometimes only to their own members. More wide ranging than this are the Clarion Awards, First Fandom's Hall of Fame Award (usually made at worldcons), the H. G. Wells Society's Award, and the SFRA's Pilgrim Award made to 'a science fiction personality'. Some publishers occasionally give awards to prizes for science fiction. One such prize was the $5000 given by *The Magazine of Fantasy and Science Fiction*, Pyramid Books and Irwin Allen to Piers Anthony for the best sf novel of 1967 (*Sos the Rope*). In the UK, however, the Orbit Awards from Futura, first made in October 1976, are intended to become annual presentations at the Eastercon from 1978. They are expected to be in two classes, the British Science Fiction Award for the best sf book first published in Britain, and the Orbit Science Fiction Award for the best unpublished sf novel (not given in 1976).

The nature of awards varies from a certificate to a money prize and trophy. The International Fantasy Awards consisted of trophies only. The Hugos are in the form of trophies, too, each of which takes the shape of an upright rocket ship on a base, the design having varied slightly over the years. The Nebulas are also trophies, each being a metallic-glitter spiral nebula and a specimen of rock crystal embedded in a clear Lucite block. The World Fantasy Awards take the form of busts of H. P. Lovecraft, while the John W. Campbell Memorial Award consists of a mounted bronze Möbius Strip and a monetary prize ($600, in 1973). The Orbit Awards consist of $500 in each class.

Several of the continental European conventions give major awards, often for translations of English-language works. Notable among them is the Prix Apollo in France, which has been won by Norman Spinrad, Roger Zelazny, John Brunner and Ian Watson, among others. Europa Awards (made at the Eurocon) and the Italian Hugo have also been won by English-speaking writers, publishers and film-makers.

Recently, several sf writers have won awards not specifically associated with the genre. In 1972 Ursula Le Guin received one of the leading prizes for children's literature, the National Book Award, for the last volume of her *Earthsea* trilogy. The other volumes have also won non-sf awards, the second being runner-up for the 1974 Newberry Gold Medal to another sf children's book, Robert C. O'Brien's *Mrs Frisby and the Rats of Nimh*. This medal was also won by another sf writer, Susan Cooper, in 1975, and in the same year the equally prestigious Caldecott Medal for illustration of children's books was won by sf illustrators Leo and Diane Dillon. In 1974 the Writers' Guild Awards were made to Harlan Ellison for 'Phoenix without Ashes', and to Ray Bradbury 'for bringing honour and dignity to writers everywhere'. Major science fiction writers are thus being recognised by awards outside as well as inside the sf world.

LIST OF AWARDS

Most bodies draw up short-lists of nominations, though without consistent policies. Short-listed works are often given a place, though again not always consistently. The following list includes only those prizes and trophies given to the winner of each class.

HUGO AWARDS

Classifications, chosen by con business meetings, have varied. At present they are: novel – 40,000 + words; novella – 17,500 to 40,000 words; novelette – 7,500 to 17,500 words; short story – up to 7,500 words.

1953
Novel: Alfred Bester, *The Demolished Man*
Professional Magazine: *Galaxy; Astounding Science Fiction* (tie)
Interior Illustrator: Virgil Finlay
Cover Artist: Ed Emshwiller; Hannes Bok (tie)
Excellence in Fact Articles: Willy Ley
New Science Fiction Author or Artist: Philip José Farmer
No 1 Fan Personality: Forrest J. Ackerman

1954 none made

1955
Novel: Mark Clifton and Frank Riley, *They'd Rather Be Right*
Novelette: Walter M. Miller Jr, 'The Darfstellar'
Short Story: Eric Frank Russell, 'Allamagoosa'
Professional Magazine: *Astounding Science Fiction*
Illustrator: Frank Kelly Freas
Amateur Publication: James V. Taurasi, *Fantasy Times*

1956
Novel: Robert A. Heinlein, *Double Star*
Novelette: Murray Leinster, 'Exploration Team'
Short Story: Arthur C. Clarke, 'The Star'
Professional Magazine: *Astounding Science Fiction*
Illustrator: Frank Kelly Freas
Feature Writer: Willy Ley
Most Promising New Author: Robert Silverberg
Amateur Publication: Ron Smith, *Inside & Science Fiction Advertiser*
Critic: Damon Knight

1957
Professional Magazine (American): *Astounding Science Fiction*
Professional Magazine (British): *New Worlds Science Fiction*
Amateur Publication: James V. Taurasi, *Science Fiction Times*

1958
Novel: Fritz Leiber, *The Big Time*
Short Story: Avram Davidson, 'Or All The Seas With Oysters'
Professional Magazine: *The Magazine of Fantasy and Science Fiction*
Illustrator: Frank Kelly Freas
Motion Picture: *The Incredible Shrinking Man* (based on the story by Richard Matheson)
Most Outstanding Actifan: Walter A. Willis

1959
Novel: James Blish *A Case of Conscience*
Novelette: Clifford D. Simak, 'The Big Front Yard'
Short Story: Robert Bloch 'The Hell-Bound Train'
Professional Magazine: *The Magazine of Fantasy and Science Fiction*
Illustrator: Frank Kelly Freas
Amateur Publication: Terry Carr and Ron Ellik, *Fanac*
Most Promising New Author: Brian W. Aldiss

1960
Novel: Robert A. Heinlein, *Starship Troopers*
Short Fiction: Daniel Keyes, *Flowers for Algernon*
Professional Magazine: *The Magazine of Fantasy and Science Fiction*
Illustrator: Ed Emshwiller
Amateur Publication: F. M. Busby, *Cry of the Nameless*
Dramatic Presentation: *The Twilight Zone* (based on the story and produced by Rod Serling)
Special Award: Hugo Gernsback (The Father of Magazine Science Fiction)

1961
Novel: Walter M. Miller Jr, *A Canticle For Leibowitz*
Short Story: Poul Anderson 'The Longest Voyage'
Professional Magazine: *Analog* (formerly *Astounding*)
Illustrator: Ed Emshwiller
Amateur Publication: Earl Kemp, 'Who Killed Science Fiction?'
Dramatic Presentation: *The Twilight Zone*

1962
Novel: Robert A. Heinlein, *Stranger in a Strange Land*
Short Fiction: Brian W. Aldiss, the 'Hothouse' series
Professional Magazine: *Analog*
Amateur Magazine: Richard Bergeron, *Warhoon*
Professional Artist: Ed Emshwiller
Dramatic Presentation: *The Twilight Zone*

1963
Novel: Philip K. Dick, *The Man in the High Castle*
Short Fiction: Jack Vance, 'The Dragon Masters'
Professional Magazine: *The Magazine of Fantasy and Science Fiction*
Amateur Magazine: Dick Lupoff, *Xero*
Professional Artist: Roy Krenkel
Special Awards: P. Schuyler Miller (Best Book Reviews); Isaac Asimov (Distinguished Contributions to the Field)

1964
Novel: Clifford D. Simak, *Way Station*
Short Story: Poul Anderson, 'No Truce With Kings'
Professional Magazine: *Analog*
Professional Artist: Ed Emshwiller
Book Publisher: Ace Books
Amateur Publication: George Scithers, *Amra*

1965
Novel: Fritz Leiber, *The Wanderer*
Short Fiction: Gordon R. Dickson, 'Soldier, Ask Not'
Professional Magazine: *Analog*
Professional Artist: John Schoenherr
Book Publisher: Ballantine Books
Amateur Publication: Robert and Juanita Coulson, *Yandro*
Dramatic Presentation: *Dr Strangelove* (based on the story by Peter George)

1966
Novel: Frank Herbert, *Dune*; Roger Zelazny, *And Call Me Conrad* (tie)
Short Fiction: Harlan Ellison, '"Repent Harlequin!", Said the Ticktockman'
Professional Magazine: *If*
Professional Artist: Frank Frazetta
Amateur Magazine: Camille Cazedessus, *ERB-dom*
Best All-time Series: Isaac Asimov, the 'Foundation' series

1967
Novel: Robert A. Heinlein, *The Moon Is a Harsh Mistress*
Novelette: Jack Vance, 'The Last Castle'
Short Story: Larry Niven, 'Neutron Star'
Professional Magazine: *If*
Professional Artist: Jack Gaughan
Dramatic Presentation: 'The Menagerie' (*Star Trek*)
Amateur Publication: Ed Meskys and Felice Rolfe, *Niekas*
Fan Artist: Jack Gaughan
Fan Writer: Alexei Panshin

1968
Novel: Roger Zelazny, *Lord of Light*
Novella: Philip José Farmer, 'Riders of the Purple Wage'; Ann McCaffrey, 'Weyr Search' (tie)
Novelette: Fritz Leiber, 'Gonna Roll the Bones'
Short Story: Harlan Ellison, 'I Have No Mouth and I Must Scream'
Dramatic Presentation: 'City on the Edge of Forever' (script by Harlan Ellison for *Star Trek*)
Professional Magazine: *If*
Professional Artist: Jack Gaughan
Amateur Publication: George Scithers, *Amra*
Fan Artist: George Barr
Fan Writer: Ted White

1969
Novel: John Brunner, *Stand on Zanzibar*
Novella: Robert Silverberg, 'Nightwings'
Novelette: Poul Anderson, 'The Sharing of Flesh'
Short Story: Harlan Ellison, 'The Beast That Shouted Love at the Heart of the World'
Drama: *2001: a Space Odyssey* (script by Arthur C. Clarke and Stanley Kubrick)
Professional Magazine: *The Magazine of Fantasy and Science Fiction*
Professional Artist: Jack Gaughan

04.01 FANDOM

Amateur Publication: Dick Geis, *Psychotic (SF Review)*
Fan Writer: Harry Warner Jr
Fan Artist: Vaughn Bodé
Special Award: Armstrong, Aldrin and Collins (The Best Moon Landing Ever)

1970
Novel: Ursula K. Le Guin, *The Left Hand of Darkness*
Novella: Fritz Leiber, 'Ship of Shadows'
Short Story: Samuel R. Delany, 'Time Considered as a Helix of Semi-Precious Stones'
Dramatic Presentation: Television coverage of Apollo XI
Professional Magazine: *The Magazine of Fantasy and Science Fiction*
Amateur Magazine: Dick Geis, *SF Review*
Fan Writer: Wilson Tucker
Fan Artist: Tim Kirk

1971
Novel: Larry Niven, *Ringworld*
Novella: Fritz Leiber, 'Ill Met in Lankhmar'
Short Story: Theodore Sturgeon, 'Slow Sculpture'
Professional Artist: Leo and Diane Dillon
Professional Magazine: *The Magazine of Fantasy and Science Fiction*
Amateur Magazine: Charles and Dena Brown, *Locus*
Fan Writer: Dick Geis
Fan Artist: Alicia Austin

1972
Novel: Philip José Farmer, *To Your Scattered Bodies Go*
Novella: Poul Anderson, 'The Queen of Air and Darkness'
Short Story: Larry Niven, 'Inconstant Moon'
Dramatic Presentation: *A Clockwork Orange* (based on the story by Anthony Burgess)
Amateur Magazine: Charles and Dena Brown, *Locus*
Professional Magazine: *The Magazine of Fantasy and Science Fiction*
Professional Artist: Frank Kelly Freas
Fan Artist: Tim Kirk
Fan Writer: Harry Warner Jr

1973
Novel: Isaac Asimov, *The Gods Themselves*
Novella: Ursula K. Le Guin, 'The Word for World Is Forest'
Novelette: Poul Anderson, 'Goat Song'
Short Story: R. A. Lafferty, 'Eurema's Dam'; Frederick Pohl and Cyril M. Kornbluth, 'The Meeting' (tie)
Dramatic Presentation: *Slaughterhouse five* (based on the story by Kurt Vonnegut Jr)
Professional Editor: Ben Bova
Professional Artist: Frank Kelly Freas
Amateur Magazine: Michael and Susan Glicksohn's *Energumen*
Fan Writer: Terry Carr
Fan Artist: Tim Kirk
Special Award: Pierre Versins for *Encyclopedie de l'Utopie et de la Science Fiction*

1974
Novel: Arthur C. Clarke, *Rendezvous With Rama*
Novella: James Tiptree Jr, 'The Girl Who Was Plugged In'
Novelette: Harlan Ellison, 'The Deathbird'
Short Story: Ursula K. Le Guin, 'The Ones Who Walk Away from Omelas'
Amateur Magazine: Dick Geis, *The Alien Critic*; Andy Porter, *Algol* (tie)
Professional Artist: Frank Kelly Freas
Professional Editor: Ben Bova
Dramatic Presentation: *Sleeper*
Fan Writer: Susan Wood
Fan Artist: Tim Kirk
Special Award: Chesley Bonestell

1975
Novel: Ursula K. Le Guin, *The Dispossessed*
Novella: George R. R. Martin, 'A Song for Lya'
Novelette: Harlan Ellison, 'Adrift Just Off the Islets of Langerhans'
Short Story: Larry Niven, 'The Hole Man'
Professional Artist: Frank Kelly Freas
Professional Editor: Ben Bova
Amateur Magazine: Dick Geis, *The Alien Critic*
Dramatic Presentation: *Young Frankenstein*
Fan Writer: Dick Geis
Fan Artist: William Rotsler

1976
Novel: Joe Haldeman, *The Forever War*
Novella: Roger Zelazny, 'Home Is the Hangman'
Novelette: Larry Niven, 'Borderland of Sol'
Short Story: Fritz Leiber, 'Catch That Zeppelin'
Dramatic Presentation: *A Boy and His Dog* (based on the story by Harlan Ellison)
Fanzine: *Locus*
Professional Artist: Frank Kelly Freas
Professional Editor: Ben Bova
Fan Writer: Dick Geis
Fan Artist: Tim Kirk

NEBULA AWARDS

Classifications: novel – 40,000+ words; novella – 17,500 to 40,000 words; novelette – 7,500 to 17,500 words; short story – under 7,500 words

1966
Novel: Frank Herbert, *Dune*
Novella: Brian W. Aldiss, 'The Saliva Tree'; Roger Zelazny, 'He Who Shapes' (tie)
Novelette: Roger Zelazny, 'The Doors of His Face, the Lamps of His Mouth'
Short Story: Harlan Ellison, '"Repent, Harlequin!" Said the Ticktockman'

1967
Novel: Samuel R. Delany, *Babel 17*; Daniel Keyes, *Flowers for Algernon* (tie)
Novella: Jack Vance, 'The Last Castle'
Novelette: Gordon R. Dickson, 'Call Him Lord'
Short Story: Richard Mackenna, 'The Secret Place'

1968
Novel: Samuel R. Delany, *The Einstein Intersection*
Novella: Michael Moorcock, 'Behold the Man'
Novelette: Fritz Leiber, 'Gonna Roll the Bones'
Short Story: Samuel R. Delany, 'Aye, and Gomorrah'

1969
Novel: Alexei Panshin, *Rite of Passage*
Novella: Ann McCaffrey, 'Dragonrider'
Novelette: Richard Wilson, 'Mother to the World'
Short Story: Kate Wilhelm, 'The Planners'

1970
Novel: Ursula K. Le Guin, *The Left Hand of Darkness*
Novella: Harlan Ellison, 'A Boy and His Dog'
Novelette: Samuel R. Delany, 'Time Considered as a Helix of Semi-Precious Stones'

Westercon Program Book, *1971: front cover by George Barr, back cover by Tim Kirk.*

Short Story: Robert Silverberg, 'Passengers'

1971
Novel: Larry Niven, *Ringworld*
Novella: Fritz Leiber, 'Ill Met in Lankhmar'
Novelette: Theodore Sturgeon, 'Slow Sculpture'
Short Story: not awarded

1972
Novel: Robert Silverberg, *A Time of Changes*
Novella: Katherine Maclean, 'The Missing Man'
Novelette: Poul Anderson, 'The Queen of Air and Darkness'
Short Story: Robert Silverberg, 'Good News from the Vatican'

1973
Novel: Isaac Asimov, *The Gods Themselves*
Novella: Arthur C. Clarke, 'A Meeting with Medusa'
Novelette: Poul Anderson, 'Goat Song'
Short Story: Joanna Russ, 'When It Changed'

1974
Novel: Arthur C. Clarke, *Rendezvous with Rama*
Novella: Gene Wolfe, 'The Death of Dr Island'
Novelette: Vonda N. McIntyre, 'Of Mist, and Grass, and Sand'
Short Story: James Tiptree Jr. 'Love Is the Plan, the Plan Is Death'
Dramatic Presentation: *Soylent Green* (based on *Make Room! Make Room!* by Harry Harrison)

1975
Novel: Ursula K. Le Guin, *The Dispossessed*
Novella: Robert Silverberg, 'Born with the Dead'
Novelette: Gregory Benford and Gordon Eklund, 'If the Stars Are Gods'
Short Story: Ursula K. Le Guin, 'The Day Before the Revolution'
Dramatic Presentation: *Sleeper*
Grand Master Award: Robert A. Heinlein

1976
Novel: Joe Haldeman, *The Forever War*
Novella: Roger Zelazny, 'Home Is the Hangman'
Novelette: Tom Reamy, 'San Diego Lightfoot Sue'
Short Story: Fritz Leiber, 'Catch that Zeppelin'
Dramatic Writing: *Young Frankenstein*
Special Awards: Special plaque to George Pal for pre-Nebula-dates film work; Grand Master Award to Jack Williamson

JOHN W. CAMPBELL MEMORIAL AWARD

(for best novel of the year)

1973
Barry Malzberg, *Beyond Apollo*
Special trophy for excellence of writing: Robert Silverberg, *Dying Inside*

1974
Arthur C. Clarke, *Rendezvous with Rama*; Robert Merle, *Malevil* (tie)
Special non-fiction award: Carl Sagan, *The Cosmic Connection*

1975
Philip K. Dick, *Flow My Tears, the Policeman Said*

1976
Wilson Tucker, *The Year of the Quiet Sun* (retrospective)

JOHN W. CAMPBELL AWARD

(for best new writer)

1973
Jerry Pournelle

1974
Spider Robinson; Lisa Tuttle (tie)

1975
P. J. Plauger

1976
Tom Reamy

GANDALF AWARDS

1974
J. R. R. Tolkein

1975
Fritz Leiber

1976
L. Sprague de Camp

INTERNATIONAL FANTASY AWARDS

1951
Fiction: George R. Stewart, *Earth Abides*
Non-fiction: Willy Ley and Chesley Bonestell, *The Conquest of Space*

1952
Fiction: John Collier, *Fancies and Goodnights*
Non-fiction: Arthur C. Clarke, *The Exploration of Space*

1953
Fiction: Clifford D. Simak, *City*
Non-fiction: Willy Ley and L. Sprague de Camp, *Lands Beyond*

1954
Theodore Sturgeon, *More than Human*

1955
Edgar Pangborn, *A Mirror for Observers*

1956
not awarded

1957
J. R. R. Tolkein, *Lord of the Rings* trilogy

AUGUST DERLETH FANTASY AWARDS

1972
Novel: Michael Moorcock, *The Knight of the Swords*

1973
Novel: Michael Moorcock, *King of the Swords*
Short Story: L. Sprague de Camp, 'The Fallible Fiend'
Film: *Tales From the Crypt*
Comic: *Conan*
Special Award: Robert Howard, *Marches of Valhalla*

1974
Novel: Poul Anderson, *Hrolf Kraki Saga*
Short Story: Michael Moorcock, 'Jade Man's Eyes'
Film: *Legend of Hell House*
Comic: *Conan*

1975
Novel: Michael Moorcock, *The Sword and the Stallion*
Short Story: Karl Edward Wagner, 'Sticks'
Film: *The Exorcist*
Comic: *The Savage Sword of Conan*

1976
Novel: Michael Moorcock, *The Hollow Lands*
Short Story: Fritz Leiber, *The Second Book of Fritz Leiber*
Film: Terry Jones and Terry Gilliam, *Monty Python and the Holy Grail*
Comic: *The Savage Sword of Conan*

JUPITER AWARDS

1975
Novel: Ursula K. Le Guin, *The Dispossessed*
Novella: Norman Spinrad, 'Riding the Torch'
Novelette: Jack Vance, 'Seventeen Virgins'
Short Story: Ursula K. Le Guin, 'The Day Before the Revolution'

FAAN AWARDS

1975
Single Fanzine Issues: Bill and Joan Bowers, *Outworlds 21/22*
Fan Editor: Bill Bowers
Fan Writer: Don C. Thompson
Fan Artist (Humorous): William Rotsler
Fan Artist (Non-humorous): Jim Shull
Letter-of-comment Writer: Harry Warner Jr

NOVA AWARD

1973
Peter Weston, *Speculation 32*

1974
Lisa Conesa, *Zimri 6*;
John Brosnan, *Big Scab*
(tie)

1975
Rob Jackson, *Maya 8*

AWARDS FROM ORBIT BOOKS

1976
British Science Fiction Award: Ian Watson, *The Jonah Kit*

04.01 FANDOM

NATIONAL ORGANISATIONS

The British Fantasy Society,
Jon M. Harvey, 37 Hawkins Lane,
Burton-on-Trent, Staffordshire, UK

The British Science Fiction Association Limited,
David Wingrove, 4 Holmside Court,
Nightingale Lane, London SW12 8JW, UK

The National Fantasy Fan Federation,
Rt 1, Box 364,
Heiskell, TN 36654, US

The Science Fiction Writers' Association of America,
Theodore R. Cogswell, 108 Robinson Street,
Chincilla, PA 18410, US

The Science Fiction Research Association,
Marshall Tynn, English Dept,
Eastern Michigan University, Ypsilanti,
MI 48197, US

SERCON ORGANISATIONS

The Fantasy Foundation,
Forrest J. Ackermann, 2495 Glendower
Avenue, Hollywood, CA 90027, US

The New England Science Fiction Association,
Box G, MIT Branch PO,
Cambridge, MA 02139, US

The Science Fiction Foundation,
North-East London Polytechnic,
Longbridge Road, Dagenham,
Essex RM8 2AS, UK

The Science Fiction Writers' Association of America, and the Science Fiction Research Association
(See above for addresses)

PRINTED SOURCES

Asimov, Isaac (ed). *The Hugo Winners 1955–1961*, Doubleday (US) 1962

Asimov, Isaac (ed). *The Hugo Winners 1963–1967*, Doubleday (US) 1971; Sphere (UK) 1973

Asimov, Isaac (ed). *The Hugo Winners 1968–1970*, Doubleday (US) 1971; Sphere (UK) 1973

Bova, Ben (ed). *Science Fiction Hall of Fame Vol II: the Novellas*, Doubleday (US) 1973 (NB For vol I see Silverberg)

Bova, Ben (ed). *Science Fiction Hall of Fame Vol III: the Novelettes*, Doubleday (US) 1975

DeVore, Howard with Donald Franson. *A History of the Hugo, Nebula, and International Fantasy Awards*, Howard DeVore (US) 1973

McKinney, Richard L. *Nebula Award Fiction 1965–1972: Novelettes*, Literaturvetenskapliga Institutionen (Sweden) 1974

Nebula Award Stories: annual anthologies published variously by Doubleday and Harper & Row in US and by Gollancz in UK, with various editors:
1. 1966 – Damon Knight (ed)
2. 1967 – Brian W. Aldiss and Harry Harrison (eds)
3. 1968 – Roger Zelazny (ed)
4. 1969 – Poul Anderson (ed)
5. 1970 – James Blish (ed)
6. 1971 – Clifford D. Simak (ed)
7. 1972 – Lloyd Biggle Jr (ed)
8. 1973 – Isaac Asimov (ed)
9. 1974 – Kate Wilhelm (ed)
10. 1975 – James Gunn (ed)

Silverberg, Robert. *Science Fiction Hall of Fame Vol I: Short Stories*, Doubleday (US) 1970

LIST OF CONVENTIONS

1. Worldcons

YEAR	NAME	VENUE	GUESTS OF HONOUR	CHAIRMEN	
1939	Nycon I	New York	Frank R. Paul	Sam Moskowitz	200
1940	Chicon I	Chicago	Edward E. Smith, PhD	Mark Reinsberg	128
1941	Denvention	Denver	Robert A. Heinlein	Olon Wiggins	90
1946	Pacificon I	Los Angeles	A. E. van Vogt and E. Mayne Hull	Walt Daugherty	130
1947	Philcon I	Philadelphia	John W. Campbell Jr	Milton Rothman	200
1948	Torcon I	Toronto	Robert Bloch (pro) Wilson Tucker (fan)	Ned McKeown	200
1949	Cinvention	Cincinnati	Lloyd A. Eshbach Ted Carnell (UK)	Don Form	190
1950	Norwescon	Portland	Anthony Boucher	Donald B. Day	400
1951	Nolacon	New Orleans	Fritz Leiber	Harry B. Moore	190
1952	10th Worldcon	Chicago	Hugo Gernsback	Julian C. May	870
1953	11th Worldcon	Philadelphia	Willy Ley	Milton Rothman	750
1954	SFCon	San Francisco	John W. Campbell Jr	Lester Cole and Gary Nelson	700
1955	Clevention	Cleveland	Isaac Asimov	Nick and Noreen Falasca	380
1956	Newyorcon	New York	Arthur C. Clarke	David A. Kyle	850
1957	Loncon I	London	John W. Campbell Jr	Ted Carnell	268
1958	Solacon	Los Angeles	Richard Matheson	Anna S. Moffatt	322
1959	Detention	Detroit	Poul Anderson (pro) John Barry (fan)	Roger Sims and Fred Prophet	371
1960	Pittcon	Pittsburgh	James Blish	Dirce Archer	568
1961	Seacon	Seattle	Robert A. Heinlein	Wally Weber	300
1962	Chicon III	Chicago	Theodore Sturgeon	Earl Kemp	550
1963	Discon I	Washington DC	Murray Leinster	George Scithers	600

YEAR	NAME	VENUE	GUESTS OF HONOUR	CHAIRMEN	
1964	Pacificon II	Oakland	Edmond Hamilton and Leigh Brackett (pros) Forrest J. Ackerman (fan)	J. Ben Stark	523
1965	Loncon II	London	Brian W. Aldiss	Ella Parker	350
1966	Tricon	Cleveland	L. Sprague de Camp	Ben Jason	850
1967	Nycon 3	New York	Lester del Rey (pro) Wilson Tucker (fan)	Ted White and Dave Van Arnam	1500
1968	Baycon	Oakland	Philip José Farmer (pro) Walter Daugherty (fan)	Bill Donaho, Alva Rogers and J. Ben Stark	1430
1969	St Louiscon	St Louis	Jack Gaughan (pro)	Ray and Joyce Fisher	1534
1970	Heicon 70	Heidelberg	Robert Silverberg (US) E. C. Tubb (UK) Herbert W. Franke (Ger)	Manfred Kage	620
1971	Noreascon	Boston	Clifford D. Simak (pro) Harry Warner Jr (fan)	Tony Lewis	1600
1972	L.A. Con	Los Angeles	Frederik Pohl (pro) Robert and Juanita Coulson (fan)	Charles Crane and Bruce Pelz	2007
1973	Torcon 2	Toronto	Robert Bloch (pro) William Rotsler (fan)	John Millard	2900
1974	Discon II	Washington DC	Roger Zelazny (pro) J. K. Klein (fan) Leigh Edmonds (DUFF)	Jay and Alice Haldeman	4000
1975	Aussiecon	Melbourne	Ursula K. Le Guin (pro) Susan Wood and Michael Glicksohn (DUFF) Donald Tuck (Ausl)	Robin Johnson	2044
1976	Mid-American	Kansas City	Robert A. Heinlein	Ken Keller	2614

NB *The number in the end column signifies registered members, some of whom do not attend; however, some unregistered attenders are often present. DUFF: Down-Under Fan Fund. TAFF (Trans-Atlantic Fan Fund), representing subscriptions of many fans, is excepted here.*

2. British Eastercons
(previously Whitcons)

YEAR	VENUE	NAME
1937	Leeds	
1938	London	
1941	London	Bombcon
1943	Leicester	Midvention
1944	Birmingham	Norcon
1948	London	
1949	London	
1951	London	Festivention
1952	London	
1953	London	Coroncon
1954	Manchester	SuperMancon
1955	Kettering	Cytricon I
1956	Kettering	Cytricon II
1958	Kettering	Cytricon III
1959	Birmingham	Brumcon
1960	London	
1961	Gloucester	LXIcon
1962	Harrogate	Ronvention
1963	Peterborough	Bullcon
1964	Peterborough	Repetercon
1965	Birmingham	Brumcon II
1966	Yarmouth	Yarcon
1967	Bristol	Briscon
1968	Buxton	Thirdmancon
1969	Oxford	Galactic Fair
1970	London	Scicon 70
1971	Worcester	Eastercon 22
1972	Chester	Chesmancon
1973	Bristol	Ompacon 73
1974	Newcastle-upon-Tyne	Tynecon
1975	Coventry	Seacon
1976	Manchester	Mancon 5

04.02 SCIENCE FICTION ART

04.02 SCIENCE FICTION ART

When primitive man began scratching in clay and daubing coloured mud on his cave walls, he was making his first attempts at representing some sort of order in his precarious existence. He began with drawings of the hunt, followed by the first crude fertility figures and what can be interpreted as attempts to depict his own gods. When he began to draw what he couldn't see, smell, hear or touch, his pictures entered the realm of fantasy.

For thousands of years man has continued in his efforts to illustrate the products of his imagination. He has invented many weird and wonderful creatures, often in connection with his religious beliefs, such as men with heads of birds, lions with wings, unicorns, gargoyles and many others. Such artists as Hieronymus Bosch have created their own fantasy worlds peopled with strange, perverse beings, and these in turn have influenced other artists.

In 1844 Isidore Grandville attracted attention with *Un Autre Monde*, a book he lavishly illustrated with his bizarre creations, including his famous 'doublivores' (an animal devised from two others). His creations and his inventive spirit had considerable impact upon the illustrations of many early science fiction novels. Late in the nineteenth century another artist, Albert Robida, came into his own as one of the first true science fiction illustrators. Robida produced many illustrations of a futuristic nature in a series of his own books entitled *Le Vingtième Siècle* (1883), and he may be properly credited with anticipating the wide perspective and predictive elements of science fiction art in his drawings of weapons and inventions of the future.

Cover by A. Robida for La Guerre Infernale.

Robida's visions were coloured by nineteenth-century social attitudes. It took someone raised outside his influence to give science fiction illustration its proper place as a medium for visions of the unknown and the future. Modern sf illustration, it has been suggested, begins with one man – Warwick Goble. Goble was charged, in the late 1890s, with illustrating the works of a new, young writer, Herbert George Wells. He reached his peak with Wells's novel, *The War of the Worlds*, throwing off virtually all of the artistic restrictions of the past and starting fresh and unsullied. He was able to infuse his illustrations with a fluid grace and a freshness that later illustrators of Wells seemed unable to equal.

Illustration by J. Allen St John for Tarzan and the Golden Lion *by Edgar Rice Burroughs.*

Early in the twentieth century, there appeared another artist of note. His name was John Allen St John and his career was closely connected with the rise of Edgar Rice Burroughs. He blended the imagery of Burroughs with his own delicate style so well that, to this day, he is considered by many to be the most successful illustrator of Tarzan, John Carter, Pellucidar and the many other visions of Edgar Rice Burroughs. His style has influenced illustrators right up to the present, particularly those concerned with ERB reprints.

The work that links the early illustrations of Goble and St John to modern sf art can be attributed substantially to one man. His name was Frank R. Paul, and he could easily be called 'the father of modern sf illustration'. He was closely associated with 'the father of magazine science fiction', Hugo Gernsback; like Gernsback, he was a European immigrant to the US. An architect by training (which was evident in his work), Paul provided cover illustrations for Gernsback's factual *Electrical Experimenter* and *Science and Invention* long before the launch of *Amazing Stories*. When Gernsback decided to start the first science fiction magazine in 1926, Paul was the cover illustrator (he was also responsible for the interior illustrations). In fact, he became the magazine's sole illustrator for many issues.

Frank R. Paul exerted an influence on science fiction illustration that has spanned the half-century from the initial issue of *Amazing Stories* to the present day. The characteristics of his work – the attention to detail, the garish colours, the penchant for gadgetry, embellishments and decoration – are still present in many sf illustrations. He was the first, the man whose presence others felt when they picked up brush and paint. A highly prolific artist, his work appeared in such magazines as *Wonder Stories, Amazing Stories, Fantastic Adventures* and *Science Fiction Plus*, to name but a few. Although he illustrated endless subjects, his cities were his forte. Drawing on his background in architecture, he was able to add a depth and breadth to alien cities rarely equalled since. Though critics delight in pointing out his obvious inability to portray the human figure, they have to admit his considerable talent for portraying aliens, alien scenery, futuristic gadgets and alien (or future) cities.

The second man to enter the world of science fiction magazine illustration was Leo Morey. Although he was never to gain the fame that Paul did (and none of the artists ever gained a fortune), he was admired and respected by the followers of science fiction. He added the human element to the cover art of the late twenties and the thirties, not only portraying the human face and figure more effectively than Paul, but also including more people in his cover designs. Where

Hugo Gernsback's Electrical Experimenter *1920.*

IN CANADA 30 CENTS

AMAZING STORIES

MAY

25 Cents

The Cerebral Library
by David H. Keller, M.D.

Beings of the Boundless Blue
by Walter Kateley

Through the Vibrations

Across the Void, Part II

Cover by Leo Morey for 'The Great Catastrophe' by Wood Peters, Amazing *May 1931.*

Paul's colours were quite flat, Morey added a liquid sheen for a striking effect.

In the early thirties, *Amazing Stories* was faced with several competitors, the most important of which were *Science Wonder Stories* and *Astounding Stories of Super-Science*. The former was started by Gernsback after he had lost control of *Amazing*, and featured covers and interior illustrations by Paul and other artists. At the same time, the work of two new, important contributors began appearing on the covers of various pulp and science fiction magazines.

The first was Wesso (real name: Hans Waldemar Wessolowski). When *Astounding Stories of Super-Science* began in January 1930, Wesso was the cover artist, and when Clayton relinquished the publication thirty-four issues later, he was still the cover artist, a remarkable tribute to his skills as an illustrator. After *Astounding* changed hands in 1933, Wesso continued his work for the magazine, though not with the same regularity. He continued to remain productive for many years, contributing to *Amazing, Astounding, Marvel Science Stories* and others.

The second artist, Howard V. Brown, first appeared in the science fiction field in 1933, when the Street & Smith pulp chain re-launched *Astounding*. Although his early covers were awkward and crude, his style matured rapidly and by the late thirties he was the equal of anyone practising the art. He produced illustrations for a variety of sf magazines, but some of his best work appeared on the covers of *Startling Stories* just before the Second World War. When compared with those of Paul or Morey, his colours seem to be slightly washed-out or faded, but he used a better balance of colour than his predecessors. One of his techniques, employed on several covers, was to put a glowing line around the outline of robots, giving them a unique and effective life of their own.

The period from January 1930 to the start of the war was a busy one for the writers, publishers, artists and readers of science fiction. New magazines were created almost every year; old ones folded or were killed by their publishers without warning. In such a climate fresh artists emerged almost overnight. Many stayed to gain some reputation in the field, but many more dropped out in order to survive (the pay rates were not particularly good at this time in pulp history).

Alex Schomburg was among the illustrators of this period. He had already worked for Gernsback before *Amazing Stories* was started, providing several covers for *Electrical Experimenter* in 1925 and 1926. When science fiction magazines were blooming in the thirties, however, he was relatively unknown to the readers and fans, in spite of his work for such pulps as *Thrilling Wonder Stories*. Nevertheless, he was destined to become one of the most recognised of sf artists in a later period.

A few other illustrators of note can be recorded during the years from 1926 to 1938. One of the most artistically dynamic was Robert Fuqua, whose jewel-like effects for *Amazing* and *Fantastic Adventures* added a new dimension to cover illustrations. Another deserving mention is Elliot Dold. Dold undertook the majority of his work for *Astounding*, and some of his black-and-white illustrations for the 'Skylark' series of stories by E. E. ('Doc') Smith are regarded as legitimate classics of the early days of the genre. A third artist, who began illustrating in the waning years of the thirties, was to become a legend among the enthusiasts of sf art. This was Virgil Finlay, whose work is considered later.

Illustration by Virgil Finlay Wonder Stories *1963.*

Other artists in the thirties, who were destined to fade almost entirely from view, included H. W. McCauley, William Juhre, Julian S. Krupa, Mark Marchioni, Jack Binder, S. R. Drigin – all now largely forgotten. Their work tended to be overshadowed by the better illustrators in the field, a field that was not large enough or rich enough to afford artists whose work was unable to gain the support of the fans.

Shortly before the outbreak of war, science fiction was beginning a new phase, one signalled by the appointment of John W. Campbell as editor of *Astounding*. This next period, roughly from 1938 to 1950, is referred to by some as the Golden Age of Science Fiction. It could also easily be known as the Golden Age of Science Fiction Illustration, for many notable artists reached their peak during those years.

Frank R. Paul was illustrating less in this period, and actually left the field for some while (he returned in the early fifties to produce some covers for Gernsback's *Science Fiction Plus*). The quality of his work remained high, but was less in keeping with the new art styles that were coming into vogue. Leo Morey continued to produce noted illustrations, but gradually he, too, dropped from the scene. Wesso, Brown and Fuqua had also more or less vanished by the end of the Golden Age.

Virgil Finlay began his illustrating in the last years of the thirties. He was active in sf illustration for more than twenty years, and worked virtually until the day of his death in 1971. He is best known for his black and white illustrations, which graced the interiors of *Thrilling Wonder Stories, Startling Stories, Fantastic Novels, Famous Fantastic Mysteries, Galaxy, Amazing Stories* and many other magazines. He also painted some excellent colour covers, but his reputation rests on his inimitable, painstakingly stippled, interior illustrations. His contribution to the field is often the standard by which the works of newer artists are judged.

Illustrations by Albert A. Neutzell for Vertex *April 1973.*

At about the time the United States was entering the war, another legendary figure had begun a remarkable career. An artist of demonstrable integrity, Hannes Bok was heavily influenced by Maxfield Parrish and A. Merrit. Their influence, plus his own skill, help to account for his totally unmistakable style. While it might be possible to confuse a Paul with a Wesso, or a Dold with a Marchioni, it is quite impossible to mistake a Bok for anyone else's work. Where others dealt in realism, Bok was a stylist, a master of the weird and macabre. His first professional work was for the December 1939 issue of *Weird Tales*, and his art subsequently appeared in more than three dozen different science fiction and fantasy magazines. He also wrote a number of tales for *Future* and *Unknown* as well as half-a-dozen other magazines; they were generally well received. While, like Finlay, most of his renown came from his black and white illustrations, he also produced cover illustrations, although many thought his colours were too subdued for the magazine stands.

Alex Schomburg became more active during and following the war, mostly with interior illustrations and the occasional cover. His skill with the airbrush was slowly being appreciated, and culminated in a flurry of activity in the early fifties. During the early forties, another name had come into prominence, that of Hubert Rogers. By 1942, Rogers was one of the leading artists in the field, illustrating mainly for *Astounding*. Like Bok, his colours were relatively drab, yet he managed to instil an aura of depth and excitement into his work.

There were many other artists during this period, of varying ability. A. Leydenfrost was among the better practitioners; his style might be described as a blending of Finlay and Bok. Charles Schneeman was another, noted for his interior illustrations; unfortunately, his

Cover by Alex Schomburg for Everyday Astrology *April 1945.*

career effectively ended with the war, as did several other careers. Earle K. Bergey became one of the best known of all science fiction illustrators, even though very few people outside science fiction knew his name. It was his renderings of the brass-brassiered female in the clutches of a tentacled monster which did much to saddle science fiction with a reputation for garishness among non-readers. Rod Ruth, as typified by some of his work in *Fantastic Adventures*, was a very capable artist of black and white illustrations, but his name is almost unknown today.

Edd Cartier is perhaps more fortunate, and is remembered for his illustrations to such stories as de Camp and Pratt's *Castle of Iron* and Williamson's *Darker Than You Think* in 1940. He ended the decade by illustrating de Camp's *The Hand of Zei* in *Astounding*.

Around 1950, at about the same time that *Galaxy* and *The Magazine of Fantasy and Science Fiction* were attracting readers and acclaim, a new era of science fiction illustration was beginning. It was hardly an instant happening, but rather a blossoming of talent over a period of years during which some of the older artists reached their peak of skill and imagination, and other young, gifted artists joined the field.

Alex Schomburg probably produced his best work in the decade and a half following 1950. In addition to many covers for *Startling Stories, Fantastic Universe, Thrilling Wonder Stories* and others, he also produced cover art for the noted Winston series of 'juvenile' sf novels that began appearing in the early fifties (in all, he painted some 40 per cent of them). Once again, his skill with the airbrush proved unmatched, and his life-like figures seemed almost to leap from the page.

Among the newcomers of the fifties was one who rapidly became respected in his profession and who was to carry away more awards than any other artist in the field. By 1976, Frank Kelly Freas had won ten Hugo awards. His combination of skill and humour have enabled him almost to dominate science fiction cover illustration, and his work has featured in many magazines, although he is best known for his contributions to *Astounding/Analog*. Noted for its use of dominant foregrounds, his style of painting is also characterised by its individual treatment of colour.

Early in 1951, *Galaxy* introduced another newcomer of real merit whose talents bore favourable comparison with those of Freas. With his first few illustrations (crude by the standard of his work of only a few years later), Ed Emshwiller demonstrated craftmanship of a high order. Signing his illustrations 'Emsh', he often worked his signature into the background, so that the readers might enjoy the puzzle of discovering 'where Emsh hid his name *this* time'. His intricate covers intrigued the eye, and his paintings appeared on the covers of almost all of the magazines extant in the fifties. In 1964, Emshwiller quit the sf illustration field in favour of experimental videotapes, an area in which he has also become well known.

Of the other leading post-war artists, Jack Gaughan began his long career in the fifties, and by 1959 had become one of the principal illustrators for *Galaxy* and *Astounding*. Although known in science fiction mainly for his black and white illustrations, his imaginative use of colour and design for covers won him much acclaim and three Hugo awards.

many illustrators passed briefly across the scene, then vanished. One of those who stayed was Richard Powers, spending much of his time and talents painting for the covers of the growing paperback book industry in the early fifties. His work for the magazines was infrequent (he contributed a number of illustrations to *Beyond* in 1953); he still produces the occasional book cover. His style seems to be heavily influenced by the Surrealists

Cover by Bruce Pennington for The Green Brain *by Frank Herbert.*

Chesley Bonestell came to the ranks of sf illustrators by a roundabout route; he began his career as an artist specialising in astronomy. His illustrations for Willy Ley's *Conquest of Space* (1949) won him nationwide recognition. He produced some work for *Astounding* and many covers for *F&SF* in the early fifties. His paintings regularly adorned the pages of *Life* magazine. He is particularly noted for the set designs on *Destination Moon* (1950), a movie based on Heinlein's *Rocket Ship Galileo* (1947).

John Schoenherr has been long regarded as the most 'painterly' of modern sf illustrators. After graduating from the Pratt Institute in 1956, he approached *Astounding*'s editor, John W. Campbell, with a folio of his work. He was soon to become an *Astounding* regular, and that publication remains the only magazine outlet for his science fiction work. In 1965, he won a Hugo for Best Professional Artist.

During the fifties and sixties, a great

(Yves Tanguy in particular), but his skill is very much his own.

A major contribution to British readership was provided by reprints of American magazines. The relatively small indigenous UK magazine market has also enjoyed its share of talented artists. In the early 1950s the pages of *Authentic SF Monthly, Science Fantasy, New Worlds* and *Nebula* bore evidence of the able work of Gerald Quinn, Bob Clothier, John Richards and Brian Lewis. Walter Gillings's pre-war *Tales of Wonder* carried the artwork of W. J. Roberts; while Ted Carnell's early post-war publications displayed the notable illustrations of R. M. Bull, a female artist whose period of work in the field was regrettably brief. In more recent years, the work of Charles Platt and Malcolm Dean (in *New Worlds)*, Bruce Pennington's vivid illustrations for *Science Fiction Monthly*, Chris Foss's paintings of space hardware and David Pelham's highly stylised book covers, have attracted critical praise. Another noted British artist is David Hardy, who,

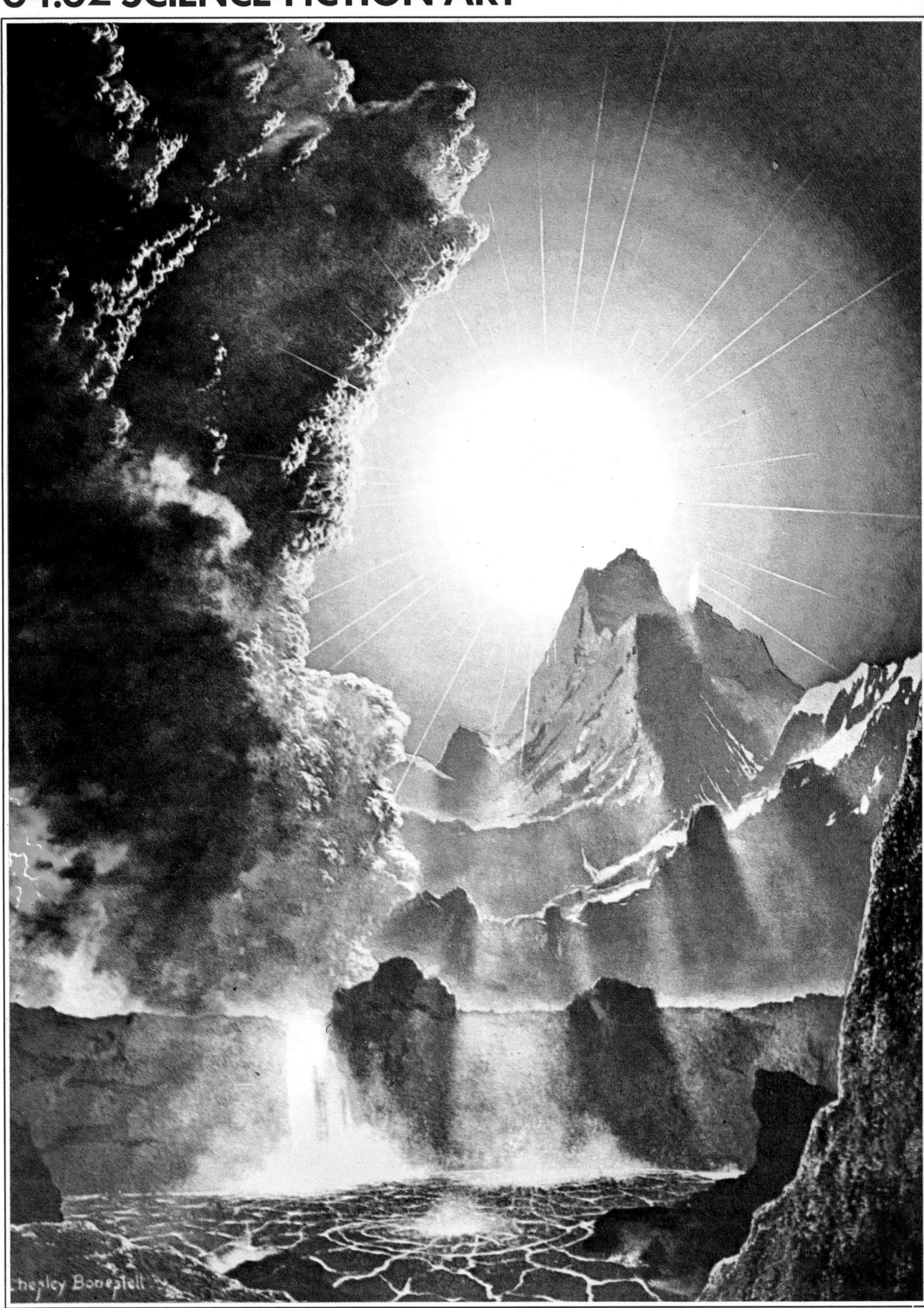
Chesley Bonestell

Left: Illustration by Chesley Bonestell from Beyond the Solar System *by William Ley.*

with astronomer Patrick Moore, wrote *Challenge of the Stars* which he illustrated himself, combining scientific accuracy (the details were checked by NASA) with a powerful sense of imagination.

With the decline of *New Worlds* and the demise in 1976 of *Science Fiction Monthly*, UK artists have mainly directed their talents to the covers of novels and anthologies more noticeably in the paperback market. Their work has also been seen in the commercial advertising field, on record jackets and in the colour pages of the quality newspapers' magazine supplements.

Other notable US illustrators in the period 1950–70 include Mel Hunter, whose smooth, slick style was sometimes mistaken for Alex Schomburg's, and Malcolm Smith, whose work for *Imagination* and *Other Worlds*, suggested that he was the man to carry on where Earle Bergey left off. Henry van Dongen graced the covers of *Astounding* with his rather oddly shaped humans for several years from the early fifties. R. G. Jones proved a skilful artist whose covers for *Amazing Stories* and *Fantastic Adventures* might be described as a bridge between the styles of the forties and those of the fifties. Ed Valigursky provided a multitude of covers for Ace Books in the fifties and sixties, in addition to his work for *Amazing* in the fifties.

What of the future? Many of the artists of the recent past (with a few notable exceptions) have either died or ceased working in the field. Fortunately, a new type of talented young illustrator is moving into the field – artists who seem to have recaptured the 'sense of wonder' that

Cover by R.M. Bull for Science-Fantasy *Winter 1951-2.*

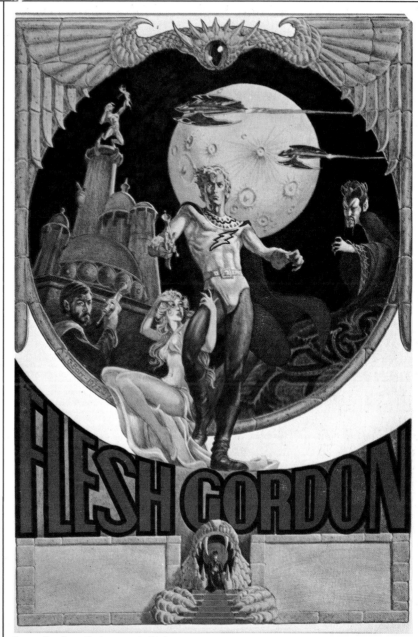

George Barr's preliminary study for the movie poster.

appeared to have been diminishing in the last few years. They are well-trained, highly skilled, and their work holds out the promise of continuing visual excitement.

One of the most notable of the American new breed is Stephen E. Fabian, a very prolific artist whose work has been favourably compared with Finlay's. Equally at ease in colour or black and white, he has provided illustrations mainly for *Galaxy*, where his covers, embodying a striking use of colour, have attracted much attention. Another recent arrival is Rick Sternbach, whose work for *If*, *Galaxy* and *Analog* has received acclaim. Like Schomburg, he is a master of the airbrush, and his covers reflect his background in astronomical art. George Barr, who came to the ranks – to a large extent – through fandom, is one more young illustrator endowed with talent. His works bring a gentleness of colour to sf illustration that has too often been missing in the past. The super-bright colours of the earlier era have appeared to fade as science fiction expands its readership to a wider audience. Other up-and-coming artists of merit include Tim Kirk, Vincent Di Fate, Mike Gilbert and the British illustrator, Eddie Jones.

Looking aside from the newcomers, one may still note the continuing contributions of Freas, Gaughan, Schoenherr and Schomburg. Their long-standing reputations are, if anything, enhanced by their most recent work. Their illustrations, coupled with those of their younger colleagues, are a useful indication that the state of sf art is not merely healthy, but also rising to meet the challenge of a more sophisticated and demanding audience.

Science fiction art has broken the bounds of its original sf magazine format and, by doing so, has accomplished a jump comparable to the influence which sf writing itself is now exerting beyond the traditionally accepted confines of the genre. The application of sf illustration techniques confronts the public from poster hoardings, product packaging, and the television and cinema screens alike, not to mention those areas already noted in the consideration of British artists. The process seems likely to continue.

PRINTED SOURCES

Science Fiction Art

Aldiss, Brian. *Science Fiction Art*, New English Library (UK) 1975

Aldiss, Brian. *Science Fiction Art* (Chris Foss illustrations), Hart-Davis, MacGibbon (UK) 1976

Ballantine, Betty (intro). *The Fantastic Art of Frank Frazetta*, Charles Scribners and Sons (US) 1975

Carter, Lin. *Imaginary Worlds. The Art of Fantasy*, Ballantine (US) 1973

Del Rey, Lester. *Fantastic Science Fiction Art 1926–1954*, Ballantine (US) 1975

Freas, Frank Kelly. *1975 Kelly Freas Selections*, privately printed (US) 1975

Frewin, Anthony. *One Hundred Years of Science Fiction Illustration*, Jupiter Books (UK) 1974

Gunn, James. *Alternate Worlds. The Illustrated History of Science Fiction*, Prentice-Hall (US) 1975

Kyle, David. *A Pictorial History of Science Fiction*, Hamlyn (UK) 1976

Rottensteiner, Franz. *The Science Fiction Book: an Illustrated History*, Thames and Hudson (UK) 1975

Sacks, Janet (ed). *Visions of the Future*, New English Library (UK) 1976

Sadoul, Jacques. *Hier, L'An 2000*, Editions Denoel (France) 1973; Souvenir Press (UK) 1975

04.03 SCIENCE FICTION IN THE CINEMA

To many discerning enthusiasts, the history of science fiction films can be read as a catalogue of disasters, with the occasional highlight to relieve the unremitting paucity of talent unhappily displayed in countless 'B' features. The fact is that a number of excellent sf movies *have* been made during the last seventy years (and those seven decades are not quoted lightly – some of the very first films to be shot were based on science fiction stories, and proved almost universally better than their latter-day counterparts).

The following outline concerns itself with the more impressive offerings in the cinema's development. The very nature of science fiction invites cinematic treatment. With growing finesse in the filming of special effects, there is little in the sf author's imagination which cannot be translated on to the wide screen – given an adequate budget and a producer prepared to have faith in his writer's script. To review the progress of the sf film from its beginnings, it is necessary to look briefly at the cinema's own birth-pangs; the two are irretrievably linked. Rather than arrest the text with an exhaustive account of directors and producers' names and production dates, the required details are given in a comprehensive listing at the end.

When films began in the late nineteenth century, they were already science fiction. A black box emitted a dazzling ray of light, and images moved where they had no right to be. On the one hand, those images aped reality; they resembled familiar places, costumes and faces. On the other, they demanded the willing suspension of disbelief. What, after all, was 'real' about a monochrome two-dimensional square of reflected light? Yet the first audiences to encounter the documentary Lumière programmes in France in 1895 could persuade themselves without difficulty that they 'saw' trains, and factory workers, and a baby having tea. They believed that their eyes recorded movement; what they were actually observing was an arrested process of change – the minute difference between one still picture and the next.

It was the shortest of directoral steps from documentary films to fantasy, and the first was taken by Georges Méliès. A professional French conjurer, he used films to extend his magic – to turn girls into demons, to remove limbs and replace them in the wrong order, to change sizes and shapes, to subvert normality or compel it to disappear completely. If the Lumières attempted to preserve the world as it was (and their cameramen roamed everywhere in the five years up to 1900), finally to give up in disillusionment with the human scene, Méliès responded to the new century with the certainty that nothing was going to be the same again. His output of films was prodigious, and their range was equally extraordinary, from adaptations of Shakespeare to Cinderella, from Berlioz to Verne. His scripts were littered with explorers, voyaging 20,000 leagues under the sea, soaring to the North Pole in a flying machine with an eagle's head – or to the Moon in a bullet. Usually he acted the leading roles himself; a notable type-cast, for within a decade he had explored and instituted almost everything the cinema was later to depend on – a studio, colour, sound, and even a distribution organisation.

It would be inaccurate to suggest that Méliès was the only filmic innovator at work at the turn of the century; the Edison studios were breaking new ground in the US; Robert Paul's team were learning the art of trick photography in Britain; and there were many other celluloid explorers in Denmark, Japan, and

A Voyage to the Moon *1902*.

Frankenstein *1910*.

a dozen more countries. Their films portrayed an environment of speculative elasticity, in which the flattened victim of a steamroller could be restored with a bicycle pump, a jalopy could ride around the rings of Saturn, and the Moon could lean from the sky to interrupt a courting couple. If the science fiction classics of the time are usually given as Méliès' *A Trip to the Moon* (1902) and Paul's *The ? Motorist* (1906), it is only because so few of these early prints have remained in circulation or have survived at all. The writings of Verne and Wells impressed the pioneer film-makers so profoundly that the first movies of this century were a wonderland of flying machines, electric laboratories, and invisible men. What has been lost in the neglect of the earliest reels is a matter of speculation and regret, but we do know that a 1909 version of *The Invisible Man* was filmed as *An Invisible Thief* in France.

The screen's first *Frankenstein* in 1910, offers, like its literary original, a useful punctuation point in our survey. Directed for Edison in the startlingly rich colours and simple special effects originated in the Méliès tradition, it nevertheless looked ahead to the perpetual dialogue between man and his darker self which identifies a particular area of science fiction. Such a dialogue, given literary voice by Mary Shelley, has been chorused by Poe, Hawthorne, Verne and Wells; but the film-makers required to understand their art more extensively before they could take up the full refrain in the second and later decades of the cinema.

The monster in *Frankenstein* was originally screened as an emaciated, vaguely leonine figure, invading its creator's wedding night at a time when the Italian film-makers were flooding the market with Odyssean miracles, and when D. W. Griffith, quite independently, was learning that more than one individual story could be told in a single film. Griffith discovered how, with editing, it was possible to alter time itself; hoping as the next step to alter man, he gave the cinema a conscience. History sees his effort as too late; by the time his classic *Intolerance* appeared, the First World War was already threatening the Edwardian view of progressive civilisation.

It is tempting to summarise the effect of the Great War on the cinema by conjuring up one title: *Caligari*. To do so is to give that arguably awkward film a weight that it probably bears with ease: it is a rich political allegory, the tragic tale of a passionate zombie who embodies the makings of *Frankenstein* and *King Kong* in one. But the zombie was also German, and while this identifies him with Mary Shelley's succession of Gothic imitators, it probably links him more directly with the concept of the alter-ego – part soul, part-demon – that found particular favour in the writings of Goethe, Hoffmann and von Chamisso.

In 1914, Paul Wegener filmed the first *Golem*, a story from Jewish mythology of the magical creation of artificial life; and in 1920, under the influence of *Caligari*, he remade it. His clay giant, eyes glittering with malice, served as a model for Boris Karloff's monstrous appearance and cumbersome movements as Frankenstein's monster in the 1930s; but it is remarkable how closely the film, in common with the contemporary work of Lang, Pabst, and Murnau, echoed the Hoffmannesque dramas of ambiguity and horror. Hoffmann's stories placed their dominant characters on the edge of the supernatural, easy victims to the evil clutches of demonic visitors from the underworld. As a parallel with the potent but abhorrent attractions of Nazism, both the writings of Hoffmann and the science fiction films of the 1920s appear strikingly prophetic in a present-day context.

The underworld, in most senses, was the dark foundation for many of the early German productions. From these gloomy forebodings emerged the chillingly unhuman vampire of *Nosferatu* (1922), the criminal master-mind of *Dr Mabuse* (1922), the warped talent of *The Hands of Orlac* (1924), the seven deadly sins of *Faust* (1926), and the erotic evil of *Alraune* (1928). In the films of Fritz Lang, the dank subterranean caverns became a crucible of revolutionary energy, from which there seemed to flow a torrent of gnome-like Huns (*Kriemhild's Revenge*), an army of gangsters (*Spione*), or, most renowned of all, the dispirited and programmed ranks of identical workers who tended the power-houses of *Metropolis* (1926).

The importance of *Metropolis* in the development of the science fiction film can be considered in several ways. It was architecturally spectacular, with sets derived from Lang's impressions during a visit to New York in 1924, to which he added the dramatic use of crowd 'shapes'. The film's handling of politics was generally humanitarian, but the implications of the union between the overlord of the city and his 'proles' at the story's close are difficult to reconcile with his earlier dictatorial megalomania. Although robots had crossed the screen before, *Metropolis* was the first visual scenario to give serious treatment to the Wellsian 'man-versus-machine' debate. Since then, science fiction in the cinema has embraced one or more of the obligatory identification marks: the 'city' sequence (*Soylent Green* and *Logan's Run*), the revolt of the underdog (*Fahrenheit 451* and *THX 1138*), and the berserk machine (*2001: a Space Odyssey* and *The Terminal Man*). By 1926, Lang's only oversight was space travel; he corrected the deficiency in 1928 with *The Woman in the Moon*, a production based on existing knowledge but allowing the Moon to enjoy an atmosphere.

In contrast to European film-making, which before the onset of the sound era moved towards the introspective or experimental, American directors

Metropolis *1926*.

04.03 SCIENCE FICTION IN THE CINEMA

The Woman in the Moon *1928.*

favoured a more out-going approach, applying their gifts to the visually dramatic productions of *The Hunchback of Notre Dame* (1923), *The Thief of Bagdad* (1924), *The Phantom of the Opera* (1925), and *The Lost World* (1925). Such films illustrate the dominant characteristics of the 1930s flights of fantasy – the deformed human derelicts that fascinated Tod Browning and James Whale, and the exotic 'lost culture' adaptations of Schoedsack and Cooper. Willis O'Brien's dinosaurs in *The Lost World* survived to endure the extravagances of *King Kong* in 1933; while Universal, inspired by the success of *Hunchback* and *Phantom*, financed both *Dracula* and *Frankenstein* in 1931, launching a golden age of horror classics, that decreased in quality in an almost direct ratio to the collection of minor directors who endeavoured to mount the bandwagon. It was the time of *Dr Jekyll and Mr Hyde* (the Oscar-winning Frederic March version of 1931), *The Mummy* (1932), *The Island of Lost Souls* (1932), *The Mystery of the Wax Museum* (1933), and *The Vampire Bat* (1933). Most harrowing of all was *Freaks* (1932), with its authentic array of unimaginably distorted humans, that was denied a UK showing for more than three decades. Every bit as ingenious was *Devil Doll* (1936), in which Lionel Barrymore used miniaturised beings for murderous ends. All these were noted classics; the dross is beyond mention.

So much was extraordinary about the flood of baroque, brutal, and often brilliant melodrama of the immediate pre-war era, that it appears unjustly overshadowed by the 'great' film of the decade, Alexander Korda's Wells-scripted *Things to Come* (1936), which came near to being a pompous bore in its occasional scenes. That it can retain its fascination, even today, is once more a measure of the elements offered uniquely by science fiction; the baleful prophecy (world war, and the bombing of London), the images of anarchy (ruined palaces and casual murder) which entertain a surrealist potency, the visions of progress (flying wings, giant television screens, the space gun) which inevitably present themselves as attainments within our current reach, all the more for having been filmed already. It was an ungainly, declamatory epic, in keeping with the later writings of Wells, but it remains an epic. Earlier adaptations of Wells's works had included a silent version of *The First Men in the Moon* (1919), James Whale's noted *The Invisible Man* (1933) and *Man Who Could Work Miracles* (1936), another Korda production. Further Wellsian films followed in the 1950s and 1960s: *The Door in the Wall* (1953), George Pal's *The Time Machine* (1959) and *The First Men in the Moon* (1964).

Descending from the sublime to the arguably ridiculous, *Flash Gordon*, the memorable US serial that began in 1936 under the direction of Frederick Stephani, carried no pretensions, yet in the long run it has paradoxically influenced the development of sf movies more substantially than *Things to Come*. Granted the advent of 'pure' sf magazines ten years earlier, *Flash Gordon* can be regarded as the cinema's enthusiastic adoption of their more lurid aspects. It epitomises pop-culture space opera, swarming with charm and nonsense. In its time it counter-balanced the morbid gloom of the 1930s horror output, but it did inflict on science fiction cinema an imprint of simplicity and ingenuous action that has taken years to remove. It also contributed on the lighter side of the balance, a sense of fun that did a world of good. Much the same can be said of the *Buck Rogers* serial, directed by Ford Beebe and Saul A. Goodkind, which began life in 1939.

The Second World War, with its acceleration of technical research and its sudden unwelcome opportunities for travel, loomed as a macabre illustration of the naïve moralistic patterns of the 1930s serials, which continued in the 1940s to incorporate a frequently militant xenophobia. Characters and adventures from the screen were re-run in the comics and pulp magazines, those of them which succeeded in remaining in circulation, and in turn the comics fed the screen. The first *Batman* serial appeared in 1943, *Superman* followed in 1948. The horror favourites of the previous decade having degenerated into encounters with Abbott and Costello, a brief return to vitality was marked by Val Lewton's productions for RKO: *Cat People* (1942), *I Walked with a Zombie* (1943), *The Leopard Man* (1943), and his two most noted films, *Isle of the Dead* (1945) and *Bedlam* (1946). More stories of darkness and suspicion than of science, they nevertheless bear close association with the preoccupations of such writers as Sturgeon and Bradbury; the latter's first collection of tales (*Dark Carnival*) being published in 1947.

Flash Gordon *1936.*

Superman *1948.*

With the advent of the atomic age, the Cold War, and the ensuing arms and missile race, horror and science fiction on the screen became more appropriately connected. The castles and forests of the Gothic stories gave way to the open desert, into which there began to fall a hail of rockets whose occupants ranged from the dangerous to the merely grotesque. The widespread speculation regarding the existence of flying saucers reached its height in the early 1950s – a further sign of the general insecurity of the international scene. The effect on the movies of the period is evident – films of invasion, alien intervention, and monstrous mutants abounded. The decade became the most prolific, although only occasionally inspired, era of the science fiction film.

The upsurge of interest owed much to George Pal's *Destination Moon* (1950), based on Robert A. Heinlein's *Rocketship Galileo*, which spelled out for cinema audiences what Heinlein's readers had been hearing for years – that space was the final frontier, an idea explicit in the conclusion of *Things to Come* and elsewhere in the work of Wells. It is not a film which has worn well (although still memorable for the designs of Chesley Bonestell's backgrounds), but at the time it stated clearly and simply a message that mankind's future – both logical and inspirational – lay in the stars. It was succeeded almost immediately by a welter of alien invasions, another view of man's likely retribution if he thought he was fit to venture beyond his homeground. They featured among many others, *When Worlds Collide* (1951), *The Day the Earth Stood Still* (1951), *The Thing from Another World* (1952), *Invasion USA* (1952), *Red Planet Mars* (1952), *It Came from Outer Space* (1953), *Invaders from Mars* (1953), and the technically brilliant Byron Haskin updated adaptation of Wells's tale *War of the Worlds* (1953).

The Incredible Shrinking Man *1956*.

First Men in the Moon *1964*.

If an overriding theme can be recognised in the films of the 1950s, it may be seen in their studies of helplessness, depicting man as powerless before the immense forces of the universe – its rogue planets, its superior alien brains, its cosmic disdain for human weakness. At the same time, almost instinctively, they demonstrated the human capacity for survival: the bloodthirsty 'Thing' is at last burned to a crisp by Howard Hawks's resourceful team; love (earthly, if not divine) proves a match for Pal's Martians, helped by a little terrestrial bacteria; and the criminal mind of Feist's *Donovan's Brain* (1953) is defeated. But as the 1950s wore on, confidence appeared to dwindle. Nature on man's own world was conceived as being in revolt, and humanity was terrorised by the likes of *The Beast from 20,000 Fathoms, The Creature from the Black Lagoon, Tarantula*, and *The Monolith Monsters*; with *The Incredible Shrinking Man* (1956), there came an allegorical but specific statement of the recognition of man's true insignificance, yet still ending on an equivocal expression of hope.

The most distinguished films of this later 1950s period are consistent in their underlying mood of near defeat. In Fleischer's *20,000 Leagues under the Sea* (1954), it was apparent that Verne's misanthropic hero of a century before was still an apposite creation. Elegantly and spectacularly produced, the film supported its leading character's view that man and the marvellous may hardly belong together. In Siegel's *Invasion of the Bodysnatchers* (1956), the replacement of humans by emotionless substitutes was – and still is – the more chilling for its comment on a possible outcome of social trends. The same theme dominated Michael Anderson's *1984* (1955), although Orwell's tale was a political comment. The two great space adventures of the period, *This Island Earth* (1955) and *Forbidden Planet* (1955), portrayed life in the furthest reaches of space as obsessed with genocide and defeat, however magnificent the alien landscapes.

The growing mastery of technical effects added an illusion of reality to many productions. After the giant ants of *Them!* (1954), invasions became increasingly bizarre; they included fifty-foot women, a deadly mantis, black scorpions and giant leeches. But such creations paled into insignificance in the shadow of a greater and more immediate danger: the Bomb.

The world started ending on film as early as 1951, with Arch Oboler's *Five*; by 1959 few members of an audience were prepared to question the credibility of Stanley Kramer's *On the Beach*, which employed a well-known cast to bring visual power to Nevil Shute's story of civilisation's destruction by radiation. Almost gentle in its basic approach, it was followed by increasingly shocking warnings: in the form of Kubrick's *Dr Strangelove* (1963), Sidney Lumet's *Fail Safe* (1964), and – in Britain – Peter Watkins's harrowing pseudo-documentary *The War Game* (1965). Less important expressions of the same note of insecurity were *The Day the Earth Caught Fire* (1961) and *Crack in the World* (1965). Two British productions, *Lord of the Flies* (1963) and *Day of the Triffids* (1962), echoed a similar theme – the latter failing to achieve anything near the acting and technical quality of the former. Pure adventure offerings of the time included *Fantastic Voyage* (1966) and *Planet of the Apes* (1967), although it could be argued that the latter is to some extent allegorical.

2001: A Space Odyssey *1968*.

With *Strangelove*, many commentators felt that Kubrick had got it right; the paranoia of the nuclear age was destroying man's rational abilities. The hysteria of Peter Sellers's performance at the beginning of the 1960s was well balanced by Spike Milligan's at their close in the livid settings and wrecked characters of his *The Bed Sitting Room* (1969). Hysteria seemed acceptable; the fatalistic mood was neatly caught in Roger Corman's *Gas-s-s!* (1970), where everyone over twenty-five died of instant old age as a result of planetary pollution! The threat of nuclear annihilation lived on, but the human capacity for the psychological acceptance of danger reduced its significance in shock value. Other threats to the well-being of society have subsequently lent themselves to the film-maker's art in an equally compelling, if less devastating way. They were heralded by the Frankenheimer/Axelrod comedy *The Manchurian Candidate* (1962), in which brainwashing and political assassination were illustrated in precise detail. The film's oppressive and anti-utopian concepts were developed and reflected in Godard's *Alphaville* (1965), Truffaut's *Fahrenheit 451* (1966), George Romero's *Night of the Living Dead* (1968), and Lucas's *THX 1138* (1970). Of these four directors probably the most adventurous was Godard, whose work in the 1960s included the noted portrayal of the collapse of society in *Weekend* (1967) and *Sympathy for the Devil* (1968). His French compatriot, Truffaut, shifted his attentions to stylish domestic drama, while in the US Romero became preoccupied with the new explicit horror cycle for which the factual Manson murders paved the way. George Lucas appears to have abandoned the present to its fate and resurrected the innocence of Flash Gordon in the style of *The Star Wars* (scheduled for 1977).

The last few years have been marked by the arrival of two singularly influential films. In 1968, Stanley Kubrick completed *2001: a Space Odyssey*, and introduced a new element into science fiction cinema, the multi-million dollar budget. His breath-taking production, which he jointly scripted with Arthur C. Clarke, is probably the richer for its ambiguities. Its space shots, challengingly realistic, give little clue as to how they were achieved, and the film's closing sequences provide no clear answer as to why. The echoes of *2001* are still sounding – not only in such parodies and imitations as *Dark Star* and *Silent Running*, but also in the budgets allotted to *Slaughterhouse Five* (1971), *Rollerball* (1975), *Logan's Run* (1976), and *The Star Wars*. The 'quickie' science fiction second-features, shot in a week with a cast of five, no longer appear to be marketable commodities – for the time being.

Lord of the Flies *1963*.

04.03 SCIENCE FICTION IN THE CINEMA

Any summary of the most important science fiction films must, in addition to *2001*, include Kubrick's *Clockwork Orange* (1971). Based on Anthony Burgess's novel, which caused little stir when it first appeared in the UK in 1962, the movie caused a storm of disapproval in Britain by its stylistic but concentrated emphasis on violence. John Boorman's *Zardoz* (1973) is equally renowned for having irritated a large number of audiences, and the argument continues regarding its merit. For many sf enthusiasts its persistent use of symbolism was applied to no very good purpose.

Symbolism also finds a place in the Russian Tarkovsky's *Solaris* (1972), possibly the nearest the cinema has yet come to capturing the complexities of contemporary speculative fiction by its intermingling of time and memory, its dark undertow of uneasiness, its emphasis on elegance and style. Based on the novel by Stanislaw Lem, *Solaris* explores both inner and outer Space. With images of hallucinatory splendour it speaks of change, and the human reluctance to contemplate the self-knowledge that change implies. The twin peaks of *2001* and *Solaris*, demonstrate two of the major pre-occupations of writers in the sf genre – the technical prowess of man, and his rising awareness of the psychological gulfs he must bridge on his way to the fulfilment of his abilities.

In the final analysis it seems that even the enormous critical and financial success of *Clockwork Orange* and *2001* may be eclipsed by Lucas' *The Star Wars*. This mythological odyssey of an intergalactic struggle will most likely become a multi-million dollar milestone. The most notable special effects include a dramatic deep space 'dogfight' between spacecraft, duels with laser-beam sabers, believable mechanical robots and non-humanoid creatures.

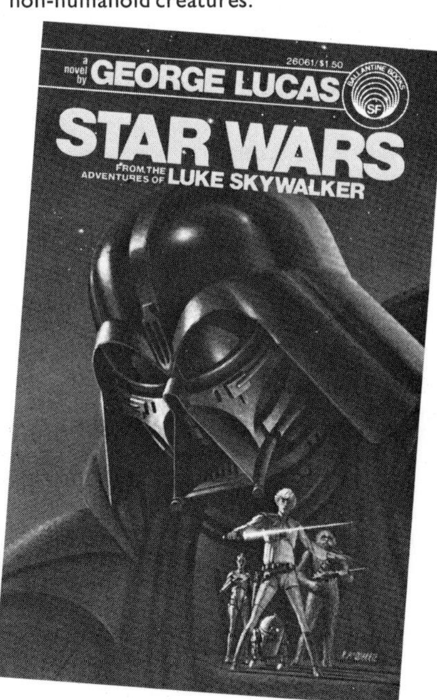

Film List

All films listed below appear in 04.04

1902
A Voyage to the Moon directed by George Méliès

1906
The ? Motorist directed by Walter Booth

1909
An Invisible Thief directed by Ferdinand Zecca for Pathé

1910
Frankenstein directed by J. Searle Dawley for Edison

1914
The Golem directed by Paul Wegener and Henrick Galeen for Deutsche Bioscop GmbH, Berlin

1916
Intolerance directed by D. W. Griffith for Wark Producing Company

1919
The Cabinet of Dr Caligari directed by Robert Wiene for Decla
The First Men in the Moon directed by J. L. V. Leigh for Gaumont

1920
The Golem directed by Paul Wegener and Karl Boese for UFA

1922
Nosferatu directed by F. W. Murnau for Prana Film
Dr Mabuse directed by Fritz Lang for UFA

1923
The Hunchback of Notre Dame directed by Wallace Worsley for Universal/Jewel

1924
The Hands of Orlac directed by Robert Wiene for Pan Film
Kriemhild's Revenge directed by Fritz Lang for UFA
The Thief of Bagdad directed by Raoul Walsh for Fairbanks-United Artists

1925
The Phantom of the Opera directed by Rupert Julian for Universal/Jewel
The Lost World directed by Harry Hoyt for First National

1926
Faust directed by F. W. Murnau for UFA
Metropolis directed by Fritz Lang for UFA

1928
Alraune directed by Henrik Galeen for Ama-Film
Spione directed by Fritz Lang for Fritz Lang Film GmbH
The Woman in the Moon directed by Fritz Lang for Fritz Lang Film GmbH

1931
Dracula directed by Tod Browning for Universal
Frankenstein directed by James Whale for Universal
Dr Jekyll and Mr Hyde directed by Rouben Mamoulian for Paramount

1932
The Mummy directed by Karl Freund for Universal
The Island of Lost Souls directed by Erle C. Kenton for Paramount
Freaks directed by Tod Browning for MGM

1933
King Kong directed by Ernest Schoedsack and Merian C. Cooper for RKO
The Invisible Man directed by James Whale for Universal
The Mystery of the Wax Museum directed by Michael Curtiz for Warner Bros
The Vampire Bat directed by Frank Strayer for Majestic

1936
Devil Doll directed by Tod Browning for MGM
Things to Come directed by William Cameron Menzies for London Films
Flash Gordon directed by Frederick Stephani and Ray Taylor for Universal
The Man Who Could Work Miracles directed by Lothar Mendes for London Films

1939
Buck Rogers directed by Ford Beebe and Saul Goodkind for Universal

1942
Cat People directed by Jacques Tourneur for RKO

1943
Batman directed by Lambert Hillyer for Columbia
I Walked with a Zombie directed by Jacques Tourneur for RKO
The Leopard Man directed by Jacques Tourneur for RKO

1945
Isle of the Dead directed by Mark Robson for RKO

1946
Bedlam directed by Mark Robson for RKO

1948
Superman directed by Spencer Bennett for Columbia

1950
Destination Moon directed by Irving Pichel for Universal-International

1951
When Worlds Collide directed by Rudolf Mare for Paramount
The Day the Earth Stood Still directed by Robert Wise for Twentieth Century-Fox
Five directed by Arch Oboler for Columbia

04.03 SCIENCE FICTION IN THE CINEMA

1952
The Thing from Another World directed by Christian Nyby for Winchester Pictures
Invasion USA directed by Alfred Green for Columbia
Red Planet Mars directed by Harry Horner for Donald Hyde-Anthony Veiller Productions

1953
War of the Worlds directed by Byron Haskin for Paramount
Donovan's Brain directed by Felix Feist for Dowling Productions
It Came from Outer Space directed by Jack Arnold for Universal-International
Invaders from Mars directed by William Cameron Menzies for National Pictures Corporation
The Beast from 20,000 Fathoms directed by Eugene Lourie for Warner Bros

1954
The Creature from the Black Lagoon directed by Jack Arnold for Universal-International

20,000 Leagues under the Sea directed by Richard Fleischer for Walt Disney Productions
Them! directed by Gordon Douglas for Warner Bros

1955
The Door in the Wall directed by Glenn H. Alvey for A. B. Pathé in association with the British Film Institute
Tarantula directed by Jack Arnold for Universal-International
This Island Earth directed by Joseph Newman for Universal-International
Forbidden Planet directed by Fred McLeod Wilcox for MGM
1984 directed by Michael Anderson for Holiday Productions

1956
The Incredible Shrinking Man directed by Jack Arnold for Universal-International
Invasion of the Body Snatchers directed by Don Siegel for Allied Artists

1957
The Monolith Monsters directed by John Sherwood for Universal-International

1959
On The Beach directed by Stanley Kramer for Stanley Kramer Productions (Lomitas)
The Time Machine directed by George Pal for Galaxy Films

1960
Village of the Damned directed by Wolf Rilla for Ronald Kinnoch MGM

1961
The Day the Earth Caught Fire directed by Val Guest for Melina

1962
The Day of the Triffids directed by Steve Sekely for Security Pictures
The Manchurian Candidate directed by John Frankenheimer for George Axelrod-John Frankenheimer Productions/Essex Productions

Poster advertising The Time Machine.

1963
Dr Strangelove or How I Learned to Stop Worrying and Love the Bomb directed by Stanley Kubrick for Hawk Films
Lord of the Flies directed by Peter Brook for Allen Hodgdon Productions/Two Arts

1964
Fail Safe directed by Sidney Lumet for Max E. Youngstein-Sidney Lumet
First Men in the Moon directed by Nathan Juran for Columbia

1965
The War Game directed by Peter Watkins originally for BBC TV (but not transmitted)
Crack in the World directed by Andrew Marton for Security Pictures
Alphaville directed by Jean-Luc Godard for Chaumiane Production Film Studio

1966
Fantastic Voyage directed by Richard Fleischer for Twentieth Century-Fox
Fahrenheit 451 directed by Francois Truffaut for Anglo-Enterprise Vineyard

1967
Barbarella directed by Roger Vadim for Marianne Productions/ Dino de Laurentiis/Paramount
Planet of the Apes directed by Franklin Schaffner for Apjac Productions/ Twentieth Century-Fox

1968
2001: a Space Odyssey directed by Stanley Kubrick for MGM
Night of the Living Dead directed by George A. Romero for Image Ten

1969
The Bed Sitting Room directed by Richard Lester for Oscar Lewenstein Productions

1970
THX 1138 directed by George Lucas for Zeotrope Productions
Gas-s-s; or it became necessary to destroy the world in order to save it directed by Roger Corman for San Jacinto/American International Pictures

1971
Silent Running directed by Douglas Trumbull for Universal
Slaughterhouse Five directed by George Roy Hill for Universal Film/Vanadas
Clockwork Orange directed by Stanley Kubrick for Warner Bros/Polaris

1972
Solaris directed by Andrei Tarkovsky for Mosfilm

1973
Soylent Green directed by Richard Fleischer for MGM
Zardoz directed by John Boorman for John Boorman Productions/Twentieth Century-Fox

1974
The Terminal Man directed by Michael Hodges for Warner Bros
Dark Star directed and produced by John Carpenter

1975
Rollerball directed by Norman Jewison, for Alonguin/United Artists

1976
Logan's Run directed by Michael Anderson for MGM

04.03 SCIENCE FICTION IN THE CINEMA

PRINTED SOURCES

Agel, Jerome (ed). *The Making of Kubrick's 2001*, Signet (US) 1970
Amelio, Ralph J. *Hal in the Classroom: Science Fiction Films*, Pflaum Publishing (US) 1974
Annan, David. *Movie Fantastic: Beyond the Dream Machine*, Bounty Books/Crown Publishers (US) 1974
Anderson, Poul. 'The Worth of Words', *Algol* No 22, May 1974
Baxter, John. *Science Fiction in the Cinema*, A. S. Barnes (US) 1970
Baxter, John. 'Memories of the Future, Part 2: Writers vs Hollywood', *Vision of Tomorrow* August 1970
Bergman, Andrew. *We're in the Money: Depression America and Its Films*, Univeristy Press (US) 1971
Bloch, Robert. 'Men, Myths and Monsters', *Algol* No 22, May 1974
Curtis, David. *Experimental Cinema: A Fifty Year Evolution*, Universe Books (US) 1971
Daniels, Don. 'A Skeleton Key to 2001', *Sight and Sound* Winter 1970, pp 28-33
Geduld, Harry M. 'Return to Méliès: Reflections on the Science Fiction Film', *The Humanist* November-December 1968, pp 23-28
Gifford, Denis. *Science Fiction Film*, Studio Vista/Dutton (UK) 1971
Gutkind, Lee Alan. 'George Méliès: Forgotten Master', *Arts in Society* Summer-Fall 1973
Harryhausen, Ray. *Film Fantasy Scrapbook*, A. S. Barnes (US) 1972; The Tantivy Press (UK) 1974
Houston, Penelope. 'Glimpses of the Moon', *Sight and Sound* April-June 1953, pp 185-188
Hutchinson, Tom. *Horror and Fantasy in the Movies*, Crescent Books/Crown Publishers (US) 1974
James, Clive. '2001: Kubrick vs Clarke', *Film Society Review* January 1970, pp 27-34
Jensen, Paul M. *The Cinema of Fritz Lang*, A. S. Barnes (US) 1969
Jensen, Paul. 'H. G. Wells on the Screen', *Films in Review* November 1967, pp 521-527
Johnson, Dennis. S. 'The Five Faces of George Pal', *Cinefantastique* Fall 1971, pp 5-27
Johnson, William (ed). *Focus on the Science Fiction Film*, Prentice-Hall (US) 1972
Kagan, Norman. *The Cinema of Stanley Kubrick*, Holt, Rinehart, Winston (US) 1972
Kawin, Bruce F. 'Peter Watkins: Cameraman at World's End', *Arts in Society* Summer-Fall 1973
Kracauer, Siegfreid. *From Caligari to Hitler: A Psychological History of the German Film*, Princeton University Press (US) 1947
Lee, Walt (ed). *Reference Guide to Fantastic Films: Science Fiction, Fantasy, and Horror*, Chelsea-Lee Books (US) 1972
Maynard, Richard. 'A Galaxy of Science Fiction Films', *Scholastic Teacher* Nov 1973, pp 27-28
Melville, Douglas. *A Historical and Critical Survey of the Science-Fiction Film*, Arno Press (US) 1975
Nye, Russell. 'The Future as History: Science Fiction', *The Unembarrassed Muse: the Popular Arts in America*, Dial Press (US) 1970
Panshin, Alexei. 'A Basic Science Fiction Collection', *Library Journal* June 1970, pp 2223-2229
Panshin, Alexei. 'Science Fiction Bibliography & Criticism', *American Libraries* Oct 1970, pp 884-885
Phillips, Gene. *Stanley Kubrick*, Curtis Film Series (US) 1974
Pohl, Frederick. '2001: a Second Look', *Film Society Review* February 1970, pp 23-27
Rice, Susan. 'Stanley Kubrick's *Clockwork Orange*', *Media and Methods* March 1972, pp 39-43
Rilla, Wolf. 'The Boundary of Imagination', *Algol* No 22, May 1974
Rovin, Jeff. *A Pictorial History of Science Fiction Films*, Citadel Press (US) 1975
Shaheen, J. G. 'The War Game', *Film Society Review* March-May 1972, pp 85-92
Sragow, Michael. '*2001: a Space Odyssey*', *Film Society Review* January 1970, pp 23-26
Steinbrunner, Chris (with Burt Goldblatt). *Cinema of the Fantastic*, Saturday Review Press (US) 1972
Strick, Philip. *Science Fiction Movies*, Octopus (UK) 1976
Vardac, A. Nicholas. *Stage to Screen*, Benjamin Blom (US) 1968
Wood, Robin. *Howard Hawks*, Doubleday (US) 1968
Youngblood, Gene. *Expanded Cinema*, E. P. Dutton (US) 1970

Magazines

American Cinematographer
Cinefantastique with special reference to 'Planet of the Apes' Summer 1972
Extrapolation: Journal of Science Fiction and Fantasy with special reference to 'Three Perspectives of a Film: *2001*' December 1968

Clockwork Orange *1971*.

04.04 SCIENCE FICTION ON TELEVISION

04.04 SCIENCE FICTION ON TELEVISION

04.04.1 United States

The technical and financial limitations of television naturally meant that science fiction tended to be overlooked in the early days of the medium. Science fiction could be left to the cinema. Eventually, though, the greater facilities available to American television resulted in the earliest science fiction television programmes being produced in the US.

American producers and directors had already had much experience in science fiction in both films and radio. The notorious Orson Welles' production of H. G. Wells's *The War of the Worlds* had been broadcast between 8 and 9 pm on 30 October 1938 and had caused widespread panic among many citizens of New York who, having missed the start of the programme, mistook it for a news broadcast. But by and large radio science fiction in the States was for juvenile audiences, with programmes like *Buck Rogers* (begun in 1932) and *Superman* (1938). It was at the juvenile audience that the first television science fiction programme, *Captain Video*, was aimed. First televised in June 1949 at 7 pm, five evenings a week, the programme proved extremely popular and reached an estimated $3\frac{1}{2}$ million children. By today's standards the programme looked cheap and hastily produced; but it was broadcast live and proved a pioneer in its field, and as such can be viewed sympathetically. Certainly, Captain Video and his Video Rangers, operating from a secret base on Earth from which they emerged to spin around space in rocket *X–9* on errands of peace, were not only popular but highly influential among the young viewers, many of whom would become part of the next generation of sf writers.

Naturally, success begot imitations, and in October 1950 there followed *Tom Corbett: Space Cadet*, a 15-minute programme broadcast at the same time as *Captain Video* and little different in format. However, it was the *Space Cadet* production team who really pioneered the use of special effects, particularly in the way they superimposed monsters on the live action. Some of their success in this area must almost certainly be due to the choice of Willy Ley as technical adviser.

Other juvenile programmes followed in their steps, including *Phantom Empire*, which was set in a future city underneath the Earth and starred famed cowboy actor, Gene Autry!

In time, television studios began to experiment with adult science fiction, and the precursor of many productions was ABC's *Tales of Tomorrow*. It was not a serial; instead, each half-hour programme consisted of a complete story, often an adaptation of such well-known sf tales as Robert A. Heinlein's 'Green Hills of Earth'.

All these programmes were broadcast in the early 1950s, and during that decade television came of age. The more sophisticated technical equipment, plus the maturing of style and technique by producers and writers, brought the new medium to a high standard of craftsmanship. The stage was set for an entirely adult and serious sf series, and it came by courtesy of Emmy Award-winning scriptwriter Rod Serling.

Serling had been a boxer in the army during the Second World War and had drawn from experience on his script *Requiem for a Heavyweight*, which placed him in the front-line of Hollywood script-writers. He had already won an Emmy for his script for *Patterns*, and he now found himself in a commanding position. Hitherto Serling had not concerned himself with science fiction, although he had produced a script for John Christopher's *No Blade of Grass* which was never used. Then, in November 1958, he wrote *Time Element* for Desilu Playhouse, concerning a man who relived the Japanese attack on Pearl Harbor. The episode was a success, and served as a pilot film for *The Twilight Zone*. Serling not only scripted most of this series (his contract stated that he had to write 80 per cent of the first two seasons' shows), but he was also executive producer and thus responsible for much of the behind-the-scenes activity. Serling achieved considerable success, and produced a series that remains in the memory of many as one of the best television science fiction programmes to date. The format varied with each season, but it was originally a half-hour programme consisting of one or two short tales, either written originally for the programme or adapted from well-known stories. Richard Matheson also wrote for

The Bionic Woman *1976*.

the series, adapting some of his own tales – such as 'Steel', about robot-boxers. Later the series was extended to a full hour. Initially, the sponsors of the programme felt it was not successful, and decided it was to be dropped after the first season. Serling appealed to viewers and received 2500 cards and letters in support of its continuance. The sponsors were convinced, and *The Twilight Zone* went on to win three Hugo Awards, plus several Emmys and the Screen Producers Guild Award as Best Produced TV Series; it was also voted Best New Programme and Best Filmed Series.

After the success of *The Twilight Zone*, anything in its wake was likely to seem poor by comparison, and for this reason *The Outer Limits* is not so well remembered. This was the brain-child of producer and scriptwriter Joseph Stefano (the man who adapted Bloch's *Psycho* for Hitchcock's film), and like *Zone* it consisted of hour-long episodes, either original or adapted from known stories. The first, 'The Galaxy Being', was broadcast in September 1963 and involved a monster snared from space by TV signals. A subsequent episode, 'The Sixth Finger', starred the actor David McCallum as a man who is accelerated through evolution and ends up with an exceptionally enlarged brain. The first season of thirty-two episodes ended in May 1964. The programme recommenced in September that year with Harlan Ellison's 'Soldier', and by and large the second series was of a higher standard than the first. It included Ellison's Writers Guild Award-winning episode, 'Demon with a Glass Hand'. But the series suffered from poor ratings, and was dropped in January 1965.

Thereafter, American television science fiction sank for a while to an innocuous low. It was virtually monopolised by Irwin Allen, today the revered name behind such financial bonanzas as the movies *The Poseidon Adventure* and *Towering Inferno*. Allen had co-scripted a film, *Voyage to the Bottom of the Sea* (1961), which tells of a nuclear submarine crew attempting to destroy a radiation belt which threatens the Earth. The book of the film was written by Theodore Sturgeon. Allen now adapted the basic theme of the film to television format, with the submarine *Seaview* and its crew weekly undergoing no end of astonishing adventures and still remaining as naïve and gullible as ever. Nevertheless, the series had its moments and provided an hour's harmless entertainment. Allen would occasionally overcome production problems by cutting in scenes from his own films. In one *Voyage* episode, the crew discovered a hidden world in the Antarctic inhabited by prehistoric monsters. In fact, the bulk of the episode consisted of scenes from Allen's production of Conan Doyle's *The Lost World* (1960), which had co-starred David Hedison, who also played second-in-command of the *Seaview*.

Allen's subsequent productions proved less and less palatable to most adult science fiction enthusiasts. *Time Tunnel* (1967) involved two men who were transported to various key incidents in time. Adaptations of several of the episodes were incorporated by Murray Leinster into the books *The Time Tunnel* (1967) and *Timeslip* (1967). Concurrently, Allen was producing *The Land of the Giants*, featuring a group of characters stranded on a planet where everyone and everything was colossal. The series was extremely well filmed, but was otherwise dull. Allen next produced *Lost in Space*, a series involving the Robinson family who, lost in space, try to set up home on an alien planet. The family were equally dull, though amusement was provided by the antics of the cowardly stowaway, Dr Smith, in his attempts to sabotage any constructive plans, and by the fact that the series included the 'robot' which had been Robbie in the film *The Forbidden Planet* (1956).

Allen's subsequent series proved abortive, and it was clear that any future TV offerings would have to be of a higher standard. There followed *Star Trek*, first broadcast in late 1965. The phenomenal success of the series requires little description here. For a while, the show was the epitome of what good television science fiction should be. It was excellently handled by Gene Roddenberry and his production crew, and many skilled sf practitioners turned out scripts, not least Harlan Ellison, who again culled a handful of awards for the episode 'The City at the Edge of Forever'. Briefly, the series related the adventures that befell the crew of the Star-Ship *Enterprise* on its explorations in the depths of space. Besides the formation of many Star Trek clubs and societies, there has also been a profusion of books transcribing the *Star Trek* episodes, by Alan Dean Foster in the US and by the late James Blish in the UK, in addition to new adventures related by Jacqueline Lichtenberg and others. The series also brought into the limelight the new writer, David Gerrold, who scripted the episode 'The Trouble with Tribbles', and has since gone on to achieve a growing reputation in the science fiction literary field. While from among the actors, Leonard Nimoy, who played the emotionless Vulcan, Mr Spock, has become well known, and has recently begun to write books, including poetry, reaching an audience that only his association with *Star Trek* made possible.

Star Trek was finally dropped in 1968, despite its appeal, and most subsequent attempts at sf series have proved meagre. These have included *The Invaders* (1967), about the lone efforts of a human to convince the authorities that aliens are among us. (A book of the theme was written by Keith Laumer.) Gene Roddenberry has tried to initiate further series, which have unfortunately advanced little further than their pilot films. Harlan Ellison's own science fiction dream series, *The Starlost*, met a dismal fate when his script was so badly mangled that the final result proved disastrous. (The original screenplay is included in Jack Dann and George Zebrowski's anthology, *Faster Than Light*, 1976, and it was also novelised by Ed Bryant as *Phoenix without Ashes*, 1975).

All that remained after *Star Trek* were adaptations for television of famous films or books. The success of the *Planet of the Apes* movies, based on Pierre Boulle's novel (1963) and adapted for the screen by no less than Rod Serling, with Michael Wilson, resulted in a companion television series, but it died after one season. David McCallum appeared (occasionally!) as *The Invisible Man* in a new series that has nothing remotely in common with H. G. Wells's classic novel, to which it is credited (for title copyright reasons).

Probably the most popular series is *The Six Million Dollar Man*, based on Martin Caidin's best-selling *Cyborg* (1972). It features an astronaut who returns to Earth badly injured, and is rebuilt as half-machine to give him the power of a superman. The complaints received from viewers, when a female companion for the hero was killed off, have resulted in a sequel series, *The Bionic Woman*. None of these recent series reaches much above the mediocre. Currently, however, Harlan Ellison is promoting several highly suitable ideas to American companies, and it is conceivable that the time is near when a new and, perhaps, different, science fiction television series will be seen in the US.

04.04 SCIENCE FICTION ON TELEVISION

04.04.2 United Kingdom

In general, American TV science fiction began by aiming at the lower age groups and worked its way up; however in Britain the TV productions began with an adult audience and erratically worked their way down. This parallels to some extent the development of readership in both countries.

British fans were initially delighted to hear on BBC radio Charles Chilton's *Journey into Space* serial, broadcast in 1953, while Radio Luxembourg similarly began transmitting juvenile *Dan Dare* episodes. But for those fortunate enough to own a television in 1953, 18 July marked the broadcast of the first of six episodes of *The Quatermass Experiment*, scripted by Nigel Kneale. Transmitted late in the evening, with the warning that the programme was considered 'unsuitable for children and those of a nervous disposition', the serial was obviously intended for a mature adult audience, and it struck a responsive chord. The story of a sole survivor of a space trip captivated British audiences, and the very name of Quatermass passed into common parlance in the UK.

Nigel Kneale can be described as Britain's counterpart to Rod Serling, and some have considered him the superior of the two. His plays for television have proved the backbone of most British visual science fiction for the last two decades. In the 1950s alone, he produced two more Quatermass serials, *Quatermass II* (1955) and *Quatermass and the Pit* (1958–59), also a chilling adaptation of George Orwell's *Nineteen Eighty-four* that brought considerable response from viewers because of its violent torture scene (though tame by today's standards).

Nigel Kneale's work aside, most other science fiction television productions in the 1950s were transmitted during 'children's hour'. These included Angus MacVicar's adaptations of his own highly readable children's tales, *The Lost Planet* (1954) and *Return of the Lost Planet* (1955). A novel innovation was *The Stranger from Space* (1953), which was scripted by Hazel Adair and Peter Ling from suggestions sent in each week by children as to how the serial should continue. This often resulted in a patchy and inconsequential plot, but it was a challenging concept.

The arrival of commercial television in the UK resulted in a new series of serials starring Gerald Flood and beginning with *Pathfinders to the Moon* (1959). By and large, the acting and production values were poor, but the series proved popular.

The commercial channel also produced a filmed series, as opposed to live studio productions. This was *The Invisible Man* (1958), which bore as little relationship to Wells's novel as the American descendant seventeen years later. It was entertaining nonetheless. The commercial stations' productions outshone those of their rival in the early 1960s. The regular series, *Armchair Theatre*, occasionally featured science fiction, and it included an adaptation of John Wyndham's science fiction love story 'The Dumb Martian', which served as a pilot for a new series, *Out of this World*. Created by story editor Irene Shubik, the programme was again obviously aimed at an adult audience, being transmitted at 10 pm on Saturday nights. Bizarre radiophonic music would give way to Boris Karloff, who introduced all thirteen plays, starting with Rog Phillips's 'The Yellow Pill', adapted by Leon Griffiths. Next in the series was Leo Lehmann's adaptation of Isaac Asimov's 'Little Lost Robot', and then Clive Exton's version of Tom Godwin's 'The Cold Equations'. The stories chosen were often sf classics, and adult audiences were able to view an excellent cross-section of the better work in the genre.

Some of the stories were original scripts, and included 'Botany Bay' by Terry Nation, who had also adapted Philip K. Dick's 'Imposter'. The combination of Nation and Shubik was seen to good effect a year later, but on the BBC channel. November 1963 marked the first transmission of *Dr Who*. This was the brain-child of Sydney Newman, who had also produced *Out of This World*, in addition to having started *The Avengers* on the commercial channel. The first episode concerning the time-travelling Doctor (then played by William Hartnell) was set in the Stone Age and proved uninspiring, but when Terry Nation took over the script for the closing scene of 'The Dead Planet', British children were introduced to the Daleks. The success of these emotionless machine-aided aliens can be measured by their constant reappearance in many subsequent episodes. Dr. Who himself underwent various metamorphoses when actors grew tired of playing the part, but the series remains the longest running sf programme on British television.

It is interesting to note that, in the UK, TV series have frequently served as the basis for sf films, for example *Quatermass* and *Dr Who*; in the US the reverse is usually true – witness *Voyage to the Bottom of the Sea* and *Planet of the Apes*.

While *Dr Who* entranced young audiences during the 1960s, the BBC continued to cater for their adult viewers. Eminent astronomer Fred Hoyle, assisted by John Elliot as scriptwriter, produced the memorable *A for Andromeda* (1962), a serial about the receipt of a message from the Andromeda galaxy containing instructions on the creation of a living being, played by Julie Christie. A sequel, *The Andromeda Breakthrough* (1964), was not as successful (in common with most sequels), though the part of the created being provided a leading role for Susan Hampshire.

Nigel Kneale also remained active in the 1960s. He provided two striking sf plays, both touched with a tinge of horror. In September 1963 came *The Road*, which involved the scientific investigation of a psychic phenomenon in a wood. *The Year of the Sex Olympics*, transmitted in July 1969, portrayed the upper-class élite making sport of the lower-class masses. Both plays received high critical praise.

Much the same team that produced the commercial series *Out of This World* provided BBC with *Out of the Unknown*, which first went out in October 1965 with John Wyndham's 'No Place Like Home'. It was followed by Alan E. Nourse's 'The Counterfeit Man'. Twelve episodes were broadcast in all, including Isaac Asimov's 'The Dead Past' and 'Sucker Bait', William Tenn's 'Time in Advance', J. G. Ballard's 'Thirteen to Centaurus', and, perhaps the best realised of all, John Brunner's 'Some

The crew of the starship Enterprise *from* Star Trek.

Tom Baker as Dr Who *May 1976.*

Lapse of Time'. The popularity of the series prompted a second batch of twelve, beginning with a striking adaptation of E. M. Forster's noted 'The Machine Stops', broadcast in October 1966. Another BBC programme later the same evening featured Brian Aldiss discussing the production. The series was, if anything, better than the first, and included 'Lambda 1' by Colin Kapp, 'Level 7' by Mordecai Roshwald, 'Tunnel under the World' by Frederik Pohl and 'Satisfaction Guaranteed' by Isaac Asimov.

The period 1965–66 saw the transmission of other popular series which sometimes verged on science fiction, in particular *The Man from U.N.C.L.E.*, imported from the United States, and the indigenous *The Avengers*. Most of the science fictional episodes in the latter were scripted by Philip Levene, and included 'The Cybernauts' (1965), 'Man-Eater of Surrey Green' (1966), featuring carnivorous plants, 'From Venus with Love' (1966), concerning the British Venusian Society, 'The See-Through Man' (1966), 'Never, Never Say Die' (1966), about a man who could not be killed, and inevitably 'The Return of the Cybernauts' (1967), starring Peter Cushing.

Another borderline series was *Adam Adamant*, first broadcast on New Year's Eve 1966, which depicted the adventures of a suave, Victorian-style avenger who was frozen in his own times and thawed out alive in the 1960s.

By the end of the 1960s, however, few British-made productions were being shown, and the only high spot was Patrick McGoohan's often puzzling, always intriguing *The Prisoner*, set around a secret agent who had tried to resign and subsequently found himself trapped in a mysterious village where every attempt to escape was foiled.

The bulk of science fiction transmitted after the mid-sixties was intended for juvenile audiences, and was usually in the form of superior puppet programmes such as *Fireball X.L.5*, *Stingray* and *Thunderbirds*. These were masterminded by Gerry Anderson, who turned his talents to human actors with *UFO*, a series depicting a special agency set up to deal with flying saucers. The series failed because the actors proved less effective than the puppets. However, Anderson's talents were later put to better use in *Space 1999*, a series with all the faults bequeathed it by those who call the genre 'sci-fi', but strong on special effects. Set on the Moon, which has been blasted out of orbit and is wandering through space, it has contained much questionable science but has also shown some story potential.

Christmas Day 1972 saw the transmission of Nigel Kneale's scientific ghost story, *The Stone Tape*, a noted production about attempts to release 'recorded' information from the stone walls of an old building. Kneale also scripted a cycle of six plays entitled *The Beasts* for transmission at the end of 1976. His three plays, *The Road*, *The Stone Tape* and *The Year of the Sex Olympics*, have been published in book form under the last title (1976).

Terry Nation turned his thoughts in 1975 to the inadequacy of civilised man in *The Survivors* (1975), which dealt with the few scattered humans who are either immune to, or recover from, a deadly virus that wipes out most of the world's population.

'Get off my Cloud' Out of the Unknown *August 1968.*

This post-catastrophe series, which began in 1975 and which Terry Nation has also explored in a novel, *The Survivors* (1976), is reminiscent in some ways of *Doomwatch* (1970–71), scripted by Kit Pedler and Gerry Davies. This last series made viewers aware of the many potential dangers inherent in an over-reliance on science, and the hazards which could result from human error. Kit Pedler, who had earlier scripted the 'Cybermen' episodes of *Dr Who*, has since transferred his talents to writing sf novels, such as *Mutant 59*, which also underline the perils arising from the applications of science.

The restrictiveness of television budgets in the UK has often hampered the production of science fiction. Bearing this in mind, it is understandable that both rival channels should have had their failures; but they have also produced some notable successes.

A Dalek from Dr Who.

04.04 SCIENCE FICTION ON TELEVISION

'Re-Entry Forbidden' Doomwatch *February 1970.*

Books from TV Series

United States TV Series

Blish, James. *Star Trek*, vols 1-11, Bantam (US) 1967-75

Bryant, Ed (with Harlan Ellison). *Phoenix without Ashes* (Starlost 1), Pyramid (US) 1975

Foster, Alan Dean. *Star Trek Log*, vols 1-5, Bantam (US) 1972-76

Gerrold, David. *The Trouble with Tribbles*, Ballantine (US) 1974

Gerrold, David. *The World of Star Trek*, Ballantine (US) 1974

Laumer, Keith. *The Invaders*, No 1, Pyramid (US) 1967

Enemies from Beyond, No 2, Pyramid (US) 1967

Leinster, Murray. *The Time Tunnel*, Pyramid (US) 1967

Timeslip!, Pyramid (US) 1967

Lichtenberg, Jacqueline (with S. Marshak & J. Winston). *Star Trek Lives*, Bantam (US) 1975

Marshak, Sandra (with Myrna Culbreath) eds. *Star Trek: the New Voyages* (9 stories), Ballantine (US) 1976

Serling, Rod. *Stories from the Twilight Zone*, Bantam (US) 1960

More Stories from the Twilight Zone, Bantam (US) 1961,

New Stories from the Twilight Zone, Bantam (US) 1962

Sturgeon, Theodore. *Voyage to the Bottom of the Sea*, Pyramid (US) 1961

United Kingdom TV Series

Adair, Hazel (with R. Marriott). *Strangers from Space*, Weidenfeld and Nicolson (UK) 1963

Ball, Brian, N. *The Space Guardians*, 'Space: 1999' series, No 3, Orbit (UK) 1975

Disch, Thomas M. *The Prisoner*, Ace (US) 1969

Hoyle, Fred (with John Elliot). *A for Andromeda*, Souvenir Press (UK) 1962

The Andromeda Breakthrough, Souvenir Press (UK) 1964

Kneale, Nigel. *The Quatermass Experiment*, Penguin (UK) 1959

Quatermass II, Penguin (UK) 1960

Quatermass and the Pit, Penguin (UK) 1960

The Year of the Sex Olympics (3 plays), Ferret Fantasy (UK) 1976

Nation, Terry. *The Survivors*, Weidenfeld and Nicolson (UK) 1976

Rankine, John. 'Space: 1999' series:

2 *Moon Odyssey*, Orbit (UK) 1975

5 *Lunar Attack*, Orbit (UK) 1975

6 *Astral Quest*, Orbit (UK) 1975

8 *Android Planet*, Orbit (UK) 1975

Tubb, E. C. 'Space: 1999' series:

1 *Breakaway*, Orbit (UK) 1975

4 *Collision Course*, Orbit (UK) 1975

7 *Alien Seed*, Orbit (UK) 1976

04.05 SCIENCE FICTION MAGAZINES

Detailed research into sf magazines today depends largely on the indexes and checklists compiled by early fans. Recently their work has been supplemented and extended by better-trained bibliographers, notably H. W. Hall for the Gale Research Company, and the New England Science Fiction Association. Original research among the magazines is hampered by several factors, including the use of pseudonyms by authors and editorial staff; non-sequential volume and issue numbering, and different numbering systems for some foreign reprint editions; non-accreditation of publishing or editorial staff; absent or ambiguous dating; and often rapid title changes. The most comprehensive history of sf magazines has come from Michael Ashley in his articles in the UK magazine *Science Fiction Monthly* and in the first volumes of his history.

Science fiction stories appeared in popular literary magazines from the 1830s, and after 1880 formed a proportion of the contents of many publications in Britain and America. Several journals with literary pretensions carried both Verne and Wells, but in America other authors also appeared in the cheaper boys' adventure magazines. The Frank Reade 'invention' stories in *Boys of New York* from 1876 were so popular that a novel series under the title *Frank Reade Library* ran from September 1892 to August 1898.

"Noname's" Latest and Best Stories are Published in This Library.

FRANK READE LIBRARY

No. 54. Vol. III

The Mystic Brand; or, Frank Reade, Jr., and His Overland Stage Upon the Staked Plains.

By "NONAME."

The magazines carrying the largest number of American sf stories in the early 1900s were owned by Frank Munsey. They were pulps, that is, they were printed on cheap paper and usually had a 7 in × 10 in format. Munsey's *Argosy* was the first adult-adventure pulp, and in his *All-Story* magazine he published the early influential stories of writers like E. R. Burroughs and A. Merritt. Seeing the popularity of this

Hugo Gernsback's Science and Invention.

sort of story, Street & Smith planned to bring out a magazine devoted to science fiction, but *The Thrill Book* (March to October 1919) was little different from the Munsey magazines and soon folded. (Arguably the world's first all-sf magazine was Otto Witt's *Hugin*, launched in Sweden in 1916. It ran for eighty-five issues and was written largely by Witt himself. It had little merit, and it is generally ignored in studies of the history of sf magazines.)

More successful was Jacob Henneberger's *Weird Tales* (March 1923), the first wholly fantastic fiction magazine, though it almost struck disaster in 1924. But once Edwin Baird was replaced by Farnsworth Wright, 'the great editor' (Williamson), *Weird Tales* became very popular, and the major market for sf writers. In this it was to be superseded at the beginning of the 'Gernsback years' (1926–36).

Hugo Gernsback began publishing popular science journals in 1908 with *Modern Electrics*, believing in the efficacy of disseminating scientific knowledge and ideas. The magazine's first story was Gernsback's own *Ralph 124C 41+*, serialised from April 1911 to March 1912. Thereafter, much scientifically based science fiction was published in the magazine, and in August 1923 it produced a specialist 'Scientifiction Issue' (by this time it was called *Science and Invention*). The following year, Gernsback sent a flier to his subscribers about a proposed sf magazine, *Scientifiction*, but response was poor. When the first specialist sf magazine did appear it was unannounced.

Amazing Stories (Amazing) appeared on 5 April 1926, but it was not a standard pulp magazine: its size was the same 8 in × 11 in of Gernsback's science journals. The first two issues consisted wholly of reprints, mostly from Wells, Poe and Verne, but as manuscripts began arriving from interested and stimulated readers Gernsback and his managing editor, T. O'Conor Sloane, were able to include an increasing amount of original material. The circulation quickly rose to a claimed 100,000. (Readers will note that changes of title are not indicated, except where particularly important. In general, at first mention the magazine's initial title is given, followed in brackets by a generic title which will then be used throughout. The parent name of publishing companies is given here, but many of them employed a different publishing name for their sf magazines.)

Gernsback kept in close touch with his readers, and in response to demand his Experimenter Publications put out one issue of a considerably thicker *Amazing Stories Annual* in June 1927. This was such a success that popular novel-length fiction was presented more frequently, from the following January, in *Amazing Stories Quarterly (Amazing Quarterly)*. Only one of its stories was a reprint.

By 1928 many of the influential early sf writers were making their debuts in *Amazing*, and its popular success was undoubted. But in early 1929 a bankruptcy suit was filed against Experimenter, organised (according to Moskowitz) by jealous rivals, Macfadden Publishing, who were producing *Ghost Stories*. Gernsback had to sell his company to B. A. Mackinnon (later Teck Publications), who continued the sf titles, Sloane remaining in charge, and Arthur Lynch as the editor. However Gernsback was already challenging strongly. His close links with his readers paid off, as he received sufficient advance subscriptions to establish Stellar Publishing. He came out with the first issue of *Science Wonder Stories*, a scant month after his last *Amazing*, in May (dated June) 1929.

To make the break with Experimenter complete he dropped the term

First issue January 1930.

'scientifiction', used in the *Amazing* subtitles, and adopted (some say coined) the phase 'science fiction' to describe the stories. A second title, *Air Wonder Stories* (sub-specialised, as the name indicates), followed in July, and in October came *Science Wonder Quarterly* for the lengthier fiction. All these magazines were in the larger format and under the editorial direction of David Lasser.

First issue July 1929.

The following year saw Gernsback's first true sf failure. Street & Smith had started specialist fiction magazines in 1915 with a detective title, and other publishers (including Henneberger of *Weird Tales*) had followed the lead. With *Scientific Detective Monthly* Gernsback tried to capture both specialist readerships, but attracted neither. The failure (January–November 1930) must have owed something to the pulp invasion of the sf field.

Astounding Stories of Super Science (Astounding) came out in January 1930 as the first sf magazine not initiated by Gernsback. Editor Harry Bates had suggested it to publisher William Clayton 'to fill a blank spot on a large sheet of color proofs of pulp magazine covers' (Bates). Backed by a large pulp-magazine company, *Astounding*'s challenge was fourfold: better terms for writers; better distribution facilities; cheaper stand price; and more popular format (this often has a considerable effect, as we shall see). The challenge came just as the Depression was hitting magazine publishers hard, and *Astounding*'s immediate success forced Gernsback to amalgamate his two main titles into *Wonder Stories (Wonder)* in June.

Two other fantasy or weird mixtures with science fiction had only short runs in 1927–28 and 1931, and Clayton themselves failed to encroach much on the *Weird Tales* market with *Strange Tales* (September 1931–January 1933). Then in April 1933 the Depression caught up with them, and their titles were bought by the previous

04.05 SCIENCE FICTION MAGAZINES

publishers of *The Thrill Book*, Street & Smith. The effect was fortuitous and immediate. The December issue of *Astounding* introduced new editor F. Orlin Tremaine's 'thought-variant' policy, encouraging originality and feasibility in writers. Tremaine 'transformed science fiction in the thirties' (Ashley) and ensured the dominance of *Astounding* for years to come. Indeed, it is the only sf magazine to have maintained a regular monthly schedule from that time to this.

Wonder Stories *July 1930.*

Irregularity was hitting all the other magazines as the Depression bit deeper. The renamed *Wonder Stories Quarterly* died in January 1933, and *Amazing Quarterly* ceased eighteen months later, the last two issues having been composed of reprints. *Amazing* itself barely weathered the storm, reducing to pulp size in October 1933. At Stellar, Lasser resigned, and Gernsback replaced him with seventeen-year-old fan Charles Hornig. At the same time, he finally brought *Wonder* down to the popular pulp size, following a year's experiment with the format in 1930–31. Hornig matched Tremaine with a 'New Policy' which also attracted good material, but *Astounding* increased its wordage in 1934 and thus its share of the market, too.

The few new American magazines of the early 1930s were juveniles concerned with mystery and adventure themes, or with space opera (eg *Terrance X. O'Leary's War Birds* in 1935). Most of them were swift failures. Nor were events among the established magazines much more encouraging. To keep going, Gernsback tried to undercut his rivals by reducing *Wonder*'s price in June 1935. This was unsuccessful, and following a move to bi-monthly schedule he tried to remove the magazine from cut-throat news-stand distribution by instituting a post-receipt subscription scheme. The idea was a flop, and Gernsback sold *Wonder* to Standard Magazines in April 1936, withdrawing himself for the time being from regular involvement with science fiction.

At Standard, N. L. Pines changed the title to *Thrilling Wonder Stories (Thrilling Wonder)*, and appointed fan Mort Weisinger as editor under the direction of Leo Margulies. Their efforts, and Standard's distribution network, brought the magazine back into close competition with *Amazing* and *Astounding*. From this time, *Weird Tales* provided less and less competition, gradually phasing out sf stories in favour of the sex and sadism of its weird-fiction rivals.

The American magazines had been distributed and reprinted in Britain from the earliest days, and in 1934 came the first native British magazine. *Scoops* (10 February–23 June) was unfortunately inferior in story quality, but has the distinction of being the only weekly professional sf magazine in the English language. The first British sf pulp came in June 1937 with *Tales of Wonder*. Editor Walter Gillings had persuaded World's Work to publish it, but had to fill it increasingly with reprinted American stories. Nevertheless, it was popular enough to last until half-way through the war (April 1942), though in depleted form. The war also put an end to *Fantasy* from Newnes (July 1938–June 1939), and to Gerald Swan's two magazines of reprints (one, amazingly, in 1944).

By 1938 Sloane was well into his eighties, and a slow and inefficient editor. *Amazing*'s circulation fell to around 27,000, and Teck finally sold the title to Chicago-based Ziff-Davis. In February a well-known Chicago fan was appointed as editor. Raymond A. Palmer revitalised the magazine, introducing new writers, reducing cover price, and catering more to the fans. He had a penchant for sensationalism which increased through the 1940s, but attracted younger readers from the start. Moskowitz has contrasted this audience with the late-teenage readers of *Thrilling Wonder* and the more adult readership of *Astounding*. The latter magazine was certainly attracting the best writers, including John W. Campbell Jr, who was soon converted to Tremaine's policies and was hired as junior editor in 1937.

Most commentators date the start of 'The Golden Age of *Astounding*' variously between 1938 and 1940 (others deny its existence). Ashley links it with Street & Smith's decision to dispense with editorial directors in May 1938, and the consequent

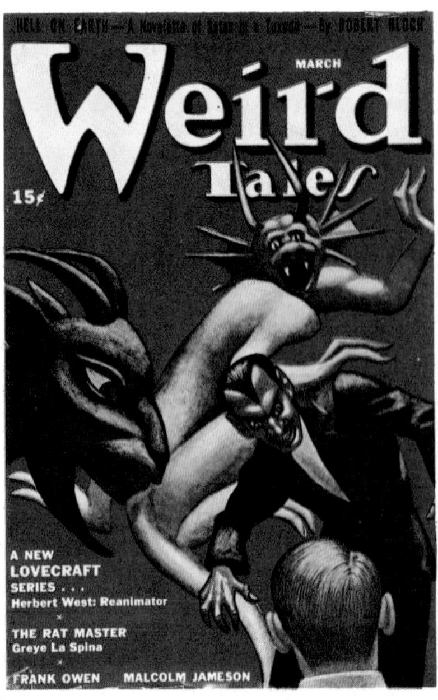

March 1942, cover by Hannes Bok.

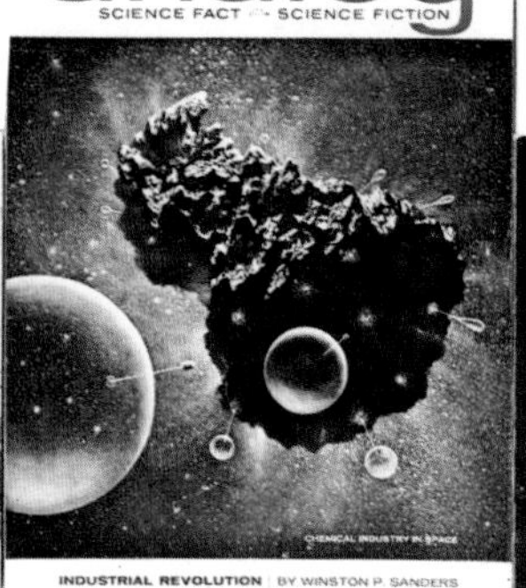

These examples of Astounding show significant stages in the development of the magazine, from change of publisher through change of format to change of name.

ascendancy of Campbell. 'The greatest of the editors' (Williamson) had an enormous influence on science fiction generally, not least due to his excellent relations with his writers, whom he often advised and inspired. With his 'nova' policy (not much different from Tremaine's thought-variants) he phased out space opera (except for the super-popular Doc Smith's), insisted on the highest standards of writing, and turned attention from the glorification of technology towards a more considered exploration of its relationship with humanity.

Many of the best-known names in the genre were introduced through the pages of *Astounding* in the late 1930s and 1940s, including Asimov, de Camp, del Rey, Heinlein, Sturgeon and van Vogt. Campbell's rejection of all but the best meant that many stories by leading writers became available for the large number of new magazines which appeared in the American pre-war boom.

In the February 1938 *Thrilling Wonder*, Weisinger asked for reactions to the idea of a companion magazine for longer works of fiction. The resulting enthusiasm led to *Startling Stories (Startling)* appearing in November that year (though dated January 1939).

Doubtless Weisinger's suggestion and the reaction to it helped to get the boom under way, but an event which must have been well into the planning stage by February 1938 was the real stimulus. This was the launching of *Marvel Science Stories* by Red Circle in May (dated August), and its first issue sold a reputed 60,000 copies. The effect on publishers was apparent the following year, when ten new titles appeared, most of them companions to existing sf magazines. This companion system either divided long and short original material between sister magazines, or else used one of the titles for fantasy and/or weird fiction, leaving the other for science fiction alone.

The only immediate failure among the companions was, ironically, Red Circle's *Dynamic Science Stories* (two issues from February). The most successful one was, predictably, Campbell's *Unknown* for Street & Smith. From March 1939 it revolutionised the weird and fantasy fields. Campbell excluded the prevalent sadistic horror, published much science fantasy, and introduced whimsical and humorous stories, later copied by other magazines. As always, he took only the best stories. Palmer's *Fantastic Adventures* (May 1939) using good authors, too, though it was rather more juvenile in tone than *Unknown*, and surprisingly took the 'bedsheet' format ($8\frac{1}{2}$ in $\times$ $11\frac{1}{2}$ in).

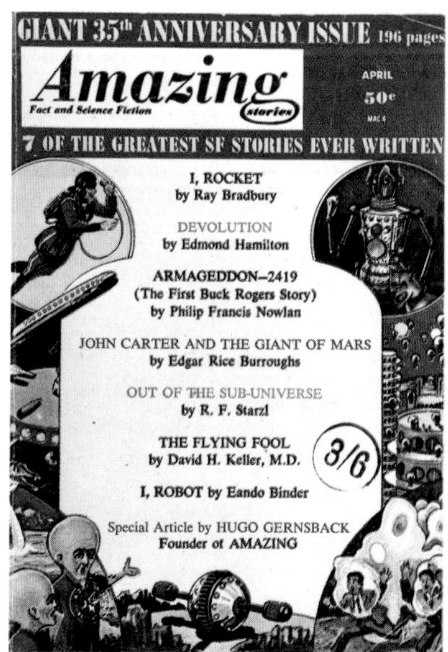

April 1961, cover by Frank R. Paul.

Other pulp publishers rushed to jump onto the sf bandwagon. Blue Ribbon (later Columbia Publications) entered the field with *Science Fiction* in March 1939 and *Future Fiction* that November. Both were edited by Hornig, who aimed to provide mature reading from less popular authors. *Science Fiction Quarterly* joined them in July 1940. The Munsey Group recognised a demand for reprints of earlier sf stories, the rights to many of which they held, and cashed in with *Famous Fantastic Mysteries (FFM)* (edited by Mary Gnaedinger). So popular was the first issue (September/October 1939), that it changed to monthly at once, presenting a mixture of weird, fantasy and sf stories. A longer fiction companion, *Fantastic Novels Magazine (Fantastic Novels)* lasted only a year from July 1940. Love Romances came into the race with *Planet Stories (Planet)* from December 1939, with editor Malcolm Reiss aiming at a juvenile space-story interest.

Most attempts to build a magazine round a single character like Street & Smith's *Doc Savage* (March 1933–June 1949) failed quickly, but Standard's *Captain Future* was an exception. Almost wholly consisting of Edmond Hamilton's stories, it started in January 1940 and outlasted Standard's weird title *Strange Stories* (February 1939–January 1941) by three years. Just as popular were the titles Frederick Pohl persuaded Popular Publications to issue, with him as editor, in February and March 1940. *Astonishing Stories (Astonishing)* and the longer-fiction *Super Science Stories (Super)* were, at a dime, the cheapest sf magazines ever, and published good-quality material by New York writers.

The boom had a revivifying effect on *Amazing Quarterly* (December 1940), but on examination the magazine proved to consist of unsold monthly copies bound three to a volume. It must have appealed to a separate audience, however, since it continued for three years, while the similar *Fantastic Adventure Quarterly* ran for ten years from 1941. Other attempts to join the money-making were not so lucky, however. The first title from H-K Publications, *Comet Stories*, lost editor Tremaine seven months after starting, as a result of the company's financial policies, and folded. Wollheim's *Stirring Science Stories* and *Cosmic Stories* suffered from similar problems with Albing's co-operative-payment scheme, and folded within thirteen months.

By this time (1941) a glut had levelled off the boom, and as many magazines were folding as starting. At the same time, the rise of comics provided competition for the magazines in readership, and in staff too. Weisinger, for instance, left Standard for National Comics in June, to be replaced by Oscar J. Friend with his juvenile letter columns. *Wonder* began to lose quality. Elsewhere a pulling-in of horns began. At Columbia, *Future* was combined with *Science Fiction* in the Fall, when the unfortunate Hornig was replaced by Lowndes. But the end of the boom had been signalled in April, when *Marvel* closed down.

Meanwhile it had had minor effects in Canada, with three titles appearing. The longest running was *Uncanny Tales* (December 1940–August 1943). This was not a reprint edition of the *Marvel*'s weird companion of the same name (Summer 1939–May 1940), but it did consist mostly of reprints. *Science Fiction* (October 1941–June 1942) also contained many reprints.

The war came to the United States in December 1941, bringing to the magazines printing and supply restrictions, and to editorial staff and writers enlistment and the draft. All magazines suffered infrequency, irregularity or shrinkage (or all three), though Palmer's titles actually increased in size in 1942 as Ziff-Davis concentrated its forces on science fiction. Many companions were axed, and many changes made in desperate attempts to corner the dwindling market. *FFM* defied the trend to quarterly publication by going monthly in June 1942, a bad decision leading to a mere three issues in 1943. At *Planet*, Reiss moved to become editorial director, his first editor, W. S. Peacock, vitalising the magazine with new writers; and Campbell also brought in new names to replace his war-serving top-flight authors.

Many magazines, and many publishers, could not survive the wartime situation. In March 1943 sf pioneers Munsey Publications were taken over by Popular Publications. Seven magazines died that year, including *Astonishing*, *Super*, *Future* and *Unknown*. By Spring of 1944 only seven of the eighteen magazines existing during the height of the boom remained.

There were some chinks of light, however. In late 1944 and early 1945, Standard replaced Friend on *Startling* and *Thrilling Wonder*, and the new editor, Sam Merwin Jr, gradually turned them towards a more mature audience. And in 1945 the man who had started specialist science fiction, Hugo Gernsback, reappeared on the scene. Having produced the first sf comic (*Superworld Comics*, 1939), he now presented *Tame*, the first in a series of science fiction humour annuals (the others ran from 1949 to 1951).

In Britain, the incipient pre-war boom had been smothered by events, but it burst forth almost as soon as hostilities ceased. The year 1946 saw no fewer than seven British magazines come on to the market, with another in 1948. Most of these were one-off or limited-run productions full of reprints, but the most important one still continues (after a fashion, and only just).

New Worlds had been projected in 1940 as a professional continuation of a fan magazine, but the three issues prepared had to be abandoned. In April 1946 editor

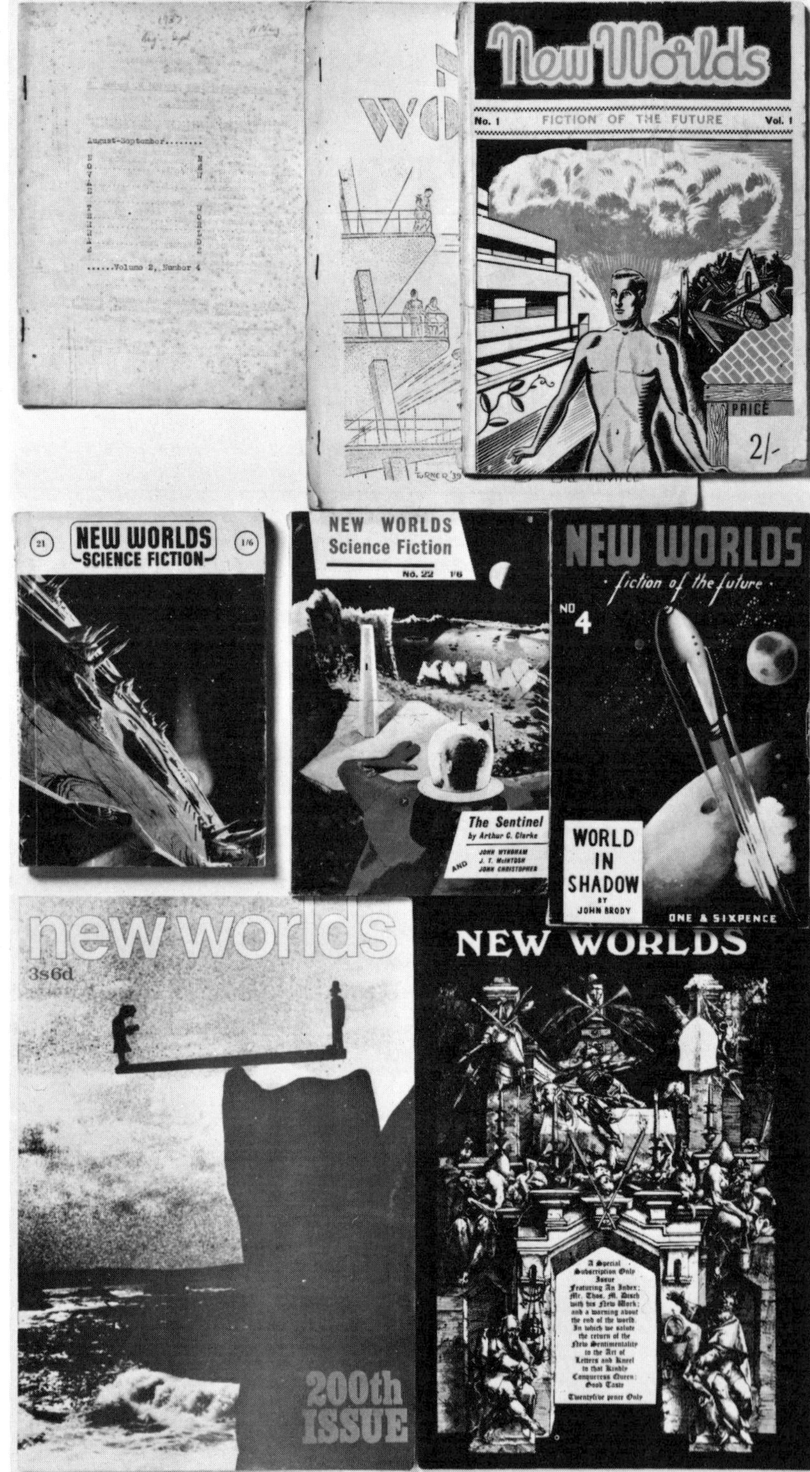

Examples of New Worlds *showing significant stages, from the first issue to the last.*

Carnell brought out the first issue for a different publisher, Pendulum Publications. The magazine was a success following a restyled cover for No 2, but Pendulum themselves failed just after the third issue came out. A fan consortium soon formed under the name of Nova Publications, and *New Worlds* continued with the Summer 1949 issue (appearing in April). The publishing name was retained when Nova was absorbed into Maclarens in early 1954, and Carnell continued as editor, introducing and encouraging many new authors.

Walter Gillings edited two of the other magazines in the British boom, including

Fantasy (this time from Temple Bar), which carried a high class of original material. Like the boom itself it was ended by paper shortages.

By contrast with Britain, the immediate post-war years in America were quiet for the sf magazines. The major events were Wollheim's return to professional publications with his well-produced digest-sized magazine of reprints, *Avon Fantasy Reader* (Avon Publishing), in February 1947, and William F. Crawford's *Fantasy Book* in July. Soon, *Amazing Quarterly* and *Fantastic Novels* reappeared, while August Derleth's *Arkham Sampler* published some excellent fiction between January 1948 and Autumn 1949. It was not until 1949 that America saw the beginning of the new boom, but this was also the beginning of the end for the pulps. Some were now revived, but none survived for long in their old format. For these were the years of the ascendancy of the digests.

Campbell was in the vanguard as usual, having taken *Astounding* down to digest size ($7\frac{3}{4}$ in × $5\frac{1}{2}$ in) in November 1943. But the real herald of the revolution was *The Magazine of Fantasy and Science Fiction (F&SF)*, which flashed on to the scene (as *The Magazine of Fantasy*) in October 1949. Published by Mercury Press and edited by Anthony Boucher (with J. Francis McComas until 1954), it set new rules by excluding letter columns and aiming at wider audiences than the ghetto readership of pulp. Starting quarterly, it was soon on a monthly basis, leading the field 'in wit, style, and sheer literary quality' (Williamson).

A year after *F&SF* launched the attack, the second new-style digest appeared. *Galaxy Science Fiction (Galaxy)* was published by World Editions Inc and later bought by Robert M. Guinn. Editor Horace Gold was as strict in his selection of material as Campbell, and quickly took *Galaxy* into the prominent position it occupied for many years. He preferred stories dealing more with social and psychological speculation than with purely technological evolution, using writers like Blish, Kornbluth, Nourse, and Sheckley.

The third of the long-lasting new digests appeared at the height of the second boom in March 1952. *Worlds of If Science Fiction* (or *If: Worlds of Science Fiction* – the preference is left to the reader) came from J. L. Quinn, who also edited when the first editor, P. W. Fairman, moved to Ziff-Davis. *If* survived free of non-fiction sections at a time when this was considered unpopular, which gives a measure of the standard of its fiction. Closely following on its heels came a digest-sized companion magazine from Ziff-Davis, *Fantastic* (July 1952). Howard Browne had taken over from Palmer at Ziff-Davis in January 1950, following the latter's sensational espousal of Shaverism, but associate editor Fairman was given too much control over *Fantastic* and its early achievements were soon forgotten. After March 1953 it absorbed *Fantastic Adventures*, but continued at low ebb until the late 1950s.

Many magazine publishers did not at first appreciate the power of the digest form and the increasing importance of good fiction. Those pulps which did not change form went to the wall. In 1951, *Fantasy Book* folded in January, *Fantastic Adventures Quarterly* in March, *Super* (restarted in January 1949) in August, and *Amazing Quarterly* in December. New pulp titles soon faded away, many of them lasting for fewer than five issues. Between 1950 and 1953 there were six of this sort in Britain, and fourteen appeared in the USA from 1949 to 1958, most of them in the first half of the decade. John Raymond, for instance, entered the field with four titles in 1952 and 1953, but editor del Rey resigned after a disagreement, and they all soon folded, only *Science Fiction Adventures* lasting until May 1954. In Britain, John Spencer brought out five titles (one weird) in 1950, but the sf titles folded one by one in 1954.

Of the companions resurrected during the boom, the only ones to last until 1960 were Columbia's *Science Fiction* (restarted as a digest, December 1953) and *Future* (May 1953, converting to digest June 1954). Others, such as Red Circle's *Marvel*, changed too late and died with the first digest issue. New companies had similar fates: Popular's reprint-stories *A. Merritt's Fantasy Magazine* (December 1949) saw only five issues; Crawford's *Spaceway* ran from December 1953 to June 1955; Reiss's *Two Complete Science-Adventure Books* had a $3\frac{1}{2}$-year run from December 1950, but another attempt failed in two issues in 1953; while another Columbia pulp lasted little more than a year in 1952–53.

Amalgamations could not defer the death of pulps, which increased from 1953. *FFM* reabsorbed *Fantastic Novels* in April 1952, but died in June 1953. Avon brought out a science fiction companion to Wollheim's fantasy title in April 1951, but a merger of the two in 1953, the replacement of Wollheim by Sol Cohen, and the inclusion of original stories all came too late. Avon's two other attempts at companions folded quickly in 1950–51.

Standard also tried changing editors, with Sam Mines replacing Merwin in 1951–52. *Thrilling Wonder* and *Startling* came up with the front runners when iconoclastic writers like Farmer were published, but the pulp format was stubbornly retained, and both died in 1955. Attempts at other magazines failed in 1950 and 1952, though the pulp *Fantastic Story Quarterly* lasted a respectable five years from April 1950.

A change took place at Ziff-Davis in December 1949, when Palmer left following the sensationalism of his 'Shaverism' policy in *Amazing*. He started Clark Publishing even before he left, producing *Other Worlds Science Stories*. This was joined by *Imagination* in October 1950, Beatrice Mahaffey being brought in to run them both with some valuable science fiction among the fantastic tales. *Imagination* went to Palmer's former Ziff-Davis colleague, William L. Hamling, who had set up Greenleaf Publishing. *Other Worlds* split in 1953 but recombined two years later, when Mahaffey left and the magazine drifted towards Palmer's occult interests. In 1957 it became entirely a flying saucer magazine, and Palmer had left sf publishing after nearly twenty years in the field. *Imagination* folded in 1958.

Gernsback tried another comeback in 1953 with *Science Fiction Plus*, edited by Sam Moskowitz. A multi-colour slick, it survived only seven issues, and Gernsback quit the field for good.

The boom was at its height in 1952–53, but by 1954 the ratio of new American magazines to dying ones was 3:10. The longest-surviving pulp, Columbia's *Science Fiction Quarterly* (restarted as a new series in May 1951) led a lonely existence after 1955, ending in February 1958. Margulies' consistently good *Fantastic Universe Science Fiction*, started in Summer 1953, unaccountably reverted to pulp size in October 1959 and suffered the hero's fate the following March. The pulps were gone for ever.

However, the digest market was now over-saturated, distribution pattern upheavals caused chaos, and the expansion of paperback publishing brought unwanted competition. Of the eight new American titles forming a small surge in late 1956–early 1957, none survived to the end of the decade, and eight established magazines folded by 1960. At the end of that year, only six American titles remained.

Britain was in a similar decline, having progressed through the boom with less verve but correspondingly fewer catastrophes. *Authentic Science Fiction Series (Science Fiction Fortnightly* for part of its life) had come from Hamilton & Co in 1951, and under later editor H. J. Campbell introduced several new authors, but ended in 1957. A Scottish magazine, *Nebula Science Fiction*, came out in September 1952, and was successfully run by Peter Hamilton to June 1959. *Vargo Statten Science Fiction Magazine* endured two publishers, two editors, and three title changes in two years (1954–56). Nova brought out *Science-Fantasy* as a companion to *New Worlds* in July 1950. This, too, was a professional continuation of an amateur publication, editor Gillings being replaced by Carnell in 1951, and it survived the slump of 1960. So did Nova's *Science Fiction Adventures* (January 1959–May 1963), a conversion of the reprint edition of the American magazine to original fiction.

Australia had taken part in the boom too, though of the eight magazines produced between 1949 and 1958 only one carried more than a modicum of original fiction. This was *Thrills Incorporated* (March 1950–June 1952).

Many American magazines tried to beat the slump with editorial changes. Damon

Knight, as editor of *If* from October 1958, could not lift it out of the doldrums, and Quinn sold it to Galaxy in February 1959. At Ziff-Davis, Fairman was replaced as editor by previous assistant Cele Goldsmith in December 1958, and the longed-for improvements in *Amazing* and *Fantastic* began almost at once. The 'New Wave' was presaged by her publication of Farmer, Aldiss and Ballard from 1961. Campbell updated *Astounding*'s name to *Analog* in October 1960. In February 1962 Street & Smith were taken over by Condé Nast.

From 1963 new magazines began appearing again. *Gamma* came in April, a good reprint-and-originals mixture from Charles E. Fritch and Jack Matcha, but saw only five issues. Guinn, having taken on Sol Cohen in December 1962 to run Galaxy's magazines, brought out *Worlds of Tomorrow* in April 1963. Pohl, who had taken over as editor from Gold in October 1961, wrought improvements in *If* and maintained *Galaxy*, but failed to make a lasting hit with the new magazine, which was absorbed by *If* in August 1967. Health Knowledge, where Lowndes was editor, brought out the weird *Magazine of Horror* in 1963. Gerald Levine's *Bizarre Mystery Magazine* had some fine stories, but only three issues from October 1965.

The most prolific publisher of the time was Sol Cohen. Leaving Galaxy in 1965, he formed Ultimate Publishing and bought *Amazing* and *Fantastic* from Ziff-Davis, along with reprint rights to the old stories. With Joseph Ross as editorial director, he began to fill the magazines with increasingly poor reprints and they predictably slipped downhill. After rapid editorial changes, Ted White came in as editor in 1969. He gradually reduced the proportion of reprints to zero and revitalised the magazines, reintroducing fan features and employing the best writers.

To exploit his reprint store, Cohen began to publish an increasing number of usually short-lived titles. By 1970 he had fourteen, four of them one-shots. But perhaps because he paid no royalties to the writers, his personal boom ended suddenly, and by the end of 1971 only three of the new magazines remained. They all ended in 1975.

Lualdi's Popular Library, with Jim Hendryx Jr as editor, had tried to enter the sf field with an unsuccessful exhumation of *Wonder Stories* in 1957 and again in 1963. Lualdi tried two other titles from 1964 and 1967, but neither lasted five issues. *Galaxy* also tried two new titles during this time, with equal lack of success, and then sold their sf magazines to UPD, where Ejler Jakobsson took over as editor in 1969. After an unpromising start, Jakobsson managed somewhat to revive *Galaxy* and *If*, and even attempted to restart two dormant titles. But these soon failed, and in 1971 the falling sales of magazines caused the reabsorption of *Worlds of Tomorrow* by *If*, which itself was absorbed by *Galaxy* in 1975, a year after James Baen became editor.

Attempts to revive Mercury's *Venture* and Crawford's *Spaceway* failed, too, the latter in 1970. The following year saw the end of eleven magazines, and also, more sadly, the death of Campbell. Ben Bova then took over at Condé Nast.

Some of the most influential magazine writing of this time was going on in Britain. In 1964 Roberts and Vinter acquired the Nova titles and Carnell left. Bonfiglioli became editor of *Science-Fantasy*, introducing new authors such as Keith Roberts; and Moorcock took over *New Worlds*, both magazines becoming pocket-book size. *New Worlds* published writers like J.G. Ballard, and Langdon Jones. When Roberts and Vinter had to give up the magazines in 1966, it absorbed its companion (by then called *SF Impulse*) and continued in slick format with the aid of an Arts Council grant, under the guidance of Moorcock. It was to become the centre of the 'new wave', presenting work by American as well as British experimental sf writers. It had an influence on mainstream literature, and 'there is no doubt that *New Worlds*' experiments will have been crucial in shaping the future of science fiction the world over' (Cordesse). The magazine's features were often critical of 'Golden Age' writers. This and the explicit sexual content of some stories led to unpopularity inside and outside the sf world, and after a hiatus its last issue came in 1971. Moorcock continued it as a quarterly paperback, but as this is a non-subscription publication, it is not generally considered a magazine. Even in the new form, it was thought likely to end in 1977.

Of influence in Britain was *Vision of Tomorrow*, a slick-format magazine edited by Philip Harbottle but lasting only one year (1969–70).

A new-style British venture came from New English Library in January 1974: *Science Fiction Monthly*, edited by Aune Butt. In eye-catching but floppy slick-newspaper format, it survived on a mixed-value diet of fandom and stories, also relying heavily on striking artwork, until 1976. Then a change of format and name (to *SF Digest*) endured one issue before NEL wound down their magazine section.

An equally important venture in

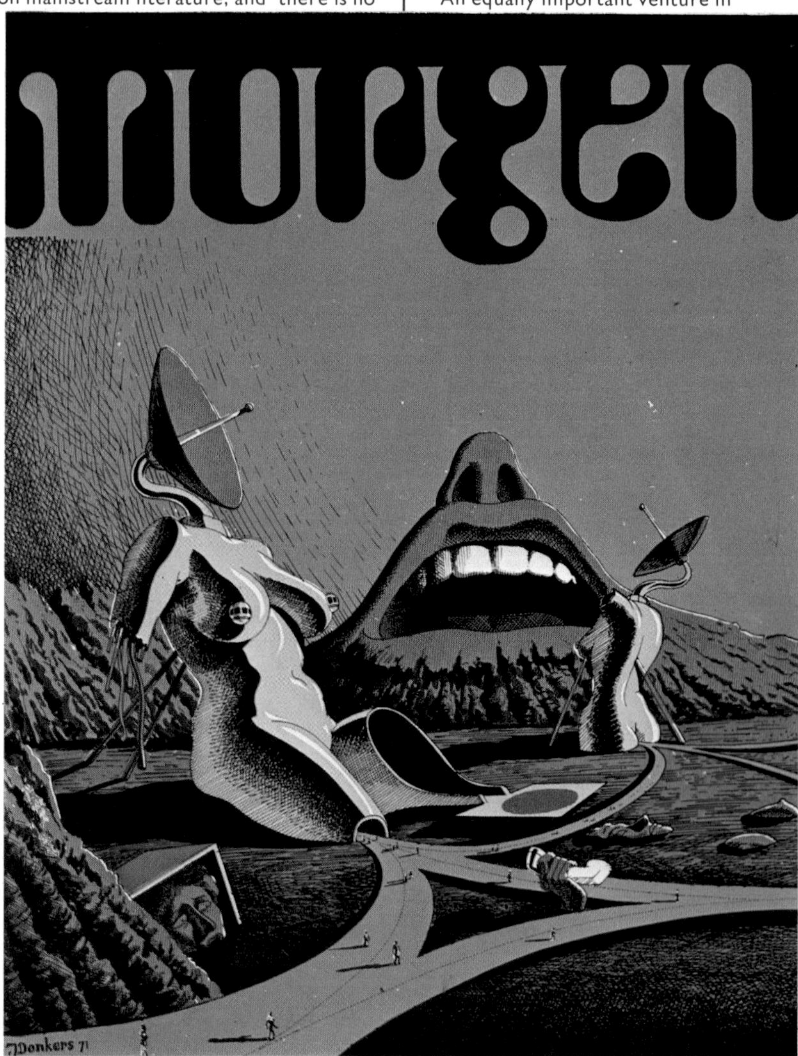

The last issue of the Dutch magazine, Morgen, *January 1973.*

America was the run of *Vertex*, published by Mankind from April 1973. In slick format, it was edited by Don Pfeil with Forrest J. Ackerman as a contributing editor. With fine fiction and a large feature section, it should have been a success, but editorial changes were followed by a disastrous switch to a newspaper format, which survived a mere three issues in early 1975.

Since the beginning of the sixties, original anthology series have encroached on the sf market, and by 1970 they began to look like a flood. Novels and collections in book form are also much more popular than in the early days of the magazine, making an increasing drain on the readership. The magazines never survived solely on regular subscribers, relying also on casual news-stand sales to a floating and constantly changing fringe readership. There is evidence that this fringe is now buying its science fiction in other forms, and subscriptions are becoming much more important for the magazines. Since the late sixties, all of them have suffered losses in circulation, except for *Analog*, which has improved its dominant position so that it now has double the circulation of its nearest rival, *F&SF*. This last is the only magazine to consistently improve its share of the market since 1973.

These two seem likely to be the only survivors into 1977. The longest runner of all, *Amazing*, has always had the smallest proportion of subscribers and is now faring worst in loss of circulation. There is doubt whether *Fantastic* is still being published, and *Galaxy* seems likely to fold at any time. Two new magazines appearing in 1976, *Odyssey Science Fiction* and *Galileo*, have limited circulations, and the latter appears to be only semi-professional, at least at the outset.

To the exhausted climber through the ranges of sf magazine publishing, 1976 seems a true watershed. On the newly revealed slopes dropping down to the eighties, the valleys may be dry indeed.

Covers from the French magazine, Métal Hurlant, *launched in January 1975.*

PRINTED SOURCES

Ashley, Mike (ed). *The History of the Science Fiction Magazine: Part 1: 1926-1935*, New English Library (UK) 1974; *Part 2: 1936-1945*, NEL (UK) 1976; *Part 3: 1946-1955*, NEL (UK) 1976

Cockroft, T. G. L. *Index to the Weird Fiction Magazines*, privately printed (New Zealand) 1962, 2 vols

Day, Bradford M. (ed). *The Complete Checklist of Science Fiction Magazines*, Science Fiction and Fantasy Publications (US) 1961

Day, Donald B. (compiler). *Index to the Science Fiction Magazines 1926-1950*, Perri Press (US) 1952

Durie, A. J. L. (compiler). *An Index to the British Editions of the Magazine of Fantasy and Science Fiction with a Cross-reference to the Original American Edition*, privately printed (UK) 1965

Goodstone, Tony. *The Pulps: Fifty Years of American Pop Culture*, Chelsea House (US) 1970

Goulart, Ron. *An Informal History of the Pulp Magazines*, Arlington House (US) 1972

Jeeves, B. T. *A Checklist of Astounding to 1959*, privately printed (US) c 1959-60, 3 parts

Lupoff, Dick and Thompson, Don (eds). *All in Color for a Dime*, Arlington House (US) 1970

Metcalf, Norm. *The Index of Science Fiction Magazines, 1951-65*, J. Ben Start (US) 1968

Moskowitz, Sam. *Science Fiction by Gaslight: a History and Anthology of Science Fiction in the Popular Magazines, 1891-1911*, World Publishing (US) 1968

Moskowitz, Sam. *Under the Moons of Mars: a History and Anthology of 'The Scientific Romance' in the Munsey Magazines, 1912-20*, Holt, Rinehart & Winston (US) 1970

NESFA. *Index to the Science Fiction Magazines 1966-1970*, New England Science Fiction Association (US) 1971

Rogers, Alva. *A Requiem for Astounding*, Advent (US) 1964

Speer, Jack (with Bill Evans). *The Index of Science Fiction Magazines*, Robert Peterson (US) 1946

Stone, Graham (compiler). *Australian Science Fiction Index 1925-1967*, Australian Science Fiction Association (Australia) 1968

Strauss, Erwin S. *The MIT Science Fiction Society's Index to the SF Magazines, 1951-65*, MIT Science Fiction Society (US) 1966

04.06 BOOKS AND ANTHOLOGIES

04.06 BOOKS AND ANTHOLOGIES

04.06.1 Books

The conception of science fiction as a separate entity from other literature began with the birth of the first specialist publication, *Amazing Stories*, in 1926. Hitherto science fiction had not been treated as a different category of fiction, being published alongside all other forms of general literature, many of which (detective stories, westerns, war adventures) have now also been pigeon-holed. Therefore, there were no specialist science fiction book publishers in those early days, nor were any of the books specifically labelled 'SF' or something similar on their spines. This had its advantages and disadvantages. It meant that those readers who enjoyed tales of scientific adventure could not immediately isolate their favoured fiction other than by investigating likely sounding titles, or seeking out those writers whom they knew produced such stories. But it also meant the books were not isolated from that section of the reading public who entertained a bias against science fiction and thus steered clear of such works on principle. Every novel enjoyed a fair chance. Paradoxically the arguments which applied then, again apply equally today. In fact, as it is often the case, events have turned full circle and now many sf novels are being published as general fiction.

Printed books date back as far as the history of printing, and the argument over who first invented mechanical printing has yet to be resolved. It is a good starting point to note that the first book printed in English was an historical fantasy, William Caxton's translation of a French romance *The Recuyell of the Historyes of Troye* (*c*1473). Another early printed book noted in the development of speculative fiction was Sir Thomas More's *Utopia* (1515/16).

The major growth of book publishing did not really begin until the early eighteenth century. Before then most writers paid for their own manuscripts to be printed, and printers acted as their own publishers. In 1724 Thomas Longman established his own publishing and bookselling business in Paternoster Row, London, which for many years remained the hub of the publishing industry until it was destroyed by bombing during the Second World War. No one firm, however, could be labelled as specialising in speculative fiction, not even when Edgar Allan Poe began to produce his many tales. It was not until scientific adventures became a vogue in the 1890s that any form of specific publishing could be seen. This was due in no small measure to the emerging talents of George Griffith, H. G. Wells and Arthur Conan Doyle, and at the same time, the ability of publishers to produce well-printed, sturdy books selling at a relatively low price.

The popularity of the future-war novel which had flared with the success of Sir George Chesney's *The Battle of Dorking* (1871) brought about a flood of imitations, the bulk of which were published either by Sampson Low (who also published many British editions of Jules Verne's work) or F. V. White. It was White who became the main publisher of George Griffith, but Griffith's early novels (all future-war), including *The Angel of the Revolution* (1893), were published by the new firm of Tower Publishing Co. This company acquired other future-war novels by such writers as William Le Queux (*The Great War in England in 1897*, 1894) and Fred T. Jane (*Blake of the 'Rattlesnake'*, 1895), and during the 1890s could be regarded as a publisher that regularly featured science fiction among its books. But no single publisher could claim to handle science fiction exclusively, not even Heinemann, who published most of H. G. Wells's early works.

The situation was similar in the United States. The Chicago firm of McClurg published the novels of Edgar Rice Burroughs, but otherwise ventured only occasionally into the sf field, although they were responsible for the book edition of George Allan England's *The Flying Legion* in 1930, Victor Rousseau's *The Messiah of the Cylinder* (1917) and several of the books of

Illustration by H. Lanos for When the Sleeper Wakes *by H. G. Wells.*

Ray Cummings. What is interesting about the Cummings novels is that they all originally appeared in the pulps, and the fourth published, *Brigands of the Moon* (1931), had originally been serialised during 1930 in *Astounding Stories*.

It requires only a brief consideration of the early sf magazine serials to realise just how few saw immediate book publication. In the early days of conventional magazine publishing a serial was written concurrently with its publication in a periodical, the novelist often fighting to meet deadlines, and almost always subsequent book publication was secured beforehand. The early serials in *Amazing Stories* were all reprints, and the first new serialised novel was A. Hyatt Verrill's *Beyond The Pole* (1926). Despite Verrill's popularity and his reputation as an eminent archaeologist, that serial never saw book publication. The second new serial, E. E. Smith's *The Skylark of Space* (1928), now ranks as one of the best known of all, but it had to wait till 1946 before it saw a book edition. Much the same applies to the other early serials, and Cummings's achievement arose solely because of his earlier sales to McClurg on the strength of his success with *Argosy*. The Munsey publications, of which *Argosy* was one, had an excellent rights section that secured prompt book publication of their successful serials; and Cummings, having made his name, could be assured of subsequent deals. With that one exception, few publishers were interested in science fiction, and most of the new writers wrote solely for the magazines, with little prospect of book publication.

The growth of specialist sf book publications owed its origins not to the big-name publishers, but to science fiction fans. By the early 1930s a host of fan publications, or fanzines, already existed, and fan groups were emerging throughout the US and spreading to Britain and beyond. The early fanzines were roughly produced from various forms of stencils, but in 1932 sf fan Conrad H. Ruppert made his printing facilities available for fandom publishing, beginning with the fanzine *The Time Traveller*. As a result several fanzines took on a professional appearance, and any special projects, such as the round-robin *Cosmos* (1933–34) later printed in a special edition, were given the Ruppert treatment. Another highspot became one of the rarest of all sf books, *Dawn of Flame*, a memorial volume of stories by Stanley G. Weinbaum published in 1936, the year after the author's death. Only about 250 copies were ever circulated, but even among so small a number there could be said to be two editions – the early copies carried a foreword by Raymond A. Palmer which was later replaced by another foreword by Lawrence Keating, at the request of Weinbaum's widow.

It was the same desire to perpetuate the work of a deceased author that resulted in the first major specialist book publishing firm, Arkham House. H. P. Lovecraft, one of the leading names in *Weird Tales*, had died in 1937. August Derleth thought his stories should be preserved in a more durable form and, putting together a selection of the best, he offered it to two leading publishers, but to no avail. Consequently Derleth, together with his colleague Donald Wandrei, established their own publishing house for the sole purpose of collecting Lovecraft's fiction into a book, issuing *The Outsider and Others* in a limited edition in 1939. The volume sold slowly but steadily, and encouraged by its success Derleth and Wandrei began to experiment, publishing further collections of work by Clark Ashton Smith, Lovecraft and Derleth himself. Arkham House quickly established itself, and whilst its main criterion was the publication of horror/fantasy and not science fiction, it was supported by many sf fans and can therefore be regarded as the first true specialist publisher in the field.

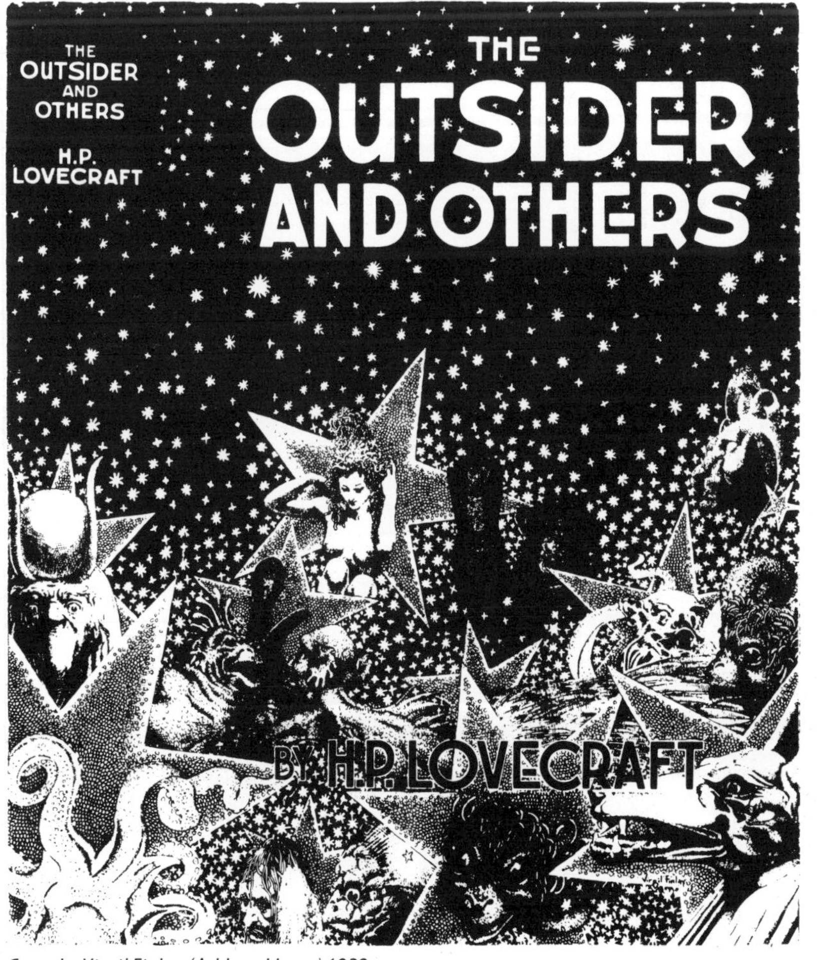

Cover by Virgil Finlay (Arkham House) 1939.

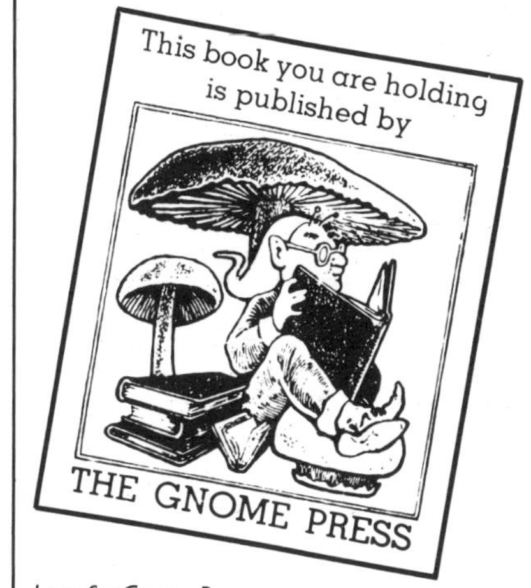

Logo for Gnome Press.

The Second World War delayed the further development of such ventures. But shortly after its end, when fans returned from the forces complete with sizeable gratuities, several of them decided to invest their capital in publishing. Others found money by alternative means, and such was their dedication that for a period fan publishers flourished. One of the earliest was Shasta Publishers in Chicago, formed by Erle Korshak, Mark Reinsberg and Ted Dikty. The original idea was to produce serious reference works on science fiction, and this was pursued ambitiously with Everett Bleiler's landmark work, *Checklist of Fantastic Literature* (1948). But later they included fiction in their lists and published some noted sf works: John W. Campbell's collection *Who Goes There?* (1948), L. Ron Hubbard's *Slaves of Sleep* (1948) and the first three books in Robert Heinlein's future-history series, ending with *Revolt in 2100* (1953). Thereafter, Shasta declined during the publishing boom when faced with large-scale competition.

Another early specialist fan publisher was Thomas P. Hadley, who actually preceded Shasta. In 1946 he issued the first book edition of *The Skylark of Space*, which sold out at an astonishing rate, and repeated his success with John W. Campbell's *The Mightiest Machine* (1947). Subsequently, Hadley's list was taken over by Lloyd Arthur Eshbach, a renowned pre-war writer, who established Fantasy Press in 1947, starting with E. E. Smith's *The Spacehounds of IPC*. In time, Eshbach published all of E. E. Smith's novels, in addition to most of John W. Campbell's works, including a new novel *The Moon Is Hell* (1950). He also edited and published an important symposium of articles by leading authors on the writing of science fiction entitled *Of Worlds Beyond* (1947). In 1952 Eshbach established a second publishing house, Polaris Press, intended to revive the lesser-known classics.

04.06 BOOKS AND ANTHOLOGIES

Cover by Hannes Bok (Shasta) 1948.

Not to be confused with Fantasy Press was William L. Crawford's Fantasy Publishing Co Inc, in Los Angeles. Crawford had produced two printed semi-professional magazines in the mid-1930s (*Marvel Tales* and *Unusual Stories*), in addition to such booklets as H. P. Lovecraft's *The Shadow over Innsmouth* (1936), now a very scarce item. Establishing the FPCI after the War, Crawford published several interesting books, including *The Omnibus of Time* (1950) by Ralph Milne Farley, Stanton Coblentz's 1929 novel *After 12000 Years* (1950) and Darrell C. Richardson's exhaustive *Max Brand: the Man and His Work* (1952). Unlike most other speciality publishers, the FPCI is still at work, issuing Emil Petaja's *Stardrift* in 1971, and currently publishing the irregular magazine *Witchcraft & Sorcery*.

Among those many others were Prime Press of Philadelphia, which first published George O. Smith's *Venus Equilateral* (1947); the New Era Publishing Co of Philadelphia, which issued David H. Keller's *The Solitary Hunters & The Abyss* (1948); and the New Collector's Group, which had published two of A. Merritt's unfinished novels completed by Hannes Bok, *The Fox Woman* (1946) and *The Black Wheel* (1947). But by far the most successful was the Gnome Press, established in 1948 by Martin Greenberg who was joined by David Kyle. Gnome published many of the sf classics of the day, including Isaac Asimov's *I, Robot* (1950) and his *Foundation* trilogy (1951–53); *Seetee Ship* by Jack Williamson (as Will Stewart) in 1951; Raymond F. Jones's *Renaissance* (1951) as well as the first collections of Robert E. Howard's Conan stories, among them *King Conan* (1953) and *Tales of Conan* (1955). In 1958 Greenberg bought up the stock of Fantasy Press and FPCI, and was able to expand Gnome Press.

While Gnome was able to survive the 1953 boom, most other speciality publishers went to the wall. Strictly speaking, their services were no longer required. They had existed to fill the gap created by the major publishers who had earlier ignored science fiction. However, by 1950 science fiction was in demand, and nearly all the leading US publishers began to include a regular sf programme in their

Who Goes There? *by John W. Campbell. Cover by Hannes Bok (Shasta) 1948).*

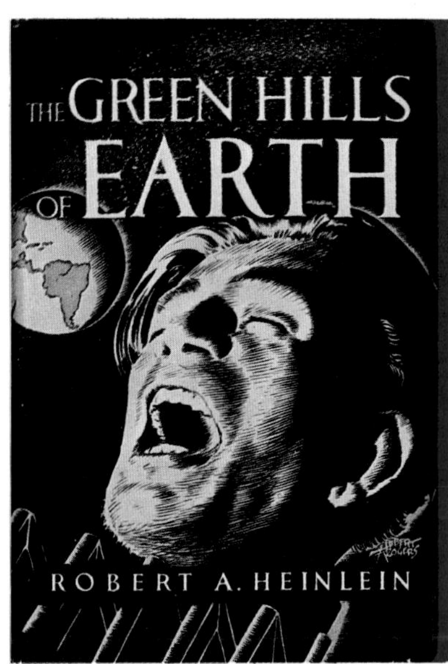

The first three books in Robert A. Heinlein's future-history series (Shasta) 1951-53. Covers by Rogers.

lists. One of the first was Frederick Fell of New York, who began to publish the regular annual *The Best Science Fiction Stories*, originally compiled by E. F. Bleiler and T. E. Dikty in 1949. But soon to overtake Fell as the leading US sf publisher was Doubleday & Co in New York, which in 1950 bought Asimov's previously unpublished novel *Pebble in the Sky*.

Thereafter, the genre became increasingly accepted, especially with the mushrooming of the paperback market. However, there was a major difference between the development of the paperback field in the US and in Britain. The US already enjoyed the bulk of the writing talent; consequently its expanding book market carried first-class material by all the major names. Stories from the much-maligned pulps suddenly found a wider and appreciative audience. In Britain, a similar rise in the popularity of science fiction books found the writers wanting. As a result, many of the 1950s publishers eager to exploit the paperback bandwagon instructed their various regular authors, who were producing gangster thrillers, westerns or spicy love stories, to write science fiction as well. With nothing more than the slightest knowledge of the field, the hacks rushed out an almost unreadable flood of the most inane stories, characters and plots. The few genuinely competent UK writers included in this scramble, John Russell Fearn, E. C. Tubb, Kenneth Bulmer and Bryan Berry among them, struggled to produce some good novels against almost impossible time limits, but their better work of the period tends to be overlooked in the morass of tenth-rate verbiage which swamped the British market, often under publishers' house pseudonyms. The consequence was that science fiction acquired a low reputation in the UK which took years to overcome. Today, most of Britain's major paperback publishers, together with many hardcover firms, recognise the speculative merits of science fiction as much as its sales value. Such publishers as Gollancz, Sidgwick & Jackson, New English Library and Weidenfeld & Nicolson, as well as Granada Publishing (whose Panther Books have the largest sf list), Sphere, Futura (with its specialist Orbit imprint), Coronet, Corgi, Pan and many others, regularly issue sf novels, collections and anthologies. The same holds true in America, on an even grander scale. In 1952 Donald Wollheim had become science fiction editor for the Ace paperback line; he was to develop it into the largest sf publishing enterprise yet seen. Ballantine Books also began publishing in 1952 and rapidly earned a reputation as a producer of 'quality' sf paperbacks. In 1972 Wollheim established his own specialist sf publishing company, DAW Books, which, together with Ballantine, Avon and Berkley, leads sf publishing in the US.

In spite of the major publishers' acceptance of science fiction, there still remains a place for the specialist semi-professional. The leading US contender for this title is Advent Publishers Inc, in Chicago, which continues the work originally envisaged by Shasta, namely, the publication of serious reference works.

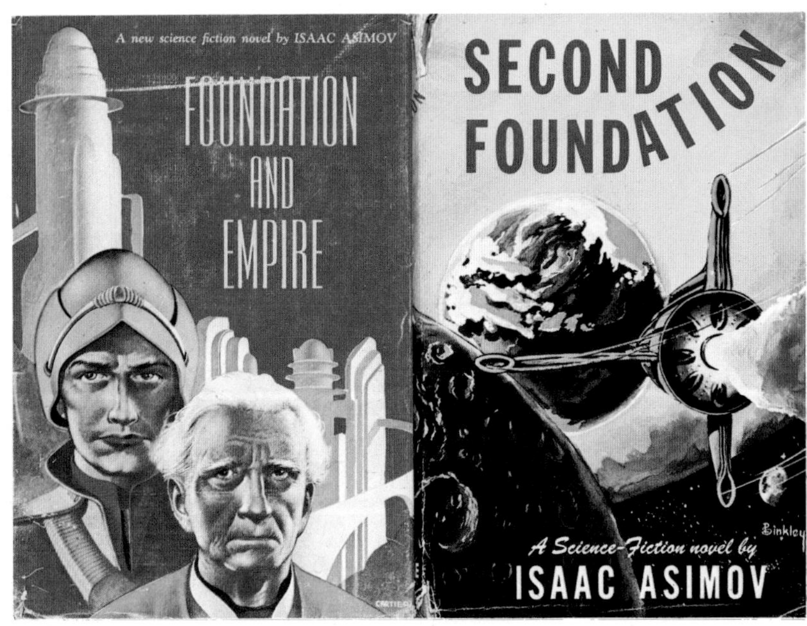

Two books from Isaac Asimov's Foundation *trilogy (Gnome Press) 1952, 1953. Covers by Cartier and Binkley.*

04.06 BOOKS AND ANTHOLOGIES

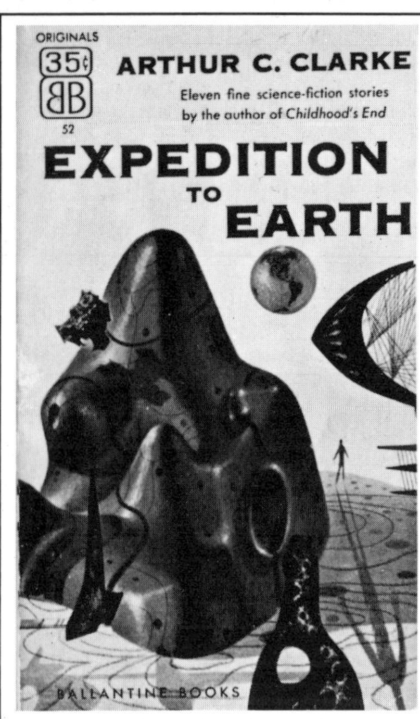

ORIGINALS
35¢
BB
52
ARTHUR C. CLARKE
Eleven fine science-fiction stories by the author of Childhood's End
EXPEDITION TO EARTH
BALLANTINE BOOKS

Among its volumes have been *A Requiem for Astounding* (1964), Alva Rogers's definitive look at the history of that magazine; *All Our Yesterdays* (1969), Harry Warner's history of sf fandom; Damon Knight's penetrating collection of sf criticism, *In Search of Wonder* (1956); Alexei Panshin's exhaustive study of Robert Heinlein, *Heinlein in Dimension* (1968); and most recently the first volume of Donald Tuck's *Encyclopedia of Science Fiction and Fantasy* (1974).

The same upsurge of interest which invigorated science fiction in the late 1940s is today revitalising fantasy fiction, and Ballantine Books, Donald M. Grant, Carcosa and others have begun issuing long-neglected or hitherto unpublished works by the great names of fantasy: Robert E. Howard, H. Warner Munn and many more. In the course of this work, much early science fiction is also being unearthed, and such publishers as the Arno Press, Hyperion and the Newcastle Publishing Co are resurrecting a host of previously rare or unobtainable works. There are now more specialist publishers at work than during the entire history of sf publishing, one more indication that the genre is reaching out to an increasingly wider readership.

04.06.2. Anthologies

A science fiction anthology is a collection of stories written by more than one author, usually assembled by a specific editor. The stories may have seen prior publication or they may be new, so making a distinction between a reprint and an original anthology, although hybrid volumes also appear.

Unlike the horror anthology, which has enjoyed a long and spine-chilling history, the sf anthology is in general a relatively new venture. One of the earliest such collections was *The Moon Terror & Other Stories*, compiled by the publishers of *Weird Tales* and containing four weird-scientific stories from that publication. It appeared in 1927. Shortly afterwards Hugo Gernsback introduced his Science Fiction Series of pocket-book short novels. In some instances the novels were so short that it needed more than one to fill out a book, thus technically a number of issues rank as anthologies. One such was number seven in the series, which featured *The Mechanical Man* by Amelia Reynolds Long and *The Thought Stealer* by Frank Bourne (1929).

Following these admittedly dubious contenders, the first true sf anthology, which also consisted entirely of new stories, was *Adventures to Come* (1937), edited by J. Berg Esenwein and containing juvenile tales by writers totally unknown in science fiction. Consequently, it had little effect on the field. Today most historians date the birth of the sf anthology from *The Other Worlds* (1941), edited by Philip Stong. Twelve of the twenty-five stories came from *Weird Tales*, and among the authors included were Theodore Sturgeon, Lester del Rey, Eando Binder and H. P. Lovecraft.

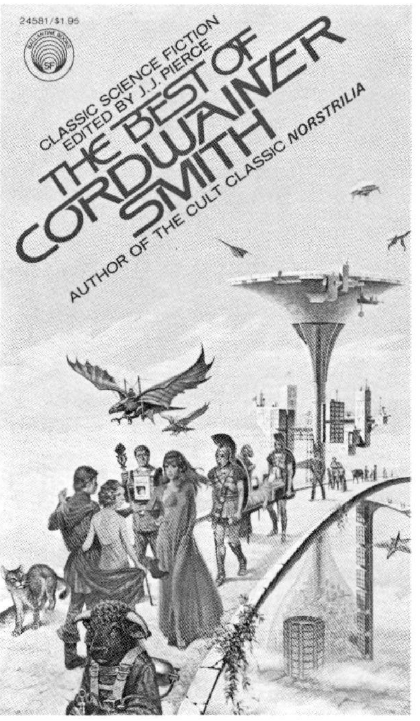

24581/$1.95
CLASSIC SCIENCE FICTION
EDITED BY J.J. PIERCE
THE BEST OF CORDWAINER SMITH
AUTHOR OF THE CULT CLASSIC NORSTRILIA

The book sold well, seeing a second edition in 1942, and despite the wartime paper restrictions publishers were beginning to appear more receptive to sf anthologies. The next Important contributions were the two collections

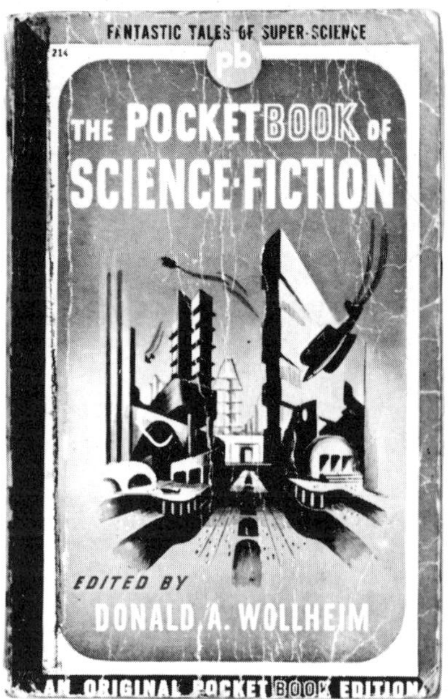

compiled by Donald Wollheim, *The Pocket Book of Science Fiction* (1943) and *The Portable Novels of Science* (1945). These did much to pave the way for publishers' interest in sf anthologies, and with the war over several more were launched in rapid succession. To readers accustomed to the slim anthologies of today, mostly under 200 pages, these early anthologies would seem almost gargantuan. Wollheim's *Portable Novels* ran to 737 pages. Groff

Conklin, who became one of the most respected of US anthologists during the 1950s, appeared with *The Best of Science Fiction* (1946), consisting of 785 pages and 40 stories by writers of the calibre of Heinlein, Simak, Sturgeon, Gallun, Campbell and Wells. In the same year there arrived *the* landmark publication, *Adventures in Time and Space* edited by Raymond J. Healy and J. Francis McComas. Its 997 pages carried 33 stories by virtually every leading name. A genuine *tour-de-force*, together with Wollheim's and Conklin's books it gave the uninitiated reader a thorough cross-section of all that was good in science fiction. (A reprint of the Healey and McComas anthology by Ballantine Books is currently still available.)

The success of such books created a favourable climate for future anthologies, and almost certainly helped in the publishers' acceptance of science fiction in general. By 1949 E. F. Bleiler and T. E. Dikty had begun their regular annual choice of the year's *Best Science Fiction*, and anthologists Conklin, August Derleth, Judith Merril and Wollheim were delving back into the crumbling pages of old pulps for some overlooked classics. It was hardly surprising that by the early 1950s fans were complaining that certain stories were being reprinted too often. The growth of reprint anthologies, coupled with the emergence of many reprint sf magazines, threatened the past with the danger of being over-mined.

One method of lending an anthology more coherence and making it less a random selection was to provide it with an over-riding theme, an approach developed particularly by Groff Conklin and Martin Greenberg. Conklin offered *Science Fiction Adventures in Dimension* (1953), *Science Fiction Thinking Machines* (1954), *Science Fiction Adventures in Mutation* (1955) and more recently *Great Science Fiction by Scientists* (1962), *Great Stories of Space Travel* (1963) and *Great Science Fiction about Doctors* (1963). Greenberg perhaps pursued a more logical sequence in his theme anthologies, so that the selected stories followed each other naturally. His compilations include *Men against the Stars* (1950), concentrating on the conquest of space; *Journey to Infinity* (1951), on the history of man; and *The Robot and the Man* (1953), which speaks for itself.

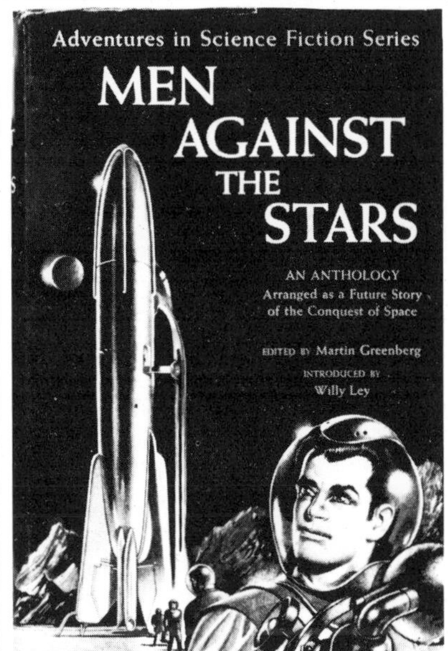

An anthology by Martin Greenberg concentrating on the conquest of space (Gnome Press) 1950. Cover by Cartier.

Another way of attempting to avoid the stereotyped anthology was to invite authors to choose their own favourite stories and supply a brief note explaining their choice, although in the outcome the final selection often owed more to the anthologist's choice than the authors'. Leo Margulies and Oscar J. Friend started this trend in 1949 with *My Best Science Fiction Story*, which produced an odd motley of tales, among them Isaac Asimov's 'Robot AL76 Goes Astray', John W. Campbell's 'Blindness' and Clark Ashton Smith's 'The Uncharted Isle'. Two years later August Derleth adopted the same ploy in *The Outer Reaches*, which not surprisingly produced a totally different crop, including Asimov's 'Death Sentence' and C. A. Smith's 'The Plutonian Drug'. More recently, Harry Harrison revived the theme for *Backdrop of Stars* (1968), in which Asimov then chose 'Founding Father'.

Several variations on the theme have also been employed. In 1954 Sam Moskowitz invited a number of magazine editors to nominate their favourite story among those they had published. The resulting *Editor's Choice in Science Fiction* included a bizarre cross-section, with Howard Browne picking Eando Binder's 'I, Robot' which appeared in *Amazing* before he edited it; Dorothy McIlwraith choosing Robert Barbour Johnson's 'Far Below' from *Weird Tales* July 1939, then edited by Farnsworth Wright; and *Blue Book* magazine somehow succeeding in gaining a mention. Several years later Laurence M. Janifer modified the theme by asking several authors to nominate their favourites by other writers, and this culminated in *Masters' Choice* (1966). Much the same ploy was used in the recent

A series of anthologies by Ballantine.

04.06 BOOKS AND ANTHOLOGIES

anthology group *Science Fiction Hall of Fame* (1972), edited by Ben Bova and Robert Silverberg. In these two later anthologies, the original selections of authors, ultimately decided by votes, were basically followed.

The selection of an annual 'year's best' anthology was begun in 1949 by Bleiler and Dikty. August Derleth employed the same tactic in *Portals of Tomorrow* (1954), all sixteen stories having first appeared in 1953. Similarly, Wollheim's *Prize Science Fiction* (1953) was a selection of the best stories of 1952. But these were one-off ventures, while the Bleiler and Dikty series continued, edited jointly till 1954, and then solely by Dikty until 1958. By then, Judith Merril had already begun her own annual series, *The Year's Greatest SF & Fantasy*, starting in 1956. Her own selections, culled from a huge array of sources, and often arguably not science fiction, thus infusing the series with an air of controversy, lasted until 1969. From the mid-1960s other editors had also been selecting science fiction annuals, resulting in a great confusion of titles. In 1965 Donald Wollheim and Terry Carr began *World's Best Science Fiction*, which ran until Wollheim left Ace Publishers. Wollheim continued with his own *Annual World's Best SF*, while Terry Carr brought out *The Best Science Fiction of the Year*, Lester del Rey: *Best Science Fiction Stories of the Year*, Harry Harrison with Brian Aldiss: *Best SF* and, for a while, Forrest Ackerman: *Best Science Fiction for 1966*. Add to this the now regular appearance of *Nebula Award Stories*, a similar culling of the year's best stories, plus individual magazines' own selections, such as *The Best from F&SF, The Best from New Worlds, Analog* and others, and the reader could be forgiven for speculating on what percentage of new stories each year fail to find their way into some anthology or another.

Annuals, thematic collections and author's choices all belong under the heading of the reprint anthology, but original compilations, consisting of stories specially written for the occasion, merit separate consideration. The first modern original anthology was Donald Wollheim's *The Girl with the Hungry Eyes* (1949), its title taken from the lead story by Fritz Leiber. It came about by accident, however, Wollheim having acquired the stories for a new pulp magazine from Avon which was never launched. Rather than lose them, Wollheim – as Avon's sf editor – issued them in paperback form instead. Several one-off original anthologies followed, including Raymond J. Healy's *New Tales of Space and Time* (1951) and Fletcher Pratt's experimental *The Petrified Planet* (1952). But the turning point came in 1953 with the appearance of *Star Science Fiction Stories* edited by Frederik Pohl. At the height of the sf boom it sold well, and Ballantine Books gave the go-ahead for a second volume, *Star SF 2* (1954). Both these anthologies contained entirely new stories, including Arthur C. Clarke's memorable 'The Nine Billion Names of God' and Jerome Bixby's 'It's a *Good* Life'. *Star SF 3* followed in December 1954, together with *Star Short Novels* in the same year, and then came a pause. In 1957 it was revived as a magazine but following a lull in the market, the series reverted to book format with *Star SF 4* (1958), continuing until *Star SF 6* (1960). The series sold well, and remains the first of the all-original sf anthology series.

That the second series of original anthologies should appear in Britain is surprising. Until the mid-1960s British sf anthologies which had not consisted of American reprints were relatively insignificant, due to some extent to the bad reputations indigenous stories had acquired by dint of the paperback pot-boilers in the early 1950s. E. J. Carnell had succeeded in producing several good anthologies with the aid of publisher Tom Boardman, the majority of their contents being selected from Carnell's own *New Worlds*. The most popular anthologies to appear in the UK were Edmund Crispin's *Best SF* series, which began in 1955 and saw five volumes up to 1963; the *Spectrum* series edited by Kingsley Amis and Robert Conquest, with five volumes from 1961 to 1966; and Brian Aldiss's *Penguin SF* series, with three volumes between 1961 and 1964. All these reprinted science fiction well known in America but which proved good introductory material for those British readers unacquainted with the US magazines.

When Carnell left the editorial chair of *New Worlds* in 1964 he had made arrangements with Corgi Books to produce a regular new quarterly anthology of original stories – the result was *New Writings in SF*. It did not always follow its quarterly schedule, but its constant appearance was a boon to British science fiction. Carnell published twenty-one volumes up to the time of his death in 1972. The series then continued under the hand of Kenneth Bulmer, and in 1976 reached number 28, with more issues than any other original anthology series. Ironically, *New Worlds*, which subsequently failed as a magazine in 1970, is now also a paperback anthology series, with volumes running into double figures.

In America the series idea was also developed by Damon Knight, who introduced *Orbit* in 1966, and has continued it into its second decade. However, the success of the original anthology also owes much to the mammoth volume *Dangerous Visions* (1967) edited by Harlan Ellison. In the year after its appearance, two of its stories won Nebula awards and two won Hugos, Ellison himself receiving a special citation at the 1968 World SF Convention as editor of the most significant and controversial sf book published in 1967. He enjoyed a similar award in 1972 for the sequel, *Again, Dangerous Visions*, which sold over 36,000 copies in one month as a special Science Fiction Book Club selection. At the time of writing, it is not known what possible records the third and final book in the series, *The Last Dangerous Visions*, might achieve.

The success of *Orbit* and Ellison's *Dangerous Visions* prompted other US publishers to bring out regular original sf anthology series. The year 1970 saw *Infinity 1* edited by Robert Hoskins, *Quark 1* by Samuel Delany and Marilyn Hacker, and *Nova 1* by Harry Harrison; followed in 1971 by *New Dimensions 1* by Robert Silverberg and *Universe 1* by Terry Carr. The Silverberg and Carr selections have also produced their own clutch of Hugo and Nebula winners; both were still running in 1976.

It is interesting to note just how many awards have been won for stories in anthologies rather than magazines since 1967. Richard Wilson's 'Mother to the World', a 1968 Nebula winner, came from *Orbit*, as did Robert Silverberg's 1969 winner, 'Passengers'. Gene Wolfe's 1973 Nebula winner, 'The Death of Dr Island', appeared in *Universe*. 'The Word for World Is Forest', Ursula Le Guin's 1973 Hugo Winner, came from *Again, Dangerous Visions*, while James Tiptree's 1974 winner, 'The Girl Who Was Plugged In', was published in *New Dimensions*. There is no better evidence than these awards that original anthologies are a force to be reckoned with by the magazines.

Robert Silverberg is an indefatigable anthologist; in addition to his *New Dimension* series he has also produced a regular annual series of original anthologies, each containing three short novels written around a basic theme, as well as a host of reprint collections. But even his prolific output pales beside the sheer volume of compilations undertaken by Roger Elwood (often with the aid of Sam Moskowitz). Beginning in 1964 with a few reprint anthologies, by 1972 Elwood had begun to compile more and more original anthologies which flooded the bookshelves in early 1973 and continued throughout 1974, 1975 and 1976 with others yet in store, although Elwood himself had moved on to other things. Most of these anthologies were based on themes, the compiler often requesting new stories to order. *Flame Tree Planet* (1973) and *Strange Gods* (1974) were woven around religious motifs; *Demon Kind* (1973) and *Children of Infinity* (1973) were based on talented children; others like *Future City* (1973), *The Wounded Planet* (1973) and *The New Mind* (1973) are self-explanatory. Sixteen original anthologies came from his editorship in 1973, twenty-four in 1974 and surprisingly only five in 1975, but during that period he was responsible for more anthologised stories than nearly all the other editors combined. Probably his most original contribution to the field was the set of four *Continuum* books (1974–75), in which the tales in each new volume were developed from the previous ones.

The overall impression is that most sf anthologies cannot be expected to sell as well as successful novels; but their continuing appearance shows that there is a steady market for them. Above all, their original influx just after the war clearly did much for the furtherance of science fiction and helped to accelerate its more widespread acceptance by the general public.

Cover by Diane and Leo Dillon (Doubleday) 1967.

THIS SYMBOL IS YOUR ASSURANCE OF QUALITY – LEADERSHIP – APPEAL

04.06 BOOKS AND ANTHOLOGIES

PRINTED SOURCES

Aldiss, Brian W. *Best Fantasy Stories* (10 stories), Faber (UK) 1962
Aldiss, Brian W. *Introducing SF* (12 stories), Faber (UK) 1964
Aldiss, Brian W. (with Harry Harrison). *All About Venus* (7 stories; 6 articles), Dell (US) 1968; revised as *Farewell, Fantastic Venus!* (21 stories), MacDonald (UK) 1968
Aldiss, Brian W. (with Harry Harrison). *Best SF*, annual series, starting with *Best SF: 1967* (15 stories), Berkley (US) 1968; nine volumes published to date
Aldiss, Brian W. (with Harry Harrison). *The Astounding-Analog Reader* (15 stories), Doubleday (US) 1972
Aldiss, Brian W. *Space Opera* (16 stories), Futura (UK) 1974
Aldiss, Brian W. *Space Odysseys* (15 stories), Futura (UK) 1974
Aldiss, Brian W. *Evil Earths* (14 stories), Futura (UK) 1976
Ashley, Michael. *The History of the Science Fiction Magazine*:
Part 1: 1926–1935 (10 stories), NEL (UK) 1974
Part 2: 1936–1945 (10 stories), NEL (UK) 1975
Part 3: 1946–1955 (10 stories), NEL (UK) 1976
(two further volumes are to be published to complete the series)
Asimov, Isaac. *Before the Golden Age* (26 stories), Doubleday (US) 1974
Asimov, Isaac. *The Hugo Winners*
Volume 1: 1955–1961 (9 stories), Doubleday (US) 1962
Volume 2: 1962–1970 (14 stories), Doubleday (US) 1971
Asimov, Isaac. *Tomorrow's Children* (18 stories), Doubleday (US) 1966
Asimov, Isaac. *Where Do We Go from Here?* (17 stories), Doubleday (US) 1971
Bailey, Hilary. *New Worlds 7* (24 stories), Sphere (UK) 1974 (with Charles Platt)
New Worlds 8 (13 stories), Sphere (UK) 1975
New Worlds 9 (10 stories), Corgi (UK) 1975
(earlier volumes edited by Michael Moorcock)
Bearne, C.G. *Vortex: New Soviet Science Fiction* (7 stories), MacGibbon & Kee (UK) 1970
Boardman, Tom. *An ABC of Science Fiction* (26 stories), Four Square (UK) 1966

Boardman, Tom. *Connoisseur's SF* (10 stories), Penguin (UK) 1964
Boardman, Tom. *SF Horizons No 1* (10 stories), Dobson (UK) 1968
Boardman, Tom. *The Unfriendly Future* (6 stories), Four Square (UK) 1966

Boucher, Anthony. *A Treasury of Great Science Fiction* (2 vols: 24 stories), Doubleday (US) 1959 (note: Boucher also edited the first 8 volumes (1952 to 1959) of *The Best from F&SF*)
Bova, Ben. *Analog Annual* (1 novel, 4 stories), Pyramid (US) 1976
Campbell, John W. Various anthology selections from *Astounding/Analog*:
The Astounding SF Anthology (22 stories), Simon & Schuster (US) 1953
Prologue to Analog (10 stories), Doubleday (US) 1962
Carnell, Edward John. *Gateway to the Stars* (9 stories), Museum (UK) 1955
Carnell, Edward John. *Gateway to Tomorrow* (10 stories), Museum (UK) 1954
Carnell, Edward John. *Lambda 1 and Other Stories* (7 stories), Berkley (US) 1964
Carnell, Edward John. *No Place Like Earth* (10 stories), Boardman (UK) 1952
Carr, Terry. *Science Fiction for People Who Hate Science Fiction* (9 stories), Doubleday (US) 1966
Conklin, Groff. *Another Part of the Galaxy* (6 stories), Gold Medal (US) 1966
Conklin, Groff. *The Big Book of Science Fiction* (32 stories), Crown (US) 1950

Conklin, Groff. *Crossroads in Time* (18 stories), Permabook (US) 1953
Conklin, Groff. *Dimension 4* (4 stories), Pyramid (US) 1964
Conklin, Groff. *Elsewhere and Elsewhen* (9 stories), Berkley (US) 1968; retitled *Science Fiction Elsewhere* (4 stories), Rapp & Whiting (UK) 1970, and *Science Fiction Elsewhere* (5 stories), Rapp & Whiting (UK) 1970
Conklin, Groff. (with Isaac Asimov). *50 Short SF Tales*, Collier (US) 1963
Conklin, Groff. *Five-Odd* (5 stories), Pyramid (US) 1964
Conklin, Groff. *5 Unearthly Visions* (5 stories), Gold Medal (US) 1965
Conklin, Groff. *Four for the Future* (4 stories), Pyramid (US) 1959
Conklin, Groff. *Giant's Unleashed* (12 stories), Grosset & Dunlap (US) 1965
Conklin, Groff. *Invaders of Earth* (22 stories), Vanguard (US) 1952
Conklin, Groff. *The Omnibus of Science Fiction* (43 stories), Crown (US) 1952
Conklin, Groff. *Operation Future* (19 stories), Permabooks (US) 1955
Conklin, Groff. *Possible Worlds of Science Fiction* (22 stories), Vanguard (US) 1951
Conklin, Groff. *The Science Fiction Galaxy* (12 stories), Permabooks (US) 1950
Conklin, Groff. *Science Fiction Oddities* (19 stories), Berkley (US) 1966
Conklin, Groff. *Science Fiction Terror Tales* (15 stories), Gnome (US) 1955
Conklin, Groff. *Seven Come Infinity* (7 stories), Gold Medal (US) 1966
Conklin, Groff. *17 X Infinity* (17 stories), Dell (US) 1963
Conklin, Groff. *A Treasury of Science Fiction* (30 stories), Crown (US) 1948

Crossen, Kendall Foster. *Adventures in Tomorrow* (15 stories), Greenberg (US) 1951
Crossen, Kendell Foster. *Future Tense* (14 stories), Greenberg (US) 1952

Derleth, August. *Beachheads in Space* (14 stories), Pellegrini & Cudahy (US) 1952
Derleth, August. *Beyond Time and Space* (32 stories), Pellegrini (US) 1950
Derleth, August. *Far Boundaries* (20 stories), Pellegrini (US) 1949
Derleth, August. *The Other Side of the Moon* (20 stories), Pellegrini (US) 1949
Derleth, August. *Strange Ports of Call* (20 stories), Pellegrini (US) 1948
Derleth, August. *Time to Come* (12 stories), Farrar Straus & Young (US) 1954
Derleth, August. *Worlds of Tomorrow* (19 stories), Pellegrini (US) 1953; UK edition divided as *Worlds of Tomorrow* Four Square 1963, and *New Worlds For Old* Four Square 1963
Disch, Thomas M. *The Ruins of Earth* (16 stories), Putnam (US) 1971; different version, Hutchinson (UK) 1973
Elder, Joseph. *Eros in Orbit* (10 stories), Trident (US) 1973
Elder, Joseph. *The Farthest Reaches* (12 stories), Trident (US) 1968
Evans, I.O. *Science Fiction through the Ages* (2 vols: 24 stories/extracts), Panther (UK) 1966
Farmer, Philip José. *Mother Was a Lovely Beast* (8 stories), Chilton (US) 1974
Ferman, Edward L. (with Barry N. Malzberg). *Final Stage* (13 stories), Charterhouse (US) 1974 (edition apparently grossly amended by publishers); full edition, Penguin (UK) 1975
Franklin, H. Bruce. *Future Perfect* (21 stories), Oxford (US) 1966
Ginsburg, Mirra. *Last Door to Aiya* (9 stories), Phillips (US) 1968
Ginsburg, Mirra. *The Ultimate Threshold* (13 stories), Holt, Rinehart, Winston (US) 1970

Goldin, Stephen. *The Alien Condition* (12 stories), Ballantine (US) 1973
Greenberg, Martin. *All about the Future* (7 stories), Gnome (US) 1955
Greenberg, Martin. *Travellers of Space* (14 stories), Gnome (US) 1951
Harrison, Harry (with Leon E. Stover). *Apeman, Spaceman* (26 stories), Doubleday (US) 1968
Harrison, Harry. *Astounding: John W. Campbell Memorial Anthology* (13 stories), Random House (US) 1973
Harrison, Harry. *The Year 2000* (13 stories), Doubleday (US) 1970

Healy, Raymond J. *9 Tales of Space and Time*, Holt (US) 1954
Hoskins, Robert. *The Liberated Future* (12 stories), Fawcett (US) 1974
Knight, Damon. *A Century of Science Fiction* (26 stories), Simon & Schuster (US) 1962
Knight, Damon. *Cities of Wonder* (11 stories), Doubleday (US) 1966
Knight, Damon. *First Flight* (10 stories), Lancer (US) 1963
Knight, Damon. *One Hundred Years of Science Fiction* (21 stories), Simon & Schuster (US) 1968
Knight, Damon. *13 French SF Stories*, Bantam (US) 1965
Kornbluth, Mary. *Science Fiction Showcase* (12 stories), Doubleday (US) 1959
Margulies, Leo (with Oscar J. Friend). *From off this World* (18 stories), Merlin (US) 1949
Margulies, Leo. *Three from Out There* (3 stories), Crest (US) 1959
Margulies, Leo. *Three in One* (3 stories), Pyramid (US) 1963
Margulies, Leo. *Three Times Infinity* (3 stories), Gold Medal (US) 1958
Mills, Robert P. *The Worlds of Science Fiction* (15 stories), Dial (US) 1963

Moorcock, Michael. (Besides the regular series, *Best SF Stories from New Worlds*, which he stopped editing at no 8.)
The Best of New Worlds (15 stories), Compact (UK) 1965
The Traps of Time (10 stories), Rapp & Whiting (UK) 1968
Before Armageddon (6 stories), W.H. Allen (UK) 1975
Moskowitz, Sam. *The Coming of the Robots* (10 stories), Collier (US) 1963
Moskowitz, Sam. *Exploring Other Worlds* (8 stories), Collier (US) 1963
Moskowitz, Sam. *Futures to Infinity* (10 stories), Pyramid (US) 1970
Moskowitz, Sam. *Masterpieces of Science Fiction* (18 stories), World (US) 1967
Moskowitz, Sam. *Modern Masterpieces of Science Fiction* (21 stories), World (US) 1966
Moskowitz, Sam. *Science Fiction by Gaslight* (26 stories), World (US) 1968
Moskowitz, Sam. *The Space Magicians* (7 stories), Pyramid (US) 1971

Moskowitz, Sam. *Three Stories*, Doubleday (US) 1967; retitled *A Sense of Wonder*, Sidgwick and Jackson (UK) 1967
Moskowitz, Sam. *Under the Moons of Mars* (9 stories/extracts), Holt, Rinehart, Winston (US) 1970
Nolan, William F. *Almost Human* (14 stories), Sherbourne (US) 1965
Nolan, William F. *3 To the Highest Power* (3 stories), Avon (US) 1968
Nolan, William F. *A Wilderness of Stars* (10 stories), Sherbourne (US) 1969
Pohl, Frederik. *Assignment in Tomorrow* (15 stories), Hanover (US) 1954
Pohl, Frederik. *The Expert Dreamers* (16 stories), Doubleday (US) 1962
Pohl, Frederik. *Star Short Novels* (3 short novels), Ballantine (US) 1954
Pohl, Frederik and Carol. *Jupiter* (9 stories), Ballantine (US) 1973
Pohl, Frederik. *Nightmare Age* (13 stories), Ballantine (US) 1971
Pratt, Fletcher. *World of Wonder* (19 stories), Twayne (US) 1951
Santesson, Hans Stefan. *The Fantastic Universe Omnibus* (19 stories), Prentice-Hall (US) 1960
Santesson, Hans Stefan. *Gods for Tomorrow* (10 stories), Award (US) 1967

Santesson, Hans Stefan. *Crime Prevention in the 30th Century* (10 stories), Walker (US) 1969
Sargent, Pamela. *Women of Wonder* (13 stories), Vintage (US) 1975
Silverberg. Robert. *Four Futures* (4 stories), Hawthorn (US) 1971
Silverberg, Robert. *Chains of the Sea* (3 stories), Nelson (US) 1973
Silverberg, Robert. *No Mind of Man* (3 stories), Hawthorn (US) 1973
Silverberg, Robert. *Threads of Time* (3 stories), Nelson (US) 1974
Silverberg, Robert. *The Day the Sun Stood Still* (3 stories), Nelson (US) 1972
Silverberg, Robert. *The New Atlantis* (3 stories), Hawthorn (US) 1975
Suvin, Darko. *Other Worlds, Other Seas* (16 stories), Random House (US) 1970
Wilson, Robin Scott. *Clarion*, original series lasting from No 1 (21 stories), Signet (US) 1971, to No 3 (21 stories), Signet (US) 1973
Wollheim, Donald A. *Adventures in the Far Future* (5 stories), Ace (US) 1954
Wollheim, Donald A. *Adventures on Other Planets* (5 stories), Ace (US) 1955
Wollheim, Donald A. *The Earth in Peril* (6 stories), Ace (US) 1957
Wollheim, Donald A. *The End of the World* (6 stories), Ace (US) 1956
Wollheim, Donald A. *Flight into Space* (12 stories), Fell (US) 1950
Wollheim, Donald A. *The Hidden Planet* (5 stories), Ace (US) 1958
Wollheim, Donald A. *Men on the Moon* (5 stories), Ace (US) 1958; revised Ace (US) 1969
Wollheim, Donald A. *Tales of Outer Space* (5 stories), Ace (US) 1954
Wollheim, Donald A. *The Ultimate Invader* (4 stories), Ace (US) 1954

04.07 JUVENILES, COMICS AND STRIPS

04.07 JUVENILES, COMICS AND STRIPS

04.07.1 The Boys Papers

From 1825 to 1855 some ninety publishing houses in London issued weekly magazines and penny part novels with such evocative titles as *Legends of Horror* (1825–26) and *The Skeleton Clutch; or the Goblet of Gore* (1842). The best known of these, and still reprinted today, are *Varney the Vampire; or, the Feast of Blood* (1847) and *Wagner the Wehr-Wolf* (1847).

Many such titles contained some elements of science fiction, but these were attributed to supernatural occurrences. With John Frederick Smith's *Stanfield Hall* (1849), however, a change of content was discernible. Although basically an historical novel, gas bombs, plastic surgery, electrolysis and even an anticipation of the cinema were introduced into the story, all explained as products of science. However, it was several more years before a fully fledged juvenile sf story appeared, and it happened in America.

The dime novel, a cheap weekly publication generally issued under a series heading, offered full-length novels to the American public at five cents a time. In August 1868 the first sf story appeared as No 45 of *Beadle's American Novels. The Steam Man of the Prairies* by Edward S. Ellis describes how a robot, built on the principles of the steam engine, sets out across the prairies and triumphantly engages the Red Indians in a series of running fights. Instantly popular, the story was later reprinted as *The Huge Hunter; or, the Steam Man of the Prairies*, No 40 of Beadle's Pocket Novels, in 1876.

Frank Tousey, a rival publisher, seeing the success of his competitor, commissioned Harry Enton to imitate Ellis's tale. Enton created Frank Reade, a philanthropic industrialist whose own robot featured prominently in *Frank Reade and His Steam Man of the Plains* (1876), which appeared serially in *Boys of New York*.

Three sequels followed: *Frank Reade and His Steam Horse* (1876), then . . . *His Steam Team* (1880), and finally . . . *His Steam Tally-Ho* (1881). Tousey then prevailed on Enton to vary his formula, but they were unable to agree and Enton left to work elsewhere. Luis P. Senarens was signed to continue the series, his stories appearing serially in *Boys of New York* under the byline of 'Noname'.

Senarens perfunctorily retired Frank Reade and succeeded him with his son, Frank Reade Jr, an inventor who excelled his father in the variety and complexity of his inventions. He fought Apaches with electrically operated armoured cars, equipped with pneumatic-electric guns. In his electric submarine, he travelled under the Arctic ice to the North Pole. Numerous airships and helicopters were to come from his workshops.

So popular were his adventures that they were soon reprinted as a complete novel in *The Wide Awake Library*. By the 1890s Senarens was the best-selling dime-novelist in America, and imitators were beginning to appear.

Street and Smith ran a Tom Edison Jr story in *Good News* under the pen-name of Philip Reade. Eight such tales, featuring heavier-than-air craft and submarines, appeared in the *Nugget Library* as complete novels during 1891 and 1892, others appearing in *The New York Five Cent Library*. A new 'invention' series featuring Electric Bob also began.

Spurred by the competition, Tousey encouraged Senarens to write another series for *Young Men of America* in 1892, featuring Jack Wright. The plot-cum-invention mix was much as before.

Frank Reade Jr made his first British appearance in *Boys of London and Boys of New York* and was duly reprinted in novel form in the *Aldine Romance of Invention, Travel and Adventure Library*, a periodical which later included stories about Jack Wright. Two-hundred-and-seventy-two issues appeared during the period 1894–1906, with some forty of them being reprinted during 1910–12, sparked by Samuel Clarke Hook's introduction of a Steam Man in his popular adventure series *Jack, Sam and Pete*, then running in *The Marvel*.

Jules Verne, who had established a world-wide reputation with his *voyages extraordinaires*, was also being serialised for the juvenile market. The year 1880 saw the commencement of his authorised translations in *The Boy's Own Paper*. Beginning with *The Boy Captain*, sixteen in all were published, including *The Star of the South* (1884–85) and *The Clipper of the Clouds* (1886–87).

Gradually, the Frank Reade series was supplanted in America by the rise of cheaply priced hard-cover editions which found favour with parents. Among them were the Tom Swift juveniles by Victor Appleton. The byline was a house name, the first thirty-five titles generally being attributed to H. R. Garis. They continued the proven Senarens formula of marvellous inventions by a boy inventor. Starting in 1910, the Appleton books included such titles as *Tom Swift and His Airship* (1910), and *Tom Swift and His Photo-Telephone* (1914). Even more imaginative were the *Great Marvel* series by Roy Rockwood which included journeys to the planets.

When he died in 1939, Luis P. Senarens had more than earned the soubriquet 'The American Jules Verne'; he had created an entire phase of juvenile fiction whose readership later moved on to adult science fiction magazines.

Many British authors also excelled at futuristic ideas and juvenile imaginative romances. In *Two Boys' Trip to an Unknown Planet* (1890), Albert R. Booth took his heroes aloft in a balloon, and told how they were picked up by an alien spacecraft. Franklyn Wright, better known as Henry Farmer, literary editor of *The Daily Express*, wrote (in collaboration) four stories about airships for *The Marvel*.

In *The Union Jack*, George C. Wallis described a journey to the Moon and Venus in a tale entitled *In Trackless Space* (1902). He later became a regular contributor to *Amazing Stories* and *Tales of Wonder*.

One of the more popular authors was Frank Atkins Jr, writing as Fenton Ash, Fred Ashley and F. St Mars. Atkins produced several lost-race serials, including *The Radium Seekers* (1903) and *The Black Opal* (1904), before turning to the inter-planetary novel with *A Son of the Stars* (1907–08).

In the early part of the twentieth century, the predominant science fiction theme in British juvenile magazines was represented by accounts of aerial and naval battles between Britain and various foreign powers, particularly Germany. It stemmed mainly from the propaganda of Alfred C. Harmsworth (Lord Northcliffe), the head of Amalgamated Press, one of the world's largest publishers of juvenile periodicals.

The campaign was conducted in periodicals edited by Hamilton Edwards: *The Boy's Friend, The Boy's Herald* and *The Boy's Realm*. Edwards himself wrote *Britain in Arms* and *The Russian Foe*, both published in *The Boy's Friend*, while Sidney Gowing wrote of a German invasion and occupation in *Britain Invaded* (1906).

Other magazines exploited the trend. Albert Bradley's *King of the Clouds* (1904) appeared in *True Blue*, J. Verney Adams's *In Days of Peril* (1912) in *The Boy's Best Story Paper*, and John G. Rowe's *The Aerial War, a Tale of What Might Be* (1911) in *The Boy's Own Library*.

When the First World War eventually broke out in 1914, many papers ceased publication or combined with others; but activity resumed soon after the armistice, with many new titles appearing. In 1919 the growth of the motion-picture industry induced Amalgamated Press to publish *Boy's Cinema Weekly*, featuring story adaptations of popular films, most notably the various Tarzan stories of Edgar Rice Burroughs.

Burroughs appeared again in a new series of *Pluck* beginning in 1922. Subtitled *The Boy's Wireless Adventure Weekly*, *Pluck* published several fantasy and sf serials during its first year. The launching issue featured Paul Quinton's *The School in the Air*, which he followed with *Wings of Adventure*. Burroughs then contributed *At the Earth's Core*, its publication presumably justified because the account of David Innes's adventure was transmitted up through the Earth by wireless.

Boy's Magazine, launched in 1922, was to provide stiff competition for *Pluck*, eventually forcing it to switch to sports stories. *Boy's Magazine* began fairly conservatively, until it published *The Raiding Planet* early in 1923. In this imaginative tale, Brian Cameron told how the planet Thor approached Earth and then attacked it with spaceships. For the next eleven years, many similar stories appeared in its pages.

Boy's Magazine ended its days obsessed with prehistoric monsters. It was succeeded in February 1934 by C. A. Pearson's *Scoops*,

RESULT OF OUR FOOTBALL PUZZLE COMPETITION THIS WEEK.
The Boys' Realm 1d.
A POPULAR PAPER FOR ALL BRITISH BOYS AND YOUNG MEN.
EVERY SATURDAY ONE PENNY.
REGINALD WRAY'S NEW STORY.
A WORLD AT STAKE!
MIND YOU START IT TO-DAY.
A GRAND STORY OF BRITAIN'S FIGHT FOR THE COMMAND OF THE AIR.
"THE JUNGLE TALES OF TARZAN."
BOY'S CINEMA Weekly
TWOPENCE.
THRILLS IN SCREEN SERIAL.
The Raiders of Robot City by MURRAY ROBERTS
Latest Amazing Adventure of Captain Justice
No. 573 6-5-37 The BOYS' FRIEND LIBRARY 4d

The MYSTERY PLANET by MURRAY ROBERTS
4d
BOYS' FRIEND LIBRARY
6-10-38

READ THE BOYS OF NEW YORK. FOR SALE BY ALL NEWSDEALERS.
THE FIVE CENT
WIDE AWAKE LIBRARY
No. 633.
Frank Reade, Jr.'s Marvel
ABOVE AND BELOW WATER

READE LIBRARY
Frank Reade Jr.'s "Sea Serpent;" Or, The Search for Sunken Gold.

FREE! THE WORLD'S FASTEST 'PLANE. DAZZLING SCIENCE PLATE INSIDE.
Boys' Magazine
2D EVERY SATURDAY
STUPENDOUS STORY OF THE STARS
THE MONSTER OF MARS
FREE GIFTS WITHIN

WAR STORY—£5 A WEEK—3 COMPLETES.
THE BOYS' BEST 1d. STORY PAPER
EVERY THURSDAY—ONE PENNY.
DAYS OF PERIL
BY J. VERNEY ADAMS
BELFAST CITY HALL.
A TALE OF FERRERS LORD AND CHING-LUNG!
WOLVES OF THE DEEP
THE STIRRING STORY OF A GREAT CONSPIRACY.
By SIDNEY DREW.
STOP! ANY MAN OPENING THIS DOOR WILL BE SHOT
Ferrers Lord
3D.
THREEPENCE.
No. 32. "THE BOYS' FRIEND" 3d. LIBRARY.

No. 226.—"THE BOYS' FRIEND" 3d. COMPLETE
DEEP SEA GO
A Thrilling, Long Complete Adventure Story, By REGINALD WRAY.
3d
No. 74. THE "BOYS' FRIEND" 3d. LIBRARY.
THE AIRSHIP'S QUEST
A STORY OF THRILLING ADVENTURE by L. J. BEESTON
3D.
A MAGNIFICENT LONG, COMPLETE STORY.

the first boys' magazine devoted exclusively to publishing science fiction. Printed weekly in a larger format than the *Boy's Magazine*, with some striking red-and-black cover illustrations by S. R. Drigin (an artist who later appeared in the adult British sf magazine *Fantasy* in 1938–39), *Scoops* published a wide variety of sf stories. The editor (Haydn Dimmock, also editor of *The Scout*) was interested in soliciting frank opinions on the magazine from its readers; he found to his surprise that many of them were grown men. Accordingly, certain minor refinements were made to its contents. Philip Cleator, founder of the British Interplanetary Society (BIS), contributed a small but regular column. Bylines began to appear, including that of John Russell Fearn, which had already appeared in *Astounding* in the US. Although it lasted a mere twenty weeks, *Scoops* gave evidence of an intelligent and informed following, many of whom identified themselves as devotees of the American sf magazines.

Later, in 1937, Pearson's were to issue a boy's annual, *The Boy's World of Adventure*, in an attempt to recoup their losses. It included colour plates and line drawings by Drigin, and reprinted five stories from *Scoops* in addition to eight new tales. But the venture was not repeated.

However, the failure of *Scoops* did not prevent sf stories from continuing to appear sporadically in general boys' magazines. The adventures of Captain Justice, authored by Murray Roberts, were to appear regularly in *Modern Boy*, while Odhams launched *Modern Wonder* in 1937, produced in photogravure and designed to appeal to the adult and juvenile market alike.

The Scottish firm of D. C. Thomson and Co Ltd likewise continued to publish sf and fantasy stories in their 'Big Five' boys' story weeklies: *Wizard, Hotspur, Rover, Skipper* and *Adventure*. The most popular creations were *Adventure*'s 'Morgyn the Mighty', a Tarzan-type hero, and *Wizard*'s story of a super-athlete, 'Wilson'. In due course, both characters were carried over into picture-strips, featuring on the covers of the story papers as cartoon heroes. Finally the time would come, years later, when the 'Big Five' themselves were converted from story papers into comics.

The comic strip, in fact, was to revolutionise the whole field of juvenile publishing; and once again the trend began in the United States.

THE BOY'S PAPERS

Bibliography

Bailey, J. O. *Pilgrims through Space and Time: Trends and Patterns in Scientific and Utopian Fiction*, Argus Books (US) 1947

Blythe, Robert C. *A Bibliography of the Writings of Edwy Searles Brooks*, privately published (UK) 1963

Gillings, Walter 'The Impatient Dreamers No.4', *Vision of Tomorrow* Jan, 1970

James, Louis *Fiction for the Working Man*, Oxford University Press (UK) 1963

Lofts, W. O. G. and Adley, Derek *The Men behind Boy's Fiction*, Baker (UK) 1970

Moskowitz, Sam *Explorers of the Infinite: Shapers of Science Fiction*, World (US) 1963

Moskowitz, Sam *Strange Horizons: the Spectrum of Science Fiction*, Scribners (US) 1976

Norton, Ray and Lay, Vernon 'Imagination Unlimited', *Collectors' Digest Annual, 1967*, Fayne (UK) 1967

Summers, Montague *A Gothic Bibliography*, Fortune (UK) 1941

Turner, E. S. *Boys Will Be Boys*, Joseph (UK) 1947

04.07.2 Comic Strips

The comic strip owes its ancestry to the caricature and the political cartoon, whose flair and satirical verve were apparent as early as the sixteenth century. In mid-nineteenth-century Britain, the tradition of visual satire was sustained by the famous periodical *Punch*, and the trend towards the use of cartoons led to the publication in 1874 of *Funny Folks*, the first comic-strip paper. By the turn of the century several such periodicals were in circulation in Britain, while in America newspapers were offering full-colour comic sections with their Sunday editions. It was there, in the *New York Herald* and the *Evening Telegram*, that the first fantasy strips began.

During the period 1904 to 1911 these two papers featured strips by various author/artists whose primary influences were the works of Edward Lear and Lewis Carroll. The most notable contributors were Winsor McCay and George Verbeck. McCay became the luminary of the *Herald* school of fantasy. He first appeared in the *Evening Telegram* in 1904 with 'Dreams of the Rarebit Fiend', a strip which dealt with a form of nightmare which would not have been out of place in the later psychedelic era. The same approach was adopted in 1906 by Peter Newel in 'The Naps of Polly Sleepyhead', while McCay remained busy with his most memorable dream-fantasy strip 'Little Nemo in Slumberland'. This last appeared each Sunday in the *New York Herald* from 1905 to 1911. In its conception McCay drew extensively on prevailing cinematographic techniques to create unusual perspectives. His preoccupation with the cinema, however, led him into movie-making (his 'Gertie the Dinosaur',

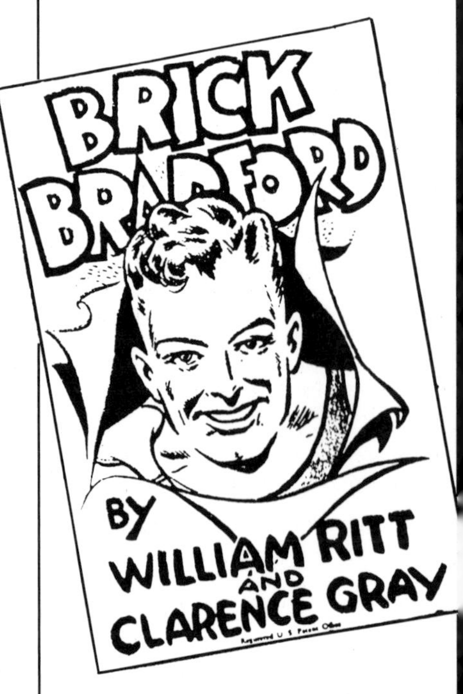

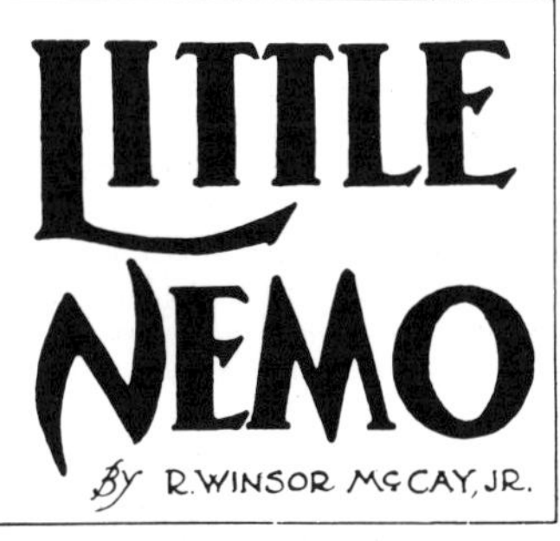

One of the most popular early comic strips.

1909, being the first commercial animated film), and the initial era of the fantasy strip came more or less to an end.

From the beginning, comic strips were seen as vehicles for humour and entertainment; and entertain they did until the depression in the 1920s created a demand for a more adventurous form of escapism.

John Flint Dille, president of the National Newspaper Syndicate and a keen reader of the Gernsback pulps, conceived the idea of a strip portraying the world of the future. In 1927 he contracted Philip Francis Nowlan, author of 'Armageddon 2419 A.D.' in *Amazing Stories*, to write the script. Changing the name of his hero to Buck Rogers, Nowlan recounted the adventures of a First World War flying ace who awoke in the future to find the America of 2430 AD overrun by the hordes of the Red Mongols. Drawn by Dick Calkins, himself a former war pilot, the naïve primitivism of artistic style, coupled with an imaginative and humorous story-line, made the strip immediately popular. Inevitably, its commercial success attracted imitators. In 1933 'Brick Bradford', illustrated by Clarence Grey and scripted by William Ritt, portrayed the adventures of a war ace taken into the past or the future by a time machine, a device also prominent in Vince Hamlin's stone-age saga 'Alley Oop'. In the meantime, Winsor McCay's son, Robert, had resurrected 'Little Nemo', adopting a more science fictional approach; but it was in Alex Raymond's 'Flash Gordon' (beginning January 1934) that a competitor of greater stature arrived.

Raymond, a staff artist for the King Features Syndicate, had won an inter-departmental competition to find the best artist for a science fiction strip. In doing so, he created Flash Gordon, another space-hopping hero who trailed an ever-loyal girl-friend in his wake, but the strip lacked the humour of the 'Buck Rogers' series. In his skilled approach and attention to detail, Raymond proved himself a leader in the modern school of comic artists. His creation was carried over into film serialisations and a single-issue science fiction pulp title, *Flash Gordon Strange Adventures* – the only fantasy magazine of the time to use full-colour interior illustrations.

As the comic strips improved in artistic techniques, so too did their marketing approaches. In 1933 M. C. Gaines brought out *Funnies on Parade*, which reprinted Sunday strip pages in a full-colour comic book similar to those published today. Initially conceived as a give-away promotional premium, it was found to be commercially marketable, and a new industry began.

At first comic books were limited to reprints from the Sunday pages. 'Buck Rogers' appeared in *Famous Funnies* No 3 in September 1934. April 1936 saw the publication of both 'Flash Gordon' and 'Brick Bradford' in the first issue of *King Comics*. But newspaper strips could provide only so much material; fresh and additional creative sources had to be found if the comic-book industry was to expand. To meet this aim came *Detective Comics*, the first completely original comic-strip book, in March 1937. The curtain was being raised on the golden age of comics – the era of the super-hero was close. As with the origins of 'Buck Rogers', much of the inspiration was to derive from the world of the science fiction magazines and fanzines.

In October 1932, a mimeographed fanzine laconically entitled *Science Fiction* appeared under the editorship of Jerome Siegel, a young sf fan who had secured his readership by advertising in *The Time Traveller*, an established fanzine. From its second issue, *Science Fiction* featured cartoons by Siegel's friend, Joseph Shuster, an admirer of Philip Wylie's widely read novel *Gladiator* (1930). This admiration found creative outlet in the fifth and final issue of *Science Fiction*, which featured a two-page strip under the heading 'Superman'.

For the next five years Siegel and Shuster struggled to sell their concept of Superman, receiving many rejection slips in their attempts to place it as a newspaper strip. By fortunate coincidence, a sample of the proposed story-line was sent to M. C. Gaines (then working as an agent for the McClure Syndicate) at about the same time that Harry Donenfield had asked him for material to fill out a new comic in the National group. Gaines showed Siegel and Shuster's strip to Donenfield who accepted it immediately, introducing the first issue of

The birth of 'Superman' by Jerome Siegel and Joe Shuster, 1939 and 'Captain America' by Joe Simon and Jack Kirby, 1941.

Action Comics in June 1938, with Superman in action on the cover. Every copy of the comic was sold. A rapid marketing survey revealed that it was indeed Superman who had been responsible for the sales success, and from then on he was to appear emblazoned on the cover of every issue of *Action Comics*. He also featured in his own quarterly comic book, *Superman*, which began in the summer of 1939.

To boost sales of *Action Comic*'s companion paper, *Detective Comics*, another 'caped crusader' arrived in issue No 27, dated May 1939. Illustrated by Bob Kane, this new character, Batman, was loosely based on a short-run series of detective stories written by Murray Leinster for *Black Bat Detective Mysteries*, a pulp magazine published in 1934. Like Superman he proved equally popular, and began appearing in his own quarterly comic, *Batman*, in the spring of 1940. The costumed hero had arrived and was to be exploited to the full.

Marvel Publishing Company entered the field in November 1939 with *Marvel Mystery Comics*, a spin-off from their magazine *Marvel Science Stories*. 'The Human Torch', a synthetic man who spontaneously ignited when the covering protecting him from contact with the air was removed, and 'The Submariner', the prince of an undersea kingdom, were both to make their debut in the opening issue. Later, in May 1941, Marvel published their most popular creation, *Captain America*.

Numerous imitations began to appear in competition with the more popular characters, the most successful of all being Captain Marvel, who appeared in *Whiz Comics* No 2 in February 1940 and in *Captain Marvel* in 1941. The product of the skilled teamwork of artist Clyde Beck and sf author Otto O. Binder, who introduced humour into the stories, *Captain Marvel* was selling nearly 2 million copies of each issue by 1948 and was the subject of a lawsuit brought by National for infringement of copyright. They claimed his characterisation was too close to that of Superman.

To combat the growing competition, Mort Weisinger, formerly an editor of *Thrilling Wonder Stories*, was approached by National's editorial director, Whitney Ellsworth, to take over the editorship of *Superman*. Under his guidance *Superman* was to develop a fuller and broader background; new characters were introduced and other series created, with sf authors recruited to write the scripts. Manly Wade Wellman worked on *Aquaman*, while Alfred Bester and Henry Kuttner wrote *Green Lantern*. Edmond Hamilton also contributed some of the *Superman* stories in 1946.

By no means all comic books were devoted to the costumed hero. Science fiction of a different kind had begun appearing under many other titles. Better Publications, who published *Startling Stories* and *Thrilling Wonder Stories* had introduced a full range of comics. 'Captain Future', then a successful science fiction pulp title, ran in *Startling Comics* from June 1940 to July 1946, with some intermittent appearances in *America's Best* in 1942 and 1943, illustrated by sf artist Alex Schomburg. The same illustrator also worked for the companion paper *Thrilling Comics*. Street and Smith entered the field with comic strip adaptations of their most popular pulp-heroes, *Doc Savage* and *The Shadow*, the latter featuring strips by *Unknown Worlds* artist Ed Cartier.

Fiction House, who published the fantasy and science fiction pulps *Jungle Stories* and *Planet Stories*, issued *Planet Comics*, a title devoted exclusively to science fiction. Even Hugo Gernsback entered the lists with *Superworld*, featuring cover and interior art by Frank R. Paul.

By the late forties many science fiction comic titles were appearing in the US. Among the most popular were those published by William Gaines, son of M. C. Gaines, under the EC imprint. Using such first-rate artists as Al Williamson, Wallace Wood, Roy Krenkel and Frank Frazetta, his titles, which included *Weird Fantasy* and *Incredible Science Fiction*, drew heavily on the sf magazines, often without acknowledgement.

During the same period, crime and horror comics were becoming notorious for their depiction of torture and sadism. Public outcry grew to the point where the Comics Code was established to set a

The first appearances of 'Batman' by Bob Rane, 1939 and 'Captain Marvel', 1940.

standard. As in the parallel case of film censorship, comics both good and bad were subject to rejection. Sales decreased and many titles disappeared – the golden age of the US comic book was over.

In Britain, the comic strips developed along the lines laid down at the turn of the century, and basically contained situation comedies aimed at young children. By the late thirties, however, American comic books were being imported. Some of their strips were also reprinted in the boys' papers and other weeklies. By 1938, Superman's adventures from *Action Comics* were appearing in *The New Triumph*, Flash Gordon stories were being reprinted in full colour on the back page of *Modern Wonder* and Buck Rogers was entertaining the adult readers of *Everybody's*. When the war broke out in 1939, importation of US comic books and sf magazines abruptly ceased. British publishers attempted to fill the gap with such American-style comics as *Slick Fun* and *Thrill Comic*. These, however, carried very little science fiction and their quality was poor.

One noteworthy exception from this period was 'Garth', which made its debut in the *Daily Mirror* newspaper in July 1943. Written and illustrated by Steve Dowling, Garth bore some resemblance to Tarzan and Brick Bradford, being both muscle-bound and able to travel through time and space in a never-ending battle against the forces of evil. The strip is still running daily.

By the late 1940s American comics were again being imported into Britain or published in reprint form. T. V. Boardman, who later published many hard-cover sf novels, reprinted *Blackhawk*, *Plastic Man* and *The Spirit* in 1947 at the same time as publishing an original sf series, *Swift Morgan*, illustrated by Dennis McLaughlin. Concurrently, several other original strips were appearing in Britain. *Oh Boy Comics* featured 'The Tornado', written and drawn by Bob Monkhouse, who later became famous as a radio and television comedian, while Dennis Gifford illustrated 'Captain Climax' for *Climax*.

The UK, however, was not to come into its own as a producer of sf comic strips until the appearance of Dan Dare on the front cover of the first issue of *The Eagle* in April 1950. Illustrated by Frank Hampson, backed by a good team of assistants, and with Arthur C. Clarke as science consultant, 'Dan Dare' became the most popular British comic strip of the 1950s. The accounts of a daring space captain's adventures and battles against green-skinned Venusians and others were followed avidly. Other strips of a similarly high standard began to flourish. *The Lion*, first issued in February 1952, likewise featured a space hero, Captain Condor, written by Frank S. Pepper, on its front cover. In *The Sun*, Jet Ace Logan made his debut, the serialisations being reprinted in paperback form in *Thriller Picture Library*. In similar paperback format, *Super Detective Library* published the adventures of Rick Random, while a companion series to *The Tit-Bits Science Fiction Library*, a non-comic periodical, was similarly publishing sf comic books. In February 1954, the *Daily Express* newspaper introduced Sidney Jordan's 'Jeff Hawke', a long-running sf strip; its companion paper, the *Junior Express*, also ran the strip in full colour a year later.

In the early 1950s, the protracted court case between National and Fawcett in the US over the copyright of Superman was finally resolved in National's favour. *Captain Marvel* ceased publication in both America and Britain, though Miller, who held the British reprint rights, were reluctant to let such a valuable property go. Under the editorship of Maurice (Mick) Anglo the next issue of the comic in the UK, already set for publication, was quickly transformed into *The Marvelman* with a story-line nevertheless very similar to the original.

In 1959, the American DC titles began to be imported into Britain in bulk, while publishers on both sides of the Atlantic began reprinting the better material from the late 1940s and early 1950s. The same year saw the commencement of an excellent adaptation of Burroughs's *Princess of Mars* in the British boy's paper *The Comet*, and a year later *Marvel Comics* were to herald a new era of the super-hero with the appearance of *The Fantastic Four*. One by one, the early wartime characters, Captain America, the Submariner, the Human Torch and many others, began to re-emerge. DC and Marvel engaged in a massive struggle for supremacy on the news-stands and brought out many additional titles. Comic fandom came into being, conventions abounded both in America and Britain, and maturing fans increasingly joined the ranks of adult sf fandom.

In Britain, *The Eagle* began to decline, meeting serious rivalry with the emergence of such titles as *T.V. Century 21* which adapted popular television series into strip form. *Fireball XL-5*, *The Thunderbirds*, *Doctor Who* and, later, *Star Trek* and *Space 1999* became the staple diet of the young.

Most recently, the comic industry appears to be undergoing a further lull, and seeking a fresh direction. In 1976 *Starstream*, a new series published by the Western Publishing Co in America ran strip adaptations of stories by Larry Niven, Isaac Asimov, Robert Silverberg and other leading sf authors, but it met with little success. Whichever way the industry does develop in the future, however, there is little doubt that its connections with the field of adult science fiction will remain as strong as they have been up to now.

COMIC STRIPS

Bibliography

Anon. 'Supersuit: Rights to Superman', *Newsweek* 14 April 1947

Bester, Alfred 'King of the Comics', *Holiday* June 1958

Gifford, Dennis *The British Comic Catalogue 1874–1974*, Mansell (UK) 1975

Gifford, Dennis *Discovering Comics*, Shire (UK) 1971

Gifford, Dennis *Stap Me! The British Newspaper Strip*, Shire (UK) 1971

Hogben, Lancelot *From Cave Painting to Comic Strip*, Chatnicleer (US) 1949

Moskowitz, Sam *Seekers of Tomorrow: Masters of Modern Science Fiction*, World (US) 1966

Murrell, W. A. *A History of American Graphic Humor*, Macmillan (US) 1933

Sheridan, Martin *Comics and Their Creators: Life Stories of American Cartoonists*, Hale (US) 1944

Steranko, James *The Steranko History of Comics*, Supergraphics (US) 1970

Waugh, Coulton *The Comics*, Macmillan (US) 1847

Wertham, Frederick *The Seduction of the Innocent*, Rinehart (US) 1954

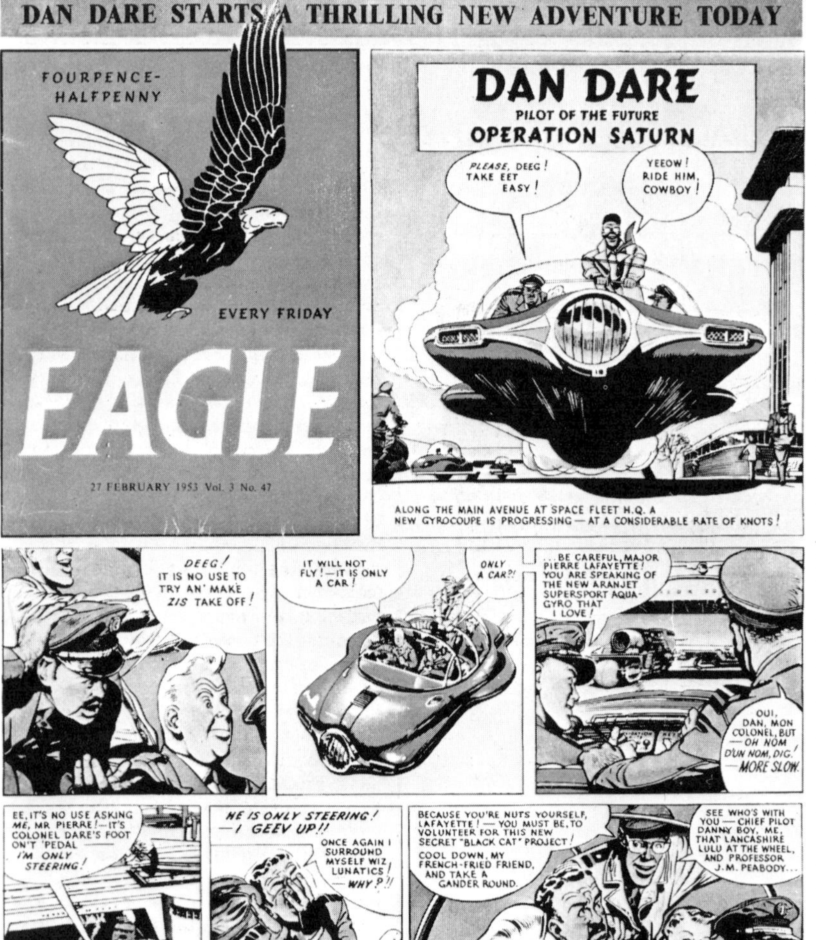

'Dan Dare' by Frank Hampson from Eagle *27 February 1953.*

04.08 COMMENTATORS AND COURSES

Few branches of literature have been taken so seriously in their relative infancy as science fiction. The genre has already given rise to a host of critical studies and commentaries, and is attracting serious attention in the academic field. It is becoming recognised more and more as a pertinent area of study in schools and universities.

No better commendation can be offered than to let the facts of the courses and studies reviewed in the following outline stand for themselves.

04.08.1 The Educational Field

In the October 1953 issue of *Science Fiction Plus* (which was actually published that August) there appeared an advertisement for a twelve-week evening-class course at the City College of New York. The course's title was 'Science Fiction Writing', and the study involved is now recognised as the first regular curriculum dealing with any aspect of science fiction to be taught at a college. Sam Moskowitz and Robert Frazier conducted it, and guest lecturers included Isaac Asimov, Algis Budrys, John W. Campbell Jr, Lester del Rey, Robert A. Heinlein, Murray Leinster, Robert Sheckley and others. The course continued each semester with Hans Stefan Santesson substituting for Moskowitz when the latter withdrew.

Earlier, single lectures or short lecture series had been held occasionally at colleges, and they subsequently continued with increasing frequency, sometimes carrying credit towards a degree. A notable example of this activity occurred in 1957, when three Chicago fans arranged a series of lectures at the University of Chicago given by Alfred Bester, Robert Bloch, Robert A. Heinlein and Cyril M. Kornbluth. The talks were taped and published, with an introduction by Basil Davenport, under the title of *The Science Fiction Novel* (1959).

Extending beyond the extra-mural, the first full-time college course was organised by Mark Hillegas at Colgate University in the Fall of 1962. This is often cited as the first fully academic series, taught by a full-time member of staff and emphasising literary qualities and social criticism. Two years later Jack Williamson followed suit with a course at Eastern New Mexico University, and since then there has been a rapid increase in the number of college sf studies in the US, particularly during the 1970s. Estimates of their number in the US and Canada in the early 1970s varied from 150 to 200. However, Williamson, who in 1971 published a survey of college courses (*Science Fiction Comes to College*), believes that there may now be over a thousand.

At the high school level, sf studies have also become extremely popular – Williamson estimates that at least 100,000 North American students, and perhaps several times that number, may now be involved in them. By contrast, science fiction features little in the education field throughout the rest of the English-speaking world. In the UK, some activity, which appears to be growing, can be recorded. Philip Strick began an extension (evening-class) course for London University in 1969, and it has continued regularly since, pursued by various instructors including Strick, Christopher Priest and Peter Nicholls. Ian Watson until recently ran a course at the City of Birmingham Polytechnic, and there is evidence that some science fiction is taught in UK schools. During 1975–76, a few British universities have accepted a handful of students for post-graduate work in sf topics, mainly with a sociological slant.

The principal centre of educational interest outside North America is the Science Fiction Foundation at the North-East London Polytechnic in the UK, founded in 1970. One of the Foundation's specific aims is to promote the educational use of science fiction, and its staff teach the subject at the Polytechnic and elsewhere, usually at post-graduate and diploma levels. A science fiction case-study can also be found in one of the Polytechnic's BSc courses. The Foundation carries out and encourages research into the genre at every level.

A body with broadly similar aims also exists in the US. The Science Fiction Research Association was set up at the Secondary Universe convention in 1970. Physically uninvolved in teaching itself, it aims to promote the serious study and consideration of the genre, and its *Newsletter* carries a certain amount of critical and bibliographical material. A more recent organisation is the Instructors of Science Fiction on Higher Education, which fosters and co-ordinates the teaching of college-level science fiction in the US.

An indication of the recent upsurge of academic interest is the establishment of several summer schools of instruction in the teaching of science fiction held in the US, a number of which are now run annually – among them James Gunn's classes at the University of Kansas. The various writers' workshops now operating might also be loosely described as courses, though with a creative rather than research or instructive intent. The first formed was Damon Knight's Milford Science Fiction Writers' Workshop, named after the town where Knight lived for many years. An annual event, it runs at various locations. Several other workshops gather annually, supported by established writers – notably the Clarion Writers' Workshop, originated at Clarion State College, Pennsylvania, but now peripatetic. However, the Milford event is still regarded as the most important. Knight was also the leading light behind the founding of the Science Fiction Writers' Association, a body which aids writers both critically and practically; and much of the serious approach to the writing of science fiction can be traced to him. (Some workshops are held several times a year, e.g. the Windy City SF Writers' Conference, which has been held in Chicago eight times since 1972.)

Outside the US, the only regularly held workshop is the annual Milford Writers' Workshop UK, organised in Milford, Hampshire, since 1972. As the name suggests, it was first set up by American expatriates (James and Judith Blish) along the lines of the US counterpart. Its membership extends beyond UK writers. A World SF Writers' Conference, reported as highly successful, took place in Dublin in September 1976, mainly organised by Harry Harrison, but it is not expected to be an annual event.

Several sf conferences of a more or less academic nature are held in North America each year, usually at colleges or universities. The Secondary Universe gatherings have already been referred to, but more local meetings, such as the Bay Area SF Seminar in California, are worthy of mention. The Modern Languages Association maintains a standing seminar on science fiction, and there is a strong sf content in the annual MLA conferences. Close links exist between this body and the Science Fiction Research Association.

Volume 11, No. 1
Whole No. 56
JANUARY 1976
SFWA
THE BULLETIN OF THE SCIENCE FICTION WRITERS OF AMERICA

04.08.2 Criticism, Reference and General

Pilgrims Through Space and Time
A HISTORY AND ANALYSIS OF SCIENTIFIC FICTION
J. O. BAILEY

The earliest major historical survey of science fiction, (1947).

The earliest research in science fiction was carried out by largely untrained fans, who produced science fiction and fantasy bibliographies and magazine indexes as amateur publications. Although these were frequently inconsistent or unreliable, their existence went a great way to stimulating a serious approach to science fiction and provided an essential background for much of the more professional work which followed. The more careful and detailed compilations were first published by semi-professional publishing houses, the larger publishers only later becoming interested in works of criticism or history. Professional competition notwithstanding, many fans still happily – and usefully – publish indexes, checklists and other items of interest in fanzines or independent booklets, either individually or in groups, the New England Science Fiction Society (NESFA) being particularly active in magazine indexing.

Among the book-length studies of the genre, several of the earliest were more concerned with an examination of its forebears, including Philip B. Grove's *The Imaginary Voyage in Prose Fiction* (1941), which looked at eighteenth century flights of imagination, Marjorie Nicolson's *Voyages to the Moon* (1948) and Roger L. Green's *Into Other Worlds* (1957). I. F. Clarke's later *Voices Prophesying War* (1966), to date the most authoritative work on the future-war theme, also delves back into the preceding century. Several works embark on critical investigations of utopian or dystopian literature, reflecting a continuing academic interest in this area, one of the most notable being Mark Hillegas's *The Future as Nightmare: H. G. Wells and the Anti-Utopians* (1969). More

04.08 COMMENTATORS AND COURSES

Two studies by James Blish, author turned critic.

recently a tendency to concentrate on the works of an individual writer, either critically or less objectively, has been observed.

The earliest major historical survey of the genre was J. O. Bailey's *Pilgrims through Space and Time* (1947), considered by many, until recently, as definitive. In 1953 Reginald Bretnor edited a largely thematic anthology of essays on *Modern Science Fiction*, including pieces by Isaac Asimov and John W. Campbell, which helped to establish the viewpoint of the, then, modern writer. Damon Knight's collection of critical reviews, published under the title *In Search of Wonder* in 1956, was also influential in its time.

Until 1956, the major critical studies had been written by people already working in the sf field. The trend was interrupted by the popular UK astronomer, Patrick Moore, whose *Science and Fiction* (1957) provided a general history and thematic survey of the genre. Three years later the work of another UK writer established a benchmark in the critical field. Kingsley Amis published his influential *New Maps of Hell* in 1960. Based on a series of lectures which the author had given at Princeton during the previous year, the book took a wide historical perspective, but emphasised the social aspects of science fiction, both satirical and cautionary. Its importance can be judged by the degree of critical attention it attracted outside the sf genre, even though the quality of its contents has since been surpassed. James Blish also provided sharply critical insight in the 1960s, publishing *The Issue at Hand* (1964) and *More Issues at Hand* (1970) under his pseudonym 'William Atheling Jr'. These collections were based on magazine reviews and were notable for their constructive, and often astringent viewpoint. In 1968 came one of the most academic historical surveys, W. H. G. Armytage's *Yesterday's Tomorrows*, tracing the use of the future in myth and literature generally.

Less intellectual criticism than Armytage's continued to be published in the 1960s and 1970s, for example Sam Moskowitz's two volumes covering individual writers: *Explorers of the Infinite* (1963) and *Seekers of Tomorrow* (1966), both based on original magazine articles. *Of Worlds Beyond*, edited in 1964 by Lloyd Arthur Eshbach, brought together contributions from John W. Campbell, Robert A. Heinlein, John Taine, Jack Williamson and others. A noted forerunner of such compilations was Reginald Bretnor's *Modern Science Fiction: Its Meaning and Its Future* (1953), which gave voice to an array of viewpoints ranging from those of Asimov and Boucher to de Camp and Philip Wylie. His later studies include *Science Fiction Today and Tomorrow* (1974) and *The Craft of Science Fiction* (1976). In 1971 Donald Wollheim offered his own inimitable view of sf future history in *The Universe Makers*, drawing on his long experience in the field. Another thoughtful collection of expanded magazine articles by editor Robert W. Lowndes, *Three Faces of Science Fiction*, appeared in 1973. The same year saw the overshadowing of Bailey's historical survey by Brian Aldiss's *Billion Year Spree* – a work containing much insight in its dealing with the early and middle years but neglectful (probably by sheer lack of space) in its consideration of more recent writers. It stands mid-way between the academic and popular approaches.

In 1975 Brian Ash produced *Faces of the Future*, an introductory work aimed at a humanist and rationalist readership, and Brian Aldiss and Harry Harrison edited *Hell's Cartographers*, an anthology of autobiographical sketches by a number of sf authors which seems likely to enjoy a continuing appeal. James Gunn's authoritative but selective history, *Alternate Worlds*, also appeared in the same year – a required companion to *Billion Year Spree*. In 1976 David Kyle, whose Gnome Press had at one time helped to stimulate sf book production, recorded his own interpretation in *A Pictorial History of Science Fiction*.

An increasing amount of academic and intellectual studies have been published in the 1970s. Such approaches are epitomised by Robert M. Philmus's developmental survey: *Into the Unknown* (1970). In an allied context, Lois and Stephen Rose's *The Shattered Ring* (1970) examined science fiction's view of the human condition vis-à-vis the spiritual aspirations of man. Willis McNelly's *Science Fiction: The Academic Awakening* outlines the growing interest which its title describes. In 1974 Martin Harry Greenberg (not to be confused with Martin Greenberg of Gnome Press repute), Patricia Warwick and others began compiling anthologies of stories, prefaced by critical essays and introductions. Each of their collections is designed to aid the teaching or learning of a particular subject, enhanced by the extrapolations of speculative writers. In a similar vein David Ketterer's *New Worlds for Old: the Apocalyptic Imagination, Science Fiction and American Literature* (1974) examines specific themes and the work of certain authors, in addition to adopting a general explanatory approach.

Present-day academic studies of science fiction owe much to the considerable amount of bibliographical detail already in print. An early widely published bibliography can be found in Everett Bleiler's *The Checklist of Fantastic Literature*

(1948). Several comparable lists have been produced, many of them devoted to particular authors or individual themes. I. F. Clarke's *Tale of the Future* (1961, revised 1972) is an annotated checklist reaching back to the seventeenth century (unfortunately inaccurate in many details). In the last few years, several small publishers or specialist bookshops have produced chapbooks of bibliography and criticism, among them the Mirage Press in the US, Ferret Fantasy Ltd in the UK and Norstrilia Press in Australia. There are indications that the trickle of these small but useful works will continue.

In the general reference field, Robert Reginald has compiled *Stella Nova* (1970), a biographical and bibliographical listing of living sf authors. Another highly annotated author listing appears in the single volume so far issued of Donald Tuck's *Encyclopedia of Science Fiction and Fantasy*, which is the first part (A–L) of a 'Who's Who'. A similar work by, Brian Ash, appeared in 1976: *Who's Who in Science Fiction*. In the area of anthologies, a useful bibliography of stories collected up to 1968 can be found in Frederick Siemon's *Science Fiction Story Index*.

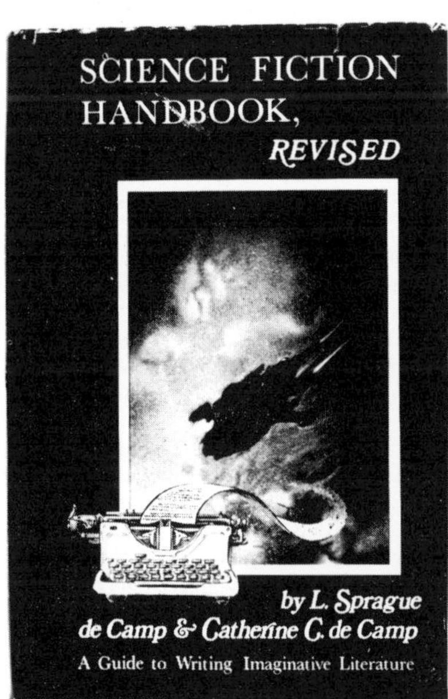

Several bibliographies of critical works have also been compiled. In 1970 H. W. Hall began a serial publication entitled *Science Fiction Book Review Index*; in 1975 a book edition incorporated the first issues of the series, together with a retrospective listing. An annotated checklist under the heading *Science Fiction Criticism* came from Thomas D. Clareson in 1972; while Robert Briney and Edward Wood went to the lengths of issuing in the same year an annotated bibliography of *SF Bibliographies*! Many useful critical and bibliographical treatments (often theses and dissertations) are not generally available on the open publications market, although they can be found in the libraries of research bodies such as the Science Fiction Foundation.

Several books introducing science fiction to select audiences are currently in print. Brian Ash's *Faces of the Future* has already been mentioned. L. Sprague de Camp's *Science Fiction Handbook*, revised by the author and his wife in 1976, concentrates on guidance for the aspiring writer, as does Ben Bova's *Notes to a Science Fiction Writer* (1975). L. David Allen's *Science Fiction Reader's Guide* provides background material in addition to instruction, while Elizabeth Calkins and Barry McGhan's *Teaching Tomorrow* (1973) and Beverly Friend's *The Classroom in Orbit* (1974) are specifically aimed at high school teachers. Recently, several 'coffee-table' books surveying science fiction, or a section of it, have been published – usually with a strong pictorial bias and often exploring the art rather than the literature of the genre. Other than to the committed devotee of sf art, they are of little value.

In the audio-visual field, a set of documentary films on sf writers has been prepared by James Gunn at the University of Kansas. Such an area of communication, still largely untapped, promises considerable development.

Some of the regular fanzines publish criticism of a high, if not always consistent, standard, but only three journals set their sights on the level of an academic approach. The most erudite of these is *Science Fiction Studies*, edited by Darko Suvin and R. D. Mullen at Indiana State University. *Extrapolation* is published as the Newsletter of the Conference of Science Fiction of the MLA, but also serves as an outlet for the SFRA. It is published at the English Department of the College of Wooster, Ohio. The North-East London Polytechnic in the UK publishes *Foundation: the Review of Science Fiction* for the SFF, aiming at a combination of scholarly criticism and more general observations.

These three journals circulate largely among academics, teachers, writers and critics. They are also sent to many libraries. While of limited appeal in the realms of fandom, their existence provides a continuing stimulus to the serious consideration of science fiction on a more intellectual level, and encourages the study of the genre on a widespread educational basis.

Bibliography

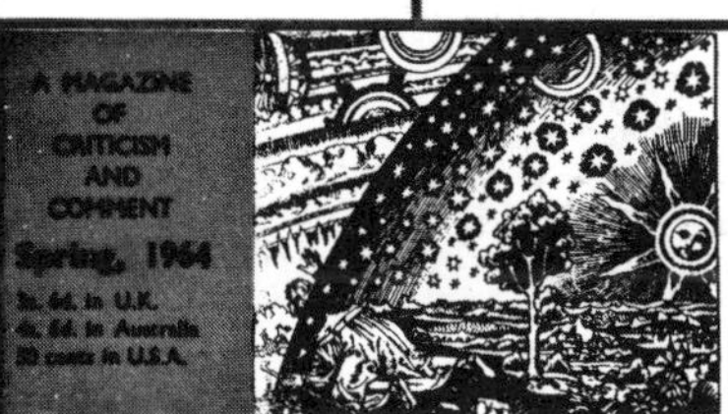

Aldiss, Brian W. *Billion Year Spree: the History of Science Fiction*, Doubleday (US) 1973
Aldiss, Brian W. *The Shape of Further Things*, Faber & Faber (UK) 1970
Aldiss, Brian W. *Science Fiction Art*, New English Library (UK) 1975
Aldiss, Brian W. (with Harry Harrison). *Hell's Cartographers*, Weidenfeld & Nicolson (UK) 1975
Aldiss, Brian W. (with Harry Harrison) eds. *SF Horizons* (reprint of a two-issue semi-professional journal), Arno Press (US) 1975
Aldiss, Margaret. *Item Eighty-Three: Brian W. Aldiss, a bibliography 1954-1972*, SF Horizons (UK) 1972
Allen, L. David. *Science Fiction Reader's Guide*, Centennial Press, Lincoln, Nebraska, 1974; previously published as *Science Fiction; an Introduction*, Cliff's Notes (US) 1973
Allen, L. David. *The Ballantine Teachers' Guide to Science Fiction*, Ballantine (US) 1975
Amis, Kingsley. *New Maps of Hell: a Survey of Science Fiction*, Harcourt Brace (US) 1960
Appel, Benjamin. *The Fantastic Mirror: Science Fiction across the Ages*, Random House (US) 1969
Armytage, W. H. G. *Yesterday's Tomorrows: a Historical Survey of Future Societies*, Routledge & Kegan Paul (UK) 1968
Ash, Brian. *Faces of the Future: the Lessons of Science Fiction*, Elek/Pemberton (UK) 1975; Taplinger (US) 1975
Ash, Brian. *Who's Who in Science Fiction*, Elm Tree Books (UK) 1976; Taplinger (US) 1976
Ashley, Mike. *The History of the Science Fiction Magazine Part 1: 1926-1935*, New English Library (UK) 1974; *Part 2: 1936-1945*, New English Library (UK) 1975; *Part 3: 1946-1955*, New English Library (UK) 1976
Atheling, William, Jr (James Blish). *The Issue at Hand*, Advent (US) 1964
Atheling, William, Jr (James Blish). *More Issues at Hand*, Advent (US) 1970
Bailey, J. O. *Pilgrims through Space and Time*, Argus Books (US) 1947
Barron, Neil, *Anatomy of Wonder: Science Fiction*, R. R. Bowker (US) 1976
Bergonzi, Bernard. *The Early H. G. Wells, a Study of the Scientific Romances*, Manchester University Press (UK) 1961
Biamonti, Francesco (ed). *Harry Harrison: Bibliographia (1951-1965)* (annotated by Harry

Harrison), privately printed (Italy) 1965
Bleiler, Everett F. *The Checklist of Fantastic Literature*, Shasta (US) 1948
Borello, Alfred. *H. G. Wells, Author in Agony*, Southern Illinois University Press (US) 1972
Bova, Ben. *Notes to a Science Fiction Writer*, Scribner's (US) 1975
Bretnor, Reginald. *SF, Today and Tomorrow*, Harper & Row (US) 1974
Briney, Robert (with Edward Wood). *SF Bibliographies: an Annotated Bibliography of Bibliographical Works on Science Fiction and Fantasy*, Advent (US) 1972
Calkins, Elizabeth & McGhan, Barry. *Teaching Tomorrow: a Handbook of Science Fiction for Teachers*, Pflaum/Standard (US) 1973
Carter, Lin. *Imaginary Worlds: the Art of Fantasy*, Ballantine (US) 1973
Carter, Lin. *Lovecraft: a Look behind the 'Cthulhu Mythos'*, Ballantine (US) 1972
Carter, Lin. *Tolkein: a Look behind the Lord of the Rings*, Ballantine (US) 1969
Chauvin, Cy (ed). *A Multitude of Visions*, T-K Graphics (US) 1975
Chesneaux, Jean. *The Political and Social Ideas of Jules Verne*, Thames & Hudson (UK) 1972
Clareson, Thomas D. *Science Fiction Criticism: an Annotated Checklist*, Kent State University Press (US) 1972
Clareson, Thomas D. *SF: a Dream of Other Worlds*, Texas A & M University Library Miscellaneous Publication 6 (US) 1972
Clareson, Thomas D. *Symbolic Worlds of Science Fiction*, Bowling Green Popular Press (US) 1974
Clareson, Thomas D. (ed). *SF: the Other Side of Realism*, Bowling Green Popular Press (US) 1971
Clarke, I. F. *Voices Prophesying War*, Oxford University Press (UK) 1966
Clarke, I. F. *The Tale of the Future; from the Beginning to the Present Time*, The Library Association (UK) 1961
Cole, Walter R. *A Checklist of Science Fiction Anthologies*, privately printed (US) 1964
Davenport, Basil. *Inquiry into Science Fiction*, Longmans Green (US) 1955
Davenport, Basil (ed). *The Science Fiction Novel: Imagination and Social Criticism*, Advent (US) 1959
Day, Bradford M. *The Checklist of Fantastic Literature in Paperbound Books*, Science Fiction & Fantasy Publications (US) 1965
Day, Bradford M. *The Supplemental Checklist of Fantastic Literature*, Science Fiction & Fantasy Publications (US) 1963
De Camp, L. Sprague. *Lovecraft: a Biography*, Doubleday (US) 1975; New English Library (UK) 1976
De Camp, L. Sprague and Catherine. *Science Fiction Handbook: the Writing of Imaginative Fiction* (revised edition of 1953 original by L. Sprague de Camp alone), Owlswick Press (US) 1975
Del Rey, Lester (ed). *Fantastic Science Fiction Art, 1926-54* Ballantine (US) 1975
Doherty, Geoffrey D. (ed). *Aspects of Science Fiction*, John Murray (UK) 1959
Elliott, Robert C. *The Shape of Utopia: Studies in a Literary Genre*, University of Chicago Press (US) 1970
Eshbach, Lloyd Arthur (ed). *Of Worlds Beyond: the Science of Science Fiction Writing*, Advent (US) 1964
Evans, Hilary and Dike. *Beyond the Gaslight: Science in Popular Fiction 1895–1905*, Frederick Muller (UK) 1976
Evans, Robley. *J. R. R. Tolkein*, Warner Paperback Library (US) 1972
Franklin, H. Bruce. *Future Perfect: American Science Fiction of the Nineteenth Century*, Oxford University Press (US) 1966
Frewin, Anthony. *One Hundred Years of Science Fiction Illustration*, Jupiter Books (UK) 1974
Friend, Beverly. *Science Fiction: the Classroom in Orbit*, Educational Impact Inc (US) 1974
Gerber, Richard. *Utopian Fantasy: a Study of English Utopian Fiction Since the End of the Nineteenth Century*, Routledge & Kegan Paul (UK) 1955
Gillespie, Bruce (ed). *Philip K. Dick: Electric Shepherd*, Norstrilia Press (Australia) 1975
Goble, Neil. *Asimov Analysed*, The Mirage Press (US) 1972
Goddard, James. *J. G. Ballard: a Bibliography*, Cypher Press (UK) 1970
Gove, Philip Babcock. *The Imaginary Voyage in Prose Fiction*, Columbia University Press (US) 1941
Griffith, George. *The Raid of 'Le Vengeur' & Other Stories* (with a critical biography by Sam Moskowitz and bibliography by George Locke), Ferret Fantasy (UK) 1974
Green, Roger Lancelyn. *Into Other Worlds: Space-Flight in Fiction, from Lucian to Lewis*, Abelard-Schuman (US) 1957
Greenberg, Martin Harry (with Carol Mason and Patricia Warrick) eds. *Anthropology through Science Fiction*, St Martin's Press (US) 1974
Greenberg, Martin Harry (with John W. Milstead, Joseph Olander and Patricia Warrick) eds. *Sociology through Science Fiction*, St Martin's Press (US) 1974
Greenberg, Martin Harry (with Patricia Warrick). *The New Awareness: Religion through Science Fiction*, Delacorte Press (US) 1975
Greenberg, Martin Henry (with John W. Milstead, Joseph D. Olander and Patricia Warrick) eds. *Social Problems through Science Fiction*, St Martin's Press (US) 1975
Greenberg, Martin Harry (with Harvey A. Katz and Patricia Warrick) eds. *Introductory Psychology through Science Fiction*, Rand McNally (US) 1974
Gunn, James. *Alternate Worlds: An Illustrated History of Science Fiction*, Prentice Hall (US) 1975
Gunn, James. *The Discovery of the Future: the Ways of Science Fiction Developed*, Texas A&M University Library (US) 1975
Hall, H. W. (ed). *Science Fiction Book Review Index, 1923–1973* (annual supplements since 1974), Gale Research Company (US) 1975
Harbottle, Philip. *The Multi-man: a Bibliographic Study of John Russell Fearn*, privately printed (UK) 1968
Heins, Henry Hardy. *A Golden Anniversary Bibliography of Edgar Rice Burroughs*, Donald M. Grant (US) 1964
Hillegas, Mark R. *The Future as Nightmare: H. G. Wells and the Anti-Utopians*, Oxford University Press (US) 1969
Hillegas, Mark R. (ed). *Shadows of Imagination: the Fantasies of C. S. Lewis, J. R. R. Tolkein, and Charles Williams*, Southern Illinois University Press (US) 1969
Hutchinson, Tom. *British Science Fiction and Fantasy* (annotated checklist), The British Council (UK) 1975
Isaacs, Neil D. (with Rose A. Zimbardo) eds. *Tolkein and the Critics*, University of Notre Dame Press (US) 1970
Ketterer, David. *New Worlds for Old: the Apocalyptic Imagination, Science Fiction, and American Literature*, Anchor Books (US) 1974
Klinkowitz, Jerome (with John Somer) eds. *The Vonnegut Statement*, Dell (US) 1973
Knight, Damon. *In Search of Wonder*, Advent (US) 1956
Kocher, Paul. *Master of Middle-Earth: the Achievement of J. R. R. Tolkein in fiction*, Houghton Mifflin (US) 1972
Kyle, David. *A Pictorial History of Science Fiction*, Hamlyn (US) 1976
La Conte, Ronald T. and Ellen. *Teaching Tomorrow Today*, Bantam (US) 1975
Lewis, C. S. *Of Other Worlds: Essays and Stories*, Harcourt, Brace & World (US) 1966
Locke, George. *Voyages in Space: a Bibliography of Interplanetary Fiction 1801–1914*, Ferret Fantasy (UK) 1975
Lowndes, Robert A. W. *Three Faces of Science Fiction*, NESFA Press (US) 1973
Lundwall, Sam J. *Science Fiction: What It's All About*, Ace (US) 1971
Lupoff, Richard A. *Edgar Rice Burroughs: Master of Adventure*, Canaveral Press (US) 1965
Mackenzie, Norman and Jeanne. *H. G. Wells: a Biography*, Simon & Schuster (US) 1973
McKinney, Richard L. *Science Fiction as Futurology: Tomorrow's World as Presented in and Suggested by Selected Works of Science Fiction*, Framtidsstudieprojektet Sveriges internationella villkor (Sweden) 1976
McNelly, Willis E. (ed). *Science Fiction: the Academic Awakening*, College English Association, Centenary College of Louisiana (US) 1974
Manuel, Frank E. (ed). *Utopias and Utopian Thought*, Houghton Mifflin (US) 1966
Manson, Margaret (ed). *Item Forty-Three: Brian Aldiss, a Bibiography 1954–1962* (annotated by Brian Aldiss), privately printed (UK) 1962
Miller, Marjorie M. *Isaac Asimov: a Checklist of Works Published in the United States, March 1939–May 1972*, Kent State University Press (US) 1972
Moore, Patrick. *Science and Fiction*, George Harrap (UK) 1956
Morse, A. Reynolds. *The Works of M. P. Shiel*, Fantasy Publishing (US) 1948
Morton, A. L. *The English Utopia*, Lawrence and Wishart (UK) 1952
Moskowitz, Sam. *Explorers of the Infinite; Shapers of Science Fiction*, World Publishing (US) 1963
Moskowitz, Sam. *Seekers of Tomorrow: Masters of Modern Science Fiction*, World Publishing (US) 1966
Nicolson, Marjorie. *Voyages to the Moon*, Macmillan (US) 1948
Nohan, William F. *The Ray Bradbury Companion*, Gale Research (US) 1975
Owings, Mark. *James H. Schmitz: a Bibliography*, Croatan House/The Mirage Press (US) 1973
Owings, Mark. *Robert A. Heinlein: a Bibliography*, Croatan House/The Mirage Press (US) 1973
Owings, Mark (with Jack L. Chalker). *The Index to Science-Fantasy Publishers*, The Anthem Series (US) 1966
Owings, Mark (with Jack L. Chalker). *The Revised H. P. Lovecraft Bibliography*, The Mirage Press (US) 1973
Panshin, Alexei. *Heinlein in Dimension*, Advent (US) 1968
Parrington, Vernon Louis, Jr. *American Dreams: a Study of American Utopias*, Russell & Russell (US) 1964; 2nd edition (enlarged) Brown University Press (US) 1974
Philmus, Robert M. *Into the Unknown: the Evolution of Science Fiction from Francis Godwin to H. G. Wells*, University of California Press (US) 1970
Plank, Robert. *The Emotional Significance of Imaginary Beings: a Study of the Interaction between Psychotherapy, Literature, and Reality in the Modern World*, Charles C. Thomas (US) 1968
Porges, Irwin. *Edgar Rice Burroughs: the Man Who Created Tarzan*, Brigham Young University Press (US) 1975
Raknem, Ingvald. *H. G. Wells and His Critics*, Universitetsforlaget (Oslo) 1962
Ready, William. *The Tolkien Relation: a Personal Inquiry*, Henry Regnery (US) 1968
Reed, Peter J. *Kurt Vonnegut Jr*, Warner Paperback Library (US) 1972
Reginald, Robert. *Stella Nova: the Contemporary Science Fiction Authors*, Unicorn & Son (US) 1970; revised as *Contemporary Science Fiction Authors*, Arno Press (US) 1975

Rose, Lois and Stephen. *The Shattered Ring: Science Fiction and the Quest for Meaning*, John Knox Press (US) 1970
Rottensteiner, Franz. *The Science Fiction Book: an Illustrated History*, Thames & Hudson (UK) 1975
Sadoul, Jacques. *Hier, L'an 2000*, Editions Denoel (France) 1973; Souvenir Press (UK) 1975
Scholes, Robert. *The Fabulators*, Oxford University Press (US) 1967
Scholes, Robert. *Structural Fabulation: an Essay on Fiction of the Future*, University of Notre Dame Press (US) 1975
Siemon, Frederick. *Science Fiction Story Index 1950–1968*, American Library Association (US) 1971
Swigart, Leslie Kay. *Harlan Ellison: a Bibliographical Checklist*, Williams Publishing (US) 1973
Taylor, Angus. *Philip K. Dick and the Umbrella of Light*, T-K Graphics (US) 1975
Tuck, Donald H. *The Encyclopedia of Science Fiction and Fantasy: vol. 1: Who's Who A-L*, Advent (US) 1974
Tuck, Donald H. *Handbook of Science Fiction and Fantasy*, privately printed (Tasmania) 1954; 2nd edition (revised in 2 vols) 1959
Van Vogt, A. E. *Reflections of A. E. van Vogt*, Fictioneer Books (US) 1975
Walsh, Chad. *From Utopia to Nightmare*, Harper & Row (US) 1962
H. G. Wells Society. *H. G. Wells, a Comprehensive Bibliography*, H. G. Wells Society (UK) 1966; 2nd edition (revised) 1968
Whyte, Andrew Adams (ed). *The New SF Bulletin Index to SF Books 1974*, Paratime Press (US) 1974
Williamson, Jack. *H. G. Wells: Critic of Progress*, Mirage Press (US) 1973
Williamson, Jack. *Teaching SF*, privately printed (US) 1972; revised from author's *Science Fiction Comes to College*, 1971
Williamson, Jack. *Science Fiction: Education for Tomorrow*, Mirage Press (US) 1976
Wilson, Robin Scott (ed). *Those Who Can: a Science Fiction Reader*, New American Library (US) 1973
Wollheim, Donald A. *The Universe Makers: Science Fiction Today*, Harper & Row (US) 1971

Journals

Extrapolation The Journal of the MLA Seminar on Science Fiction, Thomas D. Clareson (ed); published twice-yearly since May 1968 at the English Department (Box 3186), the College of Wooster, Wooster, Ohio 44691, US

Foundation: the Review of Science Fiction Peter Nicholls (ed); published thrice-yearly since March 1972 at the Science Fiction Foundation, North-East London Polytechnic, Longbridge Road, Dagenham, Essex RM8 2AS, UK

Science-Fiction Studies R. D. Mullen and Darko Suvin (eds); published thrice-yearly at the Department of English, Indiana State University, Terra Haute, Indiana 47809, US

04.09 FRINGE CULTS

Like any other speculative endeavour, science fiction enjoys its ample share of fringe cults, and not all of them of a lunatic variety, even if many of them might appear to the outsider as distinctly odd. In this section we review the three which have probably attracted the most attention in their time. The theories of Charles Fort, while frequently bizarre, have provided the inspiration for some noted sf stories, and Ron Hubbard's concept of Dianetics has also found its place in various works in the genre. The Shaver Mystery Cult, on the other hand, belongs far more in the category of the irrational, but it created a stir of some note and merits consideration here.

04.09.1 The Fortean Influence

Though he never wrote a science fiction story himself, Charles Hoy Fort, the world's first ufologist, left a mark on the genre which has continued since his death in 1932. His influence is reflected in the work of many well-known writers who borrowed his ideas and subscribed to his peculiar philosophy. Regarded by orthodox scientists as a meddlesome crank and by his disciples as something akin to a genius, he spent half a lifetime collecting printed records of mysterious happenings for which science, in his view, had no adequate explanation and offered his own fantastic hypotheses to account for them.

Such was his scepticism that he consistently cast doubt on his own conclusions, which he presented in a series of four fact-filled books written in prose as

IMPOSSIBLE BUT TRUE
THE RAIN OF FISH
There are hundreds of instances on record of a rain of fish from the sky. Many of them cannot be explained away in any logical manner. Details of this mystery appear on page 175

Amazing *December 1947.*

04.09 FRINGE CULTS

Magazine appearance of 'Lo!' in Astounding *August 1934.*

startling as his findings. *The Book of the Damned* (1919), *New Lands* (1923), *Lo!* (1931) and *Wild Talents* (1932) were eventually combined in *The Books of Charles Fort* (1941), published on behalf of The Fortean Society – founded in New York on 26 January 1931 by several prominent literary men who encouraged his questioning attitude. Among his admirers were Theodore Dreiser, Booth Tarkington, John Cowper Powys and Ben Hecht; but his most devoted follower was Tiffany Thayer, a publicist and novelist who was the mainspring of the society and editor of its journal, *Doubt*.

Born in Albany, New York, in 1874 Fort wanted to be a naturalist, but instead became a newspaper reporter before settling down to write short stories about city life. Turning to novels, he wrote prodigiously but published only one – *The Outcast Manufacturers* (1909), a tedious tale about a mail-order business. Frustrated, he abandoned fiction for the role of researcher into the strange phenomena which obsessed him for the rest of his life. For twenty-six years he pored over books and newspapers in the New York Public Library and, later, the British Museum, amassing and classifying data on earthquakes, lost planets, lights in the sky, coloured rains, falls of frogs, sea serpents, vanished ships, missing persons, poltergeists and a thousand other marvels.

'Whoever said the pen is mightier than the sword forgot the scissors', he wrote; and to some 40,000 clippings he added scribbled notes as he formed his own provocative theories to substitute for the explanations he rejected. But he did not insist that his ideas were any nearer the truth; only that the scientists were not always right and sometimes – though they might not admit it – completely at a loss. 'I offer the data. Suit yourself', was his constant cry; and 'I believe nothing of my own that I have ever written.'

Among Fort's regular correspondents was the noted journalist and author, the late Miriam Allen deFord, who since the 1950s contributed extensively to the sf magazines. According to her, Fort was 'shy, introverted', and 'the least dogmatic of men. The last thing he wanted was to set himself up as a dictator or a pundit . . . But he was stung, and rightly so, by too much experience of being ignored and dismissed by the very people to whom his findings should have been of fundamental importance.' He also possessed a mischievous sense of humour which he used to considerable effect.

Though the science fiction writers could not ignore him, it was some time before they realised how much he had to offer. Mathematical-puzzle expert Martin Gardner has recorded that Theodore Dreiser once tried to persuade H. G. Wells that Fort's ideas offered scope for fictional treatment, without success: 'Wells never regarded Fort's speculations as more than amusing scientific rubbish.' Gardner, too, doubts that Fort's influence on science fiction was as strong as some have suggested. Miriam Allen deFord, on the other hand, said: 'His impact on science fiction is tremendous.' And Fort's biographer, Damon Knight, maintains that 'Fort's influence on other writers is incalculable; his ideas have diffused so widely that compiling a list of examples would be a hopeless task.'

First to find in Fort a source of inspiration was Edmond Hamilton, who started writing in 1924. By 1926, having read his books, he was corresponding with Fort and sending clippings to him in London. But four years elapsed before Hamilton's account of 'The Space Visitors' appeared in *Air Wonder Stories* (March 1930), with an editorial reference to *The Book of the Damned* and the evidence it offered that 'over the past 150 years there has been strange extra-terrestrial activity, presumably from sentient beings'.

Taking its cue from Fort's surmise, 'I think we're fished for', Hamilton's story told how the world was terrorised by the mysterious occupants of passing space-vessels who, to satisfy their curiosity, were dredging up samples of Earth's surface with enormous scoops, much as men would trawl the ocean deeps. It was also Hamilton who first capitalised on Fort's most intriguing notion, which he expressed in the disturbing phrase, 'I think we're property'. In 'The Earth Owners', which appeared in *Weird Tales* (August 1931), mankind is threatened with extinction by invading clouds of black gas which suck the life-force from their victims. But humanity is saved by its guardians, alien life-forms which appear as globes of light and which are protecting the planet until its inhabitants are competent to deal with such intrusions.

Though many more writers played with similar notions, science fiction remained mostly insensitive to Fort's speculations, perhaps because they did not allow for the accepted findings of the astronomers at whom his sharpest barbs were directed.

Reviewing his books in *Amazing Stories*, literary editor C. A. Brandt, an expert in the genre, dismissed his opinions as founded on unreliable reports and advanced out of pure pique. Then, in 1934, *Astounding Stories* found it expedient to present *Lo!* as a series of feature articles, three years after its initial appearance in book form; and many thousands of sf readers were made aware of Fort and his fancies.

At that time, the magazine was outdoing its rivals by encouraging audacious 'thought-variant' concepts; and editor F. Orlin Tremaine's motive was clear when he declaimed: 'Here is the most astounding collation of factual data ever offered to a large audience. This book has been read by 3000 people – mostly writers seeking plots! We can offer it to the one group in America which can digest it.' But the response was not impressive, either from writers or readers, many of whom had lost their appetites long before the last of eight monthly helpings. 'To read Fort is to ride on a comet!' *New York Times* reviewer Maynard Shipley enthused. But Fort's style was such that, for many, the ride was inclined to be bumpy.

Not until 1939 did a significant Fortean concept emerge in fictional form, with such dramatic impact that it established the author and his inspirer firmly in the sf tradition. It also provided a successful send-off for a new magazine called *Unknown* (later *Unknown Worlds*). Looking for a suitably off-beat story to head the first issue, editor John W. Campbell found it in *Sinister Barrier*, the novel which British writer Eric Frank Russell based on the same idea Hamilton had developed in

'The Earth Owners'. Russell's aliens are detectable only as blue globes of pure energy that feed on the emotions of men while manipulating them for their own ends; hence wars and other disasters which cause large-scale human distress. The story gains in suspense by a detective-thriller treatment rare in this medium at the time.

Russell, a Liverpool salesman who helped to establish the pre-war British Interplanetary Society, was an active proselytiser for the Forteans, contributing to their official magazine while bombarding editors with articles and letters in praise of the man who he claimed had liberated human minds. Though he wrote no more stories directly relating to Fortean ideas, his contributions to *Astounding* and other magazines often bore the marks of his adherence to Fortean philosophy; and he traced Fort's influence in other leading authors' tales, such as 'None But Lucifer' by H. L. Gold and L. Sprague de Camp (*Unknown*, September 1939), dealing with a man who inherits the world's sorrows; Jack Williamson's 'classic' story of lycanthropy, *Darker Than You Think* (*Unknown*, December 1940); and 'The Children's Hour' by Lawrence O'Donnell (C. L. Moore, a pseudonym also shared on one occasion with Henry Kuttner), (*Astounding*, March 1944), in which the hero discovers the girl he loves is an immature member of a superior race.

'Iridescent blue closed upon him and formed a satanic nimbus behind his head.' Sinister Barrier *by E. Frank Russell (Fantasy Press). Illustration by Edd Cartier.*

Assessing the influence of Russell himself in all this, Sam Moskowitz concludes: 'For good or ill, the astonishing bulk of science fiction plastered around Fortean phenomena . . . stems from him.' Elsewhere, he attributes many stories concerning teleportation (the ability to move objects by will-power) to Fort's supposition of such 'a transportary force'; and he nominates 'What Thin Partitions' by Mark Clifton and Alex Apostolides (*Astounding*, September 1953), as the most entertaining story ever written on this theme. He also instances 'Burning Bright' by John S. Browning (Robert Moore Williams) (*Astounding*, July 1938), in which a man acquires the ability to make objects disappear after exposure to radiation. But there are scores of such tales, not forgetting Wells's *The Man Who Could Work Miracles*, which dates back to 1898 – twenty years before Fort's first book appeared.

In his biography, Damon Knight specifically mentions H. Beam Piper's story, 'He Walked around the Horses' (*Astounding*, April 1948), which he based on Fort's account of the disappearance of the British courier Benjamin Bathurst on the road to Hamburg in 1809. Charles L. Harness, author of 'The New Reality' (*Thrilling Wonder*, December 1950), which plays with the notion that man's universe has been fashioned by his own imagination, is another writer he considers 'strongly influenced by Fort'. Even astronomer R. S. Richardson, who besides writing factual pieces for *Astounding* also wrote fiction under the name of Philip Latham, has not been immune.

Fort and his followers find a place in *Jack of Eagles* (1952), a novel dealing with ESP by the late James Blish – a Fortean Society member – who based one of its characters on secretary Tiffany Thayer. Other members of the society were Nelson S. Bond, who wrote fantasy stories with a light touch of humour; R. DeWitt Miller, who assembled a book of *Forgotten Mysteries* (1947); L. Taylor Hansen, a writer on 'Scientific Mysteries' of archaeological interest featured by *Amazing* throughout the 1940s; and Vincent H. Gaddis, another writer for *Amazing* on similar subjects, and author of *Mysterious Lights and Fires* (1967).

In an article in *Amazing* for June 1965, Sam Moskowitz contended that Fort and his disciples had been confounded by the march of events. Space research had proved the wrongness of Fort's ideas about a pancake-shaped Earth surrounded by a shell in which the stars were merely holes, and planets that were only a few thousand miles distant. 'Fort', he maintained, 'came close to being wrong all the time . . . Had Fort succeeded in gaining more attention, he could only have *retarded* progress.' And he joined Miriam Allen deFord and Martin Gardner in condemning the use of the society's journal to espouse causes far removed from Fort's area of dissent.

By then, however, *Doubt* and its editor, Tiffany Thayer, had been dead for six years. Deprived of its mainspring, the Fortean Society had run down; although Eric Frank Russell still argued that since it had not been dissolved it still existed. It has been succeeded by the International Fortean Organisation, based in Arlington, Virginia, USA, which claims more than 500 members throughout the world and publishes *INFO Journal*, carrying articles on Fortean topics and studies of Fort's source material.

PRINTED SOURCES

Fiction

Blish, James. 'Let the Finder Beware', *Thrilling Wonder* December 1949
Bond, Nelson S. *The 31st of February*, Gnome (US) 1949
Bond, Nelson S. *Nightmares and Daydreams*, Arkham (US) 1968
Browning, John S. (Robert Moore Williams). 'Burning Bright', *Astounding* September 1953
Clifton, Mark (with Alex Apostolides). 'What Thin Partitions', *Astounding* September 1953
Fort, Charles. *The Outcast Manufacturers*, Dodge (US) 1909
Fort, Charles. *The Book of the Damned*, Liveright (US) 1919; Sphere (UK) 1973
Fort, Charles. *New Lands*, Liveright (US) 1923
Fort, Charles. *Lo!*, Kendall (US) 1931; Gollancz (UK) 1931; abridged version, *Astounding* April-November 1934
Fort, Charles. *Wild Talents*, Kendall (US) 1932
Fort, Charles. *The Books of Charles Fort*, Holt (US) 1941
Gold, H. L. and de Camp, L. Sprague. 'None But Lucifer', *Unknown* September 1939
Hamilton, Edmond. 'The Space Visitors', *Air Wonder Stories* March 1930; *Tales of Wonder* Winter 1938 (as 'The Space Beings'); *Startling Stories* September 1939
Hamilton, Edmond. 'The Earth Owners', *Weird Tales* August 1931
Harness, Charles L. 'The New Reality', *Thrilling Wonder Stories* December 1950
O'Donnell, Lawrence (C. L. Moore). 'The Children's Hour', *Astounding* March 1944
Piper, H. Beam. 'He Walked around the Horses', *Astounding* April 1948
Russell, Eric Frank. *Sinister Barrier, Unknown* March 1939; World's Work (UK) 1943; Fantasy, Reading, Pa., 1948
Russell, Eric Frank. 'The Bronx Jeer', *Fantasy Review* August-September 1948
Williamson, Jack. 'Darker Than You Think', *Unknown* December 1940; Fantasy, Reading, Pa., 1948

Commentaries

Brandt, C. A. 'Again – Mr Fort' (review of *Lo!*), *Amazing* July 1931
Brandt, C. A. Review of *Wild Talents, Amazing* March 1933
Clouser, Frederick. 'Charles Fort – Apostle of the Impossible', *Fate* Fall 1948
deFord, Miriam Allen. 'Charles Fort: Enfant Terrible of Science', *Fantasy & SF* January 1954; British edition, May 1954
Gaddis, Vincent H. *Mysterious Lights and Fires*, McKay (US) 1967
Gardner, Martin. *Fads and Fallacies in the Name of Science*, Dover (US) 1957
Knight, Damon. *Charles Fort, Prophet of the Unexplained*, Doubleday (US) 1970; Gollancz (UK) 1971
Miller, R. De Witt. *Forgotten Mysteries*, Cloud (US) 1947
Moskowitz, Sam. 'Lo! The Poor Forteans', *Amazing* June 1965
Moskowitz, Sam. *Seekers of Tomorrow*, World (US) 1966
Russell, Eric Frank. Review of *The Books of Charles Fort, Tomorrow* December 1941

04.09.2 Shaver and the Gods on Earth

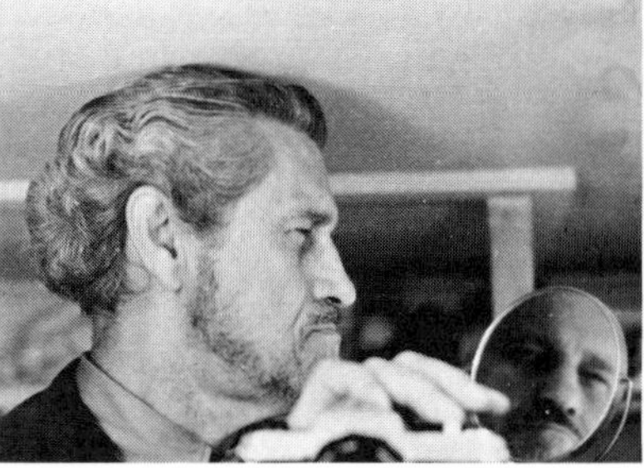

Richard S. Shaver.

Today there is a ready market for the theories of writers like Erich von Däniken, who in *Chariots of the Gods?* (1968), *Return to the Stars* (1968) and later volumes poses the question that, in its prehistory, this Earth may have been visited by alien intelligences who became the gods of mythology. Such arguments are an extension of the Fortean theme 'We are property', especially as von Däniken suggests that *Homo sapiens* may have been specially bred by such aliens.

But twenty-five years before von Däniken's theories were published, the science fiction fraternity was faced with the precursor of all such mysteries – the now infamous Shaver Hoax.

In a series of stories that began with '"I Remember Lemuria"' (1945), Richard S. Shaver (1907–75) put forward the theory that long, long ago this Earth was the home of several races, of which the major two were the Titans and the Atlans. Both were god-like immortals who had created tremendous civilisations. Over the centuries, the sun began to emit harmful radiation, so the super-beings built massive underground caverns, there to escape the rays. But to no effect: the rays were causing them to age and die. There was no answer but to leave the Earth,

Other Worlds *November 1949.*

abandoning their civilisations, and leaving behind the inferior race of humans. Some of the humans found their way down to the underground caverns and discovered the wonderful machinery built by the super-beings; but meddling released harmful energy from the machines. The radiation affected the explorers, making them degenerate. Shaver called these humans 'deros' (detrimental robots), and it was they who came to control the underground machinery whose harmful rays are the direct cause of all evil. Thereby Shaver explains away all the mysteries of this world – the wrecks, disasters and accidents; they are all the work of the deros, who continue to operate in the caverns to this day. In addition, Shaver claimed that the Titans and Atlans continue to keep a watch on the Earth and periodically visit the planet – thus explaining the mysteries of flying saucers and UFOs.

'*The Lost Continent of Lemuria' illustrated by H.R. Hammond*, Amazing *May 1940.*

Richard Shaver had originally written a letter in 1943 to Raymond Palmer, the editor of *Amazing*, which detailed a lost alphabet – the key to the Mantong language. Palmer requested more details, and the result was the manuscript 'A Warning to Future Man'. What happened afterwards has been wreathed in mystery, but the result was a sensation. According to Palmer, he rewrote the manuscript, titled it '"I Remember Lemuria"', and ran it in the March 1945 *Amazing*, together with the article 'Mantong, the Language of Lemuria'. By a coincidence, that issue of *Amazing* had an increased print run, but even that did not account for the unprecedented response from readers. Many wrote upholding Shaver's theories – they had had similar experiences of contact with the deros and the well-intentioned teros. Initially sceptical, Palmer investigated Shaver and finally admitted there had to be something in it. Consequently, over the next three years *Amazing* virtually became the Shaver journal, and the June 1947 issue was devoted entirely to the Shaver mystery. Shaver's following snowballed, and *Amazing*'s circulation rocketed. Only when an irate reader wrote direct to the publisher, William B. Ziff, complaining that the theory contradicted Einstein, was the mystery dropped. But Shaver's stories continued to appear, and when in 1948 Palmer began to publish his own magazines, the Shaver mystery reappeared and continued to bubble sporadically through the 1950s, though the science fiction field had long since washed its hands of the affair.

Diehard science fiction fans were initially in an uproar. They claimed the Shaver Theory, which had attracted the attention of editors of big-circulation magazines like *Harper's*, was lowering the standard of science fiction, and because of its apparent success all science fiction was being measured by that standard. What was more, science fiction fans were being looked upon as lunatics. The result proved a running battle between Palmer and science fiction fandom, in and out of the letter columns of *Amazing* and its companion, *Fantastic Adventures*.

What is less known is the animosity between Palmer and Shaver themselves. Over the decades since the Shaver mystery caused a major furore in *Amazing*, the truth has become distorted and facts lost. Much of this was the result of deliberate mis-reporting by Palmer, who constantly contradicted himself. One of the major bones of contention has been who actually wrote the Shaver stories. Was it Shaver, or was it, as many believe, Palmer? In 1961 Palmer published a special issue of his occult magazine *The Hidden World* which

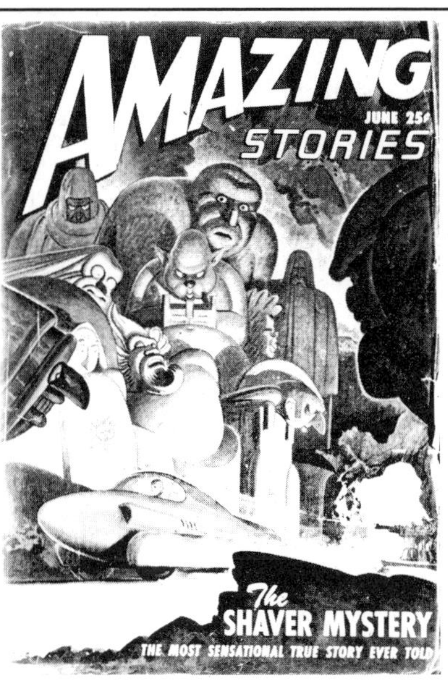

purported to be the 'True Story of the Shaver Mystery'. In that he said: 'While it is true that a great deal of the actual writing of the stories published under Mr Shaver's name has been mine, the context has only been *rewritten* by me in an editorial and revisional capacity . . .' In a letter written just before his death, Shaver emphasised this point. He said: 'I would like to point out that Palmer never plotted even one Shaver story . . .' Shaver never collaborated with Palmer, and he denied that his writing needed reworking.

By the end of the 1950s, Palmer had drifted right away from the science fiction field, and the Shaver mystery went with him. To the new generation of readers, the name Shaver meant little other than a shudder of fearful recollection down the spines of elder fans. But Shaver was far from finished. The Shaver mystery had not been a deliberate sensation-seeking plot, not by Shaver anyway. He steadfastly believed all that he had written, and right up to his death worked solidly on substantiating his facts. His greatest research went into rock books.

Shaver maintained that before the biblical Flood, when the Atlans and Titans were departing from Earth, the races recorded all the events that took place on rocks and stones. After the Flood and by reason of the Moon shifting closer to the Earth, these rocks were strewn all over the Earth, many far inland. Gradually, he pieced together many of these rocks to show a detailed record of life on Earth thousands of years ago. The pictures are not seen immediately. Many are now embedded within the stone, which must be very carefully sliced. Then, only by photographing the cross-section, magnifying it and looking at it from every conceivable angle, will one be able to see the original picture. Shaver compiled thousands of pictures and published several handbooks on the subject, but never again received the recognition he had had from the science fiction fraternity in the 1940s. He died on 5 November 1975, scorned and rejected.

Where had Shaver's inspiration for his theories come from? He claimed his beliefs originated when one night he was reading Lord Byron's poem 'Manfred', and realised he was not alone, that he had been joined by a presence. This he initially believed was a spirit – but it was a telepathically controlled ray from the underworld. He found thereafter that he was in mind-contact with the underground caves, and thereby he learned the secrets that he detailed in his series. But one must wonder how much of Shaver's theories were embellished by other influences. He was a voracious reader, and had certainly encountered the theories of Charles Fort. He must almost certainly have known of the 'theosophy' of Mme Blavatsky. It is possible he had also read the writings of H. P. Lovecraft, whose Cthulhu Mythos has much the same basis as Shaver's theories. In the Cthulhu stories, Lovecraft suggested that Earth had once been inhabited by the Ancient Ones, hostile super-beings who were conquered and exiled to Space by the Elder Ones. Mortals, tampering with the restraints set upon the Ancient Ones, sometimes release these evil deities. There is a definite similarity between the Shaver and Lovecraft concepts.

Shaver's influence on science fiction was not as direct as Fort's. Fort undeniably influenced writers, and he no doubt played a part in Shaver's theories. Shaver similarly inspired other writers to join in the Shaver mystery, and perhaps the most notable was Rog Phillips, who became a popular writer during the 1950s with such stories as 'From This Dark Mind' (1953) and 'The Yellow Pill' (1958). But Shaver's greatest influence was the direction in which he led Ray Palmer.

Palmer, crippled since a serious car accident in his youth, was one of the foremost early fans in the science fiction movement that followed the birth of the science fiction magazines in 1926. He was instrumental in organising sf clubs and publishing amateur magazines (fanzines), and wrote fiction of his own. In 1938 he succeeded to the editorship of *Amazing Stories*, a dream come true, and he immediately transformed it from the cerebral, rather stuffy publication that it had become under T. O'Conor Sloane, to an all-action, all-adventure magazine aimed at a young audience. Palmer rode high right through the war years, with *Amazing* often enjoying the highest circulation of any sf magazine, including *Astounding*. When the Shaver mystery erupted, Palmer became alienated from fandom, though he made some amends by inaugurating a special column in *Amazing*, 'The Club House', where Rog Phillips reviewed all the current fanzines. But the Shaver mystery had interested Palmer in the occult, and from that time he took less and less interest in science fiction. His editorial duties were assumed more by his assistants

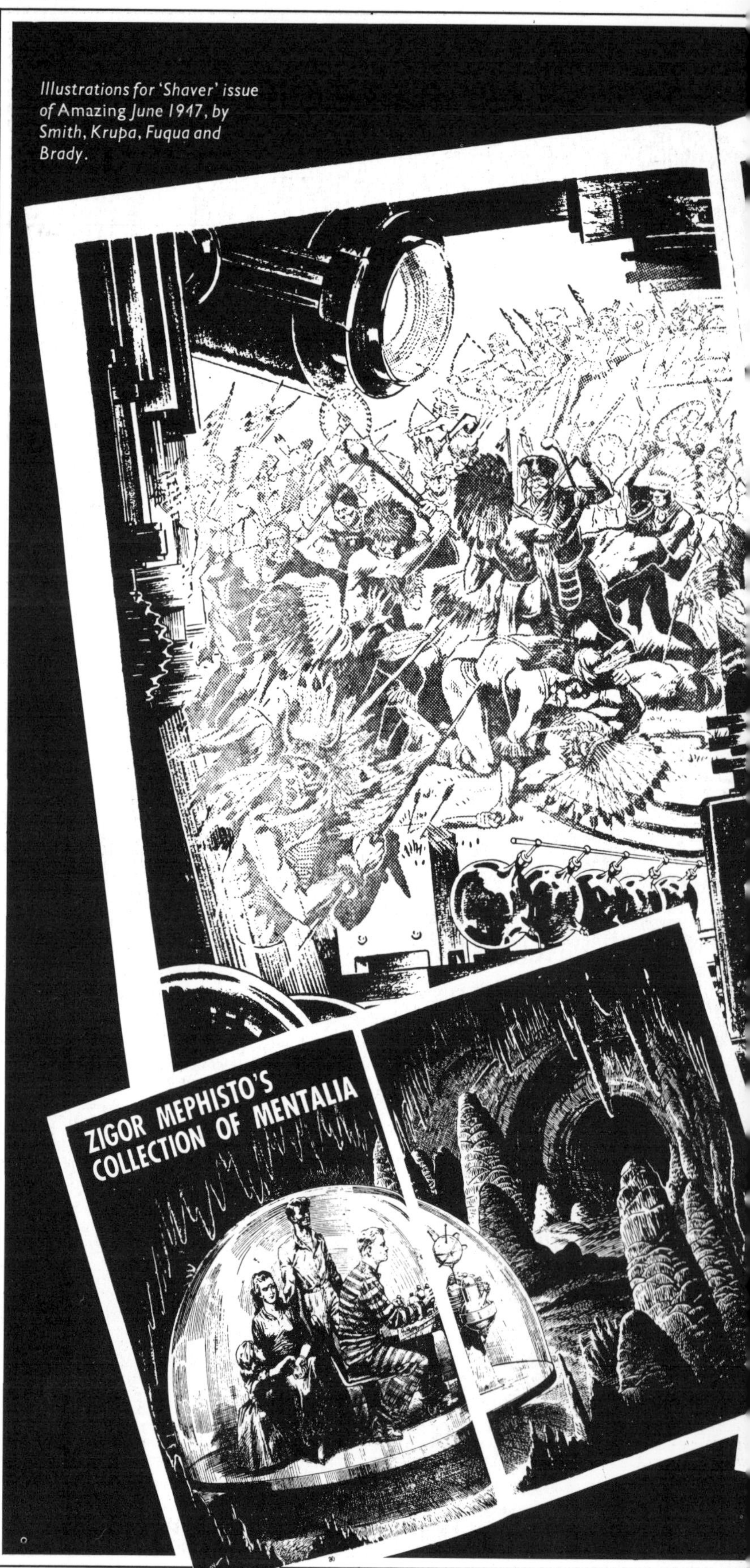

Illustrations for 'Shaver' issue of Amazing June 1947, by Smith, Krupa, Fuqua and Brady.

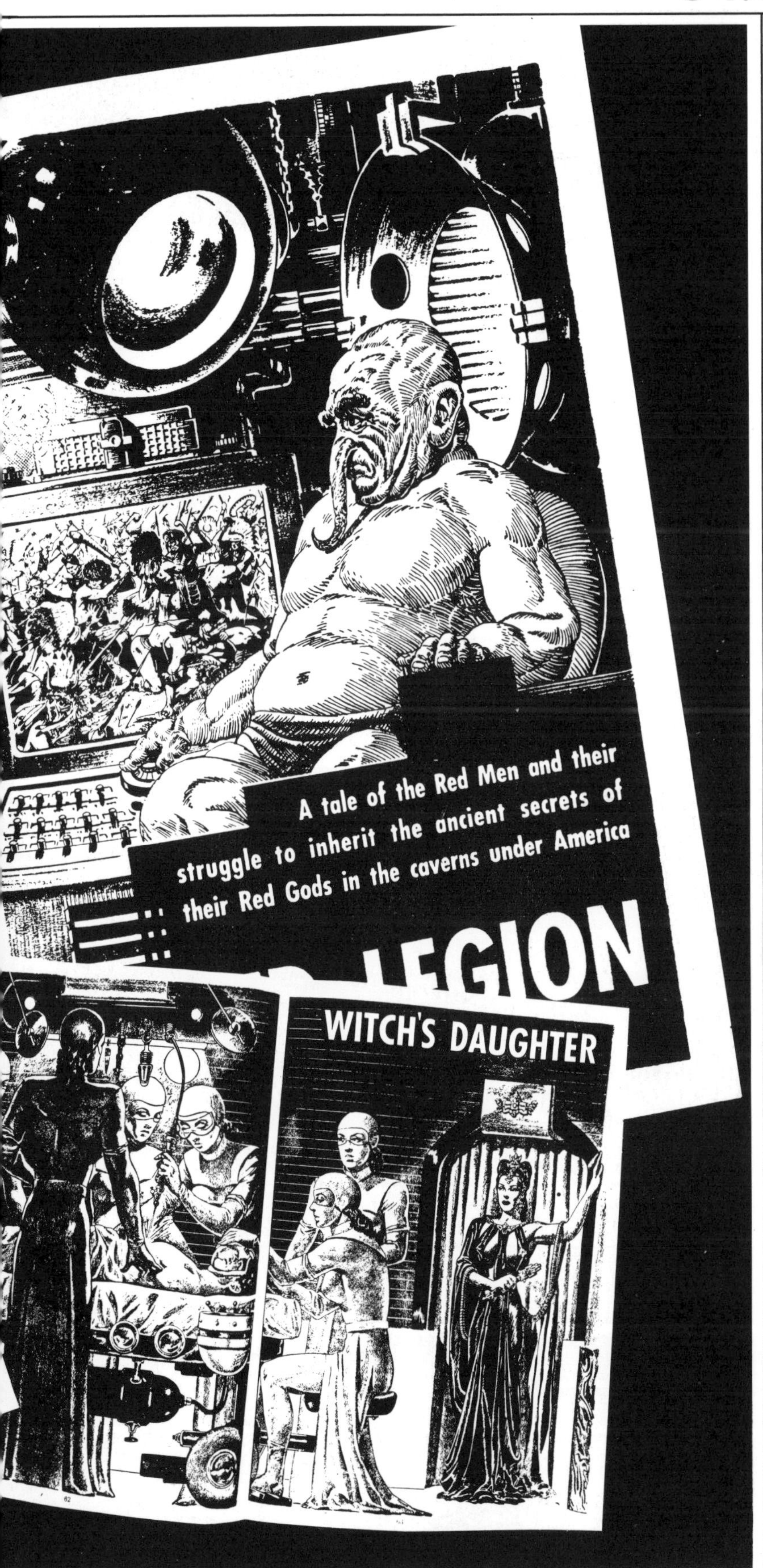

and, initially incognito, Palmer established his own publishing company and issued a magazine devoted to the strange and inexplicable, *Fate*.

A tale of the Red Men and their struggle to inherit the ancient secrets of their Red Gods in the caverns under America
LEGION
WITCH'S DAUGHTER

Fate proved a highly successful venture, and it continues to this day, though not under Palmer's guidance. It was in *Fate* that Palmer gave space to all and any wild theories, and devotees of Shaver and Fort found it a haven. Amongst its leading contributors was Vincent H. Gaddis, who has carried out much Fortean research into every form of bizarre phenomenon, and was the man who coined the term 'the Bermuda Triangle' for that area in the North Atlantic where ships and planes apparently vanish. Palmer also took under his wing Kenneth Arnold, and between them they carried out the bulk of the early work on Flying Saucers and other Unidentified Flying Objects. In Arnold's article 'The Real Flying Saucer' (1952) he relates how in June and July 1947 he was piloting his plane over Washington State when he noticed a group of strange objects in the sky. His attempts to discover the identity of these objects was inconclusive, and thus began the flying-saucer mystery. Palmer championed the cause of UFO investigations, publishing Arnold's book *The Coming of the Saucers* (1952) and devoting much space to articles and discussion on the subject in the pages of *Fate* and *Mystic* (later *Search*). In fact, Palmer's involvement became so great that in 1957 he changed the title of his science fiction magazine *Other Worlds* to *Flying Saucers from Other Worlds*. The fiction was phased out, and in 1958 the magazine became simply *Flying Saucers*. The flying-saucer cult exercised some hold over the sf magazines during the 1950s. The October 1957 *Amazing Stories* was devoted to articles on the subject, including contributions from Palmer, Shaver and Arnold. *Fantastic Universe* published a regular series of articles about UFOs by Ivan T. Sanderson and an organisation known as Civilian Saucer Intelligence. The February 1957 *Fantastic Universe* was also a special UFO issue, though besides articles it also featured specially written fiction centred on UFOs, such as 'Invasion' by Harlan Ellison, which highlighted the danger of attacking the flying saucers.

Certainly, the flying-saucer mystery would have emerged with or without Palmer, but equally it was Palmer who gave the mystery most of its initial publication and promotion, and it is quite conjectural that Palmer's interest in the whole of this field was as a result of the theories of Richard S. Shaver. But there is one other connection which is quite bizarre. Those who have read Erich von Däniken's *The Gold of the Gods* (1972) will know of the many underground tunnels in South America. These passages were purportedly discovered by Juan Moricz in 1965, though they were of course known to the Peruvian Indians. Von Däniken goes on to tell of other underground tunnels and the mysteries they contain. But to readers of *Amazing Stories* between 1945 and 1949 nothing was new about such facts. The letter column was crammed with details from readers about deep caves and tunnels, many of which supposedly proved Shaver's theories about the underground deros. These were supported by articles by Vincent H. Gaddis and archaeologist L. Taylor Hansen. In one issue of *Amazing*, Palmer reported that Hansen, then in South America, had set off to investigate further mysterious underground tunnels, and that no further word had been heard from him. Coincidentally, the last article by Hansen appeared in the December 1948 *Amazing*, and nothing was printed thereafter. Was this another example of a Palmer sensation?

The identity of L. Taylor Hansen has always been a mystery. The L. stood for Louise, and a lady of that name attended the Los Angeles fan gathering in 1939. But she claimed that she had only placed the contributions under her name. They were actually written by her brother, who was a world traveller. This is quite probable, since Palmer referred to Hansen as a man. And Hansen eventually returned. In fact, he wrote several books on archaeology, including *He Walked The Americas* (1965) specially published by Palmer. But whether it was the brother or sister Hansen who wrote the science fiction published in *Amazing* in the early years is still unresolved.

It is interesting that one of the stories, 'Lords of the Underworld' (1941), involves an archaeologist who finds himself back in the past in South America and discovers vast underground caves. Had Shaver read this story? Or had he read any of the other many novels of underground civilisations, including Edgar Rice Burroughs's *Pellucidar* series, Stanton Coblentz's *In Caverns Below* (1935) and Arthur J. Burks's 'Survival' and 'Exodus' (1938)? All could have had as much of an influence on the Shaver mystery as any of the writings of Charles Fort, or Colonel James Churchward's series that began with *The Lost Continent of Mu* (1931). Shaver may even have read the science fiction of archaeologist A. Hyatt Verrill, who in the 1920s contributed many stories to *Amazing* set in lost cities discovered in South America.

It is all conjectural, but it is interesting to look at the many sources that could be attributed to the most explosive of all mysteries to appear in the science fiction field, the Shaver mystery. Today, if anyone cites the theories of von Däniken and others, the science fiction reader may well merely sigh and say that he has read it all before, long ago.

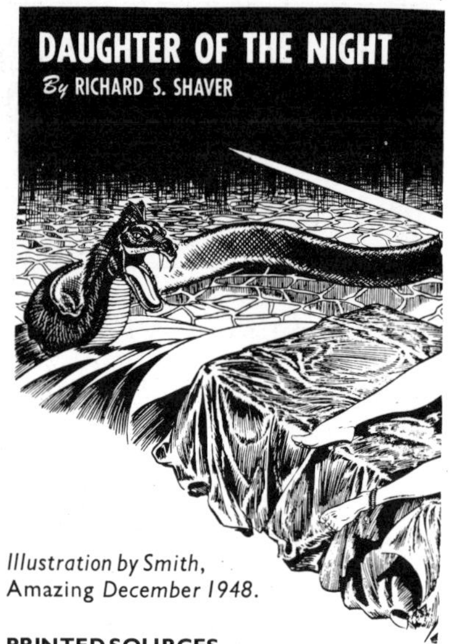

Illustration by Smith, Amazing December 1948.

PRINTED SOURCES

Palmer, Raymond A. 'The Devil's Empire', *Mystic* January 1954

Palmer, Raymond A. 'Invitation to Adventure' (non-fiction), *The Hidden World* Spring 1961

Palmer, Raymond A. 'The Facts behind the Mystery' (non-fiction), *Fantastic* July 1958

Shaver, Richard S.: The 'Lemuria' Series runs as follows:

'"I Remember Lemuria"', *Amazing* March 1945
'Thought Records of Lemuria', *Amazing* June 1945
'Cave City of Hel', *Amazing* September 1945
'Quest of Brail', *Amazing* December 1945
'Invasion of the Micro-Men', *Amazing* February 1946
'The Masked World', *Amazing* May 1946
'Cult of the Witch-Queen', *Amazing* July 1946
'The Sea People', *Amazing* August 1946
'Earth Slaves to Space', *Amazing* September 1946
'The Return of Sathanas', *Amazing* November 1946
'The Land of Kui', *Amazing* December 1946
'Joe Dannon Pioneer', *Amazing* March 1947
Special Shaver issue: four stories ('Formula from The Underworld', 'Zigor Mephisto's Collection of Mentalia', 'Witch's Daughter', 'The Red Legion'), *Amazing* June 1947
'Mer-Witch of Ether 18', *Amazing* August 1947
'When the Moon Bounced', *Amazing* May 1949
'The Fall of Lemuria', *Other Worlds* November 1949
Beyond the Barrier, *Other Worlds* November 1952–February 1953
The Dream Makers, *Fantastic* July 1958
The entire Shaver affair is detailed in *The Hidden World* issue A1, Spring 1961.
His handbooks on the rock records are:
Mysterious Shaver!, privately printed, (US) 1970
The Finding of Adam, privately printed, (US) 1970
Giant Evening Wings, privately printed, (US) 1970
Blue Mansions, privately printed, (US) 1970

It is not intended to list here all the books published in connection with UFOs, etc, but those closely connected with the science fiction world include:

Adamski, George (with Desmond Leslie). *The Flying Saucers Have Landed*, Werner Laurie (UK) 1953

Arnold, Kenneth (with Raymond Palmer). *The Coming of the Saucers*, privately published, (US) 1952

'The Real Flying Saucer' (non-fiction), *Other Worlds* January 1952

Barker, Gray. *They Knew Too Much about Flying Saucers*, University Books (US) 1956; retitled *The Unidentified*, Badger (UK) 1960

Heard, Gerald. *Riddle of the Flying Saucers: Is Another World Watching?*, Carroll (UK) 1950

Keyhoe, Donald E. *The Flying Saucers Are Real*, Gold Medal (US) 1950

In addition, the October 1957 *Amazing* was devoted to UFOs and was reprinted in 1974 as *The Special 1975 UFO Annual*

04.09.3 Origins of Dianetics

Proponents of the 'science fiction is *real*' school tend to support their case by arguing that H. G. Wells's Martian heat-ray has come true in the form of the contemporary laser, or that Huxley's *Brave New World* (1932) has shown itself in the evils of behaviourist psychology. These arguments have much to be said for them, but they share one weakness: the developments in question were turned from ideas into hardware by people other than those who entertained the original notions. Yet it is possible to identify at least one writer who not only conceived an idea, but also put it into practice. Lafayette Ron Hubbard (born 1911) began writing adventure stories in 1934 and turned to science fiction in 1938 (his first story 'The Dangerous Dimension' appeared in the July issue of *Astounding* in that year). Thereafter, he became one of editor John W. Campbell's more prolific sf authors.

During the Second World War, he served with the US Navy as commanding officer of escort vessels, and returned to writing science fiction after leaving the service. According to those present in Campbell's circle at the time, Hubbard became fascinated by hypnotism, frequently using Campbell as a subject. At about the same time he began making statements to the effect that any writer who really wished to make money should drop writing and develop religion, or devise a new psychiatric method. Harlan Ellison's version (*Time Out*, UK, No 332) is that Hubbard is reputed to have said to Campbell 'I'm going to invent a religion that's going to make me a fortune. I'm tired of writing for a penny a word.' Sam Moskowitz, a chronicler of science fiction, has reported that he himself heard Hubbard make a similar statement, but there is no first-hand evidence.

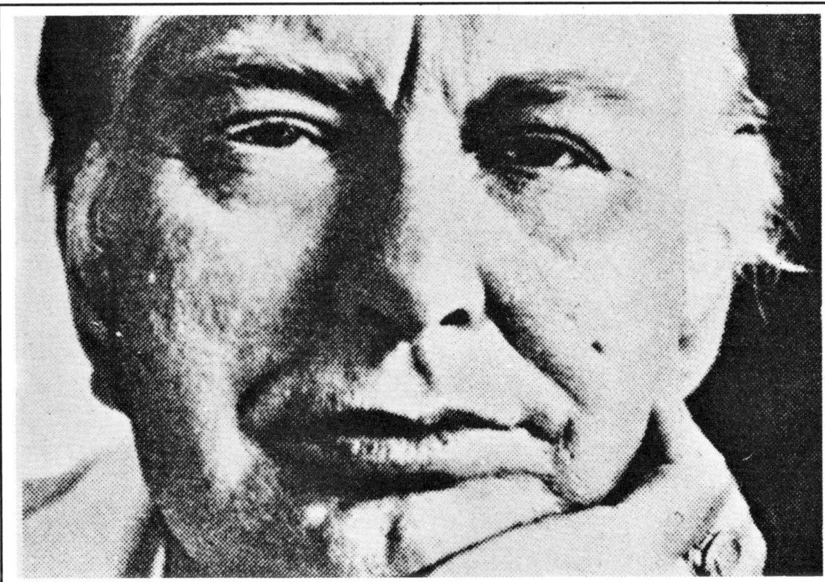

L. Ron Hubbard.

In 1950 Hubbard brought out *Dianetics*, which he acclaimed as 'a new science of the mind'. Numerous passages stressed that it was the outcome of the application of engineering methods to the study of the mind, but to the discerning observer it was fairly clear that the theory of dianetics was a random conglomeration of existing psychological concepts (some generally accepted, and others largely abandoned) and a variety of ideas lying on the fringes of professional psychological thought. Essentially, the argument suggested that the human mind forgets nothing, and hears all – even when the conscious areas of the brain are either asleep or anaesthetised. The traumatic experiences, dating back to birth, and even earlier, which affect the individual psyche are imprinted in the neuronic memory pattern in the forms of blocked pathways, to the overwhelming detriment of the individual concerned. Hubbard called such psychic blocks 'engrams'; and his concept of dianetics was designed to remove such synaptic inhibitions by a process of psychotherapy (which he chose to call 'auditing').

Auditing could be carried out by arranging for someone to guide the conversation while the person involved was totally relaxed. (Hubbard claimed that hypnotism was not involved; but in fact the method of auditing can be said to have produced a first-level form of hypnotism.) The auditor, who could be a friend, would persuade the subject to continually relive painful experiences and talk of them until they were 'discharged'. When all 'engrams' were discharged, the man became a 'clear', supposedly gifted with a perfect memory and free of all psychological traumas.

Illustrations by Miller, from L. Ron Hubbard's 'Dianetics', Astounding *May 1950, showing the evocation of ancestral memories.*

04.09 FRINGE CULTS

There was little new in such a method of therapy, beyond the extreme insistence on the influence before birth and the necessary regression to recall it. But Hubbard had discovered two basic concepts in which he departed from all previous and existing ideas – at least in his emphasis. First was the contention that no individual is really responsible *himself* for his faults (which were all produced by the careless talk of parents, and so on), an appealing argument to anyone who might find himself not all he desired. Second, it was unnecessary to consult a specialist; with Hubbard's book, any two people could easily treat each other.

The established professional reaction was to reject the book with scorn. (The ideas were hackneyed and many of them of doubtful value. Also, the method was of potential danger to border-line psychotics. Its claims were grotesquely exaggerated.) In some respects the controversy resembled that concerning Velikowsky's books. And the counter-reaction from readers was equally vehement.

Hubbard subsequently set up a foundation in New Jersey, where he hoped to gain tax-free status for his 'research'. There he ran courses in 'auditing' for a substantial fee – despite the fact that the book indicated that anyone could audit. Eventually, the tax-free plan failed, and accumulated tax debts became due. He left the United States thereafter.

Later, he developed Scientology, which he claimed was a religion and thus its organisation was not subject to taxation. The first evidence of its inception was an advertisement for a book entitled *Excalibur*. But Scientology had little to do with science fiction, whereas dianetics produced a marked if temporary effect.

Before the book *Dianetics* was published, Campbell bought an article from Hubbard: 'Dianetics, the Evolution of a Science' which appeared in the May 1950 issue of *Astounding*. (Some of the details and terminology of the article differed considerably from those given in the book.) In the following January *Astounding* featured 'Dianometry', purporting to be a study of the measured results, but appearing suspiciously like propaganda for dianetics. (A further article, 'The Analytic Mind', had already appeared in the same magazine in October 1950.)

Campbell became deeply converted to dianetics, as had been Dr Joseph Winter, MD, who joined Hubbard for a time at the 'Foundation' and had written several stories for *Astounding*. Campbell devoted considerable attention to Hubbard's ideas in his editorials, and the reader's column was almost fully occupied by the subject. The editor also sent innumerable letters to his writers and circle of friends, propagating the same views.

For a time, dianetics created a furore among readers and many writers. Katherine MacLean became immersed in auditing. James Blish expressed enthusiasm, but later opposed the theory. Van Vogt abandoned writing to run a West Coast dianetics institute. A regional sf conference held in New York on 4 July 1950, devoted an afternoon to the subject. It drew the largest audience.

'Dianetics' by L. Ron Hubbard, Astounding May 1950. Illustration by Miller.

Marvel Science Stories also took up the controversy, featuring a dissenting article by Lester del Rey, followed by a rebuttal by Hubbard – and re-rebuttal by del Rey. Hubbard had already incorporated dianetics in several of his stories, and a number of other writers followed suit (some examples are listed in the bibliography). Raymond F. Jones utilised the theory in much of his fiction. Parts of his series of novelettes, beginning with 'Tools of the Trade' in *Astounding*, November 1950, were heavily dianeticised.

Subsequently, Campbell himself began to discourage the use of dianetics, and he rejected many stories as being too biased in that direction. While dianetics cannot be compared in the length of time it endured with either the Shaver Mystery or Campbell's later obsession with psi-onics, there is little doubt that the impact it caused on its introduction rivalled those of the others, and perhaps exceeded them.

PRINTED SOURCES

Clifton, Mark and Frank Riley. *They'd Rather Be Right, Astounding* August to November 1954

Hubbard, L.R. 'The End Is Not Yet', *Astounding* August to October 1947

Hubbard, L.R. *Final Blackout*, Providence (US) 1948

Hubbard, L.R. *The Kingslayer*, Fantasy (US) 1949

Hubbard, L.R. 'Dianetics, a New Science of the Mind', *Astounding* May 1950

Hubbard, L.R. 'The Analytical Mind', *Astounding* October 1950

Hubbard, L.R. 'Homo Superior, Here We Come', *Marvel Science Stories* May 1951

Hubbard, L.R. *Return to Tomorrow*, Ace (US) 1954; published as 'To the Stars', a two-part serial in *Astounding* from February 1950

Hubbard, L.R. *Fear and the Ultimate Adventure*, Berkley (US) 1970

Huxley, Aldous. *Brave New World*, Chatto (UK) 1932; Doubleday (US) 1932

Jones, Raymond F. 'Noise Level', *Astounding* August to November 1954

Jones, Raymond F. 'Trade Secret', *Astounding* November 1953

Jones, Raymond F. 'Tools of the Trade', *Astounding* November 1950

Jones, Raymond F. 'The School', *Astounding* December 1954

INDEX

AUTHORS AND TITLES*

*excluding bibliographies and caption material